Democracy and Counterterrorism:
Lessons from the Past

Democracy and Counterterrorism: Lessons from the Past

Robert J. Art
Louise Richardson

UNITED STATES INSTITUTE OF PEACE PRESS
Washington, D.C.

United States Institute of Peace
1200 17th Street NW, Suite 200
Washington, DC 20036-3011

First published 2007

Printed in the United States of America

The paper used in this publication meets the minimum requirements of American
National Standard for Information Sciences—Permanence of Paper for Printed
Library Materials, ANSI Z39.48-1984.

Library of Congress Cataloging-in-Publication Data

Art, Robert J.
  Democracy and counterterrorism / Lessons from the the past
  Robert J. Art, Louise Richardson.
      p. cm.
  Includes index.
  ISBN-13: 978-1-929223-93-0 (pbk. : alk. paper)
  ISBN-10: 1-929223-93-5 (pbk. : alk. paper)
  ISBN-13: 978-1-929223-94-7 (hardcover : alk. paper)
  ISBN-10: 1-929223-94-3 (hardcover : alk. paper)
  1. Terrorism--Case studies. 2. Terrorism--Prevention--Case studies.
  3. Democracy--Case studies. I. Richardson, Louise, 1957- II. Title.
  HV6431.A79 2007
  363.325'16--dc22

                        2006016054

We have dedicated this book to
Robyn Art and David Art
and to the memory of
Keith Matthew Richardson (1974–1997).

CONTENTS

FOREWORD

Democracy and Counterterrorism: Lessons from the Past delivers what its succinct title promises: an analysis of how democratic states have fought groups employing political violence and terrorism, and lessons learned from these experiences that can be applied toward present and future counterterrorism campaigns. Given the current threats and challenges faced by the United States and its allies, the significance of such a volume is self-evident. After all, if we are to successfully wage the "global war on terror," we need to consider the policies, strategies, and instruments that have been employed by other democratic states in their fights against terrorist groups. While this seems like an obvious observation, more than five years after 9/11 this volume is the first to examine the subject in any kind of systematic, methodical fashion. If for no other reason, then, this assessment is of singular importance for addressing a glaring deficiency in current counterterrorism literature. Editors Robert J. Art and Louise Richardson are due credit for recognizing and filling this lacuna.

Art and Richardson enlisted a team of world-class scholars and practitioners to examine fourteen cases for the volume, focusing on thirteen states and sixteen major terrorist groups. Each case chapter includes a brief overview of the situation presented, a detailed analysis of the policies and techniques employed by the government under discussion, and an assessment of the measures that proved most effective in combating terrorism. While these individual cases in themselves are quite instructive, perhaps the volume's most valuable contribution rests with its final chapter, in which Art and Richardson synthesize the case findings, examine patterns, and tease out clear and precise lessons for the United States in its fight against al Qaeda and other terrorist organizations.

If the lessons Art and Richardson offer are not novel, they are nonetheless significant. This work has done something past studies have not: it has unequivocally demonstrated the fundamental importance of high-quality intelligence gathering, seamless international coordination, and the judicious use of political instruments in combating terrorism. While political gamesmanship and partisan bickering too often divide and distract critical actors from the task at hand, this work serves as a reminder that our wisest strategy in the war on terror is to focus on the basics. The message is clear: if such strategies have worked for democracies in the past, they can work again.

While the lessons themselves offer sound guidance for combating the transnational jihadist network and for ultimately diminishing the physical threat of terrorism, it also suggests that the United States consider ways to dampen the fuel that stokes the fire of terrorism: fear. If one considers terrorism a form of psychological warfare targeting a society's morale and seeking to win political concessions through public pressure, then perhaps the greatest danger lies not in isolated acts of indiscriminate violence, but in the damage it causes to the collective psyche. In short, the "good guys" are not the only ones trying to influence hearts and minds. Just as the United States needs to positively affect feelings and thoughts in the Muslim world, so too does it need to combat terrorists' efforts to adversely change attitudes within the United States and among our allies. If the war on terror is a generation-long war, as Art and Richardson and many others argue, it is critical to educate and engage the public to distinguish between rational and irrational fear. While we cannot control the actions of terrorists, we can ultimately control our own, sometimes illogical, psychological responses to terrorism and the threat it poses.

While Art and Richardson remind us that many democratic states have defeated terrorist groups—a heartening message in these turbulent times—the volume also makes clear a sobering fact: many other states have not succeeded in thwarting terrorist groups that threaten their societies. Put simply, terrorism often works. It is important to acknowledge this truth so that success and failure can be properly defined. Whether one believes we are facing a short-term tactical threat or one that is long-term and existential, this volume helps us understand the stakes and sets forth strategic policies for success.

That said, much more scholarship is needed. Using this study's findings as a point of departure, future studies should continue to examine the question of tactics. If *Democracy and Counterterrorism* makes plain what the focus in a fight against terrorism needs to be, future studies must define how to improve intelligence, secure international cooperation, and make better use of political instruments.

Great strength is gained in understanding not only the nature of the enemy, but also the effects, both negative and positive, of our policies toward that enemy. *Democracy and Counterterrorism* is only the latest in a long line of Institute publications to enlist, marshal, and deploy the highest level of scholarship in the service of national security concerns. Past Institute volumes have similarly contributed to our understanding of the hazards we face and the best means to combat terrorism, including *Terror on the Internet: The New Arena, the New Challenges*, by Gabriel Weimann, which examines terrorism and counterterrorism in the digital age; and *The United States and Coercive Diplomacy*, edited by Robert J. Art and Patrick M. Cronin, which offers a broad policy analysis of the emerging marriage between diplomacy and military might.

Willingness and freedom to think about the root causes of terrorism and to discuss appropriate solutions to it may explain one of the more curious observations made by Art and Richardson: over time, the counterterrorist policies of democracies get better and more effective, no matter the country implementing them or the terrorist group being fought. Art and Richardson chose not to examine how authoritarian or totalitarian states fight terror for the simple reason that democratic states are constrained in the strategies they can employ—by the need to observe human rights and the rule of law, among others. But it is clear from their conclusions that non-democratic states are at a significant disadvantage compared to democracies in confronting terrorism. While democracies might be constrained in their methods, they are also strengthened by the legitimacy granted by fighting terrorism, by the inclusive vision and respect it offers, and by the freedom democratic societies provide for innovative thinking, constructive debate, and policy adaptation. At the core of this volume thus rests a deeper truth about the present global war on terror and the need to protect and maintain democratic principles and values.

In short, *Democracy and Counterterrorism's* most important lesson may ultimately be as simple as its title: our greatest weapon against terrorism lies in democracy itself.

RICHARD H. SOLOMON, PRESIDENT
UNITED STATES INSTITUTE OF PEACE

PREFACE AND ACKNOWLEDGMENTS

The idea for this book originated in several conversations among Robert Art of Brandeis University, Louise Richardson of the Radcliffe Institute for Advanced Study at Harvard University, and Paul Stares of the United States Institute of Peace in spring 2003. In the course of those conversations, it became clear to the three of us that there was a real need for a study that systematically analyzed and compared how democracies had dealt with terrorist groups in the years since decolonization. It was also clear to us that such a study had to be a multiauthored volume because no individual possessed sufficiently detailed knowledge of a large enough number of cases to bring the project to fruition in a timely fashion. Consequently, Art and Richardson put together a research team of country experts who were also well versed in the terrorism literature, and Stares agreed to fund it. The result is this volume.

Since this book was conceived, the landscape of terrorism has been significantly altered. The tactic of suicide terrorism has expanded in scale, intensity, and geographic scope. Europe has produced the first of its own home-grown suicide bombers. British-born jihadists have attacked the London Underground system, Moroccan immigrants have murdered commuters in Spain, and eager young Muslims, radicalized by the American occupation of Iraq, have flocked to join the insurgency in Iraq. The political landscape has been altered, too. Relatively moderate parties have been replaced by more extreme parties on both sides of the sectarian divide in Northern Ireland, and in the Palestinian Authority the PLO has been replaced by Hamas as the largest political party. On a more positive note, the IRA, one of the oldest extant terrorist groups, has declared an end to its operations and it now looks as though ETA is following suit. In spite of these changes, the two fundamental challenges faced by democratic governments remain: how to respond effectively to terrorism without compromising democratic liberties, and how to deal effectively with the current generation of terrorists without creating more in the process. We conceived this book in the conviction that there is much the United States can learn from the experiences of other governments. We still think so.

Art and Richardson thank Paul Stares for having faith in this project, for funding it, and for contributing significantly to it intellectually. We also thank all our authors for their commitment to this project. They convened twice in Washington, in fall 2003 and spring 2004, to think through the implications of their work and to comment on one another's papers. They have put up with numerous requests for clarification and revisions, and many worked through four drafts of their chapters. Whatever merit the conclusions of this book have is due in large part to their extensive and generous efforts to meet our demands. We also thank Richard Solomon, president of the Institute, for his support of this project. Many other individuals contributed to the project along the way. Steve Stimon, Daniel Benjamin, Dan Byman, and Bruce Hoffman gave us the benefit of their thoughts at the project definition stage. Elise Murphy and Kelly Campbell efficiently and cheerfully took care of all the administrative and logistical tasks that such a project requires. Micah Zenko provided research assistance. Rachel Chaplin and Or-Corinne Chapman provided research and logistical support. Nigel Quinney shepherded the book through the editorial phase, and Amy Benavides saw it through to production. We are deeply grateful to each of them.

CONTRIBUTORS

Robert J. Art is Christian A. Herter Professor of International Relations at Brandeis University, a faculty associate at Harvard University's Olin Institute, a research associate at MIT's Security Studies Program, and director of MIT's Seminar XXI program. Among his most recent publications are *A Grand Strategy for America* (Ithaca, NY: Cornell University Press, 2003); and, with Patrick Cronin, eds., *The United States and Coercive Diplomacy* (Washington, DC: United States Institute of Peace Press, 2003).

Louise Richardson is executive dean of the Radcliffe Institute for Advanced Study at Harvard University. Her recent publications include *What Terrorists Want* (New York: Random House, 2006); *The Roots of Terrorism,* ed. (New York: Routledge, 2006); "State Sponsorship—a Root Cause of Terrorism?" in *Root Causes of Terrorism*, ed. T. Bjorgo (New York: Routledge, 2005); and "Fighting against Terrorism and for Justice," in *Liberty and Power: A Dialogue on Religion and Foreign Policy in an Unjust World*, ed. Bryan Hehir (Washington, DC: Brookings, 2004).

■ ■ ■

Rogelio Alonso is a lecturer in politics and terrorism at Universidad Rey Juan Carlos of Madrid and coordinator of the Unit for Documentation and Analysis on Terrorism at this university. He is the author of three books on terrorism, one of them based on the most extensive sample of in-depth interviews with IRA activists ever carried out. Among his most recent publications are *Northern Ireland: Una historia de guerra y la búsqueda de la paz* [Northern Ireland: A History of War and the Search for Peace] (Madrid: Editorial Complutense, 2001); and *Matar por Irlanda: El IRA y la lucha armada* [Killing for Ireland: The IRA and the Armed Struggle] (Madrid: Editorial Alianza, 2003).

Henri J. Barkey is the Bernard L. and Bertha F. Cohen Professor in International Relations and International Relations Department chair at Lehigh University. He served as a member of the U.S. State Department Policy Planning Staff (1998–2000). He is the author, with Graham Fuller, of *Turkey's Kurdish Question* (Lanham, MD: Rowman and Littlefield, 1998). His recent article-length publications include *Turkey and Iraq: The Perils (and Prospects) of Proximity*, Special Report no. 141 (Washington, DC: United States Institute of Peace, July 2005); "The Endless Pursuit: Improving U.S.-Turkish Relations," in *Friends in Need: Turkey and the United States after September 11*, ed. Morton Abramowitz (New York: Century Foundation, 2003), 207–49; and, with Ellen Laipson, "Iraqi Kurds and the Future of Iraq," *Middle East Policy* 12, no. 4 (December 2005): 66–76.

Daniel Byman is the director for the Center for Peace and Security Studies and the Security Studies Program at the Edmund A. Walsh School of Foreign Service at Georgetown University and a nonresident Senior Fellow at the Saban Center for Middle East Policy at the Brookings Institution. He writes widely on terrorism, Middle East security, and issues related to U.S. national security. His most recent book is *Deadly Connections: States That Sponsor Terrorism* (New York: Cambridge, 2005).

Peter Calvert is professor emeritus of comparative and international politics at the University of Southampton, England, and coeditor of the journal *Democratization*. Among his recent publications are, with Susan Calvert, *Politics and Society in the Third World*, 2nd ed. (New York: Prentice Hall, 2001); *Comparative Politics: An Introduction* (Hemel Hempstead: Longman's, 2002); and *A Political and Economic Dictionary of Latin America* (London: Europa Publications, 2004).

Audrey Kurth Cronin is director of studies for the Oxford Leverhulme Program on the Changing Character of War and a member of the international relations faculty of Oxford University (England). Among her recent publications are, with James Ludes, eds., *Attacking Terrorism: Elements of a Grand Strategy* (Washington, DC: Georgetown University Press, 2004); "How al Qaeda Ends," *International Security* 30, no. 4 (Spring 2006, forthcoming); "Behind the Curve: Globalization and International Terrorism," *International Security* 27, no. 3 (Winter 2002–3): 30–58; and "Rethinking Sovereignty:

American Strategy in the Age of Terrorism," *Survival* 44, no. 2 (Summer 2002): 119–39.

Katsuhisa Furukawa is a Senior Fellow of the Research Institute of Science and Technology for Society (RISTEX) in Japan's Science and Technology Agency, in charge of research projects on counterterrorism and homeland security for Japan. Among his most recent publications are "London Terror Attacks and Policy Implications for Japan's Counter-terrorism Strategy," *Keisatsugaku Ronshu* [Journal of Police Science] (January 2006); "Making Sense of Japan's Nuclear Policy: Arms Control, Extended Deterrence, and the Nuclear Option," in *Japan's Nuclear Option: Security, Politics, and Policy in the 21st Century,* ed. Benjamin Self (Washington, DC: The Henry L. Stimson Center, 2003), 95–147; and "Tairyou Hakai Heiki to Terorizumu no Juyou Kadai" [Critical Issues of Proliferation of Weapons of Mass Destruction and Terrorism], in *Atarashii Nihon no Anzen Hoshou wo Kangaeru* [Thinking about Japan's New National Security], eds. Masahiro Sakamoto and Tadamasa Fukiura, Toranomon DOJO Books (Tokyo: Jiyu Kokumin-sha, 2004), 141–98.

Boaz Ganor is the deputy dean of the Lauder School of Government Security and Diplomacy, head of the homeland security program at the Interdisciplinary Center, Herzliya Israel, and the founder of ICT (The International Policy Institute for Counter-Terrorism) and ICTAC (The International Counter-Terrorism Academic Community). Among his most recent publications are *The Counter-terrorism Puzzle: A Guide for Decision Makers* (New Brunswick, NJ: Transaction Publishers, 2005); and *Post-Modern Terrorism: Trends, Scenarios, and Future Threats* (New Brunswick, NJ: Transaction Publishers, 2006).

Thomas A. Marks is professor of insurgency, terrorism, and counterterrorism at the School for National Security Executive Education of the U.S. National Defense University, as well as an adjunct professor at the Joint Special Operations University. Among his most recent works are *Colombian Army Adaptation to FARC Insurgency* (Carlisle, PA: Army War College, 2002); *Insurgency in Nepal* (Carlisle, PA: Army War College, 2003); and *Sustainability of Colombian Military/Strategic Support for "Democratic Security"* (Carlisle, PA: Army War College, 2005).

David Scott Palmer is professor of international relations and political science at Boston University. Among his most recent publications are "Citizen Responses to Conflict and Political Crisis in Peru: Informal Politics in Ayacucho," in *What Justice? Whose Justice?* ed. Susan Eckstein and Timothy Wickham-Crowley (Berkeley: University of California Press, 2003); *U.S. Relations with Latin America during the Clinton Years: Opportunities Lost or Opportunities Squandered?* (Gainesville: University of Florida Press, 2006).

John V. Parachini is a senior policy analyst at the RAND Corporation and the director of RAND's Intelligence Policy Center. Among his recent publications are "Aum Shinrikyo," in *Aptitude for Destruction*, vol. 2, *Case Studies of Organizational Learning in Five Terrorist Groups*, ed. Brian A. Jackson and others (Santa Monica, CA: RAND, 2005); with Sara Daly and William Rosenau, *Aum Shinrikyo, al Qaeda and the Kinshasa Reactor: Implications of Three Case Studies for Combating Nuclear Terrorism* (Santa Monica, CA: RAND, 2005); and "Putting WMD in Perspective," *Washington Quarterly* 26, no. 4 (Fall 2003): 37–50.

Fernando Reinares is professor of political science at Universidad Rey Juan Carlos in Madrid, contributing editor of *Studies in Conflict and Terrorism*, and a member of the international advisory board of *Terrorism and Political Violence*. His recent books include the Spanish best seller *Patriotas de la muerte: Quienes han militado en ETA y por que* [Patriots of Death: Who Joined ETA and Why] (Madrid: Taurus, 2001); *Terrorismo global* [Global Terrorism] (Madrid: Taurus, 2003); and *El nuevo terrorismo islamista: Del 11-S al 11-M* [The New Islamist Terrorism: From 9/11 to 3/11] (Madrid: Temas de Hoy, 2004).

Jeremy Shapiro is a Fellow and director of research at the Center on the United States and Europe at the Brookings Institution. Among his recent publications are, with Philip Gordon, *Allies at War: America, Europe, and the Crisis over Iraq* (New York: McGraw-Hill, 2004); with Benedicte Suzan, "The French Experience of Counterterrorism," *Survival* (Spring 2003); and, with Lynn Davis, eds., *The U.S. Army and the New National Security Strategy* (Santa Monica, CA: RAND, 2003).

Paul Wallace is professor emeritus of political science at the University of Missouri, Columbia. In September 2003, Professor Wallace served as the expert witness on Sikh violence at the Air India trial in Vancouver, British Columbia. He has been a consultant on South Asia to government agencies in the United States and Canada, as well as to defense lawyers and private institutions. He is the author or editor of seven books and forty book chapters and articles. His most recent book, with Ramashray Roy, eds., is *India's 1999 Elections and 20th Century Politics* (New Delhi and Thousand Oaks: Sage Publications, 2003).

Peter Waldmann is professor emeritus of sociology at the University of Augsburg, Germany. His main research fields are political sociology, especially of Latin America, social change and development, and sociology of law and deviant behavior. Among his most recent publications are *Der anomische Staat: Über Recht, öffentliche Sicherheit und Alltag in Lateinamerika* (Oplanden: Leske + Budrich, 2002); translator, *El estado anomico* (Madrid: Vervuert 2005); *Terrorismus: Provokation der Macht*, 2nd ed. (Hamburg: Murmann Verl., 2006); and, with Rolf Kappel and Hans Werner Toberler, eds., *Rechtsstaatlichkeit im Zeitalter der Globalisierung* (Freiburg: Rombach, 2005).

Leonard Weinberg is Foundation Professor of Political Science at the University of Nevada, Reno; a Fellow of the National Security Studies Center at the University of Haifa; and senior editor of the journal *Democracy and Security*. His recent books include *Global Terrorism* (Oxford: Oneworld, 2005); with Ami Pedahzur, *Political Parties and Terrorist Groups* (London and New York: Routledge, 2003); and, with Ami Pedahzur, eds., *Religious Fundamentalism and Political Extremism* (London: Frank Cass, 2003).

GLOSSARY OF TERRORIST GROUPS

Acronym	Full Name	Country
AIS	Armée Islamique du Salut (Islamic Salvation Army)	Algeria
	al-Aqsa Martyrs Brigades	Palestine
	al Qaeda	Global
ASG	Abu Sayyaf Group	Philippines
	Autodefensas Unidas de Colombia (United Self-Defense Forces of Colombia)	Colombia
	Aum Shinrikyo	Japan
BK	Babbar Khalsa	India
BR	Brigate Rosse (Red Brigades)	Italy
BTF	Bhindranwale Tiger Force	India
	Chechen rebels	Russia
DFLP	Democratic Front for the Liberation of Palestine	Palestine
ELN	Ejercito de Liberación Nacional (National Liberation Army)	Colombia
EPL	Ejercito Popular de Liberación (Popular Liberation Army)	Colombia

ACRONYM	FULL NAME	COUNTRY
EPRLF	Eelam People's Revolutionary Liberation Front	Sri Lanka
EROS	Eelam Revolutionary Organization of Students	Sri Lanka
ETA	Euskadi ta Askatasuna (Basque Homeland and Freedom)	Spain
FALN	Fuerzas Armadas de Liberación Nacional (Armed National Liberation Forces)	Venezuela
FARC	Fuerzas Armadas Revolucionarias de Colombia (Revolutionary Armed Forces of Colombia)	Colombia
FATAH	Harakat al-Tahrir al-Watani al-Filastini (Palestine National Liberation Movement)	Palestine
FCF	Fighting Communist Formations	Italy
GAL	Grupos Antiterroristas de Liberación (Liberation Antiterrorist Groups)	France, Spain
GIA	Groupe Islamique Armé (Armed Islamic Group)	Algeria
GSPC	Groupe Salafiste pour la Prédication et le Combat (Salafist Group for Call and Combat)	Northern Africa
HAMAS	Harakat al-Muqawamah al-Islamiyyah (Islamic Resistance Group)	Palestine
	Hizballah (Party of God)	Lebanon
HM	Hizbul Mujahideen	Kashmir
HUA	Harkat-ul-Ansar	Kashmir
IMU	Islamic Movement of Uzbekistan	Uzbekistan
INLA	Irish National Liberation Army	Northern Ireland
ISYF	International Sikh Youth Federation	India

Acronym	Full Name	Country
IRA	Irish Republican Army	Northern Ireland
IRSP	Irish Republican Socialist Party	Northern Ireland
JEM	Jaish-i-Muhammad	Kashmir
JI	Jemaah Islamiya	Southeast Asia
JKLF	Jammu and Kashmir Liberation Front	Kashmir
JVP	Janatha Vimukthi Peramuna (People's Liberation Front)	Sri Lanka
KCF	Khalistan Commando Force	India
KLF	Khalistan Liberation Force	India
LeT	Lashkar e-Tayyiba	Pakistan
LJ	Lashkar I Hhangvi	Pakistan
LTTE	Liberation Tigers of Tamil Eelam (Tamil Tigers)	Sri Lanka
M-19	Movimiento 19 April (April 19 Movement)	Colombia
MIR	Movimiento de Izquierda Revolucionaria (Movement of the Revolutionary Left)	Venezuela
MRTA	Movimiento Revolucionario Tupac Amaru (Tupac Amaru Revolutionary Movement)	Peru
NAP	Nuclei Armata Proletari (Nuclei of Armed Proletarians)	Italy
PCP-SL	Partido Comunista del Perú–Sendero Luminoso (Communist Party of Peru–Shining Path)	Peru

Acronym	Full Name	Country
PFLP	Popular Front for the Liberation of Palestine	Palestine
PFLP/GC	Popular Front for the Liberation of Palestine/General Command	Palestine
PIJ	Palestinian Islamic Jihad	Palestine
PIRA	Provisional Irish Republican Army	Northern Ireland
PKK	Kurdistan Workers' Party	Turkey
PL	Prima Linea (Front Line)	Italy
PLA	Palestine Liberation Army	Palestine
PLF	Palestine Liberation Front	Palestine
PLF/GC	Palestine Liberation Front/General Command	Palestine
PLO	Palestine Liberation Organization	Palestine
PLOT	People's Liberation Organization of Thamileelam	Sri Lanka
PWG	People's War Group	India
RAF	Red Army Faction	Germany
RIRA	Real Irish Republican Army	Northern Ireland
TELO	Tamil Eelam Liberation Organization	Sri Lanka

1

INTRODUCTION

Democracy and Counterterrorism: Lessons from the Past

Robert J. Art

Louise Richardson

The subject of this book is democracy and counterterrorism. Its purpose is to survey, and then to assess, the policies and practices democracies use to combat groups that use terrorism to achieve their goals. Our ultimate objectives are to identify the counterterrorism measures and policies that have proved most effective and to suggest which of them could most help the United States and its allies in dealing with al Qaeda and al Qaeda–affiliated groups—what we call "the transnational jihadist network"—and other such groups that may emerge in the future and employ terrorism to achieve their goals.

Terrorism is both a tactic and a strategy. According to Bruce Hoffman, a longtime student of the subject, terrorism means at its core "the deliberate creation and exploitation of fear through violence or the threat of violence in the pursuit of political change."[1] In today's world, terrorism involves the deliberate and often random maiming and killing of noncombatants for political effect by subnational groups and nonstate actors. For the purposes of this volume, therefore, combating or countering terrorism means devising methods and policies to cause nonstate groups that employ this technique to stop using violence to achieve their political objectives. In this volume, we

1

concentrate on counterterrorism policies that a selected set of democratic governments have used against nonstate actors that have resorted to terrorism. Our focus is on which policies worked, which did not, and why.

To identify these policies, this volume addresses two fundamental questions: How have thirteen democratic states fought groups employing terrorism, and what lessons for counterterrorism campaigns might we derive from their collective experience? The case studies in this book deal with the first question; the conclusion, with the second question. The purpose of this introduction is to set the context for the case studies that follow.

WHY THIS STUDY?

The overwhelming majority of terrorism studies fall into one of two groups: separate monographs on the history and evolution of individual groups, or studies of terrorism in general. Such studies are useful for helping us understand the nature of specific groups that employ terrorism and the policies that particular governments have used to deal with terrorist threats. Comparative studies of counterterrorism, both cross-national and cross-temporal, are rare, however. As Martha Crenshaw, another longtime student of terrorism, remarked in 2002, scholars are "just beginning to sort through many issues regarding what lessons could be learned for U.S. policy from other cases."[2] Consequently, there are few comparative studies that analyze counterterrorist campaigns conducted by democracies.

Among the best of the studies that do exist are *Western Responses to Terrorism* (Alex Schmid and Ronald Crelinsten, eds.), *The Deadly Sin of Terrorism: Its Effect on Democracy and Civil Liberties in Six Countries* (David Charters, ed.), *A Strategic Framework for Countering Terrorism and Insurgency* (Bruce Hoffman and Jennifer Morrison Taw), *Urban Battle Fields of South Asia: Lessons Learned from Sri Lanka, India, and Pakistan* (C. Christine Fair), and *Combating Terrorism: Strategies of Ten Countries* (Yonah Alexander, ed.).[3]

Each of these studies has its merits and deficiencies. The Schmid and Crelinsten volume contains seven case studies, but it is confined to Europe and includes the Netherlands, Switzerland, and Austria—states that have had little experience with terrorism to date. The Charters volume examines six cases (the United Kingdom, Germany, France, Italy, Israel, and the United States), but the focus is on the nexus between security and civil liberties—an important issue to be sure, but only part of what concerns us here. The Hoffman and Taw study is comparative, but because it includes both terrorism and counterinsurgency cases, it draws conclusions based on only three counterterrorism campaigns (Northern Ireland, Germany, and Italy). The Fair volume systematically analyzes urban terrorist campaigns in Sri Lanka, India, and Pakistan and the respective government efforts to deal with them, and consequently it provides insights for counterterrorism, even though it is confined to three states. The Alexander volume covers a relatively large number of cases (the United States, Argentina, Peru, Colombia, Spain, the United Kingdom, Israel, Turkey, India, and Japan) and concentrates explicitly on democratic counterterrorism efforts, but the studies are not as systematic as the ones in this volume, nor are the lessons drawn from the cases and applied to America's campaign against today's global jihadist threat.

In sum, although valuable for their knowledge and insights, these studies do not exhaust the subject of democracy and counterterrorism. The purpose of this volume is to build upon these prior comparative studies and, in the process, add to the collective picture of how democratic states have combated, and should combat, terrorism.

CASE SELECTION

The case studies in this volume cover thirteen democratic states and sixteen major groups that have resorted to terrorism against these states. We employed four criteria to select our cases: the nature of the democratic government targeted, the duration of the government's counterterrorist campaign, the type of terrorist organization involved, and the degree to which the government's counterterrorist campaign succeeded or failed.

Nature of the Democratic Government. Our case studies include only democracies, but they encompass three types of democracies: fully democratic states, partially democratic states, and new or fragile democracies. (For analytical purposes, we group the second and third types into one category.) We have included these three types to increase the number of cases and their geographic range. We have avoided using authoritarian or totalitarian governments as "control states" for the simple reason that democratic states are more constrained in their ability to deploy military force domestically.

Authoritarian states eradicate insurgent terrorism from below by employing state terrorism. This practice is generally not an option for democracies, although two governments we studied did employ ruthless methods that fully mature democracies have not used.

Duration and Extent of the Counterterrorism Campaign. We have included some of the biggest and longest-lasting terrorist groups, in part because we are interested in applying lessons learned from these groups to al Qaeda and like groups. By terrorist group standards, al Qaeda is a very large, albeit loose, organization; consequently, assessing counterterrorist campaigns against large organizations is appropriate. Moreover, the campaign against al Qaeda and its affiliated groups is likely to be long, and there may be much to learn from campaigns of long duration. During such campaigns, both terrorist groups and governments have to adapt and change their techniques over time. Large and long-lived groups are likely to yield lessons especially suitable for dealing with al Qaeda.

Type of Terrorist Organization. We have included a range of terrorist groups: revolutionary, ethnonationalist, and religious or millenarian. Revolutionary groups aim to change the nature of the society in which they live, usually with the goal of redistributing resources from the rich to the poor. Ethnonationalist groups aim for separation in the form of a distinct state, for a high degree of local autonomy from the central government that rules over them, or to join another state. Religious or millenarian groups are those that either seek to establish theocratic states or hold to quasi-religious beliefs about a radical transformation of the entire world.

Success and Failure. Finally, our cases include successes and failures. We have included failures as well as successes to enhance our chances of separating what does not work from what does. Success means that attacks from the group employing terrorist tactics have ceased because the group has been destroyed as an effective force, or that the attacks have been reduced to a low level of frequency and destruction because the group has been significantly weakened and its appeal has been severely diminished or it has entered into a peace process. Failure means that the group remains potent and capable of mounting deadly attacks, or that the group continues to operate, mount attacks when it so chooses, and appeal to a larger sympathetic audience. We do not code a simple cease-fire as a success if the group remains intact and is capable of resuming its terrorist campaign, although clearly a cease-fire can be a first step on the road to governmental success.

On the basis of these criteria, we selected a group of thirteen states to examine. Clearly, this group does not include every government that has faced a major terrorist threat in the past forty-five years, but it is representative of the types of counterterrorist campaigns that democratic and quasi-democratic governments have conducted during this period. For geographic spread, we have chosen cases from Europe (Italy, the United Kingdom, Spain, and France); Latin America (Venezuela, Peru, and Colombia); the Middle East (Israel and Turkey); South Asia (India and Sri Lanka); East Asia (Japan); and Russia—almost a region unto itself. The cases include mature and fully democratic states—Italy, the United Kingdom, Spain, France, Israel, India, Japan, and Sri Lanka—and partial, new, or fragile ones (at the time they faced major terrorist challenges)—Venezuela, Peru, Colombia, Russia, and Turkey.

Finally, our cases include the three types of groups resorting to terrorism. There are ethnonationalist groups: Harakat al-Muqawamah al-Islamiyyah (Hamas), Harakat al-Tahrir al-Watani al-Filastini (Fatah), and Hizballah against Israel; Euskadi ta Askatasuna (ETA) against Spain; the Irish Republican Army (IRA) against the United Kingdom; the Sikhs—the Khalistan Commando Force (KCF), the Babbar Khalsa (BK), the Khalistan Liberation Force (BLF), and the International Sikh Youth Federation—against India; the Kashmiri Jihadis—the Jammu and Kashmir Liberation Front (JKLF), Lashkar e-Tayyiba (LeT), and the Hizbul-Mujahideen (HM)—against India; the Chechen rebels against Russia; the Liberation Tigers of Tamil Eelam (LTTE, or Tamil Tigers) against Sri Lanka; and the Kurdistan Workers' Party (PKK) against Turkey. There are revolutionary groups: the Brigate Rosse (Red Brigades, or BR) against Italy; the Fuerzas Armadas de Liberación Nacional (Armed National Liberation Forces, or FALN) against Venezuela; the Partido Comunista del Perú–Sendero Luminoso (Communist Party of Peru–Shining Path) against Peru; and the Fuerzas Armadas Revolucionarias de Colombia (Revolutionary Armed Forces of Colombia, or FARC) against Colombia. Finally, there are religious or millenarian groups: the Groupe Islamique Armé (GIA) against France and Aum Shinrikyo against Japan.

Table 1-1 lists the states under consideration, the group or groups that have employed terrorist techniques against them, and the nature of the groups. (In table titles, we use the phrase *terrorist groups* as shorthand for groups employing terrorism.) Not all the groups under study fall neatly into one category. Hamas and Hizballah, for example, want to reclaim Israel for the Palestinian state, but both also have religious agendas. The Chechen rebels are largely Muslims fighting against a Russian Orthodox state, the various Kashmiri Jihadis are Muslims fighting against a largely Hindu India, and the Sikh rebellion against India had religious overtones. Nonetheless, we have classified these groups as ethnonationalist principally because they seek their own state and are fighting against another state or their own government to get it. Religion obviously plays a role in these situations, but we believe that the primary motivation of these groups is to acquire control over their own political fates. Similarly, the GIA, which we classify as a religious group, wanted to gain control over the Algerian government, but it does not represent a separate ethnic group within Algeria; the state it wanted to establish was an Islamist or theocratic one, and our concern with the GIA is the terrorist challenge it posed to the French government in the mid-1990s. Finally, although today the FARC is concerned with retaining the territory it controls in Colombia and the narcotics trade there, it began as a revolutionary group and still claims to be one. Thus, although seven of our groups do not fall quite so neatly into one category, there are valid reasons to put them in the categories we have.

These sixteen groups differ in a number of other dimensions that make them useful for thinking about how democracies can deal with the terrorist threats of today and tomorrow. For example, the IRA, ETA, Fatah, and the PKK are among the longest-lasting terrorist organizations. Hizballah nearly rivals al Qaeda in its international reach (it is reputed to have cells around the world) and has never been vanquished by Israel, the democratic state with probably the world's most sophisticated, experienced, and extensive counterterrorism apparatus. LTTE is one of the most successful and powerful terrorist organizations of the past thirty years. It even possesses its own navy, and although it did not pioneer suicide terrorism in the contemporary world, it has made extensive use of this technique to great effect. The FARC, Hizballah, PKK, Sikh, and Kashmiri Jihadi cases are useful to look at in part because of the scale of the threat they have posed and in part because they spill out beyond the borders of their respective states and have interna-

Table 1-1. The Government Targeted and Type of Terrorist Group

Government Targeted	Terrorist Group	Type of Group
Italy	Red Brigades	Revolutionary
United Kingdom	IRA	Ethnonationalist
Spain	ETA	Ethnonationalist
France	GIA	Religious
Venezuela	FALN	Revolutionary
Peru	Shining Path	Revolutionary
Colombia	FARC	Revolutionary
Israel	Hamas and Fatah; Hizballah	Ethnonationalist
Turkey	PKK	Ethnonationalist
Russia	Chechen rebels	Ethnonationalist
India	Sikhs; Kashmiri Jihadis	Ethnonationalist
Sri Lanka	Tamil Tigers	Ethnonationalist
Japan	Aum Shinrikyo	Millenarian

tional implications. Aum Shinrikyo had vast sums of money and considerable scientific expertise at its disposal and is the only known terrorist organization to have used weapons of mass destruction (sarin and anthrax) with even a modicum of success. The Red Brigades came closer to success—to bringing down the Italian government—than is commonly thought, and the Italian government's campaign against them teaches much about how a democracy can effectively fight terrorism against a tough opponent. The French campaign against the GIA, which along with Lashkar e-Tayyiba (a Kashmiri Jihadi group) is closest in ideology and association with al Qaeda, teaches a lot about the effective marrying of judicial and intelligence systems. The campaign against the FALN was almost a textbook case of how an emerging democracy could successfully defeat a counterinsurgency group that also employed terrorist tactics. Finally, Russia has fought against groups that have received help from al Qaeda or the involvement of al Qaeda elements. In sum, although our cases do not include every group that has employed terrorist techniques against every democratic state in the past forty-five years, they do include the major ones, with the exception of current challenges such as al Qaeda and its affiliated groups.

Finally, when their tactics are taken into account, the groups we studied fall into two categories: those groups that relied solely or primarily on terror tactics, and those groups that resorted to both terror and guerrilla tactics.[4] Both terror and guerrilla tactics are weapons used by a weaker party against a stronger one. Terrorism, let's recall, is the deliberate use of violence, more often than not against noncombatants, to induce political change through fear. Guerrilla warfare refers to tactics that an irregular army uses to fight a state's regular armed forces. Whereas terrorism relies on the fear induced by random violence and killing to produce desired political results, guerrilla tactics are designed to attack and wear down governmental forces while avoiding set-piece battles with the state's regular army units, since guerrilla groups are inferior in size to regular armies and poorly equipped compared to them. Hit-and-run tactics aim to grind down regular forces and bring about their eventual military defeat through attrition and loss of will, or to pose such huge costs to a military effort that a government will seek negotiations and compromise. There is admittedly a gray area between terrorism and guerrilla warfare because guerrilla forces can and do resort to terror tactics, especially against civilian governmental officials and police forces. Despite the considerable gray area, guerrilla forces are generally much larger than those of "terror-only" groups; they usually concentrate on attacking military forces as opposed to noncombatants (although they do kill noncombatants); and they often try to seize and hold territory rather than simply attack innocents randomly.[5] Table 1-2 illustrates the breakdown of our groups by the tactics used.

In our cases, all seven groups that relied solely or primarily on terror tactics were fighting against wholly democratic states (see table 1-3). The only qualification to this statement concerns ETA, which was formed in Franco's authoritarian Spain, survived Spain's transition to democracy, and continued to operate in a fully democratic Spain. (For the GIA, we are concerned with its operations in France, not Algeria.) For the nine groups that employed both guerrilla and terror tactics, five—the FALN, the FARC, Shining Path, the Chechen rebels, and the PKK—operated against new, fragile, or partially democratic states. Of the remaining four groups, two—Hizballah and the Kashmiri Jihadis—established their base of operations within a fragile or partially democratic state. Hizballah operated from Lebanon against Israel and waged both a guerrilla war and a terrorist campaign to force Israel to end its occupation of Lebanon. The Kashmiri Jihadis

Table 1-2. Terrorist Groups and Guerrilla-Terror Tactics

Group Uses Both Guerrilla and Terror Tactics	Group Uses Primarily or Only Terror Tactics
FARC	GIA
Chechen rebels	Aum Shinrikyo
FALN	IRA
Hizballah	Red Brigades
Fatah	Sikhs
Shining Path	ETA
PKK	Hamas
Tamil Tigers	
Kashmiri Jihadis	

Table 1-3. Democratic States and Terrorist Groups

Nature of Democratic State Attacked	Ethno-nationalist Terrorist Groups	Revolutionary Terrorist Groups	Religious or Millenarian Terrorist Groups
Fully Democratic States	Hamas and Fatah (Israel) Hizballah (Israel) ETA (Spain) IRA (United Kingdom) Sikhs (India) Kashmiri Jihadis (India) Tamil Tigers (Sri Lanka)	Red Brigades (Italy)	Aum Shinrikyo (Japan) GIA (France)
New, Fragile, or Partially Democratic States	PKK (Turkey) Chechen rebels (Russia)	FALN (Venezuela) Shining Path (Peru) FARC (Colombia)	

resorted to both terror and guerrilla tactics against India, infiltrating from
Pakistan and employing terror tactics against Indian civilians but also targeting Indian military units, often with the help of Pakistani military units
that shelled Indian military forces across the border with large artillery
pieces. The third group, Fatah, operated against Israel proper and against
Israeli forces occupying Palestinian territory, using terror tactics within Israel
and a combination of guerrilla and terror tactics within occupied Palestinian
territory. The fourth group, the Tamil Tigers, was the only one of our sixteen that used both terrorism and an extremely effective insurgency war
within a democratic state.

Why did groups that used primarily terror tactics operate in only mature
democracies, and why did five of the eight guerrilla groups (the FARC, the
Chechen rebels, the FALN, Shining Path, and the PKK) emerge within
new, fragile, or partially democratic states? A definitive answer to each question is beyond the scope of this volume, but some speculation is in order,
and the discussion concerns the nature of the democracy within which, or
against which, the group was operating. In genuinely mature democratic
states, a dissatisfied group usually can do well if it has a broad base of support, because it has an electoral option that enables it to put pressure on the
government to respond to its interests. In general, therefore, we are not likely
to see broad-based groups resorting to guerrilla tactics and insurgency warfare against governments within well-established and fully functioning
democracies. LTTE is an exception to this generalization because it is a
broad-based group that has used both guerrilla and terror tactics and operates within a functioning democracy. Fatah, Hizballah, and the Kashmiri
Jihadis are anomalies because they operated against democratic states, but
from bases outside those states. So, too, is the IRA, because the movement
emerged not in mainland Britain but in the Protestant province of Northern
Ireland, where British standards of democracy were not practiced. Similarly,
revolutionary groups in well-established democracies with large middle
classes are not likely to attract large numbers of people who want to overthrow the government but are more likely to operate as fringe groups. In
well-established democracies, therefore, terror is normally the tactic of
choice for ethnonationalist and revolutionary groups.

In contrast, in new, fragile, or partial democracies, where the rules of the
game are not fully settled and well accepted and where the law and the
courts may not be objective, dissatisfied groups—both ethnonationalist and

revolutionary—have less confidence that the government will fairly address their demands, and governments often have bad track records that support the dissatisfied groups' views. Consequently, such groups are able to attract large numbers of adherents willing to fight the central government, or to support those willing to do so, in order to overthrow the government, create their own sovereign territory, or claim a high degree of regional autonomy.

Finally, religious or millenarian groups are the wild card in this analysis, because religion can be a powerful motivator, as can cult worship, which the case of Aum Shinrikyo shows. The group had more than nine thousand members in Japan alone and, according to some observers (see the Parachini and Furakawa chapter), as many as thirty thousand members altogether. Moreover, the tactics these groups resort to are more difficult to predict, although in both our cases (the GIA and Aum Shinrikyo), terror was the tactic of choice.

OVERVIEW OF THE CASES

Table 1-4 provides some important statistics about the sixteen groups under study here. Columns one and two detail the groups employing terror tactics, their nature, and the governments targeted. Column three details the strength of the hard-core active members of each group—those who actually carry out the attacks or provide the wherewithal to make them happen—not the larger number of respective supporters and sympathizers. For example, the IRA had a core of active members only in the hundreds, but its active supporters numbered in the thousands, while its sympathizers—those willing to vote for its political wing—numbered in the tens of thousands. Similarly, Hizballah has always been quite choosy about who can join the hard-core active membership, but its supporters arguably number in the thousands or even tens of thousands. Column four provides the dates during which the group operated (or still operates). Not all groups that are counted as still active, however, operate with the degree of effectiveness and potency that they once showed (see below). Column five displays the number of people killed by the group, or by both the group and the government. When people killed by both the group and the government are listed, the figure generally includes noncombatants, group members, and government security forces.[6]

Table 1-4. Profile of Terrorist Groups

Terrorist Group	Government Targeted	Approximate Member Strength	Approximate Dates of Effective Operation	People Killed
Red Brigades (revolutionary)	Italy	800	1970–82	150 by the Red Brigades; 351 by all revolutionary leftists and fascist bands
IRA (ethnonationalist)	United Kingdom	Several hundred	1970–2005	3,365 on all sides
ETA (ethnonationalist)	Spain	Hundreds	1959–present	850 by ETA
GIA (religious/ millenarian)	France	Thousands in the 1990s; 30–100 today	1992–2006	12 French citizens killed in France; 100 expatriates killed in Algeria; several thousand Algerians killed
FALN (revolutionary)	Venezuela	2,000–3,000	1963–67	6,000 on both sides
Shining Path (revolutionary)	Peru	7,500–10,000 in the 1980s; 400–600 today	1980–present	69,280 people—civilians and government forces—killed or disappeared
FARC (revolutionary)	Colombia	16,000–20,000	1964–present	41,000–60,000 on all sides

Table 1-4, continued

Hamas and Fatah (ethnonationalist)	Israel	1987–present	500-plus Hamas; 1,000-plus Fatah	1,322 killed on both sides in the first intifada (1987–93); 622 killed on both sides from 1993 to April 1999; 4,390 killed on both sides in the second intifada (September 29, 2000–January 31, 2005)
Hizballah (ethnonationalist)	Israel	1982–present	5,000 in mid-1980s; hundreds–2,000 today	More than 900 Israeli soldiers killed by Hizballah in Lebanon between 1978 and 2000; 1,237 Hizballah fighters killed between June 1982 and May 2000
PKK (ethnonationalist)	Turkey	1984–99	10,000 in mid-1990s; 4,000–5,000 today	30,000 on both sides
Chechen rebels (ethnonationalist)	Russia	1994–present	2,000–3,000	40,000–70,000 on both sides
Sikhs (ethnonationalist)	India	1980–93	Hundreds–2,000	19,359 civilians, police officers, and terrorists
Kashmiri Jihadis (ethnonationalist)	India	1989–present	3,500–4,000	35,000–65,000 killed on all sides
Tamil Tigers (ethnonationalist)	Sri Lanka	1976–present	8,000–10,000	60,000–65,000 killed on both sides
Aum Shinrikyo (religious/ millenarian)	Japan	1987–present	9,000 claimed in 1990s; 1,500–2,000 today	12 killed in 1995 Tokyo subway attack

We must stress that reliable figures on group membership and numbers of people killed are difficult to come by. For obvious security reasons, the groups studied in this volume did not make their membership lists public, and member strength varied over time for each group. In table 1-4, we have provided our best estimates of peak member strength when the group was most active, and, where available, current membership figures. Figures on the numbers of people killed are especially hard to come by, particularly for conflicts that involved counterinsurgency operations. In such conflicts, both the groups and the governments involved had political incentives either to exaggerate or to minimize the numbers of deaths that occurred.

Finally, the figures on people killed mix apples and oranges to a degree because we have relied on several databases that are not consistent with one another. In four cases—the Red Brigades, ETA, the GIA, and Aum Shinrikyo—we provide data only for numbers of people killed by terrorists, because the differences between those numbers and the total numbers killed (including killing by the government) is very small. In the other cases, with the exception of Hizballah, we have figures for the total number of people killed by both the terrorist groups and the governmental forces arrayed against them, and this total generally includes terrorists, governmental forces, and civilians. The case of Hizballah appears to have the greatest difference between the number of people killed by terrorists and the total number killed by both terrorist and governmental forces. A large number of civilians were killed as a result of Israeli defense activities against Hizballah in southern Lebanon, but it is difficult to know exactly how many.[7] For all these reasons, the data in columns three and five in particular should be treated as rough estimates rather than definitive and exact numbers. The appendix at the end of this volume details the sources for the figures provided in columns three and five.

Four important conclusions emerge from table 1-4. First, nearly all the groups operated for long periods, and all but six—the Red Brigades, the FALN, the Sikhs, the ETA, the IRA, and Aum Shinrikyo (which no longer engages in terrorism)—are still actively operating today, even though some—ETA, the PKK, and Shining Path—are doing so with severely reduced effectiveness. Counterinsurgency wars against guerrilla groups that also employ terrorism are generally drawn-out affairs because counterinsurgency efforts by nature take a long time. The government's quick dispatch of the FALN in Venezuela in the 1960s is the exception, not the rule, for

Table 1-5. Terrorist Groups by Member Strength

2,000 or Fewer	More Than 2,000
Red Brigades	FALN
IRA	PKK
ETA	Chechen rebels
GIA (in France)	Shining Path
Hamas and Fatah	FARC
Sikhs	Kashmiri Jihadis
	Hizballah
	Tamil Tigers
	Aum Shinrikyo

counterinsurgency campaigns. However, even small groups such as the Red Brigades, the IRA, or ETA, which employ only terror tactics, can bedevil governments for years. The obvious lesson here is that campaigns against groups that employ terrorism are not short-lived affairs. Usually, progress must be measured in decades, not years.

Second, there is a nearly perfect correlation between the size of the group, on the one hand, and the tactics employed, on the other. (Table 1-5 breaks out groups according to member strength.) The groups with smaller memberships (Fatah being the exception)—the Red Brigades, the IRA, ETA, the GIA, Hamas, and the Sikhs—primarily used terror tactics. The groups with larger memberships (more than two thousand members)—the FALN, the PKK, the Chechen rebels, Shining Path, the FARC, the Kashmiri Jihadis, Hizballah, and the Tamil Tigers—resorted to both terror and guerrilla tactics. The larger groups had more members because the insurgency wars they waged required larger forces than did terror-only tactics. Aum Shinrikyo is the other exception to this generalization: it had a very large membership but used only terror tactics.

Third, there is no correlation between groups with large memberships, on the one hand, and the nature of the democratic states they targeted, on the other. Five of the nine groups with large membership—the FALN, the FARC, Shining Path, the Chechen rebels, and the PKK—operated against new, fragile, or partial democracies. The remaining four groups with large memberships—Aum Shinrikyo, Hizballah, the Kashmiri Jihadis, and the Tamil Tigers—fought against more mature democracies. It appears that both mature and not-so-mature democracies can suffer groups with large memberships that resort to a combination of terror and guerrilla tactics.

Finally, not surprisingly, the biggest death tolls (more than ten thousand) occurred in those states that battled large groups employing both guerrilla and terror tactics. Hizballah is an exception because it operated mainly outside Israel and mostly against the Israeli army in Lebanon, not against Israeli civilians in Israel (except for rocket attacks into Israel).[8] The medium and low death tolls (fewer than ten thousand) occurred mostly in those states with groups that relied solely or primarily on terror tactics, with two exceptions—Hizballah and the FALN, both of which also resorted to guerrilla tactics. Table 1-6 breaks out the death toll into low, medium, and high categories.

Table 1-6. Terrorist Groups and the Death Toll

Low (Fewer Than 2,000)	Medium (2,000–10,000)	High (More Than 10,000)
ETA	IRA	PKK
Red Brigades	FALN	Chechen rebels
Aum Shinrikyo	Hamas and Fatah	Shining Path
GIA	Hizballah	Tamil Tigers
		FARC
		Kashmiri Jihadis
		Sikhs

COUNTERTERRORISM POLICIES AND THE CASES

A state can use a range of counterterrorism policies, strategies, and instruments to combat groups resorting to terror. For purposes of this volume, we have grouped these measures into three categories: political measures, legislative and judicial measures, and security measures.

- **Political measures** include negotiations with groups (in which the government makes compromises and concessions) to bring about the end of resistance; socioeconomic and political reforms to win the "hearts and minds" of people from whom the terrorists draw both armed adherents and more general support; and international cooperation to cut off funds to terrorists, extradite terrorists, police borders, and provide intelligence to the state under siege.

- **Legislative and judicial measures** include emergency and other special legislation to expand the government's power to arrest, detain, and incarcerate suspects and to gain intelligence about them in ways that involve infringements on citizens' privacy; use of the courts to empower the state and special magistrates and prosecutors to undertake broad investigative actions; legislation to disrupt the finances of groups employing terrorism; and amnesty and repentance measures designed to wean active armed members from such groups and to reintegrate them into society.

- **Security measures** include military deployments to protect the population and to seek out and destroy terrorist groups; intelligence operations, especially the use of counterterrorist units to penetrate terrorist networks and disrupt their logistics and support networks; new organizational machinery to coordinate the security instruments and disparate units of government dealing with terrorism; and preventive actions for defense, such as the hardening of facilities, control of access, and the like.

Not all of the thirteen governments studied in this volume employed every one of the above measures, and each government had its own particular way of utilizing the measures. Furthermore, the relative importance of the measures adopted differed across the cases, although good intelligence was critical to every case in which the government enjoyed success. In most cases, the government employed a large number of the measures, and in the conclusion we analyze the commonalities and the contrasts among the cases with respect to how governments used the above counterterrorism instruments.

In order that these comparisons could be drawn and lessons for counterterrorism extracted from them, the authors were asked to keep a set of questions in mind in writing about their cases. Every case study treats the questions in a different manner because the cases by necessity differ, but all the cases deal with the questions in one form or another. These are the questions the contributors were asked to keep in mind:

- What were (are) the nature, the modus operandi, and the aims of the group fighting the government, as well as the dynamics of the conflict?
- What were (are) the elements of the government's counterterrorist policy?

- Which policies used by the government worked, which did not work, and why?
- How adaptable was (is) the terrorist group to policies the government employed, and how adaptable was (is) the government in return?
- How did (has) the terrorist-counterterrorist struggle change(d) over time?
- What were the key factors enabling the government to prevail, if indeed it did prevail, and if it failed, what were the key factors for failure?
- Did (has) the government make (made) significant concessions to the terrorists' demands?
- Did the international environment contribute to the success or failure of the government's counterterrorist campaign, and if so, how?

The fourteen case-study chapters appear in the order in which they are listed in table 1-4, which is presented geographically. Each chapter begins with a brief overview of the facts of the case, followed by an in-depth analysis of the policies and techniques that the government in question employed against the groups it faced. Finally, each author draws lessons from his or her particular case and assesses which of the counterterrorist instruments seemed to prove most effective in combating the terrorist threat. We now turn to the case studies.

Appendix: Sources for Table 1-4

Red Brigades

- Member strength: William Eubank and Leonard Weinberg, *The Rise and Fall of Italian Terrorism* (Boulder, CO: Westview, 1987), 77–103.
- People killed: Donatella della Porta and Maurizio Rossi, *Cifre crudeli: Bilancio dei terrorismi italiani* (Bologna: Istituto Cattaneo, 1984), 67–71.

IRA

- Member strength: U.S. Department of State, Office of the Coordinator for Counterterrorism, *Patterns of Global Terrorism: 2003* (hereafter cited as *PGT: 2003*), Appendix C (April 2004).

- People killed: Northern Ireland, Department of Finance and Personnel, "Deaths and Injuries as a Result of the Security Situation, 1969 to 2003–04," *Northern Ireland Annual Abstract of Statistics 2003* (Belfast: Northern Ireland Statistics and Research Agency, 2004), 81.

ETA

- Member strength: *PGT: 2003,* Appendix B.
- People killed: *PGT: 2003,* Appendix B.

GIA

- Member strength: Agence France Presse, "Algeria's Deadliest Armed Group Virtually Wiped Out: Government," January 4, 2005; *PGT: 2003,* Appendix B; and International Institute for Strategic Studies, *The Military Balance: 2003–2004* (hereafter cited as *TMB: 2003–2004*) (London: Oxford University Press, 2003), 364.
- People killed: "France Puts Muslim Militants on Trial for Bombings That Killed Eight," *Independent,* November 25, 1997, 12; and *PGT: 2003,* Appendix B.

FALN

- Member strength: Norman Gall, "Teodoro Petkoff: The Crisis of the Professional Revolutionary, Part 1: Years of Insurrection" (American Universities Field Staff Report, January 1972), www.normangall.com/venezuela_art4.htm.
- People killed: Peter Calvert, "Terrorism in Venezuela," in *Encyclopedia of World Terrorism,* eds. Martha Crenshaw and John Pimlott (Armonk, NY: M. E. Sharpe, 1997), 455.

Shining Path

- Member strength: David Scott Palmer, "The Revolutionary Terrorism of Peru's Shining Path," in Martha Crenshaw, ed., *Terrorism in Context* (University Park: Pennsylvania University Press, 1995), 273–306; *PGT: 2003,* Appendix B; and *TMB: 2004–2005,* 374.
- People killed: Comisión de la Verdad y Reconciliación Perú, *Informe final,* vol. 1, *Primera parte: El proceso, los hechos, las víctimas* (Lima: Navarrete, 2003), 169.

FARC

- Member strength: Eduardo Pizarro, *Kolumbien: Aktuelle Situation und Zukunftsperspektiven für ein Land im Konflikt,* Analysen und Berichte, no. 4 (Rio de Janeiro: Konrad-Adenauer-Stiftung, November 2001), 29; and Heidrun Zinecker, *Kolumbien: Wie viel Demokratisierung braucht der Frieden,* Report 2/2002 (Frankfurt am Main: HSFK, 2002), 9.
- People killed: Monty G. Marshall (principal investigator), "Major Episodes of Political Violence, 1946–2002" (Center for Systemic Peace; Center for International Development and Conflict Management, University of Maryland, updated January 15, 2005); and Stockholm International Peace Research Institute, *SIPRI Yearbook 2004: Armaments, Disarmament and International Security* (London: Oxford University Press, 2004), 102, 140.

Hamas and Fatah

- Member strength: *TMB: 2004–2005,* 366–67.
- People killed: B'Tselem, The Israeli Information Center for Human Rights in the Occupied Territories, Statistics, "Israelis Killed in the Occupied Territories (including East Jerusalem)," B'Tselem, Publications, "Olso: Before and After, the Status of Human Rights in the Occupied Territories" (May 1999); and B'Tselem, Statistics, "Intifada Fatalities," www.btselem.org.

Hizballah

- Member strength: Magnus Ranstorp, *Hizb 'allah in Lebanon: The Politics of the Western Hostage Crisis* (New York: St. Martin's, 1997), 53; and A. Nizar Hamzeh, "Islamism in Lebanon: A Guide," *Middle East Review of International Affairs* 1, no. 3 (Spring 1997), http://meria.idc.ac.il/journal/1997/issue3/jv1n3a2.html. Other experts report that Hizballah had five thousand fighters and five thousand more reservists by the end of the 1980s. See Carl Anthony Wege, "Hizbollah Organization," *Studies in Conflict and Terrorism* 17, no. 2 (April–June 1994): 155; *PGT: 2003,* Appendix B; and *TMB: 2003–2004,* 346.
- People killed: William Stewart, "How Many Must Die?" *Time,* February 17, 1997, 43; Dilip Hiro, *Lebanon: Fire and Embers* (New York: St. Martin's, 1992), 105; Roula Khalaf, "A Guerilla with Charm: Sheikh

Hassan Nasrallah," *Financial Times,* May 27, 2000, 15; and Clyde R. Mark and Alfred B. Prados, *Lebanon,* no. 1B89118 (Congressional Research Service, updated June 10, 2005).

PKK

- Member strength: Ismet Imset, *PKK: Ayrilikci Siddetin 20 Yili (1973–1992)* (Ankara: Turkish Daily News, 1993), 188; *PGT: 2003,* Appendix B; and *TMB: 2004–2005, 362.*
- People killed: John B. Grant, "Turkey's Counterinsurgency Campaign against the PKK: Lessons Learned from a Dirty War" (unpublished thesis, Faculty of the Joint Military Intelligence College, June 2002), 1; and *SIPRI Yearbook 2002,* 142.

Chechen rebels

- Member strength: *TMB: 2004–2005, 364.*
- People killed: *SIPRI Yearbook 2004,* 142; and "Group Claims 25,000 Russian Soldiers Have Died in Chechnya," *Eurasian Daily Monitor* 1, no. 3 (May 5, 2004).

Sikhs

- Member strength: Data compiled by Paul Wallace from interviews; *Tribune,* March 31, 1989, 1; *Times of India,* April 10, 1988, 1; *India Today,* April 20, 1988, 35–36; and *Times of India,* March 17, 1989, 7.
- People killed: Government of India, Ministry of Home Affairs, National Integration Council, Meeting December 31, 1991. Annexure-1, *Profile of Violence in Punjab,* 11; Office of the Director-General of Police, Punjab, as cited in K. P. S. Gill, "The Dangers Within: Internal Security Threats," in *Future Imperiled: India's Security in the 1990s and Beyond,* ed. Bharat Karnad (New Delhi: Viking Penguin, 1994), 118, 120.

Kashmiri Jihadis

- Member strength: *SIPRI Yearbook 2002,* 45.
- People killed: *SIPRI Yearbook 2004,* 141; BBC News, "Soldiers Killed in Kashmir Attack," March 28, 2005; Praveen Swami, "Quickstep or Kadam Taal? The Elusive Search for Peace in Jammu and Kashmir,"

Special Report no. 133 (United States Institute of Peace, March 2005), fig. 2, "Fatalities from Violence in Jammu and Kashmir, 1989–2004."

Tamil Tigers

- Member strength: *PGT: 2003,* Appendix B.
- People killed: *SIPRI Yearbook 2003,* 98, 119.

Aum Shinrikyo

- Member strength: *PGT: 2003,* Appendix B; and *TMB: 2004–2005,* 372.
- People killed: *PGT: 2003,* Appendix B.

NOTES

1. See Bruce Hoffman, *Inside Terrorism* (New York: Columbia University Press, 1998), 43. See his discussion in chapter 1 for the different meanings and evolution of the term *terrorism.*

2. Martha Crenshaw at a Congressional Research Service seminar in 2002, quoted in Nina M. Serafino, *Comparative Terrorism: Possible Lessons for U.S. Policy from Foreign Experiences, Summary of the Major Points of a Seminar* (Washington, DC: Congressional Research Service, July 24, 2002), 16.

3. See Alex Schmid and Ronald Crelinsten, eds., *Western Responses to Terrorism* (London: Frank Cass, 1993); David Charters, ed., *The Deadly Sin of Terrorism: Its Effect on Democracy and Civil Liberties in Six Countries* (Westport, CT: Greenwood, 1994); Bruce Hoffman and Jennifer Morrison Taw, *A Strategic Framework for Countering Terrorism and Insurgency* (Santa Monica, CA: RAND, 1992); C. Christine Fair, *Urban Battle Fields of South Asia: Lessons Learned from Sri Lanka, India, and Pakistan* (Santa Monica, CA: RAND, 2004); and Yonah Alexander, ed., *Combating Terrorism: Strategies of Ten Countries* (Ann Arbor: University of Michigan Press, 2002).

4. It must be noted, however, that two of our groups, LTTE and the FARC, moved beyond guerrilla warfare to the use of main-force units or regular conventional warfare.

5. See Hoffman, *Inside Terrorism,* 41.

6. We thank the authors of the case studies for their help in providing us with these figures and for suggesting where to track down the ones they could not provide.

7. The Congressional Research Service (CRS) estimates that between 1978 and 2000, twenty-one hundred Palestinian and Lebanese guerrillas lost their lives, and twenty-one thousand Lebanese civilians died in clashes with the Israeli Defense Forces (IDF) and the Southern Lebanese Army (SLA). A difficulty with the twenty-one-thousand figure is that it does not break out numbers of civilians killed by IDF and SLA operations against Hizballah and by the IDF in its general operations in Lebanon, especially in the first few years after the initial invasion and the subsequent attack on Beirut. See the appendix for the full citation for the CRS source.

8. We put Hizballah in the medium-death-toll category on the basis of our estimate that the bulk of the twenty-one thousand civilian deaths caused by IDF operations in Lebanon occurred in the early years of Israel's occupation of Lebanon, not in subsequent years during IDF operations against Hizballah in southern Lebanon.

2

THE RED BRIGADES

Leonard Weinberg

> *"We are living in terrible moments. . . . It is as though we are in the catacombs."*
> —Aldo Moro

The Brigate Rosse (BR; Red Brigades) was the most successful and enduring of the various western European revolutionary terrorist organizations that emerged from the generation of 1968. In fact, the use of the past tense needs to be qualified. A revived BR, one with a modified name (Red Brigades—Party of Communist Combatants), succeeded in assassinating two government economic advisers—professors Marco Biagi (Bologna, 2002) and Massimo D'Antona (Rome, 2003)—in the past few years. Although the BR's founders, the so-called historic nucleus, have long since passed into middle age and beyond, a new generation of *brigatisti* has appeared at the beginning of the twenty-first century to pursue the work begun more than thirty years ago.[1]

Despite the BR's endurance, the Italian government did succeed in defeating and marginalizing it in the early 1980s, to a point where the organization no longer poses a significant challenge to Italy's troubled democratic institutions. The point of this commentary is to explain how the latter brought about the BR's defeat, if not its complete demise. To accomplish this task, we need to tell the story of the BR, from its origins in the "hot

autumn" of 1969 to its devastating setbacks following the 1982 liberation of
U.S. NATO general James Dozier from his BR captors by a special unit of
the state police.

As we seek to understand the trajectory of some terrorist campaigns, it
is sufficient to explain the immediate milieu from which the terrorist organization emerged and the specific events that triggered the violence. In
these instances, it is often unnecessary to capture the picture with a wider
lens; a narrow one will do because all that needs to be explained can be
explained without reference to the general social and political conditions
prevailing within the country where the terrorist campaign was launched.
As Walter Laqueur noted many years ago, understanding the demographic
characteristics of California is neither helpful nor necessary in explaining
the career of the Symbionese Liberation Army.[2] We might add that knowing much about the structure of competition between Republicans and
Democrats in Washington, D.C., during the early 1970s would not be of
much help either.

This is not the case with the BR, however. It did not appear from thin
air or the minds of a handful of exotic, violence-intoxicated individuals. To
understand this terrorist band, we must outline at least the major characteristics of Italian political life during the late 1960s and early 1970s.[3]

Following this overview of Italian politics in these crisis-ridden years, we
describe the history of the BR, from its formation in 1970 to its defeat more
than a decade later. As part of this discussion, we offer a more general analysis of BR characteristics, including its membership, organizational attributes,
links (limited) to other terrorist groups, and the casualties it inflicted. Next,
we investigate the organizational and juridical responses of the Italian state
to the threat posed by the BR; we also pay attention to the initially hesitant
roles played by the Communist Party (PCI) and the country's trade union
movement in undermining working-class BR support. Finally, we extrapo-
late from Italy's experience in defeating the revolutionary terrorism of the
1970s to the contemporary situation, as the United States and other "cru-
sader" countries seek to end the threat posed to them by al Qaeda and other
violent Islamist groups scattered around the world.[4]

A few words about the scale of the Italian problem are required. Between
1969 and 1982, terrorist groups on both the left and the right committed a
total of 4,362 attacks on people and 6,153 bombings of property. Revolutionary leftist groups, including the BR, and various neofascist bands killed

351 people and seriously injured another 768.[5] According to a 1984 public opinion poll, a plurality of Italians selected "terrorism" as the most significant problem the country had had to confront over the preceding fifty years, an era that included the fall of the Mussolini dictatorship, the instauration of democratic rule, an economic "miracle," and the rise of the largest communist party in western Europe. Although Italian terrorism in general and the BR more specifically may not rival al Qaeda in global impact, from the point of view of many Italians, terrorism was an experience of dramatic, if not singular, significance in their collective memory.

ITALIAN POLITICS AND THE RED BRIGADES

Italian politics had been dominated by the Christian Democratic Party (DC) from the end of World War II through the era with which we are concerned. From 1963 forward, the DC had governed in a center-left coalition with the Socialist Party (PSI), as well as such small parties as the Republicans and Social Democrats. Supporters of this "cautious marriage" had hoped it would bring about important economic and social reforms. They also hoped that the parliamentary majority would be large and stable enough to slow, if not end, the procession of short-lived governments that had come and gone at the rate of one per year over the previous decade. There was also the hope, less openly expressed, that the entry of the Marxist PSI into government would weaken Italy's powerful PCI, which would become increasingly isolated and marginalized.

Polarization of Politics

By the late 1960s, none of these expectations had been realized. The reforms that were carried out were few and far between. DC-led governments were coming and going at about the usual pace. And the PCI, rather than losing support or weakening its grip on important local and national institutions (e.g., the National Federation of Italian Workers), was gaining strength and expanding the scope of its activities beyond its working-class and peasant base. The level of popular support among Italians for the country's democratic system (at least as it was seen as functioning) declined precipitously during the 1960s, as many citizens came to view their state as corrupt and incompetent.[6]

Despite the fact that the U.S. government had spent close to $70 million over the preceding decades to reduce the PCI's role in Italian political life, the party's influence continued to expand. But the PCI appeared to many observers to be a far cry from a conventional communist party. In 1968 its leaders, notably Luigi Longo and Enrico Berlinguer, openly expressed their displeasure with the Soviet invasion of Czechoslovakia as a way of ending that country's experiment with "communism with a human face." More generally, PCI spokesmen refused to accept the discipline of the Communist International. Nor did they express much enthusiasm for the Great Proletarian Cultural Revolution then underway in China.

On the domestic front, by the end of the 1960s, the PCI leadership was advancing the principles of pluralism, constitutional rights, and peaceful social and economic reform. By the early 1970s, the PCI had become the leading advocate of "euro-communism," the view that the Soviet model was totally inappropriate for conditions prevailing in the advanced industrialized democracies of western Europe. These views became music to the ears of large numbers of reform-minded middle-class Italians. The PCI benefited at the polls as a result. The party's reputation for honesty and efficiency in its administration of such local governments as those of Bologna and Reggio Emilia added to its luster.

But the PCI's effort to depict itself as a largely social democratic party in all but name came with a price attached. The cost was the disaffection of large numbers of those on the left who regarded the views of Marx, Lenin, Mao, and their disciples with utmost seriousness, and who considered the cause of proletarian revolution to be virtually sacred. In short, by the end of the 1960s, a significant "extraparliamentary left" had appeared.

At first, the latter seemed little more than a collection of small fringe groups, which published equally small-circulation magazines at irregular intervals. Each group had its own take on Italy's doomed capitalist system, but Worker Power (Potere Operaio, or POTOP), Worker Autonomy (Autonomia Operaio, or AO), Continuous Struggle (Lotta Continua, or LC), and others shared a belief in the necessity of violent revolution.[7]

Under normal circumstances, the efforts of these extraparliamentary left groups in Italy (as elsewhere) would not have amounted to much. But conditions in Italy at the end of the 1960s and beginning of the 1970s were anything but normal. By pursuing a course of moderation and democratic legitimacy, the PCI inadvertently created a political space to its left, one the extraparliamentary groups rushed to fill. The size of that space expanded dramatically in these years as hundreds of thousands of northern Italians rose in protest against declining economic conditions, the structure of the universities and education more generally, the Vietnam War, and their country's continued participation in NATO and other perceived instruments of U.S. imperialism. More specifically, there were massive student protests throughout northern and central Italy in 1967–68. These were followed by the "hot autumn" of 1969, when labor contracts came up for renewal and vast numbers of workers in Turin, Milan, Genoa, and other industrial centers staged major work stoppages and became caught up in massive waves of protest and agitation. It was against this radicalized background and near-incandescent atmosphere that the BR made its appearance.

In addition to an extraparliamentary left, whose leaders or "movement entrepreneurs" were deep in the dream of revolution, Italy, unlike most countries in western Europe, had a significant extreme right, with leaders who did not cringe at the term *neofascist* and whose own thoughts turned to the prospects of a restored "strong state," one they hoped would use whatever force was necessary to repress the "Reds" and the worldwide communist threat they represented. By the end of the decade, the immediate inspiration for some neofascist leaders was the antileftist military coup in Greece that brought the colonels to power in Athens in 1967.[8] In fact, neofascists linked to the National Front and other far-right followers of the fascist military hero Prince Valerio Borghese apparently attempted just such a coup (code name Tora! Tora! Tora!) in Rome in December 1970. At the time, allegations were widespread that the neofascists had collaborators within Italy's police and military establishment—collaborators who got cold feet at the last moment.

When the BR surfaced for the first time in Milan in 1970, Italy's neofascist scene appeared as follows. There was the Italian Social Movement (Movimento Sociale Italiano, or MSI), a party rooted in the country's fascist past and at the polls the most successful of western Europe's far-right parties in this era. For years its leaders had pursued a policy of caution, aimed at making the MSI a palatable coalition partner with other right-wing parties. This policy of "insertion" had come to nothing, and in 1968 the MSI leadership fell into the hands of Giorgio Almirante and Giuseppe "Pino" Rauti, who were committed to a more radical course of action.

The new direction was labeled the "strategy of tensions" and involved public demands by the MSI for a restoration of law and order in the country on behalf of a *maggioranza silenziosa*, a silent majority of Italians fed up with all the left-wing agitation, protest, and disruption, which by this time had achieved major magnitude, especially in the northern part of the country. While appealing for law and order, the MSI was in fact playing a double game, one that actually stimulated violence and disorder. The underlying logic behind the strategy of tensions was "the worse the better." The more violence and disorder in the country, especially if it could be blamed on the far left (the Reds), the more the Italian public would be prepared to tolerate a seizure of power by the military, with sotto voce neofascist participation.

Just as the left had its extraparliamentary organizations, so too did the right. In the years leading up to the formation of the BR, a substantial list of explicitly neofascist, or in a few instances neo-Nazi, groups appeared. Their leaders were less interested in the electoral process and more interested in violent, physical confrontations with the Reds. The most prominent of these far-right groups were the New Order (Ordine Nuovo, or ON), the National Vanguard (Avanguardia Nazionale, or AN), and the National Front (Fronte Nazionale, or FN). But Milan, Rome, and some southern cities quickly abounded with Mussolini Action Squads and local units of the National Revolutionary Front, the Black Eagles, and a number of other bands.[9]

The event that more than any other set off Italy's decade-plus period of terrorist violence was the bombing of the National Agricultural Bank in Piazza Fontana in Milan on the afternoon of December 12, 1969 (other explosions were set off in other cities almost simultaneously). Sixteen bank customers were killed and many more were injured by the blast.

The tale is extremely complicated. Suffice it to say, the police quickly arrested two Milanese anarchists and accused them of the massacre. One of the accused anarchists, Giuseppe Pinelli, then died while in custody by falling out of a window at Milan's police headquarters. The police said suicide, but the press and much of the public quickly reached the conclusion that he had been murdered to keep him quiet.

Over the course of a long judicial investigation, it became clear that the bombing was really the responsibility of neofascists, who had sought to create new political identities as left-wing revolutionaries in the months preceding the *strage* (massacre). Furthermore, members of Italy's police and military establishment were implicated in the killings. Along with key neofascist figures, they were engaged in the strategy of tensions, hoping the Italian public would be so infuriated by the Piazza Fontana killings that it would be prepared to accept a coup d'état.

The details of the case took years to uncover, but the overall pattern became clear very quickly. Those on the left promptly labeled the bombing a state-sponsored massacre involving collaboration between neofascist figures and elements within the state—the police and military in particular. By the beginning of 1970, many on the left began to see parallels between the situation and the original fascist seizure of power at the end of October 1922. The rhetoric may have been somewhat overheated, but in the year the BR was organized, some Italians had reached the conclusion that taking up arms against the system was equivalent to fighting against the return of fascism. This was the political context in which the BR was organized, a situation in which many on the left, for example Giangiacomo Feltrinelli (heir to a multimillion-dollar publishing fortune and a revolutionary friend of Fidel Castro), defined as their struggle the defeat of a state propelling itself in a fascist direction. In fact, Renato Curcio, one of the BR's founders, initially defined his organization as continuing the struggle against fascism begun by the country's World War II resistance movement, a struggle in which a beloved uncle had lost his life.[10]

The BR emerged as the result of a "strategic decision" by members of a Milanese group known as the Political Metropolitan Collective (CPM) to initiate a campaign of revolutionary violence. The CPM itself had appeared in 1969 and was composed of students from the University of Trent (Italy's first university devoted exclusively to the social sciences) and young workers belonging to various grassroots groups (Comitato Unitario di Base, or CUBs) at Pirelli, Sit-Siemens, and Alfa Romeo plants, typically individuals who found the large trade union federations too willing to compromise with the bosses. Members of the CPM were joined shortly by defectors from the PCI's Young Communist Federation in Reggio Emilia. The latter had concluded that the PCI had abandoned its historic revolutionary mission.[11] The result of this encounter was the Proletarian Left, an organization committed to a campaign of "armed propaganda." By the middle of 1971, this organization had mutated into the BR and had begun a campaign aimed at mobilizing workers in the various Milanese plants and factories for revolutionary action.

It is important to remember that during the so-called Years of Lead, the BR was the largest, most murderous, and most successful—but far from the only—far-left group engaged in an armed struggle with the state. There were, in addition, Front Line (Prima Linea, or PL), the Nuclei of Armed Proletarians (NAP), and the Fighting Communist Formations (FCF), along with a not inconsiderable list of minor, short-lived bands. The state's efforts, as a consequence, were directed not only at the elimination of the BR but also at the defeat of these other groups. The Italian government responded to this challenge, haltingly to be sure, by establishing a division of labor. Since the BR posed the greatest danger, it became the target of a special unit of carabinieri, specifically responsible for its defeat.

Phases of the Battle against the BR

Gian Carlo Caselli and Donatella della Porta divide the BR's subsequent history into four distinct periods.[12] They are the periods of "armed propaganda" (1970–74); "the attack on the heart of the state" (1974–76); "the strategy of destruction" (1976–78); and "the military confrontation with the state" (1979–82).

Phase One. During the first phase, the BR largely confined its activities to Milan and Turin, the two major industrial cities of the north. BR violence—industrial sabotage for the most part but also the kidnapping of several business executives—was largely conducted within or in the vicinity of these cities' major industries. No one was killed. The purpose behind this phase of the "armed struggle" was to catch the attention of blue-collar workers and to recruit the most militant among them to the cause. To a considerable extent, the BR succeeded. By using techniques borrowed from Uruguay's Tupamaros (e.g., "people's trials" in which hapless personnel directors were forced to wear dunce caps and confess their crimes against the proletariat), the BR was able to recruit a significant number of working-class members, particularly from the Fiat Mirafiori plant outside Turin. To be sure, the organization was also able to win new university student recruits from POTOP and the other extraparliamentary groups mentioned above, but unlike other revolutionary terrorist organizations active in the Western democracies at about the same time, the BR managed to develop a base of support among members of the social class whose interests it claimed to represent. Despite this fact, the PCI's initial view of the BR was one of skepticism. The party's press questioned the authenticity of the BR's left-wing credentials, preferring to believe that the BR was likely part of the strategy of tensions and that its members were probably crypto-fascists. It would take some time before the PCI and others on the left would come to realize that the BR was part of their own "family album."

Phase Two. The second period in the BR's career was "the attack on the heart of the state" (1974–76), and it began with the kidnapping of a right-wing Genovese magistrate, Mario Sossi. (Sossi was subsequently released after his superior, Francesco Coco, agreed to release nine BR prisoners in exchange.) This was the first time the organization deliberately targeted a representative of the Italian state. The year 1974 was also the first year in which the BR killed anyone. In this case, two MSI members were gunned down during a raid on the movement's Padua headquarters.[13] In these years, the BR spread geographically by establishing "columns" and "fronts" in Genoa, the Veneto, and Rome. Its targets expanded to include not only representatives of state authority but also "reactionary" political parties, the DC most notably. BR leaders forged what proved to be a short-lived alliance with the Naples-based NAP. The shift away from northern factories and efforts at armed propaganda within them produced a certain degree of internal opposition. A minority of brigatisti objected to the move away from the factories and toward a "military" confrontation with the representatives of state power. Appropriately enough, this phase of activity included the use of pistols and machine guns, not only to threaten and intimidate but also to injure ("kneecap") and kill political targets. Citing Lenin, resolutions of the BR's Strategic Direction asserted the need to attack the state at its weakest links and to define Italy itself as under the control of the Imperialist State of the Multinationals.

In addition to being a time of stepped-up BR violence, the period 1974–76 was also a time in which neofascist groups set off explosives on trains and in public squares, causing multiple fatalities. In response to enormous public pressure, the DC-led government of Mariano Rumor decided to act. A General Inspectorate against Terrorism and Armed Bands was created in the Interior Ministry, aimed primarily against the neofascist bands. Carlo Alberto Dalla Chiesa, a carabinieri general, was appointed to head a task force in Turin to investigate the BR in the aftermath of the Sossi kidnapping. Earlier, Dalla Chiesa, who had experience fighting the Mafia in Sicily, had developed a reputation for competence based on his reorganization of the prison system, in part by creating special high-security prisons to make it more difficult for terrorists to escape. In Turin, Dalla Chiesa was able to select a staff of forty carabinieri officers drawn from various regions.

The task of defeating the BR at this point proved less than formidable. Dalla Chiesa's unit was able to plant a spy inside the BR. He supplied the authorities with information about the organization's plans, along with the names and whereabouts of its leaders. Arrests followed. When the leading brigatisti were arrested in their hideouts, the police also uncovered a treasure trove of documents, including membership lists and important information about the BR's evolving organizational format. More arrests followed; by the middle of 1976, it appeared that the government had broken the back of the BR. By one estimate, only twelve BR "regulars" remained at large; virtually the entire "historic nucleus" of founders and leaders was in custody awaiting trial. Its task of defeating the BR having apparently been accomplished, Dalla Chiesa's unit was dissolved and its staff of carabinieri returned to their regular duties.

If this setback had proven to be the end of the BR, the organization's fate would have resembled those of other revolutionary terrorist groups active at about the same time in the Western democracies. These groups had typically appeared as the large protest movements of the late 1960s lost their momentum, waging terrorist campaigns for a few years until they either imploded or were dismantled by the authorities. Italy was different, however. The BR did not go away. In fact, during the second half of the 1970s, its membership expanded significantly, and its violent acts became both more frequent and more lethal. Furthermore, during this half decade, the BR was joined in the armed struggle by a number of newly formed revolutionary terrorist bands, the largest of which was Front Line.[14]

Phase Three. The third phase of the BR's career, which Caselli and della Porta label "the strategy of destruction," began in the middle of 1976 when a BR commando murdered Genoa's state prosecutor, Francesco Coco (who had reneged on his promise to release BR prisoners in exchange for Mario Sossi's freedom; see above), along with his two bodyguards. The third period ended in 1978 in the months following the organization's kidnapping and subsequent murder, fifty-five days later, of Aldo Moro, a former DC prime minister and one of Italy's foremost postwar political figures.

A number of events in 1976–77 helped revive BR activity. There was widespread hope on the left that the crucial June 1976 parliamentary elections would result in a PCI victory—that the party would finally "surpass" the DC at the polls and bring an end to its rule. Instead, the DC's electoral performance was better than expected; it continued to hold the reins of power and left many young people with the impression that this condition would persist in perpetuity. The PCI under Berlinguer hardly committed itself to looking for exits from capitalism. In a period of "galloping" inflation and government fragility, the Communist Party leader proposed (citing the Chilean experience under Allende) a "historic compromise" with the DC (and PSI), to share power in a coalition government. Furthermore, during the election campaign, Berlinguer had expressed support for Italy's continued membership in the NATO alliance. In other words, those on the far left defined the PCI as having committed itself to propping up the system rather than bringing about its replacement.

Against this background, there was a revival of mass agitation and protest in 1977. "Metropolitan Indians" (they painted their faces red) took to the streets of Rome. Luciano Lama, head of the PCI-dominated General Confederation of Italian Workers (CGIL), was heckled and shouted down when he attempted to deliver a speech at the University of Rome (bodyguards had to protect him from the students' wrath). In Bologna, which had had a PCI mayor continuously since 1948, university students staged massive protests against the municipality; the PCI-dominated city council called for police intervention to quell the disturbances.

The BR now attracted a whole new generation of recruits who were younger, less ideologically sophisticated, and more violent than their predecessors. Many of them flowed into the organization from the extraparliamentary left groups, LC and POTOP's successor Autonomia Operaio in particular. These ultraleft groups often engaged in violent confrontations with the authorities and street-corner scuffles with neofascist toughs. In other words, the new brigatisti had already become practiced in the use of political violence before joining the BR. As a result, the new recruits and their leaders were far less inhibited in their use of violence than the first wave of BR regulars. Attacks (which included a wave of murders) increased, along with the means to mount them. In 1978 the BR (along with PL) became the beneficiary of major arms supplies from the Palestinians (the Popular Front—PFLP—in particular) after the Moro kidnapping had convinced the Palestinians that the organization was a serious endeavor. The quid pro quo was that the BR agreed to attack NATO and Israeli targets in Italy.[15]

Of course, the single most dramatic terrorist act in the BR's career to date was the kidnapping by the group's Rome column of DC leader Aldo Moro on March 16, 1978, and then his murder fifty-five days later. Before Moro was abducted from his car when it was stopped on the Via Fani (the BR commando killed his six police bodyguards in the process), he had been engaged in negotiations aimed at bringing about greater PCI participation in the DC-led coalition government. By seizing Moro, the BR not only kidnapped one of the most important politicians in postwar Italian history but also made a highly dramatic political point. The point, the BR's opposition to a historic compromise, was reemphasized when Moro's body was left in the trunk of a Fiat 128 halfway between PCI and DC headquarters in downtown Rome on May 9, 1978.[16]

The Moro case clearly represented a "military" success for the BR but not a political one. In the short run at least, the BR's ability to seize and hold captive for fifty-five days one of the country's most eminent postwar politicians, despite a nationwide search carried out by literally thousands of police and military personnel, was a tactical achievement of the highest order. On the other hand, Moro's murder was universally condemned by Italian political parties (and trade union organizations), including those on the left. The extraparliamentary left had little sympathy for Moro and what he represented, but its spokesmen recognized that by killing him, the BR was only strengthening the regime it purported to despise. Dissent over Moro also came from within the BR itself; shortly after the killing, two members of BR's Rome column, Adriana Faranda and Valerio Morucci, made their opposition public and became involved in an open dispute with imprisoned members of the organization's historic nucleus.

The BR "military" success was short-lived. The Italian government reached the conclusion, belatedly to be sure, that the BR posed a serious threat, and it began to respond accordingly. The state's reaction involved the enactment of a series of emergency laws and the reform (already in the pipeline) of police and security agencies to enhance their ability to meet the challenge (see below).

Phase Four. The BR's fourth period (1979–82), what Caselli and della Porta call "the military confrontation with the state," was characterized

by increasing dissent within the BR and the consequent spin-off of dissident factions; the abandonment of the struggle by individual members—
"repentants"—who in exchange for clemency were willing to identify other
members of the organization (see below); and armed confrontations
between the BR and the forces of order, with mounting casualties on both
sides. One defeat followed another.

In an effort to reclaim the initiative at the end of 1981, the BR leadership
committed itself to waging a "winter campaign," aimed at kidnapping a
number of prominent figures. Previously, the BR had not attacked any U.S.
targets, unlike its revolutionary counterparts in other parts of Europe. One
of the effects of this inattention was that security provided to U.S. military
personnel stationed in Italy was relatively weak. As a result, it was not all that
difficult for a BR commando to kidnap the U.S. NATO general James
Dozier from his apartment in Verona in December 1981. Dozier was held
hostage in an apartment in Padua (owned by the daughter of a prominent
physician) until he was liberated unhurt by a special operations team of the
Italian state police on January 28, 1982.

The BR's temporary success in seizing Dozier proved to be an unmiti-
gated disaster. The large-scale hunt for Dozier's kidnappers provided the
authorities with a cornucopia of BR documents. A vast Palestinian-supplied
arms cache was uncovered. Large numbers of BR regulars were arrested.
And following Dozier's liberation, many of those arrested decided to save
themselves by naming names. There was a snowball effect; as more BR
members were arrested, some identified their confederates. The confederates
then named more confederates, until by the end of 1982, hundreds of members were in custody. The organization's revolutionary initiative had come
to an end, and the Italian state had prevailed, or so it seemed.

For Caselli and della Porta, this is the end of the story, or at least the end
of the "four periods." But the BR did not disappear completely. In 1984, for
instance, the BR assassinated the Sinai-based U.S. peacekeeper Leamon
Hunt while he was on holiday in Rome. Since that episode, the BR, or individuals employing the name and using the rhetoric, has murdered a number
of Italian officials, often academics acting as economic advisers to the
government. So instead of observing that the BR died in 1982 following
the Dozier case, we might observe more accurately that it simply entered a
quiescent period.

A Profile of the BR Campaign

This narrative by itself hardly offers a complete picture of the BR's activities over the twelve Years of Lead to which we have paid attention. There is a need, then, to fill in the blanks, to give a complete picture—or if not a complete picture, at least an account that provides a better perspective.

Actions and Casualties

During these years, the BR claimed responsibility for 499 actions, the vast majority of them in just four localities: Milan, Turin, Genoa, and Rome, the country's industrial triangle, plus its national capital. The impoverished south, the Mezzogiorno, was significantly underrepresented. Although the BR was not the only revolutionary terrorist organization active in Italy in this period, it was responsible for approximately one-quarter of the total number of attacks carried out by the left. This made it the single most active of the various revolutionary or pseudorevolutionary bands. Between 1970 and 1982, the BR killed seventy-eight people and wounded another seventy-four. Most of those victimized by BR violence were individually targeted (unless they were the bodyguards of individuals the BR wanted to attack or belonged to the forces of order that sought to arrest BR members) and included businessmen, politicians, jurists, and other public officials. In contrast, Italy's neofascist terrorists, much like today's Islamist terrorists, tended to detonate bombs in public places, for instance, on trains, in railroad stations, and in public squares, in order to kill and maim members of the public, largely at random.[17]

Membership

Newspaper accounts suggest that the BR was able to recruit more than eight hundred members during the Years of Lead. The figure does not include individuals who committed little-noticed minor infractions or completely evaded detection. Among observers of leftist revolutionary terrorist groups in Europe and the Americas, there has been a strong inclination to believe that members were drawn from the predominantly middle-class strata of society. The widespread belief is that the revolutionaries were the sons and daughters of the establishment who took up arms on behalf of exploited workers and peasants. They employed terrorist violence because they were unable to achieve much support among those whose cause they claimed to champion.

This may have been the case elsewhere, but it was not true in the Italian situation. The BR succeeded well in recruiting a substantial number of individuals of working-class and "subproletarian" backgrounds. In fact, by one estimate, well over 30 percent of BR members were drawn from this segment of society. This pattern should not be all that surprising in view of the fact that the BR made a concerted effort to recruit within the plants, factories, and prisons of Turin, Milan, and Rome.[18] To be sure, the organization did attract more than its fair share of students and teachers, including such academics as professors Giovanni Senzani and Enrico Fenzi, but it would be inaccurate to depict the BR as a band of middle-class dilettantes.[19] For every Senzani or Fenzi, there were important figures like Francesco Lo Bianco and Antonio Savasta (the leader of the band that kidnapped General Dozier), who had been metalworkers before joining the BR. To a significant extent, the BR was what it claimed to be: a party of armed proletarians.

Organization

In recent years, there has been a tendency among students of the subject to draw a sharp distinction between "old" and "new" terrorism. The latter is usually described as more difficult to defeat than the former because of its more sophisticated organizational format. While the revolutionary groups of the 1960s and 1970s, belonging to what David Rapoport labels the "third wave" of modern terrorism, were organized along strictly hierarchical lines, the "new" terrorist groups have been cagey enough to make their organizations more decentralized and more horizontal in structure, and as a result much harder to eliminate.

The reality, at least in regard to the BR, is more complicated. The BR's leadership was acutely aware of the problems involved in conducting clandestine operations while simultaneously seeking a level of visibility necessary to spread its revolutionary message in the northern factories and elsewhere. The leaders were also concerned with the dangers of police spies and turncoats who would provide the authorities with whatever they needed to know to defeat the BR. The organization's Strategic Direction was composed of Leninists, many of whom had studied the methods of their patron saint. Despite this sensitivity to the problems inherent in its situation, ultimately the BR was not able to surmount them.

The BR's organization evolved over time. During its most developed phase, members were divided into "regulars" and "irregulars." The former were full-time revolutionaries leading clandestine lives and receiving salaries from the organization; the latter were more numerous and were expected to lead normal lives of family and work but also to participate in BR terrorism as the need arose.[20]

At its base, the BR was divided into "columns" organized along geographical lines: Genoa, Milan, Turin, and so forth. The columns were in turn subdivided into "brigades" of some five to seven militants, usually responsible for carrying out attacks. In addition to this geographic framework, there were also "fronts" organized along functional lines. There was a worker front and a mass front (composed of irregulars), which were responsible for recruitment activities in the factories and elsewhere, plus a logistical front responsible for acquiring necessary supplies (e.g., false identity papers, stolen automobiles).

At the national level, the BR was controlled by a Strategic Direction, consisting of twenty-five to thirty elected members. This group, which issued the organization's communiqués and statements of ideological purpose, approximated a parliament. To run the BR on a day-to-day basis, the Strategic Direction selected an Executive Committee of five or six individuals.

The latter was not composed of fools. BR leaders were aware of the dangers posed by the organization's vertical structure and the competing needs of underground activity (for the violence) and public communication (to win the masses to the cause of revolution). They were never able to overcome these difficulties, however. The BR, though, did place strong emphasis on organizational compartmentalization. For instance, the identities of members of one brigade were kept from those belonging to others within the same column. One glaring flaw in the BR's modus operandi involved record keeping. At both the regional and national levels, BR militants kept copious written records of their activities. As a result, when the authorities discovered a BR *covo* (hideout), they often reaped a wealth of documents that were then used to locate other hideouts and other militants. There is some danger here of being excessively critical. After all, we are dealing with an organization that managed to sustain its operations at a relatively high level for more than a decade and that even in 2004 had not completely disappeared.

International Influences

Italy abounds with conspiracy theories. Many Italians believe that a conspiracy or secret cabal is behind virtually all major events.[21] Terrorism and the BR were made to order for conspiratorial interpretations. At one time or another, there were rumors and suspicions that the United States or the Soviet Union was secretly behind the BR. The communists believed initially that the BR was part of a neofascist conspiracy, part of the strategy of tensions. For their part, the neofascists thought the BR was part of a worldwide communist conspiracy that had set its sights on a weak and defenseless Italian state. In the midst of what the late U.S. historian Richard Hofstadter referred to as a "paranoid style" of politics, what were the authentic international influences on the BR?

According to the confessions of a number of brigatisti, the organization had contacts with its West German counterparts from the Red Army Faction (RAF) and a few other western European revolutionary groups. The RAF provided some material help. The BR also received supplies from the Popular Front for the Liberation of Palestine (and members of the executive may have had conversations with "Carlos the Jackal"—Illich Ramirez Sanchez—toward this end; see above) but no training in PLO camps in the Middle East. Robert Meade accurately summarizes the situation: "The BR, in short, [was] an independent group, domestically oriented for the most part. There was no . . . sinister brain running the Organization from somewhere above the Strategic Direction."[22]

DEFEATING THE RED BRIGADES

The BR's challenge to the Italian state had clearly failed by 1983. How did this failure come about? What factors contributed to the group's defeat, if not complete demise? How could the Italian state, widely regarded by its own citizens as both incompetent and corrupt, inflict a thorough defeat on an organization of strongly motivated revolutionaries?

The Role of the Communist Party

A common observation about the capacity of a terrorist organization to sustain its operations over time concerns its perceived mass constituency. The latter provides a pool of sympathizers from which to draw new generations of recruits. The constituency also provides moral support, a sea in which the terrorist fish might swim undetected. In the case of the BR, this constituency was Italy's working class. In the 1970s, the BR sought to win over this constituency, but it faced formidable opponents: the PCI and the CGIL, to which it was closely linked. Both organizations commanded the support of literally millions of Italian workers, and both came to recognize the threat the BR posed to their own interests.[23] Unfortunately, this recognition came too slowly.

During the Years of Lead, the PCI's overriding concern was in demonstrating its liberal democratic credentials to all who were willing to pay attention. If power was to be achieved, it was obviously through the electoral process and friendly cooperation with the DC and its allies. The 1974 regional and 1976 parliamentary balloting revealed that the PCI represented about a third of the Italian electorate. Moreover, the party was sufficiently strong to elect mayors in major cities from Turin to Naples. In these years, the PCI's march toward power seemed virtually inexorable, and it was in this setting that the BR made its appearance.

Following the Piazza Fontana bombing in 1969, Luigi Longo, Enrico Berlinguer, and other PCI leaders became convinced that terrorism in general was part of the strategy of tensions. They concluded that neofascists posing as revolutionary leftists were manipulating, or "instrumentalizing," the violence to prepare the way for a coup d'état, a seizure of power that would be followed immediately by a crackdown on the party. This fear was so great that PCI leaders were instructed to change their places of residence almost every night to avoid the wave of arrests thought to be imminent.

When the BR began to wage its campaign of "armed propaganda" in the early 1970s, the PCI's initial interpretation was that this avowedly revolutionary organization was part of the neofascist threat to Italian democracy. In addition to this calculation, party spokesmen expressed a seemingly genuine incredulity that people claiming a commitment to Marxist socialism could be capable of terrorist violence. The terrorists had to be on the right! Who else could do such things? Beyond astonishment and denial, if it were shown that the BR really did belong to the same communist "family" as the PCI, it would constitute a profound embarrassment to the party. At a time when Berlinguer and other PCI leaders were advocating a historic compromise with the DC and the Socialist Party in order to rule Italy, an authentically communist BR would sow seeds of doubt about the commitment of any Marxist organization to the principles of liberal democracy. In brief, the

BR would serve to challenge the PCI's democratic credentials as a future coalition partner.

In place of the PCI's early view that terrorism was an exclusively right-wing phenomenon, DC leaders offered the "opposing extremisms" interpretation.[24] They claimed that terrorism was the outcome of extremism at both ends of the ideological spectrum. The MSI had given rise to the New Order and other violent neofascist bands. Likewise, the PCI had spawned a generation of communist youth who were carrying out terrorist attacks on helpless and innocent Italian citizens. If this was true, it represented a challenge to the PCI's apparent support for liberal democracy. In short, the BR and the authenticity of left-wing terrorism more generally quickly became intertwined in the rhetoric of partisan political competition. (Not to be outdone, leaders of Italy's small laical parties of the center, along with socialists, adopted a "plague on both your houses" position by claiming terrorism to be a manifestation of *catto-communismo,* a combination of disaffected communist and Catholic youths.)

The PCI's myopia in the early phases of BR activity came at a price. According to Meade, "In the early years the PCI failed to exert its vast influence upon the working class to prevent the brigatisti from entering the factories and polluting labor-management relations, and the PCI failed to expel the brigatisti once they had entered or otherwise to discipline them. The union movement in general . . . shares the blame."[25] Meade points out that some workers left the party to join the BR as regulars, while others remained in the plants as irregulars to act as mailmen, distributing BR propaganda material and spying on factory operations.

By 1977, with the escalation of BR violence, the PCI leaders were compelled to recognize the authenticity of the left-wing origins of many brigatisti, some of whom clearly belonged to communist families from Sesto San Giovanni—Italy's "red belt"—the heavily communist suburb of Milan, and whose rhetoric oozed Marxism-Leninism. The party's position against the BR hardened. When Aldo Moro was kidnapped in 1978, the PCI counseled a position of no concessions and no negotiations with the DC leader's abductors after BR communiqués demanded an exchange of prisoners—Moro for the members of the historic nucleus waiting to stand trial.[26]

PCI and CGIL leaders Berlinguer and Luciano Lama were certainly aware of a BR presence in the northern plants and factories. In the late 1970s, for example, there were six BR brigades in the Fiat Mirafiori plant alone. Furthermore, while the national Communist Party and labor union leaders came to recognize the BR as a threat to their own institutional ambitions and political goals, this was less true for the rank-and-file membership, some of whom sympathized with the BR or were willing to look the other way. During 1977–78, the party and union leaders made a concerted effort to purge local organizations of activists reluctant to adopt a hard line toward the BR and those who continued to believe that the BR might be part of a neofascist scheme.

What was to be done to repel the BR threat? The national leaders appealed for a "campaign of vigilance" within the plants and factories. Party and union members were asked to report individuals and activities they suspected were linked to the BR. In January 1979, a union member and factory worker from Genoa, Guido Rossa, was assassinated by the BR for having reported a "mailman" to the authorities.[27] A crowd of between 200,000 and 250,000 showed up for the funeral and began chanting anti-BR slogans. In a monumental blunder, the BR had begun to attack members of the Italian working class, the very class on whose behalf it claimed to be acting and from whom it needed to receive vital support.

In a subsequent series of protests and demonstrations, the PCI and the unions seized on this opportunity to depict themselves as the BR's worst enemies and as ardent defenders of the democratic order. In this way the party, after considerable foot dragging, certainly contributed to the BR's growing isolation and defeat. In the long run, though, the PCI suffered as well. The decline of the party in the electorate began with the 1979 national elections following the Moro abduction and continued virtually unabated during the 1980s. Despite the PCI's substantial efforts to defeat the BR after the kidnapping, many voters perceived the terrorist band as ineffably linked to the communist family and punished the PCI accordingly.

The Forces of Order

Italy, like France, possesses two major national police forces: the state police (polizia dello Stato, or PS) and the carabinieri. The former is a civilian organization subordinate to the Interior Ministry, while the latter is a militarized organization whose officers normally live in barracks and whose generals report to the Ministry of Defense. The arrangement is hardly ideal. Paul Furlong observes: "The division of functions between them is confused both in theory and practice. . . . Their functions are identical, and at the practical level the two bodies tend to operate without coordination, with the result that police functions of all sorts are endlessly repeated."[28] Eventually these two forces of order came to compete with each other in the struggle to defeat the BR. Before considering how this struggle came to be waged, we need to understand the ambiguous nature of the police (especially the carabinieri) defense of Italy's democratic institutions.

In 1964 Italy's first center-left government entered into crisis. PSI leader Pietro Nenni withdrew his party's support from the DC-led coalition. Forming a new government seemed to require more concessions to the PSI than DC leaders were willing to offer. At this point, Antonio Segni, the Italian president, conferred with carabinieri general Giovanni De Lorenzo, head of the Armed Forces Information Service (Servizio Informazioni Forze Armate, or SIFAR), the country's intelligence agency. The discussion involved "Plan Solo," an emergency scheme for a seizure of power in the event of a communist insurrection. De Lorenzo was told to keep his forces prepared in case such an intervention became necessary. It did not, because Nenni, alerted to what might be in the offing, agreed to the PSI's renewed participation in the ruling coalition. When the scandal broke and a parliamentary investigation was launched in 1966, the picture that emerged was about as follows.

SIFAR had compiled dossiers on more than 157,000 left-wing politicians and labor leaders, even moderate ones, identified as potential subversives. When an insurrection seemed imminent, SIFAR officers were prepared to arrest many of the individuals who "posed a danger to national security" and place them in special carabinieri-run detention camps on the island of Sardinia.[29]

General De Lorenzo eventually resigned from the army to run for parliament, where he was elected first as a monarchist and then as a deputy for the MSI, the neofascist movement. SIFAR underwent a cosmetic name change to Defense Information Service (SID), but its organization and personnel remained largely unaffected by the scandal. De Lorenzo's link to the MSI calls our attention to the broader problem of the association between the carabinieri (and other elements in the military), its intelligence service, and neofascism.

The tale of the relationship between neofascist schemes and the police is slightly outside the field of vision absolutely necessary to understand the BR's defeat, but it helps, nonetheless, in understanding the overall atmosphere of mistrust that delayed an effective reaction to the BR's threat. Suffice it to say that both SID and its state police counterpart in the Interior Ministry, the Office for Special Affairs (Ufficio Affari Riservati, or UAR), were both involved in the Piazza Fontana and other indiscriminate bombings as part of the strategy of tensions. Members of both agencies were subsequently prosecuted for their involvement. These prosecutions included charges against the head of SID itself as well as against the director of "Office D" (on counterespionage). Further, a number of SID officers, including Admiral Eugenio Henke, followed De Lorenzo into the MSI's parliamentary delegation.

The collusion between the forces of order and the neofascists to destabilize the country and perhaps stage a coup d'état became an enormous public scandal in the early 1970s. A parliamentary investigation was launched, and almost every day the press carried headlines describing the antidemocratic conduct of those responsible for maintaining Italy's constitutional order. Demands in parliament and in the press for a thorough reform (including greater democratic accountability) of the police and the intelligence agencies were mounted at precisely the time the BR was launching its campaign of "armed propaganda," and these demands continued during its "attack on the heart of the state" phase. In other words, from the state's point of view, the BR could not have chosen a worse time to initiate its terrorist attacks.

Under these circumstances, not many militants were apprehended in the first years of BR activity. Not uncommonly, those who were imprisoned were able to escape with the assistance of BR confederates on the outside. Few minimum-wage prison guards were willing to risk their lives by shooting it out with armed BR revolutionaries there to liberate their comrades from bourgeois captivity. To make matters worse, the first waves of BR prisoners were housed among the normal inmate population in the country's regular, run-down penal institutions. This policy made it possible for BR regulars to win recruits among the "subproletarian" elements with whom they were imprisoned. It was only after the government built special maximum-security prisons and began to isolate those convicted of terrorism-related crimes that the jailbreaks came to an end.

The year 1974 was the one in which the DC-led government of Prime Minister Mariano Rumor took significant steps to deal with the problem of terrorism. It was the year in which the BR kidnapped Judge Sossi (see above) and the year of the "massacre" at Piazza La Loggia in Brescia, when neofascists detonated a bomb at a public meeting of antifascists. Public pressure on the government to do something serious to stop both neofascist and leftist terrorism increased exponentially. The Rumor government responded by creating two bodies. Emilio Santillo, a former police chief in Turin, was appointed to head a General Inspectorate against Terrorism and Armed Bands. Santillo and his organization reported to the Interior Ministry and were fundamentally responsible for the struggle against the neofascist organizations. The carabinieri general Carlo Alberto Dalla Chiesa was assigned to head a special carabinieri unit (actually a unit of the judicial police) in Turin aimed at eliminating the BR.[30]

Both organizations succeeded, or at least seemed to. Large numbers of violent neofascists, including such exotics as Mario Tuti, a half-crazy drafts-man from Empoli who specialized in derailing trains, were arrested. The two major neofascist organizations, the New Order and the National Van-guard, were formally dissolved by the courts. By 1976 Dalla Chiesa's group had managed to arrest or rearrest all but one member of the BR's historic nucleus (including BR founder Renato Curcio), although a handful of late-comers remained at large.

So by the end of 1976, it appeared to many observers that the struggle against terrorism in Italy was about to come to a successful conclusion. It was at this point that the government dissolved both the Santillo and Dalla Chiesa organizations. The reason for this action, or at least the publicly expressed one, was that the entire security apparatus of the state was under-going a thorough reorganization and that Santillo's antiterrorist organi-zation would be incorporated into a new body. And in the case of Dalla Chiesa's Turin-based task force, there was a sense that it had accomplished its goal: the BR had been defeated. In retrospect, some observers came to regard the government's decision with suspicion, believing in the possibility of dark motives.

Whatever the suspicions, the state did undertake a substantial reform of its intelligence apparatus, a process of reorganization that began in 1977. SID was dissolved and replaced by structures designed along British lines (MI5, MI6) and aimed at strengthening democratic accountability.[31] Toward this end, the law was changed to give the prime minister direct responsibility for the new security agencies. The prime minister, in turn, was required to submit reports about the activities of the new agencies to a par-liamentary committee every six months. The new agencies consisted of the

Service for Intelligence and Military Security (SISMI), responsible for foreign intelligence gathering and counterespionage and part of the Ministry of Defense; and the Service for Intelligence and Democratic Security (SISDE), responsible for domestic intelligence gathering, and consequently for the terrorist organizations, and part of the Interior Ministry.

In January 1978, the state police underwent their own reform with the establishment of the Central Bureau for General Investigations and Special Operations (UCIGOS). The UCIGOS became responsible for coordinating the activities of the Division for General Investigations and Special Operations (DIGOS), whose special antiterrorist field agencies were housed in various *questure* (police headquarters) throughout the country.

These changes were undertaken with two not necessarily compatible purposes in mind: (1) ensuring that the forces of order would be subordinate to Italy's democratic (and antifascist) institutions; and (2) creating structures that would be effective in the struggle against a revived (1977) terrorist threat. The problem with achieving the antiterrorist objective was that the reforms were barely in place when the Moro kidnapping occurred; in the midst of this crisis, the government, as one official put it, was blind and deaf as it sought to locate Moro and his BR abductors.

The enormity of the Moro case, dragging out over fifty-five days with an increasingly desperate Moro sending letters to his colleagues in the DC-led government, appealing for them to make the concessions necessary to save his life, spurred overwhelming public pressure on the government following his execution. In response, the Andreotti cabinet took the additional step of creating a new special antiterrorist strike force headed by General Dalla Chiesa, based on his earlier success in Turin, charged with the specific task of finding Moro's killers and more generally eliminating the BR. To this end, the general recruited a mixed force of carabinieri and state police officers and set up his headquarters (for security purposes) in the middle of an air force base outside Rome. He then had the members of his antiterrorist nucleus study the BR's copious body of documents (the BR's Genoa column even had its own librarian!), checking residency and personal identification records and conducting stakeouts of and tailing BR suspects, for the most part in Turin and Milan.

The Dalla Chiesa force was created on an emergency basis for a two-year period. It was also granted virtual autonomy from the kind of democratic oversight just described. The general reported directly to the minister of the interior, a fact that stimulated criticism from the opposition parties in parliament, now highly sensitive to the issue of democratic accountability.

By 1979 it was clear that the kid gloves were coming off. Parliament enacted emergency legislation (see below) to make Dalla Chiesa's work and that of the DIGOS much easier. But by creating the Dalla Chiesa antiterrorist force outside the normal bureaucratic bounds, and almost simultaneously the DIGOS apparatus inside them, the government had set up a situation where the two organizations would compete with one another in the effort to bring the BR's campaign of violence to a conclusion.

Whatever the organizational messiness, the results were impressive. Della Porta estimates that only 20 percent of left-wing terrorists (including but not restricted to BR militants) were arrested before 1980. In 1980 alone, with the antiterrorist campaign in full swing, 42 percent were apprehended, with the balance taken prisoner over the next few years.[32]

Certain changes in Italian law (see below) made a major contribution to the success, but a number of deviations from democratic practice or unlawful actions on the part of the forces of order also played a role. For better or worse, these need to be mentioned.

The use of torture proved successful in a number of instances. During the Dozier kidnapping, the DIGOS tortured or threatened to torture BR militants already in custody. These methods helped a DIGOS team headed by Salvatore Genova (himself a member of the 1968 generation) locate the apartment in Padua where the U.S. general was being held (and coincidentally find a major cache of explosives provided to the BR by the Palestinians). Following Dozier's liberation, the DIGOS tortured Antonio Savasta, the BR leader in charge of the kidnapping (and a multiple murderer), and his confederates into disclosing the names and whereabouts of many BR militants.[33] The methods employed (sleep deprivation, threats to harm loved ones, punches, kicks in the groin, the pulling out of pubic hair, cigarettes extinguished on the backs of prisoners) did not rival those used by the forces of Saddam Hussein or by the Argentine military during its "dirty war" of the late 1970s, but they certainly were torture and they certainly seemed to work. Without the use of torture, Dozier probably would have been killed.

Another apparent excess in the effort to destroy the BR involved University of Padua (and University of Paris) political philosopher Antonio Negri. On April 7, 1979, Negri and eight colleagues in Padua's Political Science Department were arrested and charged with a variety of terrorism-related crimes. Prosecutors alleged that Negri and the others were "evil teachers" (*cattivi maestri*) who had led their students down the path of terrorism. More precisely, the initial allegations asserted a direct link between Negri and the BR; more extravagantly, the press claimed the philosopher was the éminence grise behind the BR and other revolutionary terrorist bands.[34]

Reality, or what eventually appeared to be the reality for most observers, was as follows: An activist, engaged Leninist, and advocate of proletarian revolution in Italy, Negri had played a leading role in the formation of POTOP. When that extraparliamentary left group dissolved itself in 1973, Negri led many of its militants into a new group, Autonomia Operaio. In 1977 AO's militants became practitioners of what came to be known as "diffuse terrorism." Unlike the well-organized and hierarchically structured operations of the BR, AO attacks were carried out (often in and around Padua) on a relatively unplanned, spontaneous basis by part-timers who did not live underground lives. Negri (and colleagues) supervised and provided ideological direction for AO. Negri, in particular, was involved in the kidnapping and subsequent accidental death of the son of a wealthy businessman.

This *cattivo maestro* did have contacts with the BR—he had conferred with Renato Curcio, for example—but beyond his offering some advice, there was not sufficient evidence to sustain the charge that Negri was directing or even directly involved with the BR. Negri was found guilty on other AO-related charges. In a complex series of events, he eventually avoided serving his sentence by fleeing to France, where he resumed his teaching as a tenured professor at the University of Paris.

At the time, many Italian intellectuals rushed to Negri's defense on the grounds that he had been arrested and prosecuted not on the basis of what he had done but because of what he had written and spoken. Free speech was the issue, and Negri, they believed, was the victim of excessive zeal on the part of the police, acting in admittedly emergency circumstances. Perhaps, but at least two of Negri's opponents on the Padua faculty had been severely beaten by AO militants, evidently at the professor's instigation.

A still more dramatic cause célèbre involving the forces of order erupted in 1980. The highly publicized reforms of the security agencies and the police had been undertaken because of parliamentary and press disclosures of the ties between these forces and neofascists. Presumably, the ties had been severed and democratic accountability was achieved as the new structures were put in place. However, in 1980 the existence of a secret Masonic lodge, Propaganda Due (P2), became known. P2's purpose was to become a state within a state, to guide the country's institutions in an anti-communist direction. Important figures in the security agencies, the police, parliament, the cabinet, and the Christian Democratic Party were revealed to be members of this covert organization. Licio Gelli, a shady businessman with a fascist past, was identified as the leader of P2. New conspiracy theories surfaced as a parliamentary commission investigated the case.[35]

The scandal had multiple effects. Because of the participation in P2 of prominent Christian Democrats, including cabinet members, the DC was compelled to relinquish the prime minister's office for the first time since December 1945. The job was given to Giovanni Spadolini, a senior leader of the Republican Party (PRI) and a political scientist with a strong reputation for incorruptibility. Spadolini pledged to lead the struggle against terrorism within the bounds of the country's constitutional order.[36] Another effect of the P2 scandal was to cast new doubt on the honesty of the changes in the forces of order that had only recently been accomplished. Stories in the press about possible links between the BR and mysterious elements on the right surfaced or resurfaced. These tales led to additional public mistrust of the police and security agencies as they sought to curtail the BR's operations.

Changes in the Law

The enactment of certain new laws and the revision of some old ones played an important role in bringing about the BR's collapse in 1983. Before describing this legislation, though, we need to briefly review the legal environment from which the laws emerged.

First, the republican constitution that came into force at the beginning of 1948 was intended to immunize the country against a return of fascist dictatorship. Not only does the document say so quite explicitly, but it contains provisions of a liberal democratic nature that provide for the freedoms of speech and association, along with other provisions referring to the rights of personal privacy for citizens in both their domiciles and their communication with others. The constitution offers habeas corpus protections; it specifies that no one may be detained by the authorities without the approval of judicial authorities.[37]

Second, although the 1948 constitution reflected the country's democratic impulses following the defeat of fascism, Italy's criminal and criminal procedure codes were both written during the years of the Mussolini dictatorship, and these codes continued in force in the decades following the instauration of democratic rule. Some of their long-standing provisions seem incompatible with liberal democratic principles. For example, Article 270 of the Penal Code refers to the crime of "subversive association," an activity involving forming, joining, or leading a group whose aim is the establishment of the dictatorship of one social class over another by means of violence. It is not hard to detect who the drafters had in mind when they included this provision.[38] Other fascist-era code provisions criminalize membership in a group expressing "antinational" sentiments or in an "armed band" (Article 307) seeking to challenge the state through force and violence.

Although the Penal Code made no specific reference to terrorism or membership in terrorist organizations at the beginning of the Years of Lead, one hardly seemed necessary. The Code of Criminal Procedure posed a different problem. At the end of the 1960s and the beginning of the 1970s, many of its fascist-era provisions were being revised to bring the document into conformity with modern liberal democratic principles. The rights of those apprehended by the police to remain silent, to have access to an attorney, and to be granted "provisional liberty" pending trial were asserted or reinforced. The code was also amended to make it more difficult for the police to violate the right to privacy by tapping telephones and other measures. Tighter restrictions were imposed on the use of firearms by the police.[39]

The terrorist events of 1974 caused a reversal in the trend toward procedural liberalization. In 1975 parliament passed the Reale Law (named after Justice Minister Oronzo Reale), which, inter alia, doubled the time someone could be held in preventive detention and reduced the occasions on which provisional liberty (freedom pending trial) could be extended. The police were granted greater latitude in conducting searches of both property and persons. The range of circumstances in which the police were permitted to use their weapons in the line of duty was enlarged. And following the Moro kidnapping, the passage of "emergency" legislation (the so-called Cossiga Law) allowed the police to question suspects without the presence of an attorney and to tap the telephones of suspected terrorists more easily than had previously been the case. Furthermore, the emergency law required all individuals selling or renting an apartment or house to report this fact, along with the identities of the renters or buyers, to the police within forty-eight hours.[40]

The criminal and criminal procedure codes were modified in 1979 and 1980 to create the new crimes of (1) belonging to associations with terrorist aims and the subversion of the democratic order; (2) kidnapping for terrorist or subversive aims; and (3) carrying out attacks with terrorist or subversive aims.[41] If terrorism (never defined) and subversion of the democratic order were found to be the motive for the crime of kidnapping or a violent attack, this fact was to be regarded as an "aggravating" circumstance, and those found guilty were to have their sentences augmented.

These measures constituted the "sticks." But "carrots" were also used to stop the BR and other terrorist organizations at war with the Italian state. In fact, it was these measures, which provided BR members with an opportunity to leave the organization and held out the prospect of a return to normal life, that proved decisive. With the chances of being apprehended growing and the likelihood of revolution diminishing, the opportunity to get out of the organization while the getting was good became an exceptionally attractive option.

The 1980 Urgent Measures for the Protection of the Democratic Order and Public Security law contained provisions concerning those willing to (1) "abandon" terrorism (typically individuals who had only minor involvement); (2) "disassociate" themselves from terrorist organizations and confess their crimes; and (3) go further and "repent" their involvements. "Repentance" (really a kind of plea bargaining) required persons accused of terrorism-related crimes to disclose information about their former associates in exchange for receiving reduced sentences for their activities. The size of the reduction in the length of sentence was calibrated to the amount and value of the information supplied to the authorities. This initiative was so successful that a new law, which expanded the number of cases in which the opportunity to repent was made available, was enacted in 1982, following General Dozier's liberation.[42]

The 1980 and 1982 laws seemed to break the back of the revolutionary terrorist organizations, including the BR. According to Justice Ministry figures, a total of 389 individuals (78 for "major" repentance, 134 as repented, and 177 as disassociated) took advantage of the opportunity to abandon their lives as terrorists in exchange for the prospect of a return to normal life at some point in the future.

The legislation on disassociation and repentance had a cascade effect. As one terrorist repented by identifying associates, the latter were arrested (or killed), which in turn produced a new crop of *pentiti* willing to disclose the whereabouts of still more. Richard Drake describes the impact of the most important *pentito,* Patrizio Peci: "Information provided by this one time leader of the Turin column . . . brought carnage to the organization. To begin with, he informed police about the location of a major terrorist hideout in Genoa. . . . Peci's confessions eventually resulted in the smashing of numerous Red Brigade hideouts, the discovery of huge arms deposits, and the death or arrest of dozens of terrorists in Turin, Milan, Biella, and Ravenna."[43]

Feedback from the DIGOS and General Dalla Chiesa's anti-BR organization also played a role. In interrogating captured brigatisti, the police became aware of widespread disillusionment on the part of these revolutionaries. The life of clandestine violence had lost its appeal for many of them; they were looking for a way out. Some brigatisti reported feelings of relief when they were arrested. The police supplied this information to the government, which then introduced legislation in parliament to exploit the information.

Many brigatisti had joined the organization in search of action and adventure: enough theory, they wanted praxis, too. They wanted to make a revolution and bring down Italy's corrupt government and exploitative economic system. For many young people drawn to the BR, the life of a clandestine terrorist proved disillusioning. According to the memoirs of some, most of the time they were profoundly bored by living for long periods in dreary apartments with little to occupy their time between armed actions.[44] For the young men in their twenties, there were not enough young women in the BR.

Disappointing for the numerous soccer fans in the organization, attendance at the Sunday matches was prohibited because of all the police in and around the stadiums in Turin and Milan.

These depressing conditions were made worse as time passed, when it became clear that the likelihood of making a revolution was very remote, except perhaps for the fanatical few. Worse still, the chances of being arrested, or worse, were raised considerably in the years following the Moro kidnapping. Under these circumstances, the possibility of a return to normal life, even if it followed a short prison sentence, appeared attractive, a way out of an increasingly hopeless and dangerous situation. For many brigatisti, the laws on disassociation and repentance must have appeared like a lifesaver to a drowning man.

The Zeitgeist

After he was captured in Padua by a specially trained DIGOS "intervention" team in the process of freeing General Dozier, Antonio Savasta was questioned by one of the detectives leading the investigation. Inspector Salvatore Genova, a man belonging to the same generation of 1968, asked Savasta if it had ever occurred to him to look around the neighborhood in Padua where he and his fellow brigatisti had held Dozier captive.[45] The question was rhetorical because the policeman went on to say that if the BR leader had looked, he would have noticed capitalism changing and mutating in complex ways. Perhaps not always for the best, but Italian capitalism had achieved a level of innovation and vitality that would be hard to dislodge, no matter what the sacred texts of Marx, Lenin, and their disciples had to say on the matter.

In the 1960s and 1970s, Italy had clearly become an advanced industrialized society, where standards of living in the north and center of the country, precisely the regions in which the BR had been most active, were comparable to those in the world's most prosperous countries. To be sure, Italy continued to abound with cases of economic and social injustice. The *burocrazia* was inefficient and, particularly in the south, unresponsive to citizen demands. Systems of patronage ("clientelism") and outright criminality were widespread within the country's ruling political parties. These failures, however, did not add up to czarist Russia in 1917 or even to Cuba in 1959. No matter how adroit the BR leadership had become at organizing attacks on the heart of the state, no matter how able they had become in outwitting the authorities, the prospects for actually making a proletarian revolution were not only bleak but virtually nonexistent. By the late 1960s, many Italians had become available for popular protest marches. Some hundreds could be recruited by terrorist bands, but a mass insurrection could not be realized or even imagined, except by those willing to naturally suspend their disbelief.

The Costs of Defeating the BR

The price paid by Italy's democratic institutions for defeating the BR (and the other terrorist groups at war with them) was comparatively low. Democracy was not interrupted by a military coup d'état, despite some plotting along these lines. The constitution was not suspended. Martial law was not declared. Capital punishment was not restored. Large numbers of citizens were not subjected to preventive detention. The police used torture briefly to extract information in connection with the Dozier case. Emergency legislation was passed, making it easier for the authorities to engage in wiretapping and other search-and-seizure operations. Some due process protections were weakened. But these measures were short-lived. Once the crisis had passed, Italy's criminal and criminal procedure codes were rewritten to bring them into conformity with contemporary democratic standards of justice.

Before the Years of Lead, Italy's political party system was widely seen as polarized, with parties at both ends of the ideological spectrum, communists and neofascists in particular, not reconciled to the prevailing constitutional order. The BR and other terrorist organizations did their utmost to further polarize the forces of left and right. At the end of the day, however, the party system was much less polarized than it had been at the beginning of the terrorism. The PCI, in these years the largest communist party in western Europe, was drawn under the "constitutional arc" of parties committed to the maintenance of Italian democracy.

In sum, Italian democracy proved to be considerably more resilient than its critics and opponents, including the terrorists, had believed.

Lessons for Democracies

How do terrorist groups end? Martha Crenshaw, Ted Gurr, and Jeffrey Ross provide us with some answers to this question.[46] The most obvious, though not necessarily the most common, way is through *defeat*. The authorities employ some mix of force and guile to destroy groups challenging their ability to govern. Another way terrorist groups may come to an end is through a *backlash* by their constituents. Members of minority ethnic communities, for example, may become so repelled by acts of violence carried out in their name that they withdraw their emotional, financial, and logistical support. If this happens, terrorist groups may lose their ability to recruit new members and may begin to suffer bouts of demoralization and other withdrawal symptoms.[47]

Burnout is a third alternative. The groups' militants, often young people, lose hope that their violence will bring about the changes they intend, and so the struggle in which they have invested so much time and effort begins to seem pointless. Ennui sets in, and members begin to contemplate other life options. A fourth option involves a *strategic shift* or *transformation*. In this case, the groups do not necessarily disappear; rather, they change their methods from terrorism to nonviolent or at least less violent forms of behavior. In a number of cases, groups have exchanged the bullet and the bomb for the ballot box. Finally, there is always the distressing possibility that terrorist groups may achieve success and transform their terrorist campaigns into full-scale revolutions and civil wars.

In this context, the BR clearly did not succeed; nor did it undergo a transformation in the sense of abandoning violence in favor of some nonviolent form of political expression, in the manner of, say, the Irish Republican Army/Sinn Féin. The best to be said about its performance is that the BR had staying power. It lasted longer than virtually all the social revolutionary bands that waged terrorist campaigns in the Western democracies during the 1960s and 1970s, and it still has not disappeared completely. Individuals calling themselves brigatisti have continued to assassinate Italian political figures into the twenty-first century.

It is undeniable, however, that the BR's role as a force to be feared ended in the year following General Dozier's liberation in the winter of 1982. This result, achieved within a few years of the reorganization of the forces of order and the enactment of emergency laws, deserves to be labeled *defeat* in the military sense of the word. But the victory of the authorities would not have been accomplished had it not been for *backlash* against BR violence, promoted belatedly by Italy's Communist Party and its major labor union organizations, the CGIL especially. *Burnout* also made the state's ability to defeat the BR far easier. The awareness that the chances of success were becoming increasingly remote, coupled with the possibility of a return to normal life through repentance (the result of legislation on disassociation and repentance), seemed to demoralize the organization. If there was to be no revolution in the foreseeable future, if the chances of getting arrested (and possibly tortured or shot) were getting stronger and the chances of leading a normal life in exchange for a little cooperation with the authorities (betraying your colleagues) were present, then the incentives for getting out while the getting was good became very powerful. The end of the BR became "a rational choice" for many of its members. Instead of the organization undergoing a strategic shift away from violence, its members as individuals (or in some cases as couples) made the shift and by so doing brought the BR's revolutionary project to a conclusion.

Does Italy's experience in responding to the threat posed by the BR during the 1970s provide us with any insight into how the United States and the other democracies ought to react to the contemporary threat represented by groups belonging to the al Qaeda network? At first glance, the answer would seem to be negative. The brigatisti were social revolutionaries, while al Qaeda's members are, or at least appear to be, religious fanatics. Despite some international connections, the BR was a fundamentally domestic phenomenon, while the jihadist groups are international in scope, with an estimated detected presence in more than sixty countries, at least at the time of 9/11. The BR was highly selective in its targeting; in most cases it killed or kidnapped particular individuals for particular reasons. Al Qaeda–linked groups, we hardly need reminding, have been willing to kill large numbers of people on a far more indiscriminate basis. (In Italy it was not the left but the neofascist groups that adopted the practice of setting off bombs in public places.)

Despite these and other differences, the BR defeat does offer some potentially useful lessons. First, the BR was harmed by the presence of a powerful and increasingly moderate Communist Party. After prolonged hesitation, the PCI (and the CGIL) initiated a campaign aimed at creating a backlash against the BR, which weakened the organization's ability to recruit new members and to communicate with its potential working-class constituents. With the aim of promoting backlash, policymakers in the United States and elsewhere, particularly in the Muslim world, are now or certainly should be communicating with the ulema in such a way as to encourage imams and other religious leaders to stress the un-Islamic nature of al Qaeda groups' resort to indiscriminate killing. Next, in the final analysis, the brigatisti were driven by motives of personal self-interest. Islamist terrorists, on the other hand, often refer to themselves as self-sacrificers, to whom the appeals of tangible self-interest have little meaning. But interviews conducted by Jessica Stern and others suggest this is not the case.[48] Money and prestige have considerable meaning for many self-sacrificers, leaders especially. Thus restructuring the incentives of individual members to make persistence more expensive and exit potentially less expensive (less costly) would promote burnout.

Third, the BR was, to put it mildly, a substantially less formidable adversary than the al Qaeda network. But the Italian state was hardly a model of effectiveness either. Its inefficiency and corruption have become matters of legend among Italian citizens. Despite this reputation, once Italian policymakers realized the BR represented a serious challenge (after the Moro kidnapping), they were able to virtually destroy the organization within two years. This experience would suggest that even Third World states (e.g., Pakistan) possess the capacity to do likewise if they feel sufficiently threatened.

Finally there is the zeitgeist to consider. No matter how much the brigatisti wanted to believe that the forces of Italian history doomed capitalism and condemned the Imperialist State of the Multinationals (SIM) to extinction, reality could not be ignored for too long. Italian capitalism and SIM seemed to thrive despite the BR's best efforts. The scale is infinitely larger, but no matter what al Qaeda groups do, they are unlikely to succeed in restoring the world as it existed in the century following the death of the Prophet.

NOTES

1. "Terrorismo, ci sono due indagati," *Corriere della Sera,* October 10, 2003.

2. Walter Laqueur, *The Age of Terrorism* (Boston: Little, Brown, 1987), 157–58.

3. Two English-language books are especially helpful in capturing this era: Paul Ginsborg, *A History of Contemporary Italy* (New York: Penguin, 1990); and Sidney Tarrow, *Democracy and Disorder* (Oxford: Clarendon, 1989).

4. For a distinction between the different historical waves of terrorist violence, see David Rapoport, "The Fourth Wave: September 11 and the History of Terrorism," *Current History* (December 2001): 419–24.

5. Donatella della Porta, "Left-Wing Terrorism in Italy," in *Terrorism in Context,* ed. Martha Crenshaw (University Park: Pennsylvania State University Press, 1995), 106.

6. Giovanna Guidorossi, *Gli Italiani e la politica* (Milan: Franco Angeli, 1984), 58–59.

7. See Giuseppe Vettori, ed., *La sinistra extraparlamentare in Italia* (Rome: Newton Compton, 1975).

8. See Daniele Barbieri, *Agenda nera* (Rome: Coines, 1976), 115–22.

9. For a summary in English, see Franco Ferraresi, *Threats to Democracy* (Princeton, NJ: Princeton University Press, 1996), 127–48.

10. See Alessandro Silj, *Never Again without a Rifle* (New York: Karz, 1979), 72–73.

11. See, for example, Soccorso Rosso (Red Aid), *Brigate Rosse* (Milan: Feltrinelli, 1976), 35–84.

12. Gian Carlo Caselli and Donatella della Porta, "The History of the Red Brigades," in *The Red Brigades and Left-Wing Terrorism in Italy,* ed. Raimondo Catanzaro (New York: St. Martin's, 1991), 71.

13. See Robert Meade, *The Red Brigades: The Story of Italian Terrorism* (New York: St. Martin's, 1990), 56–57.

14. See, for example, David Moss, *The Politics of Left-Wing Terrorism in Italy, 1969–1985* (New York: St. Martin's, 1989), 70–75.

15. Senato della Repubblica/Camera dei Deputati, *Senato della Repubblica/Camera dei Deputati parlamentare d'inchiesta sulla strage di Via Fani* (Rome: Senato della Repubblica, 1983), 131–32.

16. See Richard Drake, *The Aldo Moro Murder Case* (Cambridge, MA: Harvard University Press, 1995), 34–35.

17. Mauro Galleni, ed., *Rapporto sul terrorismo* (Milan: Rizzoli, 1981); Donatella della Porta and Maurizio Rossi, *Cifre crudeli* (Bologna: Istituto Carlo Cattaneo, 1984), 57–73.

18. Leonard Weinberg and William Eubank, *The Rise and Fall of Italian Terrorism* (Boulder, CO: Westview, 1987), 86–88.

19. Senzani, a professor of criminology at the University of Florence and a longtime BR leader, once had one of his colleagues shot after he annoyed him at a professional meeting. Richard Drake, *The Revolutionary Mystique and Terrorism in Contemporary Italy* (Bloomington: Indiana University Press, 1989), 145.

20. For a description of the organization and its dilemmas, see della Porta, "Left-Wing Terrorism in Italy," 105–59. For a firsthand account of the life of a BR regular, see Giordano Guerri, ed., *Patrizio Peci: Io l'infame* (Milan: Mondadori, 1983).

21. During the cold war, reporters used to note that in Moscow, nothing was said while everything was understood, while in Rome, everything was said but nothing was understood. Conspiracy theories then served to enhance "understanding."

22. Meade, *Red Brigades*, 226.

23. See, for example, *Almanacco PCI '76* (Rome: Partito Comunista Italiano,1976), 110–94.

24. See, for example, Giorgio Bocca, *Il terrorismo italiano* (Milan: Rizzoli, 1980), 87–98.

25. Meade, *Red Brigades*, 138.

26. See Giuseppe Fiori, *Vita di Enrico Berlinguer* (Rome: Laterza, 1989), 354–87.

27. See Giampaolo Pansa, *Storie italiane di violenza e terrorismo* (Rome: Laterza, 1980), 112–21.

28. Paul Furlong, "Political Terrorism in Italy," in *Terrorism: A Challenge to the State,* ed. Juliet Lodge (New York: St. Martin's, 1981), 81.

29. Ginsborg, *A History of Contemporary Italy,* 278–79.

30. See Stefano Rodota, "La risposta dello stato al terrorismo: Gli apparati," in *La prova delle armi,* ed. Gianfranco Pasquino (Bologna: Il Mulino, 1984), 77–91.

31. Giorgio Battistini, "Il ministro garantisce," *La Repubblica,* August 11, 1977, 3.

32. Della Porta, "Left-Wing Terrorism in Italy," 117.

33. Richard Collin and Gordon Freedman, *Winter of Fire: The Abduction of General Dozier and the Downfall of the Red Brigades* (New York: Dutton, 1990), 167–219.

34. See Giorgio Bocca, *Il caso 7 Aprile: Toni Negri e la grande inquisizione* (Milan: Feltrinelli, 1980).

35. See Ferraresi, *Threats to Democracy,* 120–22.

36. See Leo Valiani, *I governi Spadolini e la lotta al terrorismo* (Rome: Voce, 1983), 15–46.

37. For an English-language version of the constitution, see Mauro Cappeletti, John Merryman, and Joseph Perillo, *The Italian Legal System* (Stanford, CA: Stanford University Press, 1967), 281–313.

38. For a discussion, see Ettore Gallo and Enzo Musco, *Delitti contro l'ordine costituzionale* (Bologna: Patron, 1984), 23–35.

39. See Vittorio Grevi, "Sistema penale e leggi dell'emergergenza: La risposata legislative al terrorismo," in *La prova delle armi,* ed. Gianfranco Pasquino (Bologna: Il Mulino, 1984), 17–74.

40. See, for example, Alison Jamieson, *The Heart Attacked* (New York: Marion Boyars, 1989), 193–95.

41. See Piero Luigi Vigna, *La finalita di terrorismo ed eversione* (Varese: Giuffre, 1981), 21–60.

42. See della Porta, "Left-Wing Terrorism in Italy," 118–19.

43. Drake, *Revolutionary Mystique,* 108–9.

44. See, for example, Guerri, ed., *Patrizio Peci: Io l'infame,* 105–6.

45. See Collin and Freedman, *Winter of Fire,* 202–3.

46. Martha Crenshaw, "How Terrorism Ends," paper presented at the annual meeting of the American Political Science Association, Chicago, September 1987; and Jeffrey Ross and Ted Gurr, "Why Terrorism Subsides," paper presented at the annual meeting of the American Political Science Association, Chicago, September 1987.

47. See, for example, Susan Stern's autobiography, *With the Weathermen* (Garden City, NY: Doubleday, 1975).

48. See Jessica Stern, *Terror in the Name of God* (New York: HarperCollins, 2003), 188–236.

3

BRITAIN
AND THE IRA

Louise Richardson

Few countries have had the same depth of experience in counterinsurgency and counterterrorism as the United Kingdom. As a liberal democracy with extensive societal, governmental, historical, and cultural links to the United States, Britain has long faced many of the dilemmas the United States currently faces in combating terrorism, quelling insurgents, and formulating an efficacious security policy without compromising democratic principles. For more than thirty years in Northern Ireland, the British government faced an implacable terrorist threat from the Irish Republican Army (IRA), which sought to expel British rule from Ireland and proved to be one of the best-organized and longest-lasting terrorist groups in modern times. Formed in 1970, the Provisional IRA formally declared an end to its armed campaign on July 28, 2005.[1] Two months later, on September 26, 2005, the British and Irish governments issued a joint statement indicating that they had received a report from the Independent International Commission on Decommissioning confirming that the IRA had "placed all of its arms completely and verifiably beyond use."[2] It took the British government thirty-five years to get to this point. During this time, the government adopted a range of policies, both coercive and conciliatory, to counter the IRA. Some of these policies worked; many did not. With time, experience, and a keener appreciation of the enemy, the British government finally adopted a winning strategy to contain the IRA terrorist threat. There are many lessons for effective counterterrorist strategy to be gleaned from Britain's experience.

By the end of World War I, the British Empire had 450 million inhabitants in an area of thirteen million square miles around the globe. After the war, Britain faced nationalist uprisings in many of its colonies. Given their lack of organizational, financial, and military resources, many of these insurgencies employed terrorism as a popular tactic. Initially, the British relied simply on superior military force in response, as in India, but this strategy was unsuccessful over the long term.

After World War II, the British government faced wide-ranging insurgencies in opposition to colonial rule. These occurred (in chronological order) in Palestine, Malaya, Kenya, Cyprus, Brunei, Sarawak and Sabah, Aden, and Oman. The results of Britain's counterinsurgency campaigns were mixed. Malaya and Kenya were each deemed a success; Cyprus ended in compromise; in Aden the British withdrew; and Marxist insurgents seized power in what was to become Yemen. Due largely to its success in Malaya, the British military acquired a reputation for skill in counterinsurgency warfare (COIN). Malaya became a source of counterinsurgency theory with a set of principles called the Thompson Principles, which were to dominate British military thinking for some time.[3]

The year 1968 was a watershed in British military history because it was the first year since 1945 that Britain was not engaged in warfare. Prior to 1968, British forces were engaged primarily in campaigns of decolonization, while after 1968 the campaigns were more varied. Almost all had a terrorist component. Faced with a counterinsurgency campaign on behalf of the sultan of Oman, the British military examined the lessons of its counterinsurgency campaigns and the Thompson Principles and identified six principles that were then codified into army counterinsurgency policy:

1. Political primacy and political aim
2. Coordination of government machinery
3. Obtaining intelligence and information
4. Separating the insurgent from his support
5. Neutralizing the insurgent
6. Long-term postinsurgency planning

Armed with these principles; years of experience in counterinsurgency; and a professional, highly trained, and highly respected army, the British government faced the emergence of the civil rights movement in Northern Ireland in 1968. Two years later, the provisional wing of the IRA was formed out of the turmoil generated by the civil rights movement and the reaction of the authorities in Northern Ireland to the claims of the protesters. It has taken thirty-five years and more than thirty-three hundred deaths for the British government to secure what appears to be a permanent ceasefire in the conflict. At its height, the conflict required the deployment of thirty thousand British troops. It caused the deaths of 2,404 civilians, 303 police officers, and 658 military personnel; close to fifty thousand injuries; and an annual subvention from the British treasury of $5 billion.[4]

A Brief Overview of the Conflict in Northern Ireland

The history of the conflict in Northern Ireland is familiar and does not need to be repeated in any detail here.[5] Very briefly, the island of Ireland was ruled by neighboring Britain in one form or another for many hundreds of years. The Tudor and Stuart monarchies sought to solidify Britain's claim by planting settlers on the unruly island. In much of the island, these settlers became, as the saying went, "more Irish than the Irish themselves," but the northernmost part of the island remained the most obstreperous. In the early seventeenth century, the government once again dispatched settlers from England and Scotland. But unlike earlier settlers—wealthy Protestants who received large tracts of land—the new settlers were working people with trades, who received only small plots of property. The indigenous Catholic locals were displaced to poorer regions in the west.

The Act of Union of 1800 united Britain and Ireland in the United Kingdom, but many Irish people resisted the union both peacefully and violently throughout the nineteenth and early twentieth centuries. The pressure for home rule had become irresistible by the time of World War I. The Protestant descendants of the Stuart plantations in Northern Ireland, however, wanted no part of a semiautonomous Ireland. As a result, the British government passed the Government of Ireland Act in 1922, establishing two states in Ireland. Northern Ireland consisted of six counties with a two-thirds Protestant majority, and Southern Ireland (Eire) consisted of twenty-six counties with a 90 percent Catholic majority. The south gradually severed all links with Britain and established an independent republic in 1947. The north remained part of the United Kingdom but with local government exercised by a Protestant administration operating from Stormont Castle.

THE TROUBLES

The south of Ireland did not accept the legitimacy of the new arrangement, and the constitution of the new Irish Republic claimed jurisdiction over the entire island. More importantly, the Catholics of Northern Ireland did not accept the legitimacy of the arrangement either and sought to change it. In the late 1960s, a Catholic middle class emerged. They were beneficiaries of British social legislation, especially educational reform, that was far more generous than that available in the south of Ireland.[6] Inspired by the U.S. civil rights movement, they sought not to overthrow the state, as their coreligionists had tried earlier, but rather to claim equal rights within it. It was the first time the Catholic minority accepted, albeit implicitly, the legitimacy of the state by making demands on it. The unionist population, with an insecurity bred from its minority status on the island, had established, in the memorable words of one of its leaders, "a Protestant parliament for a Protestant people."[7] Incapable of seeing the civil rights movement as an opportunity to give the Catholic population a stake in the state, Protestant leaders instead saw the civil rights movement as an attack on the state itself. They employed the Protestant police force in an entirely partisan fashion against the demonstrators. British television screens were filled with scenes of riotous police charging peaceful civil rights marchers claiming "one man one vote," in scenes quite familiar to U.S. TV viewers at about the same time, but without the color divide. The British government responded in 1969 by temporarily dispatching British troops to Northern Ireland in defense of the civil power to restore order, separate the two sides, and, in large part, protect the Catholic population. Once it became clear in 1972 that the unionist government was incapable of reforming itself, the British government dissolved the Stormont parliament and ruled Northern Ireland directly from Westminster until the 1998 Good Friday Agreement established a power-sharing local executive.

THE PLAYERS

Throughout the period of what was called direct rule, the main players on the unionist, or Protestant, side were the Ulster Unionist Party (UUP) and the Democratic Unionist Party (DUP). The UUP was the largest and most moderate of the unionist parties and was led until recently by David Trimble. The DUP was smaller and more hard-line and was led throughout this period by a colorful and charismatic fundamentalist preacher, the Reverend Ian Paisley. (In elections to the Northern Ireland Assembly held in November 2003—elections marked by the success of extreme parties— the DUP surpassed the UUP for the first time.)[8] More-hard-line unionists were known as loyalists. The main loyalist paramilitary groups were the Ulster Defence Association (UDA) and the Ulster Volunteer Force (UVF).[9] On the Catholic, or nationalist, side, the largest party was the Social Democratic and Labour Party (SDLP), led until recently by John Hume. (On the nationalist side, too, the hard-line parties prevailed for the first time in the 2003 assembly elections.)[10] More-hard-line nationalists were known as republicans. Sinn Féin, led by Gerry Adams, was the main republican party and the political wing of the IRA, the main republican paramilitary group. The IRA had a number of permutations—the Provisional IRA, the Official IRA, and more recently the Real IRA and Continuity IRA—and a few rivals, including the Irish National Liberation Army (INLA) and the Irish Republican Socialist Party (IRSP). The Provisional IRA formed in 1970 when angry young men produced by the turmoil in the streets lost patience with the more ideological Official IRA. These "provos" soon became the group's main paramilitary force.[11] Unionists and loyalists sought to maintain the union with Britain. Nationalists and republicans sought to sever that link and unite Northern Ireland with the Republic of Ireland.

THE IRA's CAMPAIGN

In 1968, in response to the civil rights movement, the police force in Northern Ireland, especially the B Specials auxiliary body, essentially ran amok in Catholic neighborhoods in an effort to put the Catholics "back in their place." In response, the Catholic community turned to its traditional defender, the IRA. But the group was not to be found. Since the partition of Ireland and the civil war that ensued in the south, the IRA had occasionally blown up a bridge or planted small bombs in England, but it was largely defunct as a fighting force by the 1960s. Its leadership, in keeping with the times, had taken on a left-wing slant. When Catholics, under attack by elements of the Protestant community, turned to the IRA, they found its leaders debating Marxist dogma. Graffiti declaring "IRA = I Ran Away" started appearing in Catholic housing estates in Belfast. The organization promptly split. A mass of new young recruits, radicalized by experiences of police brutality or being burned from their homes by Protestant mobs, joined the new Provisional IRA.[12] Over the course of the Troubles, the Official IRA declined in importance and eventually became integrated into mainstream politics.

THE IRA TAKES OFF

The arrival of the British army on the ground enormously assisted the growth of the IRA. The deployment of armed forces almost invariably requires them to side with local authorities, the forces of law and order. The problem in Northern Ireland was that law and order were perceived by the Catholic community as Protestant law and Protestant order. Rapidly, therefore, the British army—previously welcomed as protectors—became identified as the enemy of the Catholic population. Of course, a British colonial army as the enemy fit much more comfortably with republican nationalist ideology than did Protestants as the enemy. Protestants had been something of a problem for republicanism. The IRA wanted an independent, united Ireland, but its ideology could not quite accommodate Protestant objection to that goal. For Protestants or unionists who could claim ancestral residence in the province back to the seventeenth century, Northern Ireland was home. They knew no other. Republicans persisted in seeing them as deluded pawns of British imperialism, and republican leaders repeatedly insisted that if Britain would simply instruct the Protestant population to accept the republican ideal of a united Ireland, all would be well. The Protestant population was the real stumbling block to the realization of the republican ideal, but the IRA could not amend its ideology to account for this fact. Instead, it perceived Britain as the enemy and the impediment to the realization of its goals and so cast the conflict in the familiar terms of a colonial battle against an imperial power. (It required sustained exposure to

Protestant representatives during the peace talks of the 1990s to explode this essential myth of republican ideology.)[13]

Until recently, successive British governments did little to undermine this perspective. Though they often repeated what in Britain was seen as a self-evident truth, that they had no selfish interest in the province, this claim was greeted with complete incredulity by even moderates in the Catholic community of Northern Ireland. Throughout the Stormont period, Britain simply ignored the province and ignored very clear evidence that British standards of fairness were routinely violated in the province by a government loyal and answerable to Westminster. Once the Troubles began, the British government continued to consider the province "a place apart." The succession of secretaries of state appointed by Conservative governments in office from 1979 to 1997 did much to enhance the impression. For all their talent, goodwill, and good intent, these officials could not help but appear as quintessential representatives of the Raj. It took the new breed of down-to-earth, problem-solving, managerial types appointed by the Labour government in the 1990s to finally put an end to this impression.

The arrival of British troops on the ground was not the only factor that transformed a bunch of disorganized, underemployed, angry young Catholic men into a hardened terrorist organization. In response to attacks from the police and marauding mobs, Catholics barricaded themselves into "no-go" areas to keep the security forces out. This tactic permitted the IRA to organize openly. Realizing the potential danger, the British government pulled down the barricades in a massive military operation. Known as Operation Motorman, it involved thirty-one thousand troops and was the biggest military action in Ireland in the twentieth century. The British followed this act with what was probably the single biggest miscalculation of the entire period. Acting on the advice of the Stormont leadership, who insisted that the agitation was caused by known republican troublemakers, the British government ordered the introduction of internment without trial. Hundreds of republican suspects were rounded up, interrogated, and imprisoned without trial. The hope was that this single act would cut the problem off at the root. In fact, it had the opposite effect: Young recruits, outraged by heavy-handed military tactics and sectarian targeting, flocked to the IRA.

The next big recruitment bonanza for the IRA was the incident known as Bloody Sunday, which occurred on January 30, 1972. On this day, thirteen Catholics were killed when British soldiers of the Parachute Regiment opened fire on civil rights marchers. TV images of priests ducking for cover and waving white handkerchiefs as horrified youngsters carried their wounded friends from the streets outraged the Catholic population. Subsequent British claims that the marchers were armed republicans were seen as proof of British perfidy; in the small world of the Catholic ghettos of Derry, everyone knew who was in the IRA and who was not, who had arms and who did not. The Catholic community believed for certain that those killed were neither armed nor in the IRA. The subsequent Widgery Tribunal, which exonerated the soldiers involved, removed the last vestige of credibility that remained for the British. The moderate Catholic community, prepared to be persuaded that the tragedy had been an awful mistake, was stunned by the whitewash offered by the tribunal.[14] Clearly, the IRA was the only available defender in the face of this onslaught, and recruits flocked to join. Even those who had reservations about the means employed by the movement shared its aims and would not turn its members in to the discredited authorities. The year 1972 proved to be the worst year of the Troubles, with 474 killed (255 by the IRA). There were 10,628 shootings, 1,853 bombings, and 4,876 injuries in the tiny province that year.[15]

Almost a decade later, in a very different environment, the British government again unwittingly served to expand the ranks of the IRA. The death by starvation of ten IRA members in 1981 was another propaganda boon for the group. The hunger strikers died in a failed effort to secure special-category—in effect, political prisoner—status. The Conservative government of Prime Minister Margaret Thatcher was unmoved by the starving prisoners, but the Catholic population of Northern Ireland was deeply moved. They elected the first to die, Bobby Sands, to a seat in Westminster while he was on the hunger strike. Young men again flocked to the IRA to exact revenge and as an outlet for their outrage after a period of relative decline in IRA fortunes.

This pattern of fluctuating popularity was evident throughout the Troubles. After a British or loyalist atrocity, IRA popularity soared. After an IRA atrocity, its popularity declined. Support for the underlying aims of the movement, although not its means, remained widespread throughout. Overall, the periods of heaviest violence were the early stages of the conflict. The years 1968 to 1972 saw a rapid escalation of violence. This was followed from 1972 to 1976 by a sustained period of intense violence and then a quarter-century of low-intensity conflict.

TACTICS

The tactics by which the IRA sought to achieve its goal of "Brits Out" evolved over the years. The intent was to raise the costs to Britain of maintaining the province to such an extent that Britain would decide to withdraw. As with other terrorist organizations, bombing was a favorite tactic. Often, bombs were directed at economic targets. Sometimes, especially in the early days, bombs were placed in city centers, causing extensive casualties. Sometimes they were detonated on the British mainland; more often, in the streets of Northern Ireland. There were about ten thousand explosions from the early 1970s to the early 1990s, and the British exchequer paid out more than $1 billion for repairs. In the 1990s, the bombing of economic targets became much more sophisticated. A single bomb outside the Baltic Exchange in London in 1992 killed three people and caused $1.25 billion in damage. A year later, a similar bomb in the Bishopsgate section of London caused an estimated $1.5 billion in damage.

The IRA demonstrated a consistent capacity to learn and to adapt its tactics. A British intelligence assessment stated in 1978: "They are continually learning from their mistakes and developing their expertise. We can therefore expect to see increased professionalism and a greater exploitation of modern technology for terrorist purposes."[16] With ingenious and inexpensive materials, the IRA could inflict great damage and require expensive countermeasures. Throughout the Troubles, the terrorists and the security forces engaged in a relentless game of one-upmanship. Initially, for example, IRA explosive devices were rudimentary and unreliable affairs, consisting of little more than some explosives and a few nails, lit by a fuse or timed by an alarm clock. Later, the IRA devised a means of remote detonation that employed radio controls for model aircraft bought in toy shops. When the Ministry of Defence (MOD) research and development division developed electronic countermeasures, the IRA, in turn, developed more sophisticated electronic switches. MOD scientists then developed electronic scanners capable of almost instantaneous detection of radio emissions. The IRA, in turn, figured out that by using ordinary radar detectors and radar guns, it could more quickly transmit crucial signals. The IRA later devised a means of using simple flash photography to detonate bombs from a distance.[17] When a bomb was mistakenly detonated by someone dialing a wrong number on a cell phone, the detonators were adapted to require two simultaneous calls. Over the years, the IRA demonstrated considerable ingenuity in using readily available and inexpensive materials and increased both the sophistication and lethality of its bombing campaign.

Security forces were hit, too, as were prestige targets and soft targets such as pubs in Northern Ireland and England. The IRA soon learned, however, that targeting security forces was more popular with would-be supporters than targeting random civilians—even Protestant and English ones. Police officers and part-time members of the locally recruited regiment of the British army, the Ulster Defence Regiment, were popular targets; 203 were killed in the Troubles.[18] Attacks on security forces took place in both Britain and Northern Ireland. In July 1982, for example, eleven soldiers were killed by two bombs in London, including one left under a bandstand in Regent's Park. In September 1989, ten Royal Marines were killed in a bombing at a music school in Kent.

The IRA's bombing campaigns in England, which were launched throughout the Troubles, were an effort to raise the costs of the British presence in Northern Ireland. Those close to the IRA suggest that the initial decision to bomb Britain was unwittingly precipitated by Secretary of State William Whitelaw's dismissal of military deaths in Northern Ireland as being acceptable and probably fewer than the numbers of soldiers killed in accidents in Germany.[19] Paul Holmes, an IRA member ordered to plant bombs in Britain, explained the rationale to the BBC's Peter Taylor: "The fact that the bombs were going off in England was bringing home to the British people what was happening in the North. You could actually see the logic of what the IRA was trying to do, basically bring home to the British people the fact that there is a war going on here and that there is more than one participant that's going to have to suffer."[20] Among the most spectacular attacks on the British mainland was the bombing in October 1984 of the Grand Hotel in Brighton during a Conservative Party conference. The bombing came very close to killing Prime Minister Margaret Thatcher and did kill five others. In February 1991, the IRA launched a mortar attack from a van in Whitehall on the prime minister's residence, 10 Downing Street, during a cabinet meeting.

Over the years, IRA tactics evolved away from indiscriminate to more sophisticated and discriminate bombing. Along with this switch came more central control over the organization, thereby ensuring that mavericks were restrained.

ORGANIZATION

In the early 1970s, the IRA retained its old military structure of large battalions, but this structure enormously facilitated infiltration by security forces, because defectors knew the identity of many IRA foot soldiers and leaders. So in the mid-1970s, the whole structure was reorganized. The new version had a cell-based, hierarchically organized, authoritarian structure that ensured operational efficiency.[21] Membership figures varied widely, and the few hundred members of active service units obscured a much larger support network that perhaps numbered into the thousands at times.

The key body in the IRA structure was the Army Council, which was essentially the management committee. It had seven members, met a few times a month, and elected a chief of staff from among the group. The Army Council ordered specific operations and approved those proposed from below. Above the Army Council was the Army Executive, which met every six months. It was made up of twelve senior IRA veterans, whose job it was to elect members to and keep an eye on the Army Council. The pinnacle of the organization was the General Army Convention (it met only a handful of times during the Troubles). Below the Army Council was the General Headquarters, based in Dublin. It had a staff of fifty to sixty people who operated ten departments, such as finance, publications, foreign operations, and the like. The organization then broke into Northern and Southern commands. The Northern Command was the larger and more aggressive of the two; the Southern Command was primarily responsible for logistical support. The active service units (ASUs) contained IRA volunteers, the people who actually carried out military operations. The Southern Command had about seventy to eighty-five volunteers; the rest were in the north. About one-third of all full-time ASU members were in the Belfast Brigade. Each ASU was generally composed of four volunteers and one officer commanding (OC). In theory, each volunteer knew the identity of only the OC, and in theory, each OC knew the identity of only one superior. Each ASU was trained in a specific task, such as bombing or robbery. A large number of members worked part-time and held other jobs, while others received a very small salary from the organization. The institutional evolution demonstrated organizational adaptation and learning and the impressive development of a highly efficient and multidimensional support apparatus. The real strength of the IRA, however, was the popularity of its goals: its traditional appeal to nationalist aspirations, which were shared by a broad public.

FINANCING

In the early 1970s, the U.S. organization Noraid provided about 50 percent of all IRA income, but by the mid-1980s, that income had dropped precipitously.[22] Supporters in the United States sent at least $3 million, and probably much more, to the IRA in the first fifteen years of the conflict.[23] In the mid-1980s, the IRA's operating budget was estimated at about $7 million per year. In contrast, the British government was spending an estimated $6 million per day to counter the IRA. By the mid-1990s, the group's annual budget was estimated at $15 million per year. From the beginning, the IRA was involved in extensive fund-raising activities. Sources of funding included bank and post office robberies. Fraud, extortion, and trade in counterfeit goods such as CDs and videos, as well as smuggling along the border with the republic, also provided income. More legitimate operations served to raise funds and launder money. Among the IRA's portfolio of investments were about twenty pubs in Dublin and others around Ireland. The IRA also owned and operated guesthouses, hauling companies, taxi services, and video stores in the republic. Some assistance came from overseas, for instance from Irish Americans in the United States and later from enemies of Britain in the Middle East. For example, when Britain permitted the United States to use British air bases to launch a bombing raid on Tripoli in 1986, Libya's Colonel Muammar Gadhafi responded by providing several shipments of arms to the IRA with the intent of punishing Britain.

The nearby Republic of Ireland not only provided legal and illegal venues for raising funds and a place to train and organize but also allowed IRA members to flee across the border, where British security forces could not follow. During the early years of its campaign, ETA in Spain enjoyed a similar escape route to southern France. With closer political cooperation between Britain and the Irish Republic came closer security cooperation that undermined but never fully mitigated this considerable asset. In Spain, too, increased cooperation between France and the democratic government of Spain seriously undermined the ability of ETA to operate in southern France.

BRITISH POLICY

The Labour government of Prime Minister Harold Wilson and Home Secretary James Callaghan was caught completely unawares by events in Northern Ireland. The deployment of troops in 1969 was intended to be a very temporary expedient, but the troops remained in place, albeit in reduced numbers, thirty-five years later. The dissolution of the local government and assumption of direct rule by Westminster was also intended to be temporary. The British calculated that the unionists would rather share power with Catholics locally than lose all power and be ruled directly from London, but that assumption turned out to be incorrect. Power was not devolved back to Northern Ireland until 1998 and since then has been temporarily reclaimed by Britain.

In spite of these early miscalculations, successive British governments have adopted a largely bipartisan approach to the problem in Northern Ireland. This approach has been facilitated by the fact that the issue has had very little electoral salience in Britain. Britain's professional military has meant that the deaths of soldiers have not become a political issue. While British policy on the surface often appears reactive and inconsistent, both Labour and Conservative governments have consistently adhered to a set of basic principles. The first and most important goal has been to restore order; the second, to ensure conditions that enable that order to be maintained. All political parties agree that Northern Ireland is different from the rest of the United Kingdom and that therefore the same rules do not apply. Both major parties also accept the basic view that changes to the constitutional status can be made only with the consent of the majority in the province.

All British governments have also shared a commitment to devolution as well as a vague belief that social and economic conditions can influence chances for peace. After an initial period of resistance, both parties conceded that the Republic of Ireland must have some role in the province. The role of an "Irish dimension" was formally recognized in the Anglo-Irish Agreement of 1985, signed by Prime Minister Margaret Thatcher and Taoiseach (Prime Minister) Garret Fitzgerald over the heads of the divided communities in the province. The agreement was precipitated by the efforts of Irish nationalists north and south to envision a new future for the island in the New Ireland Forum, and on the British side by a sense that the horror of the Brighton bombing demanded some positive steps forward.

Successive British governments from both sides of the House have used all the traditional instruments of the state—military, police, intelligence, legal, and political—to try to bring about a permanent end to the violence.

SECURITY ARCHITECTURE

In Britain, overall political responsibility for antiterrorist legislation and policy rests with the home secretary (although the home secretary does not have authority in Scotland). In Northern Ireland, overall political responsibility for police rests with the Northern Ireland secretary, appointed by the British prime minister and a member of his or her cabinet. The Northern Ireland secretary, the chief constable of the Royal Ulster Constabulary (RUC), and the general officer commanding Northern Ireland (GOC), who is responsible for the army, used to hold regular security meetings.

The difficulty of coordination of the various bureaucracies engaged in counterterrorism remains a perennial issue. In mainland Britain, the police have set up a number of special units designed to combat and cooperate against terrorism. Initially the Metropolitan Police Bomb Squad was the lead organization, but in 1976 it was reorganized into the Anti-Terrorism Branch. The officers could call on any of seven different agencies, all falling under the Specialist Operations Department of the Metropolitan Police Service. In the 1990s, in an effort to enhance flexibility and shorten chains of command, the system was reorganized into operational command units (OCU), each under the command of a senior superintendent. In 1992 the government vested MI5, the British Security Service, with the lead role in intelligence operations against the IRA on the British mainland. The Metropolitan Police Special Branch, which had previously enjoyed this function, predictably objected, but MI5 had experience in the area, and its new director general had previously headed its counterterrorism department. Moreover, with the end of the cold war, MI5 was yet another bureaucracy in search of a threat and anxious for the role. The trial and successful conviction in the Old Bailey of an IRA unit planning to bomb six electricity substations in the south of England provided evidence of successful coordination between the various agencies—MI5, the Special Branch, and the Anti-Terrorism Branch.

Like a number of other governments, Britain lacks a national counter-terrorism police agency due to the highly fragmented local police structure. There are, in all, forty-three police forces in England and Wales alone. Each police force in turn has its own special branch, and as a result, there is no single police force with overall control of any policing matter in the United Kingdom. The system, of course, renders coordination difficult and encourages the usual bureaucratic rivalries.

Within Northern Ireland, the situation was different again. There was only one police force, the Royal Ulster Constabulary, but the same doctrine of operational independence remained. It was an inward-looking police force, drawn almost entirely from the majority Protestant population and completely unprepared to deal with the scale of the security difficulties it faced in the late 1960s.

Military Deployment

The Labour government of Prime Minister Harold Wilson deployed British troops on August 14, 1969, in response to a request from Prime Minister James Chichester-Clark of Northern Ireland. The deployment, ordered by Home Secretary James Callaghan, significantly, was intended to support the civil authorities under what was known as MACP (military aid to civil power). In this case, the military in effect worked under the authority of the relevant chief constable of the police.[24] The government felt compelled to act, not least because it feared that if it did not, others might. The Irish taoiseach, Jack Lynch, publicly declared that the republic would not stand idly by and watch its coreligionists being brutalized. The Irish government appealed to the United Nations to send in peacekeepers, but Britain objected on the grounds that the situation was a domestic British issue.

The military, even an impeccably professional and well-trained military such as the British army, is a very blunt instrument when deployed in a civilian context. Quite aside from large transformative events such as Operation Motorman, Bloody Sunday, and the introduction of internment, the daily presence of the army is very difficult for a civilian population to accept. Its very physical presence, complete with weaponry and armored vehicles, cannot help but instill fear, incite resentment, and intimidate. The heavy-handedness that is a natural part of the military style of arrest and interrogation, moreover, further served to alienate the military from the civilian population in Northern Ireland and rendered easy the military's transformation from the role of protector to that of enemy and soon to a target for terrorists. Policies such as curfews and house-to-house searches in Catholic areas and cratering of border roads to diminish insurgent activity served to swell the ranks of the IRA.

No sooner were the troops on the ground than efforts were made to remove them. In January 1970, only a few months after their arrival, three of eight major army units were withdrawn. (Later, the desire to withdraw troops was constrained by the fear that to do so might appear to be a concession to the terrorists.) The British military establishment was far from enthusiastic about the deployment. It believed that the role of the British military was to defend NATO against the forces of the Soviet Union on the plains of Bavaria, not to defend Catholics and Protestants from one another on the backstreets of Belfast. Military leaders quite reasonably feared a drain on the army's limited resources.

The British military did succeed in containing the level of violence, which never again matched the carnage of the early 1970s. Instead, the violence entered a time of prolonged military stalemate with about one hundred casualties a year. These years were punctuated by particular atrocities, such as the Enniskillen bombing in 1987, in which eleven Protestants were murdered while attending a Remembrance Day ceremony, as well as successes, such as the capture of the *Eksund* arms shipment from Libya the same year. Nevertheless, the military soon realized that in spite of the extraordinary asymmetry in manpower, it could not defeat the IRA militarily. It was this realization, reluctantly arrived at, that motivated efforts to seek a political solution. General J. M. Glover, commander of land forces in Northern Ireland, wrote a top-secret intelligence estimate of the IRA, which the organization promptly found and published. The report was bitterly criticized because of the conclusions that (a) the IRA could not be defeated militarily; (b) the IRA was not made up of mindless hooligans, as the government generally portrayed IRA members; and (c) the IRA campaign would last as long as Britain remained in the province.[25] Events were to bear out Glover's analysis. In 1973, 25,343 members of the British army were deployed in Northern Ireland supporting 4,421 members of the RUC. They faced a few hundred members of the IRA. By the time of the Good Friday Agreement in 1998, these numbers had changed to 16,934 members of the army and 8,495 members of the RUC.[26]

Just as the politicians sought to develop local institutions to assume power, so the military leadership sought to develop local security forces and to move the military into the background. The policy, known as Ulsterization, was driven by a number of factors: a recognition of the provocative potential of British troops on the ground, resistance to being drawn further and further into a policing function that could more effectively be carried out by locals, and an effort to limit the drain on military resources. The most visible sign of this policy was the creation of a locally recruited regiment of the British army, the Ulster Defence Regiment (UDR). It was created in 1970 as a replacement for the much-discredited Ulster Special Constabulary, the B Specials. As a matter of fact, 60 percent of the new recruits were former members of the B Specials. The goal initially was to recruit a force of thirty-five hundred, but by 1973 the unit had eighty-five hundred members. By the late 1970s, local Ulster forces had reached a fairly stable level of fourteen thousand to fifteen thousand men.[27] Like other components of the local security services, the UDR recruited almost exclusively from the Protestant population and had no legitimacy among Catholics. From the point of view of the Catholic community, the very community from which the British government needed to win support, the UDR was little more than a case of the British arming enemies of Catholics. UDR members soon became preferred targets of the IRA because off-duty members were so easy to kill.[28] The UDR never attained the standards of professionalism of other British forces. Between 1985 and 1989, UDR members were twice as likely to commit crimes as were members of the general public. They were four times more likely to commit crimes than members of the regular British army and ten times more likely to commit crimes than members of the RUC. By the early 1990s, 120 former members were serving prison terms for serious crimes, including seventeen murders.[29] The UDR soon became a party to the conflict, and evidence emerged of repeated instances of collusion between loyalist paramilitaries and the UDR in the murder of republican suspects. Shaken by this evidence, the British government in 1992 merged the UDR and the Royal Irish Rangers to become the RIR, Royal Irish Regiment, but the sectarian composition remained unchanged. The UDR blurred the distinction between the police and the military and seriously undermined Britain's claim to have professionalized local security forces. Peter R. Neumann argues that the British policy could more fairly be called demilitarization than Ulsterization, as the government sought not so much to shift costs to the locals as to professionalize the police in the belief that the police were more likely than the military to be effective in successfully countering terrorism.[30] This position was based on the belief, which General Glover had challenged fifteen years previously, that IRA members were hardened criminals rather than politically motivated fighters. The reliance by the British government on such clearly partisan forces seriously impaired the achievement of the broader objectives, since the security forces had so little legitimacy among the Catholic population.

POLICE

Two government inquiries, the Cameron and Scarman commissions, concluded that the Northern Ireland police force had manifestly failed in its handling of the violence occasioned by the civil rights movement. As a result, in the mid-1970s the British government sought to reorganize and professionalize the RUC and to turn the police into the vanguard of the counterterrorist campaign. The secretary of state sought to reduce the military to the role of aiding the civil power and to establish police primacy in the campaign against terrorists. Only in "bandit country" along the border was the heavy machinery of the army thought to be necessary. The rural campaign was to be left largely to the army and the Special Air Service (SAS), and urban policing to the RUC. The concept of police primacy was undermined, however, by the reality that the army was responsible for more than 300 of the 357 killings carried out by the police and military between 1969 and 1993.[31]

Accompanying the effort to Ulsterize or demilitarize the security forces was an effort to depoliticize and criminalize the terrorists. The success of this plan required serious reform of the local police to turn it into an impartial force, but this transformation did not occur, although improved training and the elimination of the large number of part-timers on the force did increase its professionalism.

The problem with this plan was that the RUC was almost exclusively a Protestant force and never obtained the trust of the Catholic community. The antagonism to the police was such that the RUC could not enter several minority areas, which then had to be policed by the army. The RUC operated its own intelligence units and its own interrogation centers, which were notorious for a time for mistreatment of Catholic/republican prisoners but later were elaborately supervised. The police force was perceived by the Catholic population to be an arm of the Protestant state. In one celebrated case in April 1997, a group of RUC members stood by and watched while a Protestant mob picked up a random Catholic man, Robert Hamill, and brutally beat him to death. Not only did the police ignore the pleas of Hamill's companion and fail to stop the beating, but one policeman phoned one of the assailants after the fact and recommended that he get rid of his clothes to dispose of evidence. The Protestant community, on the other hand, remained deeply loyal to the police force, which lost 306 members in the Troubles.

The partisanship of the RUC, never in doubt in the eyes of the Catholic community, was clearly demonstrated by the Stalker affair. John Stalker, deputy chief constable of the Manchester Police Force, was appointed to investigate allegations of a shoot-to-kill policy by the RUC. In the winter of 1982, a specialist squad of police officers shot six men dead. The circumstances indicated, as Stalker carefully pointed out, an inclination, if not a policy, to shoot suspects dead without warning rather than to arrest them. Suspicions of deliberate assassinations, he argued, were not unreasonable given the circumstances. The Stalker inquiry expressed worry that the RUC's special branch was becoming a force within a force and that, together with the Special Support Unit (SSU—a heavily armed unit trained by the SAS), it was, in fact if not in name, operating a shoot-to-kill policy. Stalker charged that officers lied to cover up their crimes, and senior members of the force obstructed his investigation. Stalker recommended prosecution of eleven police officers and requested access to further evidence that he believed would warrant additional charges of murder and attempted murder against other members of the force. The investigation was promptly squashed.[32] It was only after the 1998 Good Friday Agreement, and the Patton Inquiry to which it led, that there was thoroughgoing—and deeply painful—police reform, as the RUC was reconstituted as the Police Force of Northern Ireland (PFNI). The British experience speaks to the difficulty of depending on unreliable locals and in particular the difficulty of operating through security forces whose impartiality is in doubt.

INTELLIGENCE

The most important weapon in any campaign against terrorism is intelligence. In Northern Ireland, there was a vast array of intelligence units, each belonging to a different element of the security apparatus. The difficulty of coordinating intelligence between the police and the military, and the many subunits of both that were engaged in intelligence gathering, was a perennial issue.

While the army was relegated to a supportive role by the late 1970s, its intelligence collection function remained crucial. Battalion intelligence officers gathered intelligence from a variety of sources, including the police, and in turn provided the police with necessary information to make arrests. But the concept of police primacy led to considerable frustration within the military, which in turn gave rise to some freelance activities. Between 1976 and 1978, undercover soldiers ambushed and shot dead ten people, three of whom the military later admitted were killed by mistake.[33] By the late 1970s, sharing intelligence had become exceedingly difficult as other agencies' informants were arrested and sources were compromised by feuding between intelligence operatives.

An effort to resolve the problem by the appointment at Stormont of a director and coordinator of intelligence (DCI) was rendered ineffective on the ground due to incessant feuding between the army and the Special Branch. More successful was the creation of regional crime and intelligence units, which became the model for police-military intelligence coordination in the form of tasking and coordination groups (TCGs). Each TCG combined a Criminal Investigation Department, Special Branch, and army specialists, plus MI5 agents on an ad hoc basis, and was commanded by a Special Branch officer. The appointment of a new head of the Special Branch and the enhancement of training for members of special undercover units, the Bronze Section and the Special Patrol Group (the RUC's mobile antiterrorist unit), led to significant improvements. By 1980 the IRA was taking the risk of penetration very seriously. It set up its own security department to hunt down informers. Between 1979 and 1981, it murdered seven informers, more than the number of IRA members killed by security forces in the same period.

In spite of improved intelligence gathering, 1979 was a bad year in Northern Ireland. Airey Neave, the Conservative Party spokesman on

Northern Ireland and a close friend of Prime Minister Margaret Thatcher, was murdered by a car bomb placed by the INLA in the House of Commons parking lot. The IRA assassinated the British ambassador to the Netherlands and in the summer murdered Lord Mountbatten, an icon of the British establishment and a senior member of the royal family, along with several members of his family while they were boating in Ireland. The same day, two IRA mines killed eighteen British soldiers in County Down.

In response, the government brought Sir Maurice Oldfield, the former head of MI6, out of retirement and dispatched him to Northern Ireland as security co-coordinator to take charge of the entire intelligence operation there. He had derived two major prescriptions from his long career as a spy: taking out (killing) middle management of republican paramilitaries and turning (into informants) key figures in the IRA. He established an intelligence directorate known as the Department, which drew representatives of MI5, MI6, the SAS, the RUC, the Special Branch, and the plainclothes Bronze Section of the RUC's Special Patrol Group. Large sums of money were procured from London to improve surveillance and communications equipment and acquire sophisticated computer systems.[34] The problem of coordination and interunit rivalries was never fully overcome, but the emphasis on turning key members was to lead to the "supergrass" trials (whereby the uncorroborated evidence of a former accomplice known as a supergrass was enough to secure conviction in the 1980s). The RUC estimated that by the early 1990s, 70 percent of all planned IRA operations had been abandoned on security grounds. Of the remaining 30 percent, 80 percent were prevented or interdicted by the security forces.[35]

The protracted nature of the conflict and the relatively limited geographic area gave the myriad intelligence services time to develop a network of informers recruited in a variety of ways. This process led to some spectacular military successes, such as the ambushing of IRA active service units as they were about to launch an attack on the SAS in Coagh, Tyrone, in 1991, and the even more dramatic SAS ambush in Loughgall in 1987 that killed eight IRA members. Collaboration with intelligence agents overseas, moreover, served to disrupt funding sources and interrupt arms shipments from as far away as the United States and Libya. The chronic difficulties of coordination among so many entities were never fully overcome, however.[36]

Emergency Legislation

Public pressure on politicians to do something in the face of a terrorist atrocity invariably leads to the introduction of emergency legislation. The situation of the British in Northern Ireland was no exception. Emergency legislation, however, was nothing new in the province. The 1922 Special Powers Act had given the civil authorities quite draconian powers to, among other things, censor the printed word, ban meetings and parades, impose curfews, proscribe organizations, and detain and intern suspects. The act also allowed for extensive powers of entry, search, and seizure. The Stormont government's partisan implementation of the provisions of this act against the Catholic population became one of the injustices against which the civil rights movement of the late 1960s rallied. Initially introduced to bring law and order to the newly constituted province, the act remained on the statute books ostensibly to maintain peace by prohibiting the expression of republican or nationalist sentiment deemed critical of the unionist government of the province.[37]

In 1973 the British government prorogued the Stormont parliament, replaced it with direct rule from London, and promised to abolish the Special Powers Act. Laura K. Donohue demonstrates that, in fact, most provisions of the reviled Special Powers Act were included in the new legislation, the 1973 Northern Ireland (Emergency Provisions) Act (EPA).[38] This act was repeatedly amended throughout the Troubles, with provisions such as a ban on television appearances by representatives of terrorist movements, restrictions on an accused's right to silence, and the introduction of the supergrass system to the courts.

New legislative initiatives tended to follow rapidly on the heels of terrorist atrocities. In 1974 bombs placed in two pubs in Birmingham killed twenty-one people and injured two hundred others. The atrocity was immediately followed by the hastily constituted Prevention of Terrorism Act (PTA). This act extended the government's powers of arrest and detention and strictly controlled movement of terrorist suspects between Britain and Ireland. Similarly, in 1998, after the Omagh bombing, the Criminal Justice (Terrorism and Conspiracy) Act was hastily passed. This act allowed the testimony of a police officer to serve as evidence of membership in a specified organization; it further restricted the right to silence and enhanced powers of forfeiture. In neither case, however, did the provisions of the act help lead to the arrest and conviction of the perpetrators of the atrocities in question. In the case of the Birmingham bombs, six Irishmen were soon convicted, to the widespread skepticism of the Irish community. After the men had spent sixteen years in prison, their convictions were overturned and three detectives were charged with perjury and conspiracy in the investigation. Through an exhaustive study of the provisions of the EPA and PTA, Laura Donohue demonstrated that, terminology notwithstanding, there is nothing temporary about temporary emergency legislation.[39]

One problem for the British government and the Northern Irish authorities throughout the Troubles was the belief that convictions could not be won in jury trials. Ostensibly, the fear was that witnesses might be intimidated, but there was probably also fear of tacit Catholic community support for republican terrorists, which would make it impossible to get jurors to convict and lead instead to perverse acquittals. The introduction of internment without trial was one effort to get around this problem.

As mentioned earlier, the policy of internment as implemented was an enormous mistake. Only a handful of those interned were charged with criminal offenses. The policy was introduced in August 1971 on the recommendation of the Stormont government, in the hope that troublemakers could simply be lifted from the streets and kept out of trouble. (The failure of the policy demonstrated yet again that a search for a simple solution is rarely, if ever, successful.) The policy, unwisely, was implemented almost entirely against the Catholic population, although Catholics by no means exercised a monopoly on illegal violence. Of 918 suspects interned in the first six months, none were loyalists. By the time the policy was abandoned, more than 2,000 republicans but only 100 loyalists had been interned.[40]

Military vehicles roared into nationalist/Catholic communities in the middle of the night, where troops smashed down doors, picked up hundreds of Catholic men, and interned them without trial on a prison ship and in specially prepared World War II–era prison camps. The fact that, at least initially, only Catholics were interned generated outrage among the nationalist community. The fact that most of those interned had nothing to do with the IRA—a fact well known in the communities from which they were drawn, though not to the intelligence services—made the outrage even stronger. The intelligence services seemed oblivious to the well-known fact that key sections of the IRA leadership operated out of the Republic of Ireland, not Northern Ireland, and that a great many northern republicans, relying on their own intelligence sources, had gone on the run in anticipation of the introduction of internment. The implementation of the policy serves as a demonstration of the folly of acting on unreliable intelligence and the difficulties inherent in military implementation of security policies in a civilian context.

Moderate Catholics from groups such as the SDLP and the civil rights movement combined to organize a campaign of civil disobedience in response. Those whose outrage could not be contained by rent and rate strikes flocked to the IRA. A policy designed to stem the tide of violence by picking up ringleaders failed miserably, in part because it was based on faulty intelligence and in part because it was imposed in so partisan a manner. The result was more recruits for the republican cause. As William Whitelaw, the first secretary of state for Northern Ireland, later reflected in his memoirs: "The introduction of internment was predictably followed by heavy rioting during which twenty-one people were killed in three days. Thereafter internment did nothing to stem the deterioration of the situation. On the contrary it remained a source of discontent and a spur to more violence."[41]

Internees were considered a vital source of intelligence by the security forces. To extract this intelligence, security forces subjected internees to interrogation methods that would be completely unacceptable under normal circumstances. In *Ireland v. UK,* the European Court of Human Rights determined that the five techniques employed in the early 1970s to interrogate prisoners violated the European Convention on Human Rights. These techniques were

- Having a hood placed over the head
- Being forced to stand spread-eagled against a wall for long periods
- Being denied regular sleep patterns
- Having irregular and limited supplies of food and water
- Being subjected to white noise

These techniques might not be too bad for a hardened military activist, but to the regular civilians on whom they were most often used, they were terrifying. In the face of outraged public and international opinion, Britain was obliged to stop using these interrogation methods. In two other cases, *Brogan and Others v. UK* and *Fox Campbell and Hartley,* the European Court also found the British treatment of prisoners to be in violation of the convention, but in these instances the United Kingdom claimed the right of derogation from the provisions in view of the emergency situation in Northern Ireland.

Internment remained on the statute book until it was finally removed by the Labour government in 1998. By 1975 the British government had dropped the policy, however, in the face of its manifest failure and replaced it with what were known as the Diplock Courts, which replaced trial by jury with trial by a single judge for terrorist offenses.[42]

DIPLOCK COURTS

Accompanying trial by a single judge was an effort to stretch the time a suspect could be detained without access to a lawyer. The purpose behind such detentions was to secure confessions, but the prosecution had to prove that the confessions were obtained without torture or cruel and inhuman treatment. Diplock trials relied heavily on confessions, which were more readily admissible in terrorist trials in Northern Ireland than elsewhere in the United Kingdom. A single judge, no jury, and conviction on the basis of confession—this was a far cry from the standard trial afforded in the British courts.

When a confession was unavailable, the word of a single accomplice, known as a supergrass, sufficed to win conviction. Under this system, a former member of a terrorist group who had been broken by interrogation would turn in significant numbers of his former accomplices. During a period in the 1980s, a large number of convictions were won in this way.[43] Many of these convictions were subsequently overturned in the face of widespread criticism of the system. Between 1980 and 1993, there were thirteen supergrass trials involving charges against 245 defendants. Of these, 145 were convicted, and 69 of these convictions were based on the uncorroborated evidence of a supergrass informer. There were 78 appeals against conviction, and 66 of the convictions were quashed, leaving 79 guilty verdicts extant after appeal.[44] While both loyalist and republican paramilitary members became informants, the dramatic departure from standard legal norms and practice was enough, yet again, to undermine the confidence of the minority community in the fairness of British justice.

GOING TOO FAR

Another common pitfall of democratic governments, under enormous pressure from an aroused public to provide protection and exact revenge after a terrorist atrocity, is to ignore democratic constraints and go too far. In Europe, the most dramatic case occurred in Spain with the creation of the Liberation Antiterrorist Groups (GAL), counterterrorist death squads.[45] In Britain, the deviations from democratic practice were less extreme, but a number of instances, and many others that remain under investigation, suggest that there, too, the government and especially the security services overreacted. The costs of these overreactions are high in several respects. They damage the principles the democracy is designed to defend in the first place. They also have high reputational costs overseas and especially high political costs at home, because these overreactions render efforts to win the hearts and minds of the community from which the terrorists derive their support infinitely more difficult.

One of the most celebrated examples of British overreaction in the campaign against the IRA was the apparent RUC practice of "shoot to kill" exposed by Deputy Chief Constable John Stalker, mentioned above. Even more serious allegations of collusion between security forces and Protestant terrorist groups remain under investigation. These allegations have been supported by media investigations and have been investigated by commissioners of the London Metropolitan Police.[46] In September 1989, John Stevens, then deputy chief constable in the Cambridgeshire Constabulary, began investigating allegations of collaboration between security forces and loyalist paramilitaries. A mysterious fire at the headquarters of the Stevens team destroyed many of its files. Curiously, fire alarms, telephones, and heat-sensitive intruder alarms malfunctioned at the time of the fire. In 1993 Stevens began a second inquiry; in 1998, a third. Finally, in April 2003, Stevens's report found evidence of both police and army collusion in murder.[47] In his subsequent report, retired Canadian judge Peter Cory described how security services had deliberately frustrated the Stevens inquiry by the willful concealment of pertinent evidence.

Evidence of extensive military and police collusion with loyalist paramilitaries was also revealed in the trial of Brian Nelson, a member of the Protestant paramilitary group the UDA, who was on the army's payroll. Not only did security forces refuse to act when provided with detailed information on forthcoming operations planned against Catholics, but they also provided detailed intelligence information on the whereabouts of known republicans so that the UDA could then assassinate them. Security forces, moreover, turned a blind eye to the importation and distribution of arms to some loyalist paramilitaries.[48]

It has proven extraordinarily difficult to win convictions against members of security forces for killing civilians. In the 1970s, a dozen soldiers from British regiments (excluding the UDR) were prosecuted for murder and all were acquitted. Conviction of a British soldier for murder was won for the first time in 1984 and for the second time in 1990. In both instances, the soldiers were released from prison shortly after receiving mandatory life sentences. They each spent less than two years in prison and promptly rejoined the army on their release.

It is widely believed in the Catholic community that the murders of prominent lawyers Patrick Finucane and Rosemary Nelson, who defended republican suspects, were a direct result of collusion between security forces and Protestant paramilitaries. In July 2003, the European Court of Human Rights found that the British government had committed a human rights violation by failing to ensure an independent police inquiry into the murder of Finucane. The court ruled that in cases with allegations that the police themselves are complicit, it is not adequate for that same police force to investigate the murder.

Peter Cory was finally asked in 2001 to lead an investigation. The publication of his report was repeatedly delayed by actions of the intelligence services and the Northern Ireland Office. The Northern Ireland Office was acting under pressure from the Joint Services Group (JSG), formerly known as the Force Research Unit (FRU), which was responsible for all military intelligence matters in Northern Ireland and the republic. The intelligence services threatened to issue injunctions against the publication of the report.[49] Finally, after considerable delay, several redactions, and amendments to stress the provisional nature of the findings, on April 1, 2004, Judge Cory released his report. In the case of the murder of Patrick Finucane, a Belfast solicitor who was shot dead while having dinner at home with his family, the report found: "[T]here is strong evidence that collusive acts were committed by the Army (FRU), the RUC SB [Special Branch] and the Security Service [MI5]."[50] Cory pointed out that the police and security forces failed to draw a distinction between law-abiding solicitors such as Finucane and Rosemary Nelson and the terrorists they defended. In the case of Finucane, the murder weapon itself originated in the army. Nelson, a Catholic lawyer and mother of three, was killed in her driveway by a bomb placed under her car after receiving innumerable threats to her life from the police and Protestant paramilitaries. Cory indicated that there was some reason to suggest that police officers had incited loyalist paramilitaries to kill her, and he requested a full public inquiry into these and two other cases.

Whatever the final result of the investigations, it is already clear that the widespread belief among the minority population that the police and military were on occasion operating outside the law and colluding with loyalist paramilitaries in a manner antithetical to democratic principles was well founded. This belief, and the attendant mistrust of the political and security forces, can only have prolonged the conflict and served to increase the sense of alienation of the Catholic community, the desire for revenge, and the rejection of accommodation with the state. In short, whatever the short-term gains won by the elimination of difficult opponents, the long-term costs were surely higher.

Finally, failure to adhere closely to sound legal practice and preferring instead rapid results led to the false convictions and lengthy incarcerations of numerous innocent people for IRA atrocities. Four people were falsely convicted of the Guilford bombing in 1974, which killed seven and injured more than one hundred, and in the most celebrated case, six people were wrongly convicted of the Birmingham bombing. Six members of the Maguire family and a family friend were also falsely convicted of serious terrorist offenses in mainland Britain and served long prison terms. In each instance, it was widely known within the Catholic community that those convicted were innocent and in several cases had no connection whatsoever to the IRA. This situation again served only to undermine faith in British justice and to render more difficult a political solution. Moreover, the British government, in its haste to win convictions, lost the opportunity afforded to it by some of these horrific atrocities to make a case against the IRA. Recognizing the ongoing sensitivity on the issue, in February 2005, Prime Minister Tony Blair issued a public apology for the false convictions of the "Guilford 4" and the "Maguire 7."

TALKING TO TERRORISTS

Most governments, when faced with an enemy that employs terrorist tactics, adopt a policy of no negotiation. There are a number of reasons for the policy. First and foremost, it is generally designed to demonstrate that terrorism will not be rewarded. Second, it is adopted to demonstrate repugnance for the terrorists and to insist on a moral distance between the government and the terrorists. This was the position of the British government. Officially, there were no negotiations with the IRA, but in fact, there were a number of negotiations. The first of these took place in March 1972 in Dublin when Harold Wilson, then leader of the British Labour Party, and shadow Northern Ireland secretary Merlyn Rees met leading members of the IRA. More significantly, in July of that year, senior members of the British government, led by William Whitelaw, met senior members of the IRA in London at the home of Minister of State Paul Channon. Some IRA participants, including Gerry Adams, were released from prison and transported by helicopter for the occasion. The IRA had offered a cease-fire if Whitelaw would meet with them. He replied publicly that he "could not respond to ultimatums from terrorists who are causing suffering to innocent civilians in Northern Ireland and shooting British troops."[51] Nevertheless, when the IRA called a cease-fire, the army reciprocated, and the meeting took place. The meeting did little other than to reveal to both sides the depth of their differences, but it did demonstrate a realization by the British authorities that whatever they might be saying in public, and whatever their repugnance for the IRA, they might indeed have to talk to the group.

In 1975 British government officials again held meetings with leaders of the IRA. This time, the meetings took place over several months while the IRA maintained an extended cease-fire. Initially, the republicans were led to believe that the British were trying to find a way to extricate themselves from Northern Ireland. Republicans subsequently came to believe that the negotiations were a ruse by the government designed to gather intelligence on the movement and to encourage splits within the movement by trying to draw some of the membership into constitutional politics. Partly in response to this situation, a new, younger, and tougher cadre took over leadership of the movement and determined not to be used in this way. The Army Council of the IRA committed never to talk to the British except to discuss British withdrawal from Ireland.

Throughout the 1970s, therefore, the British government adopted a dual strategy. On the one hand, it engaged the leadership of the IRA in talks. On the other hand, through the policy of Ulsterization, criminalization, and normalization, it swelled the ranks of the prison population, which was to become the new locus of the struggle. The hunger strikes of 1981, in which ten republican prisoners slowly starved themselves to death in an effort to gain political prisoner status, were the apogee of this stage of the conflict. As in other aspects of the conflict, the government ostensibly won, in that the families of the remaining prisoners refused to allow any more to die, but it may actually have lost. The widespread popularity of the hunger strikers was demonstrated by the election to Parliament in Westminster of Bobby Sands, the first of the hunger strikers to die. The hunger strikes proved to be an enormous public relations victory for the IRA, winning it sympathy around the world and throngs of recruits at home. Again, throughout the strikes, shadowy behind-the-scenes communications took place, this time between leaders of the IRA in Belfast; the leader of the hunger-striking prisoners, Brendan Hughes; and Michael Oatley, code-named Mountain Climber, of MI6—but to no avail.[52] The talks collapsed when the British government, inspired by Margaret Thatcher's mantra that "a crime is a crime is a crime," refused to concede special-category status, and the prisoners would accept nothing less.

The official position of both the British government and the IRA is that there were no behind-the-scenes discussions leading to the Good Friday Agreement until 1990, when British intelligence opened a dialogue with Martin McGuinness of the IRA. It appears, however, that secret negotiations did take place as early as 1986. From the British point of view, their purpose appears to have been to maintain contact with the more pragmatic, or moderate, wing of the IRA led by Adams. The point was to provide incentives for abandoning violence in favor of politics, and probably also to weaken the IRA by generating internal disagreements. The Army Council of the IRA appears to have been unaware of the contacts between Adams and the London and Dublin governments. The discussions were usually conducted through intermediaries, such as the Redemptorist priest Father Alex Reid and Belfast-based businessman Brendan Duddy. The contacts were monitored at the highest levels of government by successive secretaries of state for Northern Ireland, Tom King and Peter Brooke. The prime minister, Margaret Thatcher, her tough antiterrorist credentials unimpeachable after having faced down the hunger strikers, not to mention having narrowly escaped an assassination attempt, was kept informed.[53] The negotiations involved the exchange of documents that later served as the blueprint for the Good Friday Agreement reached twelve years later.[54] The negotiations continued in spite of the capture of the *Eksund,* a ship laden with 150 tons of munitions from Libya, designed to provide the necessary arsenal for the IRA's "Tet offensive" planned for March 1988. (It is hard to imagine how the negotiations would have survived the safe landing of the arsenal and the launching of the offensive.) The contacts almost did not survive an IRA attempt to assassinate Tom King in August 1987, suggesting again that knowledge of the contacts was confined to a very small number of people in British intelligence and the IRA.

Talks took place on many other levels, too. John Hume, leader of the SDLP, the largest nationalist party in Northern Ireland and therefore the leader of the only party likely to lose politically from a decision by the IRA to place more emphasis on the ballot box, via Sinn Féin, and less on the Armalite rifle, held extensive negotiations with Gerry Adams of Sinn Féin. The British government, realizing that the problem could be solved only if they were to cede to the Republic of Ireland an "Irish dimension" to the problem, also began to negotiate constructively with the Dublin government in an effort to forge agreement over the heads of the feuding parties in Northern Ireland.[55] The 1990s witnessed negotiations, cease-fires, unanswered calls for disarmament, more violence, and more talks before finally culminating, on April 10, 1998, with the Belfast Agreement (better known as the Good Friday Agreement). The agreement brought a tenuous peace to the province and a belated end to the terrorist campaign of the IRA.

The main provisions of the Belfast Agreement include the acceptance by all parties of the principle that the constitutional future of Northern Ireland will be determined by a majority vote of the citizens of the province. The signatories also agreed to pursue their objectives through "exclusively peaceful and democratic means." The agreement established a Northern Ireland Assembly with devolved legislative powers and a "power-sharing" Northern Ireland Executive in which ministries will be allocated proportionally to the main parties.[56] The nationalist interest in an Irish dimension and the unionist interest in a British dimension were addressed by the creation of two further institutions, a North-South Ministerial Council and a British-Irish Council, to discuss issues of common concern and to further cross-border cooperation. For its part, the Republic of Ireland agreed to modify the territorial claim to Northern Ireland contained in articles 2 and 3 of its constitution. The British government promised police reform, demilitarization of British army bases, and new legislation on human rights and equality. The release within two years of paramilitary prisoners belonging to organizations observing the police cease-fire was promised, and a two-year target was set for decommissioning the weapons of paramilitaries.

The agreement was ratified by referenda in both parts of Ireland in May 1998, although nationalist votes and nationalist enthusiasm have far exceeded those of the unionist population, who fear that the agreement concedes too much and allows for "a shamrock road to unity." The agreement, however, falls far short of achieving the IRA's objective of a united Ireland. It took seven and a half years, not the two stipulated in the agreement, for the IRA to implement the destruction of its arsenal. Now that it has finally done so, the terrorist campaign of the IRA is at an end.

LESSONS

There are a number of lessons to be derived from the British counterterrorist campaign against the IRA.

The Primacy of Politics. The first lesson is the importance of never losing sight of the fact that the challenge posed is political, not military. All the strength of the British military could not defeat the infinitely weaker IRA because of the support the latter had in the community and because the threat posed was fundamentally political. The clear lesson is that political grievances that garner support for terrorists must be addressed.

The Deployment of the Military. The military did serve to keep the threat from the IRA in check and after the mid-1970s to reduce the conflict to one of military stalemate. But the deployment of the military served the interests of the IRA when it legitimized its campaign by elevating it to the status of declared enemy of the British army. It also served to swell the ranks of the IRA because of the army's heavy-handed tactics and the inevitable accidents that happen when heavily armed troops are deployed in a volatile civilian setting. The goal of using the military as a backup to civilian security forces is admirable but only feasible when those civilian forces have some legitimacy. In Northern Ireland, this legitimacy was confined to one side of the sectarian divide.

The Use of Emergency Legislation. One of the few sureties of temporary emergency legislation is that it is rarely temporary. When emergency legislation is seen as too one-sided or too far a deviation from standard practice, it is unlikely to work in the long term. Nonjury courts, for example, may be a legitimate deviation from standard practice, but the uncorroborated testimony of an informant's confession is surely not adequate to win conviction in any court for which the government wishes to acquire civilian support. By keeping in mind constantly the need to secure community support, the government can ascertain and reach a balance in each instance.

Talking to Terrorists. The Northern Ireland case suggests the importance of engaging terrorists to learn how they operate, not only to undermine them but also to influence their internal dynamics and engage them in the process of peacekeeping. It is only by engaging them that one can get an appreciation of their grievances and a sense of the priorities they attach to different objectives. It is extremely hard to imagine how the Good Friday Agreement could have come about without the long experience of behind-the-scenes negotiations, both direct and indirect, between the government and the terrorists. As a practical matter, the noble injunction not to talk to terrorists and not to reward terrorism proved to be useless. Negotiations involved more than talk, and concessions were made on all sides. It was only through these negotiations that the British government, for example, learned to appreciate the power of symbols. The government learned that it had to drop monarchical symbols such as royal emblems to have a hope of attaining minority support. The Royal Ulster Constabulary became the more neutral Police Service of Northern Ireland. Similarly, the government learned the importance of the Irish dimension and the need to codify that relationship, which had the additional benefit of enhancing cross-border security cooperation. Through the talks, the government also came to appreciate the role of prisoners and the obligation felt toward them by activist republicans. Offering amnesty for political offenses became a key ingredient of the final agreement. The clear lesson to other democracies is that there is an enormous amount to be gained by negotiating with terrorists. One can learn who the cast of characters is and how they react to incentives and force. One can gain an understanding of the issues on which terrorists are prepared to negotiate and those on which they will not. By providing incentives for moderation or pragmatism and being willing to make tangible concessions, one can influence or even manipulate the internal dynamics of the opponent. The clear lesson of the British case is that, moral repugnance notwithstanding, it is best to talk to terrorists.

Intelligence. There are lessons, too, about the importance and the difficulty of coordinating intelligence functions. Systematically and hierarchically organized intelligence functions operating under clear political supervision are essential. The most crucial weapon against terrorists is intelligence, but limits ought to be set on the price paid for that intelligence. Protecting and at times arming and abetting loyalist paramilitaries as a means of getting intelligence on republican paramilitaries seems too high a price to pay. Over the years, the British security services developed a good intelligence apparatus, but this process took time. Acting prematurely on unreliable intelligence, as in the introduction of internment, was calamitous.

Going Too Far. The Northern Ireland case also indicates the difficulty of keeping the security services in check and insisting they abide by democratic constraints. When they exceed those constraints, the community the government needs to woo if it is ultimately to be successful will be alienated. When victims appeal to outsiders, either the media or in this instance the European Court of Human Rights, to substantiate their claims of abuse, the reputation of the government is severely damaged. Had the British government been willing to demonstrate its commitment to democratic principles by investigating thoroughly the claims of abuse itself and then acting openly to redress deficiencies, the support of moderates within the minority community would have been far more readily forthcoming.

The Role of Outsiders. This case also points to the importance of managing the role of outsiders. External actors played a number of parts, both positive and negative, in the Northern Ireland conflict. Sympathizers in the United States and friends in the Libyan government provided funding and weaponry to the IRA. The European Court acted as an independent arbitrator for claims of government abuse. The government of the United States exerted its influence to bring the conflicting parties together and to keep them talking. U.S. senator George Mitchell played a crucial role as moderator of the cross-party negotiations. The inclusion of the Republic of Ireland (which did not consider itself an outsider) made a political solution more acceptable to republicans and reduced the security of the IRA's southern sanctuary.

A Multipronged Approach. The final lesson to be derived from the British experience in Northern Ireland is the importance of pursuing a coordinated multipronged approach. There is no one silver bullet that can eliminate terrorism. Instead, with a clear view to long-term political objectives, the government must ensure that its various branches are acting together in a mutually reinforcing way to achieve their shared goal.

In short, one can assess the effectiveness of the British government's counterterrorism measures by reviewing the army's original six principles of counterinsurgency mentioned earlier. It is apparent that the British government made progress on the achievement of its objectives when it focused on the first principle, the centrality of the political dimension. In Northern Ireland, it worked hard and achieved considerable success in the second and third objectives, coordinating policy and acquiring intelligence. The government never fully succeeded in the fourth and fifth, separating the insurgents from their supporters and neutralizing the insurgents, and many of its own policies impaired its ability to do so. Having achieved a cease-fire, it is now working on the sixth principle, postconflict planning.

THE NEW TERRORIST THREAT

Armed with lessons of the thirty-year counterterrorism campaign in Northern Ireland, in turn built on the experience of counterinsurgency operations throughout the world, the British government prepared to face a new terrorist threat even before September 11, 2001. Known as TACT, Terrorism Act 2000 came into force in February 2001. It was designed to respond to the changing threat from international terrorism by replacing nominally temporary antiterrorism legislation that had been designed to deal primarily with Northern Ireland. The act proscribes certain terrorist groups. It enhances police powers to "stop and search" and permits detention for up to seven days (although any period longer than two days must be approved by a magistrate). The act also creates new criminal offenses, such as inciting terrorist acts, seeking or providing training for terrorist purposes at home or abroad, and providing training in the use of weaponry.

The act is subject to independent parliamentary oversight, and it is reviewed annually by a nonpartisan legal watchdog.

The Anti-Terrorism, Crime and Security Act of 2001 (ATCSA) was passed in the immediate aftermath of September 11 and expands TACT. The most controversial aspect of the new legislation is that it permits the detention of foreign nationals suspected of involvement in international terrorism outside the normal court system and based on secret evidence. The act also increases the security of civil nuclear and aviation sites and labs containing dangerous substances. It creates tough penalties for crimes aggravated by racial or religious hatred and extends the law on hoaxes. It permits the freezing of terrorists' assets at the start of an investigation. A committee of privy councillors, headed by an appointed peer, reviews the act.

Between September 11, 2001, and January 31, 2004, 544 individuals were arrested under TACT, and 98 were charged. Six were convicted for terrorist offenses.[57] Sixteen foreign suspects were certified and detained indefinitely under part four of ATCSA. All were free to leave the country, and two chose to do so. Of the remaining fourteen, one was charged with other offenses and thirteen were detained. All of these appealed their detentions to the Special Immigration Appeals Commission (SIAC), which upheld all but one of the detentions. The legality of the detentions, and the derogation from the European Convention on Human Rights that they required, was upheld by the courts. In the court of public opinion, the detentions remain more controversial. In August 2004, a parliamentary committee, the Joint Committee on Human Rights, expressed concern for the legislation's "corrosive" long-term effect on human rights and criticized the "discrimination inherent" in the legislation as it was used "disproportionately" against Muslims and treated foreigners differently than citizens.[58] In December 2004, the Law Lords ruled by an eight-to-one majority in favor of an appeal brought by the detainees. The Law Lords argued, in the words of Lord Nicholls, that "indefinite imprisonment without charge or trial is anathema in any country which observes the rule of law."[59] The Law Lords went on to argue that the detention was incompatible with European human rights law. Three months later, in March 2005, the last eight foreign terrorist suspects were released on bail.

On July 7, 2005, four bombs rocked London's public transport system during the height of the morning rush hour. Fifty-six people were killed and more than seven hundred injured. Among the casualties were four suicide bombers, three of whom had been born and raised in Britain. It came as no surprise that Britain was bombed by radical Islamists inspired by al Qaeda. The fact that the bombers were British and that they were prepared to kill themselves in order to kill others did come as a surprise and marked a significant escalation in the threat from radical extremists.

The statement issued by the prime minister immediately after the blast bespoke his experience in dealing with terrorism. Rather than immediately adopting the language of warfare, he spoke of crime scenes and police investigations. The British public also reacted with the experience acquired during the IRA's long campaign. The prime minister also set about reconsidering Britain's counterterrorist legislation. On August 5, one month after the London bombings, he announced that "the rules of the game are changing" and outlined a range of new and much stiffer counterterrorist measures. These included more and faster deportations of foreigners preaching or justifying violence and hatred. His statement also included the warning that he was willing to change human rights law if the courts proved an impediment to implementation of the new measures. New legislation went to Parliament in the fall of 2005.

The counterterrorism policy of the British government post-9/11 and -7/7 can only be informed by its earlier counterterrorism and counterinsurgency experience. Effective counterterrorist measures have to be carefully calibrated to match the nature of the threat faced, and while both the IRA and Islamist extremists pose threats to the physical safety of UK civilians, the organizations are very different in nature. Several general principles, nevertheless, remain constant: the centrality of political objectives, the imperative of understanding the opponent, and the need to coordinate intelligence and security operations. Recent British legislation and organizational restructuring, however, have done little to address the need to separate the insurgent from his or her community and to address political grievances. On the contrary, it can be argued that Britain's role in the Iraq War has greatly undermined that effort. Nevertheless, there continues to be a healthy and admirable public debate in Britain about the way a democracy needs to balance the conflicting claims of security and liberty in the fight against terrorism.

NOTES

1. In the winter of 1969–70, the IRA split into two groups—the Official IRA and the Provisional IRA. The "provisionals," or "provos," were led by traditional nationalists who were angry at the failure of the left-wing IRA old guard to protect the Catholic community in the wake of the violent state reaction to the Catholic civil rights movement. The provisionals soon eclipsed the "officials," so the terms *provisionals* and *IRA* are used interchangeably here.

2. Northern Ireland Information Service, "Joint Statement on Decommissioning by the Taoiseach and the Prime Minister," news release, September, 26, 2005, www.taoiseach.gov.ie/index.asp?locID=446&doc ID=2174.

3. Robert Thompson, *Defeating Communist Insurgency: The Lessons of Malaya and Vietnam* (New York: Praeger, 1966).

4. Northern Ireland Statistics and Research Agency (NISRA), *Northern Ireland Annual Abstract of Statistics* (Belfast: NISRA, 2003), 81.

5. There is a vast literature on most aspects of the Northern Ireland conflict. For an excellent account of the conflict in the context of Irish history, see R. F. Foster, *Modern Ireland 1600–1972* (London: Allen Lane, 1988). For historical accounts of the conflict since the birth of the civil rights movement, see J. Bowyer Bell, *The Irish Troubles: A Generation of Violence 1927–1992* (New York: St. Martin's, 1993); and Tim Pat Coogan, *The Troubles: Ireland's Ordeal, 1966–1996, and the Search for Peace* (Boulder, CO: Roberts Rinehart, 1996).

6. In this respect, nationalism has trumped economic self-interest in Northern Ireland. Working-class Catholics in Northern Ireland who relied on the British welfare state were financially better off than they would have been in the Republic of Ireland.

7. The actual statement made by James Craig, the first prime minister, was, "All I boast is that we are a Protestant parliament for a Protestant State." See *Hansard Parliamentary Debates* (Northern Ireland), vol. 16 (April 24, 1934), col. 1091.

8. The DUP won thirty seats (26.6 percent), up from twenty seats (18.1 percent) in 1998, and the UUP won twenty-seven seats (22.7 percent), down from twenty-eight seats (21.3 percent) in 1998. This result was consistent with the 2001 Westminster elections, when the DUP increased its seats from two to five (13.6 percent to 22.5 percent), and the UUP dropped from ten seats to six (32.7 percent to 26.8 percent).

9. For an account of the loyalists, see Peter Taylor, *Loyalists: War and Peace in Northern Ireland* (New York: TV Books, 1999). For an excellent analysis of Protestant paramilitaries, see Steve Bruce, *The Red Hand:*

Protestant Paramilitaries in Northern Ireland (Oxford: Oxford University Press, 1992). See also J. Bowyer Bell, *Back to the Future: The Protestants and a United Ireland* (Dublin: Poolbeg, 1996); and Jim Cusack and Henry MacDonald, *UVF* (Dublin: Poolbeg, 1997).

10. The SDLP won eighteen seats (17 percent) to Sinn Féin's twenty-four seats (23.5 percent). In the 1998 election, the SDLP won twenty-four seats (22 percent) to Sinn Féin's eighteen (17.6 percent).

11. On the IRA, see Kevin Toolis, *Rebel Hearts: Journeys within the IRA's Soul* (New York: St. Martin's, 1996); Tim Pat Coogan, *The IRA: A History* (Niwot, CO: Roberts Rinehart, 1994); and Peter Taylor, *Behind the Mask: The IRA and Sinn Féin* (New York: TV Books, 1997).

12. For an account of the impact of being burned out of one's home, see Toolis, *Rebel Hearts.*

13. For more on the peace talks, see Louise Richardson, "A Spiral of Peace? Bringing an End to Ethnic Violence in Northern Ireland," in *Civil Wars: Consequences and Possibilities for Regulation,* ed. Heinrich W. Krumwiede and Peter Waldman (Baden Baden, Germany: Nomos, 2000), 166–85.

14. The depth of feeling on this event is such that it has been repeatedly investigated and remains under investigation today. The Labour government appointed a tribunal headed by Lord Saville, whose inquiry continues.

15. For detailed figures see Kevin Boyle and Tom Hadden, *Northern Ireland: The Choice* (London: Penguin, 1994), table 3-1; and Arthur Aughey and Duncan Morrow, eds., *Northern Ireland Politics* (Harlow, Essex: Longman, 1996), appendices 18, 1–5.

16. J. L. Glover, "Northern Ireland: Future Terrorist Trends," quoted in Coogan, *The Troubles,* 211.

17. Bruce Hoffman, "Responding to Terrorism across the Technological Spectrum," *Terrorism and Political Violence* 6, no. 3 (Autumn 1994): 379–80.

18. NISRA, *Northern Ireland Annual Abstract of Statistics,* 81.

19. Coogan, *IRA,* 300.

20. Quoted in Taylor, *Behind the Mask,* 181.

21. For an account of the reorganization and how it mirrored an earlier reorganization of the IRB, an earlier organization led by Michael Collins, see Coogan, *The Troubles,* 205–7.

22. It is, of course, enormously difficult to get accurate accounts of IRA financing and of how much money was illegally sent to Ireland. The Irish Northern Aid Committee, better known as Noraid, was forced to register under the Foreign Agents Registration Act (FARA) and had to file biannual reports of its finances. These reports hardly give the full picture, although FARA report 2239 has the group sending $312,700 to Ireland in the first six months of 1972.

See Andrew J. Wilson, *Irish America and the Ulster Conflict 1968–1995* (Belfast: Blackstaff, 1995). On this point, see also Jack Holland, *The American Connection* (Dublin: Poolbeg, 1989).

23. Adrian Guelke, "The United States and the Northern Ireland Question," in *The Northern Ireland Question: Perspectives and Policies,* eds. Brian Barton and Patrick Roach (Aldershot, England: Avebury, 1994), 191–96.

24. For detailed figures of troop strength throughout the crisis, see Peter R. Neumann, *Britain's Long War: British Strategy in the Northern Ireland Conflict, 1969–98* (New York: Palgrave, 2003), appendices 189–90.

25. For excerpts from the report and a discussion of the controversy, see Coogan, *The Troubles,* 210–15.

26. Ibid.

27. See Peter R. Neumann, "The Myth of Ulsterization in British Security Policy in Northern Ireland," *Studies in Conflict and Terrorism* 26 (2003): 365–77.

28. NISRA, *Northern Ireland Annual Abstract of Statistics,* 81.

29. Mike Tomlinson, "Walking Backwards into the Sunset: British Policy and the Insecurity of Northern Ireland," in *Rethinking Northern Ireland,* ed. David Miller (London: Longman, 1998), 108.

30. See Neumann, "Myth of Ulsterization."

31. Tomlinson, "Walking Backwards," 102.

32. John Stalker, *Stalker* (London: Harrap, 1988).

33. Mark Urban, *Big Boys' Rules: The SAS and the Secret Struggle against the IRA* (London: Faber and Faber, 1992), 81.

34. Steven Greer, *Supergrasses: A Study in Anti-terrorism Law Enforcement in Northern Ireland* (Oxford: Clarendon, 1995), 41.

35. Neumann, "Myth of Ulsterization," 157.

36. See, for example, the memoirs of Richard Needham, secretary of state for Northern Ireland, 1985–1992, on problems of coordination: Richard Needham, *Battling for Peace* (Belfast: Blackstaff, 1998).

37. For a comprehensive account of emergency legislation in Britain, see Laura K. Donohue, *Counter-terrorist Law and Emergency Powers in the United Kingdom, 1922–2000* (Dublin: Irish Academic Press, 2001).

38. Ibid. See especially chapter 7, "Temporary Permanence: Emergency Powers 1922–2000," 306–55.

39. Ibid.

40. IM Research, School of Information Management, Leeds Metropolitan University, "Data Relating to Overt Violence," www.imresearch.org/PraxisCentre/NIreland/nipdata.htm.

41. William Whitelaw, *The Whitelaw Memoirs* (London: Aurum, 1989), 78.

42. For a thorough analysis of the Diplock system, see John Jackson and Sean Doran, *Judge without Jury: Diplock Trials in the Adversary System* (Oxford: Clarendon, 1995).

43. See Eamon Collins, *Killing Rage* (London: Granta, 1997), for the chilling perspective of one such supergrass.

44. These figures are from appendix C of Greer, *Supergrasses,* 287. This book provides an extensive history and analysis of the supergrass trials.

45. GAL's death squads were implicated in the killing of twenty-seven ETA members between 1983 and 1987. Several senior government and police officials were successfully prosecuted and sentenced to long prison terms for their involvement with the group.

46. See BBC documentary, "A Licence to Murder," *Panorama,* BBC, June 19 and 23, 2002.

47. Dan Keenan, "Two Arrests in Collusion Inquiry," *Irish Times,* May 29, 2003.

48. "Spics, Stings, and Double Crosses, South Africa," *Spotlight,* BBC Northern Ireland, February 18, 1993.

49. See Chris Anderson. "Corey Block by British Intelligence," *Sunday Mirror,* December 7, 2003; and Anne Cadwallader and Maria Rice-Oxley, "Europe Slaps UK on Northern Ireland," *Christian Science Monitor,* July 11, 2003.

50. For the full report, see *Cory Collusion Inquiry Report: Patrick Finucane,* HC 470, HMSO, April 1, 2004.

51. Quoted in Richard English, *Armed Struggle: The History of the IRA* (London: Macmillan, 2003), 157.

52. This time the messenger was Redemptorist priest Father Brendan Meagher.

53. Ed Maloney, *The Secret History of the IRA* (New York: W. W. Norton, 2002), 267.

54. The most authoritative account of these secret talks is contained in Maloney, *Secret History.*

55. In the Anglo-Irish Agreement of November 15, 1985, the British government officially undertook to consult the Republic of Ireland about its policies toward Northern Ireland.

56. The assembly has been suspended on several occasions since its creation due to disagreements between the DUP and Sinn Féin.

57. David Blunkett, *Counter-terrorism Powers: Reconciling Security and Liberty in an Open Society,* Cm. 6147 (February 2004).

58. Richard Ford, "Relax Powers against Terror Suspects," *Times,* August 5, 2004; Nigel Morris, "Terror Laws Used Unfairly on Muslims, Warn MPs," *Independent,* August 5, 2004; and Alan Travis, "Blunkett Faces Revolt on Internment," *Guardian,* August 5, 2004.

59. BBC News, "Terror Detainees Win Lords Appeal," December 16, 2004, http://news.bbc.co.uk/2/hi/uk_news/4100481.stm.

4

CONFRONTING ETHNONATIONALIST TERRORISM IN SPAIN

Political and Coercive Measures against ETA

Fernando Reinares

Rogelio Alonso

The main measures implemented by successive democratic governments in Spain to counter the protracted terrorist campaign of ETA (Euskadi ta Askatasuna, meaning Basque Homeland and Freedom) exhibit patterns of continuity and change. These measures include conflict regulation initiatives, social reinsertion and penitentiary provisions, law enforcement action and enhanced intelligence capabilities, judicial and legislative innovations, and progressively reinforced international cooperation. Contrary to what is often assumed, in the case of Spain with respect to ETA, democratic governmental initiatives aimed at conflict regulation predated the decision to fully rely on law enforcement and intergovernmental collaboration. Beyond this general observation, it is worth underlining that sustained initiatives in the fight against ETA can be given diverse meaning or emphasis in different time periods. These and certainly more important variations in antiterrorist policy are better understood as a result of both evolving political conditions and party replacement in executive power deriving from competitive elections.

Once in office at the central government in Madrid, ruling elites have tended to maintain the measures against ETA already implemented and elaborated on by the preceding party in power, even if inconsistencies could be noted and even if experience demanded rethinking some of these measures. Important changes in the adoption and development of measures to counter ETA can also be explained with respect to the collective action of interest groups, in particular associations representing the victims of terrorism. But these policy changes are more easily related to the lack of any enduring antiterrorist agreement between major political parties in Spain as a whole or within the Basque Country. Interparty pacts dealing with how to counter ETA existed only between late 1987 and the early 1990s, and then from 2000 on, although the signatories of the two agreements do not exactly overlap with each other. As an overall effect of political and coercive measures adopted over time by successive governments in Spain, ETA has been in decline since the early 1980s and ever more weakened through the 1990s. To be precise, the terrorist organization was socially and politically defeated by the beginning of the new century, even if its remaining leaders and members maintained the will and capacity to kill.

ETA's TERRORISM IN CONTEXT

ETA has been the main terrorist organization active in Spain throughout the past three decades and a particularly enduring one in western Europe. The group corresponds to what is known as the third wave of modern rebel terrorism.[1] As a radicalized expression of Basque ethnic nationalism, a doctrine elaborated in traditionalistic religious and racist terms at the end of the nineteenth century, its ultimate goal has been that of turning the Basque Country into a unified and monolingual state. Whereas unification is related to the existence of Basque territories and people both in northern Spain and across the border in southwestern France, the sole language refers to the vernacular Euskera tongue. New-left ideas exerted some influence on the ideology of ETA, particularly in the beginning, with separatist and irredentist aims being at times mixed with socialism, although ethnonationalist aspirations have always prevailed inside the terrorist organization. ETA became a terrorist organization in the late 1960s, amid the crisis of a dictatorship lasting for nearly forty years, namely Francoism. But it persisted during the transition from authoritarian rule and even after a new democracy was consolidated in Spain in the early 1980s.[2] Actually, the first free elections following the authoritarian regime took place in June 1977. The then-emerging national parliament, where a centrist alliance known as UCD (Unión de Centro Democrático, or Democratic Center Union) gained a relative majority of seats and the social democratic PSOE (Partido Socialista Obrero Español, or Spanish Workers Socialist Party) became the main opposition party, consensually drafted a democratic constitution, subsequently approved in a nationwide referendum and enacted in December 1978. New general elections were then called again in March 1979, showing results similar to the previous ones. Moreover, this process of democratization was coupled with that of territorial decentralization and prospects for self-government for the nationalities and regions composing Spain.

Indeed, the Basque Autonomous Community was established shortly afterward. This new political and territorial entity was a responsive outcome designed to satisfy widespread collective demands within three provinces (Alava, Guipúzcoa, and Vizcaya). Navarre, which Basque nationalists consider an integral part of the Basque Country, remained outside the process because a large majority of its inhabitants were opposed to joining any encompassing Basque political entity. However, in a referendum held in October 1979, the citizens of the other three territories ratified the statute of autonomy agreed on by their elected political representatives, both nationalists and non-nationalists, and the central government. The statute on which Basque institutions of territorial self-government were created provides extensive powers for the autonomous authorities. Provisions include a separate fiscal system, a regional police force under the command of the Basque executive, and responsibility for education and health in their entirety, among a long list of other matters over which the regional authorities enjoy sole jurisdiction.

Citizens of the Basque Autonomous Community elected their first regional parliament in May 1980. The resulting party system has been characterized ever since by high levels of fragmentation and polarization, as well as voting behavior that consistently shows significant differences across provinces and types of elections.[3] Although the PNV (Partido Nacionalista Vasco, or Basque Nationalist Party) has often received the largest fraction of

valid votes overall, Basques remain deeply divided over their support for
nationalist and non-nationalist parties. Moreover, nationalists are a true
minority in Navarre. Radical nationalist parties or coalitions closely, if not
openly, related to ETA, such as Herri Batasuna (HB, or United People),
recently renamed Batasuna (Unity), have won between 4 and 18 percent of
the vote in the three provinces of the Basque Autonomous Community,
depending on the regional or general character of the elections. Among
French Basques, electoral support for Basque nationalist parties is quite
minimal, as demonstrated by the fact that they actually contest very few
constituencies. These parties usually win a tiny percentage of votes, amount-
ing to just 1,276 in the 2004 municipal elections.

ETA has always been organized along hierarchical lines, the number of
actual militants ranging from a few hundred in the late 1970s to several
dozen by the turn of the century. Occasional collaborators may sometimes
make these figures three to five times larger. The directorate of ETA has
always been based across the border in southwestern France, where exiled
members or gunmen known to the police in Spain have lived for years and
where newly recruited activists have been provided with training in the use
of arms and explosives. French authorities intervened as late as the mid-
1980s, increasingly disrupting the maintenance of terrorist infrastructures,
collectivities, and leadership established in this sanctuary. ETA, in addition,
has traditionally maintained close ties with parties and associations belonging to the Basque radical nationalism sector but has used conditions of
political openness and tolerance to articulate a network of entities endowed
with both the mobilization of resources in favor of the terrorist organization
and the exertion of social control within its population of reference.

As an empirical study based on judicial sources shows, the overwhelming
majority of those who joined ETA were single men. Most of them were
recruited between their late teens and early twenties and had been born and
resided in urban settings.[4] In contrast with contemporary terrorists elsewhere, at the time of their recruitment, the largest proportion of ETA
members were skilled industrial workers. The next-largest occupational category included lower-middle-class and white-collar employees. Interestingly
enough, ETA militants were not homogeneously recruited across the Basque
Country. Nearly half of them came from Guipúzcoa, although this province accounts for just a quarter of the Basque population (or less if French
territory is considered). A third of all those who were recruited by the terror-

ist organization came from localities where only a small proportion of inhabitants actually speak the vernacular language. Moreover, the number of ETA militants having only autochthonous surnames equals the number with just one local surname or no local family name at all. A great many of the latter are probably descendants of mixed families or immigrants who moved to northern Spain from less-developed regions during the 1950s and 1960s.

However, an astonishing inversion in the sociological profile of ETA members has taken place over time. As the terrorist organization evolved between the early 1970s and the present, intensifying its lethal activities and growing in size during the early decades, only to decline afterward in terms of both mobilization potential and frequency of violent operations, significant changes became evident in the social and demographic characterization of militants. Overall, the percentage of women recruited increased slightly over the years. Initially, during the late 1960s and 1970s, a majority of members joined in their early twenties, shared a common rural or semirural background, came from areas with a medium or high rate of vernacular speakers, had two autochthonous surnames, and were skilled industrial workers at the time of their recruitment. Beginning in the mid-1980s, the majority of those who joined ETA were in their late teens on average, had been born in urban and metropolitan environments, were extracted from cities with a medium or low proportion of actual Euskera speakers, and had only one or no autochthonous surname. High school or vocational students below the college level became the largest occupational category in this period.

Throughout its terrorist trajectory, ETA has caused about 850 fatalities. However, most of these killings took place after Francoism. Between 1968 and 1977, when democratic elections were held for the first time in Spain after the dictatorship, ethnonationalist gunmen assassinated an average of seven persons annually. During the transition to democracy, between 1978 and 1980, the number of yearly fatalities caused by ETA escalated to an average of eighty-one. Actually, 1978, 1979, and 1980 were the deadliest years in the history of ETA's terrorism. Figures declined during the 1980s and more so during the 1990s, a long way from the escalation that took place when Spain was undergoing a process of regime change. Between 1981 and 1990, the terrorist organization perpetrated an average of thirty-four assassinations a year, and sixteen a year between 1991 and 2000. In

2001 the group killed thirteen people. The following year, ETA caused five fatalities, followed by three killings in 2003. ETA caused no deaths during 2004 and 2005. This trend is to be properly understood as an indicator of the organization's constant decline.

ETA's decline since the early 1980s also manifested itself in the amount of resources controlled, its operational capacity, and levels of popular tolerance or support. Changing political conditions in Spain, state responses to terrorism, societal reactions, and international cooperation were all decisive factors that contributed to the decline. Measures implemented by the Spanish government to counter ETA's violence have ranged from conflict regulation to police persecution of terrorists, as well as initiatives aimed at undermining the internal cohesion of the terrorist organization, special criminal legislation, and international agreements, mainly on a bilateral basis.[5] The priority given to any of these measures or a particular combination at a given time was greatly determined by the preferences of parties endowed with the executive power, but also by more general political conditions nationwide and the dynamics of terrorism itself. Over time, as democracy consolidated in Spain, parties alternated in power and ETA weakened, and although preference was given initially to political measures, these were exhausted and ultimately replaced by coercive responses applied in accordance with the rule of law.

Pathways Out of Terrorism

Spanish citizens and political elites considered the concomitant processes of democratization and territorial decentralization, even if it was not solely or primarily understood as an antiterrorist measure, to be the factor most likely to bring about the end of ethnonationalist terrorism perpetrated by ETA. Consistent with this widely shared perception, between the death of Franco, in November 1975, and October 1977, the authorities granted full amnesty to nearly nine hundred ETA members and collaborators who had been imprisoned or exiled under the dictatorship, with the intention of facilitating their integration into the new political scenario and fostering the disappearance of the terrorist organization to which they belonged. This move coincided with the legalizing of political symbols forbidden by former authoritarian rulers, such as the Basque flag, also known as *ikurriña,* which had been designed by the founder of the nationalist movement. Persecution of Euskera speakers ceased, and Euskera was soon recognized as an official language. But political elites and the public widely perceived the establishment of the Basque Autonomous Community in 1979, immediately after the approval of a new democratic constitution and following a referendum among Basque citizens, to be the conflict regulation development most likely to exert, in the short term, a substantial reduction of ETA violence.

Indeed, aware that a large number of leaders and militants belonging to one of the two factions into which ETA had been divided since the mid-1970s did acknowledge the importance of these ongoing political transformations and might thus be ready to consider giving up arms, the central government introduced, early in 1982, more genuine antiterrorist initiatives, known as social reinsertion measures, based on individual pardons in exchange for simply renouncing violence. Undoubtedly an attractive and generous alternative to exile or prison, social reinsertion has been maintained in similar terms for twenty years, applications for the program being accepted until 2002. Meanwhile, to further facilitate individual or collective dissociation from the terrorist organization and thus promoting social reinsertion, in May 1989 authorities introduced penitentiary provisions aimed at dispersing nearly five hundred incarcerated ETA militants and collaborators across the country, instead of concentrating most of them in just two prisons, as had been the case before. The original purpose of this move was to make it more difficult for ETA leaders to exert strict control over inmates and their relatives, a task usually performed through designated lawyers and subordinate associations that claimed to assist jailed terrorists. The penitentiary dispersal measure has been maintained by successive central governments. In 1996, when the PP (Partido Popular, or Popular Party) gained access to the central executive, responsibilities for penitentiaries, traditionally ascribed to the Ministry of Justice, were transferred to the Ministry of the Interior, the core institution in governmental antiterrorist policy, where they remain.

Formal political agreements among the main parties, both nationwide and regionally, can easily be associated with the formulation and implementation of counterterrorism measures. In this respect, the so-called Pact of Madrid, subscribed to in November 1987 by a large majority of the parties in the Spanish parliament, and even more importantly the pact known as Ajuria Enea, for the pacification and normalization in the Basque Country, signed by the main nationalist and non-nationalist parties of the autonomous community in January 1988, were both highly influential in the elaboration and implementation of antiterrorist policy until the mid-1990s. Both pacts provided favorable conditions for citizens to mobilize against ETA and its supporters, although their main political effect was probably that of aligning the PNV, hegemonic in the Basque government since 1980, with other democratic parties, thus isolating undemocratic separatists. However, in the early 1990s, PNV leaders decided to look for alliances with other nationalist parties, such as Herri Batasuna, despite the latter being clearly subordinated to ETA. Shortly afterward, the PP, then a rising force among the Basque electorate and already the main opposition party in the Spanish parliament, also became critical of existing reinsertion measures, openly contradicting the interparty accords. These developments brought the pacts of Madrid and Ajuria Enea to a de facto end. The PNV would go so far as to secretly sign alternative agreements with a smaller nationalist party (Eusko Alkartasuna, or EA), and in August and September 1998, ETA itself immediately subscribed to the Agreement of Lizarra, albeit this time publicly and jointly with minor nationalist parties, trade unions, and similar associations. ETA's basic goal was to constitute a nationalist front, advancing separatist proposals and imposing them on the Basque people as a whole, allegedly in exchange for ending terrorism.

Some authors believe that moderate nationalists were motivated to pursue the no-doubt-sectarian Agreement of Lizarra with the intention of creating favorable conditions that would help ETA end its violence.[6] However, two prominent nationalists suggest a different rationale. A former member of the European Parliament for HB, subsequently close to the PNV, expressed in 1998 his fears that "ETA's military defeat" would have negative political consequences for the Basque nationalists.[7] Another leading member of the PNV admitted how, in the summer of 1997, many activists feared that without ETA, the Basque Nationalist Party would become simply "insignificant." The massive demonstrations against ETA in the aftermath of the group's kidnapping and killing of a young PP councilor, Miguel Ángel Blanco, led some nationalists to openly argue that those days were the worst for Basque moderate nationalism since 1936.[8] It is extremely significant that those who were actually in power at the Basque autonomous executive equated ETA's weakness and difficulties with a profound crisis for what had been regarded until then as moderate nationalism. To some extent this crisis had already manifested itself on the electoral map, since in the two previous legislative elections, non-nationalist parties had beaten moderate nationalist ones. These circumstances would have convinced the latter of the need to look for votes in the nationalist constituency that traditionally had given its support to ETA's political wing.

All these developments against the democratic system prompted the two main Spanish parties, the PP and the PSOE, which together account for nearly half of the electorate in the Basque Autonomous Community, to sign an agreement in defense of civil liberties and against terrorism (Acuerdo por las Libertades y contra el Terrorismo) in December 2000. Smaller parties and many civil society entities subsequently endorsed the agreement. It can be argued that this was, in fact, the first proper overall antiterrorist pact formally signed in Spain. This relevant document clearly states that the nationalist PNV can be incorporated into the agreement only if it decides to side with other democratic parties instead of aligning with undemocratic radical nationalists. Besides establishing procedures for joint decision making on antiterrorist initiatives and stimulating societal reactions to ETA, the pact solemnly commits the signatories to provide continuous assistance to the victims of terrorism. The agreement emphasizes that in a functioning democracy, terrorists can never extract political advantages or rewards of any kind. Hence political negotiations between a democratic government and the terrorist organization are ruled out. Before this agreement, and following its victory in the March 1996 general elections, the PP had already stated a clear policy of no political negotiations with terrorists.

Up until 2005, Spanish authorities have nevertheless engaged twice in significant direct talks with leaders or emissaries of ETA—first secretly with those of ETA Politico-Military in 1981 and later openly with leaders of ETA Military, in 1989. In the former case, the meeting involved agreeing on possible provisions to facilitate the abandonment of violence while ruling out political concessions, but it has been a matter of debate whether this principle was actually adhered to at the second meeting, held in Algiers. A third, quite irrelevant, meeting took place in May 1999, eight months after ETA had initiated a partial cease-fire but when the leaders of the declining terrorist organization were actually devoted to the strategy of creating a broad nationalist front. Actually, ETA proclaimed its unilateral cease-fire in September 1998, and shortly afterward the PNV, EA, the radical separatists of Euskal Herritarrok (EH, as the political branch of the terrorist organization was renamed for the occasion), and several other small nationalist groups reached the Agreement of Lizarra. However, as the nationalist front failed to gain enough electoral support among Basque citizens to overcome the institutional order, and the PNV opted for a more limited approach, ETA resumed its terrorist activities, making clear the extent to which the temporary truce was a tactical move.

In the framework of the existing antiterrorist pact signed by the PP, the PSOE, and other parties and entities nationwide, measures have also been promoted to deal with the array of groups and associations known to be providing resources to ETA. Basque radical nationalism is a sector derived from and built around the terrorist organization, the subordinate specialized structures being constantly used to mobilize the human, material, and symbolic resources ETA needs to perpetuate itself over time.[9] There is, in fact, overwhelming accumulated evidence on the relationship between Herri Batasuna, or Batasuna, and ETA. For instance, a few hundred members of the former have been sentenced in court for their proven implication as militants or collaborators with the latter. It was against this background that a major political decision was adopted in 2002, when the Spanish parliament approved new legislation on parties, allowing the central executive, upon request from the parliament, to demand judicial procedures intended to outlaw political groups unwilling to condemn terrorism or linked with a terrorist organization. Even before the law was passed in parliament, a renowned judge investigating Batasuna linkages with ETA, Baltasar Garzón, had already suspended the radical separatist party. Nevertheless, in September 2002 the central government asked the Supreme Court to make the political branch of ETA illegal. Batasuna was finally outlawed in March 2003. All these initiatives prompted some debate among politicians and citizens, particularly in the Basque Country, about the likely effects on ethnonationalist terrorism.[10]

REDEFINING COERCIVE MEASURES

Francoism, in particular during the 1960s and 1970s, confronted ETA through indiscriminate repression and the use of militarized security institutions. During the period of democratic transition and consolidation, the emerging political elites had to stop using these practices and reform security structures to comply with the rule of law and the principles of an open society. Yet many of these reforms took place rather slowly. Besides, coercive measures against terrorism were not a priority on the political agenda those days. As a paradoxical result, episodes of indiscriminate repression still happened in the Basque Country during the second half of the 1970s, while internal security structures and the legal framework were being replaced in the whole of Spain. In January 1977, the National Court (Audiencia Nacional) was created in Madrid to deal with serious organized crime and terrorist offenses. This process implied a fundamental jurisdictional change, since from then on terrorist crimes would be dealt with by ordinary tribunals and not by military courts, as had previously been the case. The National Court became one of the basic pillars of antiterrorist arrangements in Spain.

Likewise, new legal provisions progressively replaced the fragmented and confusing legislation on terrorism inherited from the dictatorship. Yet it would not be until December 1978, when ETA had already started its dramatic escalation of violence, that the first democratic law to deal with terrorism was enacted. The law, some of whose provisions were intended to facilitate police investigation, included special stipulations on increasing condemnatory sentences, extending detention periods, and establishing limitations on judicial control over searches of domiciles and the interception of private communications. Interestingly enough, a significant change in the ideological orientation of the governing party during the 1980s, from the centrist position of the UCD to the leftist but moderate orientation of the PSOE, did not initially result in a different legal approach to terrorism. In December 1984, the socialist government, thanks to its absolute majority support in the parliament after the 1982 general elections, promoted a new law along the same lines of previous legislation. This new antiterrorist act, probably the most important of its kind and highly controversial as well, applied for only two years. At the end of 1987, the Constitutional Court overturned some of its provisions, such as the extension of the detention period to ten days. This special legislation was finally derogated in May 1988, not only because of its unconstitutional character but also due to a decision adopted as part of the political consensus on antiterrorist measures reached in 1988, when the above-mentioned Ajuria Enea agreement was signed.[11]

In 2001, with the central executive and parliament controlled by the PP, the criminal code was modified to include new antiterrorist provisions. In addition to violent activities aimed at producing fear in order to subvert constitutional order and seriously threaten the public domain, terrorist offenses now included actions intended to intimidate part of a given population as well as social or political groups; terrorist acts perpetrated by individuals between the ages of eighteen and twenty-one, who otherwise would be charged in special juvenile courts; the humiliation of the victims of terrorism and their relatives; and the praise or justification of terrorism. Likewise, those condemned for terrorist offenses would be ineligible for public office for at least twenty years, and terrorist actions against elected representatives in municipalities were put on a par with those suffered by members of other state institutions. Meanwhile, judges of the National Court initiated legal action against entities providing support to terrorist organizations simply by applying the existing criminal law. As a result, some youth gangs, groups seeking to maintain control over ETA members in prison and their relatives outside penitentiaries, and even a newspaper sympathetic, if not actually linked, to the terrorist organization were decreed illegal.

Concerning the police response to ETA, it is important to remember once again that during the immediate post-Francoism and democratic transition period, security agencies and security agents were those of the previous authoritarian regime. Surely affected by conditions of uncertainty, the two existing and still-militarized law enforcement agencies, namely, Policía Nacional (the National Police) and Guardia Civil (the Civil Guard), were then quite unreceptive and even opposed to the conflict regulation initiatives adopted by the government to deal with violent nationalist antagonism in the Basque Country. In addition, information services within these state security agencies were precarious and lacked coordination. Security agents, trained and indoctrinated under the authoritarian regime, were prone to disloyalty, and some officials were directly or indirectly involved with both domestic and foreign right-wing extremists.

Police branches associated with the surveillance and persecution of political dissenters during the dictatorship were dismantled at the end of 1976. However, some of their functionaries were assigned to counterterrorism starting in 1977, when the incidence of ETA terrorism was still relatively low. Indeed, terrorism was not yet a priority on the governmental agenda, and the new authorities felt a certain distrust toward the existing security forces. Thus police responses adopted in this period were rather low-key.[12] Political elites were still thinking that the demise of ETA would be a likely outcome of democratization and decentralization. As terrorist actions perpetrated by ETA escalated at the end of the 1970s, and after a rather unsuccessful attempt to coordinate resources between law enforcement bodies, the central government finally decided to establish special police units in the Basque Country. At the same time, the minister of the interior went abroad, looking for advice on how to properly counter terrorism. In July and November 1978, he traveled to West Germany and the United Kingdom, respectively, to find out about specialized antiterrorist units and appropriate information-gathering systems.

To better fight the now clearly perceived threat of ETA, the Spanish executive wanted to increase the number of agents, articulate adequate intelligence services, and modernize technical resources within the police. However, as terrorism continued to escalate, in April 1979 the civilian minister of the interior was replaced by an army general. This change could be seen as an anomaly in the context of a functioning democracy, taking into consideration the threat of a military uprising as a result of deliberate terrorist provocation and the fact that the appointment actually lasted less than one year. During this period, a delegation of the central government for security matters, headed by a general linked to the National Police, opened in the recently constituted Basque Autonomous Community and in Navarre. Not until February 1980 were special operational groups and antiterrorist units (Grupos Especiales de Operaciones from the National Police and Unidades Antiterroristas Rurales from the Civil Guard) finally deployed in the Basque Country.

Actually, it was not until the mid-1980s that a new minister of the interior, again a civilian, decided to create a unified command for fighting terrorism, headed by a police commissioner and composed of delegates from the various security agencies and intelligence services—an effort that became rather discontinuous over nearly twenty years. Following an unsuccessful coup d'état in February 1981, four army companies were assigned to antiterrorist operations in the Basque Country, although they were strictly limited to frontier surveillance and operated only until the end of that summer, when they were replaced by units belonging to the Guardia Civil. In 1982 military personnel were assigned to the protection of public buildings and installations. Beyond surveillance and protection in these years, the government of Spain was always very cautious not to involve the military in internal security issues and the fight against ETA. When the Socialist Party acceded to the central executive as a result of the October

1982 general elections, the new ruling politicians opted initially for continuity in issues concerning police response to terrorism.

The Basque autonomous police, fully and exclusively dependent on the
Basque autonomous government, engaged in counterterrorism starting in
1986, although it was not until the end of 1989, following the Pact of
Ajuria Enea, that the Ertzaintza, as this regional law enforcement agency
is also known, proactively acted against ETA. As expected, the terrorist
organization reacted by killing autonomous police officials in the coming
years. Four autonomous police officials of the seven-thousand-member
force were killed during the 1990s. ETA's targeting of Ertzaintza members
was determined to a great extent by the attitude shown by the police force
in its response to terrorism. During periods when the Basque autonomous
police force committed itself with more dedication and efficiency to fighting ETA's violence, the terrorist organization increased its hostility toward
the Ertzaintza. It was common for leading police officials belonging to this
force to approach terrorism with some leniency, allowing youngsters
involved in urban terrorism, deployed as part of ETA's strategy of destabi-
lization, to act with impunity for some time during the 1990s. This attitude, together with Ertzaintza's relatively low record of detentions of ETA
activists when compared with those of nationwide Spanish security forces,
often fueled criticism of those politically responsible for the Basque autonomous police.

During the transition from authoritarian rule, between 1975 and 1981,
right-wing extremists, including those with Basque origins and a number of
Italian neofascists connected with reactionary members of the state security
agencies, killed ten people in France and twenty-three others inside Spain;
the victims were apparently chosen because of their presumed relationship
with ETA. Also, between 1983 and 1987, a shadowy organization known
as GAL (Grupos Antiterroristas de Liberación, or Liberation Antiterrorist
Groups) carried out a similar campaign of terrorist activity against suspected
members and supporters of ETA.[13] This terrorist organization was secretly
structured around some police officials, who recruited mercenary assassins
from among gang criminals in Marseille and Lisbon, some of them already
implicated in previous terrorist activities against ETA and its sympathizers.
GAL allegedly benefited from the passivity and allegiance of some prominent politicians and state functionaries. It targeted members and collaborators of ETA living across the border in southwestern France, although,

astonishingly, about half of the twenty-eight people killed had no links whatsoever with the ethnonationalist terrorist organization. Spain, fortunately, was by then a functioning democratic regime, and the rule of law was finally applied to the policemen, gangsters, and PSOE politicians proven by judges to be involved with GAL. They all received severe court sentences for their illegal activities. Families of their victims received monetary compensation from state budget funds, as did relatives of those killed by ETA.

RESULTS OF CONFLICT REGULATION

The question here is not only to what extent all those governmental measures weakened or strengthened ETA—that is, discussion is not limited to whether or not all these political and coercive antiterrorist initiatives debilitated, in the short, middle, or long term, the terrorist organization and its mobilization potential; constrained its ability to practice violence; and reduced the levels of popular support it eventually enjoyed. Nor is the discussion limited to which measures were or became counterproductive. Actually, the timing of the implementation of a given antiterrorist measure may be crucial in explaining its success or failure. The question, therefore, also refers to the separate effects of each political and coercive measure adopted to counter ETA, including the adaptation of ETA's organizational structures, innovations in the repertoire of terrorism, and changes observed over time in ETA's patterns of victimization.

In this sense, the twofold process of political democratization and territorial decentralization could be considered the single most efficient antiterrorist initiative implemented by central authorities in Spain with respect to ETA. As with complementary developments of conflict regulation, its impact on ethnonationalist terrorism would be substantial in the short, middle, and long run. It did foster a very intense and sustained decrease in fatalities starting in 1981, once the new democratic constitution was sanctioned nationwide, the statute of self-government for the Basque Country was approved by its own citizens in a referendum, its corresponding autonomous institutions were created, and the first territorial elections were held. Admittedly, though, the success of these measures was incomplete, since ETA did not disappear completely nor did its violence diminish as quickly as expected. The impact of political reforms is highly contingent on the degree of mobilization already achieved by a given terrorist organization, its constitutive internal tendencies, and the logic adopted with respect to other collective actors in the same political sector, as theorizing suggests.[14]

Starting in the early 1970s, ETA benefited for a long time from a large amount of sympathy and significant levels of support among its population of reference. General Franco's regime overreacted to the initial acts of deadly violence perpetrated by the emerging terrorist organization, precisely as its leaders intended. Coming while memories of the civil war were still fresh, regime repression under the dictatorship afflicted large segments of Basque society and created an environment in which ETA found it easy to recruit people and gather material resources. In the immediate post-Franco period, expectations were very high and rising among radical nationalists coalescent with the separatist terrorists. Delays in granting amnesty to all those criminalized under the dictatorship for their involvement with ETA and delays in officially recognizing cultural and symbolic elements of Basque collective identity, not to mention unrealized common hopes for the sudden advent of an independent and socialist state and even the poor performance by radical nationalist candidates in the first general elections called in June 1977, were all developments generating widespread frustration within this ideological sector. In addition, abusive and uncontrolled policing of mass demonstrations, together with rather indiscriminate responses to acts of terrorism by the security agencies during the same transitional period, created widespread anger among radical nationalists. Relative deprivation and anger prompted an unusual number of young men, having internalized the beliefs of ETA, to join the terrorist organization during the late 1970s. The organization was never stronger or deadlier than it was then.

The success of democratization and autonomous government in fostering the disappearance of ETA or attenuating its terrorist campaign was also partial, because it was highly dependent on the logic adopted by the two factions into which ETA was already divided in the second half of the 1970s and the early 1980s, namely, ETA Politico-Military, or ETA(pm), and ETA Military, or ETA(m).[15] Prominent leaders of the former faction acknowledged the importance of the ongoing political transformations and decided in 1981 not only to abandon violence altogether but to dissolve ETA's entire underground structure as well. It was precisely to lower the cost of exit from terrorism, allowing for the effective self-dissolution of ETA(pm), that the central government that same year introduced social reinsertion measures based on individual pardons. As a result, nearly three hundred former militants and collaborators of ETA, a large majority of them belonging to the politico-military faction, requested and benefited from social reinsertion measures between 1982 and 1986. Interestingly, there has been no single case of recidivism among all those who applied for social reinsertion and obtained it—a most relevant fact considering that, in contrast, the majority of ETA members who received amnesty in the early years of the transition from authoritarianism to democracy got involved again in terrorist activities. In theoretical terms, this fact would suggest a most effective outcome for this type of measure, intended to affect the internal cohesion of terrorist organizations and to facilitate eventual self-dissolution if there has previously been a significant process of conflict regulation.

The central government introduced social reinsertion measures to facilitate the self-dissolution of ETA(pm) once its leaders decided violence was no longer justified under the new political circumstances and demanded alternatives to incarceration or exile in exchange for abandoning their clandestine lives. However, the measures were subsequently maintained with the intention of affecting the internal cohesion of any remaining terrorist faction. Actually, as the leaders of ETA(m), the only faction that persisted until the present day, perceived how these social reinsertion measures had the potential to negatively affect the maintenance of their clandestine structures, they attempted to raise the cost of exit by threatening militants and collaborators who opted for reinsertion or were likely to do so. To make the threat credible, ETA gunmen killed Dolores González Katarain, alias Yoyes, in September 1986. She had been a member of the group's leadership, a rare case in an underground organization overwhelmingly dominated by male activists. Yoyes decided to accept social reinsertion measures, as a result moving from a foreign country to her native hometown in Guipúzcoa, where she was killed by her former associates.

As the effectiveness of social reinsertion measures declined, in May 1989 authorities introduced a number of penitentiary provisions aimed at dispersing imprisoned members of ETA. As a result of these initiatives, more than 112 inmates sentenced for offenses related to ETA(m) had opted for reinsertion measures by 1995. Successive central governments maintained both the reinsertion measures of 1982 and the penitentiary dispersal initiatives of 1989, until the former were amended and terminated in 2002. While reinsertion and dispersion were implemented in the context of a broad political consensus on antiterrorist matters, they seemed to prove quite effective in stimulating individual dissociation from the terrorist organization and renunciation of the use of violence. In general terms, the broader the political consensus behind governmental measures to counter terrorism, the better the results obtained throughout implementation should be. For instance, ETA itself recognized the extent to which the Pact of Ajuria Enea, and later the Agreement for Liberties and Against Terrorism, damaged its organizational structures, reduced the amount of popular support it enjoyed, and impaired its mobilization potential.

Concerning the issue of negotiating with the terrorists, as has already been mentioned, Spanish authorities have twice engaged in significant conversations with leaders of ETA—first secretly with those of ETA(pm), in 1981, and later openly with leaders of ETA(m), in 1989. In contrast to the remarkable reduction of lethal terrorist activity that followed the reinsertion of ETA(pm) activists as a result of the former, successful, conversations, negotiations with ETA(m) leaders late in the same decade proved unproductive. A third, rather unsuccessful and even more irrelevant, meeting took place in May 1999, eight months after ETA(m) initiated a new, although partial, truce, but the leaders of the declining terrorist organization were actually engaged in the strategy of creating an encompassing nationalist front to exclude non-nationalist forces and violently determine Basque politics. It was as part of this strategy that ETA proclaimed a unilateral cease-fire in September 1998. But as soon as the nationalist front failed to gain enough electoral support among the citizens of the Basque Autonomous Community to fulfill the high expectations, ETA(m) resumed its terrorist activities and made clear the extent to which the temporary truce had been simply a tactical move intended to convince the nationalist group to unite and reorganize its own clandestine structures. A return to terrorism evidenced once more the hostility of ETA leaders toward democratic principles and procedures.

A major political decision on antiterrorist policy was adopted in the middle of 2002, within the framework of the existing Agreement for Liberties and Against Terrorism signed two years earlier. The Spanish parliament approved new legislation on political parties, allowing the central executive, upon request from the Spanish legislature, to demand judicial procedures intended to outlaw political groups unwilling to condemn terrorism or maintaining links with terrorist organizations. Even before the law was passed in parliament, Judge Baltasar Garzón, a magistrate of the National

Court investigating Batasuna's links with ETA, had already suspended the former. But in September 2002 the central government asked the Supreme Court to outlaw Batasuna, which became illegal in March 2003. Despite some debate over the initiatives among politicians and the public in general, the outcomes of such measures on ethnonationalist terrorism can easily be appreciated and are very positive in democratic terms. The number of lethal terrorist actions has decreased since 2002, and ETA did not regain popular support. The dismantling of satellite structures supporting ETA, together with the increase of formal sanctions against violent activism, actually accelerated the decline of the terrorist organization and reduced levels of social control imposed by ETA's supporters. Public opinion studies conducted in November 2003, May 2004, and the end of 2005 found that each year the rejection of ETA among Basque citizens was stronger than before and, interestingly enough, a majority attitude among Batasuna's constituency.[16]

EFFICIENT RULE OF LAW?

In January 1977, the National Court was created in Madrid to deal with serious organized crime and terrorist offenses. Yet it was not until December 1978, when terrorist activity had already started its dramatic escalation, that the first democratic law to combat terrorism was enacted. This law included special provisions on increasing condemnatory sentences, extending detention periods, and establishing limitations on judicial control over searches of domiciles and the interception of private communications. As it will be argued, some of these provisions were intended to facilitate police investigations. However, the legislation resulted in a worrying number of proven cases of mistreatment, even torture, of detainees, for it was a severe measure enforced by state security agencies still unreformed and largely devoid of a professional culture adapted to the emerging democratic regime. Some legislative and coactive measures against terrorism were counterproductive and, during some critical years, contributed to significant and lasting popular support for the terrorists. In fact, nearly half of Basque adults perceived ETA members as either patriots or idealists in 1978, whereas only 7 percent of those interviewed in public opinion surveys called them plain criminals. In 1989, though, less than one-quarter of Basques referred to ETA members in more or less favorable terms, and those who portrayed members of ETA as simply criminals had more than doubled since a decade earlier.[17]

Early in 2001, the penal code was modified to include new provisions adapted to changes observed in terrorist practices since the mid-1990s. Reacting to widespread popular mobilizations against ETA inside the Basque Country, ETA leaders devised a plan to complement lethal terrorist actions perpetrated by militant gunmen with other kinds of violent activities, typically committed on weekends by some 150 teenagers socialized in a subculture of hatred and exclusion. The purpose was to systematically harass Basque citizens who declared themselves not to be nationalists, particularly elected non-nationalist representatives at local, regional, and national levels of government. In response, the penal code now defined terrorist offenses as, in addition to violent activities aimed at subverting t he constitutional order and seriously threatening the public sphere, actions intended to intimidate part of a given population as well as social or political groups; terrorist acts perpetrated by individuals between the ages of eighteen and twenty-one, who otherwise would face charges in special juvenile courts; the humiliation of the victims of terrorism and their relatives; and the praise or justification of terrorism. Likewise, those condemned for terrorist offenses would not be eligible for public office for at least twenty years, and terrorist actions against elected representatives in local institutions were put on a par with those against members of other state bodies. Meanwhile, judges of the National Court, simply by applying the penal code, initiated legal action against entities providing support to terrorist organizations. As a result, some youth gangs, groups seeking to maintain control over ETA members in prison, and even a newspaper sympathetic to ethnonationalist gunmen—all belonging to a complex network created over the years by leaders of the terrorist organization—were finally decreed illegal.

What about police efficacy and efficiency in the fight against terrorism, as these parameters evolved during the transition from authoritarian rule to a consolidated new democracy? The main purpose of police detentions during this period seems to have been obtaining information about the terrorist organization and its collaborators, to be used in subsequent police operations. It is estimated that judges prosecuted only one-third of the nearly fifty-seven hundred people state security agencies arrested between 1977 and 1987 for alleged terrorist offenses relating to ETA.[18] Although information collected from these detainees facilitated further police response and contributed to a decrease in violent terrorist acts, such policing produced widespread anger and resentment among affected sectors of the Basque population, due to cases of abuse and even of torture. Popular support for ETA increased significantly, contributing to the group's long life as a terrorist organization. Similar consequences in terms of popular discontent and lasting sympathy toward ETA could be attributed to the terrorist violence practiced by right-wing extremists and GAL during the transition from authoritarian rule.

Police counterterrorist operations became much more efficient, discriminating, and selective after 1988. No single episode of illegal killing in the state response to ETA has been documented since that time. The number of people suspected of crimes associated with the terrorist organization and detained by security agencies between that year and the end of 1997 amounts to fewer than 970, about one-fifth as many as were arrested during the previous decade. More importantly, the judiciary formally prosecuted well over 60 percent of all those arrested. Between 1999 and 2004, almost 80 percent of some six hundred individuals detained for terrorist offenses in connection with ETA were incarcerated under judicial process. Interestingly enough, as the number of suspects arrested increased and as detentions occurred on a more discerning basis, ETA's terrorist activity continued to decline after 1988. This, in turn, favored even more selective policing of terrorism, state security agency reforms, and, of course, political decisions that improved antiterrorism tactics as part of the Pact of Ajuria Enea.[19] Moreover, the Basque autonomous police—the Ertzaintza—fully and exclusively dependent on the Basque autonomous government, engaged in counterterrorism from 1986 on, although it would not be until the end of 1989 that the Ertzaintza proactively acted against the gunmen of ETA(m). As expected, the terrorist organization then reacted, killing two autonomous police officials in the first half of the 1990s.

The changes in the police response to terrorism have been crucial in emotionally dissociating important segments of the Basque population from ETA and have contributed to the progressive reduction of support for the terrorist organization. Basque public opinion of ETA's militants became increasingly negative throughout the 1980s. Throughout the 1990s, citizen mobilizations against violence generalized and became articulated in a number of associations, such as the Coordinadora Gesto por la Paz (Gesture for Peace), that became prominent social features in villages and cities across the Basque Country.[20] Since the mid-1990s, ETA and its followers have reacted to this social trend by physically and aggressively confronting demonstrations against terrorism and, as indicated some paragraphs above, particularly by targeting Basque citizens who are not nationalists—often elected political representatives at various levels of government who belong to the Basque section of either the PP or the PSOE. Between 1996 and 2000, as a matter of fact, almost five thousand episodes of street harassment and intimidation against such people and their families were reported in the Basque Autonomous Community and Navarre, constituting a variety of more limited terrorism practiced by gangs of youngsters outside formal ETA membership but in open support of the terrorist organization. In addition to this violence, more common terrorist attacks perpetrated by ETA gunmen during the same period caused forty-seven fatalities.

ETA became a terrorist organization and transnationalized its activities at about the same time, in the late sixties and early seventies. The terrorist organization has crossed the border between Spain and France since its very inception for the purpose of mobilizing resources and developing strategies. Violence has been directed at targets in Spain, while refuge has been sought in France. Therefore, antiterrorist measures implemented by Spanish governments have been objectively limited by this transnational factor and the approach to the phenomenon adopted by French authorities. ETA found sanctuary in southwestern France from the late 1960s until well into the 1980s. The terrorist organization was widely perceived among French politicians, intellectuals, segments of the public, and mass media circles as an anti-Franco armed group whose members qualified for political asylum, even after Spain successfully underwent a democratic transition and consolidation. Apparent French ignorance of the facts, particularly of the Basque autonomous institutions already functioning, as well as indifference with respect to the terrorist sanctuary, caused indignation among Spanish political elites and citizens, at both the left and right ends of the political spectrum. Cooperation against terrorism between the two neighboring states began only in the mid-1980s. Since 1983 bilateral interministerial seminars held every six months have facilitated a better knowledge of the political situation in Spain among French politicians. These meetings preceded Spain's entry into the European Community as a new member state in 1986. In July 1984, the French and Spanish ministers of the interior, both belonging to socialist parties, signed a document detailing the modalities of counterterrorism cooperation. This document, known as Acuerdos de la Castellana (Agreements of the Castellana), contained the first substantial accords reached between the two countries in fighting ETA, inaugurating a period of cooperation that would develop to mutually satisfactory degrees by the turn of the century. The outcomes of this cooperation, which security officials in Spain insist could have been much more intense, have been increasingly effective apprehension of terrorists, the dismantling of their infrastructure, and the disruption of their finances. Between 1999 and 2004, about 33 percent of all ETA members detained were apprehended in France by French law enforcement agencies.

CONCLUSIONS

During the initial five years of the newly established democracy in Spain, the centrist government emphasized initiatives aimed at a peaceful regulation of the radicalized Basque nationalist conflict as a pathway out of terrorism. Consistent with this option, social reinsertion measures were introduced and coercive responses to ETA were limited or dysfunctional for a long while. As democracy consolidated, central socialist authorities became convinced of the need to negotiate with ETA and decided to engage in sustained contacts with its leaders. This choice implied a temporarily low profile for routine counterterrorism policing, but illegal force was still used in the mid-1980s, largely as a way of exerting pressure on ETA's leadership. After the mid-1990s, once the liberal conservatives of the Popular Party won a general election for the first time, antiterrorist policy was based on law enforcement and extensive bilateral cooperation. Prospects for negotiations vanished, and social reinsertion measures were ended. Moreover, authorities applied innovative measures to deal not only with ETA but with its support networks as well. As a result of these measures, ETA, a declining terrorist organization since the early 1980s, became even more weakened, to the extent of nearing a residual stage. However, at that difficult conjuncture, ETA found some relief when the main nationalist parties in the Basque Country attempted to prevent the political defeat of the terrorist organization by offering some gains to the group and its political wing.

Whereas another terrorist organization, the IRA, decided around that time to cease its campaign of violence, ETA refused to follow the same path. As explicitly acknowledged by the Basque terrorist group after the breakdown of the truce, ETA wanted, not a "peace process," but a "process of nation building."[21] It was with that intention that the group sought and reached a pact with constitutional nationalists that preceded the cessation of violence. Subsequent developments confirmed the fears expressed by many Spanish democrats that in the Basque Country, democratic nationalists were being seduced by ETA, contrary to what happened in Ireland, where the SDLP (Social Democratic and Labour Party) won over Sinn Féin to democracy, as an Irish journalist correctly put it at the time.[22] Therefore, the different roles played by Basque and Irish nationalism in that period and the distortion of the Irish model by Basque nationalist parties and ETA were decisive in this outcome. The radicalization of constitutional nationalism in the Basque region, as opposed to the constitutionalization of radical nationalism that was a key factor in the achievement of the consensus enshrined in the 1998 Belfast Agreement, contributed to the continuation of terrorism. Contrary to the spirit of the Belfast Agreement, Basque nationalists moved away from an existing consensus with non-nationalist parties around the principle of full development of Basque autonomy, strengthening ETA's will to carry on with its campaign. Whereas the IRA accepted a political settlement that did not recognize any of its major and traditional objectives, ETA refused to replicate such revisionism.[23]

A broad antiterrorist agreement signed in 2000 between the two major parties in Spain created objective conditions for a further ETA decline. In 2005 the weakness of the terrorist organization was more evident than ever before. This situation prompted a serious debate among political elites, mass media, and civil society in general as to whether ETA should simply be eradicated by police and judicial action or induced to give up terrorism through some kind of dialogue or negotiation. This debate was also encouraged by a letter, written in the summer of 2004 by six leading members of ETA (including the head of the organization during the 1990s), then serving prison sentences, which was filtered to the media some months later.[24] These prominent activists acknowledged that ETA had been defeated by Spanish state strategies and demanded that the organization give up its terrorist campaign. The leadership of ETA subsequently expelled these dissidents from the organization in an attempt to exert tight control over the group's strategy. Nonetheless, such an unambiguous and significant acknowledgment by activists who years earlier were themselves responsible for repressing voices that had called for an end to ETA's violence demonstrated the success of the Spanish state in countering terrorism.

Unlike those who argued that terrorism could end only in exchange for concessions, dissidents such as the ones now expelled from ETA showed that it was realistic and possible to expect the conclusion of the group's campaign of violence without its achieving political gains in return. In fact, such a move came only a few years after a new political party, Aralar, was formed in 2002 by disillusioned members of Batasuna, who left the party as a result of the continuation of ETA's violence despite widespread criticism of terrorism among Basque society and even radical nationalist voters. Therefore, few people would deny that even though ETA's members still have the operational capacity to kill, the terrorist organization has so far been socially and politically defeated. It was in this context that, in July 2005, the Spanish congress approved of asking the government to enter into dialogue with ETA should the group end its terrorist campaign. The congressional proposition made conversations with ETA conditional on the terrorist group's stating "a clear willingness to end the violence" through "unequivocal attitudes that may show such a conviction," provided also that "political matters shall only be dealt with through the legitimate representatives of people's will" and, furthermore, that "violence must not be politically rewarded and Spanish democracy will never accept the blackmail of violence."[25]

The course of ETA's campaign was also affected by the brutal attacks perpetrated by Islamist terrorists in Madrid on March 11, 2004. The massacre provoked widespread outrage and criticism in the country, making it even more difficult for the Basque ethnonationalist terrorist group to return to its traditional and sustained campaign of violence. To some extent it can be argued that ETA itself fell victim to terrorism. After the murder of 191 people, the political cost of killing increased considerably. But the terrorist attacks on March 11 had other negative consequences for ETA as well, in the form of enhanced and improved antiterrorist capacities. As has been previously outlined, before March 11, Spain was very well prepared to confront the main terrorist threat posed by ETA. The emergence of a new threat forced the authorities to adapt the security system without diminishing its efficiency in the fight against ETA. Improved coordination and exchange of information between law enforcement agencies, including the creation of the Center for National Coordination of Antiterrorism (Centro Nacional de Coordinación Antiterrorista, or CNCA) and a new management system to ensure joint access to relevant databases, as well as reinforced international cooperation, most notably between France and Spain within the European Union framework, no doubt added further value to the fight against ETA.

NOTES

Fernando Reinares thanks the Spanish Interministerial Commission for Science and Technology for additional support provided to a research project underlying this chapter.

1. David Rapoport, "The Four Waves of Modern Terrorism," in *Attacking Terrorism: Elements of a Grand Strategy,* ed. Andrew K. Cronin and James M. Ludes (Washington, DC: Georgetown University Press, 2004), 46–72.

2. On the origins, evolution, and strategy of the terrorist organization, see Fernando Reinares, "Nationalism and Violence in Basque Politics," *Conflict* 8, nos. 2–3 (1988): 141–55; Fernando Reinares, "Sociogénesis y evolución del terrorismo en España," in *España: Sociedad y política,* ed. Salvador Giner (Madrid: Espasa Calpe, 1990), 354–72; Antonio Elorza, ed., *La historia de ETA* (Madrid: Temas de Hoy, 2000); Florencio Domínguez Iribarren, *ETA: Estrategia organizativa y actuaciones 1978–1992* (Bilbao, Spain: Universidad del País Vasco, 1998); and Pedro Ibarra, *La evolución estratégica de ETA, 1963–1987* (San Sebastián, Spain: Griselu, 1987).

3. Francisco J. Llera, *Los vascos y la política* (Bilbao, Spain: Universidad del País Vasco, 1994), 13–33; Juan Linz, *Conflicto en Euskadi* (Madrid: Espasa Calpe, 1986), 295–366; and José L. Barbería and Patxo Unzueta, *Cómo hemos llegado a esto: La crisis Vasca* (Madrid: Taurus, 2003), in particular 306–16.

4. Fernando Reinares, *Patriotas de la muerte: Quiénes han militado en ETA y por qué* (Madrid: Taurus, 2001); and Fernando Reinares, "Who Are the Terrorists? Analyzing Changes in Sociological Profile among Members of ETA," *Studies in Conflict and Terrorism* 27 (2004): 465–88.

5. Fernando Reinares, "Democratization and State Responses to Protracted Terrorism in Spain," in *Confronting Terrorism,* ed. Marianne van Leeuwen (The Hague: Kluwer Law International, 2003), 57–70.

6. Ludger Mees, *Nationalism, Violence and Democracy: The Basque Clash of Identities* (Houndmills, England: Palgrave Macmillan, 2003), 169.

7. Testimony reproduced in Florencio Domínguez Iribarren, *De la negociación a la tregua: ¿El final de ETA?* (Madrid: Taurus, 1998), 174.

8. A more-than-illustrative example can be found in the nationalist-oriented newspaper *Deia*, July 24, 2001.

9. José M. Mata, *El Nacionalismo Vasco Radical* (Bilbao, Spain: Universidad del País Vasco, 1993); and Peter Waldmann, "From the Vindication of Honour to Blackmail: The Impact of the Changing Role of ETA on Society and Politics in the Basque Region of Spain," in *Tolerating Terrorism in the West,* ed. Noemi Gal-Or (London: Routledge, 1991), 1–32.

10. For an analysis of the rationale behind the banning of Batasuna and its positive effects as an antiterrorist measure, see Rogelio Alonso and Fernando Reinares, "Terrorism, Human Rights and Law Enforcement in Spain," *Terrorism and Political Violence* 17 (2005): 265–78.

11. Antonio Vercher, *Antiterrorismo en el Ulster y en el País Vasco: Legislación y medidas* (Barcelona: Promociones y Publicaciones Universitarias, 1991).

12. Oscar Jaime, *Policía, terrorismo y cambio político en España, 1976–1996* (Valencia: Tirant lo Blanch, 2002), 167–217.

13. Paddy Woodworth, *Dirty War, Clean Hands: ETA, the GAL and Spanish Democracy.* (Cork, Ireland: Cork University Press, 2001).

14. Fernando Reinares, *Terrorismo y antiterrorismo* (Barcelona: Ediciones Paidós, 1988), 132–40.

15. Fernando Reinares, "The Political Conditioning of Collective Violence: Regime Change and Insurgent Terrorism in Spain," *Research on Democracy and Society* 3 (1996): 297–326.

16. See relevant data in *Euskobarómetro*, 2003, 2004, and 2005, a regular survey conducted by the Department of Political Science and Public Administration at the University of the Basque Country, www.ehu.es/cpvweb/paginas/euskobarometro.html.

17. Llera, *Los Vascos y la Política,* 97–117; and Linz, *Conflicto en Euskadi,* 617–65.

18. Domínguez Iribarren, *De la negociación a la tregua,* 201–21.

19. Fernando Reinares and Oscar Jaime, "Countering Terrorism in a New Democracy: The Case of Spain," in *European Democracies against Terrorism: Governmental Policies and Intergovernmental Cooperation,* ed. Fernando Reinares (Aldershot, UK: Ashgate, 2000), 119–45.

20. María J. Funes, "Social Responses to Political Violence in the Basque Country: Peace Movements and Their Audience," *Journal of Conflict Resolution* 42 (1998): 493–510; and Edurne Uriarte, *Cobardes y rebeldes: Por qué pervive el terrorismo* (Madrid: Temas de Hoy, 2003).

21. ETA's communiqué was published in the newspaper *Gara* on April 29, 2000.

22. "Spanish Divided on Irish Model as Way Forward," Paddy Woodworth, *Irish Times,* September 17, 1998.

23. For a detailed analysis of why the attempt to achieve the end of ETA's violence in the Basque Country during the mid- to late 1990s was unsuccessful when compared to the IRA's case in Northern Ireland, see Rogelio Alonso, "Pathways Out of Terrorism in Northern Ireland and the Basque Country: The Misrepresentation of the Irish Model," *Terrorism and Political Violence* 16 (2004): 695–713.

24. Extracts from the letter can be read in the Basque newspaper *El Correo*, November 3, 2004.

25. *Lucha contra el Terrorismo* [Fight against Terrorism], Resolution 32, approved by the Spanish Chamber of Deputies in Plenary Session. Published in the *Boletín Oficial de las Cortes Generales,* VIII Legislature, no. 206, May 20, 2005. For an analysis of this resolution, see Rogelio Alonso, Real Instituto Elcano de Estudios Internacionales y Estratégicos, *La resolución del Congreso de los Diputados sobre lucha contra el terrorismo: Un comentario desde la experiencia Norirlandesa,* ARI no. 78, 2005, www.realinstitutoelcano.org/analisis/763.asp.

5

FRANCE AND THE GIA

Jeremy Shapiro

On the night of September 29, 1995, Khalid Khelkal, a twenty-four-year-old born in Algeria and raised in a heavily Muslim suburb of Lyon, was shot to death by the French police. Khelkal was the prime suspect in a series of terrorist bomb attacks across France that had begun in July and, despite his death, continued into October, eventually killing 8 and wounding more than 110 others. The attacks, a spillover of the Algerian Civil War into France, prompted severe security measures, triggered massive roundups, and delayed the scheduled removal of border controls between France and its European Union partners.[1] Some thirty-two thousand soldiers, police, and customs officials were mobilized, and they checked the identities of nearly three million people, detaining some seventy thousand for questioning.[2]

Khelkal became a suspect when a train driver, alerted by the government's campaign to encourage vigilance, spotted an unexploded bomb on the TGV high-speed train line between Paris and Lyon. Special antiterrorism investigators were called, and rather than exploding the bomb immediately, they carefully lifted a fingerprint off the bomb, passed the print through a multitude of databases, and established that it belonged to Khelkal, who had once been arrested for burglary. Working through a prearranged system, a nationwide manhunt began on September 27. Within two days, the hunt ended when an elite paramilitary squad specially trained for antiterrorist operations found and killed Khelkal in a bus station a few miles from his home.

Khelkal's death was a national sensation in France. The bombings had terrorized France for months, plunging the country's civil and military forces into a state of mobilization that had no precedent in France's postwar experience. The manhunt took place under such intense media scrutiny that a camera crew accompanied the antiterrorism squad on the operation and caught much of it on film, including cries from unidentified voices, presumably police, "to finish him off" as he lay wounded.[3] His killing under these circumstances sparked riots in the Muslim communities of Paris and Lyon.

The Khelkal episode not only provided the most dramatic moment in the wave of terrorism that overtook France in 1995–96 but also neatly encapsulated both the strengths and the weaknesses of France's approach to counterterrorism. That the bomb was found before it exploded, despite being poised innocuously beside a stretch of monotonous train track, speaks to the effectiveness of the government's public campaign to encourage vigilance among the population, part of the so-called Vigipirate plan to mobilize society against terrorism. The specialized investigators dispatched to the bomb site immediately fit the bomb into a pattern already established by previous attacks elsewhere in France. The manhunt demonstrated how well coordinated the fight against terror had become across the myriad of internal security agencies, and its finale, orchestrated by a squad specifically established for antiterrorist interventions, spoke to the firmly repressive bent of French policy, a fairly marked shift since the early 1980s.

At the same time, the French had been unable to stop the other attacks before they happened. The massive sweeps and intense intelligence work had failed to identify Khelkal as a suspect before his fingerprint was found, and the attacks continued after Khelkal's death. The reaction in France's economically and politically disenfranchised Muslim community to Khelkal's very public death similarly demonstrated the risk of a repressive policy in a divided society.

The story of how France created within a democratic polity a capacity for counterterrorism with these specific strengths and weaknesses is fascinating and instructive. This chapter will review that story with specific reference to the 1995–96 wave of bombings and to how the French experience might inform counterterrorism policy in other democracies. The first section will detail the evolution of the French counterterrorism system beginning in the early 1980s. The second will discuss the causes of the Algerian Civil War and the creation of a group, the Armed Islamic Group (GIA), determined to extend that war to the territory of France through terror attacks. The third section will discuss how the French governmental apparatus reacted to the GIA attacks, and the fourth will detail the lessons learned from that experience. The fifth section will assess the degree to which France was able to effectively fight terrorism without sacrificing its core democratic values. Finally, an epilogue will detail how these lessons have been applied to France's part in the struggle against the international Islamist movement and al Qaeda, both before and after September 11, 2001.

THE EVOLUTION OF THE FRENCH SYSTEM OF COUNTERTERRORISM

The 1995–96 wave of attacks across France represents just one manifestation of a terrorist problem that has intermittently preoccupied and divided the country since the 1950s. During the past half century, France has confronted terrorism in nearly all its modern incarnations—anticolonial terrorism intended to force France to disengage from Algeria in the 1950s; right-wing terrorism intended to prevent France from doing just that in the 1960s; left-wing terrorism aimed at undermining the capitalist system during the 1970s and 1980s; Middle Eastern, often state-sponsored, terrorism aimed at French policy in Lebanon and Chad and toward the Iran-Iraq War during the 1980s; and finally separatist terrorism in Brittany, the Basque region, and Corsica that persisted throughout the entire period and intensified particularly in the 1980s and 1990s. Over the course of that period, the French system for combating terrorism has evolved in response to the multiplicity of challenges and, more dramatically, in response to specific events that engaged public interest and spurred politicians to action.

In the 1960s, the threat to the state, particularly from the OAS (Secret Army Organization), whose roots lay within the French military and which tried to assassinate President Charles de Gaulle, was seen as of sufficient magnitude to justify a dramatic response. In 1963 the government established a centralized system, in the form of an entirely new and special court, the State Security Court (La Cour de Sûreté de l'État), for confronting the terrorist threat to the state. However, the court was composed in part of military officers appointed to two-year terms by the government, its proceedings were secret, and it had no provision for appeal. In short, it stood completely outside the normal system of French justice.[4]

While that court was reasonably effective at its immediate task, it was very controversial and was seen as a tool of the Gaullist political party that had created it. Despite its origins as a weapon against the far right, it became associated over the course of the 1960s and 1970s with efforts by the right to persecute political opposition on the left. It became, in the words of one critic, "a political weapon of the 'power.'"[5] Opposition politicians such as then senator François Mitterrand specifically criticized it as an unconstitutional appropriation of judicial power by the executive.[6]

In part as a result of these disputes, when Mitterrand and the opposition Socialists came to power in 1981, the struggle against terrorism was highly politicized in France. Two of Mitterrand's first acts were to issue an amnesty that included many extreme-left terrorists and to eliminate the State Security Court. In a time of lower terrorist threat, his government saw little need to reconstitute any specialized judicial or police organizations for dealing with terrorism.

These decisions reflected, and indeed reinforced, a deep level of distrust between the political authorities and the police and intelligence services. After twenty-three years of right-wing rule, the Socialists viewed the security services as bastions of right-wing sympathizers determined to undermine their rule. Mitterrand himself had nearly had his political career destroyed in the 1950s by false accusations emanating from the security services.[7]

Similarly, the security services distrusted the new government and resented the Socialists' decision to undo their hard work through an amnesty program. That judgment was reinforced by the presence of four communist ministers in Mitterrand's cabinet and by the fact that one of Mitterrand's advisers, Régis Debray, had fought with Che Guevara in Latin America.[8] The security services even suspected the Socialists of harboring sympathies for some extreme-leftist terrorist groups, most prominently Action Directe—a leftist group responsible for numerous attacks against the state that had been largely subdued before Mitterrand's election.[9] As it happened, many of the amnestied Action Directe leaders returned to terrorism, and the security services had to track them down again, not managing to fully dismantle the group until 1987.[10]

The political divides between the government and the security services were mirrored by institutional feuds within French governmental structures and precluded effective coordination in the fight against terrorism. At least seven different police services in four different cabinet ministries had a variety of overlapping responsibilities in matters relating to terrorism.[11] While that sort of diffusion of responsibility is essentially inevitable in modern government, the real problem was that these agencies rarely met and often actively distrusted and misled one another. According to one agent working in the domestic intelligence agency at the time, "each agency jealously guarded its information, manipulated the other services and practiced disinformation."[12]

Along these lines, in 1981 the interior minister refused, in the presence of the prime minister, to share intelligence about terrorism with the foreign intelligence agency, the Direction Général de la Sécurité Extérieure (DGSE), because he claimed it was "a nest of Soviet spies."[13] The running joke at the time was that the domestic intelligence agency, the Direction de la Surveillance Territoire (DST), would have a better chance of obtaining information if it asked the KGB than if it asked the DGSE. In an expression of its anger at this state of affairs, the DST actively cooperated with the New Zealand police in their efforts to prove the complicity of the DGSE in the 1985 bombing of the Greenpeace ship *Rainbow Warrior* in Auckland Harbor.[14]

When a renewed series of attacks by Middle Eastern terrorists began in 1982, the state's inability to protect the French population from terrorist attacks once again became a highly fraught political issue.[15] The intense political salience of the issue, in combination with the Socialists' distrust of the existing intelligence services, convinced Mitterrand, following a long tradition in France, to create an ad hoc cell within the Élysée Palace devoted to the problem of terrorism and staffed with operatives he felt he could trust. This so-called Élysée Cell operated in close contact with the president but with little coordination with other agencies and, according to some, with little regard for legal procedures.[16] The presence of this cell, greatly resented by the established police and intelligence agencies, did little to promote coordination and trust between the numerous agencies necessary to combat the complex phenomenon that terrorism had become by the 1980s. In the end, this cell failed to improve the French counterterrorism capacity and even caused a public relations disaster when it was revealed to have planted evidence in order to arrest some suspected Irish terrorists.[17]

As a result, when yet another wave of attacks of Middle Eastern origin rocked France in 1986, the French counterterrorism apparatus was perceived to be in total disarray, generating an overwhelming public outcry for increased security. A new government from the right end of the French political spectrum took power during the wave of attacks and resolved to reform the French internal security apparatus to meet the terrorist challenge.

The main response was embodied in the antiterrorism legislation passed in September 1986,[18] which attempted to centralize all judicial and investigative proceedings relating to terrorism. In the judicial sphere, local prosecutors and investigators at the scene of the attack had previously handled terrorism cases. Unfortunately, terrorist attacks were rarely isolated incidents, and the specific location of an attack was of little relevance to its investigation or prosecution. With little contact between prosecutors of different jurisdictions who were working on related cases, there was little capacity to integrate information and to discover patterns.

The 1986 legislation did not repeat the mistake of the State Security Court of the 1960s by creating a new specialized court outside the normal judicial system. The lesson from that experience was clear: to maintain vigilance in times of decreased threat and to ensure that the system would not be undone by the next administration, the government had to create a process that existed as much as possible within the normal procedures of French justice and that could therefore have legitimacy across the political spectrum.[19]

Although the legislation did take note of the special nature of terrorist crime by providing for longer jail terms for acts committed for the purposes of terrorism and for longer periods of detention and investigation in such cases, it nonetheless left the prosecution of terrorist cases within the normal procedures of French justice. Rather than creating an entirely new court, the legislation centralized proceedings relating to terrorism in the existing Trial Court of Paris and left to normal judges the ultimate decision as to the outcome of the cases.

Under this system, a local prosecutor decides if a crime committed within his geographic area of responsibility is related to terrorism, based on a definition of terrorism as "acts committed by individuals or groups that have as a goal to gravely trouble public order by intimidation or terror."[20] If an incident meets that definition, the case belongs to the specialized prosecutors and magistrates within the Paris court. This system runs contrary to a principle of French law that holds that cases should be tried in place, but it gets around the problem of the small size of local prosecutors' offices and minimizes the dangers of reprisals against local officials (particularly a problem with separatist terrorist groups in Corsica). More important, perhaps, the system created within the Trial Court of Paris a small section of prosecutors and investigating magistrates who dealt only with terrorism cases and who eventually became established as the lead actors in the French struggle against terrorism.

The investigating magistrate, a cross between a prosecutor and a judge, has no precise analogue in the Anglo-Saxon system of justice. An investigating magistrate (an inexact translation of *juge d'instruction*) is not an advocate for the prosecution or the defense, but rather is charged with conducting an impartial investigation to determine whether a crime worthy of prosecution has been committed. Once that determination is made, the investigating magistrate hands the case over to a prosecutor and a defense attorney, who, on the basis of the magistrate's investigation, act as advocates in front of a judge (or *juge de siege*). The legislation also allowed terrorists to be tried without a jury, another exception to normal French practice, but a need brought home by the resignation en masse of a jury under threat in a case against Action Directe. Ultimately, however, terrorist trials, even without juries, take place in normal courts in front of normal judges.

Investigating magistrates are intended to be impartial arbiters. They are, at least in theory, not answerable to any political authority and are granted fairly wide powers to open judicial inquiries, authorize search warrants and wiretaps, and issue subpoenas—powers that in the United States would require specific judicial authorization. Within the French judicial system, such magistrates are not at all unique to terrorist cases. Nevertheless, this institution, which in many circumstances serves merely as an unwieldy extra step in the judicial process, has proven adaptive to the complex investigations necessary in using judicial procedures to punish and even prevent terrorist actions.[21]

The 1986 legislation also created a new specialized coordinating body within the Justice Ministry (SCLAT—Service pour Coordination de la Lutte Anti-Terroriste)[22] to complement a similar organization already existing within the Interior Ministry (UCLAT—Unité de Coordination de la Lutte Anti-Terroriste, created in 1984). The purpose of these organizations was to make connections and coordinate between the various intelligence and police services within their ministries bearing on the question of terrorism, as well as to establish solid links between the ministries. Previously, no single service even within the ministries had coordinated the fight against terrorism, and thus no one was responsible for assembling a complete picture from the various institutional sources, assuring information flows between the various agencies, or providing coordinated direction to the intelligence and police services for the prevention of terrorism.[23] According to one of the architects of the system, Alain Marsaud, this system was in part explicitly modeled on the U.S. National Security Council (NSC) and the interagency process it oversees.[24]

SCLAT and UCLAT were formed within their respective ministries rather than at the interministerial level like the NSC. Nonetheless, part of their explicit purpose was to allow for better coordination between the Interior Ministry, where most of the police and intelligence services resided, and the judiciary. The problem that interministerial cooperation needed to address, however, was more than just an absence of opportunities for meetings. There was a basic cultural divide between the two arms of government. The intelligence services tended to focus on maintaining sources of information and to operate on a long time horizon, whereas the judiciary tended to focus on achieving prosecutions and to act in a time frame dictated by court procedures and laws meant to ensure the swift application of justice. This inherent cultural difference meant that important intelligence was often hidden from the judicial magistrates, that intelligence was often not used to operational advantage, and, perhaps worse, that magistrates using their own investigative resources tended to nurture parallel sources, a practice that risked becoming a source of conflict between intelligence and the judiciary.[25]

The intent of SCLAT and UCLAT was therefore to provide a forum and a point of contact within each ministry to establish personal relationships between key officials that would give them sufficient confidence to share information, despite the inherent conflict of interest implicit in their missions. For this reason, the system actually profited from the fact that UCLAT and SCLAT operated at the working level rather than at the political level. Reflecting this fact, when the Comité Interministerial pour Liaison Anti-Terroriste (CILAT) was later formed at the policy level, the UCLAT director gained a seat on the committee and UCLAT became its secretariat and the key body for the implementation of its policy.

It took some time for this system, quite revolutionary in the French context, to mature and to develop the personal relationships on which its success was premised. Indeed, the new system appears to have had little bearing on the end of the 1986 wave of attacks. Speculation at the time and since has been that this series of attacks ended because the French government decided to deal with the state sponsors of the attacks. The French government has always denied that such deals took place, and the existence of any arrangement with state sponsors of terror attacks in France remains highly controversial to this day.[26] Nonetheless, it is clear, as Michel Wieviorka points out, that "faced with international terrorism, France, we might say, followed a policy of diplomatic activities that was guided by the will of terrorist states."[27] After years of sporadic attacks, France remained largely free of international terrorist attacks on its home soil from 1987 until 1994, although it needs to be said that in 1989, France suffered its worst-ever terrorist attack when a French plane, UTA 772, exploded over Africa, killing all 170 people on board. Nonetheless, it was the spillover of the Algerian Civil War into France, which began in 1993, that first tested the counterterrorism apparatus that France had been creating since 1986.

France and the Algerian Civil War

In 1989 the government of Algeria, in power since independence in 1962, authorized Algeria's first multiparty elections. However, in early 1992, when it appeared that an Islamist party, the Islamic Salvation Front (FIS), was going to win those elections, the army suspended the entire process and declared martial law. The FIS, outlawed by the military government, retreated into a clandestine existence and began to organize an armed struggle. Once outlawed, however, the Algerian Islamist resistance quickly splintered into a variety of factions. Moderate elements favored a return to the electoral process, while more radical elements, ideologically empowered by the government's rejection of democracy, escalated their demands for the establishment of an Islamic state.[28]

The most radical such group, the Armed Islamic Group (GIA), was formed in December 1992, in part by former mujahideen returning from the Soviet-Afghan War. By 1994 they had succeeded in rallying most of the Algerian Islamist movements under the GIA banner and in gathering external support from Islamists in Tunisia, Libya, and Morocco.[29] Unlike the

FIS, the GIA did not merely aim to seize political power in Algeria. Rather, the GIA adhered to a more extreme ideological doctrine that held that the Algerian people and their government exist in a pre-Islamic state. All Algerians are considered *takfir* (impious ones) and must therefore submit themselves to the restoration of Islam or die. Through holy war, or jihad, the GIA wanted not just to take power in Algeria but also to reestablish Islamic law, the only form of law recognized by tradition. As a matter of principle, therefore, the GIA refused to contemplate compromise or to recognize any distinction among its opponents, be they moderate Islamists, the Algerian government, or foreigners.

The radical-moderate split led to bitter interfactional violence within Algeria, and moderate and radical Islamists often concentrated their attacks more on each other (and on their supporting populations) than on the government. Between 1995 and 1998, according to scholar Mohammed Hafez, no more than 25 percent of attacks carried out by rebels targeted the government.[30] Instead, wholesale massacres of civilians became common. The Algerian security services apparently took advantage of these internal struggles to penetrate many of the splinter factions in order to stoke internal dissension and to generate domestic and international condemnation of the Islamists, perhaps even carrying out some of the massacres themselves. The end result was a massive, confusing spasm of violence that amounted to a civil war, claiming more than one hundred thousand lives between 1992 and 1998.

For the early GIA leaders, France represented "the mother of all sinners" because France had colonized Algeria, despoiled its riches for more than a century, and continued through its financial and political support for the junta ruling Algeria to reduce Algerian Muslims to slavery and to move Algeria away from religion.[31] More prosaically, France maintained close links with the Algerian security services and, perhaps most seriously from the GIA's perspective, was attempting to facilitate talks between the FIS and the Algerian government. The GIA's access to a variety of militants and potential sympathizers already residing outside Algeria, particularly within the large North African immigrant population in France, gave it the ability to attack France directly. The GIA's ideology and its desire to radicalize the conflict gave it the incentive.

In 1993 the GIA told all foreigners to leave Algeria under threat of death. On October 24, 1993, Islamists kidnapped three French consular agents in

Algiers. The message carried back by one of the hostages contained an explicit threat to the security of French citizens in Algeria and to France itself. In response, on November 9, 1993, French authorities launched Operation Chrysanthemum within France. In two days, 110 people in France were questioned, and 87 were taken into custody.

This wave of arrests was certainly motivated by the hostage taking, but the arrests also responded to a general disquiet felt by the French authorities, who since 1992 had noticed the arrival in France of numerous members of the FIS and other Algerian Islamist groups.[32] For the interior minister, Charles Pasqua, these interrogations also served the purpose of sending the message that the French government intended to suppress Islamist activity within the borders of France. Several waves of arrests followed. On November 8, 1994, the Chalabi network, the most important group in France supporting Algerian resistance against the government, was dismantled. Ninety-three people were arrested, fifteen were soon released, and seventy-eight were held over for trial.

Apparently in response, on Christmas Day 1994, an Air France flight from Algiers to Paris was hijacked. With this hijacking, the GIA announced its ability and desire to strike directly on French soil. The GIA demanded the abandonment of French aid to Algeria and financial reparations for the damages inflicted on Algerians by France between 1945 and 1962 before it would release the plane. The GIA also demanded the liberation of the leaders of the FIS and a former emir of the GIA. On December 26, French commandos assaulted the plane on the tarmac in Marseille and killed the hijackers. Documents later found in London implied that the terrorists had intended to crash the plane in Paris, probably into the Eiffel Tower.

Expecting further attacks, French authorities decided to increase the pressure on Islamist networks in France. On June 2, 1995, four hundred police officers were mobilized to arrest 131 people in Paris, Marseille, Perpignan, Tourcoing, and Orléans—dismantling a vast European network of support for the GIA and other Algerian groups. Unfortunately, the French intelligence services did not know of the existence of parallel networks in Lyon and Lille. Soon afterward, on July 11, the GIA assassinated Abdelbaki Sahraoui, the moderate imam of a Paris mosque (at the rue Myrha) and a cofounder of the FIS, who lived in France and had acted as a bridge between Algerian fundamentalists and the French government. His killing apparently served as the prelude to a series of semicoordinated attacks launched in France. Despite numerous subsequent arrests, and the death of Khelkal and his associates, the attacks continued into October (see table 5-1). In early November, French police, following up on information provided by wiretaps, arrested a cell under Boualem Bensaid, later described as a pivotal figure in the 1995 attacks, and the attacks ceased.[33] But a subsequent attack more than a year later bore the hallmarks of the same broad group of terrorists and demonstrated their continued viability.

Table 5-1. Attacks in France Attributed to the GIA, July 1995–December 1996

July 11, 1995	Assassination of Abdelbaki Sahraoui, imam of the mosque on the rue Myrha. Moderate and close to the FIS, he had protested against the use of violence on French territory.
July 25, 1995	A bomb explodes in the regional transit system at the Saint-Michel station in Paris. Eight people die and eighty-six are wounded.
August 17, 1995	A bomb laden with nuts and bolts explodes in a trash can near the Arc de Triomphe, wounding seventeen. Police increase security at public places and interview witnesses to the attack, which is believed to be related to the earlier attack at the Saint-Michel station.
August 29, 1995	Authorities discover a bomb planted on a high-speed train track north of Lyon. It fails to detonate.
September 3, 1995	A pressure-cooker bomb partially explodes in an open market near Place de la Bastille in Paris. Four people are wounded.
September 4, 1995	A potentially powerful bomb fails to explode and is found inside a public toilet near an outdoor market in Paris's Fifteenth District.
September 7, 1995	A car bomb explodes outside a Jewish school in a Lyon suburb, ten minutes before school lets out. Fourteen people are wounded.
October 6, 1995	A gas canister containing nuts and bolts and hidden in a trash can explodes near the Maison Blanche subway station in southern Paris, wounding sixteen people.
October 17, 1995	In the eighth terrorist attack or attempted attack in three months, a bomb explodes in an underground commuter train at the RER Orsay, wounding thirty people.

Table 5-1, continued

December 3, 1996 A bomb explodes during rush hour at the Port-Royal station in Paris. Two people die and forty are injured, seven seriously. Police and officials quickly conclude that the bomb had been fashioned from a gas canister similar to the ones used in the previous year's attacks.

Responding to the GIA

The wave of attacks by the GIA in 1994–96 represented the first severe test of the system France had begun to put in place in the mid-1980s to combat terrorism on its home soil. In many ways, the system responded well. Important personal links had been created between the judicial and intelligence services that allowed firm actions before a threat was even manifested; preplanned emergency responses to threats mobilized both the security forces and the wider public and undoubtedly prevented many attacks; and fairly rapid postattack investigations rounded up those responsible for the attacks in about four months.

These successes occurred because the establishment of a centralized interlocutor at the Interior Ministry, UCLAT, in combination with a small, specialized corps of antiterrorism magistrates, created over time a cross-ministerial competency that almost amounted to an intelligence service in and of itself. The individual magistrates, after years of conducting connected investigations, many of which specifically resulted from evidence gleaned in prior investigations, became the type of expert on the subject of terrorism that is difficult to create within normal judicial institutions. The individual magistrates even tended to specialize in cases related to specific classes of terrorism, such as separatist or Islamist terrorism.

The investigating magistrates usually availed themselves of the Judicial Police, essentially the French detective service, as their investigative arm. At this time, however, the Division Nationale Anti-Terroriste of the Judicial Police (DNAT, previously known as the Sixth Section of the Judicial Police) was facing an increase in Basque and Corsican separatist terrorism, culminating in the 1998 assassination of the highest French government official in Corsica, the prefect Claude Erignac. The DNAT, consequently, did not have the resources to devote itself to the Islamist dossiers in the manner the magistrates would have preferred.

Thus, as early as the 1989 UTA 772 case, magistrates working on Islamist cases began to work directly with the DST, the domestic intelligence agency in the Interior Ministry, with which they had grown familiar through the UCLAT mechanism. As the agency responsible for monitoring foreign activity within the borders of France, the DST was focused on countering Soviet espionage. It had long also had the primary intelligence responsibility for countering foreign terrorism within France. The magistrates had decided to make use of the fact that the DST officially had a dual role as an intelligence agency and a judicial police force that could be placed under the authority of a magistrate.[34] The process of investigations created a continuing relationship between specific judicial authorities and the DST, which in turn inspired a degree of confidence within the DST that its agents were dealing with people in the judicial arm who understood and shared their concerns about protection of sources and the threat that judicial procedures pose to intelligence operations. The combination of expertise, effective relationships with the intelligence services, and the judicial powers already mentioned eventually created a formidable body for combating terrorism.

As a result, intelligence agents from the DST often go directly to the magistrates and prosecutors when they have information that they feel warrants a judicial investigation. If the magistrates decide from the intelligence obtained that there has or might be a criminal act, they have the power to transform the intelligence investigation into a judicial investigation. While information acquired before a judicial investigation is opened is not admissible in French court, the opening of an official investigation provides various advantages. The agents in question can from that point on avail themselves of the magistrates' extensive powers to issue warrants, subpoenas, and wiretaps, the results of which can be used as proof in court. For the DST to secure a wiretap through nonjudicial procedures requires five different signatures from the heads of five different agencies, including the head of an independent commission.[35] This tight integration of the French intelligence and judicial systems allows the latter to act much more quickly and effectively than most judicial authorities.[36]

This system also helped to depoliticize the issue of antiterrorism, although this was probably not its original intent. As the magistrates became more publicly visible, they achieved a greater capacity to assert their statutory independence from political authorities, if necessary through resort to the media. Indeed, over time, individual investigating magistrates, such as Jean-Louis Bruguière, Jean-François Ricard, Laurence Le Vert, and Gilles Thiel, gained a public reputation for implacable opposition to terrorism that stood in stark contrast to the craven image of politicians in the 1980s. As a result, the existence of the magistrates—informed, independent, and pitiless adversaries of terrorism in all its forms—effectively foreclosed the options of playing down the threat or accommodating terrorist demands. Intelligence agencies, more deeply ensconced within the government apparatus and more distrustful of the press, could not hope to play this role, even when they shared the magistrates' views.

Thus, for example, during the 1980s, the Mitterrand government had consciously attempted to limit media exposure of terrorist attacks, both to avoid giving the terrorists the publicity they sought and to avoid public pressure for dramatic action. Consequently, although the Vigipirate plan for national emergencies existed in embryonic form at the time, it was not invoked during the terrorist attacks of the early 1980s. In the 1990s, both because of the more intense media scrutiny of the age and because of the media savvy of the magistrates, such a strategy was no longer an option.[37] Vigipirate, which involves increased operations for defense of the national territory; special protection of sites of national importance, such as the presidential palace, ports, and tourist sites; and a visible presence of the armed forces within France, as well as domestic awareness programs, was first invoked during the Gulf War in 1991.[38] In fact, Vigipirate has remained in force, at least at a low level of alert, since 1991. In 1995 the alert status was raised soon after the first attacks. In addition to the discovery of the bomb on the Paris–Lyon TGV track, the government's public vigilance campaign also arguably led to a bomb being discovered near the Paris Metro by an alert citizen.[39] The more general effect of this mobilization was to increase public awareness, and anger, over the issue of terrorism so much that accommodation to terrorist demands became politically impossible.

Previously, the Foreign Affairs Ministry had often invoked raison d'état and the need to retain amicable relations with foreign states in order to interfere in domestic terrorism investigations in France—most notably in 1987 when it allowed the alleged mastermind of the 1986 wave of attacks, Wahid Gordiji, to exit the Iranian embassy and leave France in the interests of improving relations with Iran. Of course, France's Algerian policy was quite controversial within France, and French politicians frequently hinted that France might move toward a more neutral policy in the Algerian Civil War, but there is little evidence that such considerations affected the domestic battle against terror. A poll published in October 1995 showed that 91 percent of the French population supported the government's antiterrorism policy and 61 percent wanted France to keep its Algerian policy unchanged.[40] In any case, because the terrorism of the 1990s lacked any state sponsor, it was difficult for the Foreign Affairs Ministry to even find an interlocutor that could credibly promise that specific French concessions would stop the attacks. The foreign policy tail had apparently ceased to wag the domestic security dog in France.

Similarly, the notion of proposing an amnesty to attempt to placate the terrorists or attempt to reintegrate them into French society, the notion that had inspired the 1981 amnesty, became essentially a nonstarter in France. In the presence of media-minded magistrates who saw repression as the only effective means of combating terrorism, and given the experience of the 1980s, when amnestied terrorists had returned to their old patterns, an amnesty would have been a political disaster in France in the 1990s. Although this "depoliticization" of terrorism denied French politicians a degree of control over an important aspect of state policy, it also relieved them to some extent of public responsibility for solving, and therefore blame for failing to solve, what they saw as an intractable problem.

LESSONS LEARNED FROM THE 1995–96 ATTACKS

Despite evident improvements, the very fact of the attacks demonstrated that there remained in the mid-1990s significant, even deadly, weaknesses in the French counterterrorism apparatus. In part, this was due simply to the changing nature of terrorism itself. The attacks were extraordinarily simple affairs that did not rely on traceable state support as was common in the 1980s. Rather, they used essentially homemade equipment (crude gas bombs surrounded by nails), their targets were effectively random and indiscriminate, and they often drew from loose networks of operatives submerged within France's large Algerian expatriate community. Indeed, French officials believe that some of the attacks may have been copycat attacks by religiously inspired amateurs, not connected in any fashion with the original GIA operatives.[41] To complicate matters even further, many observers have asserted that some or all of the attacks were in fact the work of the Algerian secret service attempting to provoke a French reaction against the GIA.[42] This new type of terrorism, as well as the general experience of the 1995–96 attacks, implied several lessons.

Surveillance and Support Network

Stopping such attacks requires not just intelligence but also surveillance of entire communities. According to one official, French authorities learned from their experience of finding some but not all of the Islamist networks present in France that they needed to maintain a constant operational surveillance over the wide spectrum of civil society in order to prevent terrorist networks from developing on French territory.[43] In the case of potential Islamist networks, that means surveillance of the more than fifteen hundred mosques and prayer halls, as well as the more than two thousand Islamic organizations within France.[44] This job falls primarily on the Renseignements Généraux (RG), a distinct domestic intelligence agency that is specifically intended and empowered for domestic surveillance. While the DST is tasked with protecting the territory of France from its external enemies, the RG is more generally tasked with gathering all types of information on the domestic situation within France and even includes a division that does political polling. The RG is dispersed in fairly small cells throughout France and has reputedly achieved a great deal of penetration of the various Muslim subcultures in France through the use of deep local knowledge, informants, relationships with community leaders, and electronic listening devices.

Of course, the presence of a large, semi-integrated immigrant community within France has somewhat blurred the distinction between threats emanating from abroad and domestic threats, which originally justified the existence of two domestic intelligence agencies. Thus the DST also runs an extensive network of informers within the Muslim community, many of whom are convicted felons who receive reduced sentences for their cooperation. The DST also monitors immigrants entering France, particularly those with Muslim or North African backgrounds, and attempts to track their movements within France.[45] Finally, the foreign intelligence service, the DGSE, feeds foreign-sourced information into domestic intelligence and law enforcement agencies, although the DST, apparently dissatisfied with the information obtained from the DGSE, has, since the UTA 772 investigation in 1989, begun to develop its own parallel foreign sources of information.[46]

The problem, however, beyond the obvious issues of overlap and sheer volume of information, is that anticipating the types of very simple attacks that occurred in 1995–96 required thinking less in terms of the operational terrorist organizations on which French intelligence was used to focusing and more on the mechanism of support that operatives might rely on in the community. French intelligence had tended to focus its surveillance on organizations that had a history or background of violence, in this case the networks the FIS was establishing for sending aid to guerrillas fighting in Algeria. This approach provided the intelligence necessary for the roundups that preceded the 1995 attacks, but it also meant that heretofore dormant, yet ideologically more radical groups had not been disabled and may even have been relatively empowered in the Muslim community by the roundups.

However, from the perspective of many French antiterrorism officials, this inattention to terrorist support mechanisms reflected not only an intelligence failure but also a lack of institutional capacity inherent in French law. The essential problem was that terrorism, as practiced by the GIA in France in 1995–96, did not require the maintenance of substantial operational or planning capacity. Rather, this type of terrorism required the maintenance of logistics networks that, while not directly involved in terrorist activities, could supply false papers, financing, or simply safe lodging to potential operatives; operatives could drop in from abroad or be quickly recruited from within the French Muslim community. Financially, the logistics networks of the diverse armed Algerian groups supported themselves through setting up legitimate businesses, armed robberies, and trafficking in credit cards and false documents such as passports.

Under French law, such activities either were not illegal or else did not fall under the purview of the antiterrorism magistrates or the various specialized antiterrorism units within France. Normal intelligence or police organizations, more interested in gathering information or stopping crime than in recognizing specific patterns of preterrorist activity, failed to react appropriately to what appeared to them as fairly mundane criminal or even noncriminal activity.

As a result, new legislative initiatives in 1995 and 1996 specifically targeted the logistics networks by codifying the notion that conspiracy to commit terrorism was itself terrorism. Accordingly, "the participation in any group formed or association established with a view to the preparation, marked by one or more material actions, of any of the acts of terrorism provided for under the previous articles shall in addition be an act of terrorism."[47] This notion of a conspiracy to commit a crime has ample precedent in U.S. law, but it represented something of a revolution in French jurisprudence, which heretofore had required an act to be committed before any charges could be brought, or, in a parallel fashion, that an act meeting the definition of terrorism be committed before the special cadres of laws, procedures, and organizations meant to deal with terrorism could be invoked.

This new law dramatically increased the types of investigations antiterrorism magistrates and their specialized antiterrorist interlocutors within the intelligence and law enforcement agencies could undertake, allowing them to open investigations and to deploy their expertise and judicial tools before terrorist attacks took place. In this sense, they gained the capacity not just to punish the perpetrators of terrorist attacks after they took place but also to disrupt logistics networks and to prevent attacks from happening in the first place—a fairly unique role for judicial authorities.

The Balance between Centralization and Competition

The creation of the UCLAT/SCLAT system of coordination in the 1980s represented an attempt to rationalize and centralize the French government's counterterrorism institutions. As the reactions to both the September 11 and March 11 attacks demonstrated, this is an almost reflexive response of all governments to increased public demands for action against terrorism. For the highly centralized, even Cartesian, French government, it is second nature. Nonetheless, the UCLAT/SCLAT reforms, for the usual reasons of history, bureaucratic inertia, and entrenched interests, did not succeed in completely centralizing the French fight against terrorism. They did create an important mechanism and a venue through which the various actors in counterterrorism could understand each other's capacities and coordinate their efforts, but they did not create a hierarchical organization, nor did they vest responsibility for counterterrorism in one official or one organization.

In retrospect, however, this system of coordination rather than centralization was probably a good idea. The fact that several independent organizations were involved infused the system with a competitive dynamic and ensured that the system as a whole would not become too focused on one type of threat. Terrorism constituted a multifaceted and evolving threat that required the type of dynamic response that strictly hierarchical organizations can rarely achieve. This competitive dynamic, in the French context, meant that different organizations tended to specialize in specific capabilities and threats and even to serve as "champions" of their specialties within the larger French bureaucracy. Different organizations proved useful at different times and for different tasks. The DNAT thus stepped forward to deal with the surge of Corsican terrorism in the late 1990s, while the DST concentrated on Islamist terrorism emanating from abroad, and the RG maintained broad surveillance on domestic Muslim groups.

Of course, within this competitive dynamic, cooperation was often essential. The key, however, was not just providing a venue for coordination or, even in the long term, the application of high-level political pressure for cooperation. Rather, real cooperation tended to follow either from personal contacts nurtured over long periods or from establishing a relationship in which the organizations in question needed each other to fulfill their missions. Thus the fruitful cooperation between the DST and the magistrates proceeded because the magistrates could offer the DST the investigative powers it lacked (powers of wiretaps, subpoena, detention, etc.), while the DST could offer the magistrates the intelligence and operational manpower they lacked.

International Cooperation

A further lesson of the mid-1990s attacks was the increasing need for international cooperation, particularly from France's European partners, in combating terrorism. While cooperation with foreign governments had always been crucial both for gathering intelligence and for preventing terrorists from finding sanctuary in neighboring countries, the GIA experience revealed that the need had become even more critical. In the first instance, this was because instantaneous communications, frequent travel, and increased economic interdependence meant that terrorist networks were becoming more global and transnational. What had previously required only bilateral relations now frequently involved tracing terrorist activities across several countries, both friendly and hostile. Beyond Algeria and France, Algerian extremists had established networks in Britain, Germany, Denmark, Switzerland, Sweden, Spain, and Belgium.[48] Without the ability to affect such networks in other countries, French officials were effectively battling a hydra by attacking only one head—an ultimately fruitless exercise.

An even greater impetus for international cooperation came from the elimination of internal European border controls. The French experience in

1995–96 made the government acutely aware that the elimination of border controls between France and its European Union partners would not eliminate differences in perceptions, and indeed in the reality, of terrorist threats. Many of France's neighbors were not willing to make similar types of radical changes to their laws and procedures to fend off a danger they did not feel and, at least in the short term, did not face.

In the case of the 1995–96 attacks, it quickly became apparent that the financing of the attacks had originated in London, while many of the key suspects in the attacks—people whose arrest and interrogation were considered critical for forestalling future attacks—had fled abroad across France's quite porous borders. But at the height of the 1995–96 wave of attacks, two of France's EU partners, Britain and Sweden, refused to extradite suspects in the attacks to France. In the Swedish case, the Swedish court ruled that France had not presented sufficient evidence to establish a prima facie case against the suspect. In the British case, a British court ruled that the government could not guarantee that the suspect, Rachid Ramda, considered one of the masterminds of the attacks, would be treated according to international norms of human rights, an oblique reference to the possibility that he would be tortured. Both responses infuriated French officials responsible for preventing terrorist attacks in an environment of increasingly open borders.

In the end, these very visible disputes do not represent the overall state of cooperation between France and its European partners. France did make progress in establishing effective bilateral cooperation with certain neighbors on this issue even before September 11, particularly in establishing cooperation with Spain on ETA and in breaking up Algerian Islamist cells in Germany, Britain, Italy, and Spain in 2000–2001.[49] The September 11 attacks, moreover, brought a new understanding to the problem and a new, powerful advocate for increased cooperation: the United States. In response to those attacks, the European Union established a common definition of terrorism and a common list of terrorist organizations. The European Arrest Warrant, for example, adopted immediately after September 11, should render moot extradition disputes such as those that took place with Britain and Sweden in 1995.[50] The March 11, 2004, attacks in Madrid and the July 7, 2005, attacks in London created an even greater impetus toward both bilateral and European-level cooperation. An EU counterterrorism coordinator was appointed, new committees were created to facilitate coordination among member state organizations, and the European states reiterated their commitments to establishing a greater capacity for counterterrorism at the EU level and greater cooperation among member states.

But the EU still relies on its member states to incorporate its decisions into law and into practice. As the European Commission noted after the March 11 attacks in Madrid, "the Union has already put in place a series of legislative measures to combat terrorism. But implementation of these measures [by the member states] is often slow, poor and inadequate. This is unacceptable. Action is needed to turn political agreements into legal reality."[51]

The EU also still lacks any organic intelligence, judicial, or police services of its own, making it completely dependent on its member states for information and operations. For example, Europol and Eurojust, set up in 1999 and 2002, respectively, represent embryonic EU police and judicial organizations, but they have no operational capabilities of their own and are completely dependent on the corresponding member state organizations for intelligence and implementation. Those organizations have often been jealous of their prerogatives, meaning that Europol and Eurojust have thus far served primarily as forums for coordination, communication, and analysis rather than as even embryonic operational organizations.[52]

The Issue of Civil Liberties

Another unresolved issue emerging from the mid-1990s French experience is the question of how the counterterrorism system affects civil liberties, and in particular how it affects specific target communities such as the Corsicans and the large French Muslim community. This is a question not only of justice but also of effectiveness: the French experience with counterterrorism demonstrates that measures not firmly rooted in French concepts of fairness and not shared across the political spectrum will ultimately fail, even by the standard of preventing future terrorist actions. During the 1995–96 attacks, and despite public outcries for security, the action of the counterterrorism apparatus was often fiercely criticized by the media and human rights groups.

Two areas in particular have been the object of acerbic criticisms: the preventive roundups and the associated indiscriminate detention of suspects, as well as the broad powers given to magistrates to conduct these sweeps and detentions with very little oversight. The November 1993 Operation Chrysanthemum was denounced as a sweep, using the French word *rafle*, which specifically evokes actions taken during the German occupation.[53] In any case, eighty-eight people were interrogated, but only three were incarcerated and put under investigation for "conspiracy in relation to a terrorist enterprise." A variety of media outlets, as well as the Fédération Internationale des Ligues des Droits de l'Homme (FDIH), declared the arrests "media spectacles" and "destructive of liberty."[54] Roundups have often swept up people against whom there is no preexisting evidence or people who have nothing to do with the networks but just happen to be present on the day of the sweep. The decision after the 1995 attacks to go after logistics and support networks has only increased the breadth of the sweeps, as demonstrated before the 1998 World Cup in France.

Another frequent critique heard is that there is no controlling authority over the actions of the antiterrorism magistrates and that the contents of the antiterrorist laws of 1986 and 1996 offer excessive scope for the magistrates to decide what constitutes terrorism or intent to commit terrorism. According to a January 1999 report of the FDIH, a number of jurists and lawyers have expressed reservations about the vagueness of the antiterrorist laws, notably in the Chalabi affair.[55] Not only does the 1986 law heavily concentrate the competences for fighting terrorism in the hands of a limited group of antiterrorism magistrates, but their conclusions are then usually accepted uncritically by the other actors in the judicial system with very little oversight by any outside authority. Only the Chambre d'Accusation exercises any control over the decision of the magistrates, but that court decides only on issues involving respect for the procedures of the laws, not on issues of fact, such as what qualifies as "an association of criminals for purposes of committing terrorism." Thus, of the 138 people the magistrates detained for a trial in the sweeps associated with the dismantlement of the Chalabi network, 51 were ultimately found innocent of complicity in terrorism and released, but not until they had spent more than four years in jail.

For the FDIH, the introduction of the conspiracy-to-commit-terrorism language opened the door to arbitrary enforcement, because a number of acts that are not illegal become illegal when a magistrate decides they occur in the context of intent to commit terrorism. Thus, according to the FDIH, this definition of criminal conspiracy contravenes the principle of French law, according to which laws must be certain and precise. For the FDIH, the law is all the more destructive of liberty because it fails to require the magistrate to attach the allegation of participation in conspiracy to any specific terrorist act.[56]

In the view of the authorities, arresting a large number of people makes it possible to carry out corroborated interrogations in order to maintain knowledge of networks that are in a perpetual state of evolution. Thus, for example, arrests in early 1998 permitted the authorities to prevent attacks planned on the World Cup, one of which was intended for the Stadium of France. This policy stands in contrast to normal French law, which usually insists that an infraction must have actually taken place before a judicial investigation can begin.

Interestingly, these attacks on the specialized system of antiterrorism enforcement in France have not generally emanated from Muslim civil society groups. Indeed, there has been very little talk about the degree to which this cadre of special antiterrorism legislation contributes to frictions between the Muslim community and the state—a debate that is almost glaring in its absence.[57] On the most mundane level, the explanation is that the Muslim community in France appears to have bigger issues with which to contend: issues of cultural integration and economic opportunity, the plague of "normal" criminal activity in Muslim areas, and the debate over public religious expression dominate the French domestic political agenda. In this highly contentious environment, occasional counterterrorism actions that affect the Muslim population, as well as the associated constant surveillance by the state, usually quite discreet, do not generate much public outcry from within the Muslim community.

In this sense, the outbursts over the killing of Khalid Khelkal speak more to a general frustration that the French Muslim community feels over its treatment by the police and by society than to a specific response to the surveillance and even to roundups associated with the French counterterrorism apparatus. It seems clear, however, that future dramatic episodes along the lines of the Khelkal shooting have the potential to let loose a torrent of social discontent that might find its expression in opposition to the special cadre of antiterrorism laws and methods that effectively target the North African community.

ASSESSMENT OF FRENCH COUNTERTERRORISM

That the 1995–96 attacks occurred, despite an awareness of the threat and direct attempts to avert them, demonstrates just how hard it is to stop small groups from carrying out simple yet effective attacks in a free society.

Indeed, the reason the GIA ceased its attacks remains a mystery. French authorities tend to attribute it to the apprehension of the suspects and to the destruction of support networks within France.[58] Algerian specialists tend to note that the GIA was increasingly under pressure within Algeria in this period. Its tendency toward violence against Algerian civilians alienated it from its base, while it simultaneously faced stepped-up attacks from the Algerian and French governments; from the resurgent armed wing of the FIS, the Armée Islamique du Salut (AIS); and from a newly emerged and yet more radical group called the Groupe Salafiste pour la Prédication et le Combat (GSPC).[59]

It is quite difficult to assess the balance between these two arguments. The GIA clearly lost a great deal of capacity as a result of French governmental efforts against it, but as the December 1996 attack demonstrated, such simple attacks were still quite possible in France. The overriding factor seems to have been that the GIA decided to halt attacks in France for reasons that had to do more with developments in the Algerian Civil War than with French counterterrorism efforts to prevent future attacks. France's counterterrorism apparatus had vastly improved its capacity to respond quickly and in a coordinated fashion to terrorist attacks, to alert the public and enlist its aid, and to resist the temptation to politicize the fight or accommodate terrorist demands, but it had not yet developed an effective capacity to prevent terrorist attacks, especially small-scale ones, from happening in the first place.

Moreover, even this degree of vigilance and efficacy has been dearly bought. It has entailed, at least by the American definition, massive civil liberty violations and substantial public monitoring, particularly of France's North African population. The French counterterrorism apparatus is extraordinarily repressive and intrusive, and repressions fall heavily on specific groups, particularly Muslims of North African origin. It is important, however, to judge this system by French standards and expectations. French society has long been more tolerant of these types of governmental intrusions than has American society. The French system of domestic monitoring predates the foreign terrorist threat and represents a response to the fairly constant threats of domestic subversion, internal terrorism, and even revolution that France has faced over the past two hundred years. The RG is, in fact, a direct descendant of the Napoleonic intelligence service established in 1804.[60]

Perhaps as a result, the response of French civil society to the repressive nature of French counterterrorism measures, while negative, as the Khelkal riots amply demonstrated, has nonetheless been rather tepid by American standards. This situation appears to reflect both a greater trust that the government will not, ultimately, abuse this power and a general sense that there are adequate controls in place, primarily independent commissions that monitor the government's use of information.[61] As a French leader of the LDH, the French equivalent of the ACLU, put it, he essentially "trusted the police in counterterrorism matters."[62] Moreover, what attacks there have been on French counterterrorism methods have generally not emanated from Muslim civil society groups, indicative of the fact that government surveillance is widely accepted in France. These points demonstrate that France has improved its capacity for counterterrorism without sacrificing the core values of French democracy. They also emphasize, however, that the particular content of those values is unique to France and may not translate well even into other democratic contexts.

EPILOGUE: THE AL QAEDA CONNECTION

France's struggle with the GIA led the French authorities to understand relatively early that the Islamist threat was of a new, complex, and global type. Indeed, the manner in which these investigations led to this conclusion and to al Qaeda in general is revelatory of the methods employed by the antiterrorism magistrates. Starting in 1994, the antiterrorism magistrates began to notice the departure of many hard-core GIA militants for Afghan training camps. The interrogations of people belonging to the Lyon cell of the GIA after the 1995 attacks also showed that the GIA had been sending new recruits to Afghanistan since the beginning of the 1990s.

In Afghanistan they received a military education in small arms and explosives as well as a religious education in radical Islam. French investigations also revealed that the financing for the 1995 attacks came from London. The financier, Rachid Ramda, was in turn found to have financial and other connections with Osama bin Laden and his group of Afghan veterans. Clearly, France's Algerian problem was internationalizing.

The subsequent affair of the Roubaix Gang supported this conclusion. The Roubaix affair began with several heavily armed robberies in the Roubaix region in January and February 1996 and originally appeared to have no relation to international terrorism. On the eve of the G7 Summit at Lille on March 29, 1996, the gang put a bomb in a car at a police station, but the bomb was discovered and dismantled. In the investigation that followed, one gang member was identified. A police operation the next day led to the gang's hideout and to a five-hour gun battle. The gang refused to emerge from the house even as it caught on fire, and many were burned alive.[63] Subsequent investigation determined a link to the Islamist movement, but despite this link, the members of the Roubaix Gang were not normal Algerian guerrilla fighters. Rather, they were native-born French citizens and second-generation French North Africans who had converted to radical Islam in France and made their connections with the terrorist movement in Bosnia and Afghanistan. The magistrates were beginning to develop a vision of a global, yet nebulous, Islamist international.

From an address book (actually a Sharp organizer) found on the body of the deceased leader of the Roubaix Gang, Christopher Caze, links were established with individuals in Italy, Belgium, Algeria, Great Britain, Canada, and the United States. This, according to French antiterrorism magistrate Jean-Louis Bruguière, suggested that "the structure of the organization—and the targets—had changed. The targets were not just in France or Europe."[64]

Profiting from this information, the French system evolved once again, and the magistrates began increasingly to open investigations in cases of acts of terrorism committed on French citizens or against French interests abroad. From those leads, Bruguière's investigation eventually found Fateh Kemal and Ahmed Ressam, who had formed a radical Islamist cell in Montreal. With a limited degree of Canadian cooperation, the French put the cell under surveillance, collecting evidence and repeatedly warning Canadian and U.S. authorities that the cell intended to attack targets in North America.

On December 14, 1999, Ahmed Ressam was arrested on the U.S.-Canadian border with a trunk full of explosives intended for use in an attack on the Los Angeles International Airport. Ressam had grown up in Algeria, resided in Canada, and plotted attacks against the United States, but despite his having few French connections, French authorities knew who Ressam was and they had tracked Ressam and his associates in Canada for more than three years. After his arrest, French investigators were able to provide the FBI with a complete dossier on Ressam and to aid U.S.

authorities in identifying his associates, eventually sending an official to testify at his trial.[65]

French authorities concluded from all this activity that preventing future attacks required increased cooperation with foreign governments; greater attention to the sources of terrorist support, logistics, and financing within France; tighter integration of governmental resources, particularly of intelligence, judicial, and law enforcement organizations; and an increased legal capacity to act in anticipation of terrorist actions. The resulting system, while hardly perfect, has succeeded in preventing numerous planned attacks in France since 1996, including a plot to blow up the Strasbourg Christmas Market in 2000, which could have easily resulted in more than 1,000 casualties, and a plot to attack the U.S. embassy in Paris in 2002 (see table 5-2).

Table 5-2. Major Terrorist Plots Prevented by French Authorities, 1998–Present

May 1998	In a synchronized operation, police in France, Belgium, Italy, Germany, and Switzerland detained more than eighty Islamist militants suspected of planning terrorist actions during the upcoming World Cup in France.
December 2000	Four men were arrested in Frankfurt, Germany, based on a tip from French authorities. Evidence found in their apartment showed they intended to blow up the Christmas Market surrounding the cathedral in Strasbourg, France.
October 2001	In France, the Netherlands, Belgium, and Dubai, intelligence and security services arrested fourteen men suspected of planning an attack on the U.S. embassy in Paris.
December 2002	French antiterrorism police arrested nine people planning to blow up the Russian embassy in Paris. The group's apparent motive was to avenge the deaths of several comrades killed in Chechnya.
January 2003	Based on intelligence provided by French authorities, raids on five homes in North London resulted in the arrests of seven people apparently planning terrorist attacks in Britain. Traces of the deadly poison ricin were discovered in one of the apartments.

It is important to note, however, that the internationalization of the Islamist terrorist movement has changed the nature of the threat that Islamists pose in France, making attacks potentially more lethal and yet easier to anticipate and prevent. The GIA was essentially interested in affecting only French policy in Algeria; successor groups, such as the GSPC, that are more closely affiliated with al Qaeda are aiming their message at a broader audience and, particularly since the example of 9/11, tend to attempt larger, more spectacular attacks against more symbolic and thus more obvious targets. These attacks threaten greater casualties and political damage. As a result, however, they also require greater preparation and more participants and are consequently more exposed to penetration and preemption by the authorities. Recent French successes, while they clearly demonstrate an improved and impressive capacity, have also profited from an enemy that shuns the type of smaller, more random attacks that made the 1995–96 wave of terrorism so difficult to prevent.

In any case, because there have not been any major terrorist attacks since 1996, the French counterterrorism system is now viewed as mature and enjoys broad, if perhaps fragile, public support. The French now have in place a strong institutional framework for coordinating antiterrorist operations and domestic preparedness; a vast network of domestic intelligence and surveillance that relies on local knowledge and informants; a fierce and uncompromising legal capacity to anticipate attacks and to arrest, interrogate, and detain suspects; and, uniquely, a system of implacable investigating magistrates who have the experience to work effectively with intelligence organizations and the independence and tenacity to follow through on terrorist cases wherever they may lead. Altogether, this system has achieved a level of flexibility and responsiveness to the constantly evolving nature of the terrorist threats that is usually the most difficult challenge for government antiterrorist institutions.

As a result, the basic French system has changed only slightly since 9/11. The level of Vigipirate alert was increased immediately after the 9/11 attacks, and the scope and size of Vigipirate were increased dramatically to include a new awareness of the need to prepare for biological and chemical weapons attacks, but the basic structure of the plan did not change. Although France passed new antiterrorism legislation very soon after the 9/11 attacks, the legislation in fact contained only minor updates to the power of the French police, as well as a lot of nonterrorism-related regulations, such as the right to seize unauthorized amplifying equipment.[66] But France is hardly invulnerable to terrorist attack, even large-scale attacks, and French authorities emphasize the need to continue updating the system. The current focus is on improving international cooperation, both to make up for the loss of border security implicit in the enlarged European Union's free movement of peoples and to cut off financing for terrorist organizations.

NOTES

1. This refers to the Schengen Agreement on the gradual abolition of checks at the common borders of participating countries, originally signed in 1985 in Luxembourg by Germany, France, Belgium, Luxembourg, and the Netherlands. It evolved into the Schengen Protocol to the Treaty of European Union of Amsterdam in 1997, allowing for citizens of implementing countries (EU member states plus Norway and Iceland, with special arrangements for Britain, Ireland, and Denmark) to cross the borders of implementing countries at any point without border checks.

2. Bruce Hoffman, "Intelligence and Terrorism: Emerging Threats and New Security Challenges in the Post–Cold War Era," *Intelligence and National Security* 11, no. 2 (April 1996): 207.

3. Andrew Jack and Roula Khalaf, "Row over Shooting of French Suspect," *Financial Times,* October 4, 1995.

4. Irène Stoller, *Procureur à la 14e Section* (Paris: Michel Lafon, 2002), 107.

5. Edgar S. Furniss, Jr., *De Gaulle and the French Army* (New York: Twentieth Century Fund, 1964), 151.

6. For Mitterrand's criticisms, see his speech reprinted in *L'Express,* January 10, 1963.

7. In 1954, in what became known as the Affair of the Leaks (*Affaire des fuites*), the DST accused then interior minister Mitterrand of leaking information that had brought about the fall of the French garrison at Dien Bien Phu.

8. Alain Marsaud, *Avant de Tout Oublier* (Paris: Denoël Impacts, 2002), 14–16; and Jean Guisnel and Bernard Violet, *Services Secrets: Le Pouvoir et les services des renseignements sous la présidence de François Mitterrand* (Paris: Éditions La Découverte, 1988), 41.

9. Michael Y. Dartnell, *Action Directe: Ultra-Left Terrorism in France, 1979–1987* (London: Frank Cass, 1995).

10. See Daniel Burdan, *DST: Neuf ans à la division antiterroriste* (Paris: Éditions Robert Laffont, 1990), 87.

11. At the time, these included, among others, the Police Judiciaire (PJ), the Direction Centrale des Renseignements Généraux (DCRG), the Direction de la Surveillance Territoire (DST), the Police de l'Air et des Frontières (PAF), the Gendarmerie Nationale, the Direction Général de la Service Extérieure (DGSE), the Brigade Criminelle, and the Direction de la Protection et de la Sécurité de la Défense (DPSD). For a more complete list, see Guisnel and Violet, *Services Secrets*.

12. Burdan, *DST*, 10.

13. Pierre Marion, *La Mission impossible: À la tête des Services Secrets* (Paris: Calmann-Lévy, 1991), 54.

14. Douglas Porch, *The French Secret Services: From the Dreyfus Affair to the Gulf War* (New York: Farrar, Straus and Giroux, 1995), 464.

15. See, for example, Luc Chauvin, "French Diplomacy and the Hostage Crises," in *The Politics of Counterterrorism: The Ordeal of Democratic States,* ed. Barry Rubin (Philadelphia: Foreign Policy Institute, 1990), 92–102.

16. Nathalie Cettina, *L'Antiterrorisme en question: De l'attentat de la rue Marbeuf aux affaires corses* (Paris: Éditions Michalon, 2001), 40–47.

17. This became known as the Irlandais de Vincennes Affair. For details, see the memoir of the Élysée Cell member responsible for the affair: Paul Barril, *Missions très spéciales* (Paris: Presses de la Cité, 1984).

18. Loi no. 86-1020 du 9 septembre 1986 relative à la lutte contre le terrorisme et aux atteintes à la sûreté de l'État. Available at www.legifrance .gouv.fr

19. A wide range of current and former French officials interviewed by the author expressed this opinion.

20. Loi no. 86-1020 du 9 septembre 1986, art. 1.

21. Author interview with French official, October 2002.

22. UCLAT was created in October 1984. SCLAT was later renamed the Fourteenth Section of the Parquet de Paris.

23. Author interview with French official, October 2002.

24. Alain Marsaud, "Pour un 'Conseil de Sécurité,'" *Le Monde,* December 21, 1985; and interview with M. Alain Marsaud, October 2002.

25. See, for example, Cettina, *Antiterrorisme en question,* 57.

26. For a recent example of how this controversy has persisted as an issue in French politics, see "M. Pasqua veut maintenir sa candidature à l'Élysée malgré les affaires; La Controverse sur les otages du Liban se poursuit," *Le Monde,* January 10, 2002.

27. Michel Wieviorka, "France Faced with Terrorism," *Terrorism* 14 (July–September 1991): 165.

28. Philip C. Naylor, *France and Algeria: A History of Decolonization and Transformation* (Gainesville: University Press of Florida, 2000), 189–215.

29. Gerard Chaliand, *L'Arme du terrorisme* (Paris: Louis Audibert, 2002).

30. Mohammed M. Hafez, "Armed Islamist Movements and Political Violence in Algeria," *Middle East Journal* 54, no. 4 (Autumn 2000): 247–67.

31. Ali Laïdi, with Ahmed Salam, *Le Jihad en Europe, les filières du terrorisme en Europe* (Paris: Seuil, coll. L'Épreuve des faits, 2002), 193.

32. Author interviews with French officials, October 2002 and May 2005.

33. Herve Gattegno, "Une Seule et Même Équipe a organisé la campagne d'attentats de 1995," *Le Monde,* July 26, 1996. In November 2003, Bensaid was found guilty of the July 1995 Saint-Michel attack and sentenced to life in prison.

34. Author interview with French official, October 2002.

35. On the difficulties of the DST in obtaining a wiretap through nonjudicial channels, see the interview with the head of the DST in Jean-Marc Leclerc and Jean de Belot, "Le Projet d'installer RG et DST ensemble est sérieux," *Le Figaro,* June 20, 2003.

36. Author interview with Alain Marsaud, October 2002.

37. Conversely, the magistrates have come under frequent criticism, including from the intelligence services, for making excessive use of the press and personalizing counterterrorist operations. See, for example, Cettina, *Antiterrorisme en question,* 120–31.

38. In fact, there are several emergency plans for various types of contingencies—natural disasters, biological and chemical attacks, and so on. Vigipirate, however, because its specific purpose is to communicate with the public, is the best-known mobilization plan, although perhaps not the most important.

39. Agence France Presse, Les terroristes accentuent leur pression sur la France, September 4, 1995.

40. Cited in Naylor, *France and Algeria,* 226.

41. Hoffman, "Intelligence and Terrorism," 208.

42. See, for example, Jean Pierre Tuqoui, "Des fuites impliquent Alger dans les attentats de Paris," *Le Monde,* November 11, 1997.

43. Author interview with Irène Stoller, October 2002.

44. Cettina, *Antiterrorisme en question,* 142.

45. Peter Chalk and William Rosenau, *Confronting the "Enemy Within": Security, Intelligence, and Counterterrorism in Four Democracies* (Santa Monica, CA: RAND, 2004), 18–19.

46. Author interviews with French officials, December 2002, May 2004.

47. Article 421-2-1 of the French Penal Code, adopted July 22, 1996, www.legifrance.gouv.fr/html/codes_traduits/code_penal_textan.htm.

48. Hoffman, "Intelligence and Terrorism," 218.

49. On Franco-Spanish cooperation on ETA, see Jérôme Ferret, "La Construction par le bas de la lutte anti-terroriste," in *Le Silence des armes? L'Europe a l'épreuve des separatismes violents,* ed. Xavier Crettiez and Jérôme Ferret (Paris: Documentation Française, 1999), 115–40. On cooperation to combat the Islamists, see "Le GSPC: Une Filiale d'al Qaida," *Le Nouvel Observateur,* November 29, 2001.

50. See Heather Grabbe, *The Impact of September 11 on Justice and Home Affairs in the European Union* (Warsaw: Institute of Public Affairs, 2003).

51. European Commission, *Action Paper in Response to the Terrorist Attacks on Madrid* (Brussels: European Commission, 2004).

52. See Kristin Archick, *Europe and Counterterrorism: Strengthening Police and Judicial Cooperation* (Washington, D.C.: Congressional Research Service, 2002), 1–2.

53. See, for example, Erich Inciyan, "Après les coups de filet policiers dans les milieux kurdes et islamistes en France: Le Message des operations 'Chrysanthème' et 'Rouge-Rose Monde,'" *Le Monde,* December 2, 1993.

54. Fédération Internationale des Ligues des Droits de l'Homme, "France: La Porte ouverte à l'arbitraire," no. 271 (rapport d'une mission internationale d'enquête en France sur l'application de la législation anti-terroriste, January 1999), www.fidh.imaginet.fr.

55. Ibid.

56. Ibid.

57. For an exception that sees French counterterrorism laws as reinforcing social cleavages in French society, see Didier Bigo, "Reassuring and Protecting: Internal Security Implications of French Participation in the Coalition against Terrorism," in *Critical Views of September 11,* ed. Eric Hershberg and Kevin W. Moore (New York: New Press, 2002), 72–94.

58. Numerous French officials made this point in interviews.

59. See, for example, Hafez, "Armed Islamic Movements," 572–91.

60. On this general point about the tradition of domestic monitoring in France, see Porch, *French Secret Services.* On the establishment of the French secret services, see page 20.

61. France has two quasi-independent commissions, the CNIL (Commission Nationale de l'Informatique et des Libertés) and the CNCIS (Commission Nationale de Contrôle des Interceptions de Sécurité), that monitor various government surveillance activities and respond to citizen complaints. There is essentially no parliamentary oversight of these activities, however.

62. Author interview with LDH official, December 2002.

63. Laïdi, *Le Jihad en Europe,* 217.

64. Quoted in Hal Bernton and others, "The Terrorist Within," *Seattle Times,* June 25, 2002. This article is one in an eighteen-part series published in the *Times,* June 22 to July 8.

65. On Ressam, see Judge Jean-Louis Bruguière, "Terrorism: Threat and Responses," October 2001, www.gcsp.ch/e/research/OccasPapers/Bruguière PDF.pdf; and Bernton and others, "Terrorist Within" series.

66. For one review, see Dirk Haubrich, "September 11, Anti-terror Laws and Civil Liberties: Britain, France, and Germany Compared." *Government and Opposition* 38, no. 1 (2003): 3–28. See also Shaun Gregory, "France and the War on Terrorism," *Terrorism and Political Violence* 15, no. 1 (Spring 2003): 140–41.

6

VENEZUELA

The FALN-FLN

Peter Calvert

The Venezuelan case is the earliest of the case studies analyzed here. So much seems to have changed in the past forty years that an obvious question to ask is, "Is the case still important?" There are several reasons why it is. First, Venezuelan democracy was only a few months old when it had to confront the challenge of terrorism; the fact that its response was successful, therefore, should tell us something about the way in which fragile democracies can respond to such threats. Second, the way in which the Venezuelan government did so presents an interesting contrast to other cases, particularly those of Colombia and Peru today. In Venezuela, military repression was limited and strong, and effective political organization played a major role in keeping both military and civil dissidents in check. Third, unusually, the government had to cope with challenges simultaneously from left and right, and both challenges were found within the armed forces, elements of which had originally led the move to democracy. This situation made the government's task of mounting an effective anti-insurgency and antiterrorist campaign exceptionally difficult.

In this chapter, therefore, we shall look first at the course of the insurgency: how it developed and how it ended. Why did the insurgents take to terrorism, and what form did it take? We shall then look at the various methods used to counter both the insurgent and the terrorist threat before going on to assess what worked and what did not work, and why.

INSURGENCY AND TERRORISM

In the late 1950s, Venezuela, which had been under dictatorship since independence, was regarded by many on the left as one of the most favorable areas in Latin America for successful armed struggle. In January 1958, a year before the Cuban Revolution, a popular revolt toppled the ten-year dictatorship of Marcos Pérez Jiménez, who was cordially hated on account of his cruelty and corruption. Before the December 1958 elections, the leaders of the three main democratic political parties signed an agreement, the Pact of Punto Fijo, to form a government of national unity to defend the restored democracy. The elections then gave a substantial mandate to Rómulo Betancourt, who had served as elected president from 1945 to 1948, and to his Democratic Action Party (Acción Democrática, or AD), with a plurality of more than 49 percent over the Unión Republicana Democratica (URD).[1]

The new government, however, was almost immediately confronted by the challenge of an insurgent movement and soon thereafter by a terrorist campaign. The insurgency developed in two stages. The first was led by a group calling itself the Movement of the Revolutionary Left (Movimiento de Izquierda Revolucionaria, or MIR), which emerged in May 1960 as the product of a split of the bulk of its youth movement from the ruling Democratic Action Party. This was a severe blow to AD, which lost in one fell swoop 80 percent of its youth movement and fourteen of seventy-three deputies. Although the MIR's initial intention was to be a constitutional party, the arrest of six members on charges of subversion on October 20, 1960, was followed by four days of street demonstrations. The army and marines were deployed to restore order, and one person was killed in clashes. All colleges and universities were then closed.[2]

The MIR speedily came under Cuban influence and was urged by Havana to prepare for guerrilla warfare. Meanwhile, during a series of strikes in Caracas from October through December 1960, the MIR repeatedly called for the resignation of the government. The MIR leader, Domingo Alberto Rangel, later stated that in retrospect this move came too late, after the new government had already succeeded in establishing a broad base of support. It was this situation more than anything else that helped consolidate opinion in the armed forces in favor of the government. At a mass rally at El Silencio on December 1, 1960, Betancourt defended his decision to deploy the army and marines in the capital and other cities to defend the lives and property of citizens.

In 1961, under Cuban influence, the MIR established a number of rural guerrilla groups. Before they could begin operations, however, in January 1962, the army detected one of them. As a result of this failure of security, the first of a number of small-scale ambushes of government forces began only in March. But MIR operations were dispersed over such a wide area that the government soon destroyed many of the twenty groups that had been set up. Organization was poor, secrecy inadequate, and communications unreliable. The movement suffered heavy losses at the hands of the armed forces. At this point, therefore, the main threat to the government from the left came not from the MIR but from two important military and naval revolts.

On May 4, 1962, naval captain Jesus Teodoro Molina and 450 marines seized control of the naval base of Carúpano, 250 miles east of Caracas. Referring to 1958, the group claimed in its manifesto, "Our people have been cheated of the democracy won in that memorable battle," and accused Betancourt of a "reign of terror."[3] Although openly supported by the Venezuelan Communist Party (PCV), the insurgents were forced to surrender in less than twenty-four hours.[4] Following the revolt, on May 10, the government imposed a ban on both the PCV and the MIR.

A second and larger revolt took place at Puerto Cabello just a month later, on June 3, 1962. Insurgents seized control of the country's principal naval base, some seventy miles west of Caracas, in a revolt led by the naval base's deputy commander, Pedro Medina Silva, and Captain Manuel Ponte Rodriguez. After two days of intense fighting, in which government casualties reached 200 and rebel casualties much more, most of the insurgents surrendered, although a few successfully escaped and took to the hills.

Meanwhile, from March 1962 onward, Caracas and other key cities saw constant urban terrorist violence involving, among other things, the planting of car bombs and the targeted assassination of police.[5] At the same time, there were various terrorist actions with an anti-American theme, clearly intended to attract publicity for the movement and nationalist support. These actions included the sabotage on October 27, 1962, of four power stations owned by the Creole Petroleum Corporation; attacks on U.S.-owned pipelines in November 1962; a publicity theft of a loan collection of French paintings from the Museum of Fine Arts in January 1963; and the torching of a Sears, Roebuck warehouse in Caracas in February 1963, as well as many lesser incidents. The actions were intended to suggest, as to some they in fact did, a complete breakdown of law and order and the powerlessness of government to act effectively to prevent them—a common objective of urban terrorist strategy.[6]

The terrorist campaign was still in progress on February 24, 1963, when survivors of the MIR and the Puerto Cabello revolt met in Caracas to form the Armed National Liberation Forces (Fuerzas Armadas de Liberación Nacional, or FALN). On communist insistence, a parallel political organization, the National Liberation Front (Frente de Liberación Nacional, or FLN) was formed at the same time.[7] The FALN-FLN then directed a two-pronged attack on the government, combining urban terrorism in the capital, Caracas, and other major cities with the formation of new guerrilla groups in the countryside.

On June 12, 1963, the FALN-FLN made an unsuccessful attempt to assassinate Betancourt while he visited Ciudad Bolívar. Despite sharp government reaction, further publicity actions took place later in the year, starting with the August 1963 kidnapping of the celebrated Argentine footballer Alfredo Di Stefano, who, as it turned out, was released unharmed.[8]

At the time, the FALN-FLN placed great importance on the formation of new guerrilla groups in the countryside. "What had given the guerrillas faith in the future of guerrilla warfare was the fact that, during 1963, when the urban movement had been very severely repressed, they had been able to survive in the countryside without their lifeline to the cities,"[9] wrote Régis Debray. It should be noted, however, that neither the MIR nor the PCV shared the optimism of the French-born, pro-Cuban, left-wing theoretician.

After the presidential election, in early 1964, the PCV halted the armed struggle and concentrated on trying to obtain release of prisoners. FALN-FLN, led by Douglas Bravo, continued to argue that the countryside was the most important arena for armed struggle, despite the fact that the rural population was only some 28 percent of the whole and many groups were operating so far from any center of importance that they would have been of very little use. Raúl Leoni, who succeeded Betancourt as president in March 1964, offered to lift the ban on the legal operation of the PCV on the condition that the armed struggle be abandoned. In 1965, the PCV accepted this offer, bringing the urban phase of the struggle to an end. By the end of 1965, there was an open split in the FALN-FLN. By the end of 1967, the FALN was no longer a serious force, and the FLN no longer had a figure at its head capable of rallying the shattered remains of the guerrilla movement. Most of the remaining guerrillas accepted the amnesty offered by the incoming Christian Democrat (COPEI) government of Rafael Caldera in 1969. Between 1962 and 1969, some six thousand people on both sides had been killed as a result of the combination of civil unrest, urban terrorism, and rural insurgency.[10]

OUTLINE OF THE GOVERNMENT RESPONSE

As the insurgency developed in stages, it is not possible to say that there was a clear counterinsurgency plan in place from the beginning. What is clear, though, is that there was a very speedy response to each new challenge. Betancourt claimed that this response was based on his early political experience with both the nature of the threat and its appeal, but this claim has to be treated with caution.

The first step in responding to a threat of insurgency lies in identifying the nature of the threat. Where there are a number of threats, as in this case, the secret of a successful response lies in determining which threats are the most serious (the importance of the threat) and which are the most urgent (the salience of the threat). Some elements of the government's strategy, and the points at which they were important, can therefore be identified.

First, the survival of the government was the top priority, and given the way in which the previous AD government had been deposed by a military coup in 1948, the survival of the government was synonymous with the maintenance of democratic order. Keeping military support intact as far as possible, cultivating allies among the armed forces, anticipating military/ naval revolts against the government, and suppressing them with the support of loyal troops were all vital in enabling the government to overcome the series of critical challenges it faced. Many democratic governments have succumbed to their own armed forces long before there was any serious threat to them from insurgency.

Second, although emergency powers were used, they were used with restraint, although with their recent experience of an exceptionally harsh dictatorship, Venezuelans might well have accepted much greater infringements on their civil liberties. The government made only limited use of administrative detention, and (with one exception) the press remained free. More controversially, even Betancourt negotiated with the insurgents, despite the fact that they used terrorist methods. The timely use of amnesty by his successor, Raúl Leoni, was also an important factor in bringing about the collapse of the insurgency

Third, using the police to control the initial outbreak of rioting was only partially successful, since riots and demonstrations continued for several weeks. But the police were sufficiently successful for the FALN to launch a "kill-a-cop-a-day" campaign as a key part of its urban terrorist strategy. Strengthening and supporting the police in this later stage were therefore essential to success. However, it was the role of the police at the counter-terrorism stage that was most criticized. The police were accused of systematic violations of human rights and even torture of political prisoners, and Caldera replaced them with a new national police force.

Fourth, maintaining political control in the countryside through AD control of peasant organizations, and using the armed forces to detect and destroy rural guerrilla groups, successfully isolated those groups and rendered them ineffective. There is still debate as to the importance of the labor movement in the 1958 uprising, but even left-wing writers note that "the general strike was called surprisingly late in the struggle against Pérez Jiménez and only after other sectors such as the Church, university students, the U.S. embassy, and a significant part of the military had clearly distanced themselves from the regime."[11] Labor then consolidated behind the interim democratic government, headed by Admiral Wolfgang Larrazábal, who remained well to the left of Betancourt and AD. Civil disturbances, particularly by the numerous unemployed, were not organized but became increasingly belligerent in Betancourt's first year.[12] As a result, cooperation within the labor movement had broken up by the end of 1960. A struggle between AD-COPEI and the PCV, supported by URD, went on for a year and ended with AD alone controlling almost all labor unions and all peasant unions.[13]

Finally, making extreme-left opposition illegitimate through a sustained anticommunist campaign was important in retaining civilian support for the government, both in the towns and in the countryside. Left critics argue that Betancourt's anticommunism predated the insurgency and, in the eyes of those who supported the insurgency, helped bring it about. Yet they also agree that the campaign later acted to consolidate opinion behind the government. It was important, too, that the campaign was an indigenous, nationalistic response to violence and terrorism, not something that seemed to be imposed from outside, yet was supported by the United States as part of its concurrent counterinsurgency campaign in the region.

MEANS AND ENDS

Constitutional Limits

The most controversial aspect of the government's policy, inevitably, was the extent to which the government was able to maintain a functioning democracy and stay within constitutional limits. In a letter to President John F. Kennedy in the spring of 1962, Betancourt claimed, "The impatient ones would like us to go beyond the written law—and even beyond the unwritten but overriding law of respect for human dignity. I will not, however, deviate from the course laid down for me by the fundamental law of Venezuela and by my own conscience."[14]

The suspension of constitutional guarantees of civil rights, the standard state of emergency, was first used in August 1959, and Betancourt was criticized for betraying his principles.[15] The main purpose of the measure was to facilitate the arrest and administrative detention of political opponents. Here, opinions are divided, with supporters regarding the use of detention as reasonable and limited, and opponents representing it as unreasonable and brutal. "There are certain extraordinary things," a leading historian wrote about what was then the current government, "as for example the fact that the very day after the new Constitution had been approved all constitutional guarantees were suspended, and the country was ruled for two years with no such guarantees in force. Even when they were re-instituted, the country was governed as if no Constitution existed."[16]

As so often is the case, it is difficult to tell whether excessive uses of force (of which there were certainly some) were officially condoned or were the result of excessive zeal by subordinate officials, all of whom had lived most of their lives under a dictatorship. AD vigilantes have also been blamed for using force. "The Betancourt administration and the government party dealt harshly with their leftist opponents," Steve Ellner tells us. "Security forces frequently opened fire on street demonstrators and rounded them up to send to special work colonies in remote parts of the Guayana region.

Leftist trade unionists who vied with AD and Christian Democrat (COPEI) leaders for control of individual unions received a similarly unmerciful treatment. Armed bands attacked assemblies of leftist workers and, in some cases, took over union halls by force."[17]

In the FALN-FLN phase, constitutional guarantees were again suspended and known communist sympathizers (including deputies) were arrested. This action had the hoped-for effect of forcing the PCV to abandon the FALN-FLN.

What is certain is that the formal procedures of electoral choice were not suspended and were maintained throughout the insurgency, and that the December 1963 election was successfully held despite the terrorist threat. "In spite of the threats of the far Left against the voters, over 90 percent of those who were eligible to vote did so,"[18] writes Robert Alexander. As Che Guevara himself stipulated, as long as there is the possibility of gaining power by democratic means, there is no real chance that an insurgent movement will succeed.[19] Most of the remaining guerrillas accepted the amnesty offered by the incoming COPEI government in 1969, and they would clearly not have done so had they not expected to be treated fairly and with leniency. However, Fabricio Ojeda, one of those who had made the 1958 revolution possible and had helped found the MIR, was captured in June 1966 by military intelligence; he died in custody four days later. Richard Gott says "there is little doubt" that he was murdered.[20] But was he? The fact that the FALN retaliated with an unsuccessful attack on the head of the national directorate, Gabriel José Paez, does not seem conclusive.

Anticommunism

Those who had been inspired by Betancourt's earlier radicalism were particularly unhappy at the strongly anticommunist line he took. Before his inauguration, Betancourt had regularly been able to count on support from the radical left. Carleton Beals notes: "But suddenly he called upon the Army to suppress students, workers, and other demonstrators, particularly those favoring Cuba. . . . Having started to crush popular parties, which were soon outlawed, his only sure support became the Army, the landholders, and the Church—though none was wholehearted. They tolerated him because he was anti-Communist and anti-Castro."[21] Judith Ewell believes that this situation was the result of a deliberate strategy. "In effect," she writes, "Betancourt laid a trap for the left. By excluding them from his carefully constructed political and institutional channels, he left them no choice but to remain impotent or to seize the bait of the Cuban model of revolution."[22]

However, there is also evidence that Betancourt was, in fact, quite late in realizing the threat that organized left-wing opposition might pose. Even the CIA did not regard Fidel Castro's movement as a possible threat until "the final days of 1958."[23] Of course, between 1948 and 1958 the fear of Soviet intentions had fueled anticommunism in Latin America, as in the United States, but there was particular resentment among AD supporters in Venezuela over how the Eisenhower government had hijacked the OAS meeting in Caracas in 1954 to issue a strong anticommunist manifesto (the Declaration of Caracas) and ignored the plight of Venezuela itself. The communists had subsequently helped in the overthrow of Pérez Jiménez and were included in the provisional government that was still in power when violent and sustained rioting greeted then U.S. vice president Richard Nixon as soon as he arrived in Caracas on May 13, 1958, catching the junta completely unawares. Nixon claims that when he met Betancourt on that occasion, it was he, Nixon, who told him that the riots were communist inspired and that communists would try to deny Venezuela its freedom.[24]

At that stage, Betancourt clearly still saw the main threat to democracy as coming from the right and was still hoping to organize a "Caribbean legion" to rid the area of dictatorship. In 1959 he sponsored an unsuccessful expedition to overthrow his old enemy, Rafael Trujillo of the Dominican Republic. In July 1960, Trujillo reciprocated by trying to kill Betancourt. "The attempt took place on a Caracas street when an automobile full of explosives was detonated as the President's car was passing. Only a closed rear window saved Betancourt's life; the riders in the front seats, with open windows, were killed,"[25] wrote Dwight Eisenhower.

Betancourt was more consistent than his left-wing opponents thought. Nixon, on the other hand, was the same Nixon who in 1955 had warmly embraced both Trujillo and Fulgencio Batista, the former dictator of Cuba.[26] Before 1945 Betancourt was already a forerunner of later Latin American populists, with his stress on both nationalism and a cross-class appeal to the people at large.[27] In addition, Betancourt is on record as realizing the weakness of the industrial proletariat, which at that stage his political opponents did not.[28] Between 1945 and 1948, AD had delivered on its promises to the less well-off, only to alienate significant minorities and be overthrown in a military coup. Betancourt himself was among those who concluded that the party's mass support had made its leaders overconfident and that it was essential to keep significant minorities on board through compromise and consensus. This attitude implied the exclusion of the radical left, but as it turned out, the radical left excluded itself. "Whatever stance one takes on these questions," writes Daniel Levine, "it is clear that the guerrilla insurrection was decisive in consolidating the coalition being built by AD. Pointing to the revolutionary Left (and beyond, to the example of the Cuban Revolution), AD's leaders were able to present themselves as the best, indeed the only, hope for stability."[29]

Use of the Police

Both the secret police (SN) and the regular police had been dismantled in 1958; crowds had stormed the SN headquarters and killed many of its members. Nixon records that only one police officer aided Secret Service officers in protecting his car and that afterward a senior politician told him that "after ten years of ruthless dictatorship they all abhorred the idea of developing another strong police force."[30]

However, after the farewell banquet held for the vice president at the Circulo Militar, the road to the airport was cleared and the streets flooded with troops to ensure his safety. The lesson was learned. Two weeks before the visit of President John F. Kennedy to Caracas in December 1961, Betancourt's government "began a systematic round-up of known Communists and Left-wing agitators, shut down all Communist offices and several student organizations, and suspended publication of one newspaper, *Clarion*. The airport was closed for twelve hours before the President's arrival and some 35,000 troops were deployed along the parade route,"[31] notes Nixon.

The Betancourt government rebuilt the police force and formed a new national directorate, the Dirección General de Policia (Digepol), to run it. It was not long, however, before it, too, was accused of irregular arrests and mistreatment of political prisoners (although certainly not to the extent that its predecessor under the dictatorship was denounced). "Betancourt overrode all objections and insisted that a democratic President should have all means at his disposal to counter undemocratic enemies. All things considered, Betancourt and his police force should probably not be charged with inordinate abuse of power; however, it is at least arguable that his willingness to use force gave the left the pretext to escalate their own violent tactics,"[32] writes Ewell.

It is important to recognize the scale of the terrorist campaign with which the new and largely untried police force had to cope. Beginning in March 1962, the largely harmless "spectaculars" gave way to a systematic campaign of urban terrorist violence: "Bombs exploded in cars, police were shot, civilians walking near the university were gunned down, cars and buses were burned."[33] The level of terrorist violence continued to rise well into the new year. Debray writes:

> In the spring and summer of 1963, during the fiercest phase of the urban struggle, not a day went by without simultaneous armed engagements in different ranchos. At nightfall the shooting began, to die away only with the dawn. The operations included harassing the forces of repression, ambushes, full-scale battles against the army, and even complete occupation of a neighbourhood which became for a few hours a liberated territory until the concentrations of armed groups in a small area became untenable and they evaporated. The aim was to pin down the military in Caracas, to wear them out, to divide them in order to hasten demoralization and desertion—of which there were numerous cases in the police.[34]

But although apparently carefully targeted, the FALN's "kill-a-cop-a-day" strategy was unpopular with the masses because the police were drawn from local neighborhoods. As Talton Ray notes, "Almost all the murdered policemen were barrios [shantytown] residents. In many instances, they were shot to death while walking home from work or sitting in their ranchos at night; families, friends, and neighbors were witnesses. Some of those killed were elderly men who had been working for the force for years before AD came to power and were considered about as politically harmful as traffic cops."[35] Even more, the new National Guard was seen and valued as a sign of social advancement for poor boys from the barrios.[36]

The level of violence was so great that initially police cover had to be withdrawn from the worst areas of Caracas, such as Uraneta. To maintain some measure of control in these lawless zones, troops and the National Guard were brought in to establish command posts covering key points. Areas were cordoned off and searches undertaken without warning to disrupt terrorist networks. These defensive measures in turn helped reinforce efforts to recruit a corps of informants from these areas, so that the government could have prompt and accurate information on possible developments. In this context it is highly significant that the Debray critique of urban terrorism—then called urban guerrilla warfare—is based on the Venezuelan case.[37] The critique is unintentionally revealing about both the weaknesses of the strategy and the effectiveness of the government response.

Debray notes that the terrorists were easily pinned down; they had "neither the choice of time nor of place." They were forced "to operate at night (the ranchos have very weak street lighting) to ensure the safety of the combatants." They still faced the threat of informers and the hostility of local inhabitants because there were always some innocent victims, "since bullets pierce the cardboard or wood walls of the houses." However, they had little choice, since by day the government forces enjoyed considerable advantages.

> Darkness allows the popular forces to make the most of their advantages such as knowledge of the terrain, mobility, and the enemy's difficulty in using heavy weapons. On the other hand, daylight allows houses to be searched, and cordons to be thrown around whole areas and massive reprisals to be staged. As far as choice of terrain is concerned, it is almost impossible for armed groups to move in the city, where the large avenues are closely controlled, in order to take a garrison or military detachment by surprise. Such an operation entails too many risks, because the lines of retreat are too easily cut off.[38]

Use of the Armed Forces

There is a great deal of controversy about the proper way to use the armed forces in counterterrorist operations. As Debray himself noted, terrorists are almost certain to kill significant numbers of noncombatants. Given the much greater capacity they have to deploy force, this is even truer of the armed forces. Besides, the training of the armed forces encourages them to use as much force as possible to secure the desired end, which can be counterproductive in antiterrorist operations.

Two important aspects of the armed forces in Venezuela were unusual by Latin American norms. In most Latin American countries, the army is the only significant force in politics; the other services are clearly subordinate to it. However, even at this period, the army in Venezuela was checked by the existence of interservice rivalry between the army, the navy, and more particularly the air force. The air force and loyal troops were used to crush the various military revolts; those who survived were imprisoned. As in other

Latin American states (e.g., Brazil, Chile), the navy seems to have been more liberal than the army.

The other distinctive feature is more difficult to evaluate. In most Latin American countries, the collective strength of the officer corps is greater than political loyalties since the officers, who are generally sons of the upper middle classes or military families, come from all over the country. In Venezuela, however, ever since the rise of Juan Vicente Gomez in 1908, the army had been dominated by officers from the state of Táchira, which had also provided three successive presidents. This dominance had in turn helped generate resistance to the dictatorship among junior army officers and NCOs who were not members of this closed elite. As Gott notes, the phenomenon of "progressive" groups within the armed forces is not peculiar to Venezuela; it might therefore have been worthwhile for the insurgents to try to convert the army rather than destroy it, he observes.[39]

What is clear is that as early as 1958, the officer corps was strongly imbued with a spirit of nationalism, which made some of its members receptive to anti-Americanism, and that military populism *(peruanismo),* later seen as characteristic of Peru in the late 1960s and early 1970s, was also quite widespread. In 1962 progovernment forces incurred substantial casualties putting down the two major military and naval revolts openly supported by the MIR and the PCV, which suggests a very high degree of political polarization. Significantly, Debray says the Puerto Cabello uprising was supposed to be only part of a simultaneous nationalist uprising against a government that was seen as being too subordinate to foreign influences.[40] Robert Alexander notes that at the time of the uprising, the government received strong support from both business and the public.[41] However, congress was lukewarm in its comments and criticized what it termed the "violent repression and party jobbery" of the government.[42]

Debray goes on to explain the way in which the government was able to act to neutralize the danger posed by the armed forces: "The plan was uncovered by the government security services, and the dangerous officers and regiments were either transferred or imprisoned just before the projected date."[43] This was the standard procedure by which any reasonably competent Latin American government, then or now, would try to prevent the formation of hostile groups within the services. Elsewhere, Debray says a major weakness of the insurgency was that the military's sense of honor prevented its leaders from recognizing that their cause was lost and conserving their strength for a later and better opportunity.[44] This attitude, too, is consistent with the self-image of the officer as a member of an elite with a special responsibility to guide the destinies of the nation.

Despite this history of dissension within the officer corps, the government seems to have had little difficulty using troops for routine searches in the countryside in the later phases of the insurgency. This relatively low-key activity detected many guerrilla groups; it is very hard to hide in the countryside, where low population density and extensive social links mean that strangers are easily spotted.

The Countryside

Debray noted that the guerrilla forces were made up almost entirely of students, most of them recruited at the Universidad Central. Ann Brownell, an American exchange student who was there at the time, confirms this: "Young men often of peasant origin, arriving at the university, often very naive politically, were organized by the MIR and PCV, and were given virtually military training, in which most of all they learned to take orders without questioning. Then, when they were needed for some attack on police or some other group, they went out to perform such assaults without asking why."[45] This practice is, of course, standard among terrorist movements, to get new recruits to incriminate themselves as soon as possible, the easier to control them.[46] Indeed, their own accounts confirm that these early guerrillas were young, idealistic, and ill prepared. This was one of the first examples in Latin America of the phenomenon of "weekend guerrillas": students who spent weekends in the hills,[47] later a feature of the early stages of Sendero Luminoso in Peru.

A better knowledge of the situation in the countryside would have urged caution among the founders of the guerrilla movement. Venezuela, unlike other states, for example Mexico, had a relatively small population and abundant land. In the Great Depression of the 1930s, bankruptcies had created an extensive public domain, which therefore was available to Betancourt to use to realize his favored option, a land colonization program. "In Venezuela this method of land distribution did indeed become a significant alternative to expropriation of existing estates in a country which was already under pressure to carry out reform,"[48] Shlomo Eckstein and colleagues write. Betancourt was careful to avoid making enemies of big landowners, who could be politically useful; only "unproductive and feudal lands" were to be targeted by the Instituto Agrario Nacional (IAN), and any hint of possible violent seizure of big estates was condemned. He was therefore able to defuse much potential rural unrest while retaining the support of influential backers.

For the ordinary workers in the fields, political considerations were crucial; the guerrillas were unable to promise them much since the peasant movement FCV, which was also calling for land for the landless, was linked to the AD labor central, the CTV. (This situation was also very different from that of revolutionary Mexico, where Lázaro Cárdenas had been careful to keep labor and campesino organizations separate.) In fact, "hardly any land was awarded to farmers who had not been organized by FCV."[49] In effect, therefore, through the FCV, AD acted as an agency for winning "hearts and minds" in the countryside as well as the towns in the crucial early stages of the counterterrorist campaign. However, once the threat was over, Ellner confirms, "when the land takeovers subsided, land distribution and agricultural assistance were sharply curtailed, much to the disapproval of AD peasant leaders."[50] In the long run, the failure to carry through on land reform, purely because it was no longer seen as politically necessary, was to store up trouble for the future. "There are 400,000 peasants still landless, and 4 percent of the landowners own 80 percent of the land," Carleton Beals reported in 1963. "The bulk of government rural credit goes to the big landowners," he added. "Actually, all effort to keep up with the land program was abandoned later in 1961—about the time of [U.S. president John F.] Kennedy's visit [early 1962]."[51]

Political rivalry also helps explain the later successful use of the armed forces in the countryside; as elsewhere, soldiers were ultimately concerned for their own survival. Latin American officers of this period were well aware that when Castro came to power in Cuba, many of Batista's officers were shot after a summary trial by a "people's court." Teodoro Petkoff notes:

> The armed forces strongly pursued the guerrillas. Many officers were convinced that the far-Left strategy was not so much immediately to overthrow Betancourt as to create a situation which would bring the military to oust the elected president, which would create an atmosphere much more propitious to the guerrilla campaign, since it would force into it many supporters of the Betancourt regime. Knowing that that was the objective of the far Left, the military officers were the more determined to support the regime

and suppress the guerrilla effort. They had widespread support from the peasantry.[52]

The guerrillas were able neither to appeal successfully to rural workers nor to terrorize them into supporting their cause. As Mike Gonzalez perceptively points out, it was precisely the marginality of the guerrilla movement that attracted so many young Latin American revolutionaries and was to lead to disaster.[53] Successful pressure on the guerrillas brought early disillusion. Teodoro Petkoff later said that it was his experience as a guerrilla that convinced him of the merits of democracy.[54]

How Did Government Strategy Change?

"The election results, which showed the negative results of the abstention campaign, were a major political defeat for the guerrillas. 'Very objectively,' explained the guerrilla leader Douglas Bravo later, 'it must be admitted that the triumph of Acción Democrática, supported by the oligarchy and imperialism, was the first great defeat of the popular movement.'"[55] The government, wrote Moses Moleiro of the MIR, had won "a skirmish in the long battle for national liberation." The elections were a defeat for the popular movement, commented the Communist Party's Central Committee, "and our party and the FLN shared in this defeat."[56]

As noted above, the new administration offered an amnesty, and the PCV accepted in 1964, following its failed attempts to disrupt the elections, although it took three years to make the amnesty effective. On July 24, 1966, a new group of trained guerrillas, led by Luben Petkoff, landed on the coast of Falcón from the Venezuelan Caribbean island of Margarita, but they were too far from centers of power to pose a threat. The same problem was later to arise with Che Guevara's expedition to Bolivia.

"In 1964, there had been sixteen guerrilla groups active in the country. By 1968, there were only three. Leoni continued Betancourt's strengthening of the army and had accepted more U.S. training and military assistance. He also offered to commute the sentences of a number of political prisoners as a conciliatory measure. Frustrated by the seeming impossibility of a violent overthrow of the government and encouraged by Leoni's flexibility, the PCV in 1967 decided to give up the guerrilla effort and return to peaceful political combat,"[57] explains Ewell.

THE INTERNATIONAL DIMENSION

As in many later cases, the changing international context was extremely significant. It stimulated the emergent insurgency and influenced its choice of tactics, including the decision to employ terrorism. It also influenced the reaction to these events by the government.

The MIR was originally moderate and favored the constitutional path of the parent AD; its evolution toward the left was "undoubtedly" stimulated by the Castro regime in Cuba. The question of just what help was given remains controversial. Cuba's example seems to have been far more important than any financial or military assistance other than the training of cadres. "Young MIRicos were sent to Cuba, and there they were urged, particularly by Raul Castro and Ernesto Guevara, to prepare for a guerrilla war in Venezuela. Although some argued against the idea on a variety of grounds, the Cuban leaders were insistent on its necessity,"[58] recalled Antonio Hernandez. But MIR leader Domingo Alberto Rangel later recognized that the time had in fact passed:

> He argued that in 1958 there was a real possibility of a far-Left revolution in Venezuela, since the armed forces were very demoralised, the police virtually nonexistent, and the masses were anxious for a radical change. However, by the time MIR decided to launch an urban and rural campaign to overthrow the government, the appropriate circumstances no longer existed. . . . Betancourt had been able to rebuild the structure of the state, reestablish the confidence of the military in themselves and in the government, reestablish an effective police force, and mobilise behind the constitutional regime not only wide popular support but also the backing of the most powerful economic and social elements of the country.[59]

There is no doubt that Betancourt's anticommunism long predated the Cuban Revolution. When questioned on it, he was accustomed to saying that his strong views stemmed from having once been a communist himself and therefore knowing how bad communism was from the inside. At the very first AD rally after the fall of Pérez Jiménez, on July 4, 1958, Betancourt delivered "a long and eloquent history of the party's antagonism to international Communism."[60] It was not surprising, therefore, that when he was president-elect, his name was booed when Castro mentioned it in his speech in the Plaza del Silencio during a state visit to Venezuela early in 1959.[61] Until then, Betancourt had not realized how unpopular he was in his own capital.[62] Once president, Betancourt did not include a communist in his cabinet, contrary to the spirit, if not the letter, of the Pact of Punto Fijo, and he used his inaugural address on February 13, 1959, to condemn communism.

Gott correctly says that "in the beginning the Communist party would have been happy to support him. It was Betancourt himself who declared war on the Left." However, the evidence is against Gott's claim that "although Betancourt began his rule with the formal support of every political group except the Communists, by the end he had antagonized virtually every political movement in the country and had irreparably split the party which he had done so much to build up."[63] On the contrary, not only had AD retained its dominant electoral position, but it had also retained its pact with COPEI. Even the URD, which had split from the coalition in 1960, was to rejoin under Leoni, and AD and COPEI were to dominate Venezuelan politics for the next thirty years.

Betancourt undoubtedly gained popularity in 1960 when agents of Rafael Leónidas Trujillo, the much-hated dictator of the Dominican Republic, made an unsuccessful attempt to kill him. His personal bravery on that occasion was much admired. And, ironically, Castro's personal dislike of Betancourt helped further strengthen his position, especially among his own armed forces, to whom he offered a new role as a modern, professional organization in which the lower ranks would for the first time enjoy some of the rewards that had previously been monopolized by the officer corps.

In the end, the Cuban Missile Crisis, in October 1962, was to strengthen Betancourt's position even more, as the missiles that Nikita Khrushchev had sought to place in Cuba, which could have reached Seattle, could equally well have been targeted on Caracas, or Brasília for that matter, and for the first time opinion in the Organization of American States consolidated against Cuba. Although the sabotage of oil installations after October 1962 was a sign of continued anti-Americanism in Venezuela, suspicion of Soviet intentions soon eroded public support for the left. As a supporter writes, "The existence of Cuba certainly made it difficult for movements that supported the Cuban revolution to maintain that all they wanted was a bourgeois-dominated popular front. Ojeda was one of the first people to point out this illogicality in the Communist position."[64]

The failure of the missile crisis venture was the key change in the international environment that led in October 1964 to the fall of Khrushchev, dismissed by the Central Committee of the Soviet Communist Party for "adventurism." The Kennedy administration had already established its counterinsurgency strategy and was offering strong support to democratic governments in the region. Over the next two years, almost all the guerrilla movements that had sprung up in the region in imitation of the Cuban example were successfully destroyed, and by the end of that time, the OAS had voted to isolate Cuba, making it much more difficult for it to offer effective support to insurgent movements. However, this was also the period in which the majority of Latin American governments fell to military coups and were replaced by a variety of military regimes; in this respect, Venezuela and Colombia are two notable exceptions.

What Worked?

Traditional methods, namely a frontal assault by loyal troops making use of the full range of weapons available, were used to suppress the military revolts, on both the right and the left. The government had command of the air and so was able to make full use of the air force to strafe defensive positions. This success, however, was achieved only at a heavy cost of several thousand casualties on both sides.

The weak guerrilla presence was easily disrupted by routine army patrols, backed up by the air force for ground surveillance. By the end of 1966, only one serious group was still active in the field. The guerrillas could continue to survive but not to be politically effective.[65] In retrospect it is clear that the launch of the FALN-FLN came too late—the MIR had already tried guerrilla warfare and had failed. The new guerrilla groups were too small and easily located. A series of blunders by the insurgents helped disrupt the urban campaign and kept it from winning "hearts and minds" away from the government. The attempt to assassinate Betancourt and the two naval revolts helped keep army support behind the government when the big challenge came. Efforts to disrupt the 1963 presidential election helped consolidate support behind the democratic political order.

Opponents of the regime say that the limited urban deployment of troops was highly effective in helping the police retain or restore control of the more dangerous barrios. Although the role of vigilant police work should not be underestimated, in the Venezuelan case, the use of security services formed only part of an overall situation shaped by a clear political strategy.

Controlling the towns with the aid of its affiliated trade unions and the countryside through its linked peasant organizations, while allowing other legitimate political parties to do the same where they could, AD left its militant opponents very little space to recruit civilian support. Both Betancourt and his successor showed themselves ready to act against the insurgent threat without trying to create a new dictatorship. They were both helped by the mistakes of the insurgents, especially in the use of terrorist methods in the cities. Deprived of popular support, the movement was unable to maintain itself. The democratic government retained its constituency and its support, as the results of the 1963 elections confirmed.

The country remained solvent despite high military expenditures—always a serious consideration. As with other countries in the region, the armed forces received considerable aid and assistance from the United States. The traditional view is that the availability of oil revenues also made it easy for Venezuelan governments to buy off opposition and consolidate support. However, while this idea is broadly true, the situation at the time was not entirely straightforward. Petroleum revenues fell in 1957–58. They increased in 1959, but in that year Washington instituted a quota system, and a long-term decline in oil prices set in. Faced with the unpalatable choice between making sharp tax cuts to try to keep production up and maintaining the high tax rates that had been set by the interim government, of which Betancourt did not approve, Betancourt's oil minister chose the latter and took the lead in negotiations for a worldwide quota system, which led to the formation of the Organization of Petroleum Exporting Countries (OPEC) in 1960.[66] Revenue rose again in 1961 and 1963, but there followed sharp decreases in 1964 and 1965. But overall petroleum tax revenues increased 17.2 percent from 1957 to 1965, and between 1958 and 1965 they increased 63.3 percent, a compounded average growth rate of approximately 7.2 percent per year. Venezuela's relative economic strength, therefore, seems to have been sufficient to enable Betancourt and AD to reward their supporters and so isolate the guerrillas.

Yet because of the many demands on the system, the government was unable to balance the budget until 1963, and largely because of the emergency, oil revenues were used for current expenditures to a greater degree than in the past.[67] Levine concludes that it was not the oil wealth that was important, but how it was used.[68]

The timely use of amnesty by Leoni offered the PCV a quick way out of the pit into which it had been digging itself.

WHAT DID NOT WORK

Needless to say, there are also lessons to be learned about what did not work.

The use of the air force against military insurgents appears to have been highly effective. However, the use of aircraft against the 1966 guerrilla landing had exactly the reverse effect, according to its supporters; it terrorized local peasants and lost their support.[69] But by that time, rural insurgency in Latin America generally was on the decline, and the Venezuelan movement was too fragmented and too dispersed to maintain an effective presence.

The tendency of a police force under pressure is to try to take shortcuts, particularly when threatened by imminent terrorist attack. In this way, its response to terrorism can easily compromise the wider struggle against insurgency. Digepol has been accused of systematic violations of human rights and even torture of political prisoners: "Deputy Jose Vicente Rangel in November 1965 cited a number of desaparecidos for whom Digepol was popularly believed responsible. Most shocking was the case of professor and PCV member, Alberto Lovera, who Digepol had arrested on 18 October; it had then beaten and tortured him, and wound his body with chains before tossing it into the sea. It appeared on a beach near Barcelona a little over a week later."[70] No arrests were ever made, but Caldera replaced Digepol with a new national police force, Dirección de Servicios de Inteligencia y Prevención del Estado (DISIP).[71]

COUNTERTERRORISM IN A FRAGILE DEMOCRACY

Given that there are relatively few examples of a democratic system successfully overcoming an armed challenge combining insurgency and terrorism, and that at the time Venezuelan democracy was very far from having been consolidated, there are a number of lessons for policymakers as to how to deal with a terrorist threat.

The first is the value of maintaining unity between government and constitutional opposition. This unity need not necessarily take the form of a formal agreement to maintain the democratic order, such as the Pact of Punto Fijo. In fact, the secession of the URD from the government in this case weakened it at a critical moment and shows how fragile a formal agreement can be. It is not enough simply to maintain the forms of electoral democracy; any dictatorship can do that, although not all do. But the unique value of maintaining constitutional order within a framework of due process of law is that it offers those whose hostility falls something short of total a set of possible outlets for their political demands and so acts to isolate those who for one reason or another favor terrorism. Although a government faced with a militant, armed challenge will necessarily have to resort to emergency powers, Betancourt himself was clear that the need to remain within the law and the constitution places clear limits on the range of options available to a democratic government. How well Venezuela did remain within those limits is very difficult to assess. Venezuelans had been used to decades of dictatorship, so the use of emergency powers found strong supporters as well as keen critics, and in the context of the time, the tactic could be and was defended as a necessary response to an international threat.

Betancourt's success is the more striking since at the beginning of his term of office he faced the risk of military revolt from the right as well as the left. Most democratic governments need to be concerned about only one of these hazards. However, after the Puerto Cabello revolt, the armed forces, effectively purged, were successfully used to provide reinforcements and specialized support for the police in the main phase of the antiterrorist campaign. This process was critical, since the police are the key point of contact between the government and its citizens. A weak and venal police force is a serious liability, and in Latin American countries generally there is a strong tendency for the armed forces to look down on, and indeed to despise, the police. Though the police in this case were unable to maintain a presence in the poorer districts of Caracas during the worst phase of the terror, they were able to retain the sympathy and support of the public and to successfully recruit informants. In Peru in the 1990s, it was routine police work that identified the safe house from which Abimael Guzmán operated.

The Betancourt government was fortunate in that the oil installations on which much of the prosperity of the country depended were either not targeted by the terrorists or were able to be defended. Information on this situation is lacking. Over the past two decades, the ELN in Colombia has repeatedly targeted oil pipelines, which by their nature are extremely hard to defend unless hardened or buried. Not only has this situation done serious damage to the country's economy; it has also had a psychological effect in making the government look weak. In Venezuela, too, the adverse publicity gained by terrorist "spectaculars" was politically embarrassing and contributed to the tendency of observers to overrate the threat of civil unrest. In fact, the most serious threat to the democratic order came from within, from the armed forces.

Regrettably, this success does not mean that a stable democracy may not have to face new challenges. "The violence did not end with the successful containment of the left in the 1960s. Incidents in the 1970s, including clashes between government troops and guerrillas in 1977, continued to threaten political stability," writes Richard Hillman. "Therefore the events of the 1980s . . . and 1990s . . . are not unusual."[72] Ewell gives details of 1970s incidents and notes that reports of "hit squads" being formed within the security forces to counter these threats alienated AD support at the 1978 election and led to the Copeyano victory.[73] In December 2001, Federico Bravo Melet was killed by police while allegedly resisting arrest. His father, Douglas Bravo, the former guerrilla leader, claimed that forensic evidence did not support the story put forth by police, and the detectives concerned went on trial for Bravo Melet's murder in November 2003.[74]

Epilogue

Looking back, Julia Buxton cogently argues that the very success of Betancourt and AD locked Venezuela into the quasi-democratic order its critics call Venedemocracía. This system, she avers, observed the formal requirements of electoral democracy but, by maintaining a monopoly of power shared between the two main parties, AD and COPEI, favored the elite without satisfying the rising demand for justice from the poor and dispossessed. In the 1990s, this situation was to lead to a major political upheaval. Both main parties were rejected by the electorate, though Caldera did manage to win a final term as an independent, running against the system he had helped create.

In 1998 the electorate rejected the candidates of both traditional parties in favor of Hugo Rafael Chávez Frías, a former paratrooper whose chief claim to fame was that in 1991 he had led an unsuccessful coup against the democratic government.[75] Elections to a constituent assembly resulted in a revised constitution that established a "Bolivarian state" promising greater social justice to the poor. Meanwhile, as president of OPEC, Chávez was successful in bringing both Iraq and Libya into line and raising the price of crude oil. At home, however, the reform program was opposed by vested interests using both constitutional and extraconstitutional means, and some of his proposed measures were enacted by decree.

In 2002 a faction in the armed forces tried to oust Chávez in favor of an extreme right-wing businessman who was immediately welcomed by the U.S. government. Within twenty-four hours, massive popular protest had broken out and the coup was reversed by loyal troops. Despite further attempts to oust Chávez by recall, the resulting referendum confirmed him in office in August 2004, and he has been able to continue with his plans for what he terms a democratic socialist revolution in Venezuela. As for his relations with the United States, in August 2005, Venezuela was the first foreign country to offer help to the victims of Hurricane Katrina.

Notes

1. Robert J. Alexander, *Romulo Betancourt and the Transformation of Venezuela* (New Brunswick, NJ: Transaction, 1982), 429; and Rómulo Betancourt, *La revolución democrática en Venezuela,* 4 vols. (Caracas: Imprinta Nacional, 1968).

2. Richard Gott, *Guerrilla Movements in Latin America* (London: Nelson, 1970), 103.

3. Ibid., 115.

4. Ibid., 116.

5. Alexander, *Romulo Betancourt,* 494.

6. Grant Wardlaw, *Political Terrorism: Theory, Tactics, and Counter-measures,* 2nd ed. (Cambridge: Cambridge University Press, 1989), 38–39.

7. Gott, *Guerrilla Movements,* 120–27.

8. Ibid., 128–29.

9. Ibid., 133; Gott also cites Régis Debray, "América Latina: Algunos problemas de estrategia revolucionaria," *Casa de las Americas* 31 (July–August 1965).

10. Peter Calvert, "Terrorism in Venezuela," in *Encyclopedia of World Terrorism,* ed. Martha Crenshaw and John Pimlott (London: Whitaker, 1997), 1:455–56.

11. Steve Ellner, *Organized Labor in Venezuela, 1958–1991: Behavior and Concerns in a Democratic Setting* (Wilmington, DE: Scholarly Resources, 1993), 5.

12. Ibid., 10–11.

13. Alexander, *Romulo Betancourt,* 489–90.

14. Gott, *Guerrilla Movements,* 101; and Arthur M. Schlesinger, Jr., *A Thousand Days* (London: André Deutsch, 1965), 660.

15. Alexander, *Romulo Betancourt,* 492–93; see also John Gerassi, *The Great Fear in Latin America* (New York: Collier-Macmillan, 1965).

16. Guillermo Morón, *A History of Venezuela,* ed. and trans. John Street (London: Allen & Unwin, 1964), 217.

17. Ellner, *Organized Labor,* 18.

18. Alexander, *Romulo Betancourt,* 574.

19. Ernesto 'Che' Guevara de la Serna, *Guerrilla Warfare* (New York and London: Monthly Review, 1967), 2.

20. Gott, *Guerrilla Movements,* 149.

21. Carleton Beals, *Latin America, World in Revolution* (New York: Abelard-Schuman, 1963), 219–20.

22. Judith Ewell, *Venezuela: A Century of Change* (London: C. Hurst, 1984), 133.

23. Dwight D. Eisenhower, *The White House Years,* vol. 2, *Waging Peace* (London: Heinemann, 1966), 521.

24. Richard M. Nixon, *Six Crises* (London: W. H. Allen, 1962), 223.

25. Eisenhower, *White House Years,* 519.

26. Stephen G. Rabe, *Eisenhower and Latin America: The Foreign Policy of Anti-Communism* (Chapel Hill: University of North Carolina Press, 1988), 104.

27. Daniel H. Levine, "The Transition to Democracy: Are There Lessons from Venezuela?" *Bulletin of Latin American Research* 4, no. 2 (1985): 47–61; see also Margaret Canovan, *Populism* (London: Junction, 1981).

28. Luis Ricardo Dávila, "The Rise and Fall and Rise of Populism in Venezuela," *Bulletin of Latin American Research* 19, no. 2 (2000): 223–38.

29. Levine, "Transition to Democracy," 47–61.

30. Nixon, *Six Crises,* 222.

31. Ibid., 223n.

32. Ewell, *Venezuela,* 129.

33. Alexander, *Romulo Betancourt,* 494.

34. Régis Debray, "Castroism: The Long March in Latin America," in Régis Debray, *Strategy for Revolution,* ed. Robin Blackburn (London: Jonathan Cape, 1970), 34.

35. Talton Ray, *The Politics of the Barrios of Venezuela* (Berkeley: University of California Press, 1969), 132–33, quoted in Alexander, *Romulo Betancourt,* 494.

36. Ibid., 495.

37. See Régis Debray, "Report from the Venezuelan Guerrilla," in Debray, *Strategy for Revolution,* 85–110.

38. Debray, "Castroism," 65.

39. Gott, *Guerrilla Movements,* 125.

40. Debray, "Castroism," 41.

41. Alexander, *Romulo Betancourt,* 490–92.

42. Manuel Cabieses Donoso, *Venezuela Okey!* (Santiago: Ediciones del Litoral, 1963), 242, quoted by Gott, *Guerrilla Movements,* 118.

43. Debray, "Castroism," 41.

44. Ibid.

45. Alexander, *Romulo Betancourt,* 494.

46. Wardlaw, *Political Terrorism,* 41; and A. J. R. Groom, "Coming to Terms with Terrorism," *British Journal of International Studies* 4 (1978): 62–77.

47. David Esteller, *Weekend en las Guerrillas: Memorias de un combatiente en dos epocas criticas de nuestra reciente historia* (Caracas: Editorial Fuentes, 1983).

48. Shlomo Eckstein and others, *Land Reform in Latin America: Bolivia, Chile, Mexico, Peru and Venezuela,* World Bank Staff Working Paper no. 275 (Washington, DC: World Bank, 1978), 83.

49. Ibid., 87.

50. Ellner, *Organized Labor,* 25–26.

51. Beals, *Latin America,* 225.

52. Alexander, *Romulo Betancourt,* 496, citing an interview with Teodoro Petkoff.

53. Mike Gonzalez, "The Culture of the Heroic Guerrilla: The Impact of Cuba in the Sixties," *Bulletin of Latin American Research* 3, no. 2 (1984): 65–75.

54. Steve Ellner, *Venezuela's Movimiento al Socialismo: From Guerrilla Defeat to Electoral Politics* (Durham, NC: Duke, 1988), 45–46. See also Teodoro Petkoff, *Del optimismo de la voluntad: Escritos políticos* (Caracas: Centuro, 1987).

55. Gott, *Guerrilla Movements,* 131, citing Douglas Bravo, *Avec Douglas Bravo dans les maquis vénézuéliens* (Paris: François Maspero, 1968), 43.

56. Gott, *Guerrilla Movements,* 131, citing Moses Moleiro, *El MIR de Venezuela* (Guiras: Instituto del Libro, 1967), 194.

57. Ewell, *Venezuela,* 158.

58. Alexander, *Romulo Betancourt,* 484, citing interview with Antonio Hernandez.

59. Ibid., 484–85, citing 1978 interview.

60. Gott, *Guerrilla Movements,* 97, citing John D. Martz, *Acción Democrática: Evolution of a Modern Political Party in Venezuela* (Princeton, NJ: Princeton University Press, 1966), 99.

61. Gott, *Guerrilla Movements,* 97, quoting Fidel Castro, speech at the University of Havana, March 13, 1967.

62. Régis Debray, "Problems of Revolutionary Strategy in Latin America," in Debray, *Strategy for Revolution,* 113–52.

63. Gott, *Guerrilla Movements,* 100.

64. Ibid., 146.

65. Ibid., 152, 165.

66. George Philip, *Oil and Politics in Latin America: Nationalist Movements and State Companies* (Cambridge: Cambridge University Press, 1982), 294–97.

67. Jorge Salazar-Carrillo, *Oil and Development in Venezuela during the Twentieth Century* (Westport, CT: Praeger, 1994), 194–96.

68. Levine, "Transition to Democracy."

69. Gott quoting Petkoff interview with Menéndez Rodríguez. See Gott, *Guerrilla Movements,* 162–65.

70. Ewell, *Venezuela,* 158. Barcelona lies on the coast 136 miles east of Caracas, close to the island of Margarita.

71. Ewell, *Venezuela,* 170.

72. Richard S. Hillman, *Democracy for the Privileged: Crisis and Transition in Venezuela* (Boulder, CO: Lynne Rienner, 1994), 56.

73. Ewell, *Venezuela,* 205.

74. Patrick J. O'Donoghue, "Six CICPC Detectives to Go on Trial for Alleged Execution of Douglas Bravo's Son" (online report for VHeadline News, November 5, 2003), www.vheadline.com/readnews.asp?=12243.

75. Julia Buxton, *The Failure of Political Reform in Venezuela* (Aldershot, VT: Ashgate, 2001).

7

"TERROR IN THE NAME OF MAO"

Revolution and Response in Peru

David Scott Palmer

Peru is a major South American country replete with contradictions and anomalies, past and present. The highly developed, heavily populated, and well-organized Inca Empire, with its capital in the Peruvian Andean highlands city of Cuzco and with control of what is now Peru, Bolivia, Ecuador, southern Colombia, northern Chile, and northwestern Argentina, collapsed in weeks after the arrival of a small band of Spanish conquistadors. With the coastal city of Lima as the Spanish Empire's administrative center for all of South America for more than two hundred years, until the Bourbon reforms of the 1760s, Peru was favored over the rest of the region by the concentration of the Crown's human and material resources.

Perhaps due in part to Peru's privileged position within the empire, independence came late, in the early 1820s, and reluctantly, achieved largely through military forces and leaders from the South American colonial periphery of Argentina and Venezuela. The same explanation might also apply to some degree to the late arrival in Peru of the first wave of democracy, limited as it was, that gradually spread through Latin America from the 1850s onward. Only in the mid-1890s, after a succession of military heads of state and a devastating loss in the War of the Pacific (1879–83) against Chile that contributed to further political instability as well as virtually complete economic collapse, was limited liberal democracy established in Peru. Though lasting only about two decades (1895–1919, with a brief coup in 1914), this period represents to this day Peru's only extended experience with civilian-elected rule. Augusto Leguía, the last of the elected presidents in this period, carried out a "self-coup" in 1919 to rule as a civilian dictator for the next eleven years. From the 1930s through the 1970s, anything more than a brief return to democracy was thwarted by a deep animosity between the military and the Alianza Popular Revolucionaria Americana (American Popular Revolutionary Alliance, or APRA), a well-organized and ideological but noncommunist party of the left.[1]

By the 1960s, in an ironic twist, the progressively stronger and more institutionalized armed forces took upon themselves as their core national security strategy the banner of reform once espoused by their archenemy. When the military-supported elected government of Fernando Belaúnde Terry (1963–68) and his Acción Popular (Popular Action, or AP) Party stumbled in its efforts to effect change, the armed forces took over once again, this time with a comprehensive plan, largely borrowed from APRA, to transform Peru through major social, economic, and political reform.[2] Although the twelve-year military regime (1968–80) was ultimately unsuccessful for a variety of reasons, most importantly because it attempted too much with too few resources, it was still able to bring about a number of important changes. One was to open up political space for the mostly Marxist left, which the military favored as an alternative to APRA, to organize and grow into a major political force.[3]

By the time the military government—battered, bruised, and chastened by its experience with long-term institutionalized rule—agreed to turn power back to civilians between 1978 and 1980, the multiple parties of the left were major political players, particularly in unions and universities. With Peru's first presidential elections in seventeen years in 1980, also the first ever with universal suffrage, the historical and political landscape was dramatically changed. It was into this unlikely political context that the radical Maoist guerrillas of Shining Path, formally known as the Partido Comunista del Perú–Sendero Luminoso (Communist Party of Peru–Shining Path), were also to emerge.[4]

As we know, social revolutions usually arise in a context of political polarization, repression, authoritarian rule, and economic crisis. Each of the five successful social revolutions in Latin America (Haiti 1794–1804, Mexico

1910–17, Bolivia 1952, Cuba 1953–59, and Nicaragua 1974–79) occurred under such conditions. Peru's "people's war" (1980–95), although ultimately unsuccessful, began and developed under quite different circumstances. Shining Path launched its first revolutionary operations in May 1980, at the very moment Peru was establishing the most open democracy in its long and often turbulent political history.[5]

The theory of revolution would predict the early demise of such a quixotic initiative.[6] A decade later, however, Peru's democratic government was on the verge of collapse. Political violence had become generalized, the government's responses were ineffective and counterproductive, and the economy was in a shambles. Over the first ten years of the radical Maoists' people's war, more than twenty thousand Peruvians were killed, $10 billion worth of infrastructure was damaged or destroyed, some five hundred thousand internal refugees were generated, along with an almost equal number of emigrants, and there was a decline in gross domestic product of 30 percent and a cumulative inflation of more than two million percent.[7] By 1990, such discouraging indicators suggested that a Shining Path victory was close at hand.

WHY REVOLUTION UNDER DEMOCRACY?

How can we explain such a confounding set of developments? Several forces and factors were in play. One set of explanations relates to the origins, characteristics, and dynamics of Shining Path itself; another set, to those of the policies and mindset of various Peruvian governments from the 1960s through the 1980s.

Factors Relating to Shining Path

One important factor is that the group that eventually became known as Shining Path began and took root in the early 1960s largely out of public view—in Ayacucho, a remote and isolated department (state) of highland Peru. While a very important region historically, since the final major battle securing Latin America's independence from Spain was fought there in 1824, the area had only sporadic and limited central government attention for many years. As late as the 1970s, there were no paved roads in the department, only one single-lane dirt highway connecting the city of Ayacucho to the capital city of Lima, no telephones, sporadic electricity limited to three or four urban centers, a single radio station, and one weekly newspaper. In addition, both the Belaúnde government and the military regime that followed tolerated Marxist groups among students and in teachers' and labor unions. While there were occasional police roundups of militant student and union leaders in the late 1960s and early 1970s, including in Ayacucho, the detainees were soon released. As a result, Shining Path and its leadership could operate and expand over seventeen years, almost unperceived by the outside world, before the declaration of the people's war in 1980.[8]

Second, the original ancestor of this radical Maoist group organized initially at the National University of San Cristóbal de Huamanga (UNSCH) in the department's capital. While the university dated from the 1670s, it had been closed for almost eighty years before being refounded in 1959 with a mission then unique to Peruvian institutions of higher education—the promotion of development in the region.[9] The government also provided the resources necessary to pursue that mission. This meant that the university provided an opportunity unmatched in the country at that time for faculty and students to pursue either development or political agendas in the field.

Third, the opportunity to carry out such a mission attracted a number of Peru's best scholars, as well as a few with more of a political than an academic agenda. Among the latter was the young Communist Party militant Abimael Guzmán Reynoso, later to become the head of Shining Path. Within a few months of his arrival in 1962, through his unshakable convictions and force of personality, he had revitalized the almost moribund local party organization and established his presence in the still small university (with about four hundred students and forty faculty members at the time) as a committed and charismatic professor of the left. Over the next few years, he built from the ground up a communist student association and led vanguard student elements as well as their faculty counterparts to victory in university elections in 1968. The UNSCH then served even more than before as forum, incubator, and launching platform for the expansion of Guzmán's radical organization and ideology.[10]

Fourth, given the extreme poverty and the almost entirely rural, indigenous, peasant-dominated nature of Ayacucho that provided the external context within which the UNSCH operated, it is no surprise that Guzmán sided with China after the Sino-Soviet split of 1963–64. With this new ideological commitment, he worked diligently and successfully to build a strong Maoist party both within the university and in the countryside. As a professor in the university's education program and director of its training school for several years in the 1960s, Guzmán prepared and in many cases radicalized a generation of teachers who took up positions in Ayacucho's rural communities. These teachers—often from the countryside, with Spanish as their second language, and the first generation to get a university education—in many cases became the proselytizing front line of their mentor's political organization.[11]

A fifth important factor revolved around Guzmán's relationship with the Chinese. He and his principal lieutenants made several extended trips to China beginning in 1965 in the midst of the Cultural Revolution. Over these years, they became adherents of the most radical faction in that struggle, the Gang of Four. When their Chinese mentors lost out to their more moderate adversaries in the struggle for political control in China in 1976, the Communist Party of Peru–Shining Path (PCP-SL) was cast adrift and forced to fend for itself. Totally radicalized by his Chinese experience and convinced that the world communist revolution was lost unless it could be purified and returned to its original Marxist-Leninist-Maoist ideals, Guzmán concluded that only a properly directed people's war in Peru could bring a true world communist revolution about.[12]

A sixth element was voluntarism. Even though the so-called objective conditions for the armed struggle did not exist in early 1980, as Peru prepared for the return to democracy with great enthusiasm and popular support, Guzmán concluded that Lenin's voluntarist dictum could be appropriately applied. By launching the people's war at this moment, he believed, its actions would sow disquiet, chaos, and indiscriminately repressive government responses, thereby creating over time the more favorable objective conditions required for continuing and expanding the revolution.[13]

A seventh factor concerned how Shining Path could find the resources necessary to carry out its people's war, since after 1976 the organization no longer had international patrons in its quest for power through revolution. Although the group was formally affiliated with the Revolutionary International Movement (RIM), this relationship was dictated by the ideological imperative to be connected to a worldwide communist movement and involved little, if any, financial support. In the first years, Shining Path secured guns, ammunition, and dynamite through raids on isolated police stations and the hundreds of small mines that dotted the slopes of the highlands. As the movement gathered strength, its needs increased correspondingly.[14]

By the mid-1980s, it had found a new source of both local support and significant funding in the coca producers and the drug trafficking of the Upper Huallaga Valley in north-central Peru. Although it had to compete there at first with its smaller and less-radical guerrilla rival the Tupac Amaru Revolutionary Movement (MRTA),[15] Shining Path soon achieved a dominant position in the valley. By the late 1980s, it is estimated, the guerrillas were extracting at least $10 million a year from "taxes" paid by the Colombian operators of small planes that worked out of more than one hundred clandestine airstrips in the Upper Huallaga.[16]

Shining Path was able to set up a finance committee to distribute funds to the organization's central and regional committees to buy weapons, bribe local officials, and pay cadres regular stipends. The guerrillas were also able to enlist the support of many local associations of coca growers by forcing buyers to pay higher prices for their production. So Shining Path, having decided to go it alone, was in no way dependent on always uncertain outside sources of financial and material support or the dictates of others but was able to garner substantial internal resources to finance its operations and to maintain its autonomy.[17]

Factors Related to the Government

Aiding the PCP-SL in its quest, however unintentionally, were the failed efforts of the reformist military government in Peru in the late 1960s and 1970s to effect major change in economic and political organization during its tenure. This reform was based on the principle of integrating large private estates with small peasant parcels to create new wealth through increased production. The model applied, however, was not well suited to the community-based agriculture of most of the highlands, particularly Ayacucho, the center of most PCP-SL activities, where only a very few productive private agricultural properties operated. The reform's implementation actually further degraded the already precarious position of most indigenous peasants, opening up opportunities for proselytizing and support that the radical Maoists could exploit.[18]

A second factor contributing to Shining Path's ability to expand its operations, once it declared the people's war in 1980, was the official response to the early activities of the Maoist guerrillas—the reluctance of the new democratic government to recognize the presence of an insurgency on its watch. President Belaúnde (1980–85), who had been ousted by a military coup during his previous term of office in the 1960s, was so fearful of renewed military influence in his second administration that he downplayed the problem for more than two years before committing Peru's armed forces to a military response. Although he did order specialized police forces, the *sinchis,* into Ayacucho in 1981, their extraordinarily bad comportment forced the president to withdraw them within a few months. In addition, throughout his administration, he resisted calls to provide both military and economic support, focusing the government's response almost exclusively on military actions.[19]

The sinchis' activities highlighted a significant third factor that was in play, the long history of misunderstanding and exploitation between the white and mestizo center, based in Lima, and the largely indigenous highland periphery in Peru.[20] This relationship contributed to a racist mindset among police and the military that often produced, once they intervened in the largely indigenous countryside of Ayacucho and its environs, totally inappropriate responses that amounted to state terrorism. Such actions not only served to drive indigenous peasants into the arms of Shining Path but also provided the insurgents with further justification for their armed struggle.[21]

After APRA's historic electoral victory in 1985, President Alan García Pérez (1985–90) initially suggested a shift in counterinsurgency strategy to include economic as well as military initiatives in the highlands. However, his misguided economic policies at the national level produced hyperinflation and a virtual economic implosion over the last half of his administration, not only forcing the abandonment of the highland strategy but also creating a serious erosion in both civil government and military institutional capacity.[22]

One result was a sharp decline in military and police morale, as defense budgets were cut by more than 50 percent in the late 1980s and hyperinflation reduced salaries to less than 10 percent of mid-1980s levels.[23] Exacerbating the problem was the growing number of police and armed forces casualties at the hands of Shining Path—from 31 police officers and 1 soldier in 1982 to 229 police officers and 109 soldiers in 1989, for a total of 1,196 deaths (795 police and 401 military) over the first ten years of the conflict.[24]

These developments provoked hundreds of resignations at both the officer and technical personnel levels across the armed and police services and contributed to a decline in the armed forces' readiness status from 75 percent in 1985 to 30 percent by 1990.[25]

Such corrosive dynamics played out in the field in a loss of discipline, increased corruption, and, all too often, virtually complete operational ineffectiveness. With the U.S. government increasing its counternarcotics assistance to the police in this context of institutional erosion and extremely scarce resources, and as the police force felt it was bearing a disproportionate share of the counterinsurgency burden, tensions between the police and the military grew. They reached a flash point after the army failed in March 1989 to respond to urgent calls for help from a besieged police detachment in the Upper Huallaga town of Uchiza and allowed its officers to be slaughtered by Shining Path guerrillas.[26] Although the García government undertook an organizational overhaul of the armed forces, police, and eight separate intelligence agencies by consolidating and renaming them, the lack of resources, both human and material, ensured that no effective change would be immediately forthcoming.

In summary, the insurgents were able to initiate and expand their people's war through a combination of long preparation, charismatic leadership, a remote base, a radicalized ideology, and voluntarism. They were aided in their efforts by government inaction, a belated response, massive human rights violations, and economic crisis. This combination produced a set of conditions favorable for revolution that had not existed at the outset of the people's war. The continuing ineffectiveness of elected civilian regimes, including misguided economic policies in the latter half of the 1980s that produced hyperinflation, economic crisis, and the virtual implosion of government, enabled the forces of Shining Path to make major advances toward their goal of revolutionary victory.

WHY REBEL FAILURE ON THE BRINK OF SUCCESS?

This set of considerations raises a second fundamental question. If Shining Path was poised for victory by the early 1990s, why did its revolution not succeed? Within five years, the revolutionaries were a spent force, dead, in jail, or rehabilitated, the remnants scattered and no longer a threat to the state. Part of the explanation has to do with ways in which Shining Path contributed to its own collapse, and part with major shifts in official strategies and policies.

Rebel Mistakes

One of Shining Path's problems came to be overconfidence bordering on hubris. Although the organization's leadership envisioned at the outset of its people's war a long-term revolutionary struggle, its successes against a government almost pathologically unwilling to mount effective responses gave rise to the belief that the regime was about to collapse and that Shining Path was on the brink of victory. Such overconfidence led the leadership to exercise less caution in its security and in tracking the rural support structures that had long provided its core cadre.[27]

Another problem could be characterized as ideological myopia. While Shining Path's radical Maoist ideology had been a potent unifying force for its supporters and helps explain how the group could justify even the most barbaric acts, the ideology simultaneously served to alienate most of the presumed beneficiaries of the revolution. The peasantry, initially attracted by the promise of a change in status, found cadre and local commissar alike so blinded by their convictions that they imposed on the peasantry a revolutionary organization that related to neither its heritage nor its needs, and they compounded the negative effects of their efforts by using terror and intimidation to maintain local "support."[28]

A third problem was the hydrocephalic nature of Shining Path's organization. True, at the group's height, the guerrillas had a well-developed set of national, regional, and local organizations with corresponding central and regional committees to direct and coordinate. Ultimately, however, all power flowed from a single individual, President Gonzalo (Guzmán's nom de guerre). He was the group's founder, ideologist, strategist, and internal contradiction synthesizer, and he explicitly fostered a cult of personality within the membership. All other leaders, from the Central Committee on down, were subordinate. As a result, Shining Path was particularly vulnerable as a guerrilla organization should he be killed or captured.[29]

Fourth was Guzmán's decision to initiate more systematic urban terrorism in the late 1980s, particularly in Lima. Following Lenin, he justified this terrorism as necessary to build support within the urban proletariat. Operations in the capital city sowed havoc and panic but also brought the people's war to the doorsteps of the political elite for the first time, contributing thereby to the realization at last that the very survival of the nation was at stake. The terrorist actions in Lima strengthened the resolve of the central government to find solutions. They also made the guerrillas more vulnerable to counterintelligence operations, due to the intelligence services' greater familiarity with urban surroundings than with the highlands.[30]

Government Successes

Just as much of the explanation for the ability of Shining Path to advance its revolutionary project can be attributed to government errors during the 1980s, the guerrillas' own mistakes contributed to its failure in the early 1990s. Nevertheless, it is unlikely that the Shining Path threat could have been overcome without a number of significant adjustments in the government's approach to counterinsurgency as well. These occurred over a period of several years in the late 1980s and early 1990s, when it appeared to many that Shining Path was gaining the upper hand in the conflict in a larger socioeconomic context that was rapidly deteriorating as well. Taken separately, it is doubtful that any one of the changes made would have been sufficient; together, however, they combined over time to turn the tide in the government's favor.

A New Approach to Counterinsurgency. One significant change was the top-to-bottom review by the military of its counterinsurgency strategy in 1988 and 1989. The initial result was the compilation of a comprehensive *Countersubversive Manual,* which systematically analyzed the antiguerrilla campaign to that point and developed a new strategy that included the political, economic, and psychosocial aspects of counterinsurgency as well as the military components.[31] This manual served as a guide for the progressive introduction of several major adjustments in the Peruvian armed forces' approach to dealing with the now-palpable threat of Shining Path.

Beginning in 1990, the military began for the first time a "hearts-and-minds" civic action campaign in a number of the urban neighborhoods and communities that had been most susceptible to Shining Path influence, as well as strategically important to the guerrillas in many cases. The initiatives were modest, such as free haircuts and health clinics, whitewashing and reroofing of local schools, trash cleanup campaigns, soup kitchens, and the building of access roads or trails. Very quickly, local indifference, fear, or hostility toward the military turned to support. With carefully coordinated publicity for these initiatives, the media began to convey a more positive image of the military in newspapers and newsmagazines that reached a wide Peruvian audience, helping change public perceptions as well.[32]

Another change was the attachment of a soldier or two from the community or area to the unit conducting operations in that locality. The individuals involved knew the community, spoke the local language or dialect, and often could help the military unit communicate with the local population and gather much more accurate intelligence on Shining Path sympathizers and operations. Given the physical and human diversity of Peruvian neighborhoods and rural communities, particularly in the highlands, one would have expected such procedures to be a component of military counterinsurgency strategy from the outset.

The military's long reluctance to use personnel who were native to the areas of operations stemmed from a deeply held view in a highly centralized political system that such individuals would be likely to have a greater allegiance to their friends and relatives in the community than to the organization for which they worked. With the looming specter of failure and possible government collapse, however, the military changed its approach. Once again, the result was positive in many instances—better communication with the locals and the collection of intelligence on enemy plans, personnel, and operations that had heretofore not been available.[33]

In the early 1990s, the military also began to be much more sensitive to the negative effects of indiscriminate operations and attacks on local populations. The army initiated training for its operational units so that they carried out missions in neighborhoods or the countryside with fewer human rights violations and fewer misguided attacks on noncombatants. As their counterinsurgency activities became more precisely targeted and less repressive, they began to gain the support of local populations. They also began to demonstrate the contrast between their approach and the increasingly violent and indiscriminate actions of Shining Path in its desperate attempts to retain local control through force and intimidation.[34]

In another major shift in strategy and tactics drawn from the counterinsurgency review of 1988 and 1989, the Fujimori government persuaded congress to pass legislation that enabled the army to begin to formally support the training and arming of local peasant organizations (*rondas campesinas,* or civil defense committees) as a first line of defense against Shining Path attacks. For many decades, when local highland communities found themselves threatened by cattle rustlers or attempts by neighboring communities to take some of their land by force and occupation, they would organize groups of community members into *rondas* to overcome the threat to their livelihood or well-being.[35]

Shining Path's activities in the 1980s represented to many communities one more threat that had to be resisted. Although many decided to allow the guerrillas' presence and control, thereby becoming communities of acceptance, many others organized rondas to fight them off, becoming communities of resistance.[36] Often, however, their primitive weapons of stones, slingshots, and sharpened sticks were no match for Shining Path's superior arms. Even so, for years the military resisted any initiative to support the rondas in their efforts, out of fear that training and arms could be turned against them. The army also displayed the historic racism so prevalent in Peru, which manifested itself in a lack of confidence in the ability of indigenous populations to use the assistance properly.[37]

Within a very short time after the army began its program of providing basic military training and an average of two or three rifles with a few bullets each for each ronda, ronda numbers and membership mushroomed. By 1993 more than 4,200 rondas had been organized across the highlands, with a membership of almost 236,000.[38] These civil defense committees, as the army called them, became the first line of defense against Shining Path. Examples abound of their ability to fend off guerrilla attacks long enough to enable army units to arrive on the scene and rout the invaders. Assisting the rondas may have been the single most important adjustment in the Peruvian government's counterinsurgency strategy, as it gave some measure of increased capacity for resistance to the local populations most affected by the guerrillas and with the greatest stake in overcoming the threat.[39]

Another significant change in the Peruvian government's approach to the growing threat of Shining Path was the decision in late 1989 by the APRA administration's minister of the interior, Augustín Mantilla, to create a small, autonomous police intelligence unit, the Grupo Especial de Inteligencia (Special Intelligence Group, or GEIN), with the sole mission of tracking the Shining Path leadership. After a shaky beginning, with only five members and outdated equipment, the unit was provided with resources and skilled personnel, increasing to about thirty-five by 1990 and fifty a year later.[40] The group was subject to intense political pressure in the waning weeks of the discredited García government as the APRA leadership looked for some spectacular event to restore popular support. As a result, even though its intelligence was incomplete, the group felt forced to conduct a raid on a suspected Shining Path safe house in Lima that might have harbored Guzmán, a raid that confirmed his location but missed the leader.

The newly elected government of President Alberto Fujimori (1990–2000) could have been expected to terminate the previous administration's intelligence initiative as part of a complete policy overhaul. However, after Fujimori's July 1990 inauguration, he left GEIN in place. With virtually complete autonomy and with additional resources and personnel, the intelligence group slowly advanced in its ability to identify and follow the guerrilla leadership. Over the course of 1991, GEIN operatives were able to capture Shining Path's master files and round up some second-level leaders, even as the guerrillas were carrying out ever more brazen and violent terrorist acts. The culmination of GEIN's efforts occurred on September 12, 1992, when some thirty-five of its members burst into a safe house in a Lima suburb and captured a startled and bodyguardless Guzmán, along with several other members of the PCP-SL Central Committee.[41]

With this success, soon to be followed by the roundup of several hundred other militants and cadres, the government delivered a mortal psychological and tactical blow to Shining Path. The Fujimori government milked the moment to its full extent by publicly displaying Guzmán to the media in a cage especially constructed for the occasion and then quickly tried him in a military court under new procedures that kept the identities of judges hidden. Predictably, the court sentenced him to life imprisonment.[42]

Although violent incidents declined by less than 10 percent over the six months following Guzmán's capture and then increased by some 15 percent during the first seven months of 1993, these events proved to be the last gasps of a dying movement.[43] By the end of 1994, Shining Path, while still a nuisance in some parts of the country, had ceased to pose a threat to the Peruvian state. Because of the overconcentration of the organization's power in a single individual, Shining Path could not long survive Guzmán's capture. The intelligence unit received the $1 million reward the government had offered for getting Guzmán, and its members were lionized in the press—with good reason.

The Fujimori government also undertook two other important initiatives to assist its efforts to gain the upper hand over Shining Path. One was the establishment of a military and civilian court procedure of "faceless" judges to try captured guerrillas, to ensure rapid trials and protection from reprisals. The new court procedures occurred shortly after President Fujimori's unexpected suspension of constitutional guarantees in an April 1992 *autogolpe* (self-coup). One of the major problems governments had had to that point was the long delay in bringing prisoners accused of subversion to court, with time in jail awaiting trial averaging more than seven years. Another was the systematic intimidation and even assassination of judges assigned to oversee the trials, which had a chilling effect on their willingness to convict and tended to cause them to find legal excuses to release convicted terrorists from prison.[44]

The initiative was controversial from the outset because of the courts' short-circuiting of due process (it was subsequently determined that several hundred convictions had been secured without legal justification). In fact, in 1999 the Inter-American Human Rights Court (IAHRC), of which Peru was a signatory, declared the faceless-judge procedure to be an unconstitutional violation of due process. Although the Fujimori government rejected the IAHRC decision, its democratically elected successor accepted it and has set up new trials for those convicted under the previous arrangement. The effect at the time, however, was to allow the government to quickly overcome the backlog of pending cases as well as to quickly process new ones, thereby increasing a renewed sense of government effectiveness among the public as well as making the public feel more secure.

The other important initiative of the Peruvian government was the implementation in early 1993 of a "repentance law," in effect until November 1994. It was designed to enable Shining Path cadres and sympathizers to turn themselves in with their weapons or information in exchange for support, retraining, and progressive reintegration into society. During the period the law was in effect, more than five thousand individuals availed themselves of this opportunity, although most were low-level supporters and sympathizers rather than regional or national leaders. Even so, the government gained additional intelligence in the process and offered an alternative to those who had chosen to support Shining Path. In the context of the capture of Guzmán and the clear shift in advantage to the government, the timing of the repentance law's implementation was ideal, as it came when the incentive for those who had been involved with the guerrillas to turn themselves in had increased markedly.[45]

A final government initiative, not only a component of the new approach to counterinsurgency but also a response to the economic crisis that had gutted the traditional government bureaucracy and left millions of Peruvians in desperate poverty, was the creation of a new set of small government organizations to focus on small development programs in areas of extreme poverty, mostly rural. Many of these areas were also centers of Shining Path activity.[46]

The new agencies were small (with about 300 employees each nationwide), and the employees were highly trained specialists, often engineers, who were recruited on merit criteria, paid high salaries, and given significant regional autonomy. The agencies focused on a set of small development programs that would have significant impact at the local level, among them irrigation, potable water, reforestation and soil conservation, electrification, school building, and trail or road access programs.[47]

Most projects cost $2,000 or less, with labor provided by the communities themselves and technical oversight by the agencies. In many cases, the requirement for beginning a program was for the community to decide what it most needed and to elect a small committee with responsibility for overseeing the project. Over the five years between 1993 and 1998, the agencies expended more than $1 billion on an array of programs and succeeded in reducing extreme poverty by one-half (from 31 percent to 15 percent). In addition to reducing extreme poverty in districts that had in many cases been affected by political violence, the programs also demonstrated to local citizens that the government cared about them and was able to extend its reach once again to even the most isolated parts of Peru. They also fostered new local organizations that helped re-create a measure of institutional capacity at the grass roots within civil society.[48]

Economic Recovery. Peru's economy was in a most precarious state when President Fujimori took office in July 1990. Hyperinflation was out of control at a 7,600 percent annual rate. The country had completely lost access to international credit because the previous government failed to pay Peru's foreign debt obligations for almost three years. Unemployment hovered at close to 30 percent. The GDP, down more than 20 percent during the last two years of the García government, was in free fall. Without immediate and drastic measures to turn the national economy around, it is quite unlikely that counterinsurgency initiatives alone could have stemmed the growing threat posed by Shining Path.[49]

The new president, having been briefed after his election on the seriousness of the economic situation by advisers in Peru, Washington, and New
York, turned his back on his campaign promises not to take economic measures that would be drastic or pose short-term hardship. Almost immediately
after his inauguration, President Fujimori instituted a drastic economic shock
program to break the inflationary cycle by ending government subsidies and
the indiscriminate printing of currency, among other harsh measures.

Peru also began within a few weeks to reinstate regular payments on its
$15 billion foreign debt and soon created a new domestic tax collection
agency to boost government tax revenues, which had fallen to 4 percent of
GDP. The government also reduced tariffs on exports and imports to foster
production and reduce inflation and set up procedures for the privatization
of state-owned enterprises and the opening up of the national stock market
to generate direct and portfolio foreign investment. To reduce an official
bureaucracy bloated by 40 percent during the APRA government, mostly
through political patronage, the government provided significant but one-
time financial incentives for state employees to retire.

The draconian measures instituted during Fujimori's first months in
office reversed the downward economic spiral within a year. Inflation was
cut in half, domestic tax revenues increased, and the international economic
community began to look again at restoring credit to Peru. By the second
year, the cycle of hyperinflation had been broken at last, government revenues and expenditures were almost in balance, and Peru was able to reinsert
itself into the international economic system. By 1993 inflation had been
reduced to 65 percent, employment had increased, new foreign investment
had begun, and positive economic growth had been recorded for the first
time in almost a decade. By 1994 Peru had the highest economic growth
rate in Latin America, with inflation down to 10 percent.

President Fujimori also made full use of his office as a bully pulpit to help
restore public confidence, with a frenetic schedule that took him all over
Peru, particularly to the areas most affected by the insurgency and historically least favored by the central government. In spite of the multiple problems the country was facing and the strong medicine the government was
administering to try to overcome them, the president's public approval
ratings remained consistently high. The general perception was that at last
Peru had a head of state who was taking action rather than playing politics
and was thinking about the public interest rather than personal gain.[50]

However dramatic the turnaround during these first years of the Fujimori administration, the people's war had exacted a high cost for the country and its people. Over the fifteen-year trajectory of Shining Path's revolutionary terrorism and the government's efforts to combat it, close to one million Peruvians, mostly humble highland peasants, were displaced from their homes and became internal refugees. Roughly an equal number emigrated, often the more skilled and educated, out of fear for their safety and despair of ever finding secure opportunities in their homeland. The dollar estimates of the total damage caused by Shining Path operations between 1980 and 1995 were more than $15 billion to infrastructure and $10 billion in lost production, or about half of Peru's 1990 GDP. The official estimate of about thirty-five thousand deaths and disappearances has recently been revised in a careful study by Peru's Truth and Reconciliation Commission, particularly in rural areas most affected by the insurgency, which concludes that the correct number is about sixty-nine thousand, twice the earlier figure.[51]

Sadly, democracy was also a casualty, with President Fujimori's self-coup in 1992 suspending congress and the judiciary. While pressured to restore democratic forms a year later by the Organization of American States (OAS), following his 1995 reelection, Fujimori and his advisers progressively constrained democratic procedures with a set of provisions of dubious legality. Although Fujimori was forced from office in a spectacular set of developments in 2000, shortly after his fraudulent reelection, the path to democratic reconstruction has been a difficult one.[52]

At this moment, President Alejandro Toledo (2001–06), the hero of the resistance to Fujimori, has lost most of his popular support through his vacillation and indecisiveness. Shining Path is showing new signs of life, with new recruitment efforts in universities and peasant communities, incidents of political violence, and exploitation of a more transparent and human rights–respecting government to renew contacts from prisons and seek new trials. In Ayacucho, for example, Shining Path members have established a working relationship with local organizations such as the Frente de Defensa de Ayacucho (Ayacucho Defense Front) and the Federación de Cocaleros del Apurímac (Apurimac Valley Coca Growers Federation). A violent attack on the Ayacucho city hall, local businesses, and the new Regional Government Office on July 1, 2004, has been blamed on Shining Path instigators.[53] Even so, Shining Path no longer represents a threat to the Peruvian state or to most of the population. Whatever the continuing difficulties of Peru's democracy, and they are many, it is unlikely that Shining Path will be in any position to exploit them for the foreseeable future.

CONCLUSIONS

Peru was eventually able to overcome the threat posed by the radical Maoist Shining Path, but at great human and institutional cost. Looking back, had the government taken the threat seriously during 1980–81, the first year of the group's self-declared people's war, it is likely it would have nipped the insurgency in the bud.[54] But the government's initial response was to withdraw from the more isolated police posts, which opened up additional space for Shining Path to build popular support groups in the communities and to strengthen its military capacity. When the government finally did begin to take the guerrillas seriously, it responded almost exclusively with military force, often indiscriminate. Field commanders who requested an economic development component to support their military activities were ignored or dismissed.

Although the APRA government that came to power in the 1985 elections made some initial gestures to build alliances in the highlands, it soon succumbed to military pressures to pursue the same repressive strategy followed by its predecessor. Its economic policies, furthermore, produced hyperinflation, virtual fiscal bankruptcy of the bureaucracy, and the almost total loss of vital international financial and investment support. By the end of the 1980s, then, Peru faced not only generalized political violence but also its most serious economic crisis in more than one hundred years.

It was only when the government found itself against the wall that it took the insurgency problem seriously enough to review its approach and to make a number of changes between 1988 and 1992 that significantly increased its ability to deal more effectively with Shining Path's advances. The most important steps were the creation of a specialized police intelligence unit to track the insurgent leadership, the complete overhaul of the military's counterinsurgency strategy, the implementation of approaches designed to garner local support, and the decision to train and arm community civil defense committees, or rondas. Once these measures had enabled the government to regain the initiative, the repentance law that offered guerrilla sympathizers and militants rehabilitation, retraining, and reinsertion into society became a critical instrument of pacification.

Along with such specific and significant adjustments in the government's approach to counterinsurgency, the Fujimori administration established a set of new official agencies to carry out a range of small development programs in the poorest districts of Peru, often where Shining Path had a significant presence. These programs provided significant benefits in a short period of time to three to five million of the country's neediest citizens while simultaneously reestablishing the government's presence and legitimacy in the periphery. With parallel efforts to repair the severely damaged national economy, efforts that ended inflation, generated economic growth, restored the fiscal capacity of the government, and reinserted Peru into the international economy within two to four years, the Fujimori administration was able to overcome the Shining Path threat.

Unlike the government, the insurgents did not learn or adapt. From the outset, Shining Path pursued the single objective of overthrowing the regime through the people's war. Negotiation was never an option. Convinced of the ideological correctness of their approach, which included the complete reorganization of civil society along Maoist lines, Shining Path leaders tried to impose a model in their areas of operation that in no way reflected the traditions, patterns, and needs of those they said were to be the beneficiaries of their revolution. Their ideological fervor and successes against the government for a number of years blinded them to the possibility that they could be defeated. While they often learned from failures in field operations and adjusted their military strategy accordingly, they did not do so in their relations with the civilian populations under their influence. But their greatest failure was to underestimate the capacity of government to learn from its own mistakes, which led to the single most important turning point in the insurgency, the capture of President Gonzalo.

External actors, particularly the U.S. government, became sufficiently concerned about Shining Path's advances against the beleaguered Peruvian democracy to provide significant military and intelligence support in 1991 and 1992. With Fujimori's self-coup in April 1992, however, military assistance and training were immediately suspended. However, the U.S. government did not end its specialized intelligence support at this time; it is believed that such support was critical in locating the safe house occupied by Guzmán and in enabling the Peruvian police intelligence unit to conduct its successful raid and capture Shining Path's leader.[55] The conclusion Peruvian authorities had reached—that the snaring of the head of the insurgent organization would be a devastating psychological and organizational blow—turned out to be correct. In an organization where a single individual held most of the power, removing that person was the group's death knell.

Beyond the physical and human destruction wrought by the insurgency and the government's response, another casualty was Peru's democracy. Although President Fujimori defended his self-coup as necessary to prevail against Shining Path, most observers conclude that success occurred in spite of the suspension of congress, the constitution, and the judiciary, not because of it. The military, frustrated by failures of the elected governments of the 1980s to stem the insurgency or to govern effectively, put together amid the chaos of the last months of the García government a plan for gaining greater control over the process, the so-called Libro Verde, or Green Book. This plan envisioned much stronger executive control, a comprehensive counterinsurgency strategy as articulated in the *Countersubversive Manual,* and the implementation of free-market principles to restore the economy.[56]

With the election of Alberto Fujimori to the presidency in 1990, the military saw an opportunity to accomplish the Libro Verde objectives through civilian rule. Since Fujimori did not have a strong party apparatus to support him, the military became his major pillar of institutional support and backed his decision to suspend constitutional government in April 1992. However, through patronage and careful cultivation of some top military officials, Fujimori and his close advisers, particularly Vlademiro Montesinos, and not the military itself became the controlling force in subsequent policy initiatives.

While it is not clear that Fujimori planned a coup from the outset of his administration, he certainly had no patience for the give-and-take of democratic politics with the opposition majority in congress. On balance, the formal breakdown of democracy in Peru in 1992 can be attributed primarily to the corrosive forces of the people's war and counterinsurgency that had been at work for more than a decade, along with the multiple errors of elected civilian authority in other areas of governance, most particularly economic management.

Shining Path initiated its people's war at what appeared to be a most inopportune moment, on the eve of the most democratic elections in Peru's history. However, the guerrilla organization's visionary leadership, ideological conviction, and voluntarist strategy combined to enable it to advance in the remote countryside where the central government's control was tenuous at best. The government withdrawal from less defensible positions in the countryside created a political vacuum that Shining Path quickly filled. Whether by accident or design, Guzmán and his followers found that the central government lacked both the capacity and the commitment to respond effectively and that, when under growing pressure to do something, the government reacted with the repressive and insensitive force that Shining Path's radical Maoist ideology attributed to officialdom. This process served to create a cycle of negative causation that progressively created the conditions of a weakened and vulnerable state in a climate of increasingly generalized political violence. With the multiple errors of elected government in other arenas as well, especially in economic policy, the state's capacity for effective governance was progressively eroded.

Alberto Fujimori's election—the choice of someone who was not a career politician, who might lead the country out of the morass in which it found itself—was the public's act of electoral desperation. By its vote, the public in effect gave Fujimori the leeway to do whatever he thought necessary to overcome the profound and multifaceted malaise of the moment. Such popular desperation helps explain both public support for the harsh economic measures that were most painful in the short term and the public's willingness to accept the autogolpe as a possible solution to the Shining Path threat, especially in the context of Peruvian judges' release in early 1992 of more than 200 convicted guerrilla cadres "for good behavior."

Fujimori, without a party and with only the military to provide institutional support for his government, could not have acted without the armed forces' blessing. But the overriding concern at the moment of the self-coup was how to counter the continued advance of Shining Path within a context of severely weakened civilian institutions, intimidated officials, and discredited politicians. So on balance, whatever Fujimori's antidemocratic tendencies, the primary force that motivated and justified the autogolpe can be attributed to public support as well as official perception of the imminent threat of a Shining Path victory in a larger context of frustration over Peruvian democracy's multiple missteps and progressive delegitimization as a result.

As subsequent events were to demonstrate, even after the threat of Shining Path had passed, the Fujimori government continued to manipulate the system to stifle dissent and to ensure that it would continue to run the country. So instead of receiving acclaim for the success of the counterinsurgency effort and for the significant improvement in the economic and personal security of much of the citizenry, the former president continues to be pilloried for the abuses of power that he and his closest advisers committed while in office.

Shining Path, while still a minor presence in a few isolated parts of the country, has divided into radical and moderate factions. Guzmán, with a new trial that began in late 2005, has called for the end of the armed struggle for the nonce, so the once-feared insurgent organization no longer represents a threat to the Peruvian state, or to most of the population. Democracy has been reestablished, although it is still fraught with problems and challenges. While Peru still faces many difficulties, terrorism in the name of Mao is no longer one of them. Nevertheless, the continuing fragility of democratic process and procedures, the erosion of confidence by most Peruvians in their government, and the inability of the Toledo administration to channel constructively almost constant local and regional protest movements provide a context within which another insurgency, perhaps even one led by Shining Path, could emerge.

NOTES

1. Carol Graham, *Peru's APRA: Parties, Politics, and the Elusive Quest for Democracy* (Boulder, CO: Lynne Rienner, 1992), 23–35.

2. Ibid., 37–39.

3. Philip Mauceri, *State under Siege: Development and Policy Making in Peru* (Boulder, CO: Westview, 1996), 21–25.

4. Gustavo Gorriti Ellenbogen, *Sendero: La historia de la guerra milenaria en el Perú* (Lima: Editorial Apoyo, 1990).

5. David Scott Palmer, "Rebellion in Rural Peru: The Origins and Evolution of Sendero Luminoso," *Comparative Politics* 18, no. 2 (January 1986): 128–29.

6. Cynthia McClintock, "Theories of Revolution and the Case of Peru," in *Shining Path of Peru,* ed. David Scott Palmer, 2nd edition (New York: St. Martin's, 1994), 244–45.

7. David Scott Palmer, "Peru's Persistent Problems," *Current History* 89, no. 543 (January 1990): 6–7. The casualty figures cited here have been revised

sharply upward by Peru's Comisión de la Verdad y Reconciliación (Truth and Reconciliation Commission) in its 2003 report, noted below in note 51.

8. Carlos Iván Degregori, *Ayacucho 1969–1979: El surgimiento de Sendero Luminoso* (Lima: Instituto de Estudios Peruanos, 1990).

9. Fernando Romero Pintado, "New Design for an Old University: San Cristóbal de Huamanga," *Américas* (December 1961).

10. Gustavo Gorriti, "Shining Path's Stalin and Trotsky," in *Shining Path of Peru,* ed. Palmer, 167–77.

11. Degregori, *Ayacucho 1969–1979*, 41–47.

12. Gorriti Ellenbogen, *Sendero*, 51–54.

13. Peter Flindell Klarén, *Peru: Society and Nationhood in the Andes* (New York: Oxford University Press, 2000), 369–70.

14. Simon Strong, *Sendero Luminoso: El movimiento subversivo más letal del mundo* (Lima: Peru Reporting, 1992), 106.

15. For a comprehensive overview of the MRTA, see Gordon H. McCormick, *Sharp Dressed Men: Peru's Tupac Amaru Revolutionary Movement* (Santa Monica, CA: RAND, 1993). It should be noted, however, that the MRTA was responsible for only a small proportion of incidents of political violence (less than 3 percent) and even fewer of the deaths attributed to guerrilla activity in Peru through the early 1990s (less than 1 percent).

16. José E. Gonzales, "Guerrillas and Coca in the Upper Huallaga Valley," in *Shining Path of Peru,* ed. Palmer, 123–44.

17. Gabriela Tarazona Sevillano, *Sendero Luminoso and the Threat of Narcoterrorism,* Center for Strategic and International Studies, Washington Papers, 144 (New York: Praeger, 1990).

18. David Scott Palmer, *Revolution from Above: Military Government and Popular Participation in Peru, 1968–1972* (Ithaca, NY: Cornell University Latin American Studies Program, 1973), 230–37.

19. Roberto C. Noel Moral, *Ayacucho: Testimonio de un soldado* (Lima: Publinor, 1989).

20. Julio Cotler, "La mecánica de la dominación interna y del cambio social en el Perú," *Peru Problema,* ed. José Matos Mar and others (Lima: Instituto de Estudios Peruanos, 1969), 145–88.

21. Carlos Tapia, *Las Fuerzas Armadas y Sendero Luminoso: Dos estratégias y un final* (Lima: Instituto de Estudios Peruanos, 1997), 27–43.

22. Philip Mauceri, "Military Politics and Counter-insurgency in Peru," *Journal of Interamerican Studies and World Affairs* 33, no. 4 (Winter 1991): 100.

23. David Scott Palmer, "National Security," in *Peru: A Country Study*, ed. Rex A. Hudson, Area Handbook Series, 4th ed. (Washington, DC: Federal Research Division, Library of Congress, 1993), 289, 292.

24. David Scott Palmer, "The Revolutionary Terrorism of Peru's Shining Path," in *Terrorism in Context*, ed. Martha Crenshaw (University Park: Pennsylvania State University Press, 1995), 271, table 7.1.

25. Palmer, "National Security," 292.

26. Ibid., 300.

27. Carlos Iván Degregori, "After the Fall of Abimael Guzmán: The Limits of Sendero Luminoso," in *The Peruvian Labyrinth: Polity, Society, Economy*, ed. Maxwell A. Cameron and Philip Mauceri (University Park: Pennsylvania State University Press, 1997), 179–91.

28. Carlos Iván Degregori, "Harvesting Storms: Peasant Rondas and the Defeat of Sendero Luminoso in Ayacucho," in *Shining and Other Paths: War and Society in Peru, 1980–1995*, ed. Steve J. Stern (Durham, NC: Duke University Press, 1998), 131–40; Billy Jean Isbell, "Shining Path and Peasant Responses in Rural Ayacucho," in *Shining Path of Peru*, ed. Palmer, 77–100; Tapia, *Las Fuerzas Armadas y Sendero Luminoso*, 103–4.

29. See the revealing interview given by Guzmán to Luis Borje Arce and Janet Talavera Sánchez in *El Diario*, a sympathetic Lima weekly, which they titled "La entrevista del siglo: El Presidente Gonzalo rompe el silencio." See *El Diario*, July 24, 1988, 2–48. Also, regarding the organizational structure and its vulnerabilities, see Benedicto Jiménez Bacca, *Inicio, desarrollo, y ocaso del terrorismo en el Perú* (Lima: SANKI, 2000), vol. 1.

30. Tapia, *Las Fuerzas Armadas y Sendero Luminoso*, 133–52.

31. Ibid., 43–55.

32. Orin Starn, "Sendero, soldados y ronderos en el Mantaro," *Quehacer* 74 (November–December 1991): 64–65; and Lewis Taylor, "La estratégia contrainsurgente: El PCP-SL y la guerra civil en el Perú, 1980–1996," *Debate Agrario* 26 (July 1997): 105–6.

33. David Scott Palmer, interviews with military personnel in Ayacucho, July–August 1998.

34. Orin Starn, "Sendero, soldados, y ronderos," 64; and Tapia, *Las Fuerzas Armadas y Sendero Luminoso*, 47–48.

35. Orin Starn, ed., *Hablan los ronderos: La búsqueda por la paz en los Andes*, Documento de Trabajo no. 45 (Lima: Instituto de Estudios Peruanos, 1993), 11–28.

36. Ponciano del Pino, "Family, Culture, and 'Revolution': Everyday Life with Sendero Luminoso," in *Shining and Other Paths*, ed. Stern, 161–62.

37. José Coronel, "Violencia política y respuestas campesinas en Huanta," in *Las rondas campesinas y la derrota de Sendero Luminoso,* ed. Carlos Iván Degregori and others (Lima: Instituto de Estudios Peruanos, 1996), 48–56.

38. Ponciano del Pino, "Tiempos de guerra y de dioses: Ronderos, evangélicos y senderistas en el valle del río Apurímac," in *Las rondas campesinas,* ed. Degregori and others, 181.

39. Orin Starn, "Villagers at Arms: War and Counterrevolution in the Central-South Andes," in *Shining and Other Paths,* ed. Stern, 232.

40. Gustavo Gorriti, "El día que cayó Sendero Luminoso," *Selecciones de Reader's Digest,* December 1996, 121, 123, 127.

41. Ibid.,136–42; and Benedicto Jiménez Bacca, *Inicio, desarrollo y ocaso del terrorismo en el Perú*, vol. 2, 740–56.

42. Sally Bowen, *The Fujimori File: Peru and Its President, 1990–2000* (Lima: Peru Monitor, 2000), 137–43.

43. Palmer, "Revolutionary Terrorism of Peru's Shining Path," 284, 304.

44. Comisión de Juristas Internacionales, *Informe sobre la administración de justicia en el Perú,* November 30, 1993 (typescript; International Commission of Jurists, Washington, DC, 1993).

45. Tapia, *Las Fuerzas Armadas y Sendero Luminoso,* 80–81; Bowen, *Fujimori File,* 55–57; and del Pino, "Family, Culture, and 'Revolution,'" 171, 177.

46. David Scott Palmer, "Soluciones ciudadanas y crisis política: El caso de Ayacucho," in *El juego politico: Fujimori, la oposición y las reglas,* ed. Fernando Tuesta Soldevilla (Lima: Fundación Fredrich Ebert, 1999), 285–90.

47. David Scott Palmer, "FONCODES y su impacto en la pacificación en el Perú: Observaciones generales y el caso de Ayacucho," in Fondo Nacional de Compensación y Desarrollo Nacional (FONCODES), *Concertando para el desarrollo: Lecciones aprendidas del FONCODES en sus estratégias de intervención* (Lima: Gráfica Medelius, 2001), 147–77.

48. David Scott Palmer, "Citizen Responses to Conflict and Political Crisis in Peru: Informal Politics in Ayacucho," in *What Justice? Whose Justice? Fighting for Fairness in Latin America,* ed. Susan Eva Eckstein and Timothy P. Wickham-Crowley (Berkeley: University of California Press, 2003), 233–54.

49. Much of the information derived for the economic policies of the Fujimori government is from Javier Iguíñiz, "La estrategia económica del gobierno de Fujimori: Una visión global," in *El Perú de Fujimori,* ed. John Crabtree and Jim Thomas (Lima: Universidad del Pacífico y el Instituto de Estudios Peruanos, 2000), 15–43.

50. John Crabtree, "Neopopulismo y el fenómeno Fujimori," in *El Perú de Fujimori,* ed. Crabtree and Thomas, 45–71.

51. Comisión de la Verdad y Reconciliación Perú, *Informe Final,* vol. 1, *Primera parte: El proceso, los hechos, las víctimas* (Lima: Navarrete, 2003), 169. But also see other sections of this volume for basic information and analysis of Peru's political violence.

52. Among others, Carmen Rosa Balbi and David Scott Palmer, "'Reinventing' Democracy in Peru," *Current History* 100, no. 643 (February 2001): 65–72.

53. "Estallido Vandálico," *Caretas* no. 1831, July 8, 2004, 10–15.

54. There are precedents. In 1959 the military responded quickly to a Trotskyite-organized rebellion in La Convención Valley of Cuzco, and again in 1965 to a Castro-inspired attempt to establish *focos* (small local centers of revolutionary instigators) in three isolated locations in the central Andean highlands. For La Convención, see Wesley W. Craig, Jr., "Peru: The Peasant Movement of La Convención," in *Latin American Peasant Movements,* ed. Henry A. Landsberger (Ithaca, NY: Cornell University Press, 1969), 274–96. For the Andean highlands, see Luis de la Puente Uceda, "The Peruvian Revolution: Concepts and Perspectives," *Monthly Review* 17, November 1965, 12–28. The failure of the Peruvian government to respond quickly to this new rural insurgency is puzzling, given its earlier successes. The explanation rests in part on President Belaúnde's aversion to deploying the armed forces again, as he had in 1965, because he feared a new cycle of military assertiveness and the possibility of another coup against him, as had occurred in 1968. In addition, the military itself, weakened as an institution by twelve years in power, was reluctant to get involved.

55. For this and other information on the U.S. role, see Cynthia McClintock and Fabian Vallas, *The United States and Peru: Cooperation at a Cost* (New York: Routledge, 2003), 69–73. See also Cynthia McClintock, *Revolutionary Movements in Latin America: El Salvador's FMLN and Peru's Shining Path* (Washington, DC: United States Institute of Peace Press, 1998), 145, 238, and passim. While not the focus of this study, the United States also contributed to the Peruvian military's preparations to end the dramatic December 1995 takeover of the Japanese ambassador's residence by the Tupac Amaru Revolutionary Movement. When extensive and drawn-out negotiations faltered, in mid-April 1996, Peru's counterterrorism unit mounted a spectacular and successful operation. It freed forty-two hostages, killed all fourteen MRTA guerrillas, and demonstrated the effectiveness of the counterterrorism capacity originally developed to deal with the Shining Path threat.

56. Enrique Obando, "Fujimori y las Fuerzas Armadas," in *El Perú de Fujimori,* ed. Crabtree and Thomas, 361–62.

8

COLOMBIA AND THE FARC

Failed Attempts to Stop Violence and Terrorism in a Weak State

Peter Waldmann

Colombia is a paradoxical case, probably as hard to understand for its own citizens as for foreigners. Although a country with an almost uninterrupted democratic tradition of more than 150 years, it has also been marked by periodic outbursts of violence, with hundreds of thousands of deaths. The following chapter has three purposes. First, I want to show that in cases such as Colombia, where violence has been increasing over decades, there is no "solution" in sight, at least not in the short run. This situation has much to do with the nature of the conflict in the country. Second, although the violent nonstate actors are often classified as terrorist in the political discussion, *terrorism,* in the narrow sense of the term, is only of limited significance in Colombia. The dynamics of violence are rather pushed forward by a war system that has pervaded all segments of society and penetrated all regions of the country. The third point refers to democracy. The Colombian case demonstrates that democracy not only can constitute an obstacle to effectively combating terrorism and political violence but can even, under certain circumstances, help to fuel both.

This paper is divided into two parts. The first is an introduction to the Colombian conflict setting, beginning with a brief overview of the consecutive waves of violence in the country, followed by a description of some structural features of Colombian society and politics, concluding with the presentation of the "players" of the conflict game, the state and the non-state actors, their aims, their support, and their methods. The second part is more analytical, trying to evaluate the government's strategy and methods for stopping violence, the role of the time factor and learning processes, the effect of early democratization, and, last but not least, the consequences of the "internationalization" of the conflict.

THE CONFLICT: HISTORY, STRUCTURAL CONTEXT, ACTORS, STRATEGIES

Waves of Violence

Since Colombia became independent in 1819, its history has been marked by two interconnected elements: democracy and violence.[1]

Colombia is one of the oldest democracies in Latin America; the military has never been an important power group in the country, and periods of unconstitutional authoritarian government have been the exception to the rule. This situation is due to the long-standing undisputed hegemony of the traditional parties—the Conservative Party and the Liberal Party—which were both founded in the middle of the nineteenth century. Both represented the interests of the traditional upper social class, the so-called oligarchy, but at the same time they were deeply rooted in broader segments of the population. While their programs hardly differed—as can be seen from the fact that both ratified the conservative constitution of 1886—they disagreed in one aspect: the public role of the church. The Liberals were anticlerical; the Conservatives, who lost much of their original influence during the twentieth century, defended fanatically the influence of the church. This dispute contributed considerably to a Manichaean vision of political conflicts on both sides and introduced a strong element of mutual intolerance and hate.[2]

Each party had a very particular understanding of democratic procedures and principles. Colombia was one of the first states in the Western Hemisphere to introduce universal male suffrage (1853), with elections taking place early and quite regularly. However, the winning party could never be certain to come into power, as illustrated by the following statement reportedly produced by the Conservative general Manuel Briceño in 1878: "In a country, where the votes are counted by the ruling party, the citizens who have voted must wait with a gun on their shoulders for the results of their elections."[3] In most cases, the ruling party would not abandon voluntarily the exercise of political power and the privileges associated with it. Only when the ruling party was split into rival factions would the opposition have a real chance of taking over after having won elections. Frequently, bloody civil wars were the consequence of elections. Instigated by ambitious leaders of the two hegemonic parties, civil wars stopped with the conclusion of a mutual pact or agreement, one that contained some sort of division of power and influence between the two parties involved and that granted amnesty to all those who had participated in the bloodshed. In fact, elections and the use of force were alternative instruments, employed by groups of the upper class to regulate internal conflicts related to the distribution of wealth and power.

This brings us to the second element that shaped the recent history of Colombia—violence. In general terms, four waves of violence can be distinguished since 1850.[4] The first wave occurred in the second half of the nineteenth century. During this period, there were seven civil wars, the last of which, the so-called War of the Thousand Days (1899–1902), was particularly cruel. About 100,000 people died, an extremely high death toll considering the low density of the population at the time.

The second wave is commonly known as la Violencia.[5] Between 1949 and 1958, about 250,000 people were killed in a conflict that initially bore resemblance to a party conflict in the traditional sense, then developed its own dynamics. Banditry and criminal violence expanded into the countryside and superseded the political motives of violence. To put an end to this situation, party elites first accepted a military dictatorship of five years and after that agreed on alternating with each other in government.

This was the period of the National Front, which officially lasted from 1958 to 1974—although the informal consequences of agreement politics could be felt well into the 1980s—constituting the last time order and peace could be restored, at least on an external, superficial level, by a pact between the two dominant parties.[6] I say "superficial" because, as we know today, the difficulty of forming legal opposition at the time fostered the emergence of a third wave of violence. In the 1960s, several guerrilla organizations emerged to oppose the cartel of the ruling parties. These organizations were partly inspired by the success of the Cuban Revolution and partly rooted in older local traditions, different from the Cuban model.[7] Some of these organizations abandoned the armed struggle after fighting for fifteen or twenty years; others, especially the FARC (Fuerzas Armadas Revolucionarias de Colombia) and the ELN (Ejercito de Liberación Nacional), proved to be long-lasting and successful.

Finally, the last wave of violence was triggered by the drug business in the middle 1980s. Drugs transformed the traditional value system of Colombia, which was based on relative austerity and industriousness. Also, the drug business added new patterns and goals to traditional forms of violence. Meanwhile, violence pervaded all segments and fields of Colombian society.[8] There arose a strong right-wing movement consisting of death squads and paramilitary groups that reacted against the guerrilla groups and in response to a state that many people considered too weak to defend their interests. Furthermore, a great number of individuals and groups started to employ physical force, such as guns and revolvers, as a means to get by.

Some figures may be useful to show to what extent violence became part of everyday life in Colombia.[9] While in 1984, about 10,000 people were assassinated, five years later twice as many were killed. In the 1990s, an average of 25,000 people were killed every year. The whole decade produced 250,000 victims, a death toll as high as that of the entire Violencia period, considered a period of excessive, never-ending violence. With a yearly rate of more than 70 victims per 100,000 inhabitants, Colombia reached a dreadful record. Its death toll is now three times as high as that of Brazil, nine times as high as that of the United States, and twenty times as high as that of most European countries. For "massacres" (a term reserved for cases in which four or more persons are killed simultaneously) and kidnappings, Colombia holds the world record. Kidnapping has become a widespread technique, used especially by guerrilla forces to extort money from their victims. In 2001 more than 3,000 people were abducted. Many of them never reappeared, while some were sold to other underground organizations that kept them for months or years. From 1996 to 2001, about 15,000 kidnappings were registered in Colombia, with the real number probably much higher.

The steady expansion of violence gets to the very roots of society and presents a permanent challenge for its structures and even its identity. One expression of this structural crisis is that about two million people in

Colombia, about 5 percent of the entire population, are moving constantly through the country, seeking to escape from violence.[10] Many of them leave the countryside, preferring to live in big cities, where they feel safer and less exposed. Another one million people have left the country for Europe or the United States because they were threatened or believed themselves to be in danger. Many of those who went abroad are outstanding professionals, intellectuals, and managers. The country suffers from an increasing brain drain that might reduce its capacity to resolve its problems.

To complete the picture, I must add two remarks concerning the nature of violence predominant in the country. First, it is worthwhile mentioning that most violent acts are carried out by groups and not by isolated individuals. Thus, individual emotional motives can be ruled out. Instead, we can assume that extreme rationality and planning are at work. On the other side, it would be a mistake to conclude from the organized character of most violent attacks that they are related to politics. Only about 25 percent of all violent acts seem to fall into this category. The rest are carried out for a number of other reasons, among which economic ones rank highest.[11]

The first and third waves were clearly of a political nature in terms of their origins and purposes. The second wave, which was politically motivated in the beginning, soon escaped the control of the dominant parties and took an irregular, anomic course. The actual (fourth) wave seems to bear more resemblance to the Violencia period than the others. It was pushed forward by the drug business and was accompanied by a revival of former traditions of banditry and criminal violence that relegated political considerations to second place.[12] This anomic tendency made it almost easy for the government to find a way to bring the violence to an end.

Structural Features

To better understand the rising level of violence, we need to analyze some general features of Colombian society and politics: an extremely weak state, a multitude of nonstate violent actors, the economic strength combined with the centrifugal tendencies of the nonstate violent actors, and the manner in which political actors view law and democracy. As the last feature will be touched on in a special section, we will here examine only three.

The most important feature is the extreme weakness of the Colombian state, and it has two aspects—internal and external.[13] Expressions of the structural weakness of the state include a highly corrupt and inefficient administration, a deficient judicial system, and parties that are more like ad hoc formations around leading political figures than stable political organizations. The principle of the division of powers, which is the basis of the modern state, does not work in Colombia because every power leads its own course and neglects the demands and interests of the others. Frequently, the government cannot implement projects it had promised before elections because the presidential party itself blocks its initiatives. Also, the government does not automatically control all sections and departments of the executive branch. More than once, when opening a dialogue with guerrilla groups or making substantial concessions to them, the government has confronted strong resistance from the security forces, which do not follow the orders of the president but pursue a strategy responding to their own corporate interests.[14]

What is typical for the Colombian state and its relationship to its own organs also applies to its relationship with society: it never was able to dominate society, to penetrate and control it. It is not difficult to find reasons for the never-completed process of state building in Colombia. The geographic fragmentation of the country and its lack of substantial resources (financial as well as human) are two of them.[15] The main consequence of its weak position is that the state has never managed to obtain what Max Weber considered to be the most important attribute of modern state power: the legitimate monopoly over the exercise of physical force. As a matter of fact, the political elites did not even try to obtain this monopoly; they preferred instead to arm the citizens to help to defend their cause. A good example is Law 48 of 1968, which explicitly encouraged the formation of self-defense groups by authorizing the army to give them weapons.[16] But how can a society be persuaded to renounce violent means and methods when the state promotes the idea of armed self-defense and creates conditions for putting it into practice?

A second important feature is the plurality of collective violent actors.[17] Originally, there were six guerrilla organizations of some importance. While four of them decided in the late 1980s to give up the armed struggle, two of them, the FARC and the ELN, still exist. They have their own leadership and traditions. They follow their own strategies and only occasionally coordinate their actions. There is not only conflict between the state and the guerrilla forces, however. On the extreme right, another violent movement, which pretends to defend citizens against pressures and attacks from left-wing extremists, has taken shape. Its principal actor is the AUC (Autodefensas Unidas de Colombia), an organization surrounded by many minor defense groups that act independently. Finally, myriad minor organizations—militias, professional killer groups, criminal bands, drug associations, and so on—have emerged, in addition to the main actors of the conflict (the state, guerrilla forces, and paramilitaries). All these actors use violence to pursue their (mostly materialistic) goals, thus contributing to the highly diffuse conflict situation in Colombia.

The triangular relationship among the main protagonists creates a complicated situation. The government cannot speak with only one voice to the guerrilla forces. It cannot opt between fighting them and negotiating with them, as it is confronted with two rebel organizations. Moreover, it has to take into account the third force, the paramilitary organization, when calculating the consequences of the steps and measures it takes against the guerrillas. Will paramilitaries join the political course of the government, or will they prefer to follow their own strategy to shape their own profile? Not only is it more difficult to find a common denominator for three macroactors and their diverging interests than to manage a situation in which the state is confronted with one main adversary, but also the multipolarized constellation promotes all kinds of strange alliances and maneuvers. So it can happen that the paramilitaries, the declared enemies of the guerrilla forces, may come to a tacit arrangement with them on a regional level, based on the common purpose of exploiting together the natural resources of the region without interference from the military or a state authority. There seems to be a general tendency of triangular constellations—this being predominantly the case in Colombia—to engage in limited tactical games while neglecting the overall problems of the country, which are war and peace.[18]

This tendency is further enhanced by the economic strength of the main conflict actors, combined with their lack of inner cohesion. Their strong financial situation has much to do with their involvement in the drug business, although this is not their only source of revenue. Our interest here focuses above all on the consequences of this financial power, concentrated in the hands of the leaders of these organizations. One consequence is obviously their high degree of independence from both the Colombian population and external powers or agencies.[19] It does not make much sense to try to induce Colombia's armed groups to make concessions by threatening them with international economic sanctions, because they need no support from third parties to sustain themselves economically. Another consequence is that because of their enormous financial resources, they have been able to build a powerful military apparatus. According to estimated figures, the FARC has sixteen thousand to twenty thousand men under its command; the ELN has about six thousand armed members; the AUC has around ten thousand armed men.[20] These are not little subversive groups that have to act undercover to avoid being destroyed by security forces. Instead, they act like real armies that have occupied considerable parts of Colombian territory and challenge state sovereignty while at the same time fighting with each other for power.

Although big and powerful, the armed camps are by no means homogeneous blocks with a clear hierarchical structure. As they expand their fronts over different zones of the country, inevitably some regional differentiation takes place, with local leaders showing signs of considerable local autonomy.[21] The FARC still maintains the highest degree of cohesiveness and unity, while the ELN, the other subversive organization, is marked by strong centrifugal tendencies. Such tendencies are particularly important for paramilitary organizations. Even if they succeed temporarily in forming a common platform under the leadership of H. Carlos Castaño, it remains uncertain whether this cohesion will last.[22]

The fissiparous forces of the main belligerent actors add a further degree of pluralism and incalculability to the conflict. Thus, even if the government comes to a pact or agreement with the top leaders of one group, it has to fear that parts of the force might split away and continue the fight.

In sum, Colombia is a special case in which the usual labels and schemes do not apply.[23] It is not the classic insurrection of a rebel group against a powerful state. Rather, the state is weak and the rebel groups are firmly consolidated in the national territory. Nor is it a typically "horizontal" conflict, as it would be, for example, in a civil war in which two segments of the population fought for predominance in a state. In the Colombian case, most of the population is terrified and passive. The picture that probably comes closest to the actual situation is that of a formal state competing for power with armed organizations that constitute a strange mixture of guerrillas, warlord groups, and protostates. To grasp the role of terror and terrorism within this competition, we have to cast a closer look at the aspirants to state power—the nonstate groups and their origins, aims, resources, and methods.

The Nonstate Actors: Guerrilla and Paramilitary Groups

The main part of this section will deal with the guerrilla forces. Remarks on their counterpart, the paramilitary forces, will come at the end.

In the 1970s and 1980s, six guerrilla organizations were operating in Colombian territory. Four of the weaker ones accepted, after a period of long negotiations, the government offer of amnesty and the reintegration of their members socially and politically into society. Only two of the six guerrilla organizations—the FARC and the ELN—remain and continue to fight. Each group has different origins and a slightly different ideological strategic outlook, but otherwise they exhibit similar characteristics.[24]

The FARC, the oldest surviving guerrilla organization of Latin America, has its roots in movements of rural self-defense against the ruthless expansion of landowners across extensive territories. Founded in the 1960s as the armed wing of the Communist Party of Colombia, it has as its main focus the protection of land and territory. The ELN, on the contrary, emerged from the initiative of priests and intellectuals inspired by the misunderstood success of the Cuban Revolution. This group intended to control strategic resources such as oil and electricity, specializing in sabotage against big companies and their installations, especially those owned by foreign enterprises in the northern parts of the country.

Both organizations originally shared the idea of overthrowing the government in order to create the conditions for a radical social revolution. It is hard to say to what extent they still pursue these original aims. The FARC in particular is not a very eloquent and outspoken guerrilla group. Its scarce programmatic papers point more to a nondogmatic socialist or social democratic orientation than to radical views and plans. The organizations share the conviction that only a military victory over the government and the forces of the establishment can bring about a solution to the country's problems.[25]

The emphasis put on the military side of the struggle is no coincidence. Both guerrilla organizations have turned into big war machines, with thousands of armed men and highly sophisticated weaponry at their disposal. Due to their military strength, the two groups control considerable parts of the national territory, exercising their influence in almost half of the municipalities of the country.[26] Meanwhile, a strange gap exists between the military and political roles of these organizations: while having built enormous military forces, they exhibit only low and vague ideological and political profiles. Far from trying to conquer the "hearts and minds" of the population, they prefer to control in an authoritarian and rigid way those who live in the territory they control. According to estimations based on opinion polls, the political support they can count on is slim. If there were elections, not even 5 percent of the population would give them their vote (the figure depending very much on the region).[27] One of their social functions—apart from protecting small coca farmers who make their living from this product—consists of offering regular and well-paid work within the organization to thousands of young, unintegrated, and uneducated men from the countryside who would not stand a chance of getting another job.

Are the FARC and the ELN terrorist organizations, and can their acts be classified as terrorist acts? Any approach to these questions should carefully distinguish between the "political" use of the label *terrorist* and its more or less (there are no absolute scientific standards in this field) impartial, "objective" use. If a militant group is cast into the category of "terrorist" by a government or an international political organization, its legitimacy is questioned and it risks being declared inherently bad and criminal. These are attributes that prevent society from taking a group seriously and reflecting on the aim of its fight. Colombia is a good example in this respect because, depending on the political circumstances, the guerrilla groups have at times been accepted as partners at the negotiation table and at times condemned as terrorists who deserve to be persecuted and punished.[28]

If we leave aside these political arguments and ask instead about the "real" nature of the organizations in question, we soon can conclude that neither the FARC nor the ELN is basically terrorist in its orientation and mode of fighting (although the ELN has some tendencies that could point at a terrorist direction).[29] Their primary goal is not to spread panic by carrying out spectacular attacks but to accumulate wealth and to develop military strength in order to expand their control over Colombian territory. This general statement does not preclude their occasional use of terrorist means and methods for tactical reasons. There are three ways that terrorism plays a role in Colombian conflicts.[30]

The typical scene of the first constellation is the big cities of Colombia (Bogotá, Medellín, Cali), where guerrilla forces are generally absent. When a guerrilla group feels weakened or is not being taken seriously by the authorities, it often commits spectacular acts of terror to win back the attention and respect of the government and the general public. Thus the M-19, a group that gave up the struggle in 1990, made a surprising entry into the Palace of Justice in Bogotá in 1985, taking hostage the high judges. Some time after this incident, the M-19 kidnapped a well-known Conservative politician, thus forcing the government to reopen negotiations with the guerrilla group. The FARC only sporadically made use of terrorist methods, for example when committing bomb attacks in the middle of Bogotá at the beginning of the presidency of Alvaro Uribe.[31]

The second area where terror and terrorism play a role is the regions in which guerrilla forces and paramilitary groups compete for power and influence.[32] What is at stake in this case is not so much political control over those zones but the exploitation of their economic resources. In this context, terror is the main instrument to subject people and to prevent them from supporting the enemy. It is noteworthy that the armed groups that compete for predominance in a region usually do not have direct confrontations with one another but prefer to terrorize the population. The high frequency of this sort of situation led Daniel Pécaut to describe the conflict in Colombia as a war against society.[33]

Finally, terror is employed to a minor degree to consolidate political and social control in zones where the guerrilla forces have virtually monopolized the use of violence. Sporadic sanctions, including executions, serve in this case as a form of demonstration of power. They constitute a low-cost instrument that serves to stabilize authoritarian rule, deter people from engaging in resistance or criminal acts, and secure a minimum level of compliance of a population, which, even if it does not sympathize with the rulers, at least obeys them.[34]

These three situations vary considerably from one another. Only the first one bears a resemblance to the classical model in which terrorist acts are essentially messages, employed by relatively weak groups, aimed at drawing public attention to their requests and forcing the powerful to react. In the other two cases, the situation is the other way around: by means of terror acts, powerful groups send signals to a defenseless population, making clear that the population has to either submit or move. These cases resemble the typical situation of right-wing terrorism or even state terror.

A few brief remarks about the paramilitary groups, especially the AUC, are necessary. While self-defense groups are almost as old as the guerrilla groups, they became a strong force in the 1980s and then in the 1990s developed into an organization with nationwide influence and publicity, which adopted the label AUC.[35] The main reason for creating paramilitary groups was the constant pressure exercised by guerrilla groups on big land-owners (many of whom had made their fortunes in the drug business). The self-defense groups, and later the paramilitaries, promised to fill the gap left by a weak state that was no longer able to protect its citizens and that proved to be unable to control the situation in zones far from the capital. While the guerrilla forces entered the national scene in the name of the powerless and the poor, the paramilitaries, on the contrary, sought the support of the upper classes and, even more, the middle classes. Their program consists basically of eradicating left-wing extremism and restoring order and security.

In spite of this declared antagonism, the AUC has learned a great deal from the guerrilla groups.[36] As a matter of fact, in its structures and way of functioning, it bears a striking resemblance to its adversaries. It has developed similar methods of fund-raising, especially the exploitation of the resources of rich regions; it has a symbiotic relationship with drug dealers; and it invents all kinds of "taxes" in the zones it controls. Its leaders understand that the key element of power is the occupation of territory. Its hierarchical structures are also similar to those of the FARC, and it likewise rules the zones in which it predominates in an archaic and authoritarian way. Even the men who join the AUC bear a strange resemblance to those belonging to the radical left-wing organizations; they are also young, uneducated, and unmarried, come from the hinterland, and need jobs.

Nevertheless, there is a difference between the guerrilla forces and the AUC: the AUC relies almost exclusively on terror to expand its scope of influence. The AUC commits more than 60 percent of all politically motivated assassinations and the majority of massacres, its men being systematically trained to be brutal and deterrent.[37] While this feature generates considerable approval from the broad population, especially the middle classes, it complicates the AUC's relationship with the government. This leads us to the next section.

Government Reaction

This section will not deal with the methods and measures taken by the government against violence in general but will focus on what is done to restrain politically motivated violence, which—as we pointed out—constitutes only a relatively small part of all violent acts in Colombia. First we will discuss how the government has confronted the guerrillas, and then we shall deal with its attitude toward the paramilitary groups.[38]

The government's response to the permanent presence of guerrilla organizations on Colombian territory has been ambivalent over the past twenty-five years. It has combined military and repressive measures with measures of reconciliation based on negotiation. There has been only one serious attempt to resolve the guerrilla problem by using exclusively repressive means, which happened in the first years of the presidency of C. Turbay Ayala (1978–82). We shall briefly recapitulate this experience as it helps to explain why none of the governments that followed repeated the experiment.

Turbay Ayala became president as a declared hard-liner.[39] He shared his intransigent view with Ronald Reagan, who was president of the United States at the time and saw in the guerrilla forces the extended arm of Moscow, which had tried to expand its scope of influence over Latin America. It is worthwhile remembering that this was the period when the so-called National Security Doctrine, propagated by the Pentagon, dominated the discussion on security matters within Latin American military and conservative political circles. According to this doctrine, the real threat was not some external enemy intending to attack the border but the internal "ideological" enemy, who subverted the minds of the people and the structure of society. Following this line of argument, Turbay Ayala not only declared a state of siege and passed a "statute of inner security," which gave him ample freedom to pursue radical left-wing groups, but also harassed fairly moderate groups that criticized his government by accusing them of procommunist tendencies. As a consequence of this vast repressive campaign, many young people who did not see a possibility of legally expressing their dissatisfaction ended up joining guerrilla groups, whose prestige and numerical strength were growing. The decisive moment came in February 1980 when the M-19, an urban guerrilla organization that was very popular at the time, occupied in a surprising attack the embassy of the Dominican Republic and held hostage sixteen ambassadors (among them the ambassador of the United States) who were dining there. For the government, this was a strong setback, from which it never really recovered. Even though it succeeded in liberating all the hostages after lengthy negotiations without making any substantial concession to the rebels (who were granted a safe journey to Cuba), and although it kept using martial language, its nimbus of strength was broken.

The succeeding governments concluded from this failed experiment that the guerrillas could be beaten only by repression combined with dialogue and negotiation. Possibly the experience of Turbay Ayala confirmed a deeply rooted conviction in Colombia dating back to the nineteenth century: the political enemy should never be treated just like a criminal, even if he has committed terrible atrocities.[40] Instead, at some point he should be offered a truce, whose consequences include amnesty granted for violent acts committed in the past. After 1980, all presidents who initially announced that they would make no concession to the insurgents but would fight them implacably later came up with offers of amnesty and peace. This strange juxtaposition, the never-ending war on one side and never-ending discourse of reconciliation and peace on the other, gives the Colombian situation its special significance compared with other guerrilla movements in the region.[41]

Although it is true that all governments proceeded in this dual track, when looking at it in more detail, we can recognize two variants of that strategy: the "small agenda" and the "large agenda." While some governments (those of Virgilio Barco and Cesar Gaviría) relied on the first, others (those of Belisario Betancur and Andrés Pastrana) followed the second.[42]

The small agenda consisted of offering the rebels an armistice and amnesty and asking them in return to renounce their far-reaching plans of social, economic, and political transformation. The clearest sign that the rebels accepted these conditions was that they handed over their arms. The government promised not to punish them and took a series of measures to help them reintegrate into society without making further concessions to them. On the whole, the peacemaking process and its outcome confirmed the point of view of the government—the only legitimate representative of the population and the nation—while pushing ex–guerrilla members into the role of outsiders who had unsuccessfully and illegitimately tried to question the existing order.

The alternative strategy of the large agenda started from very different assumptions. In this case, by the very fact of carrying out negotiations, the government admitted that there was something fundamentally wrong with the existing order, including its political system and its elites. The guerrilla groups, their members, and their leaders were not labeled outlaws who deserved harsh repression and persecution but were treated like political actors who had to be taken seriously and deserved fair treatment. Moreover, they had to be allowed to keep their arms. The label "large agenda" applies in this case, since the dialogue between the two sides was not limited to the personal future of the rebels but comprised all sorts of structural problems of the country. These were dealt with in a series of parallel discussions designed to lead to an elaborate and definite compromise between the conflicting parties. The broad dialogue thus initiated was based on the idea that the conflict could come to an end only with the creation of a new basic agreement, a treaty that resolved all controversial issues, thereby opening the prospect of a peaceful future.

The question arises as to which strategy was more successful. Unfortunately, neither of the two proved successful since the conflict never ended and violence never stopped. But the small agenda was more successful, leading to pacifying four of the six guerrilla groups. This partial success is related to a number of circumstances. A crucial one is the fact that those who proceeded according to the small agenda were better able to coordinate state activities and to integrate the military into their plans than those who did not. Military forces are of crucial importance for any attempt to put an end to the warlike situation in Colombia.[43]

Institutionally, the military took shape only late in the development of the country. The civil wars of the nineteenth century were almost exclusively carried out by civilians. Even during the time of la Violencia, in the middle of the last century, the army still played a minor role. Never having had to defend the country's borders against foreign enemies, the military became used to seeing its main role as solving internal conflicts. Its main objective now consists of defending the state autonomy and integrity against all forces who challenge it. Although its numerical strength—about 120,000 armed men (1998)—seems rather impressive at first sight, it must be taken into account that only about 20 percent of its members form part of combat units, the rest being mostly employed in bureaucratic jobs.[44] That means that as far as fighting strength is concerned, the regular army is just one actor among others, not superior to the FARC and smaller in size than all nonstate armies combined. Obviously, a military force of this limited size is unable to control the vast and highly fragmented Colombian territory.

The Colombian army, moreover, is known to be weak in terms of professional standards and efficiency. Only in recent years have training courses carried out by U.S. inspectors and military experts helped the Colombian army raise its fighting capacities and become a serious threat to the guerrillas.

In spite of the military's formal subordination to government orders—to ensure its loyalty, since 1991 a civilian has to be minister of defense—over the past decades it has continuously increased its institutional autonomy and political influence. Any decision made about security matters that does not have army support risks being exposed to very effective resistance.

As far as we know, the army does not draw a basic distinction between military measures and measures aimed at fighting terrorism.[45] Nor does it seem to distinguish clearly between counterinsurgency tactics and military ones. Instead of giving importance to the differentiation between military, counterinsurgency, and counterterrorist measures, the main line drawn by the security forces is between two types of politics: one based on the defense of state sovereignty, which means fighting the guerrillas, and the other based on acceptance of the guerrillas, offering them the chance to take up the role of political actor. The latter position, which is identical with the large agenda and which was put into practice by a number of presidents, is rejected by the majority of the military. In their eyes, it comes close to national treason.[46]

Let us now make a slight shift from the military to the paramilitary forces. The distance between them is not great, since, according to reliable sources, there exists a close link between the two, although the government officially denies this fact.[47] Are the paramilitary groups the allies of the government? Do their actions strengthen the authority of the state, or do they rather undermine its legitimacy? What is done by the government to stop or to control them?

These questions are hard to answer because the government maintains a relationship with these groups that is even more ambivalent than the one it has with its enemy, the guerrillas. The main reason for this ambivalence lies in the fact that self-defense groups and militias did not mushroom spontaneously but were deliberately and systematically created by the state itself. They are the child that is sometimes declared illegitimate but that in spite of causing trouble still keeps a close relationship with the parent. Since the nineteenth century, governments have been creating militias and have given them arms. This tradition, far from dead, has been taken up by the recently elected president Alvaro Uribe. Following the same device, he created an army of "informants" and encouraged peasants to build self-defense groups against guerrillas in recently colonized regions.[48] The main reason for this type of collective self-defense politics is that it turns out to be less expensive than a regular, well-equipped army. Second, these groups can do things that the official army never could without being severely criticized by the media and the NGOs. They can act in a more brutal and "efficient" way than soldiers can.[49]

As a matter of fact, there is hardly a Colombian government that has seriously tried to stop or eliminate these bands. Government behavior toward them varies from verbal rejection to explicit indifference and either hidden or open cooperation. There is no significant difference between presidents who cling to the small agenda and those who stick to the large agenda.[50] Most of the Colombian population understands the ruthless activities of the paramilitary groups. Hate and revenge are motives that are generally not rejected but respected by Colombian culture.[51] In particular, people belonging to the middle and upper classes, with family members who have been abducted or killed by guerrillas, openly cheer the existence of radical right-wing groups and accept their methods.

Therefore, the government runs no risk of losing its legitimacy within its own population (excluding small fractions of intellectuals) when tolerating the violent excesses of the paramilitary groups. There is a widespread conviction that a weak state that still has not undergone the whole process of state building is not in the position to adopt the legal and moral standards that apply to highly developed states in industrial and postindustrial societies. The problem of Colombia is that global opinion is made not by the least developed countries but by the most developed and powerful ones. And global opinion is very important for the country, as it is decisive for the financial and military support Colombia receives from abroad. For this very reason, Colombian political leaders often use a double language: they criticize the paramilitary groups or even attack them verbally while at the same time avoiding real efforts to interfere with their activities.

How to End the Conflict: Evaluation of Strategies and Measures

Successes, Failures, and Their Reasons

It is necessary to establish a criterion for success or failure before evaluating the efforts made to put an end to the conflict. This criterion cannot be abstract but has to take into account what Colombians consider to be a desirable outcome of the country's troubles. Different social groups and classes may have different ideas about the causes of the conflict and about how it can be resolved, but there are at least two desirable goals that everyone is likely to share. First, peace should be restored. Second, violence should be drastically reduced, allowing citizens to have normal lives without constant fear.

One goal does not automatically include the other. The cases of El Salvador and Guatemala show that a peace treaty between insurgents and the government does not necessarily curb violence.[52] Most Colombians think that without ending the conflict, the chances of reducing the high level of criminal violence are slim. That is why they give a certain priority to the objective of putting an end to the conflict.

As we saw, the failed attempt of Turbay Ayala to crush the guerrillas by force has led most Colombians to believe that repression on its own will not be successful but needs to be complemented with a peace agreement. Is that just an irrational belief based on the country's tradition of continuous feuds and peace treaties, or does this conviction have a rational foundation? I think it does. A weak state like Colombia that has been repeatedly humiliated by insurgents does not have the necessary strength to destroy its enemies. The military is one army among others; its numerical force does not exceed that of the armies built by the rebels. Although in the past year North American equipment and training have increased its efficiency, it is still far from able to control the whole country and beat the guerrilla groups.

Under these circumstances, a repressive campaign based on the declaration of a state of siege, along with an exaggerated martial discourse, can easily become counterproductive. In most cases, innocent citizens are persecuted, while armed criminals and rebels can more easily avoid harassment. Thus this sort of campaign generates growing indignation instead of submission, and the number of rebellious activities goes up instead of down. One of the best documented results of the "violence school" of the seventies is that nothing is worse for a government than exerting an intermediate and inconsistent degree of repression.[53] It irritates people without being able to suppress their protest. That is exactly what Colombian governments have done repeatedly in the past, especially after their negotiations with guerrilla forces failed. Their voices stiffened and their measures became harsher, thus displaying the repressive side of state power while at the same time not being able to fight seriously the enemies of the state, be they criminals or rebels.

In summary, repression did not work and does not work. On the other hand, peace negotiations have also not been successful, although they have raised many hopes. Colombian history of the past twenty-five years is not only a story of a never-ending series of conflicts but also one of permanent fruitless efforts to make peace. How can this be explained? What are the causes for these permanent failures?

Before trying to analyze them, it has to be stated that there were not only failures but also partial successes, one of them being the small-agenda negotiations carried out by Barco and Gaviría that made four guerrilla groups put down their weapons and accept their members' being integrated into society. It may be useful to sketch briefly this episode as it helps us to understand what went wrong in other cases.[54]

Barco took office without initially paying much attention to the guerrillas. He broke up the dialogue that his predecessor Betancur had initiated with the rebels and pointed out the necessity of fighting them by labeling them terrorists. Evidently, he wanted to stress the principle of state sovereignty and build up state power before beginning discussions on peace. When he finally began to negotiate with the guerrilla groups in the second half of his presidency, he proceeded in a very cautious and pragmatic fashion, which critical voices have described as "technical." He handled the negotiations by keeping their political profile low, and he left no doubt that it was up to him, the president of the republic, to define the agenda and the conditions for a possible end to the conflict. The rebel groups were promised amnesty if they handed over their arms. A special social, economic, and educational program was designed to help them reintegrate into society.

After some time, Barco announced that he would revise the national constitution, thus holding out to rebels the prospect of participation in a fundamental renovation of the political system. During the negotiations, which took place separately with each of the different guerrilla groups, Barco was careful to keep closely in touch with all important institutions within the executive branch. He was particularly concerned about coordinating his policy with the military's. Even though the peace talks could not be completed while he was in power, he had the satisfaction that under his successor, Gaviría, four guerilla groups—the M-19; the EPL; and two minor organizations, the Quintin Lame and the PRT—abandoned the armed struggle.[55]

The importance of this episode should not be overestimated, since the conflict was not definitely brought to an end. However, it contains some interesting lessons. The first and perhaps most important lesson is that negotiations with armed rebels can make sense and can lead to a successful conclusion. They can be started without granting to the insurgents the status of an acknowledged political force. There is granted the assumption that their fight has some legitimacy. It would be a contradiction in terms for the government to insist that the rebels are "terrorists" while negotiating with them at the same time.

In this case, the political culture of Colombia played a certain role, too, as it allowed this sort of agreement to take place.[56] But the nature of the conflict, centered around questions concerning distribution of power and wealth, also facilitated a peaceful outcome: conflicts for tangible and divisible goods are easier to solve than conflicts for symbolic values such as collective identity or religion.[57]

The way in which Barco started and controlled the negotiations also deserves some attention: He took his time and proceeded slowly. He first tried to strengthen his own position and never placed himself on the same level as the rebels. He had a clear and limited agenda that was consistent with the interests of other state institutions. And he did not make a big show about the negotiations, thus permitting both sides to make concessions without losing face.[58]

In the literature that deals with this episode, Barco appears in a less favorable light, and other factors explain his partial success. Generally, the line goes that the guerrilla organizations that surrendered felt weak and exhausted; that the end of the cold war encouraged them to give up their struggle; that the role of a charismatic leader, Carlos Pizarro, was decisive in the case of the M-19; and so on.[59] All these factors may have had some importance, but they were not sufficient to explain the successful end of the negotiations.

This idea becomes all the more evident if we compare the negotiations under Barco and Gaviría with those of Betancur and Pastrana, both protagonists of what we called the large agenda in the last section.[60] Betancur and Pastrana failed in their efforts to end the conflict because they neglected important questions of technical, tactical, and political nature, pinning their hopes entirely on the dynamics of the peace process itself.

Their peace agenda was not only much longer than the small agenda but also suffered from a lack of order, of establishing clear priorities. They put together a catalog of questions without reaching a consensus on the problems that had to be resolved in the first place.

The peace initiative in these cases had its roots in the promises given by the two candidates during the presidential election campaign; it was not a decision the state authorities had made. Therefore, from the beginning the peace process had strong political connotations. It generated time pressure and high expectations for its outcome and along with them the risk of great disappointments.

The whole posture adopted by Pastrana and Betancur was quite different from that of Barco. Instead of claiming to be respected as representatives of the sovereign power, they treated the rebel leaders on equal terms. They made generous concessions to them without asking for something in return, even before negotiations had started.

Those who hold that peace talks based on a large agenda are the best way to end conflict argue that the procedure was a necessary means to resolve the conflict and not an obstacle to it. They claim that the main difference between Barco's situation and that of the other two presidents was that Barco tried to finish an asymmetrical conflict, while Betancur and Pastrana faced a symmetrical one.[61] The small agenda, on which Barco and Gaviría based their negotiations in the beginning of their presidencies, basically made the demand that the guerrillas capitulate. According to those who believe in the large agenda, this posture could work only in an asymmetrical relationship, in which the rebels were in a clearly inferior position to the government. In contrast, the FARC and the ELN represent a far larger challenge to the state. Having struggled in the bush for decades and having built an impressive military machine, they will not simply give up their struggle for nothing. Therefore, supporters of the large agenda believe that in this case of a "symmetrical conflict," broader concepts of structural change and more substantial concessions will be necessary to establish peace. A small agenda will be insufficient; only a large agenda will have some chance of success.

The assumption that the state and the rebel forces have a symmetrical power relationship goes too far, in my opinion. However, I agree that the small agenda would not work in this case. Undoubtedly, the FARC and the ELN, and even the AUC, are far more powerful than the organizations that gave up the armed struggle in 1990. It is less clear whether the state should put itself on the same level as the insurgents, thus creating a sort of tabula rasa. In the course of more than 150 years of state tradition, even the fragile political system of Colombia has created concepts of law and legitimacy that cannot be abandoned suddenly. I doubt that declarations made by the state—about giving up all claims on sovereignty, negotiating on equal terms with the rebels, and anticipatory concessions—will persuade the guerrilla leaders to believe that a new foundational moment has arrived for the republic. Instead, this policy will provoke distrust or will foster the conviction that state authorities are in an extremely weak position. Both reactions are bad starting points for successful negotiations.

Instead, I hold that peace talks do not make much sense under the current circumstances of a weak state and powerful insurgent groups. The rebels do not need to negotiate since they can take by force almost all they want. This situation seems to me, as William Zartman would say, not yet "ripe for solution."[62] Negotiations that have failed are worse than negotiations that have not taken place, since they regularly lead to an increase in violence when it becomes clear that they were useless. Therefore, it is better to stop any attempt to find a peaceful outcome to the conflict. I will briefly enumerate the main arguments that support this thesis.

The first and perhaps most important one is that a weak state has no incentive to offer that would tempt rebels to make concessions. As mentioned in the beginning, the Colombian state never seriously tried to obtain a monopoly on legitimate political violence. The risk of being punished for killing a person has always been fairly negligible in Colombia. At present, the perpetrators of only 4 percent of all murders are convicted and put in jail.[63] As the state has generally failed to punish violent acts in a legal way, an offer of amnesty for rebels if they hand over arms is not very attractive. Also, on the symbolic level, it is not tempting for guerrillas to join a state and a society known as inefficient and corrupt while leaving or dissolving an organization that has accumulated power and prestige to the extent that it has become a sort of myth not only in Colombia but in all of Latin America.

While the state lacks resources to make attractive concessions to the insurgents, the latter possess almost all they need: territory, military strength to defend it, high financial capacity. The only thing they want is formal recognition of their dominant role in the zones they have occupied. The comfortable position of the guerrillas can be generalized to a certain extent for almost all nonstate actors: they feel comfortable with the conflict and have no reason to finish it. It is true that none of the main war factions has a chance to win; the overall situation can be described as a stalemate between them. But it is not a situation of "hurting stalemate," to use once more an expression coined by Zartman, that would compel them to look together for a way to solve the dilemma.[64] It is a balance of forces they can handle.

The drug business helps all parties get by under these circumstances. All of them profit from it in one way or another. The money, stemming from the production and commercialization of drugs, has created its own system. This system has its own dynamics and its own stability, which all the major partners in the conflict are interested in keeping.[65] Even the military would not be happy to stop the conflict definitely, for this would mean that soldiers would no longer receive additional pay when working in particularly dangerous regions or receive high-tech equipment and weaponry to fight the drug producers and the guerrilla forces that cooperate with them.

Third, it is very unlikely that the armed conflict will end in the near future with a peace treaty because of the technical and tactical deficiencies of negotiations—the lack of clearly defined goals at the beginning, the lack of coordination between the guerrilla organizations, the lack of coordination between the different peace talk arenas—that have taken place in the recent past. As long as the differentiated treatment of the FARC and the ELN continues, the war will go on, as it is not likely that parallel negotiations will have positive results at the same time. Meanwhile, the peace talks suffer from having become a routine that no one takes seriously anymore. Both sides tend to treat them like a tactical game while always considering the option of continuing the war. The trust between the two sides has been undermined in endless rounds of negotiation. This situation is also a reason for stopping peace efforts for a while.

But even if the conflicting parties finally subscribed to the treaty, it is uncertain whether its regulations would be fulfilled and respected. The FARC has not forgotten that after the foundation of a political party, the UP, in the mid-1980s, three thousand of its members were shot by right-wing extremists. As the state is unable to control the extreme right, it can give no guarantee that rebels returning to a normal civil life will suffer no damage. The problem could partly be resolved if external agents were in charge of controlling the implementation of the treaty,[66] but in a society such as Colombia, with strong anarchic tendencies, control and protection are never perfect.

Time Factor and Learning Process

It has been observed that governments of democratic states and guerrilla movements have contrasting notions of time.[67] The rhythm of governmental programs and actions is determined by election dates and periods. This system puts governments under constant pressure, obliging them to mobilize all their energies to get things done as quickly as possible. Guerrilla forces have no timetable. They fix a goal without giving an exact promise as to when it will be reached. Generally, the time horizon of rebels is vague; they speak of decades or generations that will pass before their goals will be fulfilled. In brief, time generally is in favor of the rebels and against democratic governments.[68]

Colombia is a good example of how these different concepts of time find their expression in political maneuvers and measures. It is no coincidence that most Colombian presidents of the past twenty-five years began their presidential period with a vigorous attempt to achieve peace. They knew that nothing would impress voters more than to succeed where their predecessors had failed. When after two years no peace was within reach, they changed their political strategy by announcing that they would fight the guerrillas and by emphasizing the harsh, authoritarian side of state power. It is risky to promise peace during the election campaign because this promise makes the president vulnerable to time pressure and extortion. Therefore, Barco's tactic is all the more remarkable. He promised nothing in the beginning, thus avoiding raising false expectations. On the whole, the rivalry between the parties and the rhythm of elections—typical features of a democratic regime—help explain the constant repetition of peace announcements and efforts in a situation of permanent warfare.

The guerrilla groups do not have this kind of problem since they are not responsible to an electorate. This situation gives them considerable space in which to maneuver and to adapt flexibly to new situations and challenges. This general statement does not apply in the same way to all organizations. The M-19, whose members were mostly students and intellectuals—people who are impatient almost by definition—was permanently under time pressure. In contrast, the FARC, an organization of peasant origin, followed its own rhythm with considerable skill and success. When necessary, it ceded territory to the security forces and moved to other areas. The mobilization of new financial resources after the breakdown of the socialist regimes, when logistically and politically the FARC and the ELN suddenly became quite isolated in the Western Hemisphere, was also an example of a successful adaptation to a new situation. Over the course of the decades, the FARC continuously expanded its scope of influence, bringing more and more regions under its control.

Recently, there are signs that the time horizons of both sides are converging. On the side of the government, leading politicians are beginning to see that peace is not just around the corner but must be understood as a long-term process. They are also becoming accustomed to the idea that the guerrillas will not disappear but instead constitute a power with which politicians will have to come to terms. As far as the guerrilla group is concerned, a comparable process seems to be taking place in the opposite direction. It has developed gradually from a movement that aspired to overthrow the government into an organization that has a marked interest in maintaining the status quo of the distribution of territory, power, and wealth.

From a more objective point of view, the plans and schedules of both sides have been overshadowed by the steady growth of violence and the never-ending emergence of new collective violent actors. Was there any crucial moment at which this process could have been interrupted? Which were the decisive elements that perpetuated it?

Let me start with the second question: Colombia is a good example of the often mentioned fact that systems of violence (in contrast to peace processes) do not need special incentives to continue. Rather, they have a tendency to perpetuate themselves.[69] In the Colombian case, two factors contributed additionally to fostering the expansion of violence. One was hate and thirst for revenge, two traits of human nature that are widely accepted in this country. The other factor was economic motive.[70] The rise of the drug business in the 1980s boosted violence in this period. Actually, the fact that armed groups compete for control over prosperous regions also stimulates violence.

It is hard to say whether this spiral of ever-increasing violence could have been stopped at a certain moment and how. Some experts think that the peace talks initiated by Betancur were a failed opportunity because at the time the level of violence was still much lower than it is today. Moreover, the number of collective violent actors was more limited. But Betancur was relatively isolated with his peace proposals; even the majority of his own party did not support him.[71] The important political actors at the time (including the guerrilla groups) were either not yet convinced of the need to end the violent conflict or not willing to make sacrifices to achieve peace.

On the other hand, it is difficult to discover fundamental mistakes on the part of the guerrilla forces. There were no evident weaknesses that, if skillfully exploited by the government, could have eased a peaceful end to the conflict.

In fact, guerrilla and terrorist groups tend to make mistakes, especially when their leaders are intellectuals or priests. This fact can be explained by a tendency rather typical for fanatical intellectuals, which consists of thinking in dogmatic, Manichaean categories, a tendency that prevents them from being realistic and pragmatic. There are plenty of examples of ideological dogmatism of insurgent groups in Latin America. The MIR in Chile, Shining Path in Peru, and the EPL in Colombia are good cases in point.

On the contrary, the FARC, the most important Colombian guerrilla organization, reflects in its strategies and tactical movements features of peasant mentality:[72] it is careful, pragmatic, and shrewd. It explores well whether something works and will not forget a lesson if it has made a mistake. It is hard to find a mistake that would have harmed the interest of the organization in the past. Perhaps in the long run, the strong emphasis placed on economic and military activities and the neglect of an ideological and political profile will prove counterproductive, but for the moment this is hard to say.[73]

With the exception of state officials, who have been losing influence continuously, the majority of the relevant actors are not convinced that stopping the fight would bring them any advantage. They understand that violence works and have learned how to use it for their corporate and individual interests.[74]

Democracy and Violence

Many analysts believe that the key to Colombia's problems lies in the relationship between democratization and violence. They hold that the cause of the conflict is a process of democratization that began early but was never accomplished, a promise that was once made but never fulfilled. The only way to restore peace, they say, is to eliminate the remaining authoritarian elements in the country's political system.[75]

There are, in fact, historical developments and events that seem to corroborate this theory. The Frente Nacional, for example, was an elite cartel formed by the two leading parties that governed the country for sixteen years but informally kept control for much longer. While it is accepted wisdom that the Frente Nacional stopped the spread of violence that had originated in the Violencia period, there is no doubt that at the same time it bred new violence. By not admitting any legal opposition, it forced dissatisfied young people to go underground. From this period stems the role of the guerrilla as a sort of substitute for legal opposition in a country where the leading parties have constituted a hegemonic bloc.[76]

On the one hand, an aborted process of democratization fostered violence. On the other, democracy itself, its principles and convictions, in some way stimulated violent behavior. Only because democratic values had already been generally accepted and internalized could nineteenth-century political leaders' call for defending the electoral victory by arms have had such a far-reaching mobilization effect. Moreover, the habit of Colombian governments of delegating the administration of public order and security to militias was based on a highly developed sense of responsibility for public duties. Civil self-defense groups and the AUC are in a way the expression of a "democratic" conviction: when the state is unable to protect its citizens, they have the right and the duty to take charge of the law by using their own means.[77]

It is difficult to know whether violence in Colombia stems from a lack of democracy or is the product of a perverted concept of democracy. Nevertheless, I argue that democratization will not help end the conflict more rapidly. There is generally no guarantee that bloodshed ends because the original causes of an internal war have been eliminated. Violent conflicts follow their own dynamics; they create actors and interests. In many cases, a peaceful solution depends much more on satisfying wishes and interests of these new armed groups than on eliminating the original evil.[78] Even if it were true that the ongoing conflict has its roots in a lack of democracy, this does not mean that a profound democratic reform would automatically bring the conflict to an end. Three main arguments contradict the assumption that there is a close link between democratization and peacemaking.

The first refers to the inner structure of collective actors who participate in peace negotiations. Negotiations turn out to be dysfunctional if groups are organized in too democratic a fashion. The more hierarchical their internal structures, the better for the process of peacemaking. This logic requires leaders who have the legitimacy to speak on behalf of the entire group, persons whose words are binding for all its members.

A similar principle obtains at the negotiation table. The talks and negotiations will progress only if the number of those who participate at the table is limited. The larger the circle of group representatives whose arguments have to be taken into account, the more difficult the task of finding a consensus and a solution that will be accepted by all participants. Some observers of the Colombian scene expressed with good intentions the idea that peace talks should be open to as many voices as possible, including NGOs and representatives of civil society. In my opinion, this point of view lacks all sense of feasibility.

The third argument is empirical. The general claim for more democracy in Colombia found its expression in programs of decentralization that have ranked high in the political reform agenda since the beginning of the 1980s. Betancur started giving more autonomy and money to municipalities, a political course that was to be cemented in the constitutional reform of 1990–91. These steps toward decentralization have by no means led to a reduction in violence. On the contrary, they generated more violence as they stimulated local conflict for control over the municipalities.[79]

Evidently, the permanent conflict has done great harm to democracy. Important political leaders who had been running for president were killed. The violent atmosphere that permeated the country produced political passivity and apathy. But even bigger were the damages suffered by the law and the principles underlying a "state of law." For decades the country was in a state of siege. Appeals to the courts of justice regarding the violation of human rights had no impact, as these institutions had neither competence nor influence. The security forces became increasingly autonomous and acted almost without any legal restrictions. At the same time, criminality grew dramatically. Colombia held the world record in number of abductions. Those unable to pay a private security service were left without protection for their lives and goods. The Colombian state became increasingly unable to keep public order and to offer a minimum amount of security to its citizens.[80]

It is ironic that the guerrilla organizations are better off than the state in this respect. In the regions they control, they guarantee peace and order. True, they do it in an archaic and authoritarian way. In the zones where they rule, there is no division of powers. One and the same person simultaneously exerts legislative, juridical, and executive functions. But from all we know, living conditions in the protostates created by the guerrillas are in a sense safer and more predictable than those in areas controlled by the "official" state.

More priority should be given to the construction of the state than to democratization. In theories of political development, the introduction of democratic reforms comes generally rather late, when the process of state building is almost completed.[81] In the case of Colombia, this process is far from having come to an end. The fact that the state never penetrated the whole national territory is an "external weakness" less alarming than the "internal weakness" of the state: the inefficiency and corruption of its cadres, the low moral standards of its politicians, and so on. Our thesis is that neither a large agenda nor profound democratization is the most relevant way to approach peace. I argue instead that the weak state should be transformed into at least a normal one, able to protect its citizens and capable of counting on their support and respect.[82]

External Events and Actors

The Colombian conflict is basically homemade. It emerged from internal tensions and structural problems that followed their own logic, hardly influenced by international developments. It was only in the 1990s that Colombia started to receive more attention from its northern neighbor, the main reason being its role in cocaine production and commerce with the United States. Simultaneously, Colombian presidents took the unprecedented step of asking other countries and international organizations to help resolve the problems of their country. Plan Colombia, designed under Pastrana and backed by the Clinton administration, was an important step in this direction. It included a bundle of projects aimed at eliminating coca production and eradicating coca plants.[83] George W. Bush adopted the politics of his predecessor while putting major emphasis on reinforcing the strength of Colombian military forces. Meanwhile, the country ranks third among countries that receive military aid from the United States (after Israel and Egypt).[84] While the bulk of the money goes into training military personnel and modernizing military equipment and weaponry, smaller sums have also been invested in social objectives.

The interests of the United States in Colombia are based on three issues: First and most important is the eradication of coca and fighting the product at its source, where it is produced. The second goal, intimately related to the first one without being openly admitted, lurks in the background. It is the elimination of Marxist guerrilla groups on Colombian ground. These groups, like the Castro regime in Cuba, represent a relic of the cold war. Third, it is likely that the United States also has some vested interest in gaining control over Colombia's huge oil reserves.[85]

Since September 11, 2001, the first two issues tend to have been treated like one. Already before that, the FARC, the ELN, and the AUC had been put on the U.S. State Department's list of terrorist organizations. The U.S. government nevertheless was in favor of Pastrana's peace endeavors and his approaching the FARC, and it insisted that it would not intervene in Colombia's internal affairs. After September 11, the atmosphere stiffened considerably; the earlier distinction between armed insurrection on the one hand and production and commercialization of drugs on the other became increasingly blurred. It was officially argued that it was impossible to separate the two areas because guerrilla troops protected coca cultivators and in return received taxes that helped them finance their political and military activities. However, it was probably more important for the changing attitude of the Bush administration that after the attacks on the Twin Towers, the FARC and the ELN were no longer considered to be armed groups with just a local radius of action. They started to be looked at as part of an international terrorist network that was expanding over the entire Andean region (or even farther). In fact, it is true that the conflict had a contagious effect on neighboring countries, especially Ecuador, Venezuela and Panama. The governments of these countries were alarmed about the expansion of violence across their borders and saw no way of preventing this from happening.[86]

Most international actors have a similar attitude. They express concern about the ongoing "war," denounce regularly the violation of basic human rights, and offer to mediate between the conflicting parties, but they refrain from exerting any form of pressure on them. The United States is the only exception to the rule, as it is more seriously involved with Colombian inner affairs. Can this involvement be successful? What will be its consequences?

Eliminating the cocaine business is an international task that cannot be resolved by Colombia on its own. It seems neither fair nor rational to stigmatize unilaterally those who are not able or willing to stop the production and commercialization of the tabooed substance, since they are only one aspect of a worldwide phenomenon. The drug problem can only be reduced or "resolved" by a joint effort of all countries and societies involved in it, those where drugs are produced as well as those where they are consumed.

Leaving the drug question aside, on an analytical level, two aspects of external influence on the Colombian situation can be distinguished. One is the aspect of peacemaking, the other that of state building.[87] In both aspects, external actors should avoid optimism about their potential to help shape the future of the country. As far as pacification is concerned, the Colombian situation is similar to that of other countries where international organizations and actors have sought to persuade the conflicting parties to give in and negotiate. The results of these multiple efforts are not encouraging.[88] Experience shows that a peaceful solution to a conflict depends on the hard-liners—the "hawks" on both sides—and not so much on the groups that seek reconciliation (in most cases the majority of the population). As long as the hard-liners cannot be persuaded that it would be more advantageous for them to come to an agreement than to continue the fight, the chances of ending the conflict are very limited. A Colombian once commented on the situation of his country, saying, "If the war is not dependent on external causes, peace is not either."[89]

Help by some external actors could on a short-term basis be quite successful. For example, if the United States intervened openly in Colombia, it could change the military balance in favor of government forces. In the long run, however, this intervention might prove counterproductive, as it would be denounced as a neoimperialist operation. Probably the FARC and the ELN would be very pleased if the United States made the mistake of openly supporting the Colombian government. This action would allow them to brush up their ideological image by declaring their profane raids to be an "anti-imperialist war," one of the most successful labels employed by insurgent groups that fight against a dominant state.[90]

As far as the process of state building is concerned, external help can be more or less useful. The weakness of the Colombian state finds its expression not only in its incomplete military and administrative control over the national territory but also in its deficient internal structures. In the vast arena of inner reforms (judicial, administrative, and so on), external advice and training might prove quite helpful. But this help has its limits: as civil wars can be ended only by the parties involved, the task of state building depends in the end on the capacities, energies, and goodwill of the autochthonous elites. A state built from outside the country has yet to be invented.

SUMMARY

As was stated in the beginning, the conflict situation in Colombia is very complicated; as far as we can see, it cannot be resolved in the short term by either negotiations or repression.

Repressive methods are not likely to end the conflict, because the government's security forces are not strong enough to defeat the rebels. Even if the current president, Alvaro Uribe, has some success in strengthening the military and throwing the guerrillas on the defensive, he is still far from establishing government control over the whole territory. The state's claim to exercise the monopoly of legitimate violence is restrained not only by left-wing insurgents but also by paramilitary organizations on the extreme right.

On the other hand, negotiations are not a promising path for the moment either. The experience of the late 1980s, when four guerrilla groups gave up the armed struggle, encouraging their members to reintegrate into civil life, was unique and cannot be repeated today. These groups were relatively weak and exhausted; moreover, the decision to abandon the fight and hand over their arms was stimulated by the government's promise to let them participate in the reform of the constitution. In contrast, the two remaining guerrilla organizations, the FARC and the ELN, are very strong, in economic as well as military terms. Having maintained themselves for decades and having considerable parts of the country's population and territory under their control, they see no reason to make major concessions to the government. In fact, if we exclude the government side, none of the important parties in the conflict seems to be seriously interested in ending the bloodshed. All have learned to profit from the war economy, which is based on kidnapping, the drug business, and the exploitation of the country's natural resources.

The thesis that at the root of the Colombian crisis is the hegemonic role of the two traditional political parties and the never-completed process of democratization is highly questionable. In fact, as a closer analysis shows, the effects of democratic persuasions and habits in the history of the country were quite ambivalent. It can even be maintained that in crucial situations it was not a lack of democracy but a perverted understanding of democratic principles that gave violence an additional impulse. Actually, a strong and responsible leadership of the main actors in the conflict would offer better chances for the settling of the conflict than the deepening and expansion of the process of democratization.

The primordial task in the present situation seems to be to strengthen state authority. Authority is more than just power; it means that the state not only tightens its external control over the people and the country but also gives more coherence, efficiency, and credibility to its inner structure—in short, that it establishes the legitimacy it has lost in the past decades. Only a strong, law-abiding, credible state will in the long run inspire trust in the people and have their backing. And only a strong state will be taken seriously by the rebels, inducing them eventually to make substantial concessions.

What can external actors do to help curb the Colombian crisis? I am afraid that their influence is quite limited, even though the last two Colombian presidents, Pastrana and Uribe, insisted very much on "internationalizing" the conflict. Whether it is possible to end a civil war by a peace agreement depends essentially on the will and the interest of the actors directly involved in it. Third parties can help prepare a dialogue and negotiations. They can assist the process of coming to consent and guarantee the fulfilment of the terms agreed on, but they cannot substitute for the conflicting parties. Something similar applies to the process of state building, which in Colombia has never really been accomplished. Here, too, the external actors' abilities to promote it should not be overestimated. They can send experts to assist local authorities, initiate training courses, stimulate reform programs, and so on, but the decisive steps have to be taken by the autochthonous elites themselves.

NOTES

1. On the history of violence and politics in Colombia, see Charles Bergquist, Ricardo Peñaranda, and Gonzalo Sánchez, eds., *Violence in Colombia: The Contemporary Crisis in Historical Perspective* (Wilmington, DE: SR Books, 1992); Gonzalo Sánchez and Ricardo Peñaranda, eds., *Pasado y presente de la violencia en Colombia* (Bogotá: Fondo Editorial CEREC, 1986); Heinrich-W. Krumwiede, *Politik und katholische Kirche im gesellschaftlichen Modernisierungsprozess: Tradition und Entwicklung in Kolumbien* (Hamburg: Hoffmann und Campe, 1980).

2. Krumwiede, *Politik und katholische Kirche,* 79–91.

3. Heinrich-W. Krumwiede, "Demokratie, Friedensprozesse und politische Gewalt: Der Fall Kolumbien aus einer zentral-amerikanischen Vergleichsperspektive," in *Politische Gewalt in Lateinamerika,* ed. Thomas Fischer and Michael Krennerich (Frankfurt am Main: Vervuert, 2000), 183.

4. Heidrun Zinecker, *Kolumbien: Wie viel Demokratisierung braucht der Frieden,* HSFK Report 2/2002 (policy paper sponsored by Hessische Stiftung Friedens- und Konfliktforschung, Frankfurt am Main), 7.

5. Thomas Fischer, "War and Peace in Colombia," in *Civil Wars: Consequences and Possibilities of Regulation,* ed. Heinrich-W. Krumwiede and Peter Waldmann (Baden-Baden: Nomos, 2000), 298–301.

6. Ulrich Zelinsky, *Parteien und politische Entwicklung in Kolumbien unter der Nationalen Front* (Meisenheim am Glan: Anton Hain, 1978); and Jonathan Hartlyn, "Civil Violence and Conflict Resolution: The Case of Colombia," in *Stopping the Killing: How Civil Wars End,* ed. Roy Licklider (New York and London: New York University Press, 1993), 39–61, 51.

7. Eduardo Pizarro, "La guerilla revolucionaria en Colombia," in *Pasado y presente,* ed. Sánchez and Peñaranda, 391–412.

8. Gonzalo Sánchez, "Introduction: Problems of Violence, Prospects for Peace," in *Violence in Colombia,* ed. Bergquist, Peñaranda, and Sánchez, 1. On the effect of the drug business on the increasing of violence, see Jonathan Hartlyn, "Civil Violence and Conflict Resolution," 51, 54.

9. The figures are based on Sabine Kurtenbach, *Durch mehr Krieg zum Frieden? Kolumbien vor dem Amtsantritt der Regierung Uribe,* no. 12/2002 (policy paper sponsored by Brennpunkt Lateinamerika, Institut für Iberoamerika-Kunde, Hamburg, June 2002); Heinrich-W. Krumwiede, "Demokratie, Friedensprozesse," 180; and Sánchez, "Introduction," 15–20.

10. Kurtenbach, *Durch mehr Krieg zum Frieden?* 121; Sánchez, "Introduction," 16.

11. Peter Waldmann, "Cotidianización de la violencia: El ejemplo de Colombia," in *Analisis político,* 32 (September–December 1997): 36; Kurtenbach, *Durch mehr Krieg zum Frieden?* 122; Thomas Fischer even maintains that murders committed for political reasons are estimated at only about 12 to 15 percent. See Thomas Fischer, "War and Peace in Colombia," 291.

12. Zinecker, *Kolumbien: Wie viel Demokratisierung,* 8.

13. Eduardo Pizarro, *Kolumbien: Aktuelle Situation und Zukunftsperspektiven für ein Land im Konflikt,* Analysen und Berichte, no. 4 (Rio de Janeiro: Konrad-Adenauer-Stiftung, November 2001), 16 and following pages; Jonathan Hartlyn, "Civil Violence and Conflict Resolution," 59; Peter Waldmann, "Friedensgespräche und Gewalteindämmung," in *Kolumbien* *zwischen Gewalteskalation und Friedenssuche,* ed. Sabine Kurtenbach (Frankfurt am Main: Vervuert Verlag, 2001), 80.

14. Adolfo León Atehortúa Cruz, "Colombie: La Place des militaires dans le conflit politique armé," *Problèmes d'Amérique Latine* 34 (July–September 1999): 75–88.

15. Pizarro, *Kolumbien,* 18.

16. Ibid., 20.

17. Heidrun Zinecker, *Kolumbien und El Salvador im longitudinalen Vergleich: Ein kritischer Beitrag zur Transitionsforschung aus historisch-struktureller und handlungstheoretischer Perspektive* (Leipzig: Manuskript Habilitationsschrift, 2002), 706–8.

18. Ibid., 707.

19. J. Zuluaga Nieto, "Das kolumbianische Labyrinth: Annäherung an die Dynamik von Krieg und Frieden," in *Kolumbien zwischen Gewalteskalation und Friedenssuche,* ed. Kurtenbach, 15–35.

20. These are estimations based, among others, on Pizarro, *Kolumbien,* 29; and Zinecker, *Kolumbien: Wie viel Demokratisierung,* 9 and following pages. The situation is changing continuously, and nobody knows exactly how many troops are at the disposal of every organization. Nevertheless, from a more structural point of view, it is unlikely that any of the major actors will be reduced to an insignificant secondary-power status the next time.

21. Zuluaga Niete, "Das kolumbianische Labyrinth," 21; Zinecker, *Kolumbien: Wie viel Demokratisierung,* 17; Francisco Legal Buitrago, "La seguridad durante el primer año del gobierno de Alvara Uribe Vélez (manuscript, Bogotá, 2003), 7.

22. In April 2004, Castaño suddenly disappeared. It is not clear whether he has been killed. That means that what will happen with the AUC in the future is quite open for the moment.

23. Pizarro, *Kolumbien,* 25–35.

24. On the roots and the development, the structure and the orientation of the guerrilla movement, see Zinecker, *Kolumbien und El Savador,* 272–363; Marc Chernick, "Negotiating Peace amid Multiple Forms of Violence: The Protracted Search for a Settlement to the Armed Conflicts in Colombia," in *Comparative Peace Processes in Latin America,* ed. Cynthia J. Arnson (Washington, DC/Stanford, CA: Woodrow Wilson Center Press/Stanford University Press, 2000), 162–68; and Pizarro, *Kolumbien,* 27–43.

25. Rafael Pardo Rueda, "The Prospects for Peace in Colombia: Lessons from Recent Experiences," *Inter-American Dialogue,* July 2002, www.thedialogue.org.

26. Gonzalo Sánchez, "Introduction," 15.

27. Pizarro, *Kolumbien,* 25.

28. Kurtenbach, *Durch mehr Krieg zum Frieden?* 124; Pizarro, *Kolumbien,* 46, 47.

29. Pizarro, *Kolumbien,* 47–49.

30. On the following Eric Lair, "El terror: Recurso estratégico de los actors armadas: Reflexiones en torno al conflicto colombiano," *Analisis Político* no. 37 (1999): 64–76.

31. Zinecker, *Kolumbien und El Salvador,* 810–25; F. Leal Buitrago, "La seguridad durante el primer año del gobierno de Alvaro Vélez Uribe," manuscripto, Bogotá, 2003," 3, 11; and Lair, "El terror," 72.

32. Lair, "El terror," 74.

33. Daniel Pécaut, *Guerra contra la sociedad* (Bogotá: Espasa Hoy, 2001).

34. Lair, "El terror," 73.

35. German Palacio, ed., *La irrupción del paraestado: Ensayos sobre la crisis Colombiana* (Bogotá: CEREC, 1990); and Fernando Cubides, "From Private to Public Violence: The Paramilitaries," in *Violence in Colombia,* ed. Bergquist, Peñaranda, and Sánchez, 127–50.

36. Cubides, "From Private to Public Violence," 132 and following pages.

37. J. Zuluaga Nieto, "Das kolumbianische Labyrinth," 24; Zinecker, *Kolumbien: Wie viel Demokratisierung,* 11.

38. This section is primarily based on the exhaustive study of Zinecker, *Kolumbien und El Salvador,* which gives a very detailed account of the successive initiatives taken by Colombian governments to end the armed conflict. Partial aspects of the never-ending peace process are treated in Socorro Ramírez and Luis Alberto Restrepo, *Actors en conflicto por la paz: El proceso de paz durante el gobierno de Belisario Betancur (1982–1986)* (Bogotá: Siglo veintiuno/CINEP, 1989); Marc W. Chernick, "Introducción: Aprender del pasado: Breve historia de los processo de paz en Colombia (1982–1996)," *Colombia International* 36 (1996): 4–8; and Jaime Zuluaga Nieto, "Antecedentes y perspectivas de la política de paz," in *Colombia Contemporanea,* ed. Saul Franco (Bogotá,[publisher?] 1996), 46–86.

39. J. Zuluaga Nieto, "Antecedentes y perspectivas," 48–54; Zinecker, *Kolumbien und El Salvador,* 786–87; and Hartlyn, "Civil Violence and Conflict Resolution," 52.

40. Sánchez, "Introduction," 11.

41. Ibid., 25.

42. Chernick, "Introducción: Aprender del pasado," 5–6.

43. Atehortúa Cruz, "Colombie: La Place des militaires," 75–87.

44. Ibid., 81. The figures relating to the numerical strength of the army must be looked at with similar precaution, as should be estimations of the size of rebel and paramilitary groups. Apparently, since the end of the past century, the number and the volume of military combat units have been considerably stepped up. Uribe claims that at present about fifty thousand armed men are fighting against the guerrilla forces.

45. A good example for this assumption is the attack of the M-19 on the Palace of Justice in the center of Bogotá in 1985. Evidently, this was a terrorist action intended to draw the attention of the whole nation to the fact that in the eyes of the rebels, the government had not fulfilled its promises. Yet the military reacted in a purely military fashion: it immediately stormed the palace, killing not only one hundred rebels but also eleven judges along with them. Zinecker, *Kolumbien und El Salvador,* 811–12.

46. Atehortúa Cruz, "Colombie: La Place des militaires," 83–84.

47. Kurtenbach, *Durch mehr Krieg zum Frieden?* 124.

48. Leal, "La seguridad," 19–23.

49. Pizarro, *Kolumbien,* 35–36.

50. Ibid., 38.

51. In his autobiography, Carlos Castaño, the leader of the AUC, openly admits that the desire to take revenge for the death of his father was his principal motive in founding a violent group. It is not by coincidence that his autobiography became a best seller in 2001–2. See Mauricio Aranguren Molina, *Mi confesion: Carlos Castaño revela sus secretos* (Bogotá: Editorial oveja negra, 2002), especially chapter 3, "El sequestro de mi padre."

52. With respect to El Salvador, see Heidrun Zinecker, *El Salvador nach dem Bürgerkrieg: Ambivalenzen eines schwierigen Friedens* (Frankfurt and New York: Campus, 2004), 3, 155–57.

53. Ted Robert Gurr, "A Causal Model of Civil Strife: A Comparative Analysis Using New Indices," in *Anger, Violence and Politics, Theories and Research,* ed. Ivo K. Feierabend, Rosalind Feierabend, and Ted Robert Gurr (Englewood Cliffs, NJ: Prentice Hall, 1972), 184–222.

54. For what follows, see Zinecker, *Kolumbien und El Salvador,* 818–58.

55. Ibid., 846–54.

56. Colombian political scientists and sociologists working on the ongoing conflict in their country, the *violentólogos,* are not exempt from this cultural influence. Their studies and essays generally reflect a deep desire to settle the armed conflict by a pacific arrangement.

57. Roy Licklider, "What Have We Learned and Where Do We Go from Here?" in *Stopping the Killing,* ed. Licklider, 303–22.

58. Zinecker, *Kolumbien und El Salvador,* 818 and following pages.

59. Chernick, "Introducción: Aprender del pasado," 5; and J. Zuluaga Nieto, "Antecedentes y perspectivas," 66–67. A more equitable judgement about Barco is given in R. Pardo, "Prospects for Peace," 4.

60. Zinecker, *Kolumbien und El Salvador,* 788–818, 911–42; S. Ramírez; and Restrepo, *Actores en conflicto.*

61. Zinecker, *Kolumbien und El Salvador,* 696, 785.

62. William Zartman, "The Unfinished Agenda: Negotiating Internal Conflicts," in *Stopping the Killing,* ed. Licklider, 20–34. The concept of "ripeness" is critically discussed by Heinrich-W. Krumwiede in his article "Possibilities for Regulating Civil Wars: Questions and Hypotheses," in *Civil Wars,* ed. Krumwiede and Waldmann, 37–60.

63. Sánchez, "Introduction," 12.

64. Zartman, "Unfinished Agenda," 26.

65. Nazih Richani, "The Political Economy of Violence: The War System in Colombia," *Journal of Interamerican Studies and World Affairs* 39, no. 2 (Summer 1997): 37–82. See also Kai-Uwe Richter Bonilla, *Kolumbien: Funktionsweise und Auswirkungen der Konfliktökonomie* (master's thesis, Erlangen-Nürnberg, 2003), especially chapter 4.

66. Barbara Walter, "Conclusion," in *Civil Wars, Insecurity and Intervention,* ed. Barbara Walter and Jack Snyder (New York: Columbia University Press, 1999), 305.

67. Peter Waldmann, *Bürgerkrieg und Terrorismus* (Munich: Gerling Akademie Verlag, 2003), 56–57.

68. Henry Kissinger described this dilemma with the following words: "The guerilla wins if he does not lose, the conventional army loses if it does not win," quoted in Zartman, "Unfinished Agenda," 25.

69. Peter Waldmann, "The Dynamics and Consequences of Civil Wars," in *Civil Wars,* ed. Krumwiede and Waldmann, 105–30; and Waldmann, *Bürgerkrieg und Terrorismus,* 214–31.

70. Pizarro, *Kolumbien,* 29–32; and N. Richani, "Political Economy of Violence," 56–58.

71. Sabine Kurtenbach, "Kann Kolumbien aus seiner eigenen Geschichte lernen? Die aktuelle Bedeutung des Friedensprozesses der Regierung Betancur," in *Kolumbien zwischen Gewalteskalation und Friedenssuche,* ed. Kurtenbach, 93–109.

72. Which does not mean that at present the FARC still consists primarily of peasants. Its rank-and-file members are often socially marginalized young men coming from uprooted families, while among its leaders there are also intellectuals. Nevertheless, the thinking and planning of the organization, its mentality and style, still strongly reflect its peasant origin.

73. On the learning processes within the FARC and the ELN, see Zinecker, *Kolumbien und El Salvador,* 950–71.

74. An uninterrupted line of imitation and "learning" in this sense runs down from the traditional elites, the "oligarchy," to the guerrilla forces and the paramilitary groups. Successively they have "learned" to handle the three key elements of power—territorial control, force, and the law—in a way that best serves their corporate interests. See Hartlyn, "Civil Violence and Conflict Resolution," 50–59; Krumwiede, "Demokratie, Friedensprozesse," 184; and Cubides, "From Private to Public Violence," 130 and following pages.

75. Two authors very representative of this line of argument are Jesus Antonio Bejarano, "Reflections," in *Comparative Peace Processes in Latin America,* ed. Arnson, 201; and Zinecker, *Kolumbien und El Salvador,* 985–1020.

76. Krumwiede, "Demokratie, Friedensprozesse," 181–82.

77. It is worth mentioning that civil self-defense groups are by no means something typical for Latin America. Death squads and cleansing commandos in this region generally stem from the public sector (retired policemen and soldiers, or policemen acting on their own account), thus reflecting the state-centered attitude of most people, including the officials. In contrast, we think it is due to the strong civil and democratic tradition of Colombia that in this country civil groups are taking the defense of order and public security into their own hands. On vigilantism, still of interest is H. Jon Rosenbaum and Peter C. Sederberg, "Vigilantism: An Analysis of Establishment Violence," in *Vigilante Politics*, ed. H. Jon Rosenbaum and Peter C. Sederberg (Philadelphia: University of Pennsylvania Press, 1976).

78. Heinrich-W. Krumwiede and Peter Waldmann, "Conclusions Regarding the Regulatory Possibilities of Civil Wars," in *Civil Wars,* ed. Krumwiede and Waldmann, 321–26.

79. Kurtenbach, "Kann Kolumbien aus seiner eigenen Geschichte lernen?" 107.

80. "As a consequence . . . the already fragile public sphere has shrunk and, in a way, has become a world of fear and force." See Sánchez, "Introduction: Problems of Violence," 14.

81. Stein Rokkan, "Die vergleichende Analyse der Staaten- und Nationenbildung: Modelle und Methoden," in *Theorien sozialen Wandels,* ed. Wolfgang Zapf (Cologne and Berlin: Kiepenheuer and Witsch, 1971), 229–52.

82. Leal, "La Seguridad," 24.

83. Thomas Fischer, "Durch mehr Krieg zum Frieden? Die USA und der Plan Colombia," in *Kolumbien zwischen Gewalteskalation und Friedenssuche,* ed. Kurtenbach, 206–27.

84. Pizarro, *Kolumbien,* 41.

85. Leal, "La seguridad," 9.

86. Pizarro, *Kolumbien,* 40–46.

87. Waldmann, "Friedensgespräche und Gewalteindämmung," 85–88.

88. Krumwiede and Waldmann, "Conclusions Regarding the Regulatory Possibilities," in *Civil Wars,* ed. Krumwiede and Waldman, 325–26.

89. Zinecker, *Kolumbien und El Salvador,* 708.

90. Charles Bergquist, "Waging War and Negotiating Peace," in *Violence in Colombia,* ed. Bergquist, Peñaranda, and Sánchez, 95–212.

9

ISRAEL, HAMAS, AND FATAH

Boaz Ganor

This chapter deals with the counterterrorism policy of Israel in its struggle against secular and radical Islamist terrorism (attacks carried out by Fatah, Hamas, Islamic Jihad, the Popular Front, and other organizations). The chapter opens with a chronological categorization of the challenges Israel has faced since the founding of the state in 1948, examining the organizations active against Israel and their characteristics and presenting a general review of counterterrorism activities carried out by Israel. The second part of the chapter focuses on Israel's counterterrorism policies between 1994 and 2005—that is, from the founding of the Palestinian Authority in the West Bank and the Gaza Strip until the disengagement from the Gaza Strip. This analysis scrutinizes Israel's offensive and defensive activities, its punitive administrative measures and their effectiveness, and the effectiveness of the various units that deal with the prevention of terrorist operations in Israel.

The chapter ends with conclusions and lessons to be learned from the Israeli operative experience in the sphere of counterterrorism and argues that Israel's goal when contending with terror has been not to eradicate the phenomenon but rather to confine the scope of the attacks and minimize damage. From this point of view, it appears that counterterrorism activity has achieved its goals. Israeli successes and failures in counterterrorism policy serve as a platform to discuss democracy's ability to efficiently cope with the spread of modern terrorism.

ISRAEL AND TERRORISM

Over the years, Israel has been perceived as one of the leading countries in the field of counterterrorism due to its long exposure to various types of terror attacks and the experience its intelligence communities, operational units, and decision makers have gained in dealing with terrorism. Ian Lesser, who made a comparison between Israel's counterterrorism policy and that of the United States, stated that the primary difference between them is that the Israeli approach is defined as "offensive," whereas the Americans can afford the luxury of being "defensive." He adds, however, that recent developments point to the fact that this distinction has lost much of its validity—if indeed it was ever really valid—because Israel's policy has become much more complex and the U.S. policy much more aggressive.[1]

In any case, few countries have suffered from so many diverse terrorist attacks resulting in so many casualties (especially relative to the number of citizens) over such a long period of time. Add to this the wide variety of terrorist organizations motivated by an even wider variety of ideologies, all operating to achieve diverse objectives and supported by numerous countries. Terrorism, understood as "the use of violence aimed against civilians for the purpose of attaining political, ideological, and religious goals," had its place in the Middle East even before the founding of the State of Israel and has indeed shadowed the creation and development of the state throughout its existence.

Phases of Terrorism

The challenge posed by Palestinian terrorism to Israel can be chronologically categorized as follows:

- **1948–58: the fedayeen period.** Sporadic and organized terrorist attacks combined with criminal activity, launched mainly by Palestinians who infiltrated Israel from neighboring Arab countries.
- **1959–73: the beginning of organized Palestinian terrorism.** The creation of the Palestinian terrorist groups—the Palestine Liberation Organization (PLO), the Popular Front for the Liberation of Palestine (PFLP), the Popular Front for the Liberation of Palestine/General Command (PFLP/GC), the Palestine Liberation Army (PLA), the Saiqa, the Democratic Front for the Liberation of Palestine (DFLP)—and the launching of "internal" terrorist attacks (from within Israel, the West

Bank, and the Gaza Strip), as well as "external" terrorist attacks (infiltration from Lebanon, Jordan, Syria, and the Mediterranean Sea) and "international" terrorist attacks (executed in foreign countries against Israeli interests).

- **1974–86: the institutionalization of terrorist groups.** The establishment of terrorist organizations in Lebanon; the formation of military units; the concentration on attacks originating in Lebanon and penetrating into Israel by land, sea, and air; and the development of artillery forces to carry out random strikes on civilian settlements in the north of Israel. After terrorist forces were shattered during the war in Lebanon, the years 1984 through 1986 saw a period of calm but resulted in the growth of Shia[book style] terror in Lebanon, with Hizballah as its center.

- **1987–93: the evolution of the intifada (popular uprising).** This period combined "personal initiative" terror attacks (usually motivated by personal reasoning, indoctrination, and incitement and mainly using "cold weapons" such as knives and axes) with "organized" attacks by terrorist organizations in order to achieve specific goals. The period saw the rise of Palestinian Islamic radical terrorist organizations: Palestinian Islamic Jihad (PIJ) and Hamas.

- **1994–2000: terrorism and the Oslo peace process.** The rise of the phenomenon of suicide attacks in Israel and terrorist activity launched into Israel from Palestinian Authority territory.

- **2000–05: the al-Aqsa intifada.** A war of attrition combining terrorist activity with guerrilla warfare. This period followed the breakdown of the Camp David Summit and included the terrorist activity of two PLO factions, the al-Aqsa Brigades and Tanzim.

In each of these periods, Israeli decision makers had to face new challenges that differed in their nature, scope, main area of attack, and identity of the perpetrating organizations. The various Israeli governments confronting these challenges had their own ideologies that affected the types and scale of counterterrorist measures they chose to use.

This section will focus on Israel's counterterrorist policies during the last two time spans: 1994 to 2005. This period marks a sharp change in the nature of Palestinian terrorism, with the emergence of suicide terrorism in Israel at the end of 1993 and its consequent escalation. This period also marks a change in the identity of the principal players in anti-Israel terrorism and a shift in preeminence from secular Palestinian groups, especially Fatah, to radical Islamic groups such as Hamas and Islamic Jihad. On the one hand, this period is characterized by Israel's almost Sisyphean attempt to cope with terrorism through the use of all possible means—offensive and defensive operations, punitive actions, and deterrence. On the other hand, and parallel with these efforts, was the attempt to neutralize the causes of terrorism and the motivation of those carrying out attacks through a political process, the Oslo Accords (1994–2000). The unique challenge of coping with terror during a peace process is particularly demanding and produces serious dilemmas that are characteristic of a variety of areas of conflict in the world.

The Palestinian Terrorist Organizations

In general, the Palestinian terrorist organizations that have acted against Israel can be classified into four main groups.

The *central group* consists mainly of the Fatah organization, the first modern Palestinian terrorist organization. It is the most established and strongest of all the organizations, founded in 1959 by a number of Palestinian students in Egypt (some of them from Gaza), under the leadership of Yassir Arafat. At the time of its founding, the ultimate aim of Fatah was to destroy Israel as an economic, political, and military entity and to replace it with Palestine.[2] As the cornerstone of its program, Fatah laid down two basic principles: independence of the nationalistic Palestinian movement from any Arab government, and the supremacy of the armed struggle as the only means for liberating Palestine. Small groups active as "satellites" of Fatah included the Palestine Liberation Front (PLF), a faction headed by Abu-el Abbas, who in 1977 had split from the PFLP/GC.

The *pro-Syrian group* includes a number of organizations dominated by Syria and acting as its puppets. In 1968 Ahmed Jibril left the PFLP, creating a new organization, the PFLP/GC. Jibril, who had served as an officer in the Syrian army, had very close ties with Syria, and the organization was soon under Syria's full sponsorship. The General Command did not adopt any specific ideologies in the social or political spheres except for its obligation to "liberate Palestine" through armed struggle. In 1969 the Syrian Ba'ath regime created another organization, the Saiqa. Syria thus undertook to strengthen its influence on the Palestinian movement, but as covertly as possible.

The *communist group* usually acted as a balance between the central and pro-Syrian groups in the Palestinian sphere and included both the PFLP and the DFLP. In December 1967, George Habash formed the PFLP. The new organization adopted an uncompromising ideological line that mixed a Marxist-Leninist approach to social and economic matters with the principle of a popular armed struggle for "Palestinian liberation." Habash saw the PFLP as a jumping-off place for the eradication of the Hashemite regime in Jordan and for the liberation of Palestine. In May 1969, against the backdrop of disagreements with Habash, the Popular Democratic Front for the Liberation of Palestine faction, headed by Na'af Hawatma, left the Popular Front. At first the Democratic Front drew up a communist ideological platform more radical than that of the Popular Front, but over the years it moderated this revolutionary stand, grew closer to Syria and Iraq, and developed close ties with communist bloc countries, especially the Soviet Union.

The *Islamic group* is the newest in the Palestinian sphere. During the mid-1980s, some activists considered the nonviolent attitude of the Muslim Brothers to be too passive. These activists split from the organization and formed several factions of Islamic Jihad in the Gaza Strip and the West Bank. These factions acted in the name of a religious mandate—jihad— to carry out terrorist attacks in Israel. The founders of the Islamic Jihad factions were very much influenced by the Islamic revolution in Iran and Hizballah activities in Lebanon. Soon the Palestinian Islamic Jihad, under the leadership of Fathi Shakaki, expanded at the expense of the other factions, which eventually disappeared. This organization enjoyed the support of several Islamic Arab countries, especially Iran, which became its patron. The outbreak of the intifada (the 1987 popular uprising) and the ascendancy of Islamic Jihad brought the Muslim Brothers to the conclusion that to preserve the relevance of the movement and prevent its activists from going over to the Palestinian Islamic Jihad, it had to change its traditional stance and take an active part in events occurring in the territories. To carry out this strategy, the Muslim Brothers created a military arm named Hamas, which took up the task of controlling the intifada in the territories. Hamas's ideology was a combination of Palestinian nationalism and aspirations for an independent state on all Palestinian territory under an Islamic sharia rule. In contrast to the Palestinian Islamic Jihad, Hamas made sure not to become a puppet of any Arab or Islamic countries, although the group did accept their support.

Israeli Counterterrorism Policy, 1948–94

Immediately following its founding in 1948, the State of Israel was forced to contend with both a wave of attacks from within the country and incursions from across its borders. The 1950s and early 1960s saw the beginning of the formation of an Israeli counterterrorism policy. Israeli security staff and decision makers regarded terrorism as a military problem requiring treatment separate from other security challenges, and therefore they created military units specializing in counterterrorism. These years saw the development of combat methods suitable to both counterterrorist and regular forces, especially the creation of Israel's retaliation policy, which focused on Arab countries that gave refuge to attacking Palestinian fedayeen cells. Israel's policy of retaliation was consolidated soon after the state was founded. Israeli occupation of the West Bank and Gaza Strip produced a challenge for Israel: control over about one million Palestinian Arabs. Israel operated concurrently to establish military rule and to safeguard civilian life and normal economic activity in the territories. These two approaches did not always go hand in hand, and the tension created between civilian life and military activities cast a shadow over the Israeli government in the territories for years to come.[3]

Post–1967 War. Immediately after the occupation of the territories, Moshe Dayan, minister of defense, formulated three basic principles that guided Israeli policy in the territories during the following years: minimal military presence in Palestinian cities and villages; minimum involvement of the military government in everyday life; and, most important, the "open-bridges" policy, which allowed residents of the territories to move freely from the West Bank to Jordan and to maintain their family and economic ties in neighboring Arab states. In addition to these principles, Israel allowed residents of the territories to join the Israeli workforce. The terrorist organizations tried to use these workers time and again for infiltration into Israel and for carrying out terrorist activities. The military government made clear to residents of the territories that they could take advantage of the opportunities offered them and maintain a normal lifestyle, but only if there were no terrorist incidents or expressions of civil disobedience. By using this two-sided approach, Israel attempted to neutralize the many attempts of the PLO to incite the Palestinian public in the territories to use terrorism. Most of the intelligence burden fell on the shoulders of the Israel Security Agency

(ISA), the Shin Bet, which after the 1967 War was handed the job of preventing terrorist activities. The ISA was quickly forced to put together from scratch an intelligence network throughout the territories. The ability of the ISA to grant or refuse various benefits to residents of the territories, including the possibility of work in Israel, passage over the bridges, and so forth, gave the ISA ideal resources for obtaining the cooperation of residents in the territories. The Israeli Defense Forces (IDF) had to contend with infiltration of terrorist cells into the territories and Israel through the nation's borders (usually from Jordan). Israel decided to establish a physical defense system along its borders, using a double line of fences with land mines between them and an electronic warning system. Israel laid a dirt road along the border and placed guard towers along its length. The IDF carried out both ground and vehicular patrols along the borders and pursued targets across them. In addition to the battle against terrorist and guerrilla attacks along the Lebanese and Jordanian borders, in the West Bank and Gaza Strip, and within the Green Line (1967 borders), Israel was forced to contend with terrorism in a new guise—attacks on Israeli and Jewish targets abroad. This new wave began in 1968 and was especially targeted against El Al planes and those belonging to foreign carriers flying into Israel. Israel's response to this type of attack fell into two main categories: offensive operations (including personal attacks against activists involved in initiating, planning, and carrying out attacks abroad) and defensive actions (developing means and methods of protection for El Al planes and Israeli representatives abroad).

The War in Lebanon (1982) and Its Aftermath. In 1982, after a series of artillery fights and failed cease-fires between Israel and the Palestinian organizations in Lebanon, the Israeli government decided to implement an operation intended to destroy the military strength of the Palestinian organizations in Lebanon, and in this regard it very quickly achieved its goal. The military and terrorist infrastructures of the Palestinian organizations in Lebanon were totally destroyed, and the leaders and operatives of the organizations were deported to eight different countries. Israel, however, actually had in mind far-reaching political goals that would have brought about an alliance with Lebanese Christians and a peace agreement with them. These goals were not realized, and as the IDF's presence in Lebanon continued, attacks against it increased, it absorbed many casualties, and Lebanese elements hostile to Israel—Hizballah—expanded. Against this background, on January 14, 1985, the government of Israel decided on a staged with-drawal from Lebanon, a withdrawal that actually ended with a pullback to the security zone in June 1985.[4]

After the war in Lebanon, Israeli policy ceased to include the "elimina-tion of terrorism" as its concrete goal and instead focused on reducing ter-rorism's scope and damage. In this regard, the 1980s saw a certain sobering of policy and a switch from an almost complete emphasis on military actions for eradicating terrorism, as had been accepted throughout the 1970s, to a more complex policy that included political initiatives toward the Palestinian people, although not yet toward the PLO itself.

The Intifada, 1987. One of the important milestones in the Israeli-Palestinian conflict was the intifada that broke out at the end of 1987. It was partly the result of Palestinian protest against the ongoing Israeli occupation of the West Bank and Gaza Strip, disillusionment with the lack of progress that terrorism had brought to residents of the territories through the years, and defiance against the dominance of Palestinians not living in the territo-ries. The uprising caught Israeli security forces unprepared. About a month after it broke out, the IDF changed its strategies, increased the number of its forces in the territories, and implemented drastic punitive measures: cur-fews, administrative detention, and so on. To avoid the use of arms, the forces also equipped themselves with cold weapons for personal defense and hand-to-hand combat—metal helmets, tear gas, rubber bullets, and clubs. Israel also began to use special forces units, Shimshon and Duvdevan, which operated undercover, close to incited mobs; the operatives usually dressed to blend in with the local population.

The intifada was significant because of the influence it had over the stra-tegic outlook of both Israel's decision makers and the public: recognition of the limitations of military force and punitive actions. This attitude resulted from disappointment in the ability of the military to overcome terrorism and political violence, and among other things it translated, though not necessarily consciously, into a change in goals for the Israeli security forces regarding anything having to do with coping with terrorism—a shift from the goal of the defeat and complete eradication of terrorism to only limiting its extent and the damage it caused.

To summarize, by 1994 the Israeli public and decision makers had considerable experience in various counterterrorist operations having both defensive and offensive components. They were, however, well aware of the limitations of these operations in overcoming terrorism. Both the Israeli failure to destroy the phenomenon in Lebanon and the Palestinian uprising made clear the need for an attempt to reach a mutually acceptable agreement.

ISRAEL AND TERRORISM, 1994–2005

Since 1994 the suicide attack has become the most common weapon in the Palestinian arsenal. In this kind of attack, explosive devices are either carried on the body, in a bag, or in a vehicle driven by the perpetrator. Suicide attacks, easy to prepare and carry out, are particularly difficult to thwart. From the moment the terrorist sets out on his mission, armed with his bomb, it is almost impossible to neutralize him without activating the bomb. More than that, the method allows the perpetrator to reach the precise location of his target at a time that will ensure the maximum number of victims. The willingness of the perpetrators to commit suicide focuses media and public attention on their zeal and dedication, inadvertently legitimizing their actions.

The Oslo Accords and the Suicide Attack Phenomenon

The first suicide attack in Israel, the West Bank, or the Gaza Strip took place on February 16, 1993. From then until the end of 2003, more than one hundred suicide attacks were carried out within Israel and in the territories, killing hundreds of Israelis and injuring thousands. Suicide attacks created a new challenge for security authorities and policymakers in Israel, and a special team was created within IDF intelligence to deal with the issue of radical Islamic suicide attacks.[5]

Yitzhak Rabin and his government quickly realized the danger inherent in this type of attack. In an appearance before the ISA, the prime minister said, "Since suicide attacks began in buses and in cars, putting into question the continuance of the political process, terrorism has effectively become a strategic threat, and most of the resources of the ISA must be devoted to the prevention of these attacks."[6]

After a suicide attack in November 1994, Rabin said, "We are facing a new type of terrorism, where the terrorist knows that he has no way of escape. If someone claims to have a hermetic solution, don't believe him. There is no choice but to cope with it in our own way."[7]

The foreign minister at that time, Shimon Peres, in explaining the complexity of the battle against suicide terrorism, listed the two problems that must be overcome to cope with terrorism as follows:

> The first is military-operational—how to fight the suicide terrorists. The second is broader—how to prevent public support for them. The correct way to fight against suicide terrorists is to discover them before they do anything, and this requires receiving intelligence both from our services and from the Palestinians. But the problem cannot be solved only through weaponry. We must produce an economic situation that will divert support for the Hamas to the alternative regime.[8]

The suicide and other attacks that resulted in mass casualties cast a shadow over the peace process and presented Israeli decision makers with a most difficult challenge. On the one hand, Rabin and his government saw the agreements formalized in Oslo and afterward as a strategic choice for Israel. But on the other hand, it was clear to Israeli decision makers that public support for the agreements depended on the level of quiet and personal security they would bring to Israel's people. In an attempt to overcome the difficulties in continuing the peace process while mass-casualty attacks were taking place, Rabin coined the following motto: "The Palestinian peace process will continue as if there were no terrorism, while the war against terrorism will be fought as if there were no peace process."[9]

On the surface, separating the peace process from the terrorist attacks allowed the government to disassociate the two, although the separation proved to be only artificial and failed to fulfill its most important goal; the public was not ready to accept a situation in which the peace process would continue while terrorist attacks were occurring, and this situation led to a gradual reduction in public support for the peace process.

Separating the peace process from the fight against terrorism also produced a situation wherein the Palestinian Authority had no motivation to strike the infrastructure of Hamas, or even to put pressure on it to abstain from attacks in Israel. In the absence of such motivation, and as long as the infrastructure of the movement was not affected, Hamas had a free hand to carry out attacks as it saw fit and to convey its objections to the peace process without putting the process and national Palestinian interests in danger. In this situation, the Palestinian Authority was able to manipulate the Islamic fundamentalists and achieve its political goals while repeatedly promising to prevent terrorist attacks in Israel. This was how it came to be that the responsibility for preventing attacks, and the failure to do so, first of all fell into the hands of a foreign body, the Palestinian Authority.

In April 1995, Prime Minister Yitzhak Rabin spelled out what Israeli policy makers expected from the Palestinian Authority regarding the war against terrorism: "The fundamental responsibility for preventing the coordination of such suicide operations, obtaining explosive materials and preparing attacks, belongs to the Palestinian Authority."[10] When it became clear that the Palestinian Authority had no intention of fulfilling its responsibilities according to the agreements, however, Israeli policy makers and the public alike were severely disappointed. In April 1995, General Shaul Mofaz, then in charge of the Southern Command, said, "For the first time in my career, my responsibility for fighting terrorism is dependent on someone else, and he is not doing his job as required, not according to our understandings, and not according to the agreement."[11]

The Palestinian Authority refrained from actually using its power to ground Hamas and PIJ military infrastructure. Instead of fighting their operational capability, the Palestinian Authority tried to weaken their motivation, using a strategy of "threats and persuasion" toward the fundamentalist Islamic organizations. Hassan Asfur, Arafat's adviser, said to an Israeli counterpart, "You fought terrorism only with force—and you failed. . . . Arafat has a different strategy, and it will prevail. Back him up, and you will see. We are negotiating with the Hamas, and many of their people are joining our side."[12]

In actuality, the agreement between the Palestinian Authority and the fundamentalists allowed them to keep their weapons and to operate and organize within Authority territory, on the condition that they not "embarrass" the PLO leadership and leave the Authority open to Israeli condemnation. In this manner, the Palestinian sides reached several "working agreements" that specified that the attacks could continue but could not originate in territories under control of the Authority. Sufian Abu Zaida, a senior PLO operative, declared in Gaza in April 1994, "Whoever thinks that the Palestinian police will attempt to stop attacks from outside the borders of the autonomy is in for a big surprise."[13] This is how Arafat was able to shirk responsibility for attacks despite the fact that all stages of the attacks, including the initiative, preparations, training, and assembling of bombs, were carried out from within the territory of the Authority.

When Palestinian autonomy was granted, intelligence became even more important to Israel. In January 1995, Chief of Staff Shahak said, "We have no solution to the suicide bombers. Eight months have passed since we withdrew from Gaza, and we have fewer sources of intelligence."[14] In September 1995, Brigadier General Amidror, head of the analysis division of army intelligence, declared, "Israel's intelligence capabilities in Gaza have gone down to zero, and the same will happen in Judea and Samaria when control is transferred to the Palestinian Authority."[15] One of the central expectations Israeli security services and decision makers had of the Palestinians after the formation of the Authority was that Authority security forces would use their intelligence-gathering capabilities to prevent attacks and cooperate with Israel. The Palestinians did develop excellent intelligence capabilities after the formation of the Authority. The large number of Palestinian security and intelligence agencies, the employment of numerous intelligence operatives in these forces, the fact that the operatives themselves were part of Palestinian society, and the clan-based nature of Palestinian society all gave the Palestinian Authority a tremendous amount of real-time intelligence on Hamas and the PIJ. In February 1995, the head of Israeli intelligence, General Sagie, told the Knesset Security and Foreign Affairs Committee, "The Palestinian police force has the intelligence and military capability to reach all terrorist command centers and homes, and they do so when they receive appropriate orders."[16]

It was expected that after the steep decline in intelligence from the autonomous areas, Israel would receive warning from its Palestinian associates of imminent terrorist attacks. This information, however, was not usually forthcoming, and the most the Authority would do was act itself to thwart an attack (if it believed such action to be in the interests of the Authority at that specific time). Sometimes the Palestinians failed to take appropriate action, even after receiving intelligence from Israel.[17]

Occasionally, when Israel had passed information on to the Palestinians regarding imminent terror attacks, the Palestinian security agencies would warn those preparing the attacks. In several cases, after receiving information from Israel, Palestinian security agencies thwarted the attacks but immediately afterward tried to identify Israel's source and neutralize him.[18]

The 1996 Elections and Netanyahu's Government

Following the Israeli elections of 1996, when the Likud Party returned to power, the new prime minister, Benjamin Netanyahu, put the issue of counterterrorism at the center of his political agenda and built his policies regarding relationships with the Palestinians around it. Against this background, the prime minister directed the security establishment to reexamine Israeli security conceptions regarding the fight against terrorism and directed the heads of the ISA and the Mossad to use more initiative when considering this sphere.[19]

One of the foundations of Netanyahu's policy toward the Palestinians was that of "reciprocity." The campaign slogan he used to conquer the electorate was "If they'll give—they'll get; if they don't give, they won't get," which became the very basis of Israeli policy toward the Palestinians.[20] The ongoing restrictions on the admission of Palestinians into Israel worsened the general condition in the territories. If, during the tenure of Rabin's government, the Palestinian Authority had no interest in stopping terrorist attacks because the government had decided that the attacks would not halt the peace process, Netanyahu's government communicated just the opposite: it made it clear that the peace process would not proceed even if there were no attacks.

Terrorism did not expand considerably during Netanyahu's tenure, as could be expected, because simultaneous to Palestinian loss of faith in the Israeli government, a new Palestinian interest was created—the establishment of strategic ties between the U.S. government and the CIA, on the one hand, and the Palestinian Authority and its security apparatus, on the other. During a visit to the United States, Arafat enjoyed the status of a head of state and ally, and senior Palestinian staff and security personnel were also treated accordingly. It was clear to them that a new wave of showcase attacks in Israel would threaten the strategic ties developing with the Americans.[21]

Barak's Government and the al-Aqsa Intifada

During the period that Ehud Barak was prime minister (1999–2000), Israel began to shift its political emphasis from the Palestinian sphere to that of Syria and Lebanon, with the twofold objective of withdrawing the IDF from Lebanon and reaching an agreement with the Syrians. This policy resulted in a unilateral withdrawal from all Lebanese territory in May 2000. The withdrawal from Lebanon caused Palestinian organizations to believe that if Hizballah could succeed in ridding itself of Israel in Lebanon, the Palestinians could do the same in the territories. As a result, the influence of Hizballah increased in the territories, and the traditional deterrent image of Israeli strength was damaged.

The most serious crisis of all, and the one that was to change the nature of violence and terrorism for years to come, was the failure of the Camp David Summit in July 2000. The main repercussion of its failure was the al-Aqsa intifada, a war of attrition involving an unprecedented number of terrorist and guerrilla attacks.

Two weeks after the breakout of the intifada, a Palestinian lynch mob slaughtered two reserve Israeli soldiers who had mistakenly entered the city of Ramallah in their car. The response was not long in coming. For the first time in many years, Israel used helicopters to carry out aerial attacks on targets in Gaza and Ramallah. Sixty-seven percent of the Israeli public, outraged by graphic TV films of the lynching, felt that the response had been too weak.[22] During the same period (November 2000), the IDF began to carry out targeted killings against Tanzim activists in the Fatah movement, as well as against those in the radical Islamic groups Hamas and Palestinian Islamic Jihad. Israel once again began to raze the houses of those suspected of carrying out terrorist attacks, and Prime Minister Barak lowered the military rank of those empowered to authorize such operations.[23]

Sharon's Government and the Disengagement from the Gaza Strip

In March 2001, the Israeli government changed hands, and the new prime minister, Ariel Sharon, declared that he would not enter into negotiations under fire. The precondition for any progress in the political process would be a halt in terrorist acts. Contrary to the policy of Israeli governments before 2000, which focused on conflict resolution in an attempt to reach a solution to the Israeli-Palestinian conflict, from then on Israel was engaged in crisis management while trying to minimize casualties to its side as much as possible. To this end, Israel used all possible means and methods: intelligence, offensive and defensive activities, deterrence, punitive actions, and so forth. During the first year of the al-Aqsa intifada, Israeli operations concentrated on incursions into the Palestinian Authority's territory, targeted assassinations, aerial attacks on laboratories producing explosive devices, and limited offensive ground actions in adjacent areas. At the beginning of 2002, as a result of a series of suicide attacks, Israel shifted its policy and reoccupied most Authority territories, stationing forces within them and limiting traffic in most areas (Operation Defensive Shield). Figure 9-1 illustrates the number of successful and unsuccessful attacks carried out against Israel during the first three years of the al-Aqsa intifada (2000–2003). This table shows that the shift in Israeli policy that took place at the beginning of 2002 did prove itself by considerably limiting the number of successful suicide attacks carried out against Israelis and by considerably increasing the number of attacks thwarted. Nonetheless, it is possible to learn from the table that during the same time, there was a considerable increase in the motivation of terrorist activists to use suicide attacks against Israel, as can be seen in the sharp rise in the monthly total of attacks and attempted attacks.

After the death of Yassir Arafat (on November 11, 2004) and the election of Mahmud Abbas (Abu-Mazen) as his successor as chairman of the Palestinian Authority, there was a crucial change in the Palestinian policy regarding the use of terrorism. For the first time ever, the elected leadership of the Palestinians believed that terrorism and violence did not pay and that terrorist activity actually threatened Palestinian national interests. As an outcome, the Palestinian Authority, with Egyptian support, reached an understanding with most terrorist groups and organizations—Hamas, the al-Aqsa Brigades, and others (excluding the PIJ), temporarily stopping terrorist activity

Figure 9-1: No. of Suicide Attacks 9/00–12/03

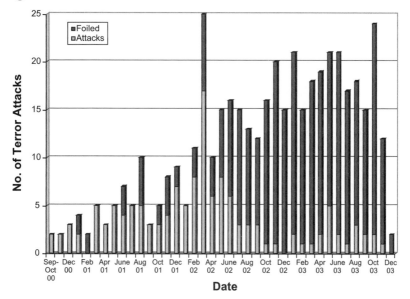

(at least until the Palestinian parliamentary elections in 2005). After the start of the U.S.-led operation in Iraq and the Sharon government's understanding that the Palestinians were not going to fulfill the preconditions of the Road Map for Peace (dismantling the Palestinian groups and removing their weapons), the Israeli government made the decision to withdraw unilaterally from the Gaza Strip and from a few settlements in the north of the West Bank. This decision was made as an outcome of a combination of calculations: the belief that there was no merit in an Israeli presence in the Gaza Strip—ideologically, strategically, religiously, or demographically—and the Israeli wish to support President Bush's initiative in fighting global terrorism by reducing international criticism extended toward America's ongoing support of Israel. The number of casualties caused to Israeli soldiers and settlers in the Gaza Strip could be considered additional factors in the reasoning process leading to the withdrawal decision. However, this last point was negligible in comparison to the initial considerations, since the number of Israeli casualties in the years before the withdrawal was very limited. In addition, the Israeli presence in Gaza never raised the same level of internal criticism that the Israeli military presence in Lebanon raised prior to the withdrawal from Lebanon (2000). Therefore, contrary to Hamas's argument in its propaganda after the Israeli unilateral withdrawal from Gaza, the Israeli decision to withdraw was not an outcome of terrorist successes in creating anxiety among the Israeli population and decision makers. Terrorist activities did not change the Israeli cost-benefit calculations.

ISRAELI COUNTERTERRORISM

Terrorism has had both direct and indirect effects on almost all Israeli government ministries, public institutions, and security and public entities. Through the years, Israeli entities that shoulder the burden of preventing terrorism developed along the lines of necessity and the characteristics of the terrorism they faced. In general, the Israeli framework involved in coping with terrorism can be divided into the intelligence, security, and civilian spheres.

Israeli Counterterrorism Apparatuses

Three intelligence organizations—Military Intelligence, the Institute for Special Operations (the Mossad), and the Israel Security Agency—are active in Israeli counterterrorism. One of the ISA's main missions is to thwart terror attacks against Israel. The ISA deals in the collection, processing, and assessment of intelligence and in the formulation of concrete warnings regarding the likelihood of terror attacks. This intelligence also helps in preparing offensive and defensive activity vis-à-vis terror organizations.

Counterterrorism tasks are imposed de facto on other security apparatuses: the Israel Police Force, the Border Police, and the Israeli Defense Forces.

The *Israel Police Force* is responsible for internal security in Israel and for preventing attacks within Israel's borders. As part of this responsibility, the police act to foil terror attacks by locating attackers on their way to the attack destination, securing sensitive facilities and crowded areas, and managing sites following terror attacks. The police force also assists in the investigation of terror attacks through its Identification and Forensic Science Division. Its Bomb Disposal Division neutralizes explosive devices.

Established in the early 1950s to protect border villages, *Border Police* forces are a division of the Israel Police Force and subordinate to it. The Border Police functions as an auxiliary force for the IDF to preserve order in the West Bank and Gaza and take part in ongoing security at the borders. The main Border Police counterterrorism unit is called Yamam. This unit carries out offensive missions such as the interception and arrest of terrorists and special missions such as liberating hostages.

The *Israeli Defense Forces* are responsible for guarding the state's borders, preventing terrorist penetration into Israel, controlling the West Bank and Gaza Strip, and conducting offensive activity against terror organizations in Palestinian Authority territory and in states that sponsor terrorism.

Both the IDF and the Israel Police Force have designated offensive units that deal with the interception and apprehension of terrorists in their areas of deployment. Their fighters are disguised as Palestinians and patrol terror organizations' deployment and activity areas.

During the 1990s, Israel created designated security units to secure schools and public transportation from possible terrorist attacks. Through the years, these units underwent changes in structure and subordination. Initially, they were founded and acted within the framework of the relevant government ministries (education and transportation), but they were subsequently transferred to the responsibility of the Israel Police, in cooperation with relevant municipalities.

Aside from these designated units, many additional institutions and government ministries are recruited for counterterrorist activities. They range from the Ministry of Health and hospitals, which have been forced to develop the special skills required to treat the hundreds of terror victims who endure injuries and trauma each month, to the Ministry of Finance and the National Insurance Institute, which are highly experienced in handling terror victims and allocating immediate and ongoing compensation to them and their families. The Ministry of Education and schools are forced to contend with the fears and anxiety of children and teens exposed to the horrors of terror, and the Ministry of Foreign Affairs is experienced in rebutting international condemnation of Israel's counterterrorism activities.

To coordinate these apparatuses, in the 1970s Israel established a special office headed by the prime minister's counterterrorism adviser. This office coordinated between the various government entities and security and intelligence agencies, translated government policy into operational activity, and supervised the implementation of government resolutions relating to counterterrorism. In 1997, the "adviser" became the "coordinator of counterterrorist activities" within the prime minister's office. Several years later, the coordinator's office was incorporated into the National Security Council, and since that time it has been a basic unit within the council. Despite the relatively senior status of the coordinator of counterterrorist activities, his actual influence over the formulation of Israel's counterterrorist policy is in fact quite limited. It is clear that the various security authorities and bodies involved in the struggle against terrorism in Israel have through the years developed strategies for cooperation, though they have never been set down in writing.

Between 1994 and 2004, the various Israeli governments used all acceptable means at their disposal—intelligence, offensive and defensive activities, deterrence, punitive actions—to fight Palestinian terrorist organizations. During the first part of this period (1994–2000), as mentioned earlier, the Israelis emphasized the political process as the way to diminish the motivation of Palestinians to carry out terrorism against Israel and to end the Israeli-Palestinian conflict with a settlement that would necessarily include an end to terrorism. During the second part of the period (2000–2004), the Israelis emphasized using all means necessary to deal with terrorism, cripple the ability of terrorists to carry out attacks, and reduce terrorism's influence on the morale of the Israeli public.

Israeli Counter- and Antiterrorism Activity

Offensive Activities. The establishment of autonomy for the territories changed the rules of the game for offensive activities against terror. In September 1994, Chief of Staff Ehud Barak said, "It was clear in advance that the IDF would not carry out preventative operations and other activities inside the autonomous territories. This task was clearly addressed to another party, and that party has lived up to the test in Gaza and in Jericho."[24]

The decision to place responsibility for counterterrorist operations within the autonomous territories in the hands of the Palestinian Authority was the result of a combination of elements: the complexity of operating in the locality (in the middle of an armed hostile population); the desire to support the sovereignty of the Palestinian Authority, which had only recently taken upon itself responsibility for security in the area; and the desire to maintain Arafat's status and image within the Authority so as not to endanger the continuation of the peace process. However, this governmental policy did not last long. When decision makers realized that fundamentalist Islamic groups were continuing their showcase attacks on Israel, and the Authority was not making use of its capabilities, Israel's policies underwent a change: security apparatuses would now operate within the autonomy, although in a discreet manner.

Undercover units and special forces concentrated on eliminating senior terrorist leaders suspected of mounting, planning, preparing, and launching terror attacks within Israel. In October 1994, after a suicide attack in the heart of Tel Aviv in which twenty-one people were killed and forty-three injured, Yitzhak Rabin announced that he had directed the security forces to eliminate terrorist leaders: "We must search for, find, and imprison or eliminate those who organize this terrorist activity."[25] In January 1995, Foreign Minister Shimon Peres repeated the commitment of the government to use offensive measures against the terrorists. He told the Knesset Foreign Affairs and Defense Committee: "It is up to us to take all measures, including those considered draconian, to locate and cripple the terrorists before they have a chance to carry out their schemes. It is up to us to act against them anywhere, without placing limitations on either the methods or the location."[26]

Carmi Gilon, former head of the ISA, notes, "During the two months between March '95 and February '96, twenty-three names were removed from the list of fugitives, of which ten were killed during shoot-outs, and the rest were captured."[27] Israeli decision makers and senior security personnel believed personal attacks to be the most effective method of fighting Palestinian terrorist organizations. The targeted killings were intended as a response to the Palestinian Authority's lack of desire and effectiveness in finding and jailing fugitives. Although in many cases Israel did not take responsibility for these actions, that did not prevent the "boomerang effect" (retaliatory terrorist attacks in response to Israeli attacks).

The most obvious example of the boomerang effect occurred in 1995 when several suicide attacks took place after the killing of "the Engineer"— Yichye Ayash. Referring to the killing, Gilon explains the rationale and effectiveness of offensive attacks against individual targets: "I felt relieved that Ayash was dead, not because of what he did, but because of what he would have done in the future. During the past three years his trademark was visible on almost all attacks, and it can be assumed that he was not about to change his bad habits . . . it is clear that when a fugitive is hit, the operational capability of the Hamas is also hit hard."[28]

During this period, Israel's offensive actions did not eliminate Palestinian terrorism or crush Hamas or Islamic Jihad, but Israel did place significant difficulties in the path of Palestinian terrorist organizations, their leaders, and operatives. They were forced to invest time and resources in defense, evasion, and escape—resources they would rather have directed toward carrying out many more attacks. In other words, Israel's offensive actions succeeded in limiting the ability of the organizations to carry out attacks and kept their capabilities low in comparison to their motivation.

Through the years, policies regarding offensive activities in Israel's fight against terrorism were based on the principle of deterrence—dissuading terrorist organizations, their activists, their leaders, and their collaborators from continuing their operations against Israel; and also deterring countries that sponsor the organizations by providing funds, weapons, safe refuge, a sympathetic environment, and the opportunity to infiltrate through their borders to targets in Israel.[29]

The wave of suicide attacks that took place in Israel from 1994 to 2004 put into question the ability of a country to deter a terrorist organization from launching attacks. In contrast to previous assessments, the argument that deterrence was impossible became more widely accepted, especially when a suicide terrorist was adamant in his objective to carry out his scheme, even at the cost of his life. A glimpse of this attitude was seen during a meeting of the government following the attack on a bus in Tel Aviv in October 1994. When Minister Shitrit suggested that Israel increase its deterrence capabilities, Prime Minister Rabin replied, "There is no deterrence capability when facing terror."[30] Benjamin Netanyahu, on the other hand, was convinced that even in the age of suicide bombers, it was possible to deter terrorists: "It is possible to deter a terrorist organization. Most of the organizations do not want to commit suicide. They are rational in character, and take into consideration costs and benefits."[31]

In spite of the debate among Israeli decision makers about the efficiency of deterring terror and suicide terrorists, they frequently justified counter-terrorist activities by citing their effectiveness in deterring terrorist organizations, attackers, and their collaborators. Nevertheless, figure 9-1 illustrates that despite Israel's impressive achievements in thwarting suicide attacks during the three years of the intifada (2000–2003), it did not decrease the level of motivation of the terrorist to attack, as reflected in the combined number of attacks and foiled attacks during this time period.

From the figure, it is reasonable to conclude that Israel's deterrent policies were not effective. While offensive and defensive actions achieved impressive successes in thwarting attacks, the total number of attempts was not reduced, and indeed it increased. If the objective of Israeli actions was to deter the organizations, their leaders, and their operatives from carrying out suicide attacks, these data show that the objective was not fulfilled. In spite of this, it is not possible to conclude from the data that it is necessarily impossible to deter terrorists or suicide bombers, only that the tactics used by Israel did not achieve this objective and that efforts must be made to tailor new methods to the unique challenges of suicide bombings.

Defensive Activities. The defensive-protective component of Israel's counter-terrorist effort includes protecting borders, sensitive infrastructure installations, symbolic targets, and locations with high population density. The foremost objective of defensive activities is to thwart terror attacks by preventing enemy infiltration, locating the terrorist on his way to carrying out the attack and stopping him, or preventing him from approaching the immediate location of his target. When these fail, the objective is to limit the damage caused. Besides the aim of actually foiling the attack, there may be other objectives, such as keeping terrorists from causing damage to the

public morale or enhancing the feeling of security within the targeted public. To fulfill these objectives, security forces carry out patrols and ambushes,
man checkpoints, and augment equipment used for guarding (fences, metal
detectors, sensors, radar, and video cameras) according to specific conditions
existing at the border or the target to be protected. Occasionally, the security
services will receive a specific warning of an imminent attack, affording
them the opportunity to reinforce security at the time and location required,
even though most defensive activities take place under conditions of intelligence uncertainty—that is, without any concrete intelligence about imminent attacks—and are based only on past experience and general assessments regarding the intentions of terrorist organizations.

Israel's relatively long borders in relation to its size, and the proximity
of the Israeli population to the Palestinian populations within the Palestinian Authority, however, make it extremely difficult to seal off Israel's borders
completely and to prevent infiltration of terrorist squads into Israeli-
populated areas.

In spite of the fact that Israel's decision makers and heads of the security
establishment continuously belittle the importance of defensive action
in thwarting terror attacks, Israel invests enormous financial resources
in equipment and personnel for defense. As soon as there is any sign of
threat, or upon receipt of specific warnings of an imminent terror attack,
police, border police, and special security forces are deployed to densely
populated areas.

In 2002, there was a change in the Israeli attitude toward the use of
defensive measures. As an outcome of the success of the fence surrounding
the Gaza Strip in preventing the infiltration of terrorists into Israel, and to
overcome the growing scale of suicide terrorism initiated and launched
from the West Bank, the Israeli government decided to build a security
barrier between the West Bank and Israel at an estimated cost of $2 bil-
lion.[32] Construction of this security fence began in the north of the West
Bank and continued southward, although the southern portion is not yet
complete. In parts of the barrier (less than 5 percent),[33] an electronic fence
was replaced with a tall wall to prevent infiltration and sniper shootings
from the Palestinian territory. The fence, accompanied with Israeli intelligence and offensive activity, has proven to be very successful in preventing
suicide attacks in Israel. By Israeli estimates, after building most of the

fence around the West Bank, Israel was successful in preventing more than 75 percent of attempts to launch suicide attacks in Israel.

Besides routine military security measures along the border and police activities within Israel, the Israeli security establishment took several other defensive measures, such as armoring buses that travel over "sensitive" routes in the territories; installing panic buttons in vehicles of Israeli civilian residents of the territories, which enable the authorities to locate and assist civilians in time of distress;[34] creating a special unit to be conspicuous on buses and at bus stops in an effort to spot terrorists and explosive devices; and augmenting security procedures at schools with special security units (these units were dismantled within a short time, and the responsibility was given to the police, who received the manpower and specialized tools needed to carry out these tasks). The amount budgeted for the protection of schools was lowered over the years. The intention was to shift from stationary (at the gates of schools) to ranging measures (mobile police patrols close to schools). With respect to public transportation, a similar process took place. At first it was difficult to find guards to serve in the units, despite the fact that the salary was relatively high.[35] In May 1995, the government decided to disband the public transportation security unit and handed responsibility over to the Israel Police, who received more manpower and an increased budget.[36] Other special units were disbanded in the same way, and the police took over their tasks.

Another form of public transportation that received special support from the government was taxi service. In August 1997, the government decided to offer taxi drivers a protection basket that included, among other things, a satellite location system for drivers in distress, transparent protective partitions to separate them from passengers, underwriting of self-defense courses for foiling terrorist acts, and personal weapons.[37] Israel also continued to invest major resources in protecting its only national airline, El Al. The cost of protecting the national airline reached $80 million during this period, with 75 percent of it funded by the government.[38]

In general, defensive actions are understood in Israel to be the last link in the chain of impeding and preventing terror. When the other links in the chain fail, the last link becomes immensely more important. But the severe terrorist attacks that occurred in Israel during the period under discussion obliged the establishment to search for appropriate defensive solutions based mainly on the civilian and police sectors, and not necessarily on the army.

Meir Dagan underestimates the importance of defensive activity in counterterrorism when he compares it with that of intelligence collection:

> It must be remembered that the number of possible targets for terrorists is
> almost infinite . . . it is impossible to place a guard at every location in
> the country. The only solution is pinpoint intelligence that leads to the ter-
> rorist about to carry out the attack, and your ability to cripple or stop him
> beforehand. . . . Most of our resources should not be invested guarding
> buses but in operational intelligence, so we can get to the terrorist before he
> places the bomb.[39]

An example of the achievement of security measures during the period
under discussion, however, was the suicide attack at the Dizengoff Center, a
mall in Tel Aviv, in March 1996. The attack, which took place during the
Purim holiday, was supposed to have taken place inside the closed area of
the mall. If that had occurred, the number of casualties would have
increased tenfold. The terrorist, however, decided to change his plans and
blew himself up outside the mall, apparently because of heavy security
placed at mall entrances.

As Brigadier General Presler, the prime minister's adviser on terrorism,
puts it, "Terrorists collect intelligence in preparation for their operations.
They send people to scout the city, and if the scout sees that we have
strengthened security it may deter them."[40]

An analysis of trends in Palestinian terror does not support the assumption that protective measures deter attackers. In some cases, defensive and
protective measures did identify attackers and foil attacks; however, these
successes were not attributable to deterrence of the perpetrators. Protective
measures, at most, disrupt the process and force operatives to change the
venue of their attacks. Of course, damage reduction must also be considered
an achievement in the struggle against terrorism. This objective is largely
obtained through the activities of the security forces and the Israel Police,
and through increased public vigilance. In Israel, civilians play a major role
in identifying suspicious objects and people, and many civilians volunteer in
the Civil Defense, an organization under the auspices of the Israel Police.
The participation of large numbers of volunteers has the effect of multiply-
ing the available forces and contributes to the success of defensive activities
by identifying and foiling some attacks and reducing the damage caused by
others. It also aids in supervision of the site after an attack has taken place.
Among other things, using volunteers in local civil guard groups raised the

morale of the public faced with terror, educated the public to be aware of suspicious objects or people and the possibility of imminent attacks, and mobilized the civilian population in the all-encompassing fight against terrorism. In summary, the cumulative experience of Israel in the defensive sphere has proven that even under prolonged terrorist threat, it is possible to conduct near-normal civilian life.

Administrative Measures against Terrorists and Their Accomplices. The special characteristics of terrorism, the elusiveness of terrorists, and the impotence of the legal and enforcement systems to cope with modern terrorism all caused Israel to frequently use administrative measures to thwart and prevent terrorism. One of the most frequently used measures was imposing a closure on villages and cities in the West Bank and the Gaza Strip out of fear that terrorist attacks would be launched from those areas. The aim of the closure was to provide maximum separation between the Israeli and Palestinian populations in the territories.

In general, it is possible to categorize the closures imposed by Israel into four types: (1) those imposed for a predetermined time frame, usually during a Palestinian memorial day or Jewish holiday; (2) those imposed for a short period of time, due to concrete intelligence warnings; (3) those imposed after a mass-casualty attack, partly to increase the feeling of security among Israeli citizens; and (4) those intended to place pressure on the Palestinian Authority to take certain security actions, for instance, jailing a fugitive terrorist.[41] The rationale behind closure was not, as many thought, punishment of Palestinian residents as a result of the attacks (though some maintained that the impact on the income of residents would generate pressure on terrorist organizations to abstain from continuing their attacks)[42] but first and foremost to stop the terrorist on his way to his target and to afford the Israeli security services a greater opportunity to spot such a terrorist as he penetrated into Israel. Security personnel and decision makers therefore maintained that closure could be an appropriate solution to terrorist attacks originated in the territories. In his address to the Knesset in April 1993, Rabin stressed the importance of closure when he said that "it returns personal security to 99.5 percent of the Israeli population."[43] Closure may have improved the feeling of security among Israeli citizens, and in certain situations it did prevent or postpone attacks, but at the same time it harmed the Palestinian economy and the livelihood of many Palestinians, occasionally producing unrest that terror organizations exploited, bringing about the escalation of violence in the territories. Rabin was also aware of the limitations of closure and said, "I told Arafat that fifteen thousand Palestinian workers would be allowed to return to their work in Israel. I did so against the security interests of Israel. I did so in order to prevent tensions that could have increased the terror in the Territories and diminished Palestinian belief that we are moving towards a solution."[44]

As a result of long-lasting closures, international organizations condemned Israel for its "starvation policies" against territory residents. These assertions illustrate the actual standpoint of international opinion regarding this subject.[45] Decision makers in Israel quickly emphasized that Israel did not use closure as a punitive measure but only as a means of prevention, imposed only when there was an immediate fear of terror attacks in Israel. Minister of Defense Yitzhak Mordecai said, "We do not use closure, heaven forbid, to punish; and when we are convinced that we can lift it, we do so, even though a certain danger is involved."[46] Minister of Finance Dan Meridor also emphasized that Israel "does not believe in closure as a permanent policy."[47]

Sometime after leaving office, Netanyahu explained the policies of his government concerning the use of closure: "I am not a big believer in using closure. Closure produces frustration in the population, and the damage caused is larger than the benefit received. Occasionally, I used closure to complement other military operations in putting pressure on the Palestinian Authority. I took a very liberal line when it came to days of closure."[48]

Nevertheless, public opinion in Israel demanded that closure remain in effect whenever there was danger of attacks within the Green Line. This attitude can be seen from the remarks of Knesset member Hagai Merom: "Past experience shows that each time we lifted the closure, the Israeli public was laid bare to attacks within the State of Israel . . . whoever removes the closure today takes upon himself the very heavy responsibility for the next attack."[49]

In an effort to resolve the dilemma inherent in deciding on a closure, Yitzhak Rabin developed a model: lifting a closure would depend on the extent to which the Palestinian Authority acted against Palestinian terror.[50]

To summarize, in spite of individual successes in preventing attacks, in most cases closure did not prevent terrorists from setting out for Israeli targets in the West Bank or in some instances even Israel itself. Some attackers found ways to avoid the closure and penetrate Israel, and some were in Israel before the closure was in place and set out from within Israeli territory.

One illustration of closure's limitations, even in instances where its aims are achieved, is that it does not prevent an attack being prepared but at most causes it to occur at a different time or place. Rabin believed that imposing a closure on the territories sometimes caused enemy terrorist targets to shift to Israelis and settlers within the territories.[51] The limited effectiveness of closure strengthened Rabin's resolution to seek, as much as possible, the absolute separation of the Palestinian population in the territories from the Israeli population in order to arrive at a satisfactory level of security and terror prevention. In January 1995, after a suicide attack at Beit Lid, the Israeli government decided that its aim was to reach a "practical" separation between Israelis in "the sovereign state of Israel" and the residents of the West Bank and Gaza.[52] This decision was manifest during the years 2003 and 2004, when Israel started to build the separation fence between Israel and the West Bank on 1967 borders.

Punitive Measures against Terrorism. One important step in designing counterterrorism policies is the creation of a punitive policy against terrorist activities. Punitive measures are intended, in part, to remove dangerous elements from society, promote public security, exact revenge from those responsible for the damage their attacks caused to society, and deter others from taking similar actions.

Punitive policies go hand in hand with enactment of laws. For example, the enactment process is essentially the preliminary stage of punitive action: decision makers define terror-related crimes that are punishable and the severity of those crimes and impose minimum punishments or a range of possible punishments for specific crimes. Enactment of laws in a democratic country—as a procedure—reflects the extent to which the public is ready to take on the burden of terror and the price it is willing to pay.[53]

During the period under discussion, Israel carried out diverse punitive actions against terror organizations and their supporters that included, in part, deportation, the razing or sealing of homes, placing limitations on admission to Israel (according to age, marital status, and so on), incarceration, administrative detention, fines, and confiscation of funds. In some cases, Israel emphasized that the actions were not used as a punishment but as a way to thwart and prevent terror.

Expulsion. Prior to the first intifada (1987), and also afterward, Israel used deportation as an administrative punitive measure against activists prominent in organizing violent protests and fermenting violence, but not necessarily against those caught carrying out acts of terrorism (see table 9-1); they were usually brought to trial and imprisoned.

Table 9-1. Deportations of Palestinians

Year	Number of Deportations	Year	Number of Deportations
1967	6	1984	1
1968	22	1985	29
1969	37	1986	10
1970–1973	785	1987	8
1974	96	1988	32
1975	40	1989	26
1976	3	1990	0
1977	0	1991	8
1978	0	1992	415
1979	1	1993–2001	0
1980	3	2002	15
1981	0	2003	14
1982	0	2004	3
1983	0		

Source: www.btselem.org/hebrew/Deportation/Statistics.asp.

Deportation was regarded as the most severe punishment and a decisive way of removing the cause of unrest. Despite the fact that the act of deportation might cause tension and temporary escalation of unrest, in the long run the benefit of deportation was greater than the temporary damage it caused. This idea is expressed in the words of IDF chief of staff Dan Shomron: "Deportation from the territories is an effective and deterrent punishment although in the short term it inflames the area. The deportation penalty will continue, but there will be no mass expulsions."[54] The use of deportation by Israel came up against the criticism of the international community and the United Nations, based on the Geneva Conventions, which ban the deportation of residents of occupied areas. However, Israel claimed that deportation was merely a focused, limited administrative step, totally unrelated to the ban against mass deportation aimed at preventing a demographic shift in occupied areas. In any case, most Israeli administrations were careful to use deportation moderately; each year only a handful of activists were exiled. The basic assumption of most decision makers in Israel was that the restricted use of this tool is the very element that ensures its effectiveness and prevents its erosion.[55] A former head of the ISA, Ya'akov Peri, has stated the following in this context: "I think that deportation is a tool that has generally proved to be effective, but not in every case. It depends on the reason for deportation, who you are deporting and the destination to which you are deporting him. If you provide good answers to these three questions then the deportation can be effective."[56]

To enable deportees to appeal the deportation decision, Israel created appeals procedures before special committees and allowed deportees to appeal decisions before the High Court of Justice. However, these procedures complicated and delayed the deportation process; this obstacle generated attempts to create new arrangements that would facilitate the deportation procedure. One proffered solution was to accelerate the appeals process by allowing deportees to exchange the right to an early plea for the opportunity to submit an appeal in absentia, through a representative.[57]

On December 17, 1992, several months after the establishment of the Rabin government and against the background of the kidnapping and murder of border guard policeman Nissim Toledano at the hands of Hamas terrorists, the Israeli government decided to deport the largest number ever of Palestinians connected with acts of terror and incitement to terror from the territories; 415 activists in Islamic fundamentalist organizations were deported to Lebanon. Most of the deportees were affiliated with the civilian infrastructure of Hamas. They were not necessarily members who were directly involved in the perpetration of attacks but served as spokespeople and political activists. Rabin defined the deportation as a strike against "the top level of the Hamas" rather than hard-core terror activists.[58] The deportation was meant to weaken the supportive environment in which Hamas functioned, thus strengthening the peace process and the PLO. In addition, the deportation was intended to signal the government's determination to combat terror and to reassure the public.[59]

The deportation was unique not only because of its unprecedented scope but also for the way it was performed. The government decided to deport hundreds of Palestinians to Lebanon for a period that would not exceed two years. The deportee was granted the opportunity to appeal deportation after being deported, through a representative before a special appeals committee. However, some deportees petitioned the High Court of Justice, and based on that court's interim injunction, buses transporting deportees to Lebanon stopped, and in the early hours of the morning, the plea hearings began. After a fourteen-hour session, the High Court decided to enable the deportation and cancel the interim injunction, and the deportees were sent to Lebanon.

The Palestinians exploited the deportation for a continuous propaganda campaign, which aroused protests and condemnations in many countries. On December 18, 1992, the UN Security Council passed Resolution 799, which condemned the deportation and demanded of Israel the immediate return of the deportees. In addition, stormy demonstrations, in the course of which several Palestinians were killed, spread throughout the West Bank and Gaza.[60] The deportees refused to leave the Marj-a-Zuhur area to which they had been deported in Lebanon and continued living there in tents under difficult conditions. Hizballah granted sponsorship to the deportees and offered them aid and operational training, including military training and instruction in the preparation of explosive devices and attack methods.[61]

In February 1993, the United States and Israel achieved an agreement, according to which the period of deportation would be shortened to only one year. On September 9, 1993, the Marj-a-Zuhur deportees were returned to the territories. Amnon Lipkin-Shahak believes that the effectiveness of the deportation tool decreased as time passed. He claimed: "During certain periods deportation was very effective. Along the time axis, it lost its effectiveness until it was even counter-effective vis-à-vis the purpose for which it was introduced."[62] In contrast, Meir Dagan maintains that deportation is "very effective." He believes that this type of penalty is far more effective than prison sentences imposed on terrorists.[63] Former prime minister Benjamin Netanyahu addressed the issue of the effectiveness of deportation by concluding, "This is a question of cost versus benefit. The international climate cost is high, therefore the benefit has to justify using it. . . . The benefit is a function of the deportee's identity."[64]

To summarize, in retrospect, selective and considered deportation of a limited number of agitators did in many cases bring about the removal of sources of incitement from the territories. The more extensively and frequently this measure was used, however, the less effective it was—in direct correlation to the level of international criticism.

Administrative Detention. One common and effective punitive measure that Israel has employed is administrative detention (see table 9-2). Like other types of administrative penalties, this detention is based on emergency defense regulations. Detention is meant to remove the inciter of violence or the initiator of an attack from an area without a public trial and without revealing evidence to the public or to the accused individual. Detention is meant to make it easier for the security apparatus to deal with cases in which the uncovering of evidence may pose a threat to state security, due to the disclosure of the identity of a source or the exposure of intelligence methods used to acquire information.

Table 9-2. Administrative Detentions of Palestinians

Number of People under Administrative Detention	Date
1,794	November 5, 1989
n/a	1990
348	December 30, 1991
510	December 30, 1992
125	December 1, 1993
163	August 3, 1994
224	December 27, 1995
267	December 25, 1996
354	December 31, 1997
82	December 26, 1998
18	December 23, 1999
12	December 13, 2000
34	December 5, 2001
960	December 8, 2002
1,007	January 1, 2003
638	January 4, 2004

Source: www.btselem.org/Hebrew/Administrative_Detention/ Statistics.asp.

The extensive use of this type of punishment obligated the judicial system (particularly the military courts) to make new arrangements and
adjustments. One of the main problems the defense system had to contend
with was the issue of "automatic supervision" over administrative detention,
according to which the detainee had to be brought before a judge, who
would examine the circumstances related to the detention within ninety-six
hours of the arrest. The inability of the military judicial system to meet this
requirement, in light of the multiple arrests, sometimes caused the release of
administrative detainees who were not brought before a judge in time. On
March 17, 1988, the order regarding administrative detentions was revised.
The requisite automatic supervision was annulled, but the detainee was
given the right to appeal his arrest before an appeals committee. The authority to issue a warrant of administrative detention was awarded to every military commander, not only to the commander of IDF units in the region.
The revised order enabled the administrative detention of thousands of Palestinians within a short period, and a special detention facility was prepared
for this purpose.[65]

Betzelem, an Israeli human rights organization, harshly criticized the
policy of administrative detentions during the first intifada. According to
the organization, international law permits the arrest of civilians without
trial only in extenuating and unavoidable circumstances, as a preventive
measure, while Israel had turned the administrative detention into a method
of punishment, changed the detention and appeals procedures illegally, and
held the administrative detainees in inhuman conditions.[66] Many decision
makers in Israel stressed that administrative detention must be regarded not
as a punitive measure but rather primarily as a necessary thwarting step due
to the sensitivity of intelligence information connected to terror organizations. Meir Dagan approached administrative detention as a necessary evil:
"It is impossible to act in the State of Israel without administrative detention.
It is one of the best tools in our possession to make use of intelligence without exposing it to the other side."[67]

Israeli experience does prove that administrative detention is indispens-
able in a democracy that must cope with terrorism. The ability to remove
for limited times those causing incitement and terror, without endangering
intelligence sources, enables the state to cope with the unique characteristics
of modern terrorism. Because of the direct and tangible damage to the rights
of the detainee, however, the use of this measure must be limited to extreme

cases—when other alternatives are not available and when the disclosure of evidence would endanger intelligence sources.

Demolition and Sealing of Houses. Prior to the first intifada, the demolition or sealing of a house was considered a severe measure and was imposed only in grave circumstances such as murder, attempted murder, the throwing of hand grenades, the planting of explosive devices, and the like. During the uprising, however, Israel made more extensive use of this measure, and it was no longer limited to the role of response to grave acts of terror but operated as a penalty for throwing Molotov cocktails—a punishment for Palestinians who acted against fellow Palestinians suspected of collaborating with Israel—and even for throwing stones. In the 1990s and early 2000s, Israel continued to impose these punitive measures, although in relatively low doses and to a decreasing extent in comparison to the previous period.[68] (In 2000 Israel did not demolish any Palestinian houses; in 2001, 10 houses; in 2002, 251 houses; in 2003, 224; in 2004, 177.)[69] In most cases, the houses of people involved in suicide attacks were demolished. The message conveyed through this punishment was that even though the suicide terrorist may go to the Garden of Eden according to his belief, he should be aware that his family will pay dearly for his deeds on earth. Former ISA head Ya'akov Peri stated, "The ISA's assessment was that the damage inflicted upon the terrorist's family and its belongings is a critical consideration among the array of considerations faced by a terrorist who is a candidate for a suicide attack."[70]

Regulation 119 of the Emergency Defense Regulations, which constitute the legal basis for the issuing of demolition orders, was actually intended to enable a military commander to maintain order and security in the area under his control. Therefore, it is doubtful whether this regulation was designed for punitive purposes beyond purely operative needs. Demolitions generated many appeals to the Israeli High Court of Justice by Palestinians— terrorists' relatives, people who had rented a house to a terrorist, neighbors residing in the same building or next door, and others—who felt they were bearing the brunt of punishments through no fault of their own. The court dismissed the majority of these applications, based on the reasoning that the issue at hand was a legal operational action in the hands of the military commander in the field.[71] The court also dismissed claims that demolition was an ineffective action, which instead of reducing terror and disorderly conduct only served to encourage it.

The punitive measure of demolishing and sealing houses was granted the court's approval. The High Court of Justice resolved that

> [the deterrent effect] must apply not only to the terrorist himself but also to those around him . . . he must know that his criminal acts will not only harm him but may also bring considerable suffering upon his family as well. From this aspect, the sanction applied to this type of demolition is no different than the prison sentence imposed on the head of a family, the father of little children, who will remain without any support or a breadwinner.[72]

The wide extent of suicide bombings during the period under discussion demonstrates that destroying the homes of terrorist operatives as a means of deterrence for potential attacks failed and has not achieved its goal. Among other reasons, this mode of punishment was made less effective because of the swift support of various, mainly Islamic fundamentalist, organizations that, under the innocent guise of educational, welfare, and religious support, paid for building new houses for terrorists' families.

Of all the punitive and administrative measures for preventing terrorism, it is apparent that administrative detention is the most important and most effective. It allows the security forces to act swiftly without endangering their sources and to neutralize terrorist activities in a manner that is not customarily used when dealing with normal criminal activities. Either this measure, like others, did not have a deterrent effect on potential attackers or its effect was negligible, although it did significantly disrupt the course of terrorist organization activities, the recruitment and training of operatives, and the ability of organizations to carry out attacks.

CONCLUSIONS AND LESSONS

Israel has never succeeded in formulating a defined policy, much less a written policy, in the area of counterterrorism. Its accumulated and abundant experience in contending with the various components of terror has enabled the country to establish a kind of oral doctrine regarding different areas of counterterrorism.

Over the years, the various Israeli administrations adopted a number of guiding principles, which represented the positions of decision makers vis-à-vis counterterrorism at any given time. In any case, new modi operandi were usually established in the aftermath of attacks perpetrated in Israel.

Assessment of Israel's Counterterrorism Policy

Assessing the degree of effectiveness of a counterterrorism activity is a complicated task. The cost-benefit considerations that make up the effectiveness equation are inevitably a by-product of goals set by the decision makers.

In the 1990s, the objective of Israeli counterterrorist activity was to minimize damage in a way that would enable the country and its citizens to go on with their day-to-day activities, without letting terror affect the peace process with the Palestinians. In general, Israeli activity sometimes brought periods of calm lasting several months or years, but it certainly did not eradicate the phenomenon. Therefore, many decision makers believe that Israel achieved partial success in its counterterrorist activity. Ariel Sharon states in this context that Israel experienced "successes over certain periods of time. A breath of fresh air for a while."[73] Shabtai Shavit says, "Israel has partially achieved its goals." He claims that the question that must be asked is not whether Israeli actions were effective but rather whether there was another way that wasn't tried. His reply to this question is, "The answer to the right or wrong policy is—there was no other way."[74]

Israel's goal when contending with terror was not to eradicate the phenomenon but rather to confine the scope of attacks and minimize damage. From this point of view, it appears that the counterterrorist activity has achieved its goals.

Intelligence. Israeli security and intelligence agencies have succeeded in thwarting many hundreds of terror attacks over the years and have prevented strikes against strategic Israeli targets. From among all the counterterrorist actions, it would appear that Israel's greatest achievement is the development of intelligence capabilities. These capabilities have enabled Israel to thwart and neutralize attacks prior to their perpetration in Israel while planning and conducting highly accurate and complex offensive activity, whether in the form of a targeted killing or an air or ground offense. These capabilities are the product of a long acquaintance with the Arab language and culture; control over the West Bank and Gaza during certain periods, which gave Israeli security entities the ability to reward Palestinians who collaborated with them; advanced technological capabilities; and so on.

Offensive Activity and Deterrence. Israeli offensive activity did not solve the terror problem, did not break up the terrorist organizations, and did not demolish their operational capabilities. Israeli offensive activity did not succeed in deterring the leaders and activists of the organizations from executing further attacks, but it was successful in causing short- and medium-term damage to the terror organizations and their leaders, limiting the scope of their terror attacks, and forcing them to invest time and resources in repairing damage.

Defensive Activity. Israel's achievements in the area of defensive prevention and obstruction were limited, which became apparent when suicide attacks intensified in Israel. The geographic and demographic structure of Israel enabled suicide terrorists to reach crowded population centers with relative ease. In certain cases, terrorists detected prior to an attack attempted to perpetrate the attack against the security forces or civilians who tried to stop them. In an attempt to overcome the limitations of defensive activities, Israel started building a partition in 2002, with the aim of making it harder for attackers to infiltrate Israel from the West Bank.

The biggest achievement of the Israeli defense system in its fight against terror was mobilizing the public to be vigilant and to warn against suspicious movements, objects, and people. It was therefore quickly possible to summon security forces to the site of an incident, receive important information from the public, and expect responsible and prudent behavior from the public as they continued their near-normal day-to-day lives. In spite of this, until the year 2000, the main failure of Israel's counterterrorist activity was its inability to develop tools to neutralize, or at least minimize, the morale-related damage caused by terrorism.

Ehud Sprinzak explains the psychological process that the Israeli public underwent in the mid-1990s that caused Rabin to define terror as a strategic threat:

> Between the months of October 1994 and January 1995, Israeli society underwent a severe shock. A series of brutal terror attacks placed terror— usually a tactical threat that does not endanger national security—in the center of national consciousness and the public agenda. Israel's citizens entered a mental "bunker" of anxiety, and public support for the government sunk in an unprecedented manner.[75]

The Israeli public, affected by the terror attacks, translated its feelings into messages and pressures addressed to decision makers, impacting the formulation of their policy.

Public opinion not only determines the range of Israeli counterterrorism activity but also affects the types of steps taken against terror—their timing, scope, and frequency—both on the level of defense, including reinforcement of the security system and the establishment of designated security units, and on the operative and offensive levels.

The extent of influence that the Israeli public has on its decision makers vis-à-vis counterterrorism efforts is reflected in the fact that resolutions regarding the establishment of security units for buses and schools, the reinforcement of the Israel Police for the purpose of thwarting terror, budget transfers, the shifting of priorities and structural changes, and so forth were in many cases made at cabinet meetings held immediately after or in the shadow of mass-casualty terror attacks. These resolutions constituted an attempt to convey a reassuring message to the public, and they also gave decision makers themselves the feeling that they were not continuing with their routine or disregarding terror attacks but were taking practical measures to thwart terror.

The Israeli Democratic Dilemma

In general, it can be concluded that Israel has proven it is possible to cope effectively with terrorism while at the same time preserving the liberal democratic nature of a country. It has done so even under the harsh and extreme conditions of the continuous threat of serious terror attacks over many years, at different sites, by numerous organizations supported by sponsoring countries. As a democratic country obliged to cope with this phenomenon, Israel is continually forced to strike a balance between effective counterterrorism activities and liberal democratic values. And, yes, Israeli citizens have been made to pay a price. Each time individuals are required to identify themselves to security personnel and have their belongings searched when entering a public place, their privacy is being impinged on. Emergency regulations that allow the army to take administrative punitive measures, although under the supervision of the High Court of Justice, do not go hand in hand with the basic values of a liberal legal system. Difficult questions regarding the rights of a suspect being questioned for plotting a terrorist attack and the need to strike a balance between the rights of individual suspects and the right of the public to defend itself created difficult situations, internal disputes, and international condemnation. In general, however, Israel has been able to meticulously preserve (largely as a result of the judicial activism of the High Court and its independence from the executive branch) the proper balance between the right to life and the freedom of its citizens. A comparison of legislation and judicial conditions in Israel, legislation enacted in the United States after 9/11 (the Patriot Act), and legislation in Britain and other Western countries clearly demonstrates Israel's achievements in protecting the balance between effective counterterrorism activities and liberal democratic values. This success most likely results from the fact that Israeli normative and judicial instruments developed during a process of evolution spanning many years, layer after layer, under internal and international scrutiny, while legislation in other Western countries was enacted under the influence of the traumatic tragedies of 9/11 as a revolutionary (as opposed to evolutionary) reflex reflecting a sharp leap from a liberal democratic orientation to the need for a tangible and immediate self-protective response to terror. Since terror is a dynamic and developing phenomenon, so too the response to terrorism must be a continually updated process that includes at all stages the relevance of the democratic dilemma.

To summarize, despite the difficulty of predicting the impact of operative Israeli steps on morale, this assessment is inevitable; in its absence, the country may win its battles against terror but ultimately lose the war. The attention focused on the psychological-morale component (offensive and defensive activity, punitive measures, information, and education) could reduce the public's anxiety level regarding terror while dealing a blow to the morale of the terror activists and their supporters, thus disrupting the strategy of their battle and thwarting their efforts to achieve their political and strategic goals.

Lessons for Other Democracies

Against the background of Israel's accumulated experience in contending with terror, and with the aim of minimizing the restrictions and damages resulting from effective counterterrorist activity on liberal democratic values, it is recommended that some hard and fast rules that will serve as the basis for counterterrorism policy be laid down.

- **A strategic threat.** It is important to recognize that the strategic threat terrorism poses to democracies stems from the physical damage terror attacks might inflict, the fear and anxiety that terrorism inspires within the democratic society, and the possibility that it will change political positions and influence political processes.

- **The goals of counterterrorism activity.** It should be made clear that the strategic goal of counterterrorism is not necessarily the eradication of terror but rather the reduction of its scope and the damage it causes. It should be emphasized that the goal is dynamic and will change according to changing circumstances.

- **Selectiveness in offensive counterterrorist activity.** Within the framework of offensive activity, it is vital to be selective when choosing the means. Offensive activity should be used for the purposes of thwarting certain attacks, disrupting the terror organization's activities, inflicting damage on its infrastructure, and deterrence, but not just for punitive reasons. It is important to ensure the use of selective offensive methods and means that will minimize damage on innocent parties as much as possible.

- **Defensive-protective activity.** Due to the fact that security activities necessitate extensive recruitment of manpower, the security system should be based at least partially on recruited volunteers. The activation of volunteers within the counterterrorist system will also help reinforce the public's morale and provide the public with psychological support when contending with terror.

- **Control.** The subordination of all security entities to ongoing and ad hoc control of the legislative body must be clearly defined. Representatives of the public must supervise the secret activities of the intelligence community and make sure they are carried out only within the framework of the law.

- **Jurisdiction.** It must be clarified that all operative actions taken in the framework of the country's counterterrorist activities are subject to jurisdiction, and it is important to establish the right of anyone who regards him- or herself as victimized by counterterrorist activity to receive remedy from the courts.

- **Administrative punitive measures.** All types of administrative punitive measures must be subject to judicial review, be as limited as possible, and be confined to a definite period of time. They must be implemented for the purpose of achieving operational goals that are defined in legislation and never for other purposes.

• **Collective punishment.** Collective punishment should be avoided at all times. It is vital to ensure that any punitive or operative activity (such as closure, curfew, or encirclement) that affects a wider population than is actually involved in terror will be used solely for operative and not for punitive goals.

NOTES

1. Ian Lesser and others, *Countering the New Terrorism* (Rand Project Air Force, 1999), xii, 120–21.

2. Yezid Sayigh, *Armed Struggle and the Search for State: The Palestinian National Movement 1949–1993* (Oxford: Clarendon, 1997), 87.

3. Schlomo Gazit, *Trapped* [in Hebrew] (Tel Aviv: Zmora-Bitan, 1999), 45.

4. Mike Eldar, *The 13th Fleet: The Story of the Amphibious Commando* [in Hebrew] (Tel Aviv: Maariv, 1993), 636.

5. *Haaretz,* February 15, 1995.

6. Carmi Gilon, *Shin-Beth between the Schisms* [in Hebrew] (Tel Aviv: Miskal-Yedioth Ahronoth Books and Chemed Books, 2000), 18.

7. *Yediot Ahronot,* December 1, 1994.

8. *Yediot Ahronot,* November 3, 1994, 13.

9. *Haaretz,* November 3, 1994.

10. *Davar,* April 10, 1995.

11. *Haaretz,* April 14, 1995.

12. Uri Savir, *The Process* [in Hebrew] (Tel Aviv: Yediot Ahronot, 1998), 194–95.

13. *Maariv,* April 25, 1995, 5.

14. *Haaretz,* January 24, 1995.

15. *Haaretz,* September 13, 1995.

16. *Maariv,* February 8, 1995.

17. *Maariv,* September 1, 1994.

18. *Yediot Ahronot,* January 27, 1995.

19. *Haaretz,* August 12, 1996.

20. *Maariv,* September 13, 1996, 2.

21. Orly Azulay-Katz, *The Man Who Defeated Himself* [in Hebrew] (Tel Aviv: Yediot Ahronot, 1999), 138.

22. Raviv Druker and Ofer Shelah, *Boomerang,* (Jerusalem: Keter, 2005) 310.

23. Ibid., 335.

24. *Hazofe,* September 19, 1994.

25. *Haaretz,* November 21, 1994.

26. *Haaretz,* January 24, 1995.

27. Gilon, 197.

28. Ibid., 360.

29. J. L. Wallach explains that a deterrent is a threat to an adversary. Should the adversary act in a specific manner, his actions will result in a harsh response. Deterrence, in effect, determines the cost of a possible terrorist act. The effectiveness of deterrence is thus dependent on the attacker realizing that the damage liable to befall him should he "cross the red line" will exceed any possible gain. Thus it must be made clear to the adversary that his tangible losses will exceed his possible gains and that the retaliation will cause such losses that it would not be worth his while to attack. It is exactly because of the special characteristics of deterrence that Martha Crenshaw doubts the effectiveness of deterrence on terror organizations. In her opinion, it is difficult to estimate what the effect of threats and punitive actions will be on adversarial decision makers. Furthermore, the leaders of terror organizations are motivated by a different set of values than those motivating the leaders of sovereign countries. The probability of misconception on the part of the deterring country is high, and a noncalculated reaction could harm that country's image, as well as involve considerable risk. See J. L. Wallach, *Kriegstheorien* [in Hebrew, translated from German], 3rd ed. (Defense Ministry Publications, June 1980), 33; Martha Crenshaw, "Terrorism: What Should We Do?" in *Terrorism,* ed. Anzovin Steven (New York: H. W. Wilson, 1986), 170.

30. *Maariv,* October 21, 1994, 7.

31. Benjamin Netanyahu, former Israeli prime minister, interview with the author, December 20, 1999.

32. ynetnews.com. www.ynet.co.il/Ext/Comp/ArticleLayout/ CdaArticlePrintPreview/1,2506,L-2936166,00.html.

33. Israel's Security Fence [in Hebrew], www.securityfence.mod.gov.il/ Pages/Heb/mivne.htm.

34. *Maariv,* August 2, 1995, 2.

35. *Haaretz,* March 24, 1996.

36. *Haaretz,* February 12, 1997, 2.

37. *Maariv,* August 22, 1997.

38. *Haaretz,* August 12, 1997.

39. *Maariv,* February 14, 1997, 17.

40. Yigal Presler, former adviser on counterterrorism to the Israeli prime minister, interview with the author, October 31, 1999.

41. Amira Hass, *Drinking the Sea at Gaza* [in Hebrew] (Tel Aviv: Hasifriya Hahadasha, 1996), 94.

42. *Maariv,* February 7, 1995.

43. *Yediot Ahronot,* April 9, 1993, 2.

44. *Davar,* February 20, 1995.

45. *Maariv,* April 13, 1995.

46. *Haaretz,* November 11, 1996.

47. *Haaretz,* January 15, 1997.

48. Boaz Ganor, *The Counter-Terrorism Puzzle: A Guide for Decision Makers.* (New Brunswick, NJ: Transaction, 2005), 197.

49. *Hazofe,* February 19, 1995.

50. *Davar,* February 20, 1995.

51. *Yediot Ahronot,* April 10, 1995.

52. *Maariv,* January 30, 1995, 9.

53. Noemi Gal-Or, "Tolerating Terrorism in Israel," in *Tolerating Terrorism in the West,* ed. Noemi Gal-Or (New York: Routledge, 1991), 159.

54. *Yediot Ahronot,* August 28, 1989, 5.

55. Shimon Peres, former Israeli prime minister, interview with author, February 11, 2000.

56. Ya'akov Peri, former head of the ISA, interview with author, November 28, 1999.

57. *Yediot Ahronot,* May 22, 1989.

58. *Haaretz,* March 31, 1993.

59. Anat Kurz, *Islamic Terrorism and Israel: Hizballah, Palestinian Islamic Jihad, and Hamas* [in Hebrew] (Tel Aviv: Papirus), 175.

60. Ronni Shaked and Aviva Shabi, *Hamas—Palestinian Islamic Fundamentalist Movement* [in Hebrew] (Jerusalem: Keter Publishing House Ltd, 2000), 21.

61. *Yediot Ahronot,* December 1, 1994, 7.

62. Amnon Lipkin-Shahak, former IDF chief of staff, interview with author, December 23, 1999.

63. Meir Dagan, former Israeli counterterrorism coordinator, interview with author, December 2, 1999.

64. Netanyahu, interview, December 20, 1999.

65. Amnon Strachnov, *Justice under Fire* [in Hebrew] (Tel Aviv: Yedioth Ahronoth Books, 1994), 66, 67, 70.

66. Betzelem, "Administrative Detentions in the Territories" [in Hebrew] (Betzelem [Israeli Information Center for Human Rights in the Occupied Territories], Jerusalem, October 1992), 7.

67. Dagan, interview, December 2, 1999.

68. Noga Kadman, "1987–1997: A Decade of Human Rights Violations" [in Hebrew] (Betzelem [Israeli Information Center for Human Rights in the Occupied Territories], Jerusalem, January 1998), 19.

69. B'Tselem: The Israeli Information Center for Human Rights in the Occupied Territories. www.btselem.org/Hebrew/Punitive_Demolitions/Statistics_Since_1987.asp.

70. Ya'akov Peri, *Strike First* [in Hebrew] (Tel Aviv: Keshet, 1999), 230.

71. Israeli High Court of Justice (4112/90), Association for Civil Rights in Israel (ACRI) v. Commander of Southern Command, 44(4) P.D. 626.

72. Israeli High Court of Justice (698/85), Daghlas, et al. v. Military Commander of the West Bank, P.D. 40(2)42.

73. Ariel Sharon, Israeli prime minister, interview with author, September 13, 2000.

74. Shabtai Shavit, former head of the Israeli "Mossad," interview with author, November 4, 1999.

75. Ehud Sprinzak, "Israeli Society Facing the Challenge of Islamic Terror" [in Hebrew] (Center for Intelligence Heritage, April 1997), 2.

10

ISRAEL AND THE LEBANESE HIZBALLAH

Daniel Byman

Israel's struggle against the Lebanese Hizballah demonstrates the many pitfalls that even a highly competent and determined democratic state may encounter when it confronts a skilled and dedicated terrorist group. For more than twenty years, Israel has fought a determined but largely unsuccessful rearguard operation against Hizballah, employing many of the tactics and methods the United States uses against al Qaeda. In 1982 Israel invaded and occupied much of Lebanon to dislodge the Palestinian presence there; in 1985 Shia guerrilla attacks spearheaded by Hizballah drove Israel back to a "security zone" along the border. After fifteen subsequent years of unrelenting Hizballah attacks, Israel suddenly departed Lebanese soil for good in May 2000. Despite Israel's technological and organizational superiority, and despite its determination to prevail, Hizballah defeated Israel through force of arms, the only Arab organization to do so.

Even after Israel departed from Lebanon, Hizballah continued to menace Israel. The Shia movement occasionally shelled settlements, engaged in cross-border raids, and kidnapped Israeli citizens. Most worrisome for Israel, Hizballah increased its training of Palestinian terrorist groups and tried to inspire them to escalate their struggle.

In combating Hizballah, Israel tried a wide range of methods, including the use of targeted assassinations, collective punishment of villages where

Hizballah supporters lived, attempts to coerce the government of Lebanon to crack down on the group, psychological operations and measures to improve intelligence collection, efforts to intimidate Hizballah's Syrian and Iranian sponsors, and the use of a security zone along the border. Together, these measures succeeded in limiting Hizballah attacks on civilians in Israel but did not stop the guerrilla campaign against Israeli soldiers in Lebanon—a confrontation in which Israel was doomed to be defeated. In addition, the measures did little to halt Hizballah's sponsorship of various Palestinian surrogates.

Israel failed to defeat Hizballah for several reasons. Most important, Hizballah proved an exceptionally skilled and determined adversary, far more so than the many Palestinian organizations Israel had confronted in the 1960s, 1970s, and 1980s. In particular, Hizballah is a large guerrilla and political movement that also employs terrorism; Israel was not able to stop the terrorism without also confronting Hizballah's other aspects. Hizballah also was far more casualty acceptant than Israel, allowing it to emerge victorious even though it suffered more losses on the battlefield. Many of Israel's measures to counter Hizballah enraged the Lebanese people, increasing overall support for the movement. Israel also proved unable to end Iranian and Syrian support for the movement. In part, Israel was unable to escalate against Hizballah and its sponsors because of international and domestic scrutiny that limited its activities.

The Lebanese Hizballah is of particular interest for democracies fighting al Qaeda today, as it is one of the few terrorist organizations in the same class as al Qaeda: Hizballah has hundreds of terrorist cadres and more than a thousand guerrilla fighters, it has literally millions of supporters in the Arab and Muslim world, and it enjoys a global network that assists with fundraising and operations. In addition to these assets, Hizballah enjoys the open patronage of both Iran and Syria, which arm, train, fund, and protect the movement.

This chapter examines the Israeli attempt to defeat Hizballah to glean lessons for counterterrorism today. It first offers an overview of Hizballah, noting how the movement has changed and describing the role of its state sponsors, Iran and Syria. It then describes the measures Israel has used against the movement, noting briefly the level of success each enjoyed. The third section takes a broader look at Israel's counterterrorism campaign, noting particular limits under which Israel labored. The chapter concludes by drawing lessons from Israel's experience for other democracies struggling to defeat terrorist movements.

THE EVOLUTION OF HIZBALLAH

Hizballah today is far different from the ragtag collection of Shia fighters that shocked the world in the early 1980s. The movement has evolved militarily, emerging as perhaps the world's most lethal guerrilla group. In addition, it has grown politically, becoming lionized in the Middle East and expanding the scope of its activities in Lebanon. Its many successes have profoundly changed the movement, transforming the threat it poses and its vulnerabilities.

For most of Lebanon's modern history, the country's Shia Muslim community from which Hizballah emerged was ignored and powerless, despite being the largest communal group in the country. Lebanon's Maronite Christian and Sunni Muslim communities dominated the country, quarreling over who would lead it but not over whether the Shias deserved a greater say. Beginning in the 1960s, the charismatic Shia cleric Musa al-Sadr challenged the traditional, politically quiescent leaders of Lebanon's Shias. Al-Sadr organized the community, demanded a greater voice in Lebanon's affairs, and, in the process, formed the Shia militia Amal (the Afwaj al-Muqwama al-Lubnaniya, or Lebanese Resistance Detachments, the acronym of which means "hope"). In 1975, in the midst of this politicization, Lebanon fell into civil war, a conflict that embroiled many of Lebanon's religious and ethnic communities, the large Palestinian refugee presence in the country, and neighbors such as Iraq, Israel, and especially Syria. The Shias and other communities that had not already formed their own militias quickly did so for self-defense.[1]

This dangerous brew grew even more toxic when Israel invaded Lebanon in 1982, trying to block Palestinian guerrillas' haven in the country. Israel's invasion of Lebanon was militarily masterful and strategically disastrous. In a lightning campaign, Israel quickly routed the Palestinian and Syrian resistance. More than 17,000 people—most of them civilians—died in the invasion of Lebanon.[2]

The Lebanese Shias in southern Lebanon, for years mistreated by Palestinian militias, initially welcomed the Israeli invaders.[3] The welcome proved short-lived. Israel showed few signs of leaving, making the liberators appear like future oppressors. As Israeli intelligence predicted, the continued occupation infuriated many Lebanese.[4] At the same time, Israel tried to establish an allied (many would say puppet) regime in Beirut that was dominated by Maronite Christian Phalangists—a move that alienated other communities and threatened Syria and Iran. As the situation in Lebanon unraveled, the United States deployed peacekeeping forces to maintain order and help ensure the smooth demobilization and departure of Palestinian fighters in Lebanon.

Nabih Berri, al-Sadr's rather lackluster successor (Imam al-Sadr himself had disappeared mysteriously in 1978 on a trip to Libya), cooperated with the Lebanese government, which was now working closely with the Israelis. Several local Shia factions, inspired in part by Khomeini's revolution, disenchanted with Berri's leadership, and already incensed over the Israeli presence in their country, rejected this cooperation, arguing that the regime was nothing more than an Israeli puppet. Iran and Syria encouraged this perception. Both countries sought to use the Shias against Israel's interests in Lebanon, and Iran also hoped to export its revolution to Lebanon. With Syria's encouragement, Iran helped organize, arm, train, inspire, and, most importantly, unite the myriad Shia groups, eventually leading to the formation of Hizballah.

Hizballah quickly became the tip of the spear in the effort to expel the Americans and the Israelis. Hizballah literally exploded into America's consciousness with devastating suicide attacks (new at the time) on the U.S. embassy in Beirut in April 1983, in which sixty-three people died, including seventeen Americans, and on a U.S. marine barracks in October 1983, which killed 241 U.S. Marines. These attacks, and the sense that the peacekeepers had little peace to keep, led to a rapid U.S. departure in February 1984.

Hizballah's use of terrorism continued after the U.S. departure. During the course of the 1980s, Hizballah took seventeen Americans, fifteen Frenchmen, fourteen Britons, seven Swiss, and seven West Germans hostage, as well as twenty-seven others of various nationalities. Ten hostages died in captivity.[5] In the 1980s and 1990s, Hizballah also worked with Iran to kill dissident Iranians, such as members of Kurdish and other opposition groups. In March 1992, Hizballah and Iran worked together to bomb the Israeli embassy in Argentina, killing twenty-nine, and in July 1994, Hizballah attacked the Jewish Community Center in Buenos Aires, killing eighty-six. Hizballah also aided other groups that shared its agenda. A Lebanese Hizballah member was indicted for helping design a truck bomb that flattened the U.S. military facility of Khobar Towers in Saudi Arabia in 1996, killing seventeen American troops.

Israel also suffered repeated truck bombings and other terrorist attacks against its facilities and officials. In November 1983, Hizballah destroyed the headquarters of the Israeli Defense Forces in Tyre, killing 141. Hizballah also began a long, bitter guerrilla war against Israel, initially carried out by local, relatively autonomous fighters in the south. Over time, these fighters became more and more effective. Many of the tactics Hizballah initially used, such as driving truck bombs into Israeli convoys and facilities, represented a mixture of terrorism and guerrilla tactics. Faced with the ferocious Hizballah attacks, in June 1985 Israel withdrew to a security zone in southern Lebanon—a buffer manned in part by Israel's ally, the South Lebanese Army (SLA).[6] Hizballah kept up the pressure and, fifteen years later, eventually drove Israel from Lebanese soil altogether.

Hizballah's size fluctuated as its struggle against Israel wore on. In the 1980s, Hizballah had perhaps five thousand fighters under arms. Several hundred of them belonged to various front organizations, such as the Revolutionary Justice Organization, the Oppressed of the Earth Organization, and Islamic Jihad, that Hizballah used for its terrorist operations.[7] This cadre shrank in the 1990s but grew far more skilled and professional. By the early 1990s, Hizballah had become an elite organization.

Hizballah realized that many of its recruits were unskilled and that large numbers made Israeli penetration of its ranks far easier. Moreover, repeated Israeli assassinations and kidnappings had demonstrated Israel's ability to gain real-time, actionable intelligence on Hizballah. A smaller size enabled Hizballah to increase the overall level of training and improve security. By the time of the Israeli withdrawal from Lebanon in May 2000, Hizballah had approximately five hundred full-time fighters and another one thousand part-time cadres.[8]

Hizballah's smaller size did not diminish its reach or its stature. Because Hizballah fighters were lionized by many Shias, it was relatively easy to gain new recruits. In addition, Hizballah worked closely with Lebanon's Shia religious network, giving it a built-in leadership base and ties to the community that went beyond the organization's narrow range of activities. Many of its recruits were bonded through kinship and regional ties, as well as through a shared ideology. Hizballah's terrorist wing in particular was able to choose among the more skilled of the organization's members, rejecting those who might in any way hinder operations.

A New Hizballah?

Success and time have fundamentally changed Hizballah. Today, Hizballah has abandoned many of its founding principles in practice if not in rhetoric. Hizballah's founding document, issued in 1985, called for replacing Lebanon's sectarian governing system with the rule of Islam, the end of Western imperialism, and the destruction of the State of Israel. Today, Hizballah has rejected the forcible implementation of an Islamic state, recognizing both Lebanon's demographic realities and the fact that few Shias support an Islamic republic in Lebanon.[9] Hizballah's secretary general, Sheikh Hassan Nasrallah, once even indicated that the movement would not actively resist any Lebanese government decision to make peace with Israel.[10] Hizballah seems to want to maximize the role of Lebanon's Shia community and its own leadership but has recognized the importance of an accommodation with other Lebanese communities and with Damascus, Lebanon's puppet master.

Hizballah still opposes the United States, but it is far more cautious. It has not been involved in an attack on a U.S. target since 1996, when a member helped Saudi Hizballah (a group that has no formal ties to Lebanese Hizballah but shares a similar ideology) hit Khobar Towers, and even then it assisted others rather than using its own capability.[11]

Hizballah has also changed, though not necessarily gentled, in its approach toward Israel. The movement was initially dedicated to Israel's destruction. The first step was the removal of Israel from Lebanon, a goal that took precedence both because of its immediacy and because of the wide support it enjoyed among Lebanese of all political stripes. Having achieved this removal, Hizballah has avoided a sustained campaign of direct strikes on Israeli territory even as it claims to be committed to ending the Zionist presence in the region. The number of direct Hizballah attacks on Israel has fallen since the May 2000 Israeli withdrawal, although shelling along the border still occurs when tension heats up. Perhaps to square this circle, the scope of Hizballah's campaign against Israel has broadened even as direct attacks have declined (as discussed further below).

The withdrawal of Syria from Lebanon in 2005 also is an important change. The political stasis that Damascus imposed on Lebanon has ended, at least for now. Although Hizballah retains goals similar to those it held before the Syrian withdrawal, it is now more focused than ever on Lebanese politics. The group has managed to further increase its influence in Lebanon, both because its political organization is unrivaled in the country (in 2005 Hizballah-backed candidates did better than those backed by any other single organization) and because its armed strength gives it tremendous "street power." As Hizballah is an important pro-Syrian voice, Damascus's support for the organization is likely to get stronger.

A Global Network

In conjunction with Iran, Hizballah also developed a truly global network. In the 1980s and early 1990s, Hizballah operatives struck in France, Kuwait, and elsewhere against Western targets. In 1992 and 1994, Hizballah attacked Israeli and Jewish targets in Argentina.

Hizballah cells have been found in Europe, Africa, South America, North America, and Asia. Operatives in these cells provide logistical support for global attacks, raise money, recruit local operatives, and collect intelligence, among other duties.[12] In Africa, for example, Hizballah has worked with the Lebanese Shia diaspora—some of whom support the movement, some of whom simply fear it—to raise money and identify potential operatives, who receive further training in Iran and Lebanon.[13] In 2001 U.S. investigators even uncovered a Hizballah cell in Charlotte, North Carolina. It was raising money for Hizballah through the arbitrage of tobacco sales tax differentials and using the profits to buy a range of sophisticated equipment for the movement, such as night-vision devices, global positioning systems, and aircraft analysis and design software.[14]

Unlike al Qaeda, which uses its network to strike at a wide range of enemies, this global network is focused primarily on one target: Israel. In the 1980s and early 1990s, Hizballah attacked several countries, often as a means of assisting Iran in achieving its objectives vis-à-vis Iraq or other countries. As the 1990s wore on, however, the network was used to attack Israeli facilities overseas and as a means of bolstering the movement in Lebanon. Even today, the global network gives Hizballah the ability to influence other countries, particularly the United States, and deter them from acting against the movement.

A Strong Political Movement

Hizballah today is a social and political organization as well as a terrorist and guerrilla movement. Popular among Lebanon's Shia plurality and respected by many non-Shia Lebanese, after the 2005 elections Hizballah holds 23 seats in Lebanon's parliament of 128 and holds two government ministries. Hizballah runs schools and hospitals and offers relatively efficient public services, in sharp contrast to the government of Lebanon.

Hizballah's social services bolster its military and terrorist activities, providing a network of sympathizers who may be called on to assist operations and also building the prestige of the guerrilla movement, demonstrating its ability to help the people beyond resistance.

Over time, Hizballah developed an extremely effective electoral machine, respected for its efficiency and, by Lebanese standards, its limited corruption. Hizballah electoral posters call for votes on behalf of the movement of martyrs. Moreover, Hizballah exploits its social service network.[15] As one Christian who voted for Hizballah explained to a would-be rival, "Where were you when we needed emergency snow removal and fuel? In this village, everyone is going to vote for Hizballah."[16]

Hizballah's political participation also led to increased moderation, as many constituents sought peace and stability, not unending conflict with Israel and its Western backers. Although the movement's leaders are still fiercely opposed to Israel, the urgency of this opposition has diminished now that Israel is no longer on Lebanese soil. Strikes on Israel that would provoke retaliation must be carefully considered, as they would anger key constituents who seek tourism, development, investment, and other benefits of stability.[17] Thus Hizballah is far more careful in striking Israel.

The "Hizballah Model"

Hizballah is not simply transitioning from a terrorist organization to a social movement. Rather, the nature of its terrorist activities is changing. Hizballah today is as much a state sponsor of terrorism as a terrorist group in its own right. Conceptually, the challenge Hizballah poses today is its effort to spread what journalist James Kitfield has dubbed the "Hizballah model." Hizballah's mix of skilled operations, willingness to sacrifice, and emphasis on a long-term struggle is widely seen as the combination that drove Israel from southern Lebanon.

Since the outbreak of the current al-Aqsa intifada in September 2000, Hizballah has stepped up its support for Hamas, the Palestinian Islamic Jihad, and other anti-Israeli groups. This support includes guerrilla training, bomb-building expertise, tactical tips such as how to use mines against Israeli armor, and propaganda from Hizballah's radio and satellite television stations. Hizballah operatives have also been caught smuggling weapons to Arabs in Israel, and its experts have helped Palestinian groups build lethal bombs.[18]

Hizballah's propaganda also bolsters terrorism. Hizballah's radio and television stations trumpet advances in the Palestinian intifada, and these broadcasts both help glorify the Palestinian struggle in the Muslim world and try to foment fear in Israel.[19] Hizballah's propaganda efforts are succeeding, with Palestinians regularly citing Hizballah as a successful model for ending Israeli occupation.

Exporting the Hizballah model while limiting actual attacks strikes a perfect balance for Hizballah today. On the one hand, Hizballah avoids alienating its Lebanese constituents, many of whom question the need for aggressive action that would risk Israeli retaliation now that Israel is gone. Syria and Iran also fear that a direct Israel-Hizballah confrontation would spiral outward and involve them in a U.S. response. On the other hand, by training other groups, Hizballah can still serve its backers' interests and its own ideology by disrupting what's left of the peace process. Because Palestinians are energized, Hizballah is able to fight to the last Palestinian and suffer few costs on its own.

September 11, 2001, and the broader concern Western states have had about terrorism due to attacks or attempted attacks on their soil, such as the July 7, 2005, attacks in London, have also had a limiting effect. The tremendous worldwide concern about terrorism, and the active U.S. campaign against al Qaeda, made Hizballah leaders cautious about any attacks that would lead them to be compared to al Qaeda. Perhaps more important, Hizballah's sponsors—Iran and Syria—both feared they would be targets of regime change and were cautious in their use of Hizballah. The U.S. invasion of Iraq further heightened these states' concerns.

Thus, in essence, Hizballah's priorities have changed. It still seeks Israel's destruction, but it will take fewer risks and endure fewer sacrifices to achieve this goal now that Israeli forces are no longer on Lebanese soil. Instead,

Hizballah sees itself as a model for and partner to the Palestinians in their own struggle against Israel rather than as the tip of the spear.

The Roles of Iran and Syria

In different ways, both Syria and Iran have played a vital role in sustaining Hizballah. For both countries, using Hizballah as a proxy allows some degree of deniability, enabling them to strike at Israel or other targets without risking a confrontation that direct military action would entail. Beyond this shared objective, the two states have very different approaches to Hizballah.

Syria provides Hizballah with weapons and logistical support. Most important, Damascus cracked down on Hizballah's rivals while for many years allowing it a haven in Lebanon and today supporting its presence there. Syria's relationship with Hizballah is intensely practical. Damascus has avoided direct involvement in international terrorism since 1986, but it still uses radical groups to put pressure on Israel and other opponents. In essence, Syria's ties to Hizballah remind Israel that it cannot end terrorism or stabilize its border without accommodating Damascus. Syrian president Bashar al-Asad confessed this open secret, noting that Hizballah was a necessary "buffer" for Syria against Israel.

Hizballah's position on the disputed chunk of turf known as Shabaa Farms is instructive. Until Syria proclaimed the Shabaa area to be part of Lebanon (as opposed to part of Syria, which Damascus had previously claimed), Hizballah ignored the issue. When Damascus sought a pretext to claim that Israel had not completed its withdrawal from Lebanon, Hizballah took up the cudgel and launched attacks on Israel, ostensibly intended to drive Israel from the Shabaa Farms area.[20] In its initial role as bystander, and its subsequent role as combatant, Hizballah has demonstrated that it often will follow where Syria leads.

Hizballah also lies low when Damascus wants to avoid a confrontation. For example, when then Syrian president Hafez al-Asad met with President Clinton in January 1994, Hizballah avoided attacks on Israel. From January until August 2003, when U.S. pressure on Syria heated up before and after the start of the war with Iraq, Hizballah also halted attacks on Israel so as not to get its patron into hot water.

As the above fluctuation in Hizballah activities suggests, Damascus appears to exercise a veto power, or at least considerable influence, over

Hizballah's military operations in Lebanon. Indeed, many observers believe that the road to southern Lebanon runs through Damascus. As Human Rights Watch notes, "By controlling Hizballah's prime access to arms, Syria appears to hold considerable influence over Hizballah's ability to remain an active military force in the south."[21] Syria's potential influence is considerable. Damascus fears unrest in Lebanon, so its intelligence on the country is superb; it knows the identity and location of Hizballah's core membership and many of its sympathizers. Moreover, Syria has repeatedly proven it will be ruthless, willing to inflict thousands of civilian casualties to root out any opposition. Syria in the past helped disarm every militia in Lebanon but Hizballah.

The recent Syrian withdrawal from Lebanon weakens Damascus's position. Even though its intelligence remains superb, its on-the-ground presence is diminished. Now far weaker politically, Syria relies more on Hizballah to represent its interests than in the past, increasing the movement's leverage.

Iran has helped build the movement from the ground up and plays a major role in sustaining it on a daily basis. After Israel invaded Lebanon in 1982, Tehran seized the opportunity and regularly deployed one thousand Islamic Revolutionary Guard Corps (IRGC) personnel—the revolutionary vanguard of Iran's military—to Lebanon's Bekaa Valley, a number that later leveled out at between three hundred and five hundred.[22] The IRGC worked with Iranian intelligence and Iranian diplomats as well as Syrian officials to create Hizballah from a motley assortment of small Shia organizations. Iran helped the fledgling movement train and indoctrinate new members in the Bekaa Valley and developed a social services and fundraising network there.[23]

These ties continue to remain strong, and Iranian sponsorship of Hizballah is much of the reason why Iran consistently heads the U.S. list of state sponsors of terrorism. Hizballah still proclaims its adherence to Iran's ideology of the *velayet-e faqih* (guardianship of the jurisconsult), and Tehran provides approximately $100 million per year to Hizballah. In addition, Iranian forces train movement members and provide intelligence. Moreover, Hizballah operatives enjoy close ties to Iranian intelligence and the IRGC, which is tied directly to Iranian supreme leader Ali Khamenei. Hizballah's senior terrorist, Imad Mugniyieh, reportedly enjoys Iranian citizenship and regularly travels to Iran. Hizballah proclaims its loyalty to

Khamenei, and he reportedly is an arbiter for group decisions. Iran is particularly influential with regard to Hizballah activities overseas. Hizballah, for example, stopped its attacks in Europe as part of a broader Iranian decision to halt attacks there.

In exchange for this aid, Iran gains a weapon against Israel and influence far beyond its borders. Because of Hizballah, Iran has defied geography and is a player in the Middle East peace process. Iran has also used Hizballah operatives to kill Iranian dissidents and attack U.S. forces, including those in Saudi Arabia and Germany. Iran also uses terrorism as a form of deterrence, casing U.S. embassies and other facilities to give it the capacity to respond should the United States step up pressure.[24] Finally, Tehran has an ideological bond with Hizballah, formed by a similar view of the role of Islam in government and by historically close ties between Lebanon's and Iran's clerical establishments.

Hizballah's foreign backers are both a source of the movement's strength and a brake on its activities. Iran and Syria both use Hizballah operations to further their own particular foreign policy objectives and, in the process, make the movement far more dangerous. Yet their close ties to Hizballah make them vulnerable to retaliation for the movement's trespasses, leading them to rein in the organization if they feel threatened.

ISRAEL'S RESPONSE TO THE HIZBALLAH CHALLENGE

Hizballah poses threats to Israel along several dimensions, not all of which are directly linked to terrorism. As the attacks in Argentina suggest, Hizballah poses a terrorist threat to Israeli personnel around the world; the movement has a global network and is willing to use it against Israel, to lethal effect. Hizballah is also a skilled guerrilla force—one of the most potent in the world. From the start it waged ferocious insurgent campaigns against Israel, and over time it proved innovative and determined. In waging this guerrilla war, Hizballah at times struck at Israeli civilian targets, sometimes using Katyusha rockets against Israeli villages and towns. Hizballah also has a strong social and political network in Lebanon. Finally, Hizballah is exporting its model to the Palestinians, the greatest current terrorist threat to Israel. Under Hizballah's tutelage, the Palestinians are becoming more deadly and have found a model to emulate that would discourage them from any negotiations with Israel.

To meet these combined challenges, Israel has used several measures, including (1) conventional military operations against guerrilla targets; (2) collective punishment to undercut Hizballah's popular and government support; (3) assassinating and kidnapping Hizballah leaders; (4) psychological warfare and improved intelligence gathering; (5) pressure on Syria and Iran; (6) using a security zone to defend against Hizballah; and (7) using other groups to act as proxies in guerrilla combat.

Conventional Military Operations

Between 1983 and 2000, Israeli forces conducted counterinsurgency operations to stop Hizballah in southern Lebanon. Israel regularly ambushed guerrillas, raided their training camps, and engaged in air strikes. For many years, these operations enjoyed considerable success on a tactical level, leading to casualty ratios of ten to one and often higher. In the 1980s, Hizballah sustained many losses while attacking the Israelis, and Israeli reprisals angered many local Shias, leading Hizballah to curtail, but not end, its operations.[25]

In 1991, however, Hizballah restructured its command, giving its guerrilla forces more local autonomy and reducing the size of the movement so it could be more professional and less vulnerable to Israeli attacks and intelligence penetrations. The fighters also increasingly specialized and improved their security and logistics capabilities. The movement learned how to better use Lebanon's broken terrain, how to plan sophisticated roadside explosives, and how to coordinate small units against Israeli forces, increasing the number of casualties it inflicted. Hizballah also attacked Israeli positions with heavier and more sophisticated weapons.[26] As a result of these changes, Hizballah became a formidable guerrilla force that increasingly began to exact a cost on the Israelis. As one Israeli officer noted, "Hizb'Allah are a mini-Israeli army. They can do everything as well as we can."[27]

Collective Punishment through Military Force

Israel attacked Lebanon in 1993 and 1996 in an attempt to destroy Hizballah's military infrastructure and, perhaps more importantly, to press the Lebanese civilian government to disarm and rein in the movement. In these operations, Israel targeted Lebanon's civilian infrastructure, trying to reverse the country's economic recovery and forcing thousands of refugees to stream from southern Lebanon into Beirut and other areas.

By 1993 Hizballah's improved military effectiveness was taking its toll, and one strike led to the deaths of seven Israeli soldiers—a political disaster for the Israeli government. For seven days in July 1993, Israel conducted Operation Accountability, which involved numerous air and artillery strikes and was intended to destroy Hizballah facilities. Perhaps 120 Lebanese civilians died in the operation, and Hizballah's retaliation with Katyusha rocket attacks on Israeli settlements killed two Israeli civilians. The operation displaced more than three hundred thousand Lebanese and Palestinians.[28]

Part of the operation was designed to undermine Hizballah's popular support. Israel targeted villages in Hizballah areas of operation, even though many civilians remained. Israel hoped that the local Lebanese population would turn against Hizballah if Israel destroyed water and electrical systems, schools, and other parts of the infrastructure.[29]

Israeli officials also hoped that the refugee flows would force the government of Lebanon to act. Prime Minister Yitzhak Rabin noted, "The goal of the operation is to get the southern Lebanese population to move northward, hoping that this will tell the Lebanese Government something about the refugees who may get as far north as Beirut."[30]

In April 1996, Israel launched Operation Grapes of Wrath, which lasted sixteen days. This operation was similar to Operation Accountability, as it again tried to put pressure on Hizballah and the Lebanese government by creating refugee flows and destroying Lebanon's infrastructure. The operation involved six hundred air raids and massive artillery barrages. Again, Hizballah responded by firing hundreds of Katyusha rockets into Israel. Human Rights Watch reports that 154 Lebanese civilians died in the operation.

Israel targeted Lebanese civilians in villages in the Hizballah theater of operations after warning them that a failure to flee would be considered proof that they were tied to Hizballah. Israel also targeted hospitals linked to Hizballah. In its public statements and those of the South Lebanese Army, Israel emphasized that it would respond to Hizballah rocket attacks by striking at Lebanese villages and emphasized that responsibility for this lay with the Lebanese government.

Israel also targeted Lebanon's infrastructure, such as Beirut's electricity infrastructure. As then deputy defense minister Ori Orr noted, "The Lebanese government can do more. It must understand that Lebanon's gross domestic product will not grow." Similarly, Uri Lubrani, who coordinated

Israel's activities in Lebanon, noted, "We have said that we are going to hit Lebanese government infrastructure just to drive the point home. . . . They should be responsible."[31]

Even after these large-scale operations ended, military pressure remained an important part of Israel's strategy for countering Hizballah. The threat of additional military strikes was always implicit, and Israel used military overflights in an attempt to intimidate the Lebanese government.[32]

These attempts at coercion failed, and even backfired, for several reasons. First, the attacks outraged many Lebanese, and they bolstered the prestige of Hizballah. Attacks on Hizballah's humanitarian infrastructure, for example, were viewed as illegitimate, even though Hizballah's humanitarian institutions contribute to the movement's overall resistance activities. As a result, much of the population, including many Lebanese Christians, rallied behind Hizballah. Hizballah exploited this anger, distributing food and medicine to civilian victims and otherwise portraying itself as a humanitarian organization.[33] Hizballah's sponsors, such as Iran, reportedly increased financial assistance to the movement after the operations.[34]

Second, the attacks did little to dent Hizballah's rather rudimentary military infrastructure. Hizballah fighters easily hid among the local population; Israel lacked the detailed intelligence necessary to separate the guerrillas from the rest of the population. The weapons Israel used—air strikes and artillery—were of little use for such a fine-grained task. Perhaps only thirteen Hizballah fighters died in Grapes of Wrath, and Israel failed to capture any Katyusha rockets.[35]

Third, the attacks increased international support for Hizballah because of the civilian death toll. On April 18, 1996, Israel shelled the UN base at Qana, killing more than one hundred men, women, and children who had sheltered in the facility. Despite Israeli claims that Hizballah was using the civilians and the United Nations as a shield for its activities, the Israeli attacks were widely criticized as deliberately striking noncombatants.[36] Israel's mistakes bolstered Hizballah's claim that it was fighting a war of liberation, not engaging in terrorism.

Most importantly, the Lebanese government was an exceptionally difficult government to coerce. From 1990 to 2005, Lebanon was a satrapy of Syria, which had deployed perhaps thirty thousand troops in the country as well as numerous intelligence officials and dominated the political system. In 2005 Syria withdrew its military and paramilitary forces, but it retains an extensive intelligence presence in Lebanon, as well as considerable influence. The Lebanese government's own forces are weak, poorly trained, and unable to rein in Hizballah.

By the 1990s, both Israel and Hizballah had routinized the conflict to the point that they were able to accept rules for their clash—a distinct shift for a movement that openly attacked Israeli civilian targets around the world and a government that readily kidnapped and assassinated Hizballah leaders. From the end of Operation Accountability in July 1993 until April 1996, there was a tacit agreement between Israel and Hizballah, brokered by the United States. Under the agreement, Hizballah would not fire Katyusha rockets into Israel proper, and Israel would not shell Lebanese villages. The conflict would instead be limited to the military and guerrilla forces fighting in the security zone.[37]

This agreement collapsed during Operation Grapes of Wrath. However, on April 26, 1996, U.S. secretary of state Warren Christopher negotiated an understanding between Hizballah and Israel—monitored by the United States and France, as well as Syria and Lebanon—whereby neither side would attack civilians. As part of these constraints, Hizballah increasingly respected "red lines" and focused only on Israel's military presence in southern Lebanon. It did launch rocket attacks on Israel, but many of these were in response to Israeli assassinations of Hizballah leaders or Israeli bombings of Lebanese villages.[38]

The role of the outsider was essential for the negotiation of the red lines. The United States and Syria had influence over Israel and Hizballah, respectively, making it harder for either party to unilaterally abrogate the agreement. Moreover, inasmuch as a limited part of the problem was different interpretations of what constituted civilian targets, the outside role helped minimize misunderstandings.

Israel accepted the red lines agreement at a time of crisis; it was not part of a long-term strategic judgment. The disastrous shelling of Qana and the ineffectiveness of the strikes generated tremendous diplomatic, and to a lesser degree domestic, pressure to halt the operation. The inclusion of outside powers and the protection promised to Israeli civilians offered a face-saving way out for Israel.

The picture from Hizballah's point of view is more speculative. In my judgment, the red lines offered Hizballah several advantages. The lines, of course, protected Lebanon's civilian population from the often harsh Israeli attacks, thus reducing any potential backlash from Hizballah's supporters. In addition, the lines allowed Hizballah to continue wearing down Israel with continued attacks in the security zone. Perhaps most important, the red lines served the purposes of Syria, enabling it to keep the cauldron bubbling while it negotiated with Israel without the risk of the attacks spiraling out of control.

Both sides usually adhered to the informal agreements, although they were imperfect. Israel and Hizballah would occasionally even apologize when one unintentionally struck outside the agreed-on areas. Israeli spokesmen at times noted that a Hizballah attack that killed Israeli soldiers in Lebanon was "within the rules."[39]

Hizballah has also successfully deterred Israel from attacks on its bases in Lebanon by increasing its ability to strike Israel proper. Hizballah is reported to have deployed long-range rockets to southern Lebanon, enabling it to reach deep into Israel and attack major urban areas. As a result, Israeli officials fear that any Israeli thrust into Lebanon would be met by a rocket attack on Israeli cities.[40]

Assassinations and Kidnapping

Israel has assassinated numerous senior and mid-level Hizballah leaders, both to hinder the movement's operations and to intimidate the organization,[41] believing that the removal of senior leaders would devastate Hizballah.[42] Among its many attacks, in February 1984, Israel assassinated Sheikh Ragheb Harb, perhaps the leading Hizballah figure in southern Lebanon. In February 1992, Israel assassinated Hizballah's secretary general, Abbas Musawi, by striking his motorcade. Israel also killed numerous Hizballah leaders at a more local level, trying to destroy Hizballah's regional network.[43]

Israel also kidnapped several senior Hizballah leaders. In 1989 Israeli commandos abducted Sheikh Abd al-Karim Obeid and several of his associates (Obeid was released in a prison exchange in 2003). In 1994 Mustafa Dirani was kidnapped. Both were senior Hizballah guerrilla leaders.[44] The kidnappings were not intended to deter Hizballah. Rather, Israel sought to use the kidnappings to gather intelligence and to disrupt Hizballah's chain of command. Even more importantly, Jerusalem sought a chit for negotiations with Hizballah over missing Israelis, such as pilot Ron Arad.

The assassinations did not hinder Hizballah operations and appear to have led the movement to increase terrorism against Israeli targets. Similarly, the kidnappings failed to hinder Hizballah operations and, if anything, hardened the determination of Hizballah to resist Israel.

Hizballah exploited the assassinations to increase its popularity within Lebanon and in the Arab world more broadly. The high-profile measures increased domestic support for Hizballah, both among Lebanese Shias and among the community in general. Hizballah played on the Shia veneration of martyrdom, lionizing its assassinated leaders and making them focal points for recruitment.[45] Indeed, by singling out Hizballah, Israel confirmed its superiority to Lebanon's other warring factions, providing grim proof of the movement's effectiveness.

Israel's level of assassinations appears to have struck an imperfect balance, causing enough pain to foster esprit among Hizballah and to enable the movement to gain politically from the attacks, but not doing enough damage to impede operations or cause a leadership struggle. As noted above, Hizballah has an experienced and broad cadre on which to draw. In contrast to the Palestinian Islamic Jihad, which was temporarily disabled by a targeted leadership attack, Hizballah had many leaders able to replace its lost cadres. With Iranian help, the Hizballah structure is highly bureaucratized, with numerous councils and specialized organizations. Thus the death of one or two individuals can be overcome by replacing them with other individuals at the same or similar levels of responsibility in the organization.

Hizballah also proved able to escalate in response to the attacks. Many of Israel's assassinations in the 1980s led to immediate Hizballah attacks on Israeli forces.[46] Many observers believed that in response to leadership attacks, Hizballah entered into a brutal tit-for-tat exchange with the Israelis, widening its target list beyond Israeli soldiers and taking actions such as shelling northern Israel outside the security zone. In 1989, probably in response to the Obeid kidnapping, Hizballah hanged Lieutenant Colonel William Higgins, who had been kidnapped in 1988.[47] The 1992 and 1994 bombings in Argentina against Jewish and Israeli targets are often portrayed as a response to Israel's assassination of Musawi and kidnapping of Dirani in the same years. As Clive Jones contends, the assassinations crossed "a Rubicon of restraint that had been tacitly acknowledged by both sides."[48]

Psychological Warfare and Intelligence Gathering

Israel used a range of psychological tactics to try to divide the Shia community, win support, or at least tolerance, for its activities, and undercut backing for Hizballah. To gain popular goodwill, Israel gave money to newspapers and funded broadcasts to dramatize its humanitarian efforts. Israel also initiated a halfhearted civil aid program. To discourage popular assistance to the guerrillas, Israel dropped leaflets warning of retaliation for any attacks.[49]

Israel's military intelligence was the primary organization responsible for collecting information against Hizballah and other targets in Lebanon. Israel also took the unusual step of deploying its domestic intelligence service, Shabak, to Lebanon in large numbers. After the 1967 War, Shabak had established a network of informers throughout the West Bank and Gaza Strip, which enabled it to disrupt many terrorist attacks and prevent anti-Israeli groups from forming in the first place. In Lebanon, Shabak officers worked with the Israeli Defense Forces, trying to re-create the set of informers, safe houses, and other intelligence infrastructure that existed in Palestinian territories. Shabak tried to recruit informers among the Shias and used harsh interrogations to dissuade potential supporters from backing Hizballah and affiliated groups.[50] At times, the levels of brutality became high. Rafi Malka, a senior Shabak official, noted about Lebanon: "In order to stay sane and stay alive, you had to do things that were unacceptable."[51]

Israel's efforts appear to have met with little success, though data are scarce on the specific effects of various projects. In my judgment, Israel's efforts failed in part because the negative effects of day-to-day counterinsurgency operations—such as arrests, detentions, collective punishment, and harassment—far outweighed the positive benefits of particular programs. With Iranian support, Hizballah also devoted considerable attention to proselytizing and spreading propaganda of its own. Lebanon is a small society, with tightly knit families and villages. Israeli attempts to discredit individuals were often offset by superior local knowledge of these individuals, making it hard to blacken their names. Hizballah also enjoyed the genuine admiration of many Shias.

A major Israeli problem was that it did not control Lebanese territory the way it controlled the West Bank and Gaza. As a result, Hizballah had far better local intelligence than the Israelis, both due to its operatives' familiarity with the territory and because it had a vast network of sympathizers. In addition, Hizballah was effectively able to coerce or intimidate those Shias who might otherwise not support its efforts, while Israeli threats were less credible because the Israeli presence on the ground was not permanent. Over time, Hizballah also developed its own counterintelligence capabilities, enabling it to weed out informers and to plant its own operatives in communities that cooperated with the Israelis.

Pressure on Syria and Iran

As noted above, both Iran and Syria use Hizballah as a proxy to strike Israel and to advance their interests in the region. Given Israel's many difficulties in striking at Hizballah directly, it has tried to use military and diplomatic pressure on Syria to force Damascus to crack down on its proxy. Throughout the 1990s, Israel participated in peace talks with the Syrian regime. Implicit in these talks was that a peace agreement would lead Damascus to end its support for Hizballah and curtail the movement's activities in Lebanon. When the peace talks collapsed, Israel tried to use limited military pressure to dissuade Syria from supporting terrorism. In 2001 Israel attacked positions in Syria to send a message to Damascus. The attack immediately led Hizballah to respond by shelling Israeli outposts in the Shabaa Farms area.[52]

Israel at times turned to Washington to press Damascus to curtail Hizballah's attacks when they proved particularly damaging. Washington was sympathetic, given its own bloody history with Hizballah, but such efforts produced mixed results. At times, Hafez al-Asad clamped down on Hizballah to please the United States and continue the peace talks. However, the situation also demonstrated Hizballah's effectiveness and the benefits Syria enjoyed from its influence over the movement. This demonstration probably increased Damascus's commitment to keeping Hizballah viable.

Diplomatic means to end Syrian support for Hizballah collapsed due to a welter of other concerns, primarily the inability of both sides to agree on exactly where the new border between the states would be after Israel withdrew from the Golan Heights—concerns not directly linked to Hizballah. However, from the Israeli point of a view, a major reason for the collapse of the talks was tremendous popular skepticism about Damascus's genuine commitment to peace. Then Syrian president Hafez al-Asad's decades of support for Hizballah and various Palestinian terrorist movements soured Israeli public opinion, making it hard for a series of Israeli leaders to finalize a deal even though many Israeli elites saw it as inevitable. By the end, negotiations focused on only a few meters of territory along the border.[53]

Militarily, Israel had an even greater challenge when confronting Syria. During the 1990s, a strike on Syria would have undermined the always fragile peace process. When the talks collapsed, Israel was in the midst of the brutal al-Aqsa intifada, which consumed many of its military resources and tarnished its already poor image in the world. Military strikes by Israel would have bolstered the regime of Hafez al-Asad's son, Bashar, by allowing him to prove his nationalist bona fides, and would have made Israel appear as an aggressor even to its remaining friends, such as the United States.

Geography makes it difficult for Israel to use direct military pressure against the Islamic Republic of Iran. Israel has instead tried to work with Turkey, which borders Iran, as one means of putting pressure on the Islamic Republic. Even more importantly, Israel has used its influence in the United States to maintain pressure on Iran.

The United States has a host of grievances against Iran, ranging from its nuclear program to its human rights record. Central to U.S. grievances, however, are Iran's support for terrorism and opposition to the Middle East peace process.[54] Israel has emphasized these points in its bilateral relations, using its powerful lobby with Congress and its close ties to successive U.S. administrations to emphasize this point. This influence contributed to U.S. decisions to maintain and strengthen sanctions against Iran, to try to isolate and contain it, and to otherwise maintain a confrontational posture.[55]

U.S. pressure has achieved at best limited results with regard to Iran's support for Hizballah. The Lebanese militia is widely popular in Iran, as is the anti-Israel struggle in general. Iran's current political paralysis and strong sense of nationalism make it difficult for any leaders to make concessions to the United States on support for Hizballah, particularly if no rewards are given.[56]

One bright spot is that Iran and Syria avoided certain types of arms transfers to Hizballah, suggesting they recognize limits to the struggle. Many of the items in Iran's and Syria's arsenals, particularly modern long-range artillery, were not passed on to Hizballah for many years. Some systems, such as chemical weapons, were never transferred. This restraint suggests that both Iran and Syria feared some form of retaliation and sought to keep the conflict active but not to have it boil over into a broader war.

The Security Zone

Because offense was not proving to be an effective defense, Israel created a security zone in southern Lebanon as a buffer against Hizballah attacks. The security zone initially began after Israel's limited foray into Lebanon in 1978. When it was re-created in 1985, Israel initially planned to maintain the zone for a short period of time, but continued Hizballah attacks led to a sense of insecurity and the belief that the zone was necessary to protect Israel. Israel deployed one thousand of its own troops to the zone and also worked with two thousand SLA militiamen. Over time these numbers fell, but Israel increasingly fortified the zone.[57]

The zone proved effective in limiting Hizballah cross-border attacks into Israel and mortar attacks on Israeli settlements. Due to Hizballah's limited armaments—Katyusha rockets' range is limited to 20 kilometers—it could strike only Israeli settlements near the border. The zone also made cross-border infiltration—a problem that had plagued Israel in the 1950s and 1960s with regard to Palestinian terrorists—far harder for Hizballah and almost certainly reduced the number of infiltrations.

The zone, however, became a source of insecurity as Hizballah steadily became far more effective in attacking the Israeli soldiers and SLA fighters stationed there. Over time, the continued casualties—almost 10 percent of those serving in Lebanon[58]—undermined domestic support in Israel for the security zone.

The security zone also undermined the legitimacy of the Israeli cause and bolstered that of Hizballah. UN forces in Lebanon, Arab governments, and many European states portrayed Hizballah's struggle against Israel in the zone as an attempt to liberate Lebanon, not as terrorism.[59] Hizballah also drew on broader Lebanese support as the defender of the country's sovereignty, making the Lebanese public (including many non-Shias) willing to support it in the face of Israeli pressure and reprisals.

Using the South Lebanese Army as a Proxy

Israel began working with the South Lebanese Army in the 1970s, as all of Lebanon's neighbors created or worked with various proxies to gain influence in Lebanon. The SLA was largely Christian originally and its fighters numbered perhaps fifteen hundred. Many of its leaders saw Israeli support as a way of propping up their own faltering position in Lebanon. Over time, many Druze and Shia Muslims joined the movement, largely because of the pay and other benefits.

After Israel's 1982 invasion and subsequent partial withdrawal, Israel relied heavily on the SLA to man the security zone. SLA forces helped Israel run checkpoints, conduct searches, and interrogate prisoners, manning forty-two of the fifty Israeli positions. Israel paid and equipped almost three hundred SLA fighters in the Jezzine enclave of the security zone and worked with them directly along the border strip.[60]

SLA fighters did die in place of Israelis, one of the primary purposes of using a proxy force. However, the SLA proved a weak ally. SLA fighters were neither as trained nor as motivated as their Israeli (or Hizballah) counterparts. They had neither the skill nor the logistics to take the fight to Hizballah. As Hizballah became more skilled, and as it was clear that Israel had no strategy for stopping the attacks, SLA morale plummeted. One SLA observer described their role as "sandbags for an Israeli bunker." Not surprisingly, defections began to increase in the mid-1990s.[61] Hizballah increased these defections by treating leniently SLA members who gave up arms.

EVALUATING ISRAELI EFFECTIVENESS

By almost any standard, Hizballah gained impressive victories in its struggle against Israel. Hizballah attacks contributed heavily to Israel's decision to withdraw to a security zone in Lebanon in 1985, and they were almost the sole reason behind Israel's decision to withdraw altogether in 2000.

Hizballah's successes enabled it to gain stature both in Lebanon and in the broader Muslim world. Many Christian and Sunni Muslims express admiration for Hizballah's successful resistance (and its relative lack of corruption). Hizballah also became the premier Shia resistance movement in Lebanon, with its once-strong rival Amal being reduced to little more than a lapdog of Syria. Hizballah is also widely admired among Palestinians and other Arabs because of its successful resistance to Israel.

Hizballah's victory and the subsequent Israeli withdrawal also created a credibility problem in the eyes of many Israelis. Many Israeli security officials opposed the withdrawal, believing it would embolden others to emulate Hizballah. More generally, they believed that withdrawal under pressure would be a direct contravention of the "iron wall" philosophy that has governed Israel's relations with its neighbors and would encourage new challenges to Israel's military supremacy, and thus to its existence.

Hizballah's successes occurred in the face of sustained, competent, and at times ruthless Israeli attempts to destroy the movement. Several of the factors that led to Hizballah's success involve the movement's own prowess. Others, however, concern the nature of Israeli democracy and its weak geopolitical position.

A Resilient and Determined Adversary

One of Israel's biggest problems in countering Hizballah is the movement's skill. In 2002 Florida senator Bob Graham, the former head of the Senate Select Committee on Intelligence, declared that Hizballah is more lethal than al Qaeda. Then deputy secretary of state Richard Armitage echoed Graham's concern, noting that "Hezbollah may be the 'A team' of terrorists," while "Al Qaeda is actually the 'B team.'"

In addition to its skill, Hizballah was an elite organization that had mass support among Lebanon's Shia community. Thus the deaths of individual fighters, while at times painful for the organization on the tactical level, did not hinder recruitment. Hizballah could replenish its losses, enabling it to sustain the conflict with Israel despite repeated blows. Few terrorist organizations in the world could lose as many cadres as Hizballah lost and still continue their struggle.

Lebanese Shia Resentment of Israel

Israel failed to gain any sympathy among Lebanon's Shia community, and its counterinsurgency measures increased Shia support—and that of other Lebanese—for Hizballah. As described above, many Shias initially welcomed the Israeli presence, but Israel was quickly seen as a brutal occupier. Although at times concerns about losing support among local residents led Hizballah to limit or temporarily suspend attacks, apparent Israeli escalations through assassinations, kidnappings, and strikes on civilians further angered many Lebanese, making them more supportive of attacks. Israel's devastation of southern Lebanon in Operations Accountability and Grapes of Wrath proved particularly damaging to its reputation. Furthermore, the Shias feared that any long-term association with Israel would tar them forever in the broader Arab and Muslim world.[62]

Lebanese Weakness

Israel should focus its wrath on the government of Lebanon, which openly tolerates and supports Hizballah, but this option is not realistic. In theory, holding a government accountable for the actions of its citizens seems sensible. Former U.S. secretary of state Colin Powell has called on the Lebanese government to stop Hizballah's attacks on Israel. The Lebanese government deploys approximately seven thousand troops along the Israeli-Lebanese border and has tens of thousands more in the rest of the country. However, it is not clear if these forces could be used effectively. Lebanon's armed forces are more a glorified gendarmerie than a true fighting force. In addition, the force is designed to reflect Lebanon's myriad ethnic communities, not to help the central government impose order. If confronted with Hizballah's dedicated and well-trained fighters, the Lebanese government forces would probably lose.

Most importantly, in the 1990s, Lebanon was in essence a Syrian satrapy, and no important decisions were made independently of Damascus. The damage Israel inflicted on Lebanon in 1993 and 1996 did not move the government in Beirut, which looked to Syrian interests before addressing the welfare of its own citizens.

No Strategy for Victory

By the mid-1990s, Israel appeared to lack any long-term strategy for defeating Hizballah. Israel's "success" in limiting the conflict to the security zone also gave it no chance of overall victory. While Hizballah could undermine popular support in Israel by killing Israeli soldiers, there were no equivalent "strategic" targets in the security zone that if destroyed would force Hizballah's capitulation. Hizballah had effectively deterred Israel from escalation.

Over time, the failure of the various Israeli efforts to stop Hizballah—and the movement's increasingly effective attacks on Israeli troops in the security zone—convinced many Israelis that pulling out of Lebanon was necessary, even though the Israeli military opposed it. Ironically, Hizballah's own restraint helped convince Israel of this course. Hizballah's willingness to adhere to red lines and its focus on military over civilian targets led many Israelis to believe that pulling out of Lebanon would not lead Hizballah to target Israel proper.[63]

Counterterrorism at the Expense of Counterinsurgency

By establishing red lines, Israel did deter Hizballah from conducting "terrorism," narrowly defined to include only direct attacks on civilians. For most of the 1990s, Hizballah focused on attacking the Israeli military in southern Lebanon. When it did attack Israeli cities, it was often as part of a tit-for-tat exchange after Israel expanded its operations. Hizballah's attacks in Argentina may also have been a response to Israeli actions against Hizballah's leaders, but in any event the last of these extraregional attacks was in 1994.

Part of the reason Hizballah abandoned civilian attacks, however, was the prestige and benefit of attacking the Israeli military directly. As Hizballah's more conventional military options increased, it was able to gain followers and influence without earning the opprobrium that came with terrorist attacks.

The price for Israel of stopping Hizballah's attacks on civilians was considerable, moreover. By creating red lines, Israel in essence institutionalized a struggle it was not able to win. Given the value Israel placed on the lives of its soldiers—and Hizballah's willingness to sacrifice its own fighters—casualty ratios would have had to be increasing rather than decreasing for Hizballah to stop its attacks.

Hizballah also shifted its involvement in terrorism to include exporting its skills and methods—the Hizballah model—but Israeli policy was not able to counter this process. By gaining a safe haven outside the immediate theater of combat, Hizballah was able to become in essence a state sponsor of terror. It helped make Palestinian groups far more lethal and inspired them to avoid any compromises.

Casualty Sensitivity

Israel was exceptionally sensitive both to the number of casualties Hizballah inflicted and to the fate of captured, kidnapped, or missing Israelis. In its conduct of war and its force posture, Israel places a tremendous premium on ensuring the safety of its soldiers. The fate of airman Ron Arad, who was downed in 1986, has long obsessed Israel, and Israeli military leaders feared the loss of another pilot or soldier into Hizballah's hands.[64]

Hizballah played on this casualty sensitivity, believing (correctly) that it could outlast Israel by being more willing to sacrifice. As Hizballah's deputy secretary general Na'im Kassem noted, "When an Israeli soldier is killed, senior Israeli officials begin crying over his death. . . . Their point of departure is preservation of life, while our point of departure is preservation of principle and sacrifice." [65]

A recent Israeli prisoner swap demonstrates the efficacy of Hizballah's position. In January 2004, Israel freed three hundred Lebanese prisoners and four hundred Palestinians in exchange for an Israeli businessman and the bodies of three IDF soldiers. Although many of the Palestinians were low-ranking members of various radical groups, this exchange represented a tremendous propaganda coup for Hizballah. The Lebanese organization demonstrated that it—in contrast to Palestinian groups and Arab states—was able to force the Israelis to make concessions. Even more importantly, Israel released former senior Hizballah officials Mustafa Dirani and Abd al-Karim Obeid.[66] If similar ratios are used for future exchanges, Israeli effectiveness would have to reach superhuman proportions to stay ahead of Hizballah's.

The Giant Fishbowl

Israel is subject to intense media scrutiny and the attention of international organizations. Although counterinsurgency efforts may benefit from targeting—or at least intimidating—civilians, this has tremendous diplomatic and political consequences.[67] Hizballah facilities were often "civilian" in nature, as is true with many terrorist movements. Israel could not target the movement's headquarters, logistics sites, or other parts of its infrastructure without killing civilians and was thus compelled to cut short its campaigns, particularly in 1996, before the pain inflicted had a chance to sink in.

The fishbowl effect had a tremendous impact in Israel itself. Any casualties Israel suffered immediately became part of an increasingly raw public debate, keeping the failure of Israel's overall strategy on the front pages of many newspapers. Moreover, Israeli society would not have supported the level of brutality needed for Israel to impose its will on southern Lebanon, and the active Israeli and world media prevented such operations from being carried out in secret.[68]

Limited Israeli Interests

The withdrawal of Israeli forces from Lebanon and the campaign against Hizballah did not pose the same political risk to Israel's government as would a similar failure against Palestinian movements. There were no Israeli settlements in Lebanon, and hundreds of thousands of Lebanese do not work in Israel. Moreover, as the 1990s wore on, Hizballah's attacks caused harm primarily to Israel's forces in Lebanon, not the rest of Israeli society. The campaign against Hizballah, in contrast to the effort against the Palestinians, did not fundamentally change the daily lives of most Israelis or require changes in Israeli laws that threatened Israel's democracy. These limited interests contributed to Israeli casualty sensitivity, but they also enabled Prime Minister Barak to pull Israeli forces out of Lebanon without major political damage.

Overall Diplomatic Isolation

Israel today faces a tremendous problem: the isolation, and indeed hostility, it suffers from much of the world. Despite Israel's close alliance with the United States, many Asian and European powers are hostile to Israel, to say nothing of Muslim and Arab states. Hizballah thus enjoys the benefit of the doubt in many capitals, an unusual arrangement for a terrorist group opposing a recognized government.

Israel's isolation makes it particularly hard to press Iran and Syria. Both governments gain prestige by supporting a terrorist group rather than suffer from the stigma that might go with backing such violence. Any Israeli military pressure is subject to particular scrutiny, even if deliberately limited in its devastation. Israel's isolation also makes it more difficult to gain cooperation on curtailing Hizballah's global financing network and on putting political pressure on the movement.

The Balance Sheet on Success

The almost-twenty-year Israeli campaign against the Lebanese Hizballah has failed to destroy the movement. Indeed, when Israel left Lebanon in 2000, Hizballah was far stronger politically and militarily than it was when it began in the early 1980s. Hizballah today enjoys a worldwide network for recruitment, funding, and logistics and is widely lauded as a model of successful resistance. In Lebanon itself, it is widely popular, both for its social welfare activities and for its resistance to Israel.

Hizballah's use of violence did not stop, although it did change. Hizballah attacked Israeli targets overseas in 1992 and 1994. Hizballah also became increasingly involved in the Palestinians' struggle against Israel, helping train and organize Palestinian movements and making them more lethal. Hizballah also increased its military campaign against Israel over time, despite the skilled and occasionally ferocious Israeli response. By the time of the Israeli withdrawal, Hizballah had greatly reduced the casualty ratio with Israel.

The perception of Israel's failure is also real and consequential. In both Israel and the Muslim world, Hizballah is perceived as having inflicted a humiliating defeat on Israel. This situation, in turn, has inspired Palestinians against Israel and been cited by al Qaeda leaders as proof of the effectiveness of terrorism.

Yet Israel's efforts were not an unqualified failure. Hizballah is directly responsible for fewer Israeli deaths than it was in the 1990s. In addition, Israel's withdrawal from Lebanon increased Hizballah's incentives for restraint. Although the movement is active against Israel in a number of ways, as discussed above, it has limited its own attacks to occasional cross-border raids, a marked decrease from its constant strikes against Israeli forces in the late 1990s. Hizballah increasingly shifted from a terrorist group that viewed civilians and soldiers as interchangeable targets to a movement that focused primarily on killing Israeli soldiers in the area of Lebanon that Israel occupied. The Hizballah of the 1980s repeatedly took hostages and conducted terrorist attacks against targets elsewhere in the Middle East and in Europe. By the late 1990s, Hizballah was refraining from such actions and operating largely as a guerrilla organization. Hizballah has used its short-range Katyusha rockets largely as part of a tit-for-tat exchange with Israel, shelling civilians in response to perceived Israeli escalation. Nor has Hizballah used all the means at its disposal. For example, Hizballah has saved the long-range rockets it possesses for use as a deterrent. Hizballah made this shift in part because it recognized that attacks on civilians that could be described as "terrorism" hurt its image among potential supporters, both in the region and outside it.[69]

LESSONS FOR OTHER DEMOCRACIES

Israel's experience with Hizballah, while unique in several ways, offers several lessons for other democracies fighting terrorist organizations. First, Israel's experience with Hizballah suggests the many difficulties of confronting a skilled terrorist group that is also a popular insurgent movement.[70]

Although Hizballah at times kept its cadre for guerrilla operations distinct from its terrorist cadre, the political leadership and many of the key personnel belonged to both groups. Thus it proved impossible for Israel to eradicate Hizballah as a terrorist movement without destroying it as a guerrilla operation as well. Hizballah simply had too many well-trained and motivated people who could be used for terrorist as well as guerrilla operations.

Second, counterterrorist measures should avoid inflaming nationalism whenever possible. When examining the interplay between terrorism and insurgency, the United States, and to a lesser degree other Western powers, also must recognize how counterterrorism measures may provoke a nationalist backlash that, in turn, generates support for the insurgency. Israel's destruction of Lebanon's infrastructure, its local intimidation campaign, and other measures designed to punish Hizballah supporters appear to have backfired, making the movement a symbol of resistance that even Christians and Sunni Muslims came to respect. Given the unpopularity of the United States in the Muslim world today, highly publicized U.S. support for many governments' counterterrorism campaigns may actually increase popular support for the terrorist.

Third, the terrorist threat often mutates, becoming less direct but no less dangerous. The Hizballah model poses a particularly disturbing challenge—one that requires new categories of analysis as well as new policies. In essence, the United States and other Western powers define involvement in terrorism very narrowly. Thus Hizballah is widely portrayed as a movement of national liberation, not simply because of its cause but because its activities are seen as focused on the Israeli military. This view is true in a narrow sense, but Hizballah's efforts to train the Palestinians suggest a much broader role that few have addressed.

Fourth, democracies such as the United States must recognize the severe limits imposed by worldwide media attention. Israel's standard of behavior in Lebanon and elsewhere had to conform to limits set by Israeli society and, to a lesser degree, by the international community. Abusive intelligence interrogations in Lebanon, the shelling of Qana, assassinations and kidnappings, and other harsh measures came under particular scrutiny. Many other Western powers would face the same mix of domestic and international attention to their actions. Even if they conducted similar activities, they might limit their numbers or otherwise be halfhearted in the process. This in turn might lead to the worst of all worlds for the government in question: widespread condemnation of a particularly harsh tactic, with few benefits accruing from it.

Fifth, democracies must be vigilant against state sponsors of terrorism. Israel's failures against Hizballah also speak to the problem of confronting state sponsors. Both Iran and Syria made Hizballah far stronger and helped the organization survive Israel's onslaught. Nevertheless, Israel has not been able to bring pressure to bear on either Damascus or Tehran. As a result, Israel can make tactical gains against Hizballah, but it is impossible for Israel to put the forces on the ground to shut the organization down once and for all.

Sixth, there is a limit to how much democracies can "outsource" their counterterrorism efforts, for reliance on proxies poses its own set of challenges. Israel found that it was hard to convince even a completely dependent proxy like the SLA to conduct dangerous operations when Israel itself was unwilling to act. Moreover, the SLA lacked Israel's skill level, making it hard to carry out more than limited defensive measures. Any U.S. efforts to rely on local regimes and even warlords to help prosecute the global war on terrorism must recognize the likely limits of these actors as well as their potential contributions.

Finally, Israel's experience suggests the necessity of maintaining a positive international image on other issues. Because much of the world condemns Israel's treatment of the Palestinians, Israel is constrained in its ability to counter other terrorist groups such as Hizballah, even though the two causes are quite distinct. Moreover, both Iran and Syria are able to escape pressure they otherwise deserve because they are backing a foe of one of the world's most reviled governments—Israel. The United States must recognize that its diplomatic success in pursuing counterterrorism objectives cannot be divorced from its overall international reputation.

As the above observations suggest, the Israeli experience with Hizballah offers many lessons about why democracies need to be cautious when confronting skilled terrorist and guerrilla groups. Israel inflicted many grievous losses on Hizballah, but the Lebanese movement weathered these and even prospered.

The past is not a necessary prologue when it comes to gauging the future of Hizballah's confrontation with Israel. Indeed, Hizballah's fortunes may have peaked. Having succeeded in expelling Israel from Lebanon, the movement now has few objectives that will rally most Lebanese, or even most

Shias, in support of its violence. For now, it has straddled the fence, engaging in politics, supporting other militant groups, conducting limited attacks on Israeli targets, and maintaining a strong latent capability to use terrorism. Over time, however, its lack of a rallying cry similar to the liberation of Lebanon may lead support for the movement to decline.

Notes

1. For valuable accounts of the collapse of Lebanon into civil war, see Dilip Hiro, *Lebanon: Fire and Embers* (New York: St. Martin's, 1992); and Michael Hudson, "The Breakdown of Democracy in Lebanon," *Journal of International Affairs* 38 (Winter 1985): 277–92. The best account of the role of the Palestinians can be found in Don Brynen, *Sanctuary and Survival: The PLO in Lebanon* (Boulder, CO: Westview, 1990). The steady politicization of the Shias is described in Augustus Richard Norton, *Amal and the Shi'a* (Austin: University of Texas Press, 1987).

2. For an excellent account of the military campaign, see Kenneth Pollack, *Arabs at War* (Lincoln: University of Nebraska Press), 524–51. See also Thomas Collelo, *Lebanon: A Country Study* (Washington, DC: Federal Research Division, Library of Congress, 1989), 204.

3. Fouad Ajami, *The Vanished Imam* (Ithaca, NY: Cornell University Press, 1986), 200; and Hala Jaber, *Hezbollah: Born with a Vengeance* (New York: Columbia University Press, 1997), 14.

4. Ian Black and Benny Morris, *Israel's Secret Wars: A History of Israel's Intelligence Services* (New York: Grove, 1991), 394.

5. Jaber, *Hezbollah,* 113.

6. Ibid., 16–27. Initially, many of the attacks were carried out by southern Lebanese affiliates of Amal, but over time these affiliates either joined or were overshadowed by Hizballah. See Black and Morris, *Israel's Secret Wars,* 451.

7. Hizballah has admitted that these organizations are not separate entities. See Magnus Ranstorp, *Hizb 'allah in Lebanon: The Politics of the Western Hostage Crisis* (New York: St. Martin's, 1997), 53. See also A. Nizar Hamzeh, "Islamism in Lebanon: A Guide," *Middle East Review of International Affairs* 1, no. 3 (Spring 1997), http://meria.biu.ac.il/journal/1997/issue3/jv1n3a2.html. Other experts report that Hizballah had five thousand fighters and five thousand more reservists by the end of the 1980s. See Carl Anthony Wege, "Hizbollah Organization," *Studies in Conflict and Terrorism* 17 (1994): 155.

8. Augustus Richard Norton, "Hizballah and the Israeli Withdrawal from Southern Lebanon," *Journal of Palestine Studies* 30, no. 1 (Autumn 2000). Other sources put the number of full-time fighters even lower, at about three hundred. See Nicholas Blanford, "Hizbullah Attacks Force Israel to Take a Hard Look," *Jane's Intelligence Review* 11, no. 4 (April 1, 1999).

9. Amal Saad-Ghoreyeb, *Hizbu'llah: Politics and Religion* (Sterling, VA: Pluto, 2002), 23–36; Jaber, *Hezbollah*, 56–77; and Judith Harik, "Between Islam and the System: Sources and Implications of Popular Support for Lebanon's Hizballah," *Journal of Conflict Resolution* 40, no. 1 (March 1996): 58.

10. Interview with Sheikh Hassan Nasrallah, "Peace Requires Departure of Palestinians," *Middle East Insight* (March–April 2000), 32.

11. *United States of America v. Ahmed al-Mughassil et al.* (Khobar Towers indictment), June 2001, paragraph 15. The full text of the indictment can be found at www.pbs.org/newshour/updates/june01/khobar.pdf.

12. See "Terrorist Group Profiles," Naval Postgraduate School, taken from the U.S. Department of State, *Patterns of Global Terrorism* (Washington, DC, various years), available at http://library.nps.navy.mil/home/tgp.hizballah.htm; and Yoram Schweitzer, "A Transnational Terrorist Organization," September 1, 2002, occasional paper by the Institute for Counterterrorism in Israel, www.ict.org.il/articles/articledet.cfm?articleid=448.

13. Matthew Levitt, "The Hizballah Threat in Africa," *Policywatch 823,* January 2, 2004.

14. *United States of America v. Mohamad Youssef Hammoud et al.,* United States District Court, Western District of North Carolina, Charlotte Division. The text can be found at www.fd.org/pdf_lib/Hammoud.pdf.

15. A. Nizar Hamzeh, "Lebanon's Hizbullah: From Islamic Revolution to Parliamentary Accommodation," *Third World Quarterly* 14, no. 2 (1993): 321–37.

16. As quoted in Harik, "Between Islam and the System," 51.

17. Steven N. Simon and Jonathan Stevenson, "Declawing the 'Party of God': Toward Normalizing in Lebanon," *World Policy Journal* (Summer 2001): 39; and International Crisis Group, "Hizballah: Rebel without a Cause?" Middle East Briefing no. 7 (Amman/Brussels, July 2003), 7.

18. Hizballah also assisted in the shipment, interdicted by Israelis in January 2002, of large amounts of conventional weaponry to the Palestinian Authority aboard the arms ship *Karine-A.* In May 2003, Israel's navy stopped a boat that had missile ignition switches and a Hizballah expert, who Israel claims was intended to help Palestinian militants increase the accuracy of their Qassam rockets. See International Crisis Group, "Hizballah," 10; and James Kitfield, "The Iranian Connection," *National Journal* (May 17, 2002): 1469.

19. Adham Saouli, "Lebanon's Hizbullah," *World Affairs* 166, no. 2 (Fall 2003).

20. For a good review of the Shabaa Farms dispute, see International Crisis Group, "Old Games, New Rules: Conflict on the Israel-Lebanon Border," November 18, 2002, www.crisisweb.org/home/index.cfm?id=1663&l=1.

21. Human Rights Watch, *Civilian Pawns: Laws of War Violations and the Use of Weapons on the Israel-Lebanon Border* (New York: Human Rights Watch, May 1996), 22.

22. Norton, "Hizballah and the Israeli Withdrawal"; Shimon Shapira, "The Origins of Hizballah," *Jerusalem Quarterly* 46 (Spring 1988): 123.

23. Initially, these included the Islamic Amal movement (a splinter of the parent Amal organization founded by al-Sadr), the Association of Muslim Ulema in Lebanon, the Lebanese Da'wa, and the Association of Muslim Students, among others. Over time, the movement spread to Beirut, where it incorporated the many followers of Sheikh Fadlallah, a leading Lebanese religious scholar who at the time endorsed many of the ideas of the Iranian Revolution. From there, the movement spread to the Amal stronghold of southern Lebanon, where it incorporated many local fighters who were battling the Israelis largely on their own. See Ranstorp, *Hizb 'allah in Lebanon,* 25–33; Shapira, "Origins of Hizballah," 124; Wege, "Hizbollah Organization," 154; and Sami G. Hajjar, "Hizballah: Terrorism, National Liberation, or Menace?" (research monograph, Strategic Studies Institute, Carlisle, PA, August 2002), 6–9, www.carlisle.army.mil/usassi/welcome.htm.

24. Paul Pillar, *Terrorism and U.S. Foreign Policy* (Washington, DC: Brookings Institution, 2001), 159.

25. Jaber, *Hezbollah,* 29–31.

26. Ibid., 37–42; and David Eshel, "Counterguerrilla Warfare in South Lebanon," *Marine Corps Gazette* 81, no. 7 (July 1997): 40–45.

27. As quoted in Clive Jones, "Israeli Counter-insurgency Strategy and War in South Lebanon, 1985–1997," *Small Wars and Insurgencies* 8, no. 3 (Winter 1997): 92.

28. See Human Rights Watch, *Civilian Pawns,* 8–16, for an overview of problems during Operation Accountability. As was clear in Operation Grapes of Wrath in 1996, there is a dispute over whether Operation Accountability deliberately sought to affect civilians or whether that result was an acceptable side effect.

29. Ibid., 12.

30. Ibid., 10n16.

31. Orr is quoted in Human Rights Watch, *Israel/Lebanon: "Operation Grapes of Wrath"* (September 1997): 15; Lubrani is quoted on page 17. See also pages 5–6 and pages 14–15 for an overview of Israeli objectives.

32. Hizballah has faced pressure to respond to these overflights, as they challenge Hizballah's self-proclaimed role as the defender of Lebanon. See Nicholas Blanford, "Diplomats Say Israel Set to Continue Overflights over Lebanon," *Washington Report on Middle East Affairs* 22, no. 8 (October 2003), www.wrmea.com/archives/October_2003/0310035.html.

33. Jones, "Israeli Counter-insurgency Strategy," 96; Jaber, *Hezbollah,* 199; and Gary C. Gambill, "The Balance of Terror: War by Other Means in the Contemporary Middle East," *Journal of Palestine Studies* 28, no. 1 (Autumn 1998): 63.

34. Michael Eisenstadt, *Iranian Military Power* (Washington, DC: Washington Institute for Near East Policy, 1996), 74.

35. Jaber, *Hezbollah,* 178.

36. For a review, see United Nations, "Report of the Secretary General's Military Advisor Concerning the Shelling of the UN Compound at Qana on 18 April 1996," S/1996/337.

37. Human Rights Watch, *Civilian Pawns,* 4.

38. Hajjar, "Hizballah," 27; and Jones, "Israeli Counter-insurgency Strategy," 90–92.

39. Norton, "Hizballah and the Israeli Withdrawal."

40. Blanford, "Israel Set to Continue Overflights over Lebanon."

41. For an overview of the strengths and weaknesses of assassinations, see Catherine Lotrionte, "When to Target Leaders," *Washington Quarterly* 26, no. 3 (Summer 2003): 73–86. For an examination of Israel's policy of targeted killings (particularly of Palestinians), see Steven R. David, "Israel's Policy of Targeted Killing," *Ethics and International Affairs* 17 (Spring 2003): 111–26. For a critique of David's work, see Yael Stein, "By Any Name Illegal and Immoral: Response to Israel's Policy of Targeted Killing," *International Affairs* 17 (Spring 2003): 127–37.

42. Jones, "Israeli Counter-insurgency Strategy," 90.

43. Black and Morris, *Israel's Secret Wars,* 397.

44. Israel also imprisoned numerous Hizballah fighters. It has tried to use imprisonment to gather intelligence, weaken Hizballah's forces, and gain additional chits for the return of its own captives and MIAs, such as downed Israeli pilot Ron Arad.

45. Jaber, *Hezbollah,* 25.

46. Jaber, *Hezbollah,* 20–25.

47. Higgins probably died of torture before being hanged. Jaber, *Hezbollah,* 37.

48. Jones, "Israeli Counter-insurgency Strategy," 91.

49. Black and Morris, *Israel's Secret Wars,* 393–94; and Jones, "Israeli Counter-insurgency Strategy," 82, 96.

50. Black and Morris, *Israel's Secret Wars,* 395–96.

51. As quoted in ibid., 399.

52. Blanford, "Israel Set to Continue Overflights over Lebanon." Israel also attacked Syria in 2003 in response to Palestinian attacks on Israel.

53. For an overview of the talks, see Jerome Slater, "Lost Opportunities for Peace in the Arab-Israeli Conflict," *International Security* 27, no. 1 (Summer 2002): 79–106.

54. For an overview of U.S. objectives, see Deputy Secretary of State Richard Armitage, "U.S. Policy and Iran" (testimony before the Senate Foreign Relations Committee, October 28, 2003), www.state.gov/s/d/rm/25682.htm.

55. Among the many U.S. measures are unilateral U.S. sanctions against Iran; the Iran-Libya Sanctions Act, which mandates U.S. sanctions against foreign companies that do business with Iran under certain circumstances; efforts to isolate Iran diplomatically; and a large U.S. military presence in the Persian Gulf region designed in part to deter Iranian adventurism.

56. For useful overviews of Iran's politics today, see Ray Takeyh, "Iran at a Crossroads," *Middle East Journal* 57, no. 1 (Winter 2003); and Jahangir Amuzegar, "Iran's Crumbling Revolution," *Foreign Affairs* 82, no. 1 (January–February 2003): 44–57. For a review of Iran's support for terrorism and how it has changed, see Gary Sick, "Iran: Confronting Terrorism," *Washington Quarterly* 26, no. 4 (Fall 2003), www.twq.com/03autumn/docs/03autumn_sick.pdf.

57. Jones, "Israeli Counter-insurgency Strategy," 88.

58. Ibid., 89.

59. Jaber, *Hezbollah,* 43.

60. Blanford, "Hizbullah Attacks"; Norton, "Hizballah and the Israeli Withdrawal from Southern Lebanon." Israel also tried to create proxy forces among local Lebanese Shias, but this effort met with little success. See Jaber, *Hezbollah,* 17.

61. Jones, "Israeli Counter-insurgency Strategy," 94.

62. Ajami, *Vanished Imam,* 201.

63. Molly Moore, "Israeli Army Engaged in Fight over Its Soul," *Washington Post,* November 18, 2003, A1.

64. Human Rights Watch, *Israel/Lebanon,* 39. For an overview of how Israel's casualty sensitivity has affected its military operations and security posture, see Eliot A. Cohen, Michael J. Eisenstadt, and Andrew Bacevich,

Knives, Tanks, and Missiles: Israel's Security Revolution (Washington, DC: Washington Institute for Near East Policy, 1998).

65. As quoted in Jones, "Israeli Counter-insurgency Strategy," 89.

66. Aluf Benn, Yoav Stern, and Yossi Melman, "Nasrallah: Kuntar, More Israelis to Be Released," *Haaretz,* January 25, 2004, www.haaretz.com/hasen/spages/386401.html.

67. Nathan Leites and Charles Wolf, Jr., *Rebellion and Authority* (Chicago: Markham, 1970), 90–109.

68. Black and Morris, *Israel's Secret Wars,* 399.

69. Judith Palmer Harik, *Hezbollah: The Changing Face of Terrorism* (New York: I. B. Tauris, 2004), 2–4.

70. Israel also was conducting a counterterrorist operation in a foreign land. Thus it lacked the automatic legitimacy that governments usually enjoy when operating in their own territory.

11

TURKEY AND THE PKK

A Pyrrhic Victory?

Henri J. Barkey

In 2006, seven years after the defeat of Turkey's longest Kurdish-inspired insurgency, Ankara's Kurdish question remains unresolved. In fact, the issue has regained much of its salience due to three interrelated factors. The first is renewed violence—still sporadic but deadly nonetheless. Some of the thirty-five hundred to forty-five hundred Kurdistan Workers' Party (PKK) fighters who took refuge in northern Iraq after the capture of their leader, Abdullah Öcalan, in 1999 have been making their way back to Turkey.[1] While the PKK no longer constitutes the kind of military or political threat it did to Turkey in the 1990s, the return to armed attacks is a powerful reminder of potential things to come.

The second and far more serious and delicate problem is the emerging autonomous Iraqi Kurdish entity in the wake of the U.S. invasion of Iraq. Turkey had adamantly opposed federalism in Iraq, which would reward Iraqi Kurds with a federal state of their own, preferring a return to centralized rule by Baghdad. Ankara's fears are grounded in the possibility of both the emergence of an independent Kurdish state at some point in the future and the demonstration effect of Kurdish federalism in Iraq on Turkey's Kurdish minority. Ankara's other card in the Iraqi mix is its support for the Turkish-speaking minority, the Turcomans, who along with the Kurds claim the oil-rich city of Kirkuk. However, Iraqi Kurds, with their steadfast support for U.S. goals in Iraq and their history of repression under Baghdad's draconian rule, have earned a seat at the Iraqi table, a fact that Turkey is finding difficult to reverse.

Third, Kurdish (nonviolent) political activism in Turkey itself has continued unabated. Over the course of the past decade and a half, many political parties proclaiming to support the aspirations of Kurds have emerged. While the authorities routinely close down or harass these parties, such activities are unlikely to disappear; if anything, they are increasing in intensity with Turkey's European Union (EU) accession candidacy.

These three problems point to the fact that after almost a century of efforts, Turkey is still struggling to come to grips with its Kurdish minority. The "Kurdish question" has manifested itself in one form or another since the founding of the republic in 1923 and the abrogation of what the Kurds thought was a deal between them and the new Turkish leadership over the nature of the new state. Throughout the twentieth century, Turkey experienced unrest among its Kurdish population; sometimes this took the form of rebellions and at other times, peaceful political activity. Only very rarely did the Turkish state offer its Kurdish citizens an olive branch. Ironically, many Turkish Kurds have today pinned their hopes for progress on Turkey's EU accession process.

The PKK insurgency was the longest rebellion the Turkish state ever had to confront. Having commenced in 1984, it came to a temporary end with a 1999 unilateral cease-fire declaration by the PKK following Öcalan's arrest and conviction. The rebellion claimed the lives of thirty thousand people, mostly insurgents, civilians caught in the middle, and security forces. Irrespective of its remaining forces in Iraq and Turkey, the PKK is a defeated military force. To be sure, the insurgency never posed a strategic threat to Turkey; the PKK had no chance of defeating one of NATO's largest armies. Therefore, the prospect of the Kurds separating from the Turkish mainland was at best a fantasy. On the other hand, the ferocity of the struggle meant that Ankara had to commit a large number of soldiers and resources to fighting it, a costly proposition for a country continuously mired in economic troubles. The struggle sullied Turkey's relations with neighbors, the United States, the European Union, and friends and foes alike. It also undermined the rule of law in Turkey, gave rise to wide abuses of power, and undermined Turkish democracy. The political costs, therefore, were quite significant.

From the beginning, the Turkish state took an uncompromising attitude toward the rebellion. Rooted in the decades-old position that the Kurds did not really exist,[2] the state sought a military solution. Still, in its early days in the mid-1980s, the insurgency was not taken very seriously; troubles in the Kurdish regions were not new. The military, which in Turkey had traditionally and especially since 1960 exercised an inordinate amount of influence, was more apprehensive about the PKK than was the civilian establishment led by Turgut Özal (prime minister, 1983–89; president, 1989–93). Özal eventually succumbed to the officers' approach and gave them carte blanche. The military's scorched-earth policy turned a considerable segment, if not most, of the inhabitants of the Kurdish regions into active opponents of the state. Village evacuations, a village guard system, and sheer repression characterized the state's policy until Özal decided to seek a different approach in the aftermath of the 1991 Gulf War. Early efforts at change in policy were abandoned after his death in 1993, and the government resumed the hardline policy with a vengeance. This policy included mystery killings at the hand of state-sponsored paramilitary groups and severe restrictions on freedom of expression. The state carried the war to the Kurdish regions and also engaged in cross-border operations, seeking to destroy the PKK's rear base in northern Iraq.

In the end, the tide turned completely against the PKK, not just because of the increased sophistication of counterinsurgency operations, but also because of the dire straits in which the region's Kurdish population found itself. Many were forced to move into regional cities, where jobs were scarce, and others into the squalor of the shantytowns of Turkey's western cities. The coup de grâce to the insurgency came when the Turkish military, having succeeded in containing and then reducing the size of the PKK, went after its leader in Damascus by threatening Syria with war. Then Syrian president Hafez al-Asad decided quickly and sent Öcalan packing. Once Öcalan was captured, the PKK, to save his life, decided to withdraw from Turkish territory into northern Iraq and announced a unilateral cease-fire.

With its forces holed up in the mountainous regions of northern Iraq, the PKK tried to come to grips with the changed international environment and remain relevant. It first changed its name to the Kurdistan Freedom and Democracy Congress (KADEK), hoping that the changing political conditions in Turkey, specifically the advent of the pro-Islam and liberal Justice of Development Party (AKP) of Recep Tayyip Erdogan would provide an opportunity for participation in Turkish politics. By the end of 2003, it had once again decided on a makeover, changing its name to the Kurdistan People's Congress (KONGRA-GEL) and hoping to get recognition as a political movement twice removed from its violent past. However, the Turkish state, having decisively defeated the PKK, is unlikely to allow any political space for former fighters, no matter how reformed they may profess to have become. This attitude was evident when the Turkish parliament passed a restrictive amnesty law designed to lure rebels back from northern Iraq. In other words, as far as the Turks are concerned, the PKK has reached the end of the road.

This chapter explores the origins and trajectory of the insurgency, the Turkish state's response, and the means deployed to successfully defeat the insurgency. The chapter concludes with an analysis of the costs to Turkey of the counterinsurgency campaign, the lessons learned, and its impact on democratic development.

The PKK

Roots

The origins of the PKK can be found in the tumultuous 1960s, a period that shook university communities throughout Turkey. This period was influenced not only by the radicalization of politics in Europe and elsewhere but also by changed domestic circumstances in Turkey itself following the 1960 military coup d'état. In overthrowing the center-right Democratic Party, the young officers gave rise to two contradictory tendencies. The coup opened the way for both military interference in politics and greater political participation and polarization. While most Turkish Kurds had spent the 1950s supporting the Democratic Party against the Republican People's Party founded by Mustafa Kemal Atatürk, a new generation of Kurds emerged from among those who had migrated to large cities and who had made the long journey to Turkish universities from their relative isolation in Turkey's eastern and southeastern provinces.

The Kurds in the universities gravitated toward the Turkish Labor Party (Türkiye Işçi Partisi, or TIP), a classic left-wing party. The TIP became the focus of intense intra-ethnic politics. For Kurds who sought to take it over, the TIP experience was disappointing. Not only was the party banned after the 1971 coup, but the Kurds also discovered that the Turkish left was unwilling to support their cause. The PKK emerged out of this twin disillusionment. Kurds gravitated toward a series of left-wing underground militant and violent groups. Some of these hoped to begin a revolution by going into the countryside à la Che Guevara, while others engaged in urban violence. The PKK itself was a natural outgrowth of these types of movements; it was formed in 1978 by Öcalan, then a student in the Political Science Faculty in Ankara. It did not start its armed activities until 1984. Ironically, Öcalan and some of his comrades escaped Turkey for Syria ahead of the 1980 coup and thus avoided the dragnet. In the intervening years, the PKK organized itself in the southeast. In an admission that antistate activities in the southeast were among the triggers for the 1980 coup, Bülent Ulusu, commander of the naval forces and one of the coup's architects, reported that when the army went on maneuvers in the Kurdish areas, it was met with chants and slogans calling for its expulsion from the region. "The East is boiling," he said. "The communists and the Kurds are in complete cooperation there."[3]

No specific event triggered the insurgency. It was, in fact, an evolutionary process in which the PKK took advantage of the general disregard for the southeast shown by successive Turkish governments. Traditionally seen as the most underdeveloped two regions of the country, the east and southeast received a minimal share of public and private investments. The relative poverty of the area also meant that these were the least desirable regions for government employment and service. In fact, both regions were places of exile for functionaries thought to be deserving of punishment. The combination of neglect and poverty, buttressed by the Turkish state's policy of assimilation and denial of Kurdish identity, made for difficult relations in the Kurdish regions. The PKK easily exploited these resentments.

Aims

The PKK started off as a Marxist-Leninist organization. It was a natural extension of the student movements that had turned violent in the 1970s. The PKK's main difference from these leftist groups was its emphasis on Kurdish identity. At the outset, the organization preached that a Marxist revolution would free the Kurds both from the bondage of the Turkish yoke and from the Kurdish *aghas* (feudal landlords) who exploited the peasantry. Marxism served three important functions for the PKK. First, it was the only discourse that the PKK leadership understood, because Turkish universities in the 1970s had come to be controlled by the hard left, intent on imposing its dogma. Radicalized students for the most part did not attend classes and spent much of their time regurgitating Marxist-Leninist thought. This was their lingua franca. Second, Marxism helped distinguish the PKK from other Kurdish groups, especially the more conservative and Iraqi-linked ones that had much sway in the southeast. Third, Marxism provided the leadership with the ideological means to indoctrinate recruits and maintain control over the organization.

While the organization was wholeheartedly committed to the Marxist-Leninist ideology, the fact of the matter was that this was not the main attraction for individual recruits in the southeast; they joined because of the appeal to Kurdish consciousness.[4] Öcalan himself, in a 1993 interview, claimed he was not a Marxist or a communist but believed in "democratic-socialism."[5]

From the outset, the PKK pronounced itself in favor of a separate Kurdish state. In fact, it even had pan-Kurdish aspirations. The scope of its objectives followed the fortunes of the insurgency; initially in favor of a uncompromising stand against the Turkish state, the PKK changed its tune first with the end of the cold war and then when it lost the initiative on the ground. It began to downplay its Marxist-Leninist roots and then sought to define its aims for the Kurds in the form of successive federations—Arab-Kurdish in Iraq, Turkish-Kurdish in Turkey, and Persian-Kurdish in Iran. When the Turkish army went on the offensive, the PKK's discourse changed dramatically. In the waning days of the insurrection, the PKK was reduced to advocating equal rights for Turkey's Kurdish citizens, a dialogue with the state, and the democratization of Turkish institutions. After his capture, Öcalan went so far as to denounce some of his former associates, claiming that he had been duped by foreign powers, and paid his respects to the Turkish people.[6]

Tactics

Following classical insurgency tactics, the PKK first tried to establish its domination over other Kurdish groups, armed and unarmed, and then proceeded to terrorize the very population it wanted to free. Its use of violence was designed to spread fear among the rural Kurdish population and establish its bona fides as a serious organization. It also made a point of targeting landlords, who had become increasingly unpopular, and not just in the southeast.[7] Kurdish areas were culturally and religiously conservative places where landlords who had been co-opted by Ankara "delivered votes" to political parties and helped maintain order. As a consequence, the PKK polarized the Kurdish regions; the landlords, with the help of the central government, organized themselves against it and formed village guard units, which in turn provoked more violence.

The PKK routinely targeted state officials. In a strongly centralized state such as Turkey, where everyone is in effect appointed by Ankara, state officials were not just governors and gendarmerie but also policemen on the beat and the teachers, who, through no fault of their own, had been sent to a Kurdish region. By assassinating officials, the PKK aimed to physically separate the Kurdish regions from the rest of the country and show that it was capable of taking on the mighty state. If schoolteachers were intimidated and refused to show up for work, or if policemen were afraid to venture out at night, then the PKK could claim success.

With time, the PKK consolidated its position and altered its tactics from the pursuit of sheer terrorism to a more conventional guerrilla style focused on targeting security forces. With large numbers of recruits joining the organization, the PKK upgraded its fighting techniques, created training bases in the countries surrounding Turkey, and fielded more disciplined forces. It focused its military activities largely in the southeast and east, with occasional forays into other parts of the country. However, in the large urban areas of Istanbul, Ankara, and Izmir, where many Kurds had migrated, its activities remained relatively weak. With the exception of a few spectacular terrorist events, it shied away from engaging in activities or investing too much military capability in the cities. It did not even follow up on its threat to wreck the burgeoning tourism industry as a means of putting pressure on the government. Good police work and the PKK's preference for concentrating activities where it was doing well and was assured of support deterred the PKK from taking the war to the cities as it had promised.[8] This situation did not mean that Kurds in the cities did not support or sympathize with the PKK, however. Quite the contrary; they raised funds for the organization and organized politically. Even Kurds who opposed the PKK for political or ideological reasons were affected by the PKK's prowess and even felt a sense of "national" pride.

In the southeast, the PKK took advantage of the terrain, relied on hit-and-run tactics, mined roads, and occasionally engaged large-scale Turkish forces. Suicide attacks were few and far between. A female member who infiltrated a police base during a ceremony carried out the most spectacular suicide attack. Unlike other Kurdish groups in the region, and unusual for the conservative cultural setting of the region, the PKK made liberal use of women, especially as fighters.

In the southeast, early success allowed the PKK to expand its influence and attempt to replace the Turkish state with its own makeshift "institutions." For instance, it created "people's courts" to mete out justice when the state was slow to react and also to adjudicate local disputes. In many respects, the PKK benefited from a perception that it had momentum on its side. During the first phase of the insurgency, it had the initiative against the security forces and local authorities. At the height of its success (1988–91), the PKK could count on as many as ten thousand fighters and had an extensive network of supporters, runners, couriers, and sympathizers.[9]

As it expanded its operations in the southeast, it also paid a great deal of attention to the political side. Öcalan recognized that the PKK could not possibly defeat the Turkish military. The armed struggle, he claimed, brought a degree of prestige.[10] The PKK strived to become more than a purely military organization, and it was careful to emphasize the importance of political activity. The PKK defined itself as a political party with component units that included military, political propaganda, and recruitment wings. It organized itself not just in Turkey and the surrounding countries but also in Europe, creating a Kurdish parliament in exile and, perhaps most importantly, keeping a close watch on political developments in Turkey. In the late 1980s and 1990s, Kurdish political parties, intent on forcing a debate on the Kurdish issue, began to emerge. The PKK did not directly control these parties, which had to constantly reinvent themselves as the authorities banned them, but there is no question that PKK sympathizers and members joined them and often assumed leadership positions. By the early 1990s, the PKK was the dominant factor in all things Kurdish in Turkey.

The organization was under the complete dominance of one person: Öcalan. He had created it, and his imprint was everywhere. His control was absolute, and he created a personality cult reminiscent of Saddam Hussein or Kim Il Sung. The worship of the leader enabled him to maintain control over the organization after his capture and imprisonment. In fact, recently the PKK has been further reduced to an organization that lives to seek its leader's freedom, in the process alienating a significant segment of Turkish Kurds.

THE INSURGENCY'S INTERNATIONAL DIMENSION

Like other insurgencies, the one led by the PKK could not have matured without a propitious international context. Turkish Kurds have historically had close ties with their Iraqi counterparts, ties that continue today. The legendary Iraqi Kurdish leader Molla Mustapha Barzani's exploits had reverberated across the region. In addition to the ethnic factor, strong family ties bind the two communities. When Saddam Hussein's regime began its post–Iran-Iraq War Anfal campaign, which culminated with the gassing of Kurdish towns to punish rebellious Kurds, Turkish Kurds took notice. Similarly, when Iraqi Kurds poured over into Turkey at the end of the 1991 Gulf War, Turkish Kurds mobilized to help them. The Turkish government's initial hesitation to extend aid to these refugees further polarized the southeast, including those who had not been pro-PKK.

The PKK took advantage of the absence of Iraqi authority in northern Iraq and set up its rear bases there. Both Kurdish factions in northern Iraq, the Kurdistan Democratic Party (KDP) and the Patriotic Union of Kurdistan (PUK), at one point sympathetic to the PKK, would be cajoled into supporting Turkish counterinsurgency incursions into their own territory in pursuit of the PKK. Still, the mountainous border areas among Iraq, Turkey, and Iran made a perfect no-man's-land for insurgent activities. The border was relatively easy to cross for small armed bands and correspondingly difficult for an organized army. The PKK used Syrian, Iraqi, and Iranian territory for strategic depth. There, it could train militants and provide them with respite far from the reach of the Turkish army.

The PKK's second most important external source of support was the Syrian regime of Hafez al-Asad. Öcalan had established himself in Damascus; he and his lieutenants enjoyed the protection of the Syrian security services as they moved freely between Damascus and the Bekaa Valley in Syrian-controlled Lebanon. Under Turkish pressure, the Syrians in the mid-1990s began to somewhat restrict Öcalan's freedom of movement and the use of Syrian training camps. Nevertheless, the fact that the organization could be run on a daily basis by its leader living unimpeded in a foreign capital was a tremendous advantage. Öcalan's presence in Damascus was the worst-kept secret; Syrian officials would routinely refuse to acknowledge his presence, yet journalists and others had no trouble meeting with Öcalan. Why Syria supported him as long as it did remains a mystery; the most-often-quoted excuse was the simmering dispute over the sharing of the waters of the Euphrates River. As long as the PKK was operational, the reasoning went, Damascus had a card to play against the massive complexes of dams and irrigation networks Ankara intended to build in the southeast.

Iran was the other country most directly involved in supporting the PKK. The PKK used Iranian territory, often in connivance with local authorities, to escape Turkish troops. It established bases across the border but more importantly in areas in Iranian Kurdistan too far for Turkish military operations, including effective air strikes. The Iranian government, just like the Syrian one, professed its innocence regarding PKK activities.

The Kurdish diaspora, especially in Europe, was an important component of the PKK's global reach. Of the 2.5 million Turks living in Germany alone, estimates put the number of Kurds at more than half a million. These Kurds, together with Kurds living in other countries, provided the PKK with three significant elements of support: a base for recruiting would-be combatants, a base for financing its operations, and a base for lobbying European governments. The financing needs of the PKK, like those of all other ethnonationalist organizations, were quite significant. In addition to making arms purchases and managing its operations, it also ran a satellite television station, Med-TV (later renamed Medya-TV and more recently ROJ-TV), which most Kurds in Turkey could pick up with relative ease provided they owned satellite dishes. This television station proved to be one of the most important consciousness-raising instruments at the PKK's disposal. In the absence of any other broadcast in Kurdish, a large number of Kurds, many of whom did not support the PKK, watched its programs.

The PKK relied on both donations and intimidation to raise funds. Although the PKK was officially banned in most European countries, many PKK-related self-help organizations provided Kurdish workers with a place to meet and stay in touch with one another. When necessary, the PKK could easily mobilize tens of thousands of Kurds in Europe for protest meetings and to influence European political opinion.

As a potential candidate for EU membership, Turkey was particularly susceptible to criticisms of human rights violations and undemocratic practices. For many in the European Union, the Kurdish issue loomed large in rendering Turkey ineligible for membership consideration. The Turkish government would continuously, and often with U.S. support, complain of the lackadaisical European approach to the PKK. Ankara would point out that while governments officially banned the PKK, many of its front organizations operated with impunity and in plain sight. Although many individuals—European political figures and others—supported the Kurdish cause in Turkey and even the PKK, most countries were careful to put some distance between themselves and the PKK. Still, the PKK managed to broadcast from studios in Brussels and London and remain a presence on European soil. Although the PKK was unwelcome in Europe, its European presence and strong European criticism of Turkish counterinsurgency policies were important sources of political support for the organization.

The Turkish State at War

For a state that had forcefully denied the mere existence of the Kurds, there was little choice but to forcefully combat the insurgency. Turkey's approach was dictated not just by the ideological character of the state but also by the interplay among the different power centers, specifically the relationship between the military and the political leadership. What differed over time was the effectiveness of the counterinsurgency campaign and the tactics employed.

Ideology and Approach

In an April 1990 meeting between journalists and publishers with the president of the republic and representatives of the military and intelligence, the secretary general of the National Security Council, General Sabri Yirmibesoglu, criticized the press coverage of the conflict in the southeast and also argued that "the struggle in the southeast is like our war of independence . . . journalism ends here."[11]

In a nutshell, General Yirmibesoglu's comments underscored the state's approach to the Kurdish insurrection. For decades, starting in the 1930s when all things Kurdish were banned, Turkish policy was anchored in the simple denial of the Kurds' very existence. While this policy was devoid of reality when it came to the Kurdish regions, for the rest of the country it perpetuated a 1930s myth.[12]

Kurds fared poorly after the Atatürkist revolution because Turkey not only became home to a very centralized state apparatus but also remained one of the more ideological states in the world. Kemalism, as most people have come to refer to the state ideology, is a "mixture of secularism and nationalism which is at the heart of most of Turkey's major policy preoccupations."[13] Secularism and nationalism were defenses set up by a modernizing elite intent on catching up with the rest of the world and unwilling to brook or accommodate dissent. Religious reaction and Kurdish nationalism were the two forces most feared by this elite.

As a result, throughout the Republican period, the central government authorities were vigilant about the possibility of ethnic violence. All took care not to refer to Kurds in public discourse and in the press. The state completely banned the Kurdish language, changed Kurdish place-names into Turkish ones, and imposed a general policy of Turkification. But the state's meager resources were insufficient to make Turks out of Kurds. Many Kurds to this day still have not learned enough Turkish to function in society.[14] By 1937 the nascent Turkish state had had to suppress at least four violent revolts. After the last rebellion, Kurds turned their attention to political activity. While most activity was surreptitious, including joining the Turkish Grand National Assembly to advocate for local economic concerns, it helped raise the level of consciousness among Kurds. This process conflicted with the state's preferred solution of assimilation. In effect, the state was torn between its distrust for the Kurdish regions and the Kurds in general and its official dogma that everyone was a Turk.

When the Kurdish issue erupted into the open once again in Iraq in the 1980s and later in Turkey, the state had difficulty adjusting to this new reality. It kept referring dismissively to Iraqi Kurds as "separatist forces in northern Iraq" or "feudal or tribal elements." Former prime minister Bülent Ecevit, a stalwart of the establishment and a member of the center-left, perhaps best exemplified the state view. He adamantly opposed any concession to Kurds; the issue was simple as far as he was concerned: Kurdish demands were nothing more than dissatisfaction with the region's underdevelopment and the feudal ties that accompanied it. Also sympathetic to Saddam Hussein, Ecevit felt that the Kurds of Iraq were undeserving of any consideration.[15]

The Turkish establishment was also seized by the fear of foreign involvement in its domestic Kurdish problem. Although Syrian, Iranian, and Iraqi involvement was clear, most of the elite worried more about the European powers and the United States. Any criticisms of human rights practices in the southeast were deemed to be supportive of the PKK cause. More importantly, because of suspicions of British involvement in the first Kurdish revolt in the 1920s, fears abounded that the imperialist powers wanted to revive the 1920 Sevres Treaty, which had contemplated a Kurdish autonomous region.[16]

The violence that ensued in the southeast with the rise of the PKK was not predetermined, but it was also a fact that difficult intra-ethnic and state-citizen relations had been deteriorating. If Ankara was slow to respond at the outset of the PKK insurgency, it was in part because it refused to acknowledge that the Kurdish question enjoyed any saliency. Having allowed these problems to simmer, the state was even less willing to accommodate or make any concessions to a revolt. Ideologically, therefore, the response of the state to the PKK-led insurrection was a predetermined one of countering violence with violence, without much of an attempt to win the hearts and minds of the local citizenry.

Civil-Military Relations

What would complicate the counterinsurgency campaign in Turkey was the delicate nature of civil-military relations. The military has traditionally been an important force, and as the country moved to genuine democracy in the 1950s, officers resented the ascendancy of civilian politicians. The 1960 coup reversed the process of civilianization and ushered in an era of heightened military involvement in politics. Two coups that followed, in 1971 and 1980, firmly established the military as the primus inter pares. A constitutional body, the National Security Council (NSC), composed of civilians and generals, was created to regularly discuss the nation's most pressing issues, which more often than not were domestic concerns. While defined as an advisory body, the NSC in reality served as a conduit or channel for the preferences of the Turkish General Staff, which could rarely be ignored.

The 1980 intervention was the most thorough; not only were all the politicians banned from participating in future political activities, but a new constitution restrictive of individual rights was introduced. The new order significantly expanded the military's prerogatives. When the military returned power to civilians, the new prime minister, Turgut Özal, proved to be a maverick intent on rolling back the influence of the military establishment.[17] Throughout the 1980s, he and the military clashed over the approach to national security and the proper role for officers. The PKK insurgency, however, prevented Özal from accomplishing a turnaround in this area. The climactic clash was over Turkey's role in the 1991 Gulf War; Özal's determination to align Turkey with the United States in the run-up to the war resulted in the resignation of the chief of staff of the armed forces, a first in Turkish history. After Özal's death, the new governments returned to the old practice of leaving policy initiatives to the generals. In fact, in 1998 it was the military that signaled the most important shift in policy, when the commander of the land forces threatened Syria with war if Öcalan was not kicked out. His pronouncement mobilized the government and public opinion, not to mention Turkey's primary ally, the United States, to pressure Syria into kicking the PKK leader out. The insurgency, especially after Özal's demise, served to reestablish the military's preeminence in domestic security and political matters.

COUNTERINSURGENCY STRATEGY AND TACTICS

Phase I: Learning the Ropes, 1984–93

Surprisingly, given the perpetual concerns the Turkish state had with respect to the Kurdish regions, it responded rather slowly to the emergence of the PKK. Perhaps because the PKK started by attacking wealthy Kurdish land-lords, it appeared to the authorities that the group was more of a bandit organization. A longtime observer of the insurgency has suggested that the state first thought this revolt resembled the ones of the early Republican period, and hence the reaction was similar to the one employed then.[18] In other words, state authorities responded with harsh measures; interrogations, torture, and detentions quickly alienated the local population from a state for which there was no great reservoir of sympathy and support. In the insurgency's initial days, villagers quickly discovered that the local gendarmerie forces proved quite unfriendly, even if they were called to defend people against the PKK.

Instead of trying to win the hearts and minds of the local population, the security forces played into the hands of the PKK. Compared to the insurgents of the 1920s and 1930s, the PKK was a great deal more sophisticated. It avoided large-scale confrontations, maintained the initiative, and paid a great deal of attention to the political side. As John Grant has argued, the initial reaction by the authorities was to assault the PKK's "fluid military infrastructure"; "[i]t took the Turks a while to learn that the PKK's true center of gravity was the support it received from the Kurdish population in the southeast, not its guerrilla army."[19] Although Ankara continuously increased its security presence in the Kurdish regions, especially in the towns, the police, with few friends to rely on, tended to be on the defensive and often retreated to fortified positions at night, which suited the PKK.

Early on, the state created the village guard system, designed to exploit preexisting rivalries among the clannish Kurdish communities of the southeast, marred by a history of intervillage disputes and feudal-like relationships that bonded villagers to local aghas. Thus it was relatively easy for Ankara to identify villages and local leaders who would contribute unemployed peasants to local militias. Sometimes villagers were not given a choice and were forcibly recruited, while at other times the monthly pay of $100, a princely sum then for anyone from that region, produced loads of volunteers. There were as many as seventy thousand village guards at the height of the system. These guards were supposed to protect their villages from PKK attacks; provide advance intelligence for the security forces, especially considering that they had a better knowledge of the land and language; and act as shock troops of a sort during the army's anti-PKK operations. As useful as they may have been to the security forces, the village guards, at least their local Kurdish bosses, were equally entrepreneurial: they often raided other villages, under the pretext of the villages' PKK leanings, only to loot them. The PKK, in turn, attacked the guards mercilessly. The system contributed to the deepening of intra-Kurdish animosities and ultimately a regionwide refugee crisis.[20]

On the administrative side, Ankara in 1987 declared a state of emergency in the southeast (OHAL State of Emergency Rule) and appointed a super-governor to coordinate government activities. Emergency rule represented an administrative extension of martial law; not only were civil liberties severely restricted and constitutional protections eliminated, but emergency rule allowed for the introduction of new police and military units better equipped to deal with the insurgents' challenge. The government hailed the effectiveness of the OHAL system, but critics have pointed out that between 1987 and 1991, the situation deteriorated considerably.[21]

Finally, the other tactic the state employed during the early phase was periodic cross-border raids into Iraq. During the Iran-Iraq War, these were conducted with the connivance of the regime in Baghdad, which had deployed most of its troops against Iran. After the 1991 Gulf War, when the Kurds established their autonomous region in northern Iraq under the tutelage of the United States, Turkey, with the help of the two Kurdish groups in the north, engaged in large-scale actions against suspected PKK locations and formations.[22] These were of some limited effectiveness because they disrupted the PKK's logistics and gained time.[23]

Overall, in the earlier phase, the government suffered from poor tactics and intelligence. Some officers criticized Prime Minister Özal for misunderstanding the nature of the challenge.[24] The Turkish military was restricted to roads and open terrain, enabling the PKK to ambush army convoys; the military telegraphed its moves well in advance and in general did not fight in the winter months.[25] In addition to poorly trained troops, the Turks suffered from low morale. General Dogan Güres, a chief of staff during the period, admitted in a 1995 postretirement interview that when he was first appointed, troops sent to the region would refuse to serve or resigned, and forces were badly equipped and trained.[26]

Phase II: Intensification, 1993–99

Alarmed by the deepening problem, Ankara in 1993 decided to increase the pressure on the PKK. It had already begun to shift greater resources into the region. It also stepped up the training of its troops and deployed elite commando units. Most importantly, it changed tactics; it adopted ones similar to those of the PKK. It dispatched small mobile units, designed to take the fight to the PKK rather than sit and wait for the insurgents to strike. It created new police strike units called special teams (Özel Timler), composed of nonuniformed fighters and police officials, to man roadblocks and blend into the countryside, dealing with the support offered to the PKK there. Many team members were drawn from the ultranationalist Nationalist Action Party, a party that espouses racialist theories. Under the nominal control of the Ministry of the Interior, the special teams were responsible for many of the human rights violations in the region. They did much of the dirty work. The military, in contrast to these special teams, starting in 1995 tried to improve its profile in the conflict areas; all soldiers were issued a small booklet advising them on how to treat and avoid abusing the local population.

The military command rethought its methods and strategy and learned from its mistakes. Aggressive ground tactics were supplemented by better air-ground coordination and activities. The military purchased a wide variety of helicopters and used them to introduce rapid-response teams. The increased mobility enabled the military to slowly take the initiative away from the PKK. Moreover, the military also decided to flood the area with security forces and soldiers. As General Güres explained, the aim was to fill every nook and cranny, block all escape routes, and deny the PKK fighters access to food and replenishment: "They [the PKK] could not operate in the winter. We are ready. We have clothing for minus 40 degree [centigrade] conditions. . . . In 1991 we would stop [operations in the winter months]. Now we never halt operations."[27] In fact, in addition to the village guards, as many as 250,000 security personnel were deployed in the region to fight the PKK.[28]

The most important shift occurred with the military assuming complete control of operations in the southeast. The death of President Özal in early 1993 eliminated the one person in the political hierarchy who still insisted on a measure of civilian control over counterinsurgency operations. This change was already in the making prior to Özal's demise. Özal had become president in 1989, and when his party lost the elections in 1991, the veteran center-right politician Süleyman Demirel assumed the prime minister's office. Demirel had always been in favor of more hard-line policies against the PKK. Upon Özal's death, Demirel became president, and a relatively unknown economist, Tansu Çiller, assumed the mantle of prime minister.

Çiller at the outset flirted with the idea of a political solution to the Kurdish issue. She quickly reversed course when the military hierarchy opposed the idea, and she decided to offer carte blanche not just to the military but also to the security services writ large. She also decided to equate all things Kurdish with the PKK.[29] The military campaign was joined by a political one at home when she decided to prosecute the representatives of the legal Kurdish party, DEP, for sedition. The number of disappearances of sympathizers, alleged or real, not just in the southeast and east but also in the major western cities, increased. In perhaps one of the more bizarre encounters of her rule, she even "tried to convince villagers that helicopters that had attacked [these] villages belonged to the PKK."[30]

The more aggressive tactics included free-fire zones, village evacuations, and the punishment of local villagers.[31] On many occasions, "the European Court of Human Rights . . . found Turkish security forces responsible for torturing, killing, and 'disappearing' Kurdish villagers and burning them out of their homes."[32] The number of villages and hamlets evacuated and burned is difficult to determine, although estimates have varied between twenty-two hundred (with five hundred thousand villagers being relocated)[33] and four thousand (with a million-plus villagers losing their homes).[34] The regional capital city of Diyarbakir swelled with refugees coming in from the countryside. In fact, urbanization in the southeast increased dramatically.[35] Many Kurds also migrated west; from the Mediterranean cities of Adana and Mersin to Istanbul and Izmir, all cities experienced a major influx of dislocated Kurds. According to a U.S. State Department report, "In an effort to deny the PKK logistical support, the Jandarma [gendarmerie] during the year occasionally rationed food and other essentials in some rural areas in the emergency region. Security forces returned to evacuated villages and burned homes, to deny the PKK, and have shot livestock, burned forests and orchards, or denied villagers permission to harvest fields."[36] To be sure, some Kurds also left because they were caught between the state and the PKK, and the fighting significantly reduced the residents' already much diminished economic standards. Government tactics eliminated the PKK's room to maneuver and most importantly reduced its ability to feed and shelter its combatants.

Although the Turkish security services and the government had come under significant criticism for not adequately dealing with the PKK problem, one area of uncontested success was the cities. Considering that in Istanbul alone, people of Kurdish extraction numbered in the millions, there were relatively few urban terrorist incidents. Kurdish activists in the main cities, while engaged in political work, seemed to refrain from violent activities. In the cities, the security forces had a great deal more training and were more experienced, largely because they had been combating a variety of subversive groups dating back to the early 1970s. Overall, the police and other security units kept a close eye on all they thought were potentially subversive. Finally, Kurds in the cities, including recent arrivals, feeling the pressure of dislocation in the harsh conditions of the slums, preferred to distance themselves from overtly Kurdish groups. To be sure, there were a number of spectacular incidents attributed to the PKK, including the fire-bombing of a department store in Bakirköy said to belong to the family of the super-governor of the southeast.

By 1995 the situation had been decisively reversed in the southeast. Not only was the PKK on the defensive, but the military and security services now controlled most of the territory. The main threat posed by the PKK—usurping or replacing state authority in the towns and villages of the southeast—was defeated. The fighting went on; the PKK could still score limited successes by ambushing troops and attacking isolated out-posts, but it also paid a heavy price as its own casualty toll increased. Even if the PKK had had no chance of achieving a separate Kurdish state, it had nevertheless developed into an organization that was a great deal more than a few brigands. But by the end of 1995, with the local population the primary victim of this struggle, the PKK had become a containable irritation—albeit an important one—for the state.

Civilian Counterinsurgency Infrastructure

Part of the success of the counterinsurgency can also be attributed to the relentless pressure exerted on the Kurdish population of the region and beyond. Here the state had also mobilized its judicial branch. It introduced a series of laws designed to combat terrorism; most of these laws allowed judges and prosecutors to liberally interpret their provisions, which allowed them to deem any type of speech subversive. As a result, tens of thousands of people were arrested and hauled in front of state security courts and other judicial bodies. State security courts were typically empowered to try cases of sedition. Emergency law in the southeast also provided the authorities with a great deal of leeway with suspects. Lawyers for defendants were also besieged, often ending up in detention; human rights organizations were subject to continuous harassment, as were doctors who treated the wounded. With few constitutional bodies willing to come to their defense, the Kurds of the region found themselves abandoned. Occasionally, local members of parliament would try to intervene to win the release of a few detainees.

It was with Çiller's appointment of Mehmet Agar to the head of the National Security Organization (Emniyet Teskilati) that the civilian coun-terinsurgency infrastructure took an ominous turn. During his command, the number of disappearances and extrajudicial killings—including that of a prominent Kurdish member of parliament—increased dramatically. An automobile accident near the town of Susurluk unleashed a scandal that revealed how the national police were linked to numerous disappearances, mysterious bombings, and other illegal activities.[37] Moreover, in the southeast, local officials co-opted an emerging Kurdish Islamist group, Hizballah, to attack PKK sympathizers and supporters.[38]

Responding to International Support for the PKK in Iraq and Syria

Turkish governments from the beginning preferred to deal with their neighbors on a diplomatic level. Capitalizing on regionwide worries about pan-Kurdish nationalism, the Turks tried to foster regional discussions on the Kurdish question. As far back as 1978, General Kenan Evren, then chief of staff of the armed forces, went to visit Saddam Hussein and suggested working together to deal with the Kurdish problem in both their societies.[39] In the 1990s, Turkish officials routinely conferred with their Syrian and Iranian counterparts to discuss the Iraqi Kurds, all the while accusing both of these neighbors of harboring the PKK.

As part of rethinking their strategy, the Turks decided to tackle the strategic depth that the PKK enjoyed in Iraq. After having engaged in only hot-pursuit operations, starting in 1992, they made more forays into northern Iraq. Turkish operations in northern Iraq evolved into bolder actions and employed up to fifty thousand troops in coordinated raids that lasted weeks at a time. Eventually, the Turks established a small but continuous military presence in northern Iraq designed to keep a better eye on both Iraqi Kurds and PKK forces.

Having contained the PKK in Turkey and scored successes in Iraq, Ankara decided to deliver its coup de grâce by threatening Syria into abandoning its support of Öcalan and the PKK leadership. The military high command decided to increase the pressure on the Syrians. In late September 1998, the commander of the land forces, Atilla Ates, while visiting troops near the Syrian border, threatened Damascus with military action if it did not desist from supporting the PKK. The menace was amplified in subsequent days, first by the chief of staff and later by the president of the republic.[40] Rumors of significant Turkish troop movements also circulated, although it never was clear whether the Turks had actually mobilized to move against Syria.[41] By that time, Turkish-Israeli relations had developed significantly, especially in the military realm, and the Arab world suspected the two of reaching a strategic alliance. Syria was defenseless against Turkey because it had no significant troops deployed north of the city of Hama. Alarmed at the prospect of a Turkish move against Syria, possibly backed by Israel, Egyptian president Hosni Mubarak personally undertook a mission to resolve the crisis.

The Syrian leadership, unwilling to risk a confrontation with Turkey, blinked. Öcalan was unceremoniously sent packing. In search of refuge, Öcalan traveled across Europe, ending up in Kenya at the Greek ambassador's residence. Once discovered there by U.S. intelligence, he was delivered to the Turks,[42] who put him on trial. It is possible that the Turks never thought they could lay their hands on Öcalan, but the chain of events that began with their saber rattling worked. Afraid that he might be executed, the PKK decided to save its leader's life by declaring a unilateral cease-fire and pulling the remnants of its forces out of Turkey and into northern Iraq.

DEALING WITH DISSENT

Critical to the success of the campaign against the PKK was the policy dealing with domestic dissent. For the Turkish state, this was as much a political struggle as a military one. As Christina Lynch Bobrow argues, the state's primary means of dealing with dissent was through "arbitrary governance." It enforced the boundaries of free expression quite arbitrarily. This approach provided it with a maximum degree of freedom to suppress dissent because "[a citizen] never knows when one will get into trouble."[43] The judiciary, therefore, could infer a crime in some citizens' behavior, while others would never be prosecuted for the exact same expression. Such arbitrariness also preserved a veneer of legality.

If insurgency initially stifled organized legal Kurdish political activity, especially in the southeast, this situation did not last long. The Social Democratic Party (SHP), looking for votes to meet the 10 percent national threshold necessary to obtain seats in parliament, concluded an electoral pact in 1991 with the first of the Kurdish parties, HEP. This process resulted in some twenty-three Kurds from the southeast with distinct nationalist leanings becoming members of parliament. Soon they defected from the SHP to form their own bloc. This led to the formation of a series of legal Kurdish political parties: HEP, ÖZDEP, DEP, HADEP, and most

recently DEHAP. In each case, the party was banned, its leaders imprisoned, and, as is the case with a banned party, its assets taken over by the
state. The reasons for proscription differed, but the fact that these parties
had links, often indirect, with the PKK or had committed transgressions
was sufficient to institute proceedings against them.

DEP was the last of the parties to have any parliamentary representation.
Once the authorities banned the party, its MPs lost their right to sit in parliament. For the most part, these parties were poorly led; they could not
sufficiently distance themselves from the PKK and committed gross political miscalculations that prevented them from making any inroads with the
Turkish public at large. Nevertheless, each time a party was banned, another
would quickly emerge in its stead. HADEP and later its successor, DEHAP,
continued to operate, often harassed by the authorities and the judiciary.
Although unsuccessful in national contests, in 1999 HADEP was quite able
to win the mayoralties of numerous southeastern municipalities, including
Diyarbakir, the largest city in the southeast. In the 2002 national elections,
it polled 6.2 percent of the vote.[44]

The state and its institutions also went after the media in an attempt to
silence pro-Kurdish newspapers and intimidate mainstream ones to limit
any criticism of the military campaign. Fundamentally, the objective was
also to minimize any discussion of the Kurdish issue so as to prevent its
legitimation as an issue at home. Journalists working for Kurdish media were
the subject of abuse, assassinations, imprisonment, and mistreatment.[45]

The mainstream media exercised a great deal of self-censorship, especially during the latter stage of the counterinsurgency campaign. Whereas
many Turkish journalists in the Özal years traveled to Damascus and the
Bekaa, after the collapse of a putative cease-fire in 1993, they shied away
from tackling the PKK problem and even the Kurdish issue. This is not to
say that the mainstream press didn't publish some important stories, but
given the magnitude of the problem, these were few and far between. After
the hardening of the policy toward the insurgency, the government deterred
journalists from visiting the southeast to investigate. Publishers who relied
on state funds, credits, newsprint, and advertising went out of their way to
please the authorities. In a blatant and notorious case, the deputy chief of
staff of the armed forces had incriminating evidence implicating two senior
journalists manufactured and leaked to the press in order to get them fired.
They both lost their jobs.[46] One of the two generals accused of having

engineered the false accusations explained in an interview that the military was worried in 1994 that the press was starting to compare the situation in the southeast to the U.S. predicament in Vietnam.[47]

It would be wrong to assume that all the Turkish press was intimidated; it is by most standards a free and raucous institution. However, many in the mainstream press viewed the Kurdish issue as the civilian and military bureaucracy did, as an existential threat for which they had little sympathy. These journalists shared the same ideological blinders and took it upon themselves to shade their reporting accordingly. Hence they could ignore many of the stories emanating from the conflict area.

Finally, there were other voices of dissent. In 1994 a report by a group of parliamentarians castigated the behavior and attitude of security forces in the southeast. While calling for more effective counterterrorism measures, they also pointed out the vagaries of government policy, the inadequacies of personnel, and the day-to-day humiliations of the population. The report avoided mentioning the Kurds but was nonetheless ignored.[48] More importantly, a number of nongovernmental organizations, such as the Human Rights Foundation and the Human Rights Association, tracked abuses of power and received political support for their efforts from the outside, most notably from the European Union and the United States. These NGOs had to endure close scrutiny by the state.

ALTERNATIVE STRATEGIES

Did the state have alternative options? The immediate answer is perhaps no. No state, especially one with the ideological underpinnings of Turkey, could have ignored an armed challenge of this magnitude and not have responded with force. A more measured answer, in the form of a hearts-and-minds campaign to reduce the PKK's bases of support, was possible. For that the state had to properly identify what it was dealing with: a resurgence of Kurdish nationalism. This process required a change of mindset that was far too difficult for many. The only exception was Özal.

Özal's Opening

Much to the consternation of the governing elites, Özal, who had initially understated the nature of the problem, began to reevaluate his thinking. In April 1990 he argued, "Since 1984 the main issue was the Kurdish question.

In addition to foreign influences, Kurdish nationalism had been increasingly accepted by a larger segment of the masses."[49] He progressively tried to move both the state and public opinion to be more accepting of the Kurdish identity. He claimed his own grandmother had been Kurdish. In 1991 he revoked a 1983 law that declared Turkish to be the mother tongue of Turkey's citizens and banned all other languages.[50]

More importantly, he seemed to be developing an integrated approach to the problem without necessarily giving up on combating the insurgency. He not only suggested that Kurdish language broadcasts and publishing be freed, but he very subtly tried to influence Turkish Kurds by making overtures to Iraqi Kurds and their leaders. He received the leaders of both the Kurdistan Democratic Party and the Patriotic Union of Kurdistan, Massoud Barzani and Jalal Talabani, at his residence. He provided them with Turkish diplomatic passports to ease their international travels. He was instrumental in approving the U.S.-led no-fly zone over northern Iraq, which provided the Kurds with a respite from Iraqi forces. Given the close relations Turkish and Iraqi Kurds enjoyed, Turkey's Kurdish population noticed these moves. Özal suggested that Turkey actively collaborate with the Kurds against both the PKK and Saddam Hussein.[51] He clearly wanted to slowly win the trust of his own Kurdish citizens in ways that the Turkish state had never tried before. In weaning Iraqi Kurds away from Hussein's grip, he saw an opportunity for increasing Turkish influence in Iraq. This approach went counter to Turkish state policy. Özal's forceful focus on the issue made even his archrival, Demirel, upon becoming prime minister in 1991, pronounce that he, too, recognized Turkey's Kurdish reality. Yet Demirel, together with most of the establishment, opposed Özal's overtures. Demirel would very quickly drop from his discourse any reference to the "Kurdish reality," in part because the military warned him not to refer to the concept again.[52]

To move ahead, Özal also understood that he had to end the war in the southeast. Using Talabani and some Turkish journalists as intermediaries, he indirectly encouraged Öcalan to declare his unilateral cease-fire in early 1993. Although the Turkish military declared that it would not recognize it, there was a visible diminution in the level of tension in the southeast and even in the rest of the country. Özal had other ideas, including a comprehensive amnesty to convince the rebels to abandon the armed struggle.[53] He died before he could push through more of his policy changes; soon thereafter, the cease-fire itself collapsed when the PKK murdered thirty-three unarmed soldiers. With that action, a point of no return was reached. There would be no other effort at searching for alternatives.

In addition to a weak media, the paucity of efforts at searching for alternatives can be traced to an underdeveloped civil society. While some intellectuals and the occasional journalist would advocate moderation, the gulf between Kurdish and Turkish groups remained quite significant. Efforts by even the most respectable of institutions—such as the Union of Chambers of Commerce and Industry, the main quasi-public business association, which sponsored a study on the southeast—were roundly and vehemently denounced. Only one political movement—the New Democracy Movement—tried to bridge the gap, but it failed to garner any votes in the 1995 elections, in large measure because it was unprepared to contest the elections.

The Kurdish regions' economic backwardness was often cited by many, especially politicians such as Ecevit, as the primary cause for local discontent. Turkish industrial and agricultural economic development in the 1950s through the 1980s had privileged the western parts of the country. In the early 1980s, Ankara began to develop the Southeastern Anatolia Project (GAP), a long-term endeavor that envisaged the building of an extensive network of dams and irrigation systems on the Euphrates and Tigris rivers. GAP did not address the poorer parts of the southeast and in some respects did more to reward large landowners who sold coveted lands to the state.

The state provided precious few economic benefits to the region to counter the economic arguments advanced for the insurgency. It argued that investments during a terrorist campaign would not be productive. Yet even after the capture of Öcalan, the state failed to deliver on its promises for public investment in the region. On March 1, 1999, for instance, Ecevit announced a two-year incentive package for the east and southeast totaling $114 million. This was the tenth such package for these regions, and, as with the others, it never materialized.[54] The Erdogan government has taken some timid steps to begin confidence-building measures for the region by slowly implementing laws passed to ease Kurdish broadcasting. This action is widely interpreted as part of adhering to EU requirements rather than a gesture to the Kurds.[55]

The AKP government introduced a limited amnesty law, with a fixed six-month duration, in July 2003. By the time the law expired in February 2004, only 140 PKK fighters had taken the offer. Pressure from the military, the main opposition party, and elements within the AKP restricted the pro-posal's conditions and thus rendered it far too tough for many to accept.[56] As one senior ruling party leader argued, the problem went beyond the restrictive nature of the actual law to its administration, which inevitably fell short because of "fixed and cliché ideas."[57] The PKK immediately denounced the amnesty, in large part because the PKK leadership was excluded from its provisions.

In the summer of 2005, Prime Minister Recep Tayyip Erdogan jour-neyed into the Kurdish heartland of Turkey to Diyarbakir and for the first time officially acknowledged the existence of a Kurdish problem that needed solving. Although he clearly had his eye on the scheduled beginning of the European Union accession negotiations in October, Erdogan nonetheless crossed an important threshold, as evidenced by the consternation he caused among hard-liners and conservatives on all sides of the political spectrum. It is important to note here that there is a good deal of difference between the government and the state apparatus. Having raised expectations, Erdogan will be under a great deal of pressure to deliver, not just from those who believe in his efforts, but also from the international community.[58]

A PYRRHIC VICTORY?

For Turkey, there could have been only two aims: to defeat the insurgency and the PKK, and to minimize the political headway made by the Kurdish cause. In view of the PKK's own initial maximalist aims, its ideology, its leadership, and the depth of Kurdish discontent, which persists to this date (albeit in a much diminished form), the Turkish state had few choices but to fight to the end and win. There is no question that Ankara has won the mili-tary campaign. Despite a slow start, it managed over the course of a decade to readjust its strategy and employ new means designed to bring the fight to the insurgents and to reduce or eliminate the cooperation they received from the local population. The coup de grâce that befell the PKK with its decapi-tation was supplemented by its decision to transfer a large majority of its combatants to northern Iraq. The remaining PKK forces in northern Iraq do not represent a grave threat to Turkey. In 2005 the PKK managed to mount a number of attacks—including some with improvised electronic devices clearly obtained from Iraq—against Turkish troops in the southeast, causing casualties. Nevertheless, not only does the PKK remain militarily weak, but its recent resumption of violence has further eroded its room to maneuver in Europe, as evidenced by Germany's September 2005 decision to close down a series of PKK-affiliated organizations, including a newspaper. Although the United States has yet to do it, it has promised the Turks that, conditions in Iraq permitting, it will rid Iraq of the organization.

Even if Ankara's military success is incontestable, there are serious questions about the efficacy of its counterinsurgency campaign. Turkey not only reacted slowly but also helped make matters worse by instituting counterproductive measures to combat the insurgency. In the process, it lost the hearts and minds of the Kurdish citizens of Turkey and thus contributed to the insurgency's resilience. To be more precise, its hearts-and-minds campaign was at best insincere. Turkish Kurds feel they have been defeated, yet they have not been won over by a state that still regards them with suspicion.

The counterinsurgency campaign did not succeed in putting the Kurdish genie back into the bottle. Despite Turkish claims that Kurds were not subject to discrimination and that denied the existence of a Kurdish question, the rest of the world increasingly came to view the situation differently. It was difficult to ignore the mobilization of Kurds in both Turkey and Europe in support of the insurgency during the 1990s. The Kurdish question became a reality, to quote former president Demirel. Moreover, the PKK insurgency was instrumental in raising the consciousness of many Kurds, even those who did not believe in the organization's methods or aims. The existence of DEHAP and the continuing political struggle over language rights and other forms of cultural expression demonstrate that, far from defeating it, the long insurgency has strengthened the idea of Kurdishness. Six years after the end of the military campaign, the level of Kurdish mobilization in Turkey and in the diaspora remains high.

This situation has to be juxtaposed with the inevitable lessening of resistance by the Turkish military high command to the legalization of Kurdish language usage in broadcasting, publishing, and private schools as the EU process forces the reform of all Turkish institutions, including civil-military relations. This does not mean that Turkey will give in to demands for group rights, but as the democratization of the political system progresses, individuals will find themselves freer to engage in activities in the name of Kurdish causes. The military will remain vigilant at the prospect of Kurdish activities, peaceful or otherwise.

The Turkish state has achieved a Pyrrhic victory. It remains to be seen whether the Turkish state will manage to navigate through the difficult waters that lie ahead. For one thing, the Turkish establishment is still very much threatened by the emerging prospect of a Kurdish autonomous or federal state in northern Iraq. Turkish fears of the contagion effect of Iraqi developments have been reinforced by developments in Syria, where Kurds and Arabs fought in the mostly Kurdish-inhabited Qāmishlī region in March 2004. The March 1, 2003, decision by Turkey not to allow the United States to open a second front against Iraq has effectively made Iraqi Kurds Washington's closest allies in the region. The United States has been supportive of the Iraqi Kurds' ambitions to build a federal Iraqi state.[59]

If, in fact, this is a Pyrrhic Turkish victory, can the PKK claim any success? Although the PKK would like to claim credit for the current saliency of the Kurdish question, one needs to remember that this was never one of its goals. Launched when the cold war was still very much part of the international order, the PKK-led insurgency was once much more ambitious in its aims. As the insurgents got stronger, their ambitions grew. Claiming credit for the current saliency of the Kurdish issue at best represents an ex post facto justification. The PKK modified its demands as it lost ground. By 1996 the aspirations for a Kurdish autonomous region in Turkey, much less the fantasy of leading a pan-Kurdish state in the region, were gone.

Would the Kurdish issue be as salient without the PKK insurgency? This is a difficult question to answer for sure, but all the elements of increased politicization were evident before the insurgency and the end of the cold war. Considering the numerous wars involving Iraq since the 1980s and the emergence of a Kurdish entity in northern Iraq in the aftermath of the U.S. invasion of the country, chances are that the Turkish Kurds would have been swept by the strong currents of ethnic revivalism. Turkey's quest for EU membership added further impetus to the process as it forced open political space. Therefore, the insurgency raised sensitivities and highlighted the problem; it was not a sufficient condition alone.

Finally, there is still the question of the legal pro-Kurdish political parties. Öcalan influenced, backed, and had his supporters infiltrate them because he saw them as potential vehicles for his entry into the political process. These parties, despite the severe hardships they have endured, ranging from banning to assassinations and continuous harassment at the hands of legal authorities, have managed to survive. Today, as it has always been, there is a great deal of tumult among the Kurdish rank and file; a diverse array of activists, ranging from die-hard supporters of Öcalan to many who seek alternative and nonviolent paths to improved conditions, are making their presence felt.

COUNTERINSURGENCY AND DEMOCRACY

The counterinsurgency campaign exacted a toll on Turkey's democracy. Not only were massive human rights abuses committed against the country's own citizens, but after the intensification of the counterinsurgency campaign subsequent to Prime Minister Çiller's ascendancy, the state brooked little if any dissent on this matter. To be sure, the military and bureaucratic elite perceived the Kurdish question as an existential matter. As a result, the insurgency ended up undermining the general, although not perfect, efforts at democratization launched by Özal.

More importantly, the need to employ the armed forces in the counterinsurgency campaign created the conditions for continued military engagement in politics. It also meant that the Turkish military, which had executed a coup and then extricated itself from power in the 1980s, could resist Özal's efforts at civilianization of the regime and limiting its prerogatives. In fact, after Özal's passing from the scene in 1993, the military became even more active in pushing political leaders and the judiciary behind the scenes to prosecute and otherwise hinder activists, journalists, and academics engaged in the Kurdish issue. The Kurdish insurrection was too important to be left to the politicians. Had it not been for the military's enhanced role, it also would have been difficult to implement what many observers called a "postmodern coup" in 1997, when officers engineered the removal of a government composed of the Islamist politician Necmettin Erbakan and the bête noire of Turkish politics, Çiller.

Throughout this period, Turkey remained an electoral democracy. Elections were held on time, and electoral manipulations were mainly restricted to the southeast, a process made easier by the destruction of many villages and hamlets. The restrictions on civil liberties and the degree of self-censorship observed by many in the otherwise relatively free media diminished the quality of democracy. Since 1980 Freedom House scores have placed Turkey in the "partly free" category, as measured by indicators relating to "political freedom" and "civil rights." Whereas there were relative improvements in Turkey's respective scores following the return to civilian rule in the early 1980s, with the intensification of the counterinsurgency campaign, the Freedom House indicators took a turn for the worse.[60]

In effect, Turkey's democracy, to use Larry Diamond's term, was "hollowed" out.[61] Turkey's politicians sanctioned or supported the use of illiberal means to undermine opposition to the basic tenets of the state: the indivisibility of the nation (the rubric under which Turkey refused to concede the existence of the Kurds) and secularism. Its legal system, while robust, was nonetheless more concerned with the preservation of regime interests than with individual rights. That "hollowed-out democracy" is on the mend, however, in part because of the defeat of the insurgency but more importantly because of the EU accession process.

Even those who had advocated a more hard-line policy against Syria, such as Sükrü Elekdag, a former ambassador and scion of the Turkish establishment, criticized the successive governments' inability to tackle some of the basic issues relating to the Kurdish problem. He argued that the Kurds' cultural differences, economic backwardness, inability to broadcast in Kurdish, and discriminatory treatment at the hands of state authorities were all issues that could have been addressed by existing institutions.[62]

Ironically, in the end, the military defeat of the insurgency, the harsh measures employed, and the costs to democracy have created the conditions for European pressure, in the context of EU negotiations, to force a reexamination of civil-military relations. It is also true that had the insurgency continued, the Europeans would not have begun accession negotiations with Ankara in 2005.

Lessons Learned

There is no question that the single-minded approach of the Turkish state in the end produced the desired result: a military defeat of the insurgency. The Turkish approach was, with the exception of the short interlude provided by the later years of Özal's presidency, based purely on a military solution.

Turkey is the case of a democratic state willing to employ illiberal practices to combat an insurgency. It could get away with such a policy because of the extraordinary degree of ideological harmony among the ruling elites, especially the military, which facilitated the imposition and maintenance of draconian measures designed to fight an ethnic insurgency. As a result, the state had no serious domestic opposition to contend with, and the press and other institutions had limited impact, if any. This sense of unity also enabled the state to bear the costs of the counterinsurgency. Although accurate numbers are hard to come by, the cost of the conflict, estimated by some at $100 billion, took a toll on the Turkish economy. Government expenditures in the southeast, in addition to direct military outlays (state personnel got danger pay), contributed to the inflationary cycle and budget deficits. The conflict undermined investor confidence in Turkey and may have also hampered the growth of the profitable tourist industry.

The Turkish case demonstrates that a state can succeed without a campaign for hearts and minds. Critical to the Turkish state's success was the severe repression of the population that supported or provided the conditions for the insurgency to flourish. The violence perpetrated by all sides, the repression, the village evacuations, the village guard system, and the myriad of special security services brought the population to its knees. It paid a terrible price for the insurgency, as the region's economy was devastated, with the livestock count halved since 1990.[63] In short, the conflict exhausted the population and reduced the number of isolated hamlets and villages where PKK fighters could seek refuge and hide. In fact, after 1996 there was a decline in the number of disappearances, and village evacuations diminished in frequency, due in part to foreign criticisms of counterinsurgency operations' toll on civilians and also due to the much diminished numbers of sympathizers. The economic side effects of the counterinsurgency have not been resolved; the effort to repopulate the countryside has been a meager one, and the cities continue to teem with the unemployed and the barely employed.

Another factor that helped make Ankara victorious over the insurgency was its ability to integrate its domestic and foreign policies in pursuit of its aims. It relentlessly and single-mindedly lobbied both the United States and the European Union to reduce the PKK's room to maneuver internationally. It subsumed all of its other foreign policy interests to this issue.

Foreign support proved critical to Ankara, which was particularly successful with Washington. The latter was unwavering in its assistance for the fight against the PKK. The United States at every turn not only characterized the PKK as a terrorist organization, a designation that validated Turkish claims, but also pushed its European allies hard to clamp down on PKK activities within their own territories. To be sure, the United States was not pleased with the human rights violations the counterinsurgency campaign entailed and kept pushing Ankara to deal also with the political aspects of the problem. The U.S. administration, specifically the Clinton one, also had to walk a tightrope at home because of criticisms of Turkey's behavior from both Congress and the NGO community.[64] At times, this meant the delay or halt of the delivery of certain weapons systems necessary for the antiterrorism struggle. Still, the United States provided critical political and moral support that was especially instrumental in cornering Öcalan once the Turks decided to confront Syria.

Initially, Ankara was not as successful with its neighbors Syria and Iran. Its condemnations of both countries failed to bring about any change in their policies. Syria, possibly because of the Oslo process and its calculations that the United States would not allow any Turkish action against it, could afford to ignore Ankara's accusations. What Damascus failed to understand was the impact of the burgeoning Turkish-Israeli relationship. Even if Israel would remain on the sidelines in the event of a conflagration, the relationship provided the Turks with critical political and psychological support, as well as many friends in Washington. Arab states in general, and Syria in particular, feared a pincer movement of sorts. This was a risky strategy; Syria could have called the Turkish bluff, in which case, having mobilized its domestic opinion, Turkey would have had no choice but to act militarily, at a minimum by launching air strikes or limited incursions. In turn, this action could have galvanized Arab public opinion and created a conflict between Turks and Arabs.

In retrospect, the Turkish generals who spearheaded the opening to Israel and became one of Tel Aviv's best customers were quite conscious of Syria's strategic isolation. Moreover, they and the foreign policy establishment proved to be diplomatically quite adept. Despite their deep anger toward Syria, they were also careful to offer Damascus a face-saving diplomatic route by starting first security and then trade negotiations between the two states. Thus they could also impress upon the rest of the Arab world their "limited" aims.

The push on Syria would not have provided the intended results had Ankara not turned the tide of the insurgency. It was clear to Damascus that with the PKK on the defensive, it no longer constituted a valuable asset to use against its northern neighbor. Still, Iran would have been impervious to such pressure. It is considerably more powerful and, unlike Syria, does not have another powerful neighbor on its borders. Moreover, the stakes were less important given that Öcalan resided in Syria and not Iran.

Unquestionably, the decapitation of the PKK was the coup de grâce. The capture of Öcalan did in the insurgency; he was the PKK's Achilles' heel. He provided it with direction, tactics, and above all charismatic authority. He succeeded in blurring the lines between the cause and his personality. Hence, after his capture, the organization could give up its larger goals in order to save him from capital punishment. The cause had become him. To date, Öcalan remains the leader of the PKK and is often the object of adulation at political gatherings, a fact that rankles the Turkish public and establishment. As long as Öcalan does not call for a complete dismantlement of the organization, especially the remnants of its military wing, the remaining leadership will keep it going.[65]

In the end, the Turkish strategy worked not only because the state was much more powerful and resourceful than the PKK, but also because, under military tutelage, the campaign became focused, earlier mistakes were corrected, and the state proved it was prepared to pay the high cost needed to prevail.

The biggest error the Turks committed was allowing a terrorist group to transform itself into an insurgency. In view of the difficult relations between the Kurdish regions and the central government, perhaps this was an unavoidable outcome, yet the state squandered its most important asset: the daily continuous and harmonious relationship between Turk and Kurd. This relationship is not a lost cause as of yet and represents an important goal for the future.

NOTES

1. The number of PKK fighters in Iraq is in much dispute. The figures range from twenty-five hundred to five thousand. In July 2005, then deputy chief of staff Ilker Basbug estimated their numbers as follows: two thousand stationed along the Turkish border and some six hundred in the Qandil Mountains deep inside northern Iraq near the Iranian border; see *Milliyet,* July 19, 2005.

2. For a detailed history of the Kurds, see David McDowall, *A Modern History of the Kurds* (London: I. B. Tauris, 1996). The Turkish state until the 1990s refused to acknowledge the existence of Kurds. Official Turkey, while always keeping a close eye on the Kurds' political ambitions, nonetheless preferred to believe that Kurds were errant Turks or that sooner or later they would be assimilated into the wider population.

3. Cüneyt Arcayürek, *Müdahalenin Ayak Sesleri, 1978–1979* (Istanbul: Bilgi Yayinevi, 1985), 272. This interview, conducted on September 6, 1979, did not see the light of day until Arcayürek published his book.

4. For an impressionistic account of PKK fighters, see Kadri Gürsel, *Dagdakiler: Bagok'tan Gabar'a 26 Gün* [Those in the Mountains: From Bagok to Gabar in 26 Days] (Istanbul: Metis Yayinlari, 1996).

5. Hasan Cemal, *Kürtler* [Kurds] (Istanbul: Dogan Kitap, 2003), 40.

6. *Hürriyet,* March 18, 1999.

7. McDowall, *Modern History of the Kurds,* 420.

8. In a series of interviews he gave to a Turkish journalist, Öcalan acknowledged that he was having a hard time putting together an effective organization in the cities. See Mehmet Ali Birand, *APO ve PKK* (Istanbul: Milliyet Yayinlari, 1992), 159. It is also clear from his interviews with the same journalist that Öcalan was completely focused on the southeast, where he thought he had a genuine advantage in confronting Turkish security forces. Nevertheless, there were occasional attacks, such as one in Antalya in June 1993, when hand grenades were thrown at a tourist spot, and a bombing in the famous Istanbul bazaar in April 1994. Ironically, in renewed violence during 2005, a new organization likely related to the PKK, the Kurdistan Freedom Hawks, targeted a number of tourist resorts, although without much effect.

9. Ismet Imset quotes this number, which he attributes to Öcalan. See Ismet Imset, *PKK: Ayrilikçi Siddetin 20 Yili (1973–1992)* [Twenty Years of Separatist Terror] (Ankara: Turkish Daily News, 1993), 188. The PKK recruited its fighters mostly from the Kurdish regions but also saw enlistments from European-based Kurds, as well as Iraqi and Syrian Kurds. It also forcibly abducted youngsters from villages, dragooning them into its "armed forces." Ten thousand fighters probably stretched the limits of the organization, which Öcalan ran with an iron hand from Damascus.

10. Birand, *APO ve PKK,* 153.

11. Cemal, *Kürtler,* 109. Yirmibesoglu was referring to the 1919–23 War of Independence led by Atatürk.

12. Speaking in parliament in October 1994, the minister of the interior, Nahit Mentese, argued, "I want to reiterate that we do not have an ethnic problem; we may have geographical problems, economic problems, but we categorically do not have an ethnic problem. In Turkey—I do not even want to pronounce it—there is no Kurdish issue, Circassian issue." *Türkiye Büyük*

Millet Meclisi Tutanak Dergisi (Turkish Grand National Assembly Record of Minutes), October 18, 1994, 401.

13. Malcolm Cooper, "The Legacy of Atatürk: Turkish Political Structures and Policy-Making," *International Affairs* 78, no. 1 (2002): 118.

14. Ironically, there are also many Turkish citizens who claim Kurdish ancestry and yet cannot speak Kurdish. Öcalan is one of them.

15. For a discussion of Ecevit's views on Kurds and the relationship with northern Iraq, please see Henri J. Barkey, "Hemmed in by Circumstances: Turkey and Iraq since the Gulf War," *Middle East Policy* 7, no. 4 (October 2000): 110–26.

16. Mesut Yegen, *Devlet Söyleminde Kürt Sorunu* [The Kurdish Problem in State Discourses] (Istanbul: Iletisim Yayinlari, 1999). Ironically, Yegen argues that the foreign connection charges, as well as the state discourse that characterized the Kurds as bandits, backward, separatists, and Islamists, while designed to destroy Kurdish identity, may have done just the opposite.

17. Özal had been miffed that on the eve of the 1983 parliamentary elections, then president Kenan Evren, author of the 1980 coup, had called on the population to vote for the two political parties created by the military.

18. Mehmet Ali Kislali, *Güneydogu: Düsük Yogunluklu Çatisma* [The Southeast: Low Intensity Conflict] (Ankara: Ümit Yayincilik, 1996), 167, 170–71.

19. John B. Grant, "Turkey's Counterinsurgency Campaign against the PKK: Lessons Learned from a Dirty War" (unpublished thesis, Faculty of the Joint Military Intelligence College, Washington, DC, June 2002), 39.

20. Other factors complicated matters; among the most notable was the drug trade. The conflict occurred at one of the major international crossroads for drug trafficking. In the murky environment of the period, a great many people, including the PKK, had their hands in that trade.

21. Kislali, *Güneydogu,* 182.

22. The PKK presence in their midst was a problem for Iraqi Kurds. The presence of large numbers of armed fighters was a source of instability and a potential threat to their control of the region, but more importantly it also threatened their relations with Turkey, which accommodated a U.S. and British air force presence, primarily responsible for the maintenance of the protective no-fly zone over northern Iraq.

23. Some questioned the effectiveness of these operations. Baskin Oran argues that, while after every operation, claims were made that the terrorists' back had been broken, the fact of the matter is that these operations were of limited success. See Baskin Oran, *"Kalkik Horoz" Çekiç Güç ve Kürt Devleti*

["Poised Hammer" Hammer Force and a Kurdish State] (Istanbul: Bilgi Yayinevi, 1996), 191.

24. Güven Erkaya and Taner Baytok, *Bir Asker Bir Diplomat* [A Soldier, a Diplomat] (Istanbul: Dogan Kitap, 2001). In interviews with a journalist, Admiral Erkaya complained that at its outset, Özal characterized the insurrection as composed of just three to five brigands (page 242).

25. Grant, "Turkey's Counterinsurgency Campaign," 40.

26. Kislali, *Güneydogu,* 222.

27. Ibid., 224.

28. Former president Demirel complained in an interview that the government had mobilized extensively, with 250,000 soldiers and 100,000 village guards fighting the PKK. See Murat Yetkin, "Demirel Sicak Gunleri Anlatti," *Radikal,* August 15, 2004.

29. Henri J. Barkey and Graham E. Fuller, *Turkey's Kurdish Question* (Lanham, MD: Rowman and Littlefield, 1998), 138.

30. Kemal Kirişçi and Gareth M. Winrow, *The Kurdish Question and Turkey* (London: Frank Cass, 1997), 131.

31. An interesting account of the conflict is given by Nadire Mater, who interviewed soldiers who fought against the PKK. The interviews reveal the suffering of both the local population and the soldiers, as well as the difficult conditions under which the soldiers had to operate. Some were disturbed by the way the locals were treated. The book was banned by the authorities, and its author was prosecuted. She was eventually acquitted. See Nadire Mater, *Memedin Kitabi* [Memed's Book] (Istanbul: Metis Güncel, 1998).

32. Human Rights Watch, *Turkey and War in Iraq: Avoiding Past Patterns of Violation* (New York: Human Rights Watch, March 2003), www.hrw.org/backgrounder/eca/turkey/turkey_violations.htm.

33. Grant, "Turkey's Counterinsurgency Campaign," 47.

34. Local NGOs put the figure of displaced persons at between one and three million. See U.S. Department of State, "Turkey Country Report on Human Rights Practices" (Bureau of Democracy, Human Rights, and Labor, February 2004), www.state.gov/g/drl/rls/hrrpt/2003/27869.htm.

35. Matthew Kocher, "The Decline of PKK and the Viability of a One-State Solution in Turkey," *International Journal on Multicultural Societies* 4, no. 1 (2002): 133–39. Kocher also argues that two to three million displaced persons is too high.

36. U.S. Department of State, "Turkey Country Report on Human Rights Practices" (Bureau of Democracy, Human Rights, and Labor, February 2000), www.state.gov/g/drl/rls/hrrpt/1999/index.cfm?docid=365.

37. Cemal, *Kürtler,* 227–31.

38. Kirişçi and Winrow, *Kurdish Question and Turkey,* 129.

39. Interview with Evren, in Kislali, *Güneydogu,* 213. Saddam Hussein was dismissive of the idea of cooperation with Turkey, arguing that Iraq's Kurdish problem was under control.

40. The decision to increase pressure on the Syrian leadership, apparently made at a National Security Council meeting, received a great deal of media coverage in Turkey, including speculation on whether a series of suspicious bombings in Damascus and other Syrian cities was the work of Turkish clandestine operations. See *Hürriyet,* October 10, 1998. Also, the supposed text of an ultimatum letter to Damascus was leaked to the press. See Metehan Demir, "Iste Gizli Baris Mektubu" [The Text of the Secret Peace Letter], *Hürriyet,* October 3, 1998.

41. Grant points out that "Turkish threats were made more credible because Turkish forces near the Syrian border were already mobilized to support just-concluded NATO exercises." Moreover, Ankara had begun to show its assertiveness earlier by bombing PKK bases in Iran. See Grant, "Turkey's Counterinsurgency Campaign," 52.

42. Then president Demirel confirmed this information. See Murat Yetkin, "Demirel: Apo'yu Bize ABD Teslim Etti" [The United States Delivered Apo to Us], *Radikal,* August 16, 2004. This is part of an insightful and detailed analysis of the crisis with Syria by Yetkin, serialized as "137 Firtinali Gün" [137 Stormy Days], *Radikal,* August 9–24, 2004.

43. Christina Elana Lynch Bobrow, "Arbitrary Governance: Managing Expression in Turkey" (unpublished Ph.D. dissertation, Georgetown University, Washington, DC, 2003).

44. In the March 2004 local elections, DEHAP attempted an electoral pact with a social democratic party; the effort backfired and the party fared relatively poorly.

45. Human Rights Watch, *Violations of Free Expression in Turkey* (New York: Human Rights Watch, 1999), 60.

46. The two journalists, Cengiz Çandar and Mehmet Ali Birand, among the most respected in their field, were accused of taking money from the PKK, according to a high-level PKK operative who had defected to the Iraqi Kurds, and were turned over to the Turkish authorities. Years later, documents describing the process of manufacturing the evidence were leaked to the press and published. The Turkish General Staff never denied the accusations. As for the two journalists, Çandar did not immediately lose his job but was sacked later when he wrote a column critical of the military.

47. Interview with General Erol Özkasnak, *Radikal,* November 7, 2000.

48. *Türkiye Büyük Millet Meclisi Tutanak Dergisi,* October 18, 1994, Report 10/116.

49. Omer Faruk Gençkaya, "Turgut Özal'in Güneydogu ve Kürt Sorununa Bakisi" [Turgut Özal's Approach to the Southeast and to the Kurdish Problem] in *Kim Bu Özal: Siyaset, Iktisat, Zihniyet* [Who Is Özal: Politics, Economics and Mentality], ed. Ihsan Sezal and Ihsan Dagi (Istanbul: Boyut Kitaplari, 2001), 116.

50. Barkey and Fuller, *Turkey's Kurdish Question,* 64.

51. Cemal, *Kürtler,* 128.

52. Ibid., 54.

53. See interview with journalist Cengiz Çandar, who was an adviser to Özal, in Rusen Çakir, *Türkiye'nin Kürt Sorunu* [Turkey's Kurdish Problem] (Istanbul: Metis Yayinlari, 2004), 113–14.

54. Derya Sazak, "Bu Kaçinci Paket?" [How Many Packages?] *Milliyet,* March 3, 1999; and Reuters, March 2, 1999.

55. Ismet Berkan argues that despite the desire to conform with the Copenhagen Criteria, which set out the political standards for EU negotiations, Ankara is lagging in implementing language and especially broadcasting reforms. See "Reformlar Sürüyor ama . . ." [The Reforms are Continuing but . . .], *Radikal,* February 23, 2004.

56. The law provided a clean bill only to those who could prove they had never participated in armed combat and could furnish information on others. For a discussion on the amnesty proposal, see Agence France-Presse, "2,000 Kurd Rebels Could Be Pardoned under Turkish Amnesty," July 2, 2003; "Amnesty, What Amnesty?" *Economist,* August 28, 2003; "Turkish Amnesty for Kurd Rebels Expires," Associated Press, February 6, 2004.

57. See the interview with Mir Dengir Firat, a deputy AKP president, in Çakir, *Türkiye'nin Kürt Sorunu,* 167.

58. For a discussion of expectations from the Turkish government in Turkey and especially in Europe, see Philip Robins, "Turkey and the Kurds: Approaching a Modus Vivendi?" in *The United States and Turkey: Allies in Need,* ed. Morton Abramowitz (New York: Century Foundation, 2003), 85–107.

59. For a discussion of the stakes in northern Iraq for Turkey, see Henri J. Barkey, *Turkey and Iraq: Perils (and Prospects) of Proximity,* Special Report no. 141 (Washington, DC: United States Institute of Peace, 2005).

60. There are signs of improvement, however, as seen in the 2004 report. For Freedom House scores, please check www.freedomhouse.org/ratings/index.htm.

61. For a discussion on the hollowing out of democracy in "third-wave" countries such as Turkey, see Larry Diamond, *Developing Democracy: Toward Consolidation* (Baltimore: Johns Hopkins University Press, 1999), 49–60.

62. Sükrü Elekdag, "Kürt Sorunu" [Kurdish Problem], *Milliyet,* August 16, 1999.

63. Grant, "Turkey's Counterinsurgency Campaign," 55.

64. Henri J. Barkey, "The United States, Turkey and Human Rights Policy," in *Implementing U.S. Human Rights Policy,* ed. Debra Liang-Fenton (Washington, DC: United States Institute of Peace Press, 2004), 363–400.

65. In the summer of 2004, the Turkish press reported divisions among the leadership between so-called more moderate elements, which included Öcalan's brother, and more hard-line members of the leadership council. On the other hand, from his prison cell on Imrali Island in the Sea of Marmara, he continues to try to control the organization and, perhaps more importantly, influence political developments. He does this through his lawyers, who visit him. See Çakir, *Türkiye'nin Kürt Sorunu,* 242–61. While divisions within the Kurdish community remain, the number of demonstrations in support of Öcalan grew dramatically in 2005.

12

RUSSIA AND CHECHNYA

Audrey Kurth Cronin

The case study of Russia in its two brutal wars in Chechnya is characterized by complex political and strategic ambiguities, and it can be analyzed through a number of perspectives. In defining the case primarily as counterterrorism, we are making a controversial judgment before we have even begun. Especially as it has recently evolved, Russia's conflict in Chechnya is indeed a case of counterterrorism and terrorism, in which Chechens who are members of terrorist organizations have killed many innocent Russian civilians in tragic surprise attacks aimed at influencing a broader audience and at generally intimidating the population. Proven links to Islamist terrorist groups implicate the Chechen conflict as a flash point in the so-called global war on terrorism. But that is not all it is. Since 1994, primarily in response to separatist activities, the Russian state has visited gross atrocities, indiscriminate targeting, and human rights abuses on Chechen civilians. These are acts of "state terror" at a minimum.[1] Such actions by the Russian state have been carried out with virtual impunity, even with respect to international opprobrium, especially since 9/11. The Chechen case is likewise a classic study in the protection of state sovereignty and territorial integrity following the cold war, with two civil wars to determine the character of post-Soviet Russia. Accurately or not, Russian leaders have viewed the Chechen wars in this way and have characterized them as vital to the survival of the state. With Russia having lost most of the Soviet empire, its efforts to cling to the remaining "Peter the Great land area" are

383

not inconsequential to this case. Finally, others in the international community have seen the wars as ethnic conflicts among competing Chechen clans as well as ethnic Russians, with clear elements of racism and even "ethnic cleansing" in the Russian military response and in the state's approach to the handling of displaced civilians who have fled to neighboring republics.

The Chechen conflicts thus have elements of all the major themes in the post–cold war study of international conflict, not least of which is the rising threat of international terrorism. Terrorism, state terror, civil war, separatist insurgency, and ethnic conflict are all labels that variously apply to this conflict; how the discussion of Russia and Chechnya is framed is not a neutral issue. But since September 11, 2001, the terrorist element has predominated, both in the presentation of the conflict and increasingly in the evolution of Chechen tactics. Indeed, this chapter argues that the growing international characterization of Chechnya as another front in the "war on terrorism" may itself be having an important effect on the evolving dynamic between Chechen tactics, Russian responses, and the status of the ongoing conflict in Chechnya. It is also arguably having a dramatic and worrisome influence on the development of post-Soviet Russian democracy. The Russian government, at least, sees the conflict increasingly through the prism of a protracted counterterrorism campaign.

From the perspective of the Chechens, the aims of the conflict have mainly been the independence of Chechen territory from Russia (especially at the outset); revenge for the killings of Chechens, particularly civilians; and the survival of the Chechen "homeland" and culture. The motivation of revenge has increased over the course of the conflict, and the alienation of the population both from Russia and from its own fighters seems to have contributed to growing rifts within the Chechen resistance movement. In recent years, the goal of the establishment of an Islamic state in the Caucasus has also been reflected in the actions of foreign fighters and small factions that are, to some degree, associated with and funded by international terrorist organizations, including al Qaeda.[2] Overall, however, the overwhelming impression is of a population exhausted by conflict and increasingly caught in a trap in which outside agendas are manipulating and dominating the course of events.

At this writing, guerrilla operations—including ambushes, mine warfare, antihelicopter operations, and other tactics of conventional warfare that kill Russian soldiers—continue in Chechnya and throughout the North Caucasus, but the role of terrorist tactics in the Chechens' strategy has dramatically increased.[3] Without dismissing the aspects of this conflict that transcend terrorism, many of which are covered effectively elsewhere,[4] the chapter will focus on the interactive terrorist and counterterrorist methods being undertaken by both sides, including the degree to which narrow and inaccurate perceptions have influenced both. This is an ongoing conflict in which conclusions about the outcome of the case study are premature. The chapter will emphasize the importance of the framing of a conflict within a state's counterterrorist response, especially when that approach is dominated by the use of military force. Perceptions are particularly important in cases of ethnonationalist/separatist terrorism,[5] in which disputes relate to control of territory and the tactics of groups commonly transition in and out of traditional insurgency, guerrilla warfare, and terrorist tactics.[6] Ethnonationalist/separatist terrorism has been the most long-lived form of terrorism in the modern era.[7] Over time, the challenge for the democratic state is to retain domestic and international political support for the often protracted counterterrorist campaign and to bring the reality on the ground into line with the perception that the state is attempting to project. More important, perhaps, the state must accomplish these things without undermining its tenuous hold on democracy and changing the fabric of the state itself—arguably the crucial element in this case study.

The chapter will proceed in six parts. First, a historical background section will lay the groundwork for the current conflict, including the deep historical antipathy between the Chechens and the Russians, especially the well-known legacy of Chechen deportation during the Stalin years. Second, the chapter will analyze the tactics used by both the Russians and the Chechens in recent conflicts, including both the first and second wars. The emphasis here is on explaining the tactics of the insurgency and counterinsurgency, increasingly overlaid and dominated by a widening terrorism/counterterrorism dynamic. The next section examines important aspects of the state's counterterrorist response, including negotiations, control of the media and public opinion, and implications for the state's evolving political system. Fourth, the narrative tackles the internationalization of the conflict, especially its alleged ties to the broader so-called war on terrorism and al Qaeda–associated operatives. Fifth, significant recent developments are briefly recounted, to cast these developments in current perspective as much as possible.[8] Finally, the concluding section of the chapter examines the broader implications of this case study for analyzing comparative state counterterrorism.

A Brief History of Chechnya and the Recent Chechen Conflicts

The post-Soviet wars for Chechen independence have been consistent with an established tradition of resistance to the Russian empire on the part of the Chechen people, a tradition that was reinvigorated by the disintegration of the USSR. Aside from the works of romantic writers such as Pushkin and Lermontov, who used liberal poetic license, there is little evidence that either the Russians or the Soviets understood or appreciated the complexities of Chechen culture. Generally, the Chechens were considered to be savage, primitive, backward, and mainly worthy of imperial domination. In the eighteenth century, the Chechens converted to a very fervent form of Sufi Islam, an evolution that compounded the alienation and antipathy of Russian Orthodox Christians. Much is made of the legendary martial character of traditional Chechen society, in which the young male warrior plays a central part and blood feuds between rival *teips,* or clans, can continue for generations. A teip is not just a group of people who belong to an extended family; the concept originated in common land ownership, as an outsider to the region could join a teip by acquiring land. Thus the deep connection between individuals, families, collective honor, and an ancestral piece of land is elemental to the Chechens. The rule of law and loyalty to a larger state entity are late arriving, poorly established, and somewhat alien to them.[9]

An extremely important unifying event for Chechnya was the brutal mass deportation of the Chechens from their homeland by the Soviet government, allegedly for (wholly unsubstantiated) collaboration with the Nazis.[10] Resettlement was a favored tool of Soviet policy, used for suppression of many "troublesome" minorities, but it was employed with particular brutality against the Chechens.[11] On February 23, 1944, special NKVD units (secret police) employed speed, secrecy, and overwhelming force to deport virtually the entire Chechen population to Central Asia, killing thousands along the way. There are no reliable census figures, but at least a quarter (probably more) of the Chechen population died either during the deportation or in the harsh living conditions that followed.[12] Contrary to its design, however, the experience of mass exile fortified a sense of unity among those who were thrown together in adverse primitive conditions. They were shunned by local populations in Central Asia, which added to their cohesiveness. When the surviving Chechens returned to their homeland following the death of Stalin, they shared an enhanced sense of national awareness, as well as a determination to perpetuate their own language, customs, and religion. The Chechens were the largest deported nationality permitted to return en masse to their homeland, and the painful memory of their treatment was fresh in the chaos that followed the Soviet years.

During the Soviet era, efforts to dilute the Chechen nation through the internal migration policies of the Soviet empire resulted in the movement of Great Russians to Chechnya but also the countermovement of Chechens to urban areas such as Moscow, which with approximately fifty thousand Chechen residents remains the second-largest Chechen city after Grozny.[13] Interestingly, the cultural antipathy (sometimes overt racism) displayed by many Russians toward Chechens is not reciprocated: virtually every Chechen speaks fluent Russian and is intimately familiar with the dominant Russian culture, habits, tastes, and society.[14] Many have served in the Soviet army or participated in other state organizations. This experience has proven useful in the recent separatist insurgencies, as well as in the terrorist operations that have accompanied them.

Finally, it is also important to realize the role of oil in the economic value of Chechnya. The discovery of oil in the region around the Caspian Sea in the nineteenth century played a major role in the economic development of Chechnya and put Grozny on the map as a major industrial center and railroad transport hub. Important oil pipelines run through Chechnya from Baku, Azerbaijan, to the Russian Black Sea port of Novorossiysk. Chechnya's geopolitical importance to greater Russia as a transit point and crucial oil refining center has been a significant factor in its unenviable fate.[15]

The First War in Chechnya (1994–96)

In the chaos of the breakup of the Soviet Union (especially the struggle between Mikhail Gorbachev and Boris Yeltsin), Chechen nationalism, an evolving cultural/religious identity, strong anticommunism, and a desire to break out of the centrally controlled economy led to a movement to establish an independent Chechen state. The first president of Chechnya, Dzokhar Dudayev, was a major general in the Soviet air force, married to a Russian woman, and an ethnic Chechen who had lived in Chechnya only briefly as a teenager. His time away from Chechnya and his relative detachment from several powerful, competing Chechen teips may have contributed to his political rise as a romantic nationalist behind whom Chechens of many clans could rally.[16] Dudayev prevailed in somewhat anarchical elections on October 27, 1991, in which almost none of the large ethnic Russian population in Chechnya voted. His first decree was to declare Chechnya an independent state. The next day, the Russian parliament pronounced the Chechen elections illegal. A few days later, Boris Yeltsin declared a state of emergency and dispatched twenty-five hundred Interior Ministry (MVD) troops to Chechnya. Gorbachev, who still largely controlled Soviet military means to crack down on Chechnya, hesitated to reinforce the MVD forces, which apparently remained at the airport near Grozny. The Russian parliament rescinded Yeltsin's order to use force, the Russian interior troops withdrew, and Dudayev gained stature as the Chechen hero who had successfully taken on the Russian empire.[17] In hindsight, this was a Pyrrhic victory, as Yeltsin and his supporters did not forget the humiliating inability to act and the embarrassing outcome.

Three years later, the first war in Chechnya was not, strictly speaking, a counterterrorist operation but a poorly planned Russian counterinsurgency operation largely carried out on the streets of Grozny. When a Moscow-backed opposition faction within Chechnya tried unsuccessfully to overthrow Dudayev's government, in late November 1994, its members were routed by forces loyal to the general.[18] Within a fortnight, Yeltsin's government decided to intervene. Some argue that the catalyst for Yeltsin's decision was a series of four bus hijackings and kidnappings in the region along the border of Chechnya in the summer of 1994, although the point is subject to dispute.[19] Given its timing, the war may also have been an effort to boost President Yeltsin's popularity in advance of his reelection. The intervention was in any case hastily assembled; some Russian military leaders, convinced that prior planning was inadequate, resigned in protest.[20]

There is evidence that those in the Russian military who supported the intervention believed it would be a simple show of force that would meet with little or no resistance—comparable, perhaps, to the driving of Soviet tanks into Prague in August 1968.[21] Contrary to expectations, however, the

Russian military operation, which began on December 11, 1994, met widespread and determined resistance from both Chechen guerrilla fighters and Chechen civilians. The highly networked Chechens showed themselves to be resilient guerrilla fighters, attempting to rid their territory of the last vestiges of the Soviet empire, and the Russian troops were humiliated and bloodied.[22] Notably, the Yeltsin government portrayed the operation as not primarily against terrorism but against a separatist movement that, if allowed to secede, might result in more demands by other republics for independence and then the eventual breakup of Russia.[23] It is also notable that Yeltsin himself, who underwent minor elective surgery on his nose as the invasion was taking place, disappeared from view for more than two weeks, leaving the military to fend for itself.

Russian losses in the first Chechen war were shocking. Troops mostly consisted of ill-trained, poorly equipped, and poorly led conscripts as well as older mercenary or contract forces *(kontrakniki)* (more on this below).[24] The war was highly unpopular among the Russian public and strongly condemned by the international community. Although the Russians did eventually gain control of Grozny, they were forced to seek a peace treaty that would ensure the withdrawal of Russian troops and the end of the war. Among other reasons for the peace treaty was the 1995 Budennovsk hostage-taking incident, in which more than one hundred people died—presaging future terrorist attacks. The first war in Chechnya ended in the negotiation of the Kasavyurt Accords, signed by Russian lieutenant general Aleksandr Lebed (Yeltsin's political rival) and Chechen leader Aslan Maskhadov on August 30, 1996.[25] According to the terms of the agreement, Russian troops were to be withdrawn from Chechnya with a promise of economic aid from the Russian government to Chechnya and a referendum on the future of Chechnya to be held five years hence (in 2001).

The Interwar Period (1996–99)

The interwar period was characterized by a dramatic expansion of criminal networks in Chechnya and the apparently increasing influence of radical Islamist movements. There was widespread kidnapping of westerners for ransom and fighting for control among rival criminal networks. The sympathy that had developed as a result of extensively broadcast images of atrocities against the Chechen people dissipated in the face of criminal behavior including assassinations, murders, and attacks on economic targets in neighboring regions.[26] Many international aid workers and journalists, targeted for kidnapping or other crimes, fled.[27] As is so often the case in Chechnya, however, the situation was complex, and things were not always as they seemed: in the wave of criminal behavior, drug trafficking, racketeering, and black market activity centered in Chechnya at this time, there was evidence of complicity on the part of Russian military officers, political figures, police officials, and even the Federal Security Service (FSB).[28]

Chechen war hero General Aslan Maskhadov was elected president in apparently fair democratic elections in January 1997,[29] but the quasi-independent Chechen republic never developed the basic skeleton of a productive state, lacking a functioning economy, basic human services, and any sign of an embryonic civil society.

The Second War in Chechnya (August 1999–Present)

The second war in Chechnya started after incursions by Chechen fighters led by Shamil Basayev into neighboring Dagestan in August 1999, ostensibly to establish an Islamic republic there. In addition, a series of bombings of civilian apartment houses in Moscow and Vologodonsk were blamed on Chechen terrorists, although there is controversy about whether Russian security forces were involved.[30] The bombs killed nearly three hundred people, offering both a need and an opportunity for a strong Russian riposte. Then premier Vladimir Putin had been put in charge of the Chechen operation by President Yeltsin. Apparently acting at the behest of the commander in chief, Putin ordered Russian forces to repel the invasion of Dagestan, which they did fairly easily, and then to bomb and begin moving ground forces into Chechnya.

The second intervention was an integral part of Putin's ascension to the presidency: he established a personal tie to the prosecution of the war in Chechnya from the outset. The apartment bombings, whatever their genesis, seemed to galvanize Russian public opinion against the Chechens. The second war was seen as an opportunity to exact revenge, restore Russian morale, and erase the national humiliation of the first conflict. Responding to the public mood, Putin was elected president in part on his promises to "flush the Chechens down the toilet"[31] and "strangle the vermin at the root."[32] Long before al Qaeda's attacks on the United States and the widespread international attention to the issue, Putin framed the second conflict in Chechnya as a war against terrorism. In the first war in Chechnya, the

Russian leadership referred to the enemy as "bandits" and "rebels"; after the Moscow bombings, they were "terrorists."[33] Indeed, by spring 2000, Putin had publicly declared "victory over terrorists," but although the Russians had quickly established dominance on the battlefield this time, war crimes and human rights abuses by Russian forces continued unabated, and the pace of terrorist attacks by Chechen operatives on traditionally Russian soil increased, especially after October 2002, as will be seen below.

FROM INSURGENCY TO TERRORISM AND COUNTERINSURGENCY TO COUNTERTERRORISM

Given the complexity of this conflict and the long history of its origins, what is surprising is the extent to which the strategy, tactics, and public image of both sides have come to be dominated by the leitmotif of terrorism and counterterrorism. This has happened in at least three ways. First, terrorism has been deliberately used as a mechanism of shock. The Chechens, having suffered tremendous brutality at the hands of Russian forces, have employed major acts of terrorism increasingly to shock the Russian people, especially in Moscow but also elsewhere in Russia. This shock seems to have been intended to draw attention to the Chechen cause and to affect both international and domestic public opinion in order to undermine the Putin government and drive it to concessions. Second, terrorist attacks on several occasions have been used during sensitive political periods as catalytic events. For example, in 1995 the Budennovsk hostage crisis helped lead to the end of the first war. The 1999 Moscow apartment bombings, whoever the perpetrators, apparently precipitated the outbreak of the second Chechen conflict. The October 2002 Dubrovka theater siege ended the search for a semblance of political legitimacy, if not actual peace, and effectively killed the moderate Chechen presidency of Aslan Maskhadov. All these events were triggers to dramatic changes in the course of the conflict. Third, terrorism has been a successful mechanism for leveling the playing field, providing a means to improve a losing position by enlarging the battlefield and expanding the potential targets—in short, a means to engage in asymmetrical warfare. The Chechens used terrorism when they were at a disadvantage on the battlefield in both wars, when the Russian counterinsurgency seemed to be prevailing. There are numerous examples of this tactic, as the next section will reveal. Each of these three themes—terrorism to shock, to act as a catalyst, and to transition to asymmetrical warfare—will be clear in the following analysis of the interaction between Chechen insurgency and terrorism, on the one hand, and Russian counterinsurgency and counterterrorist tactics, on the other.

The First War

The Russian forces' tactics in the urban combat that was at the core of the first war in Chechnya were appalling by nearly any standard. In December 1994, the Russian air force easily eliminated the small fleet of aircraft belonging to the Chechens; however, the movement across rural areas toward Grozny met resistance from the local population, which slowed the Russians down and forced a delay in the military timetable. The idea was to move to Grozny and surround the rebel forces that were presumed to be concentrated in the city center. But the Russian troops were not prepared for urban warfare.

On New Year's Eve, three armored columns closed in from the north, east, and west, but the force of some six thousand Russians met a determined enemy, entrenched and employing tunnels, hiding in the basements of buildings, and shooting from rooftops. It was much easier to defend a city that the Chechens knew well than it was to take it with a major show of force. The heavy Russian vehicles, including tanks and armored personnel carriers, instead of providing protection became easy-to-spot targets, difficult to maneuver in the urban environment. When a tank or vehicle was hit in the narrow city streets, often all the vehicles behind it were trapped; Russian soldiers did not abandon their vehicles because they either misjudged their own vulnerability or did not know where to run.[34] Most had very little training, and they were regularly ambushed. The most gruesome and telling images of this war projected by journalists were the photographs of charred corpses of Russian soldiers, some of them in grotesque positions, apparently trying to get out of their "steel coffins."[35] Fratricide among the Russian soldiers was likewise a serious problem. Casualty figures are disputed, but anywhere from fifty-five hundred to fourteen thousand Russian troops died in the first war.[36]

The Chechen fighters were outnumbered, but they operated in small groups, much less hierarchically organized.[37] Many had been trained in the Soviet army, and they knew the enemy well. They had much more mobile light weapons, including automatic rifles, machine guns, and portable anti-

tank grenade launchers. Small squads of handfuls of men were in turn organized into twenty-five-man cells that included support persons such as
medics. They divided the city into quadrants and ambushed the Russians in
coordinated attacks. Snipers operated at night and sometimes engaged in
"dirty tricks" such as booby-trapping the bodies of dead Russian soldiers,
disguising themselves as Red Cross workers, and passing themselves off as
civilians.[38] These tactics made it extremely difficult for the Russians to distinguish between combatants and noncombatants. In part as a result of these
tactics, Chechen civilians fared worse than either Russian soldiers or their
own fighters; although estimates vary, upward of fifty thousand Chechen
civilians, including ethnic Russians living in Chechnya, died in the first war,
and about a third of the Chechen population was displaced.[39]

Abuses by Russian forces also accounted for huge losses among Chechen
civilians. Undisciplined troops engaged in looting, raping, and assaulting
the civilian population. They carried out *zachistki,* or cleansing operations,
ostensibly to search for rebel fighters and arms but in effect as a means of
rounding up the male population and then looting and burning civilian
residences.[40] They set up "filtration camps" to screen and hold civilians,
especially Chechen males but also sometimes ethnic Russians. In the
camps, people were reportedly murdered, tortured, and held in the most
primitive conditions.[41] Civilians in Grozny were subjected to not only brutal bombing and artillery attacks on houses and apartment buildings but
also the destruction of the municipal water system, which led to an outbreak
of viral hepatitis and cholera that likewise infected Russian forces.[42] Alienated civilians either fled from Chechnya, joined the Chechen forces, or
hunkered down in their homes. Many provided active or passive support to
Chechen fighters.

One part of the Russian forces' problem was that Ministry of Defense,
FSB, and MVD forces were used, operating side by side. They had not
trained together, nor were they accustomed to coordinating, and the Interior
Ministry troops had no armor or heavy weapons.[43] There was virtually no
intelligence collected and poor reconnaissance. The troops did not even
have reliable maps.[44] The Russian forces moved in armored columns,
intending, for example, to capture major buildings and the railroad station
in Grozny, but the Chechens did not put up a fixed defense and instead
presented a shifting and elusive target. Gradually, the Russians learned
from their mistakes. Employing small-unit tactics and bringing in more

experienced fighters, they more or less controlled Grozny through the spring of 1995. Despite heavy losses, Russian troops occupied Grozny by late January 1995, and Chechen fighters regrouped in the mountainous highlands.

Just as Russia seemed to be prevailing, however, the Chechens upped the ante. In June 1995, rebel leader Shamil Basayev carried out a raid on Budennovsk, a town located about one hundred miles from Chechen territory in southern Russia. Apparently acting on his own and without the approval of President Dudayev, Basayev and his group of about 150 fighters sought to bring the battle directly to Russian civilians, in the same way they said it had been visited by the Russian government on the people of Chechnya. Basayev and his men stormed their way into the small provincial Russian town and took a large number of hostages, whom they marched through the center of town as human shields and then held in a hospital. About twelve hundred people were crammed into the facility. Basayev demanded that Russia stop the war in Chechnya, withdraw its troops, and negotiate with President Dudayev.

The Budennovsk hostage crisis continued for five days, and as many people died in Russian government attempts to storm the hospital as had died in the initial Chechen raid on the town.[45] The event ended when the Russian government agreed to negotiate and gave Basayev and his fighters safe passage on buses back to Chechnya, where they were greeted as conquering heroes. The Budennovsk episode was a watershed event, demonstrating the Chechens' willingness to use terrorist tactics to pursue their cause, strengthening the separatist cause just at a time when it was flagging, and forcing the Russian government into negotiations under the auspices of the Organization for Security and Cooperation in Europe (OSCE)—an organization committed to advancing fair political agreements but lacking effective means of enforcement.[46]

The Budennovsk seizure in June 1995 was a catalytic event with respect to Chechen tactics, as it initiated an increasing trend toward using terrorist tactics in Chechnya, as well as in neighboring Ingushetia, Dagestan, North Ossetia, and Russia proper.[47] It was followed by a series of bombings, notably in June and July 1996 against trains, train stations, a subway train, and a trolley in Moscow, Volgograd, and Trubnaya, and then in April through June 1997 against train stations and a train in Pyatigorsk, Moscow, and Armavir.[48] A particularly worrisome episode took place in November 1995, when Chechen separatists reportedly left about a gram of highly radioactive cesium-137 in a Moscow park. Although the very small amount posed no serious threat to the population, the event prompted widespread media attention and seemed to be intended as a warning.[49]

The shift of focus by the Chechens toward the use of high-profile terrorist tactics on traditional Russian soil was an important element in pushing the Yeltsin government to negotiate and withdraw its troops. Combined with the embarrassing performance of the Russian military in the counterinsurgency campaign, the Budennovsk incident led Moscow to sue for peace and sign the Kasavyurt Accords. The peace treaty was an object of disdain for the Russians, however, and was referred to in the press and parliament as "Great Russia's humiliation by small Chechnya." Indeed, Boris Yeltsin referred to Chechnya as the biggest mistake of his presidency.[50]

The Second War

Of the two sides in the first war, the Chechens were much more passionate and sure of their cause: to defend the homeland and perpetuate the Chechen nation. Young Russian conscripts and volunteers thrown into battle in Chechnya often had no idea what they were fighting for. The Chechen fighters suffered from no such confusion. With the humiliation of the Russian army, the withdrawal after the Kasavyurt Accords, and the bombings of the Moscow apartment buildings, however, the anger and desire for revenge drove the Russians to share in the passion that had previously been obvious only on the Chechen side. The second war was even more of a pounding slaughter of Chechen civilians, including heavy and indiscriminate Russian use of artillery and air strikes. The pace of cleansing raids *(zachistki)* and other systematic abuses of Chechen civilians was higher than ever.[51] Human rights violations continued on both sides, but they were not as widely monitored or reported. Like the first war, the second war became a long, grueling urban campaign. However, the improvement in attitude on the part of the Russian troops, who seemed to believe that they were fighting for a worthy cause, was an important change.

For the Russians, the military tactics of the second war differed markedly from those of the first. For one thing, the operation began with movements by MVD forces in Dagestan for a few weeks before they entered Chechnya. Even then they did not go directly into Grozny but first laid siege to the city with a brutal, indiscriminate aerial bombing campaign, accompanied by heavy artillery, that essentially pounded the city into rubble. Russian forces moved into the outskirts of Grozny in mid-October 1999, and the senior Russian command shifted from the MVD to the Ministry of Defense. There were Russian incursions in mid-December, and Russian authorities called on civilians to leave the city, promising safe passage. There was more elaborate preparation and planning for the storming of the city this time, as well as reconnaissance and intelligence gathering. In the second incursion, infantry storm detachments led the assault, with tanks following. Ground troops deliberately drew fire, exposing the Chechens' position and then calling in air or artillery attacks. Gradually and steadily, the Russian forces moved forward, although night raids by Chechen guerrillas continued, and, as in the first Chechen war, the Chechen fighters successfully relied on ambushes. The fighting continued to be slow, bloody, and difficult, with a high rate of casualties on both sides, but by early 2000, the Russians occupied most of Chechnya, and Chechen forces were pushed into the mountainous highlands and over the border with Georgia, into the Pankisi Gorge.

Although the Russians were much more successful tactically against the Chechen resistance from the outset of the second conflict, the Chechens were battle hardened and well prepared to fight. According to Russian reports, Chechen leaders had established a network of training camps employing some one hundred foreign instructors, largely Arab Afghans but also Pakistan-based militants.[52] Disguised in Russian uniforms, the Chechens engaged in night raids on Russian positions. Chechen treatment of Russian prisoners was so appalling that Russian soldiers and airmen were apparently terrified of capture; this situation may have worked against the Chechens, as it resulted in an increased determination by the Russians to fight. Efforts to ambush Russian tanks were not as successful as they had been in the first conflict because of the use of infantry escorts and reactive armor. Both sides relied heavily on the use of snipers, and the tallest building in Grozny, with its targeting advantage, was one of the most hotly contested sites. Although the Chechens were somewhat better equipped than they had been earlier, their guerrilla tactics had not changed dramatically between the first conflict and the second. The Russians, however, had adapted and prepared more effectively to counter them.[53]

Putin began to claim victory over the Chechens in 2000, even as operations in the country continued and casualties on both sides mounted. Those casualties continued in subsequent years: although the highest number of troop casualties occurred in the first year of the war, the Russian General Staff reported at least one hundred Russian troops killed each month during 2003.[54] While figures of troop losses range widely and are hotly disputed,[55] the total number of troops lost in both Chechen wars clearly exceeds the total number of Soviets lost in the Afghanistan conflict (1979–89).[56] Continued losses at the current pace may soon drive the total for the second war alone (1999–present) above the Afghanistan level.[57] Thus, although they are on some level prevailing, the Russians are paying a high cost for this conflict.

As they found themselves at a disadvantage, the Chechens again diverted the war into terrorist attacks carried out away from the battlefields in Chechnya. As in the first conflict, a crucial turning point was a major terrorist event—the seizure of the Dubrovka theater in Moscow on October 23, 2002, in which eight hundred civilians were held hostage for three days by Chechen militant terrorists led by Movsar Baraev. In Operation Groza, the storming of the theater by Russian special forces, an unidentified anesthetic gas was used to incapacitate the operatives.[58] All forty-nine of the Chechen operatives were shot as they lay unconscious, apparently to prevent them from detonating their explosives; but the loss of potential intelligence gained through interrogation was regrettable. Because of a lack of medical facilities on the scene, combined with the unwillingness of the Russian government to reveal to medical authorities the nature of the gas, 129 civilians died of asphyxiation during or shortly after the raid.

The Dubrovka theater episode marked a watershed in the gradual transition of the Chechens toward increasing projection of terrorist violence outside Chechen territory. It was followed by a quickening pace of terrorist attacks on Russian territory, culminating in the tragic slaughter of more than three hundred people, most of them schoolchildren, in Beslan in North Ossetia. These and other very recent developments will be discussed further below.

ASPECTS OF COUNTERTERRORISM

The Role of Negotiations

Before the Dubrovka theater incident, Putin appeared to be under pressure to negotiate with Chechen president Aslan Maskhadov. Domestic polls indicated that the Chechen conflict was beginning to undermine Putin's popularity in Russia, and with parliamentary elections scheduled for December 2003, this was potentially an important problem.[59] Representatives of Putin's government and Maskhadov's government held a series of secret negotiations during the fall of 2001 and again in August 2002. Much of the resistance to a settlement reportedly came from the Russian side, which was reluctant to negotiate with moderate Chechens represented by the Maskhadov government and instead preferred to empower Akhmad Kadyrov, Russia's handpicked candidate in the upcoming Chechen presidential elections. The idea was to turn over power to Kremlin-supported candidates and gradually transition to their control of Chechnya, a technique that became known as Chechenization. Others, however, especially members of the FSB, reportedly opposed doing anything other than pursuing the military campaign in Chechnya to a victorious conclusion, even if it took years.

Gradually, the interlocutors seemed to settle on the outlines of a plan in which Chechnya would be granted a "special status" of limited autonomy and self-government within the territorial integrity of the Russian Federation. Other peace initiatives in the fall of 2002 included an OSCE-arranged meeting between Putin's representative for human rights in Chechnya, Abdul-Khakim Sultygov, and Chechen parliamentary deputies. Events seemed to be moving in the direction of a possible settlement until right before the Dubrovka theater incident. Although President Maskhadov promptly made a statement denouncing the hostage incident, the Putin administration blamed him for it and discredited him as a negotiating partner. Unlike the apartment bombings in 1999, this crisis was clearly and very publicly carried out by militant Chechens, explosive belts strapped around their waists, carrying signs in Arabic, with the women veiled and dressed in black. The Chechens' connection to militant Islamist international terrorism, especially al Qaeda and associated groups, seemed obvious.[60] Putin treated the Dubrovka theater episode as Russia's "own 9/11."

According to journalistic accounts, during the siege, the Putin regime privately offered to begin serious negotiations on troop withdrawals from Chechnya with the Moscow hostage takers, even as preparations for the storming of the theater were moving ahead at full speed. The rebels accepted and announced to the hostages that they had "good news"—that they would not be killed. But apparently the Russian government's offer was disingenuous, and the decision to storm the theater irrevocable. On the day the withdrawal negotiations were supposed to begin, Russian troops stormed the building, killing all the Chechens as well as 129 Russian civilians. The Russian public was outraged at the Chechens. Following the Dubrovka theater incident, Putin's approval ratings increased, and domestic support for military action went up, although a significant percentage of Russians—45 and 50 percent in different polls—still supported peace negotiations.[61] After the incident, Maskhadov announced that he was "prepared for unconditional peace talks with Russia," but Putin called him a murderer. Putin's administration showed little interest in peace talks, concentrating instead on installing a Kremlin-backed regime in the 2003 Chechen "elections" and turning over governing authority to it.[62] Since the Dubrovka siege, Chechenization combined with harsh military measures has been the Russian government's approach in Chechnya.

Control of the Media and Access to Information

The Russians fared very poorly on the public relations front during the first Chechen war, and this fact seemed to clearly undermine support for the war. Chechen resistance fighters reportedly gave access to journalists, and Moscow made no attempt to constrain their movements. The first war was very thoroughly covered by intrepid journalists, who often accompanied rebel commanders at considerable risk to themselves. The Russian media in particular often questioned the official version of events, for example, when investigative reporters uncovered secret Russian military support for Chechen opposition forces. Television coverage of the first war was widespread and vivid. In part as a result of the unflinching, thorough coverage of the war, especially the pounding of Grozny and especially from Chechen civilians' perspectives, Russian opinion of the war was extremely critical: in January 1995, 52 percent of Russians opposed military actions in Grozny, and only 20 percent approved.[63] The war was so unpopular that Yeltsin was under strong pressure to finish it and conclude a peace treaty in order to be reelected in 1996.

The difficulty that the Russians had in distinguishing Chechen fighters from civilians was a source of both operational setback and huge negative publicity within the international community. The Russians seemed unable to engage in urban warfare without using massive firepower. The resulting targeting of civilians and the extensive destruction of civilian infrastructure were heavily covered in the press, contributing to widespread domestic

opposition to the war. The international community also stridently condemned the violations of human rights that the Russian army committed
in its efforts to defeat an enemy that employed the local population as a
shield. The OSCE played an important role in documenting these abuses
during the 1994–96 Chechnya conflict and also played a crucial role in the
negotiations that ended it.[64]

Tactics with respect to the media differed markedly during the second
war, with strict government control over the press.[65] Apparently learning
from British and U.S. information management during the Falklands War
and the 1991 Gulf War, or perhaps from U.S. and NATO public affairs
during the Kosovo conflict, the Russian government made a concerted
effort to manage the image of the second war and to restrict access by Russian and international media.[66] The Russian government implemented a
strict system of accreditation and escorts for journalists. The result was a
sharp drop-off in news of Russian actions in Chechnya and a dramatic
reduction in exposure of both the Russian domestic audience and the international community to the actions going on in Chechnya. Critical television coverage of the second war was essentially shut down. Where previously
there had been interviews with romanticized Chechen partisans and pictures of Russian boys burning to death in the streets of Grozny, there were
now Russian commanders and soldiers talking about fighting the "terrorist"
enemy. Much of the semantics changed: where the press had previously
referred to the conflict as a "war," it now increasingly accepted the official
description of a "counterterrorist operation." Restricted access and the conscious attempt by the Russian government to spin the information emerging
from the conflict seem to have had a clear effect on domestic public opinion,
which has been far more supportive of the second war.[67]

Implications for Russian Democracy

It is difficult to draw conclusions as this is an evolving case and the nature
of what will presumably be a uniquely Russian-style "democracy" remains
to be seen. It would be a gross oversimplification to attribute the Putin government's gradual movement toward what some Russian government officials call "managed democracy" exclusively to the impact of Chechnya.
Nonetheless, the second Chechen conflict and its accompanying counterterrorist campaign occurs within a broader context of what many consider
worrisome developments in Russia. In recent years, there has been a dra-

matic movement toward state monopolization of the levers of power, including financial, bureaucratic, political, and legal power, in the service of the Putin presidency. Researchers have also documented a widespread resurgence of state control over independent voices for human rights and civil liberties, including harassment and prosecution of environmentalists, human rights activists, members of non–Russian Orthodox religious groups, academics, and other nonstate actors. The international community's early post–cold war attention to and financial support for the establishment of democracy in Russia has diminished, concurrent with a relative disinterest in Russian military activities and human rights atrocities in Chechnya. With a post-9/11 international community focused on counterterrorism, it is difficult to sort out cause and effect; however, the so-called counterterrorist campaign against the Chechens, impelled by increasingly bloody terrorist attacks against Russian civilians, has contributed to and exacerbated a more generalized drift by the Russian state away from any semblance of Western-style, pluralized democracy.[68]

In one area, at least, the question of cause and effect seems clear. Evidence of the impact of the Chechen conflict on Russian democracy can be seen in the diminished role of the media in Russian society since the start of the second war, as described above. In addition to controls on journalists trying to cover events within Chechnya, since 2001 the Russian state has shut down and reorganized media outlets critical of the Kremlin, including the national television channel NTV, the newspaper *Segodnya,* and the magazine *Itogi.*[69] The Chechen war has contributed to the state's general control over all forms of media, often reasserted under the pretext of protecting national security. Numerous prominent journalists who had been covering the war or writing assessments critical of the government, notably Andrei Babitsky and Anna Politkovskaya, have been detained, harassed, and threatened, and many have fled to the West.[70] The government increasingly hampers the flow of information coming out of Chechnya, contributing perhaps to incentives for the Chechens to bring the war to the Russian people in other ways.

According to a prominent study of recent Russian public opinion, the lack of media coverage of the second conflict in Chechnya bears a direct relationship to Russian attitudes toward human rights.[71] Polling data from late 2001 show tepid support for civil liberties, combined with a willingness to sacrifice rights for order and national security.[72] The polls reflect a surprising degree of public apathy or ignorance regarding atrocities by Russian troops in the Chechen war. For example, only 4.2 percent of those questioned expressed shame that Russian troops violate human rights and international norms—compared to the vast majority (68.1 percent) who were much more concerned about the large losses of Russian troops.[73] Those who did express support for human rights in the abstract did not transfer that concern over to condemnation of Russian military abuses in Chechnya and opposition to the war, a situation that the authors of the study consider to be a direct result of the paucity, or perhaps manipulation, of media exposure.

The desire for order is long-standing in Russian culture, an understandable legacy of centuries of violent upheaval and instability. Moreover, polling data also led to the conclusion that Russians, many of whom have experienced severe hardships in the post-Soviet years, are generally more interested in economic issues than in questions of civil liberties, including the fate of Chechen civilians. Russian popular attitudes toward the Chechens likely also reflect a heightened anxiety caused by an increase in terrorist attacks carried out by Chechen operatives outside Chechnya.[74] In any case, the Putin government's two-part policy of limiting the public's awareness of casualty rates, human rights abuses, and the economic costs of the war through control of the media, on the one hand, and emphasizing the national security aspects of the war, on the other, is a very effective approach—as President Putin's overwhelming and essentially unopposed reelection in March 2004 seems to confirm.[75] But the approach certainly does not encourage the flowering of what most westerners would consider a pluralistic civil society. In this sense, the war in Chechnya, including the counterterrorist campaign by the government, may be having a corrosive effect on the democratization of post-Soviet Russia. And the international community's legitimate, but sometimes exaggerated, focus on international links between Chechen guerrillas and al Qaeda operatives likewise contributes.

INTERNATIONALIZATION OF THE CONFLICT

There are important links between some Chechen factions and the international jihad movement. Connections between al Qaeda and Chechnya center on the role of an associate of Osama bin Laden's known as Ibn Khattab.

According to some sources, Khattab was a Saudi national, born in about 1970 in the al-Khobar area of northeastern Saudi Arabia, and his real name was Samir bin-Salih bin-Abdallah al-Suwaylim.[76] Khattab developed an extremely close relationship with Osama bin Laden when the two were fighting Soviet soldiers in Afghanistan side by side. Khattab apparently continued the fight against the Russians in Chechnya and was involved in the first war. For example, on April 16, 1996, Ibn Khattab's force of Arab Afghan/Chechen insurgents reportedly destroyed a Russian military convoy leaving Chechnya. According to the UK-based Islamic Observation Center, fifty vehicles were destroyed and 273 soldiers killed.[77]

Khattab reportedly helped to train Chechens and Dagestanis in a camp located in the Chechen village of Serzhenyurt. Many point to his influence leading to the growing radicalism of Chechen fighters, especially reflected in the use of suicide attacks, a tactic that is almost certainly a foreign import. Khattab, who was well known for his fierceness, joined with Basayev to lead the invasion of Dagestan in August 1999, which was intended to result in the establishment of an Islamic state there. He was also implicated in the September 1999 bombings of Moscow apartment buildings that killed nearly three hundred people, although the exact perpetrators are disputed.[78] Ibn Khattab was reported killed by the Russians, in circumstances that are difficult to determine (perhaps a poisoning), on August 25, 2002.[79]

Financial support for the Chechen resistance also seems to have come directly from Osama bin Laden. According to one account, while it was based in Sudan, al Qaeda operated a satellite office in Baku, Azerbaijan, and sent fighters to Chechnya during the first war at a cost of $1,500 each.[80] Another account claims that in 1994, al Qaeda created a pipeline for fighters and matériel that ran through Ankara, Turkey, into Azerbaijan; from there, fighters were smuggled over the border into Dagestan and on to Chechnya.[81] Reportedly, bin Laden was using a bank in the Gulf to direct funds to operations in Chechnya, and he ordered an investigation after it was brought to his attention that Chechen leaders were siphoning off large sums for their personal use.[82] This report is unconfirmed.

It is worth remembering that the Taliban regime was the only government in the world to recognize Chechen independence after the first war. Reportedly, Chechens also trained in al Qaeda's Afghan camps, although numbers are hard to verify.[83] Chechen militants fought the United States in its post-9/11 war against the Taliban in Afghanistan. Other connections are

alleged. For example, Mohammed Atta, one of the hijackers who participated in the attacks of September 11, was reportedly planning to join the
fight in Chechnya instead. Recently, the United Nations for the first time
added the name of a Chechen, Shamil Basayev, to the list of individuals and
organizations with clear connections to al Qaeda whose assets should be
frozen under Resolution 1267 (which imposes sanctions on the Taliban and
al Qaeda). This is strong evidence of widely accepted links between al
Qaeda and the rebel leader.[84]

The degree to which this conflict is simply another outgrowth of the
international reach of al Qaeda should not be overstated, however. Although
there is some dispute over the numbers, most experts put the number of
foreign fighters in Chechnya at around two to three hundred—a small
proportion of the total number of Chechen rebels, currently estimated
between two and three thousand.[85] But the increasing radicalization of the
Chechen cause is evident in the increasing use of suicide tactics, the shift in
expression from separatist demands to the language of international jihad,
and the apparent growth in the relative strength of radical factions among
Chechen fighters.

More broadly, there is clear evidence of Islamic militant funding and
support for the Chechens. Al-Jazeera regularly broadcasts reports of Russian
military abuses in Chechnya, often including graphic footage of human
rights outrages against Chechen Muslims. Islamic charities such as the
Global Relief Foundation, the al-Rashid Trust, and the Benevolence International Foundation have been active in Chechnya and are reportedly a
major source of financial support for Islamist Chechen fighters.[86] These
three organizations are on the UN's list of groups with sanctions imposed
because of their connections with al Qaeda or the Taliban; they are also on
the U.S. list of individuals and organizations designated terrorists. Many
well-meaning citizens, including Saudi nationals,[87] apparently contribute
large sums to such charities, intending to provide relief to the suffering
people of Chechnya; however, some proportion of the funds is diverted to
radical Chechen fighters and operatives. The broader implications of the
conflict are important politically. Graphic pictures of atrocities committed by the Russians against Chechens published by news outlets such as
al-Jazeera have had tangible effects on public opinion among Muslim audi-
ences, which increasingly see the conflict as an example of anti-Muslim
violence in an ever more divided world.

In the West, the changed political atmosphere after September 11 contributed to an apparent lack of interest by the international community in the second conflict in Chechnya, especially compared to the first Chechen war, with Human Rights Watch labeling the international community "glad to be deceived."[88] Not only the media but also international observers were kept from Chechnya; in late 2002, the Russian government refused to renew the mandate of the OSCE Assistance Group, effectively ending the monitoring of humanitarian concerns in the region.[89]

U.S. policy toward Russia, including the attitude toward Russian forces in Chechnya, changed markedly following September 11. The conflict was now cast as part of the "war on terrorism," a perspective furthered by the naming of three Chechen fighter groups as "specially designated global terrorists."[90] Although the annual U.S. State Department's human rights report still listed extensive abuses by Russian forces in Chechnya, the Bush administration placed its emphasis on Russia's role as an ally in the war on terrorism. In practice, the U.S. government tried to distinguish between the Chechen "resistance" and Chechen "terrorists," for example by designating Shamil Basayev as a terrorist but not Maskhadov. Especially after the Dubrovka theater incident, there was ambivalence in U.S. support for a negotiated settlement, as well as in the U.S. attitude toward the elections of 2003. The apparent shift in U.S. policy, combined with the limited information coming out of Chechnya, strongly influenced how the international community viewed the conflict.

RECENT DEVELOPMENTS

As mentioned above, since the Moscow theater siege of October 23–26, 2002, the pace of terrorist attacks by Chechen operatives in both Chechen and non-Chechen areas of Russia has greatly increased. The Chechen resistance seems to be transitioning from traditional insurgent tactics to increasing use of terrorist attacks, especially suicide attacks using female operatives against innocent civilians.[91] The list of recent attacks is quite long.[92] There were nine suicide bombings in Moscow during 2003, as well as a large number of terrorist bombings in other Russian cities against targets such as cafés, trolley bus platforms, and passenger and commuter trains. And the casualty rate continues to spiral upward. In September 2004, devastating suicide bombings occurred in Moscow just outside Red Square (6 people killed, nearly 100 wounded), on the subway (41 people killed, more than 130 wounded), and just outside a subway stop (at least 10 killed, more than 50 wounded). In August 2004, female suicide bombers exploded two civilian airliners in midflight, killing eighty-nine people.[93]

A more recent tragedy, with gruesome echoes of the 1995 Budennovsk hostage crisis, was the September 2004 seizure of an elementary school in Beslan in North Ossetia by approximately thirty-one guerrillas.[94] After trapping more than one thousand innocent civilians in the school's gymnasium, the hostage takers demanded all Russian troops be pulled out of Chechnya. More than 330 people were killed, possibly when Russian special forces and vigilantes stormed the school after hearing an explosion (the order of events is disputed). Many of the victims were young children who had arrived at school for their first day of the autumn term. On Chechen rebel Internet sites, Shamil Basayev claimed responsibility for planning the Beslan siege, although he blamed the children's deaths on the Russian forces.[95] Notably, Aslan Maskhadov denied any links to the three-day siege. President Putin condemned the Chechens, introduced new security measures at home, and called on the international community to join with him in fighting international terrorism.

The increasing use of terrorist attacks, especially in areas outside Chechnya, has demonstrated a shift in tactics and an attempt by Chechen militants to bring the battle to the Russian people. In the broader global context, however, it has facilitated the Russian government's efforts to depict the conflict as another front in the war on terrorism and to involve the United States and its allies in the war against the Chechens. While the Chechens are clearly engaging in outrageous acts of terrorist violence, the oversimplification that has accompanied this "framing" of the conflict has been unfortunate, as it removes any incentive on the part of the Russian government to address the grievances of Chechen civilians who have been brutalized in the two wars, and it also polarizes the Russian population, which is understandably outraged at Chechens who attack innocent civilians in this highly publicized manner. It is hard to see how the transition to suicide attacks is benefiting the cause of Chechen independence or even self-government, especially since the influence of foreign elements such as al Qaeda radicalizes the Chechen cause and heightens the incentives for the United States and its allies to side with the Russian government in the war on terrorism.

Within the Russian government, Chechen terrorism has further rein-forced the dramatic swing toward executive power. For example, the deputy head of the Russian Federal Security Service, Vyacheslav Ushakov, address-ing newly elected members of the state Duma in February 2003, said it was unlikely that the number of terrorist acts in Russia would go down and that these acts might demonstrate that certain countries have an interest in "turning the republic into a centre of world terrorism." He then pointed to the U.S. Patriot Act as a model for giving the special services "unprecedented powers in the fight against terrorism."[96]

Indeed, the palpable influence of the counterterrorist campaign on the nature of the Russian state is one of the most worrisome aspects of this ongoing case study. In the wake of the Beslan school siege, President Putin announced a series of changes to the political system intended to strengthen the Russian state's ability to respond to Chechen terrorism. While it is too early at this writing to judge their long-term effects, Putin's clear consolida-tion of power in the executive is of concern to many seasoned observers. Included in the new measures, for example, is a fundamental change to the Russian constitution whereby the governors of Russia's eighty-nine regions are chosen by the president instead of being directly elected by the people they represent. Moreover, the Russian parliament is made up of members drawn from national party lists, eliminating the local constituency races that enabled independent candidates to win. Putin also created a new body, not unlike the U.S. Department of Homeland Security, to centralize the response to terrorist attacks.[97] Whatever the dynamic of the Chechen conflict in future months and years, it is clear that President Putin's coun-terterrorist campaign is contributing to a profound transformation of post-Soviet Russia.

It is difficult to assess Russian federal government counterterrorist mea-sures taken to prevent attacks outside the Caucasus in any depth. Press accounts are often contradictory and unreliable, and there is little effort by authorities to inform the public regarding antiterrorism efforts. One serious problem seems to be that the Russian security agencies, the FSB and the MVD, have been working against each other and are reluctant to share intelligence.[98] But some critics have argued that there is little good intelli-gence for them to share: neither organization will recruit Chechen operatives to gain an inside perspective on rebel activities on the chance that the spies will then turn against the federal authorities.[99] And intelligence gathered through electronic means, which the two organizations apparently do share, is virtually useless, because almost no one who works for the Russian security services can translate the Chechen language.[100] Some of the intelligence appears to have utility, however, as the Russians have successfully targeted numerous key separatist leaders in recent months. Assassinated leaders include former Chechen president Zelimkhan Yandarbiyev, reportedly the chief Middle East fund-raiser, who was living in Qatar and was killed by a car bomb; and Abu Walid (also known as Abdul Aziz Ghamdi), an Arab militant leader who reportedly became the top Arab field commander after Khattab's death in 2002 and was killed in a bomb blast in April 2004.[101]

In Chechnya there are reports that human rights abuses by Russian forces are worsening, with an increase in civilian deaths as a result of raids and kidnappings.[102] Usually, the abductions involve young Chechen men who are taken during zachistki, or sweeps. A recent development is the parallel launching of a series of raids preemptively targeting young Chechen women who have lost a husband, brother, or father and might fit the profile of potential suicide bombers. Often the women have no known connections to rebel groups, but they are held for months or simply disappear.[103] With limited independent press coverage, it is difficult to get objective confirmation of these events.

Another crucial and underreported element in the Russian federal government's handling of the conflict is the treatment of the large number of civilians who were displaced beginning in 1999.[104] These people found themselves targets of the government's counterterrorist and counterinsurgency tactics, as well as the increasing terrorist targeting of civilians by Chechen rebel forces. Fearing for their lives, many Chechen civilians fled, especially to camps in neighboring Ingushetia. But particularly after May 2002, Russian authorities began to pressure them to return to Chechnya by closing camps, suspending subsidies, deregistering displaced persons, and conducting sweep operations in the refugee camps.[105] While a survey conducted by the humanitarian organization Doctors Without Borders indicated that 98 percent of the displaced Chechens did not want to return to their homeland (mainly for fear for their lives), they have been nonetheless systematically pressured to do so.[106] Meanwhile, conditions in Chechnya continue to be deplorable, due not only to the deteriorating security situation but also to the scarcity of heating, electricity, and water; serious risk of injury from land mines and unexploded ordnance; and high rates of diseases such as tuberculosis, hepatitis A, and HIV/AIDS.[107] It seems that the Russian government's policy of Chechenization includes coercively repopulating Chechnya with Chechens—perhaps intending to contain the risks of Chechen-associated terrorism in other parts of Russia.

The killing of Chechen president Akhmad Kadyrov in a bomb blast in Grozny on May 9, 2004, dealt a serious blow to the Putin government's plans for turning over power to the Kremlin-sanctioned government. Also seriously wounded in the blast, which occurred at a parade commemorating the fifty-ninth anniversary of the victory over Nazi Germany, was Colonel General Valery Baranov, the top Russian field commander in charge of Russian forces in Chechnya.[108] This development had serious implications for the Kremlin's policy, as the power vacuum left by Kadyrov's assassination increased the civil strife among various factions vying for control of the Chechen government and especially the vast criminal network that has become deeply entrenched in Chechen society. The August 2004 election of Alu Alkhanov, the Kremlin's next candidate, was greeted with skepticism by the international community, and in the violent and chaotic Chechen context, the top concern of the new president, according to some news accounts, is simply to stay alive.[109]

The deceased president had reportedly been engaging in criminal activity, including kidnappings, murders, beatings, disappearances, extortion, and thefts, on a widespread scale. The Russians had largely handed over day-to-day security to the Kadyrov regime, and reports noted human rights violations on the part of Chechen security services. Kadyrov's son, Ramzan, was in charge of the presidential security force (which numbers about one thousand men), his nephews ran a new street-patrol force known as the PPS as well as the security detail for Chechen oil facilities, and a Kadyrov loyalist was in charge of the republic's police force.[110] Before the assassination, reports indicated that the Chechen population was becoming as intimidated by their own Kremlin-backed leader as they were by Russian national forces, who were rapidly transferring power to the new regime. Although there had been some minor progress in rebuilding physical infrastructure that had been destroyed by the Russians in their bombing, evidence indicates that Kadyrov and his henchmen had taken a large cut of reconstruction funds coming from Moscow and had been siphoning off oil revenues.[111] At this writing, it is difficult to predict what will happen in post-Kadyrov Chechnya, although it seems likely that there will be further factional fighting and civil strife. Hope of negotiation with rebel forces is dim: in March 2005, Russian forces killed Aslan Maskhadov, removing the only Chechen rebel leader with whom Putin might conceivably have held talks.[112] It is sadly probable that this atmosphere of instability, corruption, and violence will in turn spawn more terrorist attacks within and outside Chechnya.

CONCLUSION: A STRATEGIC FAILURE ON BOTH SIDES

Although effective in shocking public opinion, acting as a catalyst to action, and shifting the battlefield to asymmetrical warfare, the use of terrorism in the long term has proven to be massively counterproductive for the Chechens. The Chechen homeland has been devastated, the Chechen population has been dispersed and devastated, and the Chechen economy (apart from criminal enterprises) is virtually nonexistent. In the face of terrorist attacks, Putin's political will has been undiminished, despite nagging popular doubts and concerns on the part of the elite, and his popularity in Russia seems secure. If anything, terrorism has increased Putin's hold on executive power and strengthened his hand to do virtually whatever he wishes in Chechnya. In short, terrorism has exacted a cost from the Russians, but the Chechens have paid a much greater price: although some short-term gains have been realized in the past decade, ultimately the Chechens cannot win a war of attrition.

But Russian counterterrorism has been no more successful in a larger strategic sense. Despite repeated claims by President Putin that the war is over, major Russian operations and rebel attacks have continued. The total number of Russian casualties during 2003 in Chechnya was reportedly higher than it had been in any year since the start of the war.[113] The highly publicized but dubious Chechen elections of October 2003 and August 2004, in which the population had no viable alternatives to Akhmad Kadyrov and Alu Alkhanov (the Kremlin's choices), were an effort to project an image of democracy and normality in the embattled region, even as attacks continued and the living conditions of the Chechen people were deplorable. Likewise, the transition that seems to be occurring in the Chechen resistance, toward more terrorist attacks on traditional Russian territory, more apparent influence of militant Islamic fighters, and an increasing employment of suicide attacks (notably by women), is changing the character and dynamic of the conflict. In the short term, such attacks have hurt the cause and led to increased Russian domestic support for the war, but over time, it is unclear what effect they will have.

There seems to be a polarization occurring, both within Russia and within the Chechen republic. On the one hand, following each terrorist attack blamed on Chechen operatives, there is passionate Russian hatred of the Chechens. This process seems to be having a palpable influence on the evolution of the Russian state toward more executive power, more restriction of civil liberties, and increased willingness to support strong use of force. On the other hand, there is a fractionizing occurring within Chechnya itself, as the Kremlin-supported government seems to be engaging in criminal behavior against its own people and increasing numbers of Chechens appear to be swayed by militant Islamic groups. It remains to be seen whether the Putin regime's spin on Russia's withdrawal from a festering Chechen territory (now labeled a self-governing democracy) will prevail over time, especially in view of the assassination of Chechen president Kadyrov, and whether the terrorist problem that seems to be growing increasingly acute will continue to increase under the new post-Kadyrov Chechen regime. To the extent that Chechenization was the Kremlin's solution to the terrorist threat, it has thus far failed.

The history of terrorism provides little ground for optimism in this case. The state's initial bungled response to a separatist insurgency, including massive human atrocities followed by an ever more powerful military response in the second war, has resulted in a shifting of the conflict away from military confrontation and guerrilla warfare to a terrorist campaign directed at civilians. In the history of terrorism, ethnonationalist/separatist terrorist groups tied to conflicts over territory have been the longest lived in the modern era, with a staying power drawn from both the ethnic identity of the group and its multigenerational source of community support. This conflict is also apparently becoming increasingly about a militant Islamic ideology; thus it combines the longest-lived terrorist motivation in the modern era with a religious motivation—arguably the most powerful type of terrorist ideology in human history. The irony is that as the Russian government has increasingly portrayed this situation as a counterterrorist struggle, the reality is evolving to match the description. And unfortunately, if current trends continue, the victims of this ongoing tactical evolution will be Russian and Chechen civilians.

Given Russia's sovereignty over Chechen territory and President Putin's personal tie to harsh military responses, it is difficult to see how this situation will be resolved without a change in leadership in Russia or Chechnya or both. Both sides are showing too much resilience and willingness to absorb pain, and there is a stalemate. It appears that the Russians can maintain the war, because they can absorb the casualties and pay the price under the banner of counterterrorism. The Chechens have been given the trappings of political stability and a democratic state, but there is no developing civil society evident. The Chechen government appears to be deeply involved in criminal enterprises and willing to continue victimizing the Chechen people. The Chechen rebels, who are not apparently under control of the new Chechen government, seem to be able to maintain an insurgency virtually indefinitely and able to keep up their terrorist tactics, unheeding of the cost to a minority of Chechens and at a price that the Russians seem to be able to absorb. The Chechens' persistent ties to international Islamist funding and organizations, including al Qaeda, seem to enable them to operate independent of any state. Indeed, this region, if it were not under the sovereignty of Russia, would be called a failed state in anyone's lexicon. The potential for escalation to the use of more potent weapons exists, as does the possibility of a diversion of the conflict beyond Russia. The evolving counterterrorism dynamic in this case study seems headed toward escalation, not de-escalation, and certainly no one is winning. On the basis of historical experience with separatist conflicts, rational people would conclude that it is time for a peace agreement, but the will for peace is lacking. Especially in the current political environment, the terrorist and counterterrorist elements of this case have led to an undermining of rationality on both sides.

Notes

Note: This chapter has been updated as of September 2004.

1. Some commentators have gone further, labeling Russian military action in Chechnya "genocide," "ethnic cleansing," and various breaches of the laws of war. On "genocide," see, for example, Mark Waller, "Rights-Russia: Putin Accused of 'Crushing Democracy,'" *Global Information Network,* March 5, 2004; on "ethnic cleansing," see, for example, Stephen Blank, "Russia's Ulster: The Chechen War and Its Consequences," *Demokratizatsiya* 9, no.1 (Winter

2001): 5–25; on breaches of international law and the laws of war, see Matthew Evangelista, "War Crimes and Russia's International Standing," *The Chechen Wars: Will Russia Go the Way of the Soviet Union?* (Washington, DC: Brookings Institution, 2002), 139–77. These examples are illustrative, not comprehensive.

2. From the beginning, there has been much skepticism about Russian claims of ties between Chechen rebels and al Qaeda. It is important not to overstate these ties and thereby distort the essential nature of the conflict as primarily a guerrilla, separatist war. Nonetheless, within this context, evidence of connections between al Qaeda and Chechen rebels does clearly exist in open sources and takes several forms. First, data reportedly captured in Afghanistan verify the link. See, for example, Liam Pleven, "Russia: War Damaging al-Qaida, Chechen Ties," *Newsday,* January 26, 2002. Second, testimony in the trials of al Qaeda operatives has confirmed ties between Chechnya and al Qaeda. See, for example, Anton Notz and Hugh Williamson, "Court Hears 9/11 Pilots Had Links with Chechens," *Financial Times,* October 30, 2002, 7; and Richard Willing, "Defendant Aided Chechens, British say," *USA Today,* June 14, 2002. Individual Chechen rebels, such as Khattab, have been linked to al Qaeda in numerous sources. Logistical and targeting data reported after Chechen suicide attacks also provides circumstantial evidence of a link to the broader Islamist network. Finally, the United Nations 1267 Sanctions Committee issued a report in July 2003 that confirmed connections between al Qaeda and Chechen rebels. See United Nations, *Security Council Committee Established Pursuant to Resolution 1267 (1999) Concerning al Qaeda and the Taliban and Associated Individuals and Entities,* the Monitoring Group's first report, www.un.org/Docs/sc/committees/1267.

3. For an excellent discussion of these evolving military/insurgency tactics, see Mark Kramer, "Guerrilla Warfare, Counterinsurgency, and Terrorism in the North Caucasus: The Military Dimension of the Russian-Chechen Conflict," unpublished manuscript, April 2004, subsequently published as "The Perils of Counterinsurgency: Russia's War in Chechnya," *International Security* 29, no. 3 (Winter 2004–5): 5–63. From the outset
of the conflict, the Russian government described its operations as "counterterrorist operations" (*kontrterroristicheskaya operatsiya,* or KTO), but mines and explosives account for roughly 40 percent of Russian troop casualties, and ambushes account for the next-largest share. E-mail correspondence with Kramer, April 7, 2004.

4. See Kramer, "The Perils of Counterinsurgency."

5. These ethnonationalist/separatist groups are only a subset of terrorist groups, with three other types commonly identified by terrorism experts as left wing, right wing, and religious or "sacred" terrorist organizations. See Audrey

Kurth Cronin, "Behind the Curve: Globalization and International Terrorism," *International Security* 27, no. 3 (Winter 2002–3): 39–42.

6. People often struggle with distinguishing between ethnonationalist/separatist terrorism and insurgency/guerrilla warfare. On the whole, I agree with Bruce Hoffman, who argues that guerrillas or insurgents (unlike "terrorists") are numerically larger groups of armed individuals who operate as a military unit, target primarily military forces, and seize or hold territory (even if only temporarily). Generally, this is how the terms will be used here. Of course, these distinctions always have gray areas, as insurgent groups sometimes target civilians whom they consider to be friendly with the enemy government and thus sometimes engage in terrorist tactics. See Bruce Hoffman, *Inside Terrorism* (New York: Columbia University Press, 1998), 41–43.

7. In discussing the longevity of terrorist groups, Martha Crenshaw notes only three significant terrorist groups with ethnonationalist ideologies that ceased to exist within ten years of their formation (one of these, EOKA, disbanded because its goal—the liberation of Cyprus—was attained). In contrast, a majority of the terrorist groups she lists as having existed for ten years or longer, including the IRA (in its many forms), Sikh separatist groups, Euskadi ta Askatasuna (ETA), the various Palestinian nationalist groups, and the Corsican National Liberation Front, have recognizable ethnonationalist ideologies. See Martha Crenshaw, "How Terrorism Declines," *Terrorism and Political Violence* 3, no. 1 (Spring 1991): 69–87. According to David Rapoport, the average life span of 90 percent of terrorist organizations is less than a year, and nearly half of those that make it to the one-year mark cease to exist within a decade.

8. During the writing of this case study, specific events in Chechnya and Russia were evolving rapidly. The author made every reasonable effort to keep up with the day-to-day changes. However, the chapter reflects events that occurred only through September 2004.

9. Carlotta Gall and Thomas de Waal, *Chechnya: Calamity in the Caucasus* (New York: New York University Press, 1998), 20–31.

10. John B. Dunlop, *Russia Confronts Chechnya: Roots of a Separatist Conflict* (Cambridge: Cambridge University Press, 1998), 61–62.

11. According to Dunlop, the reasons for the deportation cited in the NKVD archives included "the desire to defuse ethnic tensions"; the goal of "stabiliz[ing] the political situation"; the meting out of punishment for "acts against Soviet authorities, and to liquidate banditry"; and "punishment for collaboration with the fascists." See ibid., 61.

12. According to NKVD documents, Lavrentii Beria's men crammed almost half a million people into 152 trains comprising one hundred cars each, with forty to forty-five individuals, most of them children, crammed inside each freight car. See ibid., 66–71.

13. Gall and de Waal, *Chechnya,* 31–36. Before the war, the population of Grozny was estimated at about three hundred thousand.

14. Ibid.

15. Anatol Lieven calls Grozny "formerly the greatest oil-refining centre of the largest oil-producing state in the world." See Anatol Lieven, *Chechnya: Tombstone of Russian Power* (New Haven and London: Yale University Press, 1998).

16. Emil' Pain and Arkadii Popov, "Rossiiskaya politika v Chechne," *Izvestia,* February 7, 1995, 1, 4, cited in Dunlop, *Russia Confronts Chechnya,* 98–99.

17. Matthew Evangelista, *The Chechen Wars: Will Russia Go the Way of the Soviet Union?* (Washington, DC: Brookings Institution, 2002), 19–20.

18. Ibid., 31–32. See also Lieven, *Chechnya,* 92–93.

19. See Lieven, *Chechnya,* 86. For the opposing viewpoint, see Evangelista, *The Chechen Wars,* 30–31. According to Dmitri V. Trenin, the hijackers were criminals who sought profit, not political independence. See Dmitri V. Trenin, *The Forgotten War: Chechnya and Russia's Future,* Policy Brief no. 28, The Carnegie Endowment for International Peace, 2.

20. According to Lieven, 557 military officers of all ranks were disciplined or sacked or resigned in protest against the intervention. See Lieven, *Chechnya,* 106–7, 142. For an extensive discussion of the decision making that went into the war, see Andrew Bennett, *Condemned to Repetition? The Rise, Fall, and Reprise of Soviet-Russian Military Interventionism, 1973–1996* (Cambridge, MA: MIT Press, 1999), 334–41.

21. The evidence for this viewpoint is indirect. Olga Oliker cites an e-mail exchange with retired brigadier general John Reppert, December 10, 2000, based on General Reppert's personal conversations with General Grachev. Nonetheless, given how events transpired, it seems a plausible explanation. See Olga Oliker, *Russia's Chechen Wars 1994–2000: Lessons from Urban Combat* (Santa Monica, CA: RAND, 2001), 9n13, www.rand.org/publications/ MR/MR1289/ (accessed December 12, 2003). See also John R. Pilloni, "Burning Corpses in the Streets: Russia's Doctrinal Flaws in the 1995 Fight for Grozny," *Journal of Slavic Military Studies* 13, no. 2 (June 2000): n45.

22. John Arquilla and David Ronfeldt, *Networks and Netwars: The Future of Terror, Crime, and Militancy* (Santa Monica, CA: RAND, 2001), 330.

23. Matthew Evangelista, "Chechnya's Russia Problem," *Current History* 102, no. 666 (October 2003): 316.

24. An estimated 1,146 Russian soldiers were killed in the first three months of the war, and another 374 went missing and are likely dead. These figures are from the late Russian general Dmitry Volkogonov, given to journalist Nigel Chandler and cited by Lieven, *Chechnya,* 111.

25. Maskhadov succeeded Dudayev, who was killed by a Russian missile. Maskhadov was later also killed, apparently in a Russian operation.

26. Fiona Hill, Statement to the Helsinki Commission Hearing on "The Chechen Crisis and Its Implications for Russian Democracy," November 3, 1999, www.eurasia.org/news/HillsStatement110299.html.

27. Ibid.

28. Stephen J. Blank, "An Ambivalent War: Russia's War on Terrorism," *Small Wars and Insurgencies* 14, no. 1 (Spring 2003): 127–50. According to Stephen Blank, officers in the North Caucasus Military District routinely sold soldiers to the Chechens as slaves or to become drug couriers and addicts through August 1999, but there is no way to confirm this assertion.

29. Maskhadov won 59.3 percent of the vote, and rebel leader Shamil Basayev won 23.5 percent. See Scott Parrish, "Final Chechen Election Results," *OMRI Daily Digest,* no. 23, part 1 (February 3, 1997), cited by Evangelista, *Chechen Wars,* 48.

30. The actual carrying out of those attacks is shrouded in mystery, and some argue that the Chechens may not have been responsible for the bombings. The FSB was caught carrying out a supposed "simulation" of similar explosions in Ryazan, leading to suspicion of an FSB role in the other attacks as well. The local Ryazan police found and defused a bomb that had been placed, like most of the others, in a multistory apartment building. First the Kremlin praised the police, and later the FSB said the device was a fake that they had deliberately planted. See Michael Wines, "A Film Clip, and Charges of a Kremlin Plot," *The New York Times,* March 6, 2002, A8. Stephen Blank describes confidential statements from members of the Ministry of Foreign Affairs as early as May 1999 that there would be a war in Chechnya by August, which certainly gives cause to question the coincidence—although reports of these predictions are unconfirmed. See Blank, "Ambivalent War," 134.

31. "Putin's Chechen Remark Causes Stir," BBC News, November 13, 2002, http://news.bbc.co.uk/2/hi/europe/2460305.stm (accessed February 16, 2004).

32. *Izvestia,* October 1, 1999, cited by James Hughes, "Chechnya: The Causes of a Protracted Post-Soviet Conflict," *Civil Wars* 4, no. 4 (Winter 2001): 37. Hughes reports that Putin also personally awarded hunting knives to Russian troops serving in Chechnya on the 2000 New Year's holiday.

33. Hill, Statement to the Helsinki Commission Hearing, 3.

34. Oliker, *Russia's Chechen Wars,* 12–16.

35. One photograph in particular was published on the front page of *Komsomol'skaia Pravda.* It showed the burned corpse of a Russian soldier hanging halfway out of the hatch of his armored vehicle, having desperately tried to escape. Associated Press, *Komsomol'skaia Pravda,* January 11, 1995, 1, cited by Pilloni, "Burning Corpses," 1n2.

36. "Casualty Figures," *Chechnya Weekly* 4, no. 5, Jamestown Foundation, February 20, 2003. The fifty-five-hundred figure is the official Russian government number, and fourteen thousand is the estimate of the Soldiers' Mothers of Russia organization.

37. The number of Chechen fighters is not agreed on. According to the International Institute for Strategic Studies, they number approximately two to three thousand. See International Institute for Strategic Studies, *The Military Balance, 2003–2004* (Oxford: Oxford University Press, 2003), 345.

38. Oliker, *Russia's Chechen Wars,* 21.

39. It is very difficult to get reliable casualty statistics on the Chechen conflicts. The Russian government is consistently accused of underreporting the figures. The Russian Interior Ministry claimed that twenty thousand civilians had been killed. On the basis of careful research, Sergey Kovalyov, a prominent human rights activist, estimated that more than fifty thousand had died. Chechen authorities have claimed about one hundred thousand deaths. See Human Rights Violations in Chechnya, www.hrvc.net; and "Casualty Figures," *Chechnya Weekly* 4, no. 5, Jamestown Foundation, February 20, 2003.

40. Gall and de Waal, *Chechnya,* 244.

41. Pilloni, "Burning Corpses," 54. See also Human Rights Watch, "The 'Dirty War' in Chechnya: Forced Disappearances, Torture, and Summary Executions," *Human Rights Watch* 13, no. 1 (D) (March 2001), www.hrw.org/reports/2001/chechnya/ (accessed April 24, 2004).

42. Pilloni, "Burning Corpses," 53–54.

43. Anatoly S. Kulikov, "Russian Internal Troops and Security Challenges in the 1990s," *Low Intensity Conflict and Law Enforcement* 3 no. 2 (Autumn 1994): 209, cited by Gregory J. Celestan, "Wounded Bear: The Ongoing Russian Military Operation in Chechnya" (working paper, Foreign Military Studies Office, U.S. Army, Fort Leavenworth, KS, August 1996), 3, www.fas.org/man/dod/101/ops/war/docs/sounded.htm (accessed December 12, 2003).

44. Oliker, *Russia's Chechen Wars,* 9–12.

45. Gall and de Waal, *Chechnya,* 275. Apparently, the Russian Al'fa commando force had been deployed against the Chechens in the Budennovsk hospital siege but was forced to disengage under fire when the government decided to negotiate. See Mark Galeotti, "Elite Squad Hoping to Share Expertise," www.janes.com; accessed at www.janes.com/security/law_enforcement/news/ipi/ipi0313.shtml, December 12, 2003.

46. The Budennovsk incident was followed in January 1996 by a raid by two hundred Chechen rebels, led by Salman Raduyev, on a Russian military airfield and the taking of thousands of hostages at a hospital in the town of Kizlyar in Dagestan. As with Basayev's raid, the Chechens demanded that Russian troops leave Chechnya. Most of the hostages were released the next day. However, more than twenty-four hundred Russian military, security, and police troops laid siege to the rebels, disregarding the fate of the remaining hostages and vowing to deal a "decisive blow" to terrorism. See Jim Nichol, *Chechnya Conflict: Recent Developments and Implications for U.S. Interests,* CRS Report for Congress, no. 96-193, March 1, 1996, 2.

47. Dennis A. Pluchinsky, "Terrorism in the Former Soviet Union: A Primer, A Puzzle, A Prognosis," *Studies in Conflict and Terrorism* 21 (1998): 126.

48. Ibid.

49. Richard A. Falkenrath, Robert D. Newman, and Bradley A. Thayer, *America's Achilles Heel: Nuclear, Biological and Chemical Terrorism and Covert Attack,* 4th ed. (Cambridge, MA: MIT Press, 2001), 42, 210. It is still unclear what that incident was intended to signal, but it is hard to avoid the conclusion that the Chechens could be interested in using, or threatening to use, a radiological explosive device, or "dirty bomb."

50. Hill, Statement to the Helsinki Commission Hearing, 2–3.

51. Human Rights Watch, "The 'Dirty War' in Chechnya"; Mikhail A. Alexseev, "Chechnya: 9/11, the Moscow Hostage Crisis, and Opportunity for Political Settlement" (PONARS Policy Memo 250, October 2002). Program on New Approaches to Russian Security at the Center for Strategic and International Studies, Washington, DC, www.csis.org/ruseura/ponars/pm/.

52. According to RAND, these camps included Alos Abudzhafar, focused on partisan tactics and marksmanship; Yakub, specializing in heavy weapons; Abubakar, devoted to terrorist tactics; and Davlat, devoted to teaching psychological and ideological warfare. These reports are not confirmed. See Oliker, *Russia's Chechen Wars,* 39–40.

53. Ibid., 39–50.

54. Vladimir Mukhin, "Moskva uvelichivaet voiskuyu gruppirovku v Chechne: Pod shumok teraktov Genshtab podtyagivaet v myatezhnuyu respubliku poslednie rezervy," *Nezavisimaya gazeta* (Moscow), June 9, 2003, 1; cited in Kramer, "Guerrilla Warfare."

55. It is virtually impossible to get accurate, reliable statistics on casualties in Chechnya. One reason for the widely differing estimates is a discrepancy regarding what a casualty is, with some sources claiming that official figures do not include those who died in the hospital of wounds, as well as those killed in action. There are also apparently no official statistics on those who were wounded and did not die.

56. The official number of Soviet troops lost in Afghanistan is 14,453. See G. F. Krivosheev, *Soviet Casualties and Combat Losses in the Twentieth Century* (London: Greenhill, 1997).

57. Official figures generally indicate that some five thousand Russian soldiers have died during the second war in Chechnya. However, human rights groups claim that the real figure is about three times that high (fifteen thousand). The Union of the Committees of Soldiers' Mothers of Russia estimates that about twenty-five thousand Russian soldiers and police officers have been killed in Chechnya since 1994 (in both wars), with at least fifty thousand wounded or injured. See Jamestown Foundation, "Group Claims 25,000 Russian Soldiers Have Died in Chechnya," *Eurasia Daily Monitor* 1, no. 3, May 5, 2004; www.jamestown.org/edm/article.php?article_id=236655. One crucial difference between the war in Afghanistan and the second Chechen war, however, is the level of press control that has been exercised with respect to Chechnya; the Soviet withdrawal from Afghanistan was heavily influenced by the publicity surrounding traumatic losses in the war against the mujahideen. For an excellent source of information about the factors leading to the Soviet withdrawal from Afghanistan, see Sarah E. Mendelson, *Changing Course: Ideas, Politics, and the Soviet Withdrawal from Afghanistan* (Princeton, N.J.: Princeton University Press, 1998).

58. Four days after the event, the Russian government announced that the drug was derived from fentanyl, but this assertion is open to question. According to medical literature, fentanyl's effects are not generally as powerful or fast acting as those of the gas that was used. More likely, it was an incapacitating agent that is prohibited under the 1993 Chemical Weapons Convention (CWC), thereby explaining the Russian government's refusal to disclose anything about it. (I am indebted to Mark Kramer for this observation.) The gas may have been derived from other compounds, such as halothane, etorphine, or BZ (3-quinuclidinyl benzilate), alone or possibly in some mixture with fentanyl. Speculation about the true nature of the gas seems to be partly based on scientific analysis of testing done on German citizens who were among the hostages and were flown to Germany in the immediate aftermath of the event. Among other things, this speculation has caused concern about the robustness of the CWC. See Martin Enserink and Richard Stone, "Questions Swirl over Knockout Gas Used in Hostage Crisis," *Science* 298, no. 5596 (November 8, 2002): 1150–51.

59. The All-Russia Center for the Study of Public Opinion (VTsIOM) reported on October 8, 2002, that when respondents were asked "how the situation in Chechnya has changed since V. Putin was elected president," 43 percent felt the situation had not changed and 21 percent thought it had gotten worse. Likewise, a September 2002 poll found 56 percent of the respondents favoring negotiations with the Chechens. John Dunlop, "The October 2002 Moscow Hostage-Taking Incident," reprinted in Johnson's Russia List, no. 8017, January 16, 2004.

60. According to John Dunlop, in a private conversation Russian journalist Anna Politkovskaya asked "Abubakar," leader of the Chechen hostage takers, if he knew that peace negotiations by representatives of Chechen president Maskhadov were going on. She even offered to telephone the representatives and put them on the line with him. He answered: "They don't suit us. They are conducting these negotiations slowly . . . while we are dying in the forests. We are sick of them." Dunlop, "October 2002 Moscow Hostage-Taking Event," 20.

61. Ibid., 24. Support for military action went up to 46 percent, and the number of Russians in favor of peace negotiations dropped to 45 percent. Dunlop argues that the evidence points to significant collusion between Chechen extremists and elements of the Russian leadership who wanted to put an end to negotiations with the Maskhadov government. Nichol cites a poll that indicates 50 percent support for peace negotiations. See Jim Nichol, *Russia's Chechnya Conflict: An Update,* CRS Report for Congress, no. RL31620, April 16, 2003, 12.

62. There is broad international consensus that the 2003 event was not a legitimate, fair election.

63. "Rossiiane O Chechenskoi Voine" [Russians about the War in Chechnya], *Segodnia,* January 19, 1995, 3; cited by Pilloni, "Burning Corpses," n76.

64. Rachel Denber, "'Glad to Be Deceived': The International Community and Chechnya," *Human Rights Watch World Report 2004,* 5–6, http://hrw.org/wr2k4/7.htm (accessed February 22, 2004).

65. Nichol, *Russia's Chechnya Conflict,* 11. The *Washington Post* reported on June 10, 2002: "Though Russian military forces are no closer to winning the war than they were when Putin launched it in the fall of 1999, Mr. Putin has succeeded in squelching almost all critical discussion of the conflict in the Russian media." See also "Chechnya's Refugees" (June 10, 2002), A20.

66. Hughes, "Chechnya: The Causes of a Protracted Post-Soviet Conflict," 37; and Oliker, *Russia's Chechen Wars,* 62–63.

67. Oliker, *Russia's Chechen Wars,* 63–65.

68. For much more information and specific data regarding these developments, see Sarah E. Mendelson, "Russia's Rights Imperiled: Has Anybody Noticed?" *International Security* 26, no. 4 (Spring 2002): 39–69.

69. Ibid., 47.

70. See Anna Politkovskaya, *A Small Corner of Hell: Dispatches from Chechnya* (Chicago: University of Chicago Press, 2003).

71. Theodore P. Gerber and Sarah E. Mendelson, "Russian Public Opinion on Human Rights and the War in Chechnya," *Post-Soviet Affairs* 18, no. 4 (2002): 273–74.

72. Ibid.

73. Ibid., 289. The 2001 figures changed only slightly in 2003, with 3.8 percent worried about the behavior of Russian troops and 64.6 percent focused on the loss of Russian troops. Based on unpublished January 2003 polling results provided by Sarah Mendelson to the author.

74. Notably, those who described their sentiment toward Chechens as either "hostility" or "fear" made up a total of 48 percent of those answering the poll (36 percent and 12 percent, respectively). This was the highest level of both feelings expressed toward any ethnic group, with the runners-up being Gypsies (45 percent), Azeris (29 percent), Muslims (16 percent), and Americans (14 percent). Unpublished 2003 polling data provided to the author by Sarah Mendelson.

75. Putin won 71 percent of the vote and faced no serious opposition. See Stuart D. Goldman, *Russia,* Congressional Research Service, Issue Brief no. IB 92089, April 9, 2004.

76. Peter L. Bergin, *Holy War, Inc.: Inside the Secret World of Osama bin Laden* (New York: Free Press, 2001), 219; and Nichol, *Russia's Chechnya Conflict,* 20. Some sources describe Khattab as Jordanian born. See also Daniel Benjamin and Steven Simon, *The Age of Sacred Terror* (New York: Random House, 2002), 146.

77. Michael Sheuer, *Through Our Enemies' Eyes: Osama bin Laden, Radical Islam, and the Future of America* (New York: Brassey's, 2002), 141.

78. Bergin, *Holy War, Inc.,* 219.

79. The actual date of Khattab's death is not agreed on. Some report that he was allegedly killed during a clandestine Russian operation using biological toxins in March 2002. See Nichol, *Russia's Chechnya Conflict,* 20.

80. Bergin, *Holy War, Inc.,* 86.

81. Simon and Benjamin, *The Age of Sacred Terror,* 113.

82. Rohan Gunaratna, *Inside al Qaeda: Global Network of Terror* (New York: Columbia University Press, 2002), 64. There has also been a report of a 1998 attempt by bin Laden to buy a nuclear warhead, which, according to sources, cost $30 million in cash and two tons of heroin, which were donated by the Taliban. High-level members of the Russian Mafia were involved, and the meeting that allegedly sealed the deal occurred near Grozny. Bin Laden was apparently duped, however. See Sheurer, *Through Our Enemies' Eyes,* 191.

83. Gunaratna, *Inside al Qaeda,* 135.

84. Six UN Security Council entries allege some connection with al Qaeda or the Taliban: Two links are individuals, Basayev and Zelimkhan Ahmedovish Yandarbiev, a Kazakh alleged to be involved in Chechnya; three links are organizations, the al-Rashid Trust, the Benevolence International Foundation, and the Global Relief Foundation; and one link is a terrorist organization, the Riyadus-Salikhin Reconnaissance and Sabotage Battalion of Chechen Martyrs (RSRSBCM; translates to "Requirements for Getting into Paradise"). See the UN Security Council's list of organizations and individuals subject to sanctions under Resolution 1267 (directed at the Taliban and al Qaeda) at www.un.org/Docs/sc/committees/1267. The resolution requires nations to freeze the organization's financial resources and ensure that they are not used by the group or passed on to the Taliban or Osama bin Laden.

85. The estimated number of Chechen rebels comes from the International Institute for Strategic Studies, *Military Balance, 2003–2004,* 345.

86. All three organizations are listed by the U.S. Department of the Treasury as specially designated global terrorist organizations (SDGTs), whose assets are frozen. See Office of Foreign Assets Control, www.treas.gov/offices/eotffc/ofac/sdn/index.html.

87. Benjamin and Simon, *The Age of Sacred Terror,* 288.

88. Denber, "'Glad to Be Deceived.'"

89. Ibid., 3–4.

90. Three groups are on the SDGT list (Executive Order 12334): the Islamic International Peacekeeping Brigade (IIPB), the RSRSBCM, and the Special Purpose Islamic Regiment (SPIR).

91. See, among other sources, Steven Lee Myers, "From Dismal Chechnya, Women Turn to Bombs," *New York Times,* September 10, 2004, www.nytimes.com (accessed on September 10, 2004).

92. For a list of attacks, see U.S. Department of State, *Patterns of Global Terrorism, 2003* (Washington, DC: U.S. Government Printing Office), 37–38; and Peter Baker, "Old Enemies Enlist in U.S. Terror War: Former Soviet Republics Become Allies," *Washington Post,* January 1, 2004, A18, A22.

93. Steven Lee Myers, "Explosive Suggests Terrorists Downed Plane, Russia Says," *New York Times*, August 28, 2004, www.nytimes.com (accessed August 30, 2004). The two female suicide operatives apparently bribed their way onto the two airliners, despite raising suspicions among airport authorities. Notably, a group calling itself the Islambouli Brigades of al Qaeda claimed responsibility, citing the war in Chechnya and Russian involvement in Muslim lands elsewhere.

94. Shamil Basayev, in his statement of claim for the incident, announced that there were thirty-one operatives from various ethnic regions of Russia, including twelve Chechen men, two Chechen women, and two Arabs. "Chechen Rebel Claims Beslan Seige," BBC News, September 17, 2004, http://news.bbc.co.uk (accessed October 17, 2004).

95. Ibid.

96. "Top Russian Security Official Seeks 'Additional Powers' in War on Terror," *RIA Novosti,* February 9, 2004, translated and reprinted in Johnson's Russia List, no. 8057, February 10, 2003, www.cdi.org/russia/johnson/.

97. "The Kremlin's control freak," *Economist Global Agenda,* September 17, 2004, *Economist.com* (accessed October 17, 2004); and Fred Weir and Scott Peterson, "Russian Terrorism Prompts Power Grab: New Measures Announced Yesterday Would End Direct Election of Governors in Russia's 89 Regions," *Christian Science Monitor,* September 14, 2004, http://csmonitor.com (accessed on October 17, 2004).

98. Kramer, "Guerrilla Warfare," 40.

99. Andrei Soldatov and Irina Borogan, "Spetsy po terroru: FSB prevrashchaetsya v armiyu," *Versiya* no. 49 (December 2003): 10, cited in Kramer, "Guerrilla Warfare," 40.

100. Ibid. According to the article, there was one Chechen-speaking translator on the staff of the FSB in the 1990s. See Kramer, "Guerrilla Warfare," 40.

101. Peter Baker, "Russia Moving to Eliminate Chechen Rebel Leaders; Separatists Defiant after Series of Setbacks," *Washington Post,* April 20, 2004, A13.

102. Alex Rodriguez, "Atrocities against Chechen Civilians on the Rise, Rights Groups Say," Knight Ridder Tribune News Service, May 6, 2004, 1; and David Filipov, "Shadowy Kidnappings Keep Chechens on Edge," *Boston Globe,* February 29, 2004, A10.

103. Kim Murphy, "Chechen Women Being Seized to Preempt |Bombings, Rights Groups Say; Female Kin of Suspected Rebels Are Reportedly Taken Away by Security Forces to Unclear Fates," *Los Angeles Times,* May 26, 2004, A3.

104. Estimates vary, but as many as two hundred thousand Chechen civilians continue to be displaced. See Kramer, "Guerrilla Warfare," 5.

105. Norwegian Refugee Council, Global IDP Database, *Protecting Internally Displaced Persons in the OSCE Area: A Neglected Commitment* (Geneva and Oslo: Global IDP Project, October 2003), 24–27; and Human

Rights Watch, "Into Harm's Way: Forced Return of Displaced People to Chechnya" (New York: Human Rights Watch, January 2003), especially 6–12. I am grateful to Mark Kramer for drawing my attention to both of these references.

106. Human Rights Watch, "Into Harm's Way," 25.

107. Ibid. Notably, according to the report, monitoring by human rights institutions has been seriously restricted. Human Rights Watch has been denied access to Chechnya since 1999, the mandate of the OSCE Assistance Group in Chechnya ended in December 2002, and the deteriorating security situation forced representatives from the Council of Europe to leave in April 2003.

108. Steven Lee Meyers, "Chechnya Bomb Kills President, a Blow to Putin," *New York Times,* May 10, 2004, 1; and Susan B. Glasser and Peter Baker, "Chechen President Killed in Bomb Blast," *Washington Post,* May 10, 2004, 1. According to press reports, Colonel General Baranov had a leg amputated as a result of injuries suffered in the blast.

109. C. J. Chivers, "A Priority as Chechnya's President Takes Office: Staying Alive," *New York Times,* October 6, 2004, A3.

110. Kim Murphy, "New Chechen Leader Stirs Fear, Distrust: the Kremlin-Backed Government Rules by Intimidation, Residents and Rights Workers Say," *Los Angeles Times,* February 10, 2004.

111. Ibid.

112. "Chechen Leader Maskhadov Killed," BBC News, March 8, 2005, http://news.bbc.co.uk/2/hi/europe/4330039.stm.

113. The International Institute for Strategic Studies claims that Russian forces suffered 4,749 casualties between August 2002 and August 2003, the highest figure in one year since the current Chechen conflict began. See International Institute for Strategic Studies, *Military Balance, 2003–2004,* 86–87.

13

COUNTERING TERRORIST MOVEMENTS IN INDIA

Kashmir and Khalistan

Paul Wallace

Political violence has posed threats to India since its independence in 1947. Left-wing violence began in Telangana in 1948,[1] subsequently reemerged in the Naxalbari part of eastern India in the 1970s, and since has expanded with varying names into Naxalite violence elsewhere in India.[2] In October 2003, the People's War Group (PWG) nearly assassinated Chief Minister Chandrababu Naidu in Andhra Pradesh. Left-wing terrorism also crossed the border in an even more deadly form as the Maoist movement in Nepal.[3] Tribal irredentism and violence also have a lengthy history in the northeast of India, continue to confront contemporary India, and have spilled over into the bordering independent Himalayan state of Bhutan.[4]

Nevertheless, left-wing and tribal-based violence have not posed as serious a threat to India's integrity as has the combination of insurgency and terrorism in Punjab and Kashmir. Ethnonationalism became intensified by religion in Punjab and Kashmir, with Pakistan providing a further complication. Islamic militants, abetted by jihadist groups and support from

Pakistan, have been engaged in an insurgency since 1989 in Kashmir. Resulting internal and cross-border terrorism continue. In 1980 Sikh militants began terrorist activities in Punjab that became a movement for an independent Khalistan state. Popular support had ended by 1993, but terrorists were still able to kill the chief minister in a suicide car attack in 1995, and incidents continued in 2006.[5]

Partition of India and the creation of Pakistan in 1947 served as the catalyst for the subsequent ethnoreligious nationalist movements. The ensuing migration resulted in more than five hundred thousand deaths and forced approximately fifteen million people to flee—Hindus and Sikhs to India, and Muslims to Pakistan. Punjab, split between the two countries, served as the epicenter of the tragic events. Kashmir became divided the following year. Nationalist movements as they developed in both areas continue to involve and exacerbate Indo-Pakistani relations.

Kashmir provides the most serious and costly threat to India. Approximately one million Indian and Pakistani troops were arrayed against each other following a terrorist attack on India's parliament in New Delhi on December 13, 2001. A low-intensity conflict in Kashmir has marked relations between the two neighbors for more than a decade, and terrorist actions continue within Indian-controlled Kashmir. The leaders of India and Pakistan initiated a serious dialogue in Islamabad in December 2003. Subsequently, talks about talks that include Kashmir have continued between their representatives.[6] Nonetheless, killings continue in Kashmir as major participants such as the Hizbul Mujahideen refuse to participate. Although Punjab's militant insurrection, driven by the Sikh movement for an independent Khalistan, largely ended in 1993, residual elements continue.

This chapter deals with Punjab and Kashmir. Following an overview of the two cases, I focus on the most and least effective counterterrorism efforts there. I provide historical background only to the extent that it is needed to explain the genesis and major developments of the movements that resulted in political violence and terrorism. Insurrectionary antistate movements in both cases involve groups that hit "soft" civilian as well as military targets, threaten and intimidate various sectors of society in regard to social as well as political goals, and achieve a significant degree of fear and terror among the general population. In turn, the state responds in a manner, especially in regard to interrogation methods, that is characterized as state terror.

The initial section, introducing Punjab, emphasizes the period of political violence beginning in 1980. Earlier Sikh religious traditions were reformulated in a radical manner by a new leadership emphasizing political violence and political goals. Punjab as a territorial area provided an ethnic dimension. Two major events in 1984 were especially traumatic: The Indian army action in the Golden Temple complex in June resulted in the killing of the Sikh movement's major leaders and the transformation of a unified militant movement into many contending groups. Prime Minister Indira Gandhi's assassination in October, the second major event, was immediately followed by the killing of large numbers of Sikhs. Sikh alienation and mobilization became more extreme, leading to a decade in which violent Sikh groups battled with the state until they were defeated.

Successful state efforts included more effective use of the police and military, as well as positive, rural-based, "hearts-and-minds-oriented" programs. Human rights violations by the state were counterproductive, while terrorist excesses were a major reason for the terrorists' loss of support.

An overview of Kashmir begins with differing concepts of nationalism and the basis of partition. Pakistan's "two-nations" theory, based on religious communities, versus India's secular nationalism, is the ideological basis of the discord. Kashmir as a Muslim-majority princely state ruled by a Hindu maharajah, a nationalist movement led by a largely secular Muslim leader, and regionalism in which Hindus dominate in Jammu and Buddhists in Ladakh complicate the context. Contemporary secessionist movements became activated in the 1980s. In addition to pro-Pakistani and pro-Indian groups, there is a long-existing movement for an independent Kashmir. Pro-Pakistani groups aided by jihadists—radical Islamic fighters from many countries—and assisted by Pakistan are particularly violent, with tactics ranging from attacking the legislative assembly to beheadings. Three wars between India and Pakistan involved Kashmir. Periodic peace efforts also are part of the history. Events following 9/11 and the emphasis on dealing with terrorism in Afghanistan and South Asia led to renewed peace efforts between India and Pakistan beginning in December 2003. Nonetheless, violence continues in Kashmir.

The final and key parts of the chapter deal with India's efforts to counter terrorism in Punjab and Kashmir. To provide a focus to the counterterrorism efforts and to enable a comparison between the two cases, I have selected five key areas: (1) military responses, including the deployment of regular army, police, and nonregular military; (2) special legislation; (3) human rights; (4) negotiations; and (5) closure.

Questionnaires based on these categories were sent to a select group of knowledgeable individuals. Segments of their replies are quoted anonymously, and their extended comments helped inform and provide balance to the highly volatile subject. Respondents include a former deputy head of the United Nations Mission in Kashmir, who continues to be active on Kashmir, and two retired colonels, one Indian and one American, who have extensive experience in the area and continuing knowledge of Kashmir. Indian political scientists from Amritsar and Chandigarh in Punjab, India, provide perspectives enhanced by having lived in the area during the violent period. North American political scientists in the group include one of the leading specialists on the Indian and Pakistani militaries. Another is chair of a women's studies program with two major books on India and a professional concern with human rights. Finally, the group includes two relatively new Ph.D.s who wrote major dissertations on contemporary Punjab.

A conclusion attempts to establish the most significant lessons on counterterrorism stemming from the two cases. Lessons about each of the five areas enumerated above include what appears to work well, as well as what is counterproductive.

THE SIKH AND KASHMIR CONFLICTS

Sikh political violence and terrorism in India lasted more than a decade, from approximately 1980 to 1993. Incidents continue in the twenty-first century, and the possibility of reactivation of the movement is present but unlikely in the short run. A resumption of low-intensity warfare between India and Pakistan in Kashmir could induce Pakistan to use militant Sikhs to continue their actions from Pakistan.

According to official figures, twenty thousand people were killed during the 1980–93 period by the terrorists and the mirrorlike reaction of the state. Other estimates are much higher. The "Punjab problem," as it became popularly labeled, escalated, from political confrontation between various Sikh groups and the state and central governments to increasing levels of political violence. A movement led by a charismatic religious leader with millenarian social and religious goals superseded normal political conflict. His death in violent conflict resulted in a proliferation of contending militant groups. Correspondingly, Sikh extremist political demands rose to the level of openly seeking an independent Sikh state. Failing to achieve sufficient support among the population, the insurgency degenerated into reliance on terrorism.

Normalcy seems to have returned to Punjab State, the homeland of the Sikhs and the center of the terrorism. Nonetheless, militants continue to be apprehended in the twenty-first century, and an infrastructure for terrorist activities continues in Pakistan and overseas. Terrorist groups include the Khalistan Commando Force, the Babbar Khalsa, the Khalistan Liberation Force, and the International Sikh Youth Federation. Their support within Punjab, however, has "withered away."[7] Most notable since the "end" of the Punjab insurgency/terrorist movement has been the killing of Chief Minister Beant Singh and his entourage in a suicide car attack in front of the heavily guarded state secretariat building in 1995. The accused were about to come to trial when they escaped from a high-security prison in January 2004.[8] One of the escapees, subsequently arrested by the Delhi police, is accused of involvement in Delhi cinema bomb blasts in May 2005 and of training two young Sikhs to serve as suicide bombers.[9]

Problems of identity are central to the role of Sikhs in Punjab. They are equally if not more important to the Sikh diaspora[10] in North America and the United Kingdom, where militant rhetoric feeds into indigenous Punjab dynamics. Self-identity assumes greater priority, particularly on the basis of religion, in response to perceived threats, whether real or politically manufactured.

Religion and ethnicity underlie Sikh nationalism in India. Since 1980 nationalism has taken the form of political violence, with methods ranging from terrorist hit squads to bombings of soft targets, extortion, and the targeting of police and other authorities by the militants. In turn, state terrorism has included torture and summary executions by the police under the euphemism "encounters." Violent militancy has been contained since 1993, but an infrastructure in support of violence continues in adjoining Pakistan. Periodic efforts to revive the terrorist movement in Punjab are reported, and incidents continue, such as a railway track "blast triggered by anti-national elements" in central Punjab on January 5, 2004.[11] An occasional bomb that can be attributed to either a Khalistani or Kashmiri source, as in the Delhi cinema bombings of May 2005, explodes in the nearby national capital of New Delhi.

Religious revivalism and ethnic identity are interwoven in India. Sikhs are a majority in Punjab State—63 percent compared to the Hindu 34.5 percent of the total population of 20.2 million—but still have to face minority-status issues because they constitute a small percentage of India's large population and because of the centralizing features of India's national government.[12] Nationally, Sikhs are only 1.8 percent of India's population of more than one billion, compared to 82 percent for Hindus and 12 percent for Muslims. Punjab is where Sikhs are concentrated and where Sikhism began in the fifteenth century as a new world religion founded by Guru Nanak.[13]

Two centuries later, in 1699, Guru Gobind Singh completed the transformation of the originally pietistic sect into a militant religious community in order to defend Punjab against its Mughal rulers. This tenth and last guru established the Khalsa as a distinctive community, set forth its doctrines, and completed the Sikh's holy book, the Guru Granth Sahib. His model included Khalsa initiation (a form of baptism), a prohibition against the cutting of hair, and what has been interpreted as a ban on alcohol and tobacco. At this point, Sikhs became a militant community, warriors defending their land against the Muslim rulers of the Mughal dynasty. All Khalsa males had to take the name Singh, or "lion," and wear a kirpan (sword or dagger). Women had to take the name Kaur, usually translated as "princess." Ranjit Singh's Punjab kingdom, conquered by the British in the 1840s, provided a model of Sikh political rule. The Temple Reform Movement of 1920–25[14] and the Punjabi Suba movement for a Sikh-majority state in the 1960s are examples of successful militant but nonviolent movements by the Sikhs; their opponents, however, were not necessarily nonviolent.[15]

In the late 1970s, a charismatic religious leader, Sant Jarnail Singh Bhindranwale, emerged with a thundering style and reformulation of the Khalsa model. Initially, covert support came from the Congress Party, which attempted to use him to split the Akali Dal, the dominant Sikh party in Punjab.[16] Sant Bhindranwale quickly went from unsuccessful elective politics to a violent confrontation with an alleged heretical Sikh sect in 1978. Eighteen Sikhs were killed in what one scholar has described as "provocative stage management."[17] Deliberate killings—"hits"—began in 1980 and had escalated to more than one hundred a year by 1984. The massacre of bus passengers in September 1983 was the "first of their acts to spread mass-terrors."[18] Bhindranwale combined the almost monkish and ascetic elements of his religious seminary, the Damdami Taksal, with the warrior element of Nihang Sikhs, a fanatical component of the Sikh military during the nineteenth century.

Bhindranwale demanded that Sikhs purify their community and assert themselves with violence against Hindu discrimination. Puritanical social codes were promulgated. By 1991, at the height of the killings, girls had been forbidden to wear skirts, trousers, or dresses in school, and a new curriculum had been ordered. One headmistress of a government school asked for a few weeks so that girls who came from poor factory-worker families could arrange for the traditional *salwar-kameez*. The response came in the form of "two bullets through her belly." Hindi and the national anthem were proscribed. Subtitles in the Punjabi language were even to be used for televised film songs. Journalists had to use the "new-speak of militancy": terrorists became "militants, *khadkoos* or Khalistani mujahedin."[19]

Violence increased consonant with Bhindranwale's extremist rhetoric, and his movement increasingly undercut the legitimacy of the moderate Akali Dal as well as the institutions of state government.[20] He became an authority who settled disputes in a summary fashion and instituted punishment from his base in the Golden Temple complex. A semiofficial *Encyclopaedia of Police* states that "police and civil administration" could have "effectively checked" Bhindranwale if "political interference" had not intervened. The author concludes, "Politics was used to keep the fire simmering."[21]

Bhindranwale fortified the Golden Temple complex and defended it against the Indian army's Operation Bluestar in June 1984. More than one thousand people, including religious pilgrims, Bhindranwale, and his two chief lieutenants, were killed during a religious holiday. Operation Bluestar became one of the two major symbols of repression. The other major catalytic action for Sikhs occurred almost immediately following the assassination of Prime Minister Indira Gandhi in October 1984 by two of her Sikh bodyguards. Orchestrated violence in Delhi and elsewhere outside Punjab killed more than two thousand Sikhs, enflaming Sikhs everywhere in India and the diaspora. They blamed the Congress Party.

However, the militant leadership splintered following Bhindranwale's death, resulting in four major groups and more than one hundred subgroups engaged in political violence. An independent Sikh-ruled Khalistan became the goal of this hydrocephalous movement. Moderate Akali Dal

Sikh leadership lost control of the political agenda to the militant groups. Central government rule and deinstitutionalization (suspension of the legislature and decline of other state government institutions) followed, giving way to military force. Table 13-1 provides official data on the escalation of killings beginning in 1981, not counting the deaths in the Golden Temple in 1984 or later that year in Delhi. As terrorist groups proliferated, totals increased to more than one thousand deaths per year, with a high point of almost five thousand deaths in 1991. An initial focus on killing Hindus changed as Sikhs became the major targets, as is detailed in table 13-2. Sikh-on-Sikh violence became dominant as terrorist groups operated primarily in rural areas, where the population is primarily Sikh.

Table 13-1. Violence in Punjab, 1981–94

	Civilians and Police Killed	Police Killed	Extremists Killed	Total Killed	Extremists Arrested
1981	13	2	14	27	84
1982	13	2	7	20	178
1983	75	20	13	88	296
1984	359	20	77	436	1,630
1985	63	8	2	65	491
1986	520	42	78	598	1,581
1987	910	95	328	1,238	3,750
1988	1,949	110	373	2,322	3,882
1989	1,168	201	703	1,871	2,466
1990	2,467	506	1,320	3,787	1,759
1991	2,591	497	2,177	4,768	1,977
1992	1,518	252	2,111	3,629	1,502
1993*	38	21	472	510	454
Totals	11,684	1,776	7,675	19,359	20,050

Source: Data compiled by Paul Wallace from Government of India, Ministry of Home Affairs, National Integration Council, meeting December 31, 1991, Annexure-1, "Profile of Violence in Punjab," 11. Office of the Director-General of Police, Punjab, as cited in K. P. S. Gill, "The Dangers Within: Internal Security Threats," in *Future Imperilled: India's Security in the 1990s and Beyond,* ed. Bharat Karnad (New Delhi: Viking Penguin, 1994), 118, 120. Department of State submission to the Joint Committee on Foreign Relations, U.S. Senate and U.S. House of Representatives, 1220.

*1993 data from January 1 to September 10 only.

Table 13-2. Hindus and Sikhs Killed by Terrorists in Punjab, 1981–91

	Number of Hindus	Percentage of Hindus	Number of Sikhs	Percentage of Sikhs
1981	10	77	3	23
1982	8	62	5	38
1983	35	47	40	53
1984	237	66	122	34
1985	45	73	17	27
1986	324	63	193	37
1987	425	47	478	54
1988	858	45	1,044	55
1989	442	38	734	62
1990	743	30	1,694	70
1991	744	29	1,847	71
Totals	3,871		6,177	

Source: Data reported in *Times of India,* February 9, 1992, 15, from the Ministry of Home Affairs, Government of India.

Military responses to terrorism became more sophisticated and effective. The regular army's use of overwhelming force during Operation Bluestar in 1984[22] (compared to an elephant chasing a mouse!) is to be contrasted with the police-led surgical nature of Operation Black Thunder in May 1988. Police, paramilitary, regular armed forces, and home guards were used in large numbers, as were outreach programs in villages. These dual strategies lessened popular support for the militants and were reinforced by growing resentment toward terrorist excesses.

Restarting the political process contributed significantly to the changed situation in Punjab. General and local elections in 1992 brought back regular election cycles at all levels. The moderate Akali Dal had replaced the terrorist groups as the major vehicle for rural Sikh political expression by 1997, regaining control of the political agenda. The Akali Dal also swept state and national elections until 2002, thereby temporarily replacing the Congress Party as the dominant political party in Punjab. An alliance with the Hindu upper caste–based Bharatiya Janata Party (BJP) enabled the Akali Dal to combine essentially rural Sikhs with urban Hindu support. This broad-based Sikh-Hindu coalition moderated social and political tensions. A

Times of India editorial emphasized Punjab's democratic renewal: "While security action can curb the terrorists temporarily only the democratic process can destroy the roots of terrorism."[23] Return of the Congress Party to power in Punjab in 2002 did not result in renewed violence, except for occasional acts as noted previously. Popular support for terrorism in Punjab has not returned. Both major political groups include Sikhs and Hindus; the Akali Dal does so through its alliance with the BJP, while Sikh leaders dominate the Congress Party.

Overview of Terrorism in Jammu and Kashmir

Political violence in Kashmir arose out of the partition of British-ruled India into the independent states of India and Pakistan in 1947. Radically different criteria fueled these contending nationalist movements. Pakistan arose from the two-nations theory set forth by Muhammad Ali Jinnah, the father of Pakistan, and the political party he unquestioningably dominated, the Muslim League. Simply put, the theory maintained that two nations existed in undivided India, the majority Hindus and a minority of Muslims, who would suffer discrimination in an independent India. Pakistan would be composed of the Muslim-majority areas of India and would serve to guarantee the rights of not only Muslims there but also, in some measure, Muslims remaining in India.

India's nationalist movement, led by Mahatma Gandhi and institutionalized through the Congress Party, consciously followed an accommodative, pluralist model. "Unity amidst diversity"—meaning the aggregating of all religions, regions, languages, and castes, including minorities—became a popular slogan. Prime Minister Jawaharlal Nehru sought to create an all-India nationalism and then an independent secular Indian state, of which Kashmir was set forth as an important symbol.[24] He succeeded to a significant degree during his lifetime, and the concept of a secular state continues to maintain significant support.

According to the two-nation theory, the Muslim-majority state of Kashmir should have become part of Pakistan. Pakistani politics in large measure is driven by what is almost an obsession to rectify this perceived injustice. India, on the other hand, views Kashmir through its accommodative and secular lens as an integral part of India. Partition, it maintains, was not based on religion. The United Kingdom carved out the new state of Pakistan based on various criteria. Princely states, such as Jammu and Kashmir, had the choice of accession to either Pakistan or India or, according to a few rulers, independence. Maharajah Hari Singh, a Hindu but the dynastic ruler of Muslim-majority Jammu and Kashmir State, acceded to India. Furthermore, Kashmir, as India's only Muslim-majority state, is an important symbol for India's more than 150 million Muslims, even though its total population in 2001, according to the census, was only 10,069,917, including Hindus and Buddhists. India's Muslim population is second only to Indonesia's.

It is arguable whether the maharajah delayed choosing between India and Pakistan because he sought independence for Kashmir and signed the legal instrument only under duress as tribal warriors invaded Kashmir from Pakistan. India and Pakistan have fought three wars involving Kashmir. A fourth conflict, in 1999, was limited to the Kargil sector of Kashmir. The first war took place immediately after Kashmir's accession to India; the second, in 1965; and the third, in 1971. Pakistan was dismembered as a consequence of the third war; East Pakistan emerged as independent Bangladesh. India captured approximately one hundred thousand troops.

Prime Minister Indira Gandhi's subsequent negotiations with Prime Minister Zulfikar Ali Bhutto in the 1972 Shimla Summit also involved Kashmir. The cease-fire line established under United Nations auspices, with some modifications, became the Line of Control (LoC), a de facto boundary. In time, conceivably, it could be accepted as the permanent, de jure boundary. The Indian establishment would be pleased with such an outcome. Meanwhile, India continued to integrate the two-thirds of Jammu and Kashmir that it controlled while according this territory a special status under Article 370 of the constitution. Most importantly, under this article, non-Kashmiris cannot own land in the state.

Nonetheless, movements for changing Kashmir's status in relation to India have been continuous since 1947. A nationalist movement under Sheikh Muhammad Abdullah had sought independence from the maharajah before 1947, and it continued into the postpartition period. The highly popular Muslim leader led a largely secular movement with ties to the Congress nationalist movement and Jawaharlal Nehru.[25]

However, disputes over the degree and nature of autonomy estranged Abdullah from New Delhi. Kashmir, according to Abdullah, had "a division of sovereignty" with India and, in contrast to other states in India, could "sever our relations with India."[26] Sheikh Abdullah alternated between being in power and being jailed. The National Conference, under his son Farooq Abdullah, continued as a major political party seeking more autonomy yet engaging in elections and a nonviolent political role. Managing Kashmir and electoral manipulation took precedence over deepening democratic roots and institutions for policymakers in New Delhi.

Secessionist demands developed in the 1980s, partly among youth in Kashmiri jails. A first group of young men was reported crossing over to Pakistan for arms training in 1987–88.[27] December 1989,[28] however, can be considered the catalytic month for the onset of insurgency and terrorist actions. Almost immediately after Rajiv Gandhi's Congress government lost the national elections to a coalition, the Jammu and Kashmir Liberation Front (JKLF) kidnapped the daughter of the new home minister, Mufti Mohammed Sayeed, a Kashmiri. V. P. Singh's government in New Delhi agreed to the ransom demands on behalf of its Kashmiri cabinet minister, releasing five militants.

Contemporary accounts of the Kashmiri conflict invariably compile the violence figures from this month. In 2004, estimates of the number of civilians, terrorists, and military personnel killed since 1989 ranged from thirty-five to sixty-five thousand.[29] See table 13-3.

Table 13-3. Violence in Kashmir, January 2002–July 2005

	Civilians Killed	Security Personnel Killed	Terrorists Killed	Total Fatalities	Violent Incidents	Suicide Attacks
2002	493	210	991	1,694		
2003	399	194	845	1,438		
2004	362	203	601	1,166	1,611	41
2005	313	129	645	1,087	1,217	22
Totals	1,567	736	3,082	5,385		

Source: Compiled from data in *South Asia Intelligence Review* (SAIR) 4, no. 4, August 8, 2005.

As in Punjab, the number of people killed can be compared with criminal violence statistics in states such as Bihar or metropolitan areas elsewhere in the world. Terrorism and the state response, one analyst observes, compound dislocation through transfers of population, deployment of security forces, economic effects, and the danger of a larger war, possibly involving nuclear weapons.[30]

A kaleidoscope of militant groups, ranging from terrorists directly attacking Indian military forces as well as soft targets to nonviolent militant groups joined together in the legally recognized and sometimes fractured Hurriyat Conference, have filled the Kashmir scene. The JKLF is the oldest of the militant groups, having been founded in 1976 by Amanullah Khan and Maqbool Butt. Its lineage extends back to an earlier group, the Kashmir National Liberation Front, founded by Khan, Butt, and Hashim Qureshi in 1964 in Peshawar, Pakistan. The JKLF's unit in Indian Kashmir was established in February 1988, almost two years before it dramatically kidnapped the daughter of the all-India home minister in December 1989.

The JKLF has consistently sought independence for all of Kashmir from both India and Pakistan, now primarily as a nonviolent organization related to the Hurriyat Conference. The JKLF operates in the Pakistani-controlled sector of Kashmir as well as in Pakistan, various European countries, and the United States.[31] Kashmiri nationalism is an apt characterization of the JKLF philosophy. A variety of other groups are more difficult to categorize, as is the line between insurgency and terror. Whether Kashmiri liberation in the form of an independent state or incorporation into Pakistan is the goal varies with respect to individual groups, and even within their leadership. Violent tactics range from attacking Indian military personnel to attacking "soft" civilian targets, intimidation, and occasional beheadings.

After 1991 externally directed groups marginalized the JKLF. Indeed, Pakistan's Inter-Services Intelligence (ISI) had ceased its support for the JKLF by 1990.[32] Independence for Kashmir, the JKLF goal, was replaced by an openly pro-Pakistani goal: "The *Muslim Valley* waging an *Islamic movement* against the *Hindu Indian State* in order to accede to *Islamic Pakistan*"[33] (italics in original). Hizbul Mujahideen, the largest guerrilla organization active in the first decade of the twenty-first century, is characteristic of the terrorist organizations that became dominant. It is a Pakistani-oriented organization, the militant wing of the Jama'at-i-Islami, with an estimated strength ranging from fourteen hundred to twenty thousand.[34] In contrast to the more Kashmiri and nationalist JKLF, it has a larger number of foreigners and places more emphasis on Islam.[35] The Lashkar e-Tayyiba (LeT), Jaish-i-Muhammad, and Harkat-ul-Ansar, as well as a number of other groups, reflect the increasing involvement of external

Islamic militants after the withdrawal of Soviet forces from Afghanistan and the focus of jihadists on Kashmir.

Pakistan came close to instigating a fourth war with India as its military action in the Kargil sector in 1999 escalated the low-intensity conflict in Kashmir into a major, but geographically limited, conflict that sparked an intense patriotic surge in India. Since both states had made successful nuclear tests the previous year, the possibility of a nuclear war resulted in international intervention, particularly by U.S. president Bill Clinton.

Following 9/11, Pakistan abruptly switched from support for to public opposition to the Taliban and al Qaeda. However, a month later, in October 2001, jihadists attacked Kashmir's legislative assembly in Srinagar, and in December they attacked India's parliament in New Delhi. In response, India mobilized its military along the entire frontier with Pakistan, and Pakistan reciprocated. International pressure again facilitated the reduction of tensions, but Kashmir remained the center of tensions between the two nuclear states. India demanded the cessation of what it termed cross-border terrorism. Pakistan denied direct involvement but nonetheless agreed to rein in the jihadists in Kashmir. President Pervez Musharraf and Prime Minister Atal Bihari Vajpayee personally started a peace process during their meeting in Islamabad in December 2003, followed by subsequent meetings of high-level officials in 2004.

Elections in May 2004 replaced the Bharatiya Janata Party–led government with a Congress Party–led alliance, with no apparent change regarding Kashmir. Talks continued, along with what were labeled confidence-building measures. Nonetheless, negotiations between India and Pakistan did not provide a short-term solution to the external jihadist and internal militant terrorism in Kashmir. As talks continued in August 2004, India released the results of a four-year study that attacked Pakistan's financial support for terrorists in Kashmir. Pakistan supplied about Rs.500 million (US$10.8 million) annually, the report stated. It also stated that during the preceding two years, Indian security forces had seized Rs.30 million and US$100,000 from militants in Kashmir. At the same time, the congress's minister of external affairs, Natwar Singh, charged Pakistan with cross-border terrorism in Kashmir. Pakistan denied the allegations while charging India with "gross and systematic violations of human rights in Kashmir."[36] Violence, however, decreased in 2004 to its lowest level since 1992. India's union home minister, Shivraj Patil, reported to parliament on December 8 that the daily average incidents of violence dropped to six in 2004 from nine in 2003 and eleven in 2002. That decrease of 24 percent was accompanied by a 12 percent reduction in killings.[37]

INDIA'S STRATEGIES TO COUNTER TERRORISM IN PUNJAB AND KASHMIR

Political violence clearly poses a problem to law and order, thereby inviting a *military* response ranging from police deployment to regular military intervention. A wide range of organizations fall within this spectrum. In India, these organizations include, most importantly, the Border Security Force (BSF) and the Central Reserve Police Force (CRPF). Specially trained antiterrorism groups—for example, the National Security Guards and their most elite units, the Black Cat Commandos—also have been formed to guard VIPs and to engage in operations. Other units that have been employed include the Assam Rifles, the Indo-Tibetan Rifles, and the Railway Protection Forces, and village-level forces also have been raised. In both Punjab and Kashmir, military tactics have been complemented by attempts to seal off external support through measures such as fencing.

A second type of response to the political violence has been *special legislation,* enacted by India's parliament to provide for special situations presented by unorthodox terrorist organizations and actions. The military actions and the special legislation lead to a third consideration in countering terrorism: *human rights.* A basic question here is the degree to which perceived violations of human rights by government forces, as well as by the militant organizations, operate in favor of the state or the terrorists. Human rights violations perpetrated by the state can alienate the target population, thus providing a fertile recruiting ground for terrorists. Militants face the same problem; terrorist actions, especially against the civilian population, can diminish their support base.

A fourth factor in the fight against terrorism, *negotiations* can be an important means by which the government encourages the moderate elements in militant groups, as well as lessening extremist external support. A negotiated settlement is one option. How agreements are implemented constitutes an important consideration; the negotiations themselves and their implementation become part of the political process, which in a democracy involves changing perspectives, leaders, and political situations.

Finally, there is an additional concern that receives comparatively little attention in counterterrorism situations and literature. It can be summed up as *closure*. Cessation of political violence may not deal adequately with the consequences of the violence and the scars remaining in human survivors. If a reasonable degree of closure is not secured, if the issues and situations that led to violence are not sufficiently resolved, terrorism can reappear.

Military Responses

Operation Bluestar: "An Elephant Chasing a Mouse." The military nature of Operation Bluestar at the Golden Temple complex in Punjab in 1984, with its use of overwhelming force, can be contrasted with that of Operation Black Thunder, employing appropriate military force four years later in the same place. Using the regular military in a massive manner—an "elephant chasing a mouse"—led to an increase in terrorism rather than countering it in 1984. K. P. S. Gill, who subsequently headed Punjab's police force and was in charge of Operation Black Thunder in 1988, criticizes Operation Bluestar as "an ill-planned, hasty, knee-jerk response . . . a botched operation." Instead, he advocates the model of Operation Black Thunder, which relied on "concerted police action, with suitable para-military and army backing."[38]

In June 1984, approximately seventy thousand regular army troops and paramilitary forces sealed off the city of Amritsar and the state of Punjab following three years of terrorist incidents. At least one thousand people, including almost one hundred soldiers and about four hundred pilgrims, were killed in two days of fighting around the heavily fortified Golden Temple complex.[39] Some sources extend this figure to more than five thousand.[40] A white paper issued by the government of India attempted to explain the need for the military action, which can be summed up as political violence and secessionism.[41] Table 13-2 provides official data on the number of Hindus and Sikhs killed in Punjab from 1981 through 1991. The numbers before 1984 are not large, but they do include the murders of prominent individuals, such as a leading newspaper publisher and a high-ranking police official.

Political violence coupled with a highly publicized movement based on religion and led by a charismatic leader no longer subject to central government control or influence could be interpreted as a secessionist threat, even though the demand for an independent Sikh state, Khalistan, existed more as a threat than a nonnegotiable demand. Fortifying the Golden Temple complex posed a direct challenge. The government believed that the display and use of overwhelming conventional military force would quickly end the conflict with minimum casualties and send a clear signal to other potential secessionist movements. This was a costly miscalculation; not only did political violence and terrorism not diminish, but they increased enormously in succeeding years, as documented in official figures (see table 13-1).

Sant Jarnail Singh Bhindranwale, the charismatic leader of the movement, died in the military action along with his two major lieutenants: Amrik Singh, who had secured youthful recruits through his leadership of the All India Sikh Students Federation (AISSF); and former major general Shahbeg Singh, a hero of the Bangladeshi liberation war of 1971, who had had responsibility for training and fortification. The latter had joined Bhindranwale after his dismissal from the army on charges of corruption. Eliminating this top leadership tier didn't diminish support for Sikh extremism.

Operation Woodrose followed, with the military rounding up thousands of suspected Sikh militants, including many innocents, throughout the state of Punjab. K. P. S. Gill categorizes this operation as suffering from "all the classical defects of army intervention in civil strife." He states that the army "operated blindly," as it mistrusted the local police and intelligence and lacked its own sources of information. As a consequence, Gill concludes, "the indiscriminate sweep of Woodrose pushed many a young man across the border into the arms of welcoming Pakistani handlers."[42]

Two major negative consequences in terms of counterterrorism resulted from Operation Bluestar and its immediate aftermath: an intensely negative Sikh reaction and the replacement of clear movement leadership by many contending groups. Ethnic identification sharply increased as Sikhs reacted to the destruction of their holy center. Tanks had destroyed sections of the Golden Temple complex—equivalent to the Vatican for Catholics—and participated in the destruction of the Akal Takht, second in religious importance only to the Harmindar Sahib.[43] The Sikh Library, with its priceless manuscripts and artifacts from the founders of the religion and subsequent periods, also was destroyed. The destruction wrought in the Golden Temple complex of buildings, the killing of pilgrims, and the consequent humiliation of Sikhs led to a uniform negative reaction by Sikhs.

Khushwant Singh, a notable moderate Sikh who openly opposed Bhindranwale and violence, stated in an interview:

> I said for once that I was not living in a secular India but in a Hindu India. Because, for once I discovered from the reactions, that the entire reaction—the adverse reaction—was almost entirely Sikh, that the favorable reaction was almost entirely Hindu. . . . And this is what I feared that this kind of army action would result in—a total polarisation of views between the Sikh and the Hindu and that has taken place.[44]

Kuldip Nayar, a highly respected Punjab Hindu journalist, had the same reaction. In his book coauthored with Khushwant Singh, he states dramatically, "Punjab's tragedy is that there are no Punjabis any more in Punjab—only Sikhs and Hindus."[45] Sikhs outside India, in the diaspora, also were outraged.[46] Sikh alienation from their Indian identity, and Hindu antagonism toward Sikhs, penetrated sufficiently deep to provide a recruitment context for the next wave of terrorists.

The second major effect of Operation Bluestar was the elimination of the top leadership of Bhindranwale's movement. Bhindranwale had not unequivocally called for an independent Khalistan, a state ruled by Sikhs. Nevertheless, his exhortations to Sikhs to regain their religious purity, his sharp criticism of Hindus and the government, and the terrorist acts of his followers prepared the ground for what followed. In a manner comparable to but preceding the actions of Osama bin Laden and al Qaeda, he reformulated and hijacked the Sikh religion and its traditions in a radical, militant, violent manner.[47] Two quotations from his tape-recorded speeches illustrate this theme:

> Sikhs are living like slaves in independent India. Today every Sikh considers himself a second rate citizen. . . . How can Sikhs tolerate this?[48]

> I cannot really understand how it is that, in the presence of Sikhs, Hindus are able to insult the [scriptures]. I don't know how were these Sikhs born to mothers and why they were not born to animals, to cats and bitches. . . . Whosoever insults the *Guru Granth Sahib* [Sikh bible] he should be killed then and there.[49]

Operation Bluestar created a leadership vacuum, with many groups contending for power in what became the Khalistan movement. No one leader or group emerged to replace Bhindranwale and his hierarchy and to provide the possibility of negotiations with the government. Four major groups, each with many subgroups, provided the post-Bhindranwale structure for the Khalistan movement. They were the Babbar Khalsa, the most zealously religious group, with a specialty in bombs; the Bhindranwale Tiger Force (BTF); the Khalistan Liberation Force (KLF); and the Khalistan Commando Force (KCF). The number of subgroups and their allegiances changed over time. In early 1992, the KCF reputedly had sixty-three subgroups, or bands, operating under its banner; the BTF had thirty; the Babbar Khalsa, twenty-seven, and the KLF, twenty. Another 22 groups operated independently, for a total of at least 162 terrorist groups.[50]

Motivation and organization could become more personal and complex at the village level. A research team from Guru Nanak Dev University in Amritsar District, the major center of terrorist activity, emphasized "a kind of politics of the 'personal'" in its findings. "Terror and violence" were related to "personal or family disputes, vendetta, mercenary interests, sexual gratification," and "inter-group and intra-group warfare and killings." Class and caste in the form of poor Jat Sikh youth were also emphasized.[51]

The AISSF operated within and outside this structure. A more violent version of the AISSF, the Sikh Student Federation (SSF), emerged with a different leadership.[52] In theory, a Panthic Committee provided an umbrella for all the groups. Established in 1986 as a self-constituted policy body for the movement, it set forth the goal of an independent Sikh state, Khalistan. Its five members, all wanted men, were publicly identified in 1987.[53] Its organizational efforts also included the 1987 formation of an international body, the Council of Khalistan, for the "foreign policy of Khalistan."[54] In reality, this hierarchical chain of command with stated goals and authority structures never became legitimate. Rival Panthic Committees competed for the allegiance of subgroups, which were also subject to a high level of factionalism.

A second major catalytic event shook India four months after Bluestar, exacerbating the situation. Prime Minister Indira Gandhi was assassinated by two of her Sikh bodyguards on October 31, 1984. Large-scale violence against Sikhs followed, with more than two thousand Sikhs killed and their property burned, particularly in Delhi.[55] K. P. S. Gill, who later, as Punjab's police chief, was credited with defeating the terrorist movement, describes the violence as "the pitiless massacre of Sikhs in what were perceived to be Congress government–sponsored riots."[56]

Sikh temples were systematically attacked, and approximately fifty thousand Sikhs fled to Punjab from Delhi and other parts of India.[57] The

anti-Sikh drumbeat, in which Sikhs were in essence condemned as seces-
sionists, continued during the election campaign that concluded in December 1984. An omnipresent election poster of the slain Gandhi proclaimed:
"Whenever I will die, every drop of my blood will make India strong, and
will keep alive a united India."[58]

Operation Black Thunder: Appropriate Use of the Military. Operation
Bluestar and its consequences served to fuel a many-headed terrorist movement for almost a decade. Official estimates of civilians, police, and terrorists
killed increased from twenty-seven in 1981, twenty in 1982, and eighty-
eight in 1983 to more than one thousand per year from 1987 through 1992.
Detailed data for this time period are provided in table 13-1. The military
nature of Operation Bluestar accelerated terrorism rather than containing it.
In contrast to the earlier brutish military action, the "elephant chasing a
mouse," Operation Black Thunder, from May 9 to 18, 1988, skillfully
employed surgical military tactics with maximum transparency.

Militants again occupied the Golden Temple in Amritsar, but this time
the Punjab police were in charge of the state response, and military action
served the purposes of counterterrorism. Terrorists and other militants were
cleared from the Golden Temple complex with a minimum loss of life and
a maximum amount of discredit to the terrorists in an operation led by the
well-trained Black Cat Commandos of the National Security Guards and
involving three thousand paramilitary personnel. In contrast to Operation
Bluestar, Black Thunder took place under full public scrutiny, using a minimum of force. No tanks rolled over the *parikrama,* the walkway surrounding the water. Snipers and a blockade, rather than tanks and infantry
charges, applied continual pressure. About thirty terrorists were killed, and
two hundred surrendered on the final day.

More than one hundred media personnel, including television reporters,
provided live coverage. Their highly public presence probably contributed
to the restrained use of force and certainly enhanced the government's
credibility, especially in its efforts "to preserve the sanctity of the temple."
Moreover, most Sikhs were sensitive both to military restraint and to temple desecration by the terrorists (which quickly became apparent), including torture, murder, and defecation in the Harmindar Sahib, the single
most holy building in the temple complex, which by itself is called the
Golden Temple.[59]

Terrorist legitimacy suffered as a consequence of the terrorist desecrations during Operation Black Thunder, although the violence continued at a high level. Sarab Jit Singh, a key figure in Black Thunder, served as deputy commissioner of Amritsar from 1987 to 1992 and as a key decision maker in rooting out the terrorists from the Golden Temple complex in 1988. He points out in a carefully written book that the "Army Operation of 1984 . . . had bruised the Sikh psyche,"[60] but strategy and special military action, rather than brute force, led to the surrender of the terrorists in 1988. Loss of the temple "also meant a loss of control over their cadres."[61] Sarab Jit Singh concludes that Operation Black Thunder could have led to the end of the political violence. He blames the government, particularly in New Delhi, as well as the SGPC, the managing committee of the historic Sikh temples, for losing this opportunity. Political violence, by both the militants and the state,[62] continued until 1993.

Further support for the effectiveness of Operation Black Thunder in fighting terrorism comes from an unsigned eight-page report found on the body of the self-styled "general" Labh Singh, a major leader of the Khalistan Commando Force killed on July 12, 1988. The report, analyzing reaction to Operation Black Thunder, states that the lack of Sikh protest against the operation indicated that "they have been alienated by the extortion of money, indiscriminate killings and other anti-social activities." Referring to factional fighting among militants, the document called for an end to vengeance killings.[63]

K. P. S. Gill also emphasizes the importance of Operation Black Thunder. He had become Punjab's director general of police (DGP) a couple of weeks earlier and thus was in charge of the operation. In contrast to Operation Bluestar, he writes, Black Thunder cleared the Golden Temple of the terrorists "in a clean, economical and near-bloodless action." Moreover, the "macabre exposures" meant that the Khalistan movement "could never recover the façade of religiosity that had attended it in its early years, and became increasingly and manifestly criminalised."[64]

Military pressure, most dramatically in Operation Black Thunder, and terrorist excesses appear to be the two major factors in the state's successful competition with the militants for control. Militant excesses, as described in the "General" Labh Singh report and in such popular publications as *India Today,* increasingly became viewed as terrorist acts. Popular support for the insurgents-cum-terrorists fell. Killings, however, continued at a high level and even increased in some years during the period 1988–1992. Government military actions intensified as the government employed not just more troops but more-specialized units, obtained better intelligence, and avoided the pitfalls of Operation Bluestar. In this respect, Operation Black Thunder provided a general framework for future military counterterrorism operations in Kashmir as well as Punjab.

Lessons from both Operation Bluestar and Operation Black Thunder in Punjab seem to have been applied to the Hazratbal crisis in Kashmir in 1993. It began on October 13, 1993, when militants armed with light machine guns reportedly entered the shrine in Srinagar that contains a holy relic of the Prophet. Forty years earlier, in 1953, the shrine had been the center of a crisis when the relic disappeared and then was recovered. Now, a military confrontation took place. Two companies of the BSF were initially deployed and then replaced by the regular army, which launched a siege that lasted thirty-two days. Neither the BSF nor the army engaged in a frontal assault, as had happened in Operation Bluestar in 1984. The siege, accompanied by negotiations led by the police and the divisional commissioner, resolved the situation successfully. Approximately fifty militants and twelve other supporters surrendered on November 16, 1993. Despite some reports to the contrary, the governor and his civilian and military advisers "were mostly in accord" during the crisis.[65] As in Operation Black Thunder in Punjab, the state apparently failed to take advantage of the Hazratbal success. According to a retired Indian colonel, the "security forces failed to press home the advantage in Srinagar" and adjoining areas. "Ambushes, killings, attacks on convoys, installations and pickets increased."[66]

Regular Army, Police, and Nonregular Military. Military forces continued to increase in Punjab. A force of seventy thousand police and paramilitary troops was employed against the militants in mid-1988. Twelve new BSF battalions were raised in 1989–90, the CRPF expanded rapidly, and the Indo-Tibetan Border Police raised six new battalions in 1991 for bank security in Punjab. In addition, home guards and special police officers had added another forty thousand troops by April 1992.[67] Military strategy also had to adjust to the decentralized nature of the terrorist movement; a central organization or concentration of militants no longer existed, while the extent of militant operations expanded. The best strategy consisted of "an effective intelligence backed up with swift induction of well trained committed troops . . . as well as mobile commandos." The Punjab police raised its own commando force, with the National Security Guards stationed as another commando force in the key militant area of Amritsar.[68]

K. P. S. Gill notes the difficulties he had as DGP in convincing New Delhi of the need to continue to upgrade the police. Improvements were made in communications and transport, and additional police were recruited. Requests for upgrading weaponry were slower in being filled. A counterproductive tactic led to the deployment of between 40 and 50 percent of the Punjab police in passive barricade duties that provided the "illusion of security" but resulted in the police being "easy targets for drive-by-shootings" or "weapon-snatching." After Operation Black Thunder, a reallocation increased the operational police force to about 85 percent of total personnel. These changes enabled the formation of mobile units and allowed local police stations to make independent and rapid responses to terrorist acts instead of having to call in backup paramilitary forces.[69]

Structural problems included antagonism between the Sikh-dominant Punjab police and the out-of-state and largely non-Sikh paramilitaries. Developing and sharing intelligence also posed major problems. Joint interrogation teams, the sharing of personnel, better coordination, and a system of intelligence documentation, analysis, and dissemination dealt successfully with these problems.[70]

As a corollary to military action, both the military and the police began to interact more effectively with villagers. It has to be emphasized that the villager has always been the target of the Khalistani groups, as Sikhs dominate by large majorities in rural Punjab, while Hindus are the majority population in urban areas. The regular army undertook civic action programs reminiscent of U.S. efforts to win the "hearts and minds" of villagers in Vietnam. The *Times of India* described some of these actions in an article headlined "Army Wins Hearts in Punjab." These programs provided schools, teachers, bridges, footpaths, bus service, agricultural services, sanitation systems, and even sports equipment and coaches.[71]

India Today in 1992 compared army tactics at this point with the statewide movement in 1984 that followed Operation Bluestar. The army, "having learnt the lessons of Operation Woodrose . . . is trying its best not to be rough with the villagers whose support they lost during Operation Woodrose." Serving snacks and lunch, setting up medical facilities, repairing schools and drainage systems, and other development activities complemented the more usual military role of cordon and search. This particular operation involved 394 villages, 10,961 patrols, and 4,754 ambushes; 334 top militants were killed and 1,600 arrested.[72]

The army made similar efforts in Kashmir, according to Brian Cloughley, a former military officer who served with the United Nations in Kashmir. Citing the Uri sector, where two brigade commanders had been establishing schools, he writes that the Srinagar Corps, in the most sensitive area of the state, "has got the message loud and clear . . . that cooperation with the locals pays dividends in every way."[73]

Regular police in Punjab, their reputation tarnished by charges of atrocities, followed the army's lead in 1992 with their own civic action programs and medical camps.[74] One Indian academic, focusing on the 1980s, concludes in a section headlined "Demoralised Police" that one "important factor in sustaining militancy in Punjab was the role played by police." He cites corruption, extortion, "arming the terrorist groups," and reprisal and retaliatory killings. He credits K. P. S. Gill, the new DGP, as turning around the "weak, demoralised and politicised police force" in order to combat terrorism effectively.[75]

One of the most controversial counterterrorism tactics employed by the Punjab police was the use of former terrorists to kill or capture terrorists and to extract intelligence. These "cats," as they were called, were first used by the Punjab police in the 1980s but became more central under DGP Gill in the post-1991 period. One veteran reporter wrote that cats became the "pivot" of Gill's "post-1991 anti-terrorism strategy." One major success based on such intelligence efforts was the arrest of Sukhdev Singh Babbar, leader of the Babbar Khalsa, one of the most feared and effective militant organizations. A second major terrorist group, the Khalistan Commando Force, and its chief, Gurjant Singh Budhsinghwala, were "neutralized in a 'cat' operation."[76]

On the other hand, human rights activists Ranjan Lakhanpal and Inderjeet Singh Jaijee emphasize that paying bounties to former terrorists and protecting them from criminal prosecution is a "grossly illegal practice of the Punjab Police." Some former terrorists turned to extortion, robbery, and other criminal behavior after the crisis ebbed and funds became scarce.[77] Nihang leader Baba Ajit Singh Phoola, who in the 1980s and early 1990s led the Tarna Dal in "eliminating" Sikh terrorists, provides one example. His arrest in March 2004 followed an alleged "reign of terror" in

Amritsar District. Police support had provided him with an arsenal of weapons and control of a historic Sikh temple.[78]

Another veteran reporter acknowledges the success of the cats and other tactics in killing major terrorists but notes that the "summary executions" also involved innocents, causing "seething resentments." Punjab's citizens "have been wounded by the bombs and bullets of terrorist outlaws," he emphasizes, but "so too have they been stricken by the methodical brutality of their protectors—the police—who often choose to enforce the law by breaking it."[79] Brian Cloughley doesn't credit the police along with the army in Kashmir as winning hearts and minds and specifically criticizes the "scruffy and brutal paramilitaries."[80]

Military tactics in Punjab were also adapted to provide more effective counterterrorism. The army, composed of personnel from various parts of India, largely confined its role in the Sikh-dominated countryside, reported veteran newsman Chandan Mitra, "to patrolling and cordoning" instead of directly fighting the militants, and its medical camps were particularly effective in "terrorist-infested villages" from which most doctors had fled. Moreover, the "polite firmness of the army is in stark contrast to the boorish . . . behavior of the police."[81] Punjab police, largely Sikhs, did the bulk of the fighting against fellow Sikhs. Religion, consequently, did not become an issue in the actual confrontations. A novel adaptation consisted of placing metal shields in front of tractors, to provide protection for the attacking forces without antagonizing the population by using tanks.[82]

Fencing was used along the border to counter infiltration from training camps in Pakistan as well as the smuggling of weapons. Concertina wire was placed along the seventy-eight-mile land border beginning in 1988, and a border district in Rajasthan was later added.[83] It is probably impossible to completely seal off the Ravi and Sutlej rivers, but there is some evidence of short-term success: the smuggling of gold and narcotics became significantly diverted from Punjab to Kashmir, and by 1992 Gujarat had become a major entry point for weapons smuggled from Pakistan.[84] Observers often make comparisons with the inability of the United States to seal off its borders with Mexico. Rumors also commonly maintain that military postings on the Indian side of the border are compromised by corruption, as dealing with smugglers can be lucrative for border guards.

Fencing along the 460-mile LoC dividing the Indian- and Pakistani-controlled parts of Kashmir has implications that are not present in Punjab, with its mutually recognized borders. Symbolically, successful fencing has the potential for making the LoC the international border, a desirable outcome for India but not for Pakistan. India consequently has been making a maximum effort at fence building since at least 2003. The fence is about twelve feet high and twelve feet wide; coils of concertina wire, sharp-edged metal tape, and strategic electrification make an imposing physical structure. Thermal imaging devices, motion sensors, and night-vision equipment from the United States, France, and Israel provide further barriers to infiltration.[85]

Despite the impressive barriers, the conventional wisdom about the effectiveness of the Kashmiri fencing is similar to that about the fencing dividing India from Pakistani Punjab. A particularly strong conclusion regarding fencing in Kashmir comes from the Pakistani side, from a non-Pakistani with years of experience working with the military:

> The various barriers do little to prevent border crossing in either direction. In Kashmir, I was informed by several military sources that Indian Border Security Forces were usually eager to accept bribes by *jihadis* to secure safe passage into Kashmir. The going rate apparently was the equivalent of $2000. The choice involved was simple: accept the bribe, look the other way, and live; decline the bribe, oppose infiltration, and face the possibility of violent death. On the southern side of the international border, Pakistani security forces had similar lack of success in curbing the smuggling of illegal immigrants and drugs despite the existence of modern, illuminated border fencing, although I have no info as to whether bribery was involved in these sectors.[86]

Another non–South Asian respondent with long service in Kashmir views fencing there as a "mild disruption." Then he adds: "It's difficult to see how it could be claimed that the fence along the actual border is anything like effective, given the enormous amount of smuggling that goes on. Indian 'scotch' sells well in Multan and Bahawalpur, for example." Low wages, he maintains, encourage the corruption of the guards.[87] Smuggling also continues in Rajasthan, where "despite 1,035 km of fencing . . . illegal trade is booming."[88]

A contrary conclusion comes from a retired Indian army officer who served in Kashmir, follows developments closely, and is critical of various aspects of Indian policy. He states that fencing is "very effective specially in the plains where patrolling is easier but also effective in mountains."[89] Similarly, India's home minister, Shivraj Patel, stated in late 2004 that there had been a reduction in—not a cessation of—infiltration after the installation of fencing.[90] N. C. Vij, India's chief of army staff, more precisely stated that infiltration had been reduced by one-third, even though "the number of attempts to infiltrate are double that of previous years."[91]

Two basic conclusions emerge from the information presently available about fencing. First, personnel are more important than structures. Unless the guardians are reliable, no amount of fencing or other barriers will work. Second, fencing increases the costs for smuggling, whether of terrorists or goods.

A former United Nations observer in Kashmir describes the police in Kashmir in terms similar to those used to describe their Punjabi counterparts: "It is difficult—probably impossible—anywhere in the sub-continent to eradicate the colonial legacy of the police being masters and not servants of the public . . . but the police in Indian-administered Kashmir require restructuring and, above all, better training."[92] Another longtime specialist on both sides of the border concludes: "On the police: bad training and leadership and pay made them part of the problem."[93]

Counterterrorism Military Units. Two different perspectives exist regarding the counterterrorism effectiveness of specially raised units in Kashmir. One view deals with the preexisting paramilitary forces brought in from elsewhere in India; the other, with the nature of the newly organized units. One point of view is that new units are organized as a consequence of the failure of the paramilitaries. The army organized the Rashtriya Rifles as a separate force of light infantry to handle counterinsurgency so that the army could be reserved for regular operations. The force consists of approximately thirty units of about a thousand men each.[94] An expert respondent who served with the United Nations stated that the Rashtriya Rifles were organized because "the paramilitaries were so bad."[95] Another expert respondent also strongly criticized the BSF as representing "a reminder of occupation rather than a benevolent presence intended to help and protect the civilian community." He had even more extreme criticism for the "Special Operations Group of former guerrillas" as being responsible for "anonymous identification of suspects" on the basis of "family enmity and similar non-militant activity."[96] Sumit Ganguly notes that the Ikhwan-ul-Muslimoon is the most prominent of the local counterinsurgent groups created by the central government, but in his text and

several footnote references, he criticizes them for their corruption and violation of human rights.[97]

A report on the counterinsurgents by a "Joint Fact Finding Committee
of Organisations, Bombay" is uniformly critical. An army spokesman, the
report states, describes them as "reformed militants" who are "threatened by
their former comrades and the Pakistani training agencies." They do use
their weapons against militant groups such as the Hizbul Mujahideen and
the Jama'at-i-Islami. But, the report concludes, they also "hunt down"
unarmed "human rights activists, journalists [and others who] are either
supportive of Kashmiri self-determination or critical of [the] Indian State's
brutalities in Kashmir." The report gives details on a number of cases. It
also alleges that counterinsurgents engage in criminal activities. Kashmiris,
the report states, commonly describe them as "renegade militants." The
Ikhwan-ul-Muslimoon is listed as the strongest group, but seven others are
briefly described.[98]

The Bombay report distinguishes the former militant groups from
the Rashtriya Rifles. Part of the army and a specially constituted counterinsurgency wing under the Union Home Ministry, the latter often carries
out combined operations with former militants such as the Ikhwan-ul-
Muslimoon. The report, with several examples, is equally critical of the
Rashtriya Rifles, especially personnel below the rank of lieutenant.[99]

A general conclusion is that counterinsurgent and locally raised units are
most effective in the latter stage of an insurgency, when proper training,
supervision, and support are available. Then these units can develop "a sense
of participation and identity" and "stand up against coercion to support and
feed militants," states a former Indian military officer. Their local knowledge is valuable, he adds, and they can be used for flood relief and riot control, as well as "in the Naxalite affected areas."[100] Punjab's police chief,
K. P. S. Gill, described the reluctance of villages to participate in local
defense and the efforts needed to accomplish more than a "cosmetic exercise
in morale building." By 1989, he writes, after proper preparation, village
defense forces were able to "play a significant role . . . against terrorism."[101]

Special Legislation

Special legislation for the purposes of state control extends back to the British period, when preventive detention and other measures were a part of the
colonial system. Independent India inherited and maintained some of these

measures that compromise due process, ranging from various degrees of preventive detention for individuals to Article 371 of the constitution, which enables New Delhi to establish "President's Rule" in any state of India, thereby superseding its democratic institutions in favor of central government rule. Prime Minister Indira Gandhi interpreted this constitutional provision to establish an emergency regime for all of India for a twenty-month period between 1975 and 1977.[102]

A long list of repressive ordinances and legislative acts from about 1980 on, including the National Security Act (NSA) of 1980 under Prime Minister Indira Gandhi, reflects British colonial practices. The one-year detention without charge or trial allowed under the NSA was extended to two years for Punjab in 1984.[103] Critics labeled these measures "the black laws" for their curtailing of civil rights and their draconian implementation.[104] Most prominent have been the Terrorist and Disruptive Activities (Prevention) Act of 1987, familiarly known as TADA, and the Prevention of Terrorism Act (POTA), which superseded it. Under TADA, all of Punjab was designated a "notified area" in 1988; this was followed almost immediately by the dissolution of the already-suspended state assembly. A month later, the fifty-ninth constitutional amendment empowered the government to declare a state of emergency in Punjab, thereby suspending fundamental rights. It also allowed New Delhi to extend President's Rule for a period of three years rather than six months, as stated previously in the constitution.[105]

Political authorities obviously desired these special measures to control terrorism in Punjab. An official spokesman explained that 254 people had been killed between January 1 and February 11, 1988. The dead, he pointed out, included "senior leaders and activists of the Congress, CPI, BJP and police personnel."[106] Critics emphasized the need for more rather than less democracy and criticized these measures as abetting rather than diminishing terrorism. Suspects, including many innocents, were detained for long time periods without normal procedural rights. Torture ensued for many.[107]

A similar situation in regard to special legislation may exist in Kashmir. One longtime non–South Asian observer concludes that special legislation increases terrorism. He comments: "There was already enough legislation to combat terrorism. All that TADA and POTA have done . . . is to help government to crack-down on peaceful dissidents and deter legitimate expression of disagreement with central policies, especially in regard to human rights violations."[108]

Another individual with an Indian military background in Kashmir is neutral on special legislation: "In an insurgency like Kashmir my view would be that the special legislation neither increases nor reduces terrorism."[109]

The implementation of special legislation is the key to whether it counters or results in an increase in terrorism. A basic conclusion for Punjab and Kashmir is that heavy-handed implementation created a human rights problem more than it helped combat terrorism.

Human Rights

Human rights tend to suffer during the "spiral of violence"[110] resulting from vengeance, organizational imperatives, and accompanying escalation. In Punjab a "bullet for a bullet" policy by the Punjab police, "encounters" involving illegal executions, and consistent allegations of torture detailed in a variety of sources[111] served to be counterproductive to combating terrorism.

The spiral of violence similarly and importantly includes the various militant groups employing terrorism against innocent civilians, especially in rural areas. The police became a special target in the latter stages of terrorism. In August 1992, reports K. P. S. Gill, then DGP for Punjab, of the 167 persons killed in Punjab, "100 were either policemen (37) or members of their families (63)."[112]

In this context of state and terrorist excesses, there appears to be a correlation between human rights abuses by the state and increasing popular support for militants, on the one hand, and terrorist abuses causing a loss of popular support for militants in both Punjab and Kashmir, on the other.

Several respondents support these conclusions for Kashmir. One veteran non–South Asian participant in Kashmir states that human rights violations constitute the leading counterproductive item in fighting terrorism. He cites the "security forces' brutality and refusal to properly investigate allegations of criminal activity . . . especially by irregular elements." As a consequence, young Kashmiris are "encouraged to join militant groups."[113] A U.S. academic agrees that human rights violations were a "major problem originally" and remain an important factor, as they "complicate good police and military policy." Nonetheless, he suggests that since "brute force" contains "the problem," only "by getting Pakistan out of this business can anything work."[114]

A U.S. military observer provides a Pakistani perspective. Every military briefing he attended over a period of years "included a comprehensive listing on Indian human rights abuses culled from the reporting of Human Rights NGOs [nongovernmental organizations]." The Pakistani military used the same "set of talking points and briefing slides" for foreign visitors and journalists in Pakistan, Kashmir, and the northern areas. The human rights abuse "clearly resonates within the Pakistan body politics and provides a major incentive for the various jihadi groups to seek revenge."[115]

A retired Indian officer is less critical and offers a facilitating suggestion. "The record is pretty good," he states, "keeping in view the level and duration of the insurgency." He recommends: "Human Rights organizations should be permitted to monitor the situation," an idea that is not yet "accepted by the Indian government."[116] Renewed emphasis on human rights surfaced in 2004 in negotiations between India's government and the All Parties Hurriyat Conference (APHC) of dissident groups. The APHC received what appeared to be a positive response to its demand that human rights violations in the valley be curbed. At the minimum, this is a negotiating point.[117]

A fundamental conclusion to be drawn from Punjab and Kashmir is that human rights abuses by the state provide a significant recruitment platform for terrorists and therefore are counterproductive. The same conclusion holds for terrorist abuses. "Freedom fighters" can become "terrorists" in the minds of their target population when they abuse them. As an observer of the Punjab movement from its inception, I have concluded that terrorist violations of the human rights of Sikh villagers was the single most important factor in the movement's demise. Emphasizing human rights in Kashmir could assist the major efforts being made to restore normalcy by the state and national governments.

Negotiations

To what extent are negotiations effective in counterterrorism? One perspective is that talking implies at least the beginning of confronting the problems and should reduce the level of violence. Nonnegotiable preconditions can, of course, delay or abort negotiations. In theory, talking also emphasizes the more moderate elements in the militant movement as well as the state. As moderate doves occupy more "political space," militant hawks are driven to the extremes. Violence can and usually does continue, as evidenced in the actions of the splinter Real IRA (Irish Republican Army) or the assassination of Israeli prime minister Yitzhak Rabin by an extremist Israeli.

In Punjab,[118] another consideration arose out of negotiations between the moderate Akali Dal political party, led by Sant Harcharan Singh Longowal, and Prime Minister Rajiv Gandhi following Gandhi's massive victory—401 out of 508 seats—in the 1984 elections. Rajiv Gandhi extended a "healing touch," as it became popularly labeled, toward the Akali Dal during the subsequent Punjab state elections. Akali leaders were released from internment, and "secret" negotiations regularly leaked to and reported on by the press culminated in the Punjab Accord in July 1985. Longowal declared, "The period of confrontation is over." Negotiations were successful, but implementation became the problem.

Violence did not cease during or after the negotiations. On the contrary, bombs were now implanted in transistor radio cases and exploded in bus and train stations. But moderate Akali Dal candidates won, with high levels of support, in the September 1985 state elections. Rajiv Gandhi neglected his own Congress Party to the extent that British election specialist David Butler commented that this was the only election he had ever known "where the ruling party [was] so eager to lose." Gandhi seemed to have learned an important lesson in dealing with terrorism: political initiatives have to be pursued consistently and with integrity regardless of the political violence that may be continuing. Moreover, he negotiated over a number of political issues—for example, the Anandpur Sahib Resolution, which included demands for increased decentralization for Punjab State[119]—that his mother, Prime Minister Indira Gandhi, had labeled secessionist. While his mother's policies led to Operation Bluestar, Rajiv had a moderate Sikh political party with a high degree of legitimacy in power in Punjab.

Negotiations, however, were not sufficient. Veteran BBC correspondent Mark Tully and his colleague concluded that Rajiv Gandhi "backed down on the sensible accord" when "his party told him it was damaging its electoral prospects in the crucial Hindi-speaking states of northern India."[120] Not implementing major provisions of the Punjab Accord, which included transfers of territory and establishing Chandigarh as solely the capital of Punjab rather than its being shared with Haryana State, led to an even higher level of political violence and terrorism.

Militants retook control of the Golden Temple in January 1986, and Sikh political leadership became increasingly extremist. As the *Times of*

India editorialized: "The inevitable failure of the Union government to implement the basically flawed Punjab accord has been overtaken by a renewed struggle for leadership of the Sikh community."[121] Almost another decade passed before the terrorist movement could be brought under control, at the cost of approximately twenty thousand lives.

Negotiations between Pakistan and India, including Kashmir, began again in December 2003. A number of questions arise as to the nature of the negotiations. All respondents agree that negotiations between India and Pakistan are important to counterterrorism. An academic emphasized the process that has to take place: "It will take some time" for negotiations to be successful, "but a peace process is designed to make the unacceptable eventually acceptable as both sides learn how to compromise."[122]

A former United Nations participant in Kashmir pointed out that talks have to be bilateral, as India insists, and "better some talks than no talks." India will not accept a mediator, he stated, but he strongly recommended a mediator from the Association of Southeast Asian Nations (ASEAN). He strongly opposes the United States as a mediator or a facilitator, as "this would kill the process stone dead." Both India and Pakistan distrust the United States for a variety of reasons, he maintains. The UN should have a role, he asserts, but India "simply won't have it."[123]

A retired Indian army officer offers a very different scenario. He supports multilateral talks with the United States as mediator. He states that the United States "is already playing that role from the sidelines." UN participation in "monitoring agreements and peace moves like ceasefires and withdrawals" is also important. He points out that the UN Military Observer Group for India and Pakistan (UNMOGIP) is "already in place"; that "broad-based" negotiations, "including militants but certainly not with the militant organizations themselves," are recommended; and that a "facilitator" can "play a vital role even though not publicized."[124]

A non–South Asian with long official experience in both India and Pakistan, but closest to the Pakistani side, provides an analysis suggesting that negotiations can split the insurgent movement:

> Pakistan purports to speak for the good of the Muslim Kashmiris, but finds it difficult to tolerate Kashmiris it doesn't control directly. Whether Pakistan is behind recent assassinations of moderate Kashmiris is an open question. If I were an Indian government advisor, I would certainly use this factor as an opportunity to split the ranks of my opposition.

In terms of process, he favors "direct bilateral negotiations conducted concurrently at various levels: Foreign Minister, Foreign Secretary, bilateral working groups, [m]ilitary-to-military, etc." He doubts that any mediator will be acceptable to India, but "the U.S. can be a facilitator by conducting a robust policy of talks with both sides that are not tied directly to the negotiations. Additionally, the U.S. could be helpful in confidence building measures and has in fact offered both sides a common aerial surveillance picture of LOC activity as a first step." A UN role is doubtful, he states, as India has "disdain" for what it considers "outdated UN resolutions on Kashmir."[125]

Negotiations can be the beginning of the endgame for Kashmiri terrorism, but the lessons from the failure of the Punjab Accord are clear. One lesson is that agreements are only as effective as the willingness and ability of the consenting parties to implement them. A more positive lesson is that negotiations can be pursued fruitfully even though violence continues. Thus, in August 2004, India and Pakistan exchanged prisoners of war as part of their peace talks and other confidence-building measures.[126] On the other hand, developments within Jammu and Kashmir included continued terrorism as "the instrument to silence the doves."[127]

India, Pakistan, and any other parties they can bring to the table will establish a process for Kashmir as well as for other outstanding issues. Mediators can be helpful, as in the role of Norway in the Oslo process between Israel and the PLO, and Norway again in the ongoing Sri Lanka negotiations. Facilitation operating more quietly can be a useful complementary option. Kashmir represents a complex set of issues as well as firmly held positions. Accordingly, it has spawned a cottage industry examining the various possibilities. Proposals by the Kashmir Study Group (KSG) and the BBC are particularly informative.

The KSG consists of U.S. legislators and a committee of academics and foreign policy specialists with lengthy professional experience with South Asian issues.[128] The KSG has furnished proposals to government officials in India and Pakistan, beginning with the Livingston Proposal, set forth in Livingston, New York, on December 1, 1998. It recommended a "sovereign entity," but "one without an international personality," with a special relationship to both India and Pakistan. A KSG report issued in January 2000 included three different versions of Kashmir's status, with detailed recommendations as well as general concepts that could be the basis for serious negotiations. The three versions are

- Two Kashmiri entities, each with its own government and special relationships with India and Pakistan
- One Kashmir "straddling" the LoC, with its own government and special relationships with India and Pakistan
- One entity on the Indian side of the LoC, composed of areas that choose to join it

Each of these proposals includes explanations that could become the focus of negotiations. Most difficult are issues that involve external mediators, plebiscites, and the withdrawal of military forces. In a January 2003 paper, a KSG member recommended starting with specific confidence-building measures (CBMs).[129] Some of these measures—for example, restoration of direct Indo-Pakistani trade by land, sea, and air; reinstatement of rail, bus, and air links; and cultural, athletic, and prisoner exchanges—continue into 2006.

The recommended list is quite lengthy and rich in regard to negotiable possibilities. One CBM periodically recommended centers on the demilitarization of the Siachen and Baltoro glacier area. Since 1984 a costly miniwar between India and Pakistan has been fought in this uninhabited area.[130]

Another useful set of options is provided by BBC *News Online,* which sets forth seven Kashmiri scenarios with maps, religious compositions, and succinct explanations for each of them.[131] A brief summary of each underscores the difficulties involved, but some combination conceivably could be negotiated. The scenarios are

- The status quo; unacceptable to Pakistan
- Kashmir joins Pakistan; unacceptable to India and non-Muslims
- Kashmir joins India; unacceptable to Pakistan
- An independent Kashmir; India and Pakistan would oppose this choice being offered in a plebiscite
- A smaller, independent Kashmir; not acceptable to India or Pakistan
- An independent Kashmir Valley; not economically viable
- The Chenab formula, first suggested in the 1960s, which would divide Kashmir along the Chenab River; this formula would give the vast majority of land to Pakistan and would be unacceptable to India

A wealth of experience and options are available to India and Pakistan in their negotiations. To counter terrorism in Kashmir, each side will have to compromise long-held positions. That, of course, is the key to any serious negotiations. A joint effort to counter terrorism can reduce tensions in Kashmir and thus throughout South Asia. Both Pakistan and India will have to conclude that negotiation and compromise are better options than the possibility of high-risk conflict. The worst scenario for all concerned is a spiral of violence leading to nuclear war.

Closure

During the past three decades, more than twenty nations have attempted some form of closure, primarily involving commissions and courts. A new academic discipline named transitional justice is developing, using a new language with terms such as "retributive justice," "restorative justice," "historical clarification," and "lustration."[132] War crimes trials in the Netherlands and Tanzania focus on the perpetrators, a process established in the post–World War II Nuremberg trials. An intriguing experiment with village-based, semijudicial *gacaca* proceedings in Rwanda, to try approximately one hundred thousand Hutus accused of genocide in 1994, is another kind of tribunal approach.[133] The goal is to successfully confront the violence with transparency and justice so that a reoccurrence is less likely.

There is no formula or single method for closure. Most notable is the Truth and Reconciliation Commission (TRC) of the Republic of South Africa.[134] It is a laudable effort, but there is difficulty in evaluating its success. Partly, the problem is that closure efforts inevitably necessitate compromises and may not satisfy the need for justice. Nonetheless, the TRC confronts the past, rather than adopting an ostrichlike position of ignoring it, while facilitating understanding and reconciliation. TRCs also were established in Chile in 1990[135] and Peru in 2002.[136] Argentina took until 2004 to attempt closure for the military dictatorship and terrorism of 1976–1983. The state has opened the records of the disappeared, is identifying babies taken by military families, and has opened a Holocaust-type Museum of Memories.[137]

Punjab's approaches to closure consist of deliberate efforts to deal with the social consequences of violence as well as more direct political measures. It is estimated that the violence in Punjab left 13,000 widows and "caused suffering to 88,000 children." Hostility and a desire for revenge are among the characteristics expressed by victims of the terrorist movement as well as the state.[138] A major divide tends to separate movement victims from state victims. Both groups, including those in institutions, continue to "relive the traumatic experience" of the terrorism era.[139]

Women were especially targeted by the terrorists and the police, but for different reasons. Khalsa movement values emphasized women "as reproducers of the Sikh martial race and repositories of Sikh culture."[140] In a sample of two hundred female victims, 32 percent belonged to the militant-affiliate category, and 28 percent to police families. Other victims witnessed killings, torture, or humiliation.[141]

Nongovernmental organizations and the government provide assistance to victims. State assistance, however, is not provided to those "suspected of having militant connections."[142] The Guru Aasra Trust, established in 1997, houses "children of Sikh freedom fighters" and "children of innocent civilians . . . killed in fake police encounters."[143] One major study by a senior police official in Punjab, including thirty-three recommendations, focuses exclusively on the needs of the families of "killed police personnel."[144] Victims continue to be apprehensive about the revival of militancy, with 38 percent positive and 29 percent uncertain.[145] Some efforts are being made to deal with "mistrust . . . and insecurity," psychological rather than physical problems.[146]

More direct political efforts involve the resumption of the political process, including elections at every level of the state, from local government in rural and urban areas to the state assembly and national parliament.[147] Equally important for closure is the return of many former militants, including some of the most notorious leaders. Many have retired, a few have entered politics, and most have quietly entered regular occupations.[148] Encouraging former terrorists to return was part of the political strategy of the then-ruling Akali Dal–BJP alliance announced in April 2001.[149]

Results were almost immediate. A major breakthrough occurred when Wassan Singh Zaffarwal, chief of a major terrorist group, the Khalistan Commando Force, returned to Punjab from Switzerland on April 11, 2001, after negotiating his surrender with the police. He served a two-year prison term, then became a homeopathic physician. Another militant returned from the Philippines a week after Zaffarwal's surrender.[150] Jagjit Singh Chohan also returned in 2001, after twenty-five years in exile. He was perhaps the earliest ideologue of the movement. He set up a Khalistani government in exile in London and issued Khalistani "passports," following a political career that included being elected finance minister in the Punjab government in the 1960s. After returning, he set up a charitable hospital and established a political party that advocated for Khalistan but elicited little response.[151]

Zaffarwal's and Chohan's returns encouraged many others to follow. Bhai Kanwar Singh Dhami, a political ideologue of the Akal Federation, released from jail in 1997, acknowledges that the "movement is dead." He has established a trust that runs orphanages and homes and in 2003 provided shelter for 250 women and children. He also gives financial support to 360 children of slain militants and distributes monthly pensions to widows. Orphaned children are raised in "strict adherence" to Sikh religious codes, while both boys and girls are trained in the traditional *gatka,* a Sikh martial art.[152] Manraj Grewal authored a book, published in 2004, that captures the aspirations of the returnees in its title, *Dreams after Darkness: A Search for a Life Ordinary under the Shadow of 1984.* His interviews with returned militants and accounts of survivors of those who died violently emphasize how people are rebuilding their lives.[153]

It is possible that conflicting socialization processes are under way for state versus militant victims. NGO institutions, such as those provided by ex-militants, appear to be emphasizing a set of values in contrast to those of the state. Moreover, physically separate institutions can reinforce emotionally laden stereotypes. Political groups and parties that emphasize extremist positions, especially when in the opposition, can provide channels that could once again be destructive for Punjab.

Some human rights organizations emphasize revealing what transpired as well as attempting to secure justice. In addition to the work of national and state human rights commissions, various documentary reports continue to be published. One of the most notable is a first volume of more than six hundred pages that provides extensive documentation and analysis of hundreds of cases of alleged disappearances, torture, and extrajudicial killings.[154] Khushwant Singh, in reviewing the volume, points out that K. P. S. Gill dismisses the charges against his police force as "rubbish." Singh emphasizes that the National Human Rights Commission is investigating major charges.[155]

It is too early to discuss efforts toward closure in Kashmir. Discussions between Indian and Pakistani officials, and between various groups in

Kashmir and the elected state and national governments, constitute important beginnings. Elections in 1999 and 2004 also provide elements of a meaningful political process. Fissures in Kashmir, however, run even deeper than in Punjab and involve nuclear-armed India and Pakistan in even more fundamental ways. Nonetheless, it is not too early to consider measures that can ease the healing that is so necessary for the future.

In the end, the major achievement of efforts at closure probably is understanding, rather than forgiveness, and a willingness to live with the truth. Scars will remain. It's not over until it's over. The question remains as to whether the trauma involved in periods of movement and state terrorism can ever be resolved. Closure, whatever its form, is the final stage of counterterrorism. The longer participants in actual or potential violent confrontation delay engaging in conflict resolution, the deeper become the fissures that need to be repaired.

CONCLUSION

Sikh and Muslim secessionist movements in Punjab and Kashmir, respectively, both assisted by Pakistan, have presented major challenges to India, especially since the 1980s. Normal democratic channels no longer sufficed for organized groups that became committed to terrorist tactics to achieve political goals. The Sikh Khalistani movement in Punjab did not represent a mass uprising, but it did have widespread support among the Sikh population after two catalytic events in 1984: the Indian army action in the Golden Temple and the killing of Sikhs following Prime Minister Indira Gandhi's assassination. Following the death of its charismatic leader in the Golden Temple, the movement split into many contending groups, whose excesses over time alienated their basic constituency, while government efforts became more successful. More than twenty thousand people were killed during the period 1980–1993.

Violence has been a part of the Kashmir situation since Kashmir acceded to India in 1947 following partition. Three wars between India and Pakistan mark Kashmir as the central issue between the two countries. Militant and terrorist groups, as in the Punjab situation, lack central control and direction. Pakistan has control of some groups and influence over others with the goal of a Muslim-majority state, or at least Muslim-majority areas joining Pakistan. Jihadist groups composed of radical Muslims from many countries became particularly important in the 1990s. Another irredentist stream seeks independence from both India and Pakistan, or possibly a high level of autonomy and relationships to both. There is also a pro-Indian part of the population, dominated by Muslims, with an elected government in Indian Kashmir. Conflict in Kashmir continues, along with peace talks between India and Pakistan. Between forty and sixty thousand people were killed in Kashmir between 1989 and 2006.

A first consideration in both cases is the target population. Secessionist groups as well as the government need legitimacy from the larger population in the state, as well as in India. Terrorist tactics can undermine the legitimacy of the government or be counterproductive. Similarly, government efforts to maintain law and order can counter terrorism or provide a stimulus for terrorist recruitment and loss of government legitimacy.

Five subject areas—military action, special legislation, human rights, negotiations, and closure—were delineated as being particularly important to government counterterrorism efforts. Each area is important in its own right and also interrelated with the others. To enhance this evaluation and its objectivity, a number of experts, military and academic, were asked to assist this analysis by responding to a questionnaire. My conclusions take their replies into consideration, and excerpts from their comments are included in the text.

Punjab provides the clearest case of unsuccessful as well as successful military tactics. Operation Bluestar in June 1984, which used the regular military in a massive manner—an "elephant chasing a mouse"—proved to be counterproductive, as it alienated even the most moderate Sikhs. Destruction of parts of the sacred Golden Temple complex and the killing of a large number of innocent pilgrims inflamed Sikhs. The army action led to Prime Minister Indira Gandhi's assassination by two of her Sikh bodyguards four months later, followed by an organized massacre of Sikhs in response.

New terrorist groups emerged, challenging the government even more directly with openly secessionist slogans and once again occupying the Golden Temple. Operation Black Thunder, organized and led by the Punjab police in 1988, cleared the Golden Temple of terrorists in a highly successful counterterrorism action that contrasted sharply with Operation Bluestar. Specially trained units used surgical military tactics with maximum transparency. Snipers and a restrained but effective use of force contained the terrorists within a small area, where they lacked essential services and supplies. Large numbers of media personnel covered every part of the operation, so that maximum publicity recorded the government's restraint as well as the terrorists' desecration, including torture, murder, and defecation within the holiest temple.

The military lesson for counterterrorism that comes from comparing these two actions emphasizes good planning, intelligence, specialized units used in an appropriate manner, and credible media coverage. More than one thousand people, including significant numbers of military personnel, were killed in Operation Bluestar. Four years later, approximately thirty terrorists were killed and, even more significantly, two hundred surrendered on the final day. Unlike with Operation Bluestar, terrorist excesses became public knowledge in a credible manner in Operation Black Thunder, thereby damaging terrorist legitimacy.

Nonetheless, the state continued to use an increased number of military troops in Punjab, particularly various paramilitary units provided by New Delhi. In addition, Punjab state police forces were modernized, and new units of mobile commandos were created. New tactics enabled better coordination between the regular military, the paramilitary, and the police. On the negative side, atrocities allegedly committed by the police, particularly torture during interrogation and "encounter" deaths (illegal executions), were counterproductive in terms of stimulating new terrorist recruitment to the various groups. The police also used cats—former terrorists—to kill terrorists and extract intelligence. The mixed results included the capture or killing of major terrorists, along with the killing of innocents and major situations of corruption.

Kashmir also saw an increase in numbers and kinds of military units. Regular military units are involved with guarding the borders and periodic low-intensity conflict, extending from the Siachen Glacier and Kargil conflict in 1999 to exchanges of artillery shelling. They are also involved with action against militant groups and are the subject of attacks.

Punjab's lessons on the use of the military were applied in Kashmir during the Hazratbal shrine crisis in 1993. Militants armed with rapid-firing weapons seized the shrine, which contains a holy relic of the Prophet. Rather than a frontal assault, a thirty-two-day siege, accompanied by negotiations led by the police and the district commissioner, was waged to force the surrender of the militants. As in Punjab, however, appropriate military action may have settled one crisis situation but was not sufficient in resolving the larger problems. Terrorism continued and even increased.

Paramilitary units are used extensively in Kashmir, as in Punjab, as are former terrorists. Some of the same pluses and minuses are present in terms of whether these units are seen as occupation forces or as protection for the civilian community. Former terrorists occasion the strongest criticism. Stronger criticism of these units in Kashmir than in Punjab may relate to the need for better training, supervision, and support. Punjab's greater success also may relate to its development of a strong police force composed primarily of Sikhs. Police brutality in Punjab, accordingly, did not involve different religious communities.

A less controversial military counterterrorism program in Punjab involved civic action by the regular military and the police in key rural areas. Schools, teachers, bridges, bus service, agricultural programs, kitchens, medical facilities, sanitation systems, and various sports programs appear to have been successful in establishing important links to villagers. One major program involving 394 villages reportedly resulted in a large number of top militants being killed and arrested. Comparable efforts in Kashmir have received less attention, but the counterterrorism message is clear: "Cooperation with the locals pays dividends in every way."[156]

Indian military efforts in Punjab and Kashmir also have to confront the fact of long borders with Pakistan. Training camps in Pakistan, infiltration, and smuggling have led India to construct elaborate fencing in an attempt to seal its borders. Marshland in Punjab provides problems, but they are less troublesome than those created by Kashmir's mountainous terrain. A minimum conclusion is that fencing and modern technology increase the costs for crossing the borders, but terrain and human corruption are limiting factors.

Special legislation to counter or prevent actions against the state extends back to India's colonial past. Common features of such legislation are that it curtails civil rights and can be implemented in an extreme manner with only limited checks. India's federal constitution includes emergency provisions that can empower the central government, even to the extent of suspending state governments. These provisions have been used periodically in India, along with new legislation such as the National Security Acts, TADA, and POTA. It has to be reemphasized that the government and militant groups contest for legitimacy from the larger population. From that perspective, a basic conclusion for Punjab and Kashmir is that heavy-handed implementation creates a human rights problem more than it helps combat terrorism.

Human rights also are a key area in the battle for the hearts and minds of the population. A spiral of violence took place in both Punjab and Kashmir, as both the terrorists and government engaged in the killing of innocents, torture, and other excesses. In Punjab, a "bullet-for-a-bullet" policy by the state police, encounter killings, and credible allegations of torture were counterproductive to the effort to win over the terrorist support base. Similarly, terrorist abuses, especially in rural areas, were key to a loss of popular support and the consequent demise of the movement. A comparable situation may be developing in Kashmir. Objective observers cite human rights abuses by the state as well as the militants.

A minimum conclusion for both Punjab and Kashmir is that human rights abuses by the state provide a significant recruitment tool for terrorists and therefore are counterproductive. Allowing increased access to human rights groups in Kashmir, both domestic and foreign, could provide needed transparency and a corrective influence. Improving Indian human rights behavior in Kashmir is vitally important in the battle for public support and in countering Pakistani information and propaganda. It can also lead to an emphasis on human rights violations by militants. Militant intimidation and terror became increasingly important factors in the demise of the Punjab movement. Freedom fighters can become terrorists in the minds of their target populations. Counterterrorism policies emphasizing human rights, despite provocations, are critical to these perceptions in the battle for the hearts and minds of the population.

Negotiations involve at least two major stages. First is developing a process for serious negotiations and arriving at a settlement. Second, and equally important, is implementing the agreement. Lack of trust, which is intensified when terrorism is involved, is a key factor inhibiting the first stage. Moreover, there are extreme and moderate elements within both the movement and the state. Federalism in India provides two levels of government, which at times creates a complicating factor in terms of competing political parties that alternate in power, may have different perspectives, and manifest factional differences. External support of terrorists by Pakistan in both Punjab and Kashmir further complicates the situation. It also provides the beginning of a negotiating framework, however.

India and Pakistan are the two obvious parties to any serious negotiations. What other parties, if any, are to be included in negotiations on Kashmir is an open question. Mediation by a third party, such as Norway or a notable individual such as Nelson Mandela, has been suggested. So has "facilitation" by the United States and international bodies, such as occurred in the crisis following the attack on India's parliament in December 2001. India and Pakistan have a wealth of options in peace negotiations, which resumed in December 2003. Public presentation of their nuclear readiness in 1998 and events stemming from 9/11 add pressure to reduce tensions in Kashmir. Nuclear war is the other end of this spectrum.

Implementation of an agreement may be as difficult as arriving at the compromises needed to reach the agreement. Punjab's case illustrates how the lack of trust under Prime Minister Indira Gandhi became transformed. Demands that she interpreted as secessionist became negotiable under her son and successor, Prime Minister Rajiv Gandhi. His government, as well as the moderate Sikh party with which he negotiated, withstood terrorist actions so as to successfully reach an "accord." The Punjab Accord nonetheless fell victim to interpretations of Congress Party self-interest and was never implemented. Punjab's terrorist movement ended without negotiations but at an enormous cost of at least twenty thousand deaths after the accord. Kashmir's killings since 1989 are more than twice those of Punjab. They continue at a notable level despite peace talks. Implementation will have to be effectively built into the final negotiations if counterterrorism is to be successful in Kashmir.

Closure is an ongoing concern in Punjab and an important consideration for the future of Kashmir. Scars remain after political violence has ended. Terrorism can reappear if the society has not been reconciled to past events or at least achieved a significant degree of understanding, and if the issues and situations that led to violence are not sufficiently resolved. In the past three decades, a variety of means have been used in efforts to achieve closure: the Truth and Reconciliation Commission in South Africa; transparency efforts in Argentina; war crimes commissions for Bosnia and Rwanda; and village-based semijudicial proceedings in Rwanda.

Punjab's efforts include social measures for the victims of terrorism, particularly an estimated thirteen thousand widows and eighty-eight thousand children.[157] State assistance, however, is not provided to victims suspected of having militant connections; nongovernmental organizations tend to this category. Therefore, there is danger that two different socialization processes can result in core groups bitterly opposing each other in the future. There is an awareness of this possibility in Punjab, but whether adequate measures are being taken to counter it is an open question.

There is a notable degree of success in the political arena on institutional and personal levels. Beginning in 1992, restarting the democratic political system with elections at the local and state levels resulted in new political alignments that have reduced religious and social tensions. Most notable is the coalition between the moderate Akali Dal, the major party for rural Sikhs, and the BJP, a major party for urban Hindus. Through peaceful elections, the alliance has since alternated in power with the Congress Party, which aggregates a cross-section of Punjab's population.

At the personal level, closure for former militants is taking the form of a meaningful degree of reconciliation through returning to Punjab rather than facing a Truth and Reconciliation Commission. Leading terrorists have negotiated their surrender so as to serve short sentences or none at all. Their reintegration into society includes notable social service. That situation, however, leaves unresolved the charges against them for their terrorist acts.

Neither have allegations against the state been satisfactorily investigated. In particular, there has been no closure for the massacre of Sikhs outside Punjab in 1984 and state actions in Punjab. Pakistan also remains a factor. A Home Ministry report released in August 2004 alleges that Pakistan is pressuring Sikh militant groups, whom it supports on its soil, to revive militancy in Punjab. These militants include the Babbar Khalsa, the Khalistan Commando Force, and the International Sikh Youth Federation.[158] Further incidents, arrests, and revelations of new strategies continue.[159]

A beginning toward closure has been made in Kashmir with elections to the state assembly and national parliament—which observers consider to be fair—in 1999 and 2004. That assessment contrasts with charges of managed elections in the past. Negotiations between India and Pakistan, and with various groups inside Kashmir, mark the beginnings of a long-term peace process that could lead to the end of terrorism. Closure efforts in Punjab as well as in other parts of the world can provide important lessons for Kashmir, some of which can be pertinent to the negotiating process. Indo-Pakistani relations remain central to Kashmir and also continue to be important in regard to Punjab.

NOTES

1. The Telangana region of then Madras State subsequently became one of the major regions within the new state of Andhra Pradesh.

2. In 2004 there were reports that the People's War Group and the Maoist Communist Center were discussing a merger under a new name, the All India Maoist Communist Center. For a succinct summary of their activities in central and eastern India, see Nihar Nayak, "Left Wing Extremism: Synchronized Onslaught," *South Asia Intelligence Review (SAIR)* 2, no. 28 (January 26, 2004). In 2003 Nayak reported that in the nine states in which Naxalite-related violence occurred, there were 546 incidents and 509 deaths. In Andhra Pradesh, 1154 persons, including 164 Naxalites and 990 civilians, were killed.

3. BBC News estimates that "more than 12,000 people have died over 10 years of Maoist insurgency." January 6, 2006. By one calculation, the "Maoists have an estimated strength of between 8–10,000 well-armed and trained 'regulars,'" plus 25,000 or more militia. See Saji Cherian, "Nepal: The State Retreats, the Maoists Pursue," *SAIR* 4, no. 25 (January 2, 2006). Linkages with leftist extremists in India and with groups in the Philippines, Peru, and Turkey are asserted in Samrat Upadhyay, "Dark Days in Shangri-La," *New York Times,* November 10, 2003, A23. He also points out that "the rebels model their approach after Peru's murderous Shining Path guerrilla movement." International military assistance to Nepal, including from the United States, is emphasized in Conn Hallinan, "Nepal and the Bush Administration," *Foreign Policy in Focus,* Interhemispheric Resource Center, February 3, 2004.

4. Bhutan's military closed down the Bodo Liberation Tigers training camps, and more than twenty-five hundred of its cadres surrendered in Assam on December 6, 2003. Deputy Prime Minister L. K. Advani witnessed the formation of a Bodoland Territorial Council (BTC) the following day. See *Assam Tribune,* December 7, 8, 2003. Bibhu Prasad Routray, acting director of the ICM Database and Documentation Centre in Guwahati, Assam's capital, commented: "After the Mizo Accord of 1986, the formation of the BTC could be the only and still qualified success story in the resolution of an insurgency in India's northeast." See *SAIR* 2, no. 21 (December 28, 2003).

5. Two Babbar Khalsa International (BKI) "terrorists" were arrested for bomb blasts in two Delhi cinemas on May 31, 2005. Another two BKI activists were arrested with bomb materials in Punjab. See *Hindu* and *Telegraph,* June 1, 2005. A new development is the recruiting of foreign-based Hindus and clean-shaven Sikhs. Ramesh Vinayak, "A Close Shave with Terror," *India Today,* August 15, 2005, 16–18. Similarly in Kashmir, Hizbul Mujahideen, the leading Islamic jihadist group, is recruiting Hindu youth. Ramesh Vinayak, "Now Hindu Jehadis," *India Today,* January 23, 2006, 6–9.

6. *New York Times*, February 19, 2004, 3.

7. Jugdep Chima, "Back to the Future in 2002? A Model of Sikh Separatism in Punjab," *Studies in Conflict and Terrorism* 25, no. 1 (January–February 2002): 33. For a detailed account of the external dimension, see N. G. Barrier and Paul Wallace, "International Dimensions of Sikh Political Violence," *Ethno-Nationalism and Emerging World (Dis)Order,* ed. Gurnam Singh (New Delhi: Kanishka, 2002), 282–300.

8. Reported in the *Tribune* (Chandigarh), January 23, 2004, following the escape on January 22 of Jagtar Singh Hawara, prime accused, and three others. Seven days later, the alleged "mastermind" behind the escape was arrested. Narain Singh Chaura is described as "a militant ideologue trained in Pakistan" who has been trying to "revive militancy" and "is termed as a professor of militancy." See *Tribune,* January 30, 2004. *India Today,* February 2, 2004, 18, provides details and a diagram of the ninety-four-foot-long, fourteen-foot-deep tunnel the prisoners in the high-security prison dug for their escape. Officials concede that "glaring complicity of the prison staff" had to be involved. Various militant groups are named.

9. Jagtar Singh Hawara is described as a "top" Babbar Khalsa International "terrorist." Two terrorists he allegedly trained were apprehended by the Chandigarh police in July 2005. See *Asian Age,* July 17, 2005.

10. For the best single book on this subject, see Darshan Singh Tatla, *The Sikh Diaspora: The Search for Statehood* (Seattle: University of Washington Press, 1999).

11. The "anti-national" finding is by a four-member inquiry panel. See *Tribune,* January 17, 2004, 5. Security was heightened along the highway, as well as along railroad tracks, during this period, at least partly because of the upcoming Republic Day on January 26. At about 6:30 a.m. on January 16, 2004, I was stopped at a roadblock on the national highway in this area in a clearly labeled Government of India tourist car. Our trunk was opened and searched.

12. Paul Wallace, "The Sikhs as a 'Minority' in a Sikh Majority State in India," *Asian Survey* 27, no. 3 (March 1986): 363–77.

13. W. H. McLeod, *Guru Nanak and the Sikh Religion* (London: Oxford University Press, 1968); and W. H. McLeod, *The Evolution of the Sikh Community* (Delhi: Oxford University Press, 1975). For what may be the best single source on the five hundred years of Sikh history, and very readable, see Khushwant Singh, *A History of the Sikhs,* vol. 1, 1469–1839, and vol. 2, 1839–1988 (Delhi: Oxford University Press, 1991). This is a revised, updated, and paperback version of the 1966 publication by Princeton University Press.

14. Harjot Oberoi, *The Construction of Religious Boundaries: Culture, Identity and Diversity in the Sikh Tradition* (Delhi: Oxford University Press, 1994).

15. For a contrary perspective that directly relates Sikh identity to terrorism and political violence, see Rajiv A. Kapur, *Sikh Separatism: The Politics of Faith* (London: Allen and Unwin, 1986).

16. Indira Gandhi's son Sanjay is credited with recruiting Bhindranwale to split the opposition Akali Dal "after his mother's (temporary) fall from power in 1977." See Joseph Lelyveld, *New York Times Magazine,* December 2, 1984, 43.

17. Ayesha Kagal, "Armed Coup in Golden Temple," *Times of India, Sunday Review,* December 19, 1982, 1, 6. See also Harish K. Puri, "Religion and Politics in Punjab," in *Religion, State, and Politics in India,* ed. Moin Shakir (Delhi: Ajanta, 1989), 338.

18. Ajay K. Mehra, "Insurgency and Terrorism," in *Encyclopaedia of Police,* vol. 2, ed. S. K. Ghosh (New Delhi: Ashish, 1995), 1193.

19. Shekhar Gupta, "Punjab: The Rule of the Gun," *India Today,* January 15, 1991, 14–22.

20. Simranjit Singh Mann commanded the Faridkot district police force in 1978. Bhindranwale visited him there and organized a religious ceremony. Mann also issued arms licenses to people who later formed "killer squads." He defended his decision on the weapons charge with, "Sikhs have a lust for weapons and I satisfied it through legal means." See *India Today,* February 15, 1990, 70.

21. Mehra, "Insurgency and Terrorism," 1194.

22. Kuldip Nayar and Khushwant Singh, *Tragedy of Punjab: Operation Bluestar and After* (New Delhi: Vision, 1984).

23. *Times of India,* September 8, 1992, 16.

24. In a speech to parliament on September 17, 1953, Nehru stated: "We have always regarded the Kashmir problem as symbolic for us . . . as it illustrates that we are a secular state." Ashutosh Varshney, "Three Compromised Nationalisms: Why Kashmir Has Been a Problem," in *Perspectives on Kashmir: The Roots of Conflict in South Asia*, ed. Ruju G. C. Thomas (Boulder, CO: Westview, 1992), 202.

25. Navnita Chadha Behera points out that Sheikh Abdullah realized that British imperialism served as an even greater obstacle to independence than did the princes. Thus his National Conference allied with the Congress nationalist movement under the organization established for princely states, the All-India States People's Congress. See Behera Centre for Policy Research, *State Identity and Violence: Jammu, Kashmir and Ladakh* (New Delhi: Manohar Delhi, 2000), 52–56. Excellent scholarly treatment is also provided by Sumit Ganguly

in three books: *The Origins
of War in South Asia: Indo-Pakistan Conflicts since 1947* (Boulder, CO:
Westview, 1986); *The Crisis in Kashmir: Portents of War, Hopes of Peace*
(Washington, DC: Woodrow Wilson Center Press; Cambridge: Cambridge
University, 1997); *Conflict Unending: India-Pakistan Tensions since 1947*
(New York: Columbia University Press, 2001).

26. Behera, *State Identity and Violence,* 93.

27. Ibid., 165. Sumit Ganguly also emphasizes the "political decay" as well
as the politicization of the youth: "Earlier generations of Kashmiris were not
nearly as politically aware as those that emerged in the late 1970s and early
1980s." See Ganguly, *Crisis in Kashmir,* 92–93.

28. See Ganguly, *Crisis in Kashmir,* 103ff; and Behera, *State Identity and
Violence,* chapter 7.

29. *Guardian,* January 6, 2004, used the figure of 65,000, while the BBC
News, February 6, 2004, stated that "more than 35,000" have died. A former
high-ranking member of Indian intelligence testified that from 1989 to 2003,
12,755 civilians and 4,842 Indian security personnel were killed in Kashmir. In
addition, the average number of local terrorists killed between 1994 and 1998
was 1,069 per year, while the average number of foreign terrorists killed was 172
per year. The ratio between local and foreign terrorists killed reversed from
1999 to 2003, with 726 local terrorists killed per year versus 951 foreigners per
year. The total of these figures is 32,187. See *Testimony by Bahukutumbi
Raman, Additional Secretary (retired),Cabinet Secretariat, Government of
India (GOI), New Delhi, former member (2000–2002), National Security
Advisory Board, GOI,* Committee on International Relations, Sub-committee
on Asia and the Pacific and International Terrorism, U.S. House of
Representatives, Washington, DC, October 29, 2003.

30. Tom Marks, "At the Frontlines of the GWOT [General War on
Terrorism]: State Response to Insurgency in Jammu," *Journal of Counterterrorism and Homeland Security International* 10, no. 1 (2004): 38–46.
According to his information, 33,680 persons, nearly 14,000 of them civilians,
were killed from 1990 to 2002.

31. Ganguly, *Crisis in Kashmir,* 170–71; Behera, *State Identity and
Violence,* 169–76; Sumanta Bose, *Kashmir: Roots of Conflict, Paths to Peace*
(New Delhi: Vistaar, 2003), 294; and K. Santhanam and others, eds., *Jihadis
in Jammu and Kashmir* (New Delhi: Sage, 2003), 162–74.

32. Santhanam and others, *Jihadis,* 168.

33. Behera, *State Identity and Violence,* 177.

34. Behera arrives at the figure of "13,000–20,000 men." See ibid., 177.
Ganguly, *Crisis in Kashmir,* cites one source with the figure of 4,000 (p. 170).

Bose, *Kashmir,* simply states that it is the "largest guerrilla organization active in IJK" Indian Jammu and Kashmir (p. 293). Santhanam and others, *Jihadis,* provides a "strength" total of fourteen hundred "Pak-trained" (p. 117). A more recent source states that in the early 1990s, the Hizbul Mujahideen had a strength of twelve thousand after the Tehreek-e-Jihad-e-Islami merged into it. But in 2000 its cadres declined to fifteen hundred, largely due to the effectiveness of the Indian security forces and the Ikhwans, counterinsurgents "responsible for killing many of its members . . . nearly 2000." See Suba Chandran, "Hizbul Mujahideen (HM)," in *Terrorism Post 9/11: An Indian Perspective,* ed. P. R. Chari and Suba Chandran (Delhi: Manohar, 2003), 171–72.

35. Chandran, "Hizbul Mujahideen," 177–81, 208n41; and Ganguly, *Crisis in Kashmir,* 170.

36. Separate reports from Jammu and Islamabad, *Times of India,* August 29, 2004.

37. Kanchan Lakshman, *South Asia Intelligence Review* 3, no. 26 (January 10, 2005).

38. K. P. S. Gill and others, "Endgame in Punjab: 1988–1993," in *Faultlines: Writings on Conflict and Resolution* 1, no. 1 (May 1999): 9.

39. *India Today,* June 30, 1984, 8–14; *New York Times,* June 9, 1984; *New York Times,* July 29, 1984; and Government of India, *White Paper on the Punjab Agitation* (New Delhi: Government of India Press, 1984).

40. Chand Joshi estimates that seven hundred soldiers and five thousand Sikhs were killed. See Chand Joshi, *Bhindranwale: Myth and Reality* (New Delhi: Vikas, 1984), 161.

41. Government of India, *White Paper on the Punjab Agitation,* 1984.

42. Gill and others, "Endgame," 9.

43. The Akal Takht, translated as "Throne of the Immortal," represents the temporal center of Sikhism. The Harmandir Sahib (Temple of God) is the Golden Temple, representing the religious center of Sikhism.

44. Khushwant Singh, *Choice,* September 1984, 8.

45. Nayar and Singh, *Tragedy of Punja,* 31. I personally experienced this divide between Sikhs and Hindus in Delhi and Punjab following the military actions. Hindus blamed Sikhs for the violence that preceded Operation Bluestar, while Sikhs reacted against the desecration of their holy temple and the actions against Sikhs.

46. Tatla, *The Sikh Diaspora.*

47. Bhindranwale refashioned the Khalsa Sikh model formulated by the tenth and last guru in 1699. For a detailed discussion, see Paul Wallace, "Political Violence and Terrorism in India," in *Terrorism in Context,* ed.

Martha Crenshaw (University Park: Pennsylvania State University Press, 1995), 361ff.

48. Quoted in Mark Juergensmeyer, "The Logic of Religious Violence: The Case of Punjab," *Contributions to Indian Sociology* 22, no. 1 (1988): 70.

49. Quoted in Joyce Pettigrew, "In Search of a New Kingdom of Lahore," *Pacific Affairs* 60, no. 1 (1987): 16. Ranbir Singh Sandhu provides almost five hundred pages of translated material in *Struggle for Justice: Speeches and Conversations of Sant Jarnail Singh Khalsa Bhindranwale* (Dublin, OH: Sikh Educational and Religious Foundation, 1999).

50. *Times of India,* February 9, 1992, 15.

51. Harish K. Puri, Paramjit Singh Judge, and Jagrup Singh Sekhon, *Terrorism in Punjab: Understanding Grassroots Reality* (New Delhi: Har-Anand, 1999), 184–86.

52. One militant explained the split as the AISSF remaining a legal organization, while the SSF operated underground. Interview in San Pedro, California, detention center, 1987. See also *Times of India,* June 11, 1988, 8; *India Today,* September 30, 1987, 43; and *India Today,* November 15, 1987, 44.

53. *Times of India,* September 24, 1987, 1.

54. *Sikh Herald* 2, nos. 1–4, 1987, 1.

55. The official figure of 2,717 killed represented almost entirely Sikhs. "Unofficial figures are considerably higher." See Mark Tully (BBC correspondent) and Zareer Masani, *From Raj to Rajiv: Forty Years of Indian Independence* (New Delhi: Universal Book Stall, 1988), 136–37. The single most important document in terms of its widespread distribution and impact is Rajni Kothari and Gobinda Mukhoty, *Who Are the Guilty? Report of a Joint Inquiry into the Causes and Impact of the Riots in Delhi from 31 October to 10 November 1984* (New Delhi: People's Union for Democratic Rights and People's Union for Civil Liberties, 1984). See also Amiya Rao, Aurobindo Ghose, and N. D. Pancholi, *Report to the Nation: Truth about Delhi Violence,* foreword by Justice V. M. Tarkunde (Delhi: Citizens for Democracy, 1985), 1–54.

56. Gill and others, "Endgame," 10. Harvard Law School graduate Jaskaran Kaur documents the Congress (I) Party role in "Congress (I) Party and the Delhi Administration," in *Twenty Years of Impunity: The November 1984 Pogroms of Sikhs in India* (London: Nectar, 2004).

57. S. M. Sikri (former chief justice of India), *Report of the Citizen's Commission* (New Delhi: Citizen's Commission, 1985), 35ff. See also *Times of India,* December 23, 1984, 2; and *Indian Express,* January 11, 1985, 7.

58. Personal observation during the elections in India. Eight years later, nationally prominent columnist Tavleen Singh bitterly compared the killing of

Sikhs in Delhi, which she blamed on the Congress Party, with the killing of Muslims in Gujarat, ruled by the BJP. Rajiv Gandhi, she asserts, "came to power with the largest majority in Indian parliamentary history mainly because he openly espoused the politics of hate." He justified "the massacre of the Sikhs in a speech," and his Congress Party "ran a series of newspaper advertisements in which Sikhs were depicted as terrorists and enemies of India." Thus, she concludes, it became difficult for the Congress Party to successfully oppose the BJP for its actions in Gujarat in 2002. See Tavleen Singh, "After Rajiv, before Modi," *India Today, Sunday Express,* December 15, 2002.

59. *India Today,* May 31, 1988. See especially an editorial titled "Challenge of Openness," on page 5 and extended coverage on pages 36–43. See also *New York Times,* May 23, 1988, 4.

60. Sarab Jit Singh, *Operation Black Thunder: An Eyewitness Account of Terrorism in Punjab* (London: Sage, 2000), 129.

61. Ibid., 150.

62. Ibid., 52.

63. *Times of India,* July 15, 1988, 1; and *India West,* July 22, 1988, 8.

64. Gill and others, "Endgame," 16.

65. Ganguly, *Crisis in Kashmir,* 120.

66. Colonel Ravi Nanda, *Kashmir and Indo-Pak Relations* (New Delhi: Lancer, 2001), 109.

67. *Times of India,* May 22 1988, 1. Budget information and succinct descriptions of the central police and paramilitary groups are contained in the *Sunday Mail,* July 28, 1991; and *Indian Express,* April 20, 1992, 3.

68. *India Today,* December 31, 1990, 20–21.

69. Gill and others, "Endgame," 18–21.

70. Ibid., 22–26.

71. *Times of India,* February 28, 1992, 7. A Reuter's report emphasized the civic action programs along the border with Pakistan, including stringing power lines, curbing petty crime, and operating medical clinics. See *India West*, February 28, 1992, 12.

72. *India Today,* February 15, 1992, 14–15.

73. Brian Cloughley, "What Next in the Valley?" *Daily Times* (Pakistan), January 21, 2004, 3.

74. Kanwar Sandhu, "Punjab: A Golden Opportunity," *India Today,* November 30, 1992, 38.

75. Sharda Jain, *Politics of Terrorism India: The Case of Punjab* (New Delhi: Deep and Deep, 1995), 240–44.

76. Ramesh Vinayak, "Punjab, Prowling for a Living," *India Today,* December 15, 1995, 50–53.

77. Ibid., 50–53.

78. Jaideep Sarin, *Indo-Asian New Service,* March 8, 2004; *Tribune,* March 10, 2004; and private communications.

79. Kanwar Sandhu, "Punjab Police: Official Excesses," *India Today,* October 15, 1992, 28–33.

80. Cloughley, "What Next in the Valley?" 3.

81. Chandan Mitra, *Hindustan Times,* May 26, 1992, 1.

82. Interview with a lieutenant general who served in Punjab. Conducted at international seminar, "Threat from Terrorism to Peace, Security and Human Rights," Centre for Policy Research, New Delhi, March 3–6, 1996.

83. *India West,* April 29, 1988, 1; and *Statesman,* March 18, 1989. 8.

84. Ashraf Sayed, "Gujarat Found to Be Main Entry Point for Pak Arms," *India West,* October 2, 1992, 4; and Rahul Kumar, "Smuggling of Gold Declines in Punjab," *Economic Times,* June 25, 1992.

85. Amy Waldman, "India and Pakistan: Good Fences Make Good Neighbors," *New York Times,* July 4, 2004, 3.

86. Personal communication, December 2003.

87. Personal communication, January 2004.

88. Ashish Gupta, "Smugglers of the San Dunes, *India Today,* May 30, 2005, 28–30.

89. Personal communication, February 2004.

90. *Daily Excelsior,* November 8, 2004.

91. *India Today,* September 13, 2004, 26. *India Today* reported that new Pakistani techniques included "burrowing a hole below the fences, plastic ladders, and plastic gloves."

92. Personal communication, February 2004.

93. Personal communication, January 2004.

94. Personal communication, July 2004, with a retired Indian army colonel who served in Kashmir.

95. Personal communication, December 2003.

96. Personal communication, January 2004.

97. Ganguly, *Crisis in Kashmir,* 152–53. Ganguly also cites the following critical articles about these groups: Harinder Baweja and Ramesh Vinayak, "A Dangerous Liaison," *India Today,* March 15, 1996, 52–55; and Human Rights Watch/Asia, "India's Secret Army in Kashmir: New Patterns of Abuse Emerge in the Conflict, *Human Rights Watch/Asia Report* 8, no. 4 (May 1996).

98. "The Counter-insurgents: A Report by Joint Fact Finding Committee of Organisations, Bombay," in *Counter-insurgency in Kashmir,* no. 26 (Srinagar: Institute of Kashmir Studies, 1996), 57–64.

99. Ibid., 65–67.

100. Personal communication, February 2004.

101. Gill and others, "Endgame," 32–33.

102. Paul Wallace, "Centralisation and Depoliticisation in South Asia," *Journal of Commonwealth and Comparative Studies* 16, no. 1 (March 1978): 3–21.

103. Human Rights Watch, *Human Rights in India: Punjab in Crisis,* Asia Watch Report (New York: Human Rights Watch, 1991), 148–58.

104. People's Union for Civil Liberties, *Black Laws 1984: The Terrorist Affected Areas (Special Courts) Ordinance: Ordinances Amending the National Security Act* (Delhi: People's Union for Civil Liberties, 1984).

105. *Times of India,* February 12, 1988, 1; and *Hindu,* March 1, 7, 8, 9, 1988.

106. *Times of India,* February 12, 1988, 1.

107. Detailed accounts can be found in Inderjit Singh Jaijee, *Politics of Genocide: Punjab 1984–1998* (Delhi: Ajanta, 1999). Jaijee is a noted human rights lawyer in Chandigarh.

108. Personal communication, February 2004.

109. Personal communication, January 2004.

110. This term is taken from Richard Gillespie, "Political Violence in Argentina: Guerrillas, Terrorists, and *Carapintadas,*" in *Terrorism in Context,* ed. Crenshaw, 234.

111. See Jaijee, *Politics of Genocide.* Asia Watch/International, Amnesty International, and the Punjab Human Rights Organisation sharply criticize government violation of human rights. The voluminous literature on the "Punjab problem" is replete with human rights violations by the state and the militants.

112. K. P. S. Gill in the foreword, in P. M. Das, *Terrorism: The Untold Story* (Chandigarh: Abhishek, 2002), 1.

113. Personal communication, February 2004.

114. Personal communication, December 2003.

115. Personal communication, February 2004.

116. Personal communication, December 2003.

117. *Times of India,* March 26, 2004.

118. The following section on Punjab is largely a summary from Wallace, "Political Violence and Terrorism in India," 388–91.

119. The Anandpur Sahib Resolution arose at different points in time and in various forms. See ibid., 383–84.

120. Tully and Masani, *From Raj to Rajiv,* 142.

121. *Times of India,* January 28, 1986, 8.

122. Personal communication, December 2003.

123. Personal communication, February 2004.

124. Personal communication, December 2003.

125. Personal communication, February 2004.

126. *Times of India,* August 9, 2004.

127. Praveen Swami, "The Hawks Strike Back," *South Asia Intelligence Review* 3, no. 4 (August 9, 2004).

128. Kashmir Study Group documents are available on the Web at www.kashmirstudygroup.net. See also Kashmir Study Group, "1947–1997: The Kashmir Dispute at Fifty, Charting Paths to Peace" (unpublished report on the visit of an independent study team to India and Pakistan: Professors Ainslie Embree, Charles H. Kennedy, Howard B. Schaffer, Joseph E. Schwartzberg, and Robert G. Wirsing, 1997).

129. Joseph P. Schwartzberg, "An Agenda for Peace in Kashmir and South Asia," Kashmir Study Group, January 2003, www.kashmirstudygroup.net/statements/0103_agenda.html.

130. Prime Minister Manmohan Singh endorsed a proposal that the disputed glacier area be declared a "peace mountain." Scientists from India, Pakistan, China, Canada, and the United States have been advocating that the region be declared a "science peace park." See Pallava Baglia, "Peace Mountain Can Be Science Lab," *Indian Express,* June 14, 2005, 1.

131. See the BBC News Online website, http://news.bbc.co.uk/1/shared/spl/hi/south_asia/03/kashmir_future/html/default.stm.

132. Serge Schmemann, "How to Face the Past, Then Close the Door," *New York Times,* April 18, 2001, 4

133. Marc Lacey, *New York Times,* June 20, 2002, 4.

134. Dorothy Shea, *The South African Truth Commission: The Politics of Reconciliation* (Washington, DC: United States Institute of Peace, 2000). See also the 1999 documentary film *Where Truth Lies*: *South African Truth and Reconciliation Commission,* Triumph over Terror series, no. 1835, Bullfrog Films.

135. James S. Torrens, *America* 181, no. 2 (July 1–24, 1999): 12.

136. Juan Forero, *New York Times,* February 16, 2002, 3.

137. *New York Times,* April 19, 2004, 13.

138. Pramod Kumar, Rainuka Dagar, and Neerja, *Victims of Militancy* (Chandigarh: Institute for Development and Communication, with acknowledgment to UNICEF India Country Office, New Delhi, 2001), 3.

139. Ibid., 104.

140. Ibid., 9.

141. Ibid., 14.

142. Ibid., 105.

143. Anoop Singh, *Panthic Weekly,* May 1, 2005, www.panthic.org/print.php?a=1279.

144. Das, *Terrorism: The Untold Story,* 193–202. K. P. S. Gill and M. S. Bhullar, former director-generals of the Punjab police, contribute a foreword and a preface, respectively.

145. Kumar, Dagar, and Neerja, *Victims of Militancy,* 88.

146. Ibid., 101–14.

147. For a review and analysis of Punjab's election history, see Pramod Kumar, "Electoral Politics in Punjab," in *India's 1999 Elections and 20th Century Politics,* ed. Paul Wallace and Ramashray Roy (New Delhi: Sage, 2003). Page 382ff focus on the post-terrorist period.

148. In 1996 I interviewed one former Punjab militant who worked for the State Bank of India, a government concern. He talked confidentially about his time in Pakistan with other militants and how he finally decided to return after being in Nepal and concluding that the Punjab movement no longer had any prospects. He secured his position through a relative in an important elective position in state government.

149. "Badal, BJP Offer to Ex-Punjab Militants," *Hindu,* April 6, 2001.

150. "Homecoming," *India Today,* April 30, 2001; and *Tribune,* April 15, 20, 2001.

151. Chandra Suta Dogra, "Yesterday's Obdurate Khalistani Is at Last Returning Home—Softened, If Not Chastened," *Outlook,* May 26, 2003.

152. Ibid.

153. Manraj Grewal, *Dreams after Darkness: A Search for a Life Ordinary under the Shadow of 1984* (New Delhi: Rupa, 2004). Reviewed in *Tribune,* August 15, 2004.

154. Ram Narayan Kumar, *Reduced to Ashes: The Insurgency and Human Rights in Punjab* (New Delhi: Committee for Coordination on Disappearances in Punjab, 2003).

155. *Tribune,* June 1, 2003.

156. Cloughley, "What Next in the Valley?" 3.

157. Kumar, Dagar, and Neerja, *Victims of Militancy,* 104

158. Government of India Home Ministry Report, 2003–4, reported in the *Hindustan Times,* August 18, 2004.

159. Vinayak, "Punjab: A Close Shave with Terror," 16–18.

14

SRI LANKA AND THE LIBERATION TIGERS OF TAMIL EELAM

Thomas A. Marks

A distinction must be drawn between terrorism as a *method of action* and terrorism as a *logic of action*.[1] Research demonstrates that terrorism is distinguished by the latter; insurgency incorporates the former. The key element of terrorism is the divorce of armed politics from a purported mass base, in whose name terrorists claim to be fighting. Little or no meaningful effort goes into construction of a counterstate, which is the central activity of insurgency. In contrast, insurgencies, while also armed expressions of organic, internal political disaffiliation,[2] use terroristic action principally as one weapon among many to facilitate construction of the counterstate.[3]

The problem for security forces is that early on, armed challenges to the state appear more or less the same. Hence, response of the state to "terrorism" is often inappropriate. Focusing on perpetrators of terror themselves can be effective in cases of terrorism as a logic of action, often referred to as "pure terrorism," because the perpetrators essentially are the movement. However, adopting such an approach when dealing with insurgents, those who use terrorism as a method of action, can be disastrous. In particular, a focus on rooting out "the terrorists," as opposed to emphasizing political solutions to sources of conflict, often leads to abuse of the populace. This sets in motion a new dynamic, motivated by self-defense, that allows an operationally astute insurgent challenger for state power to mobilize additional support. The situation may even mobilize for pure terrorists a mass base where none hitherto existed.

It is this process that has made the ongoing struggle of the Liberation Tigers of Tamil Eelam (LTTE) in Sri Lanka of more than passing interest. A movement labeled "terrorist" by any number of governments, it saw itself as insurgent, as representing a population, the Tamils. It desired to use terrorism as a method of action, as a tactic. Its position within a functioning parliamentary democracy, though, left it unable to recruit a mass base; thus, isolated militants lashing out at a system were judged to have engaged in oppression. Terrorism increasingly became a logic of action. Having eschewed political work among the masses, LTTE was able to emerge as an insurgent movement only through mistakes made by the democratic system, in particular a failure of the state to protect a substantial fragment of its population. Consequently, the LTTE counterstate reached considerable dimensions within the "traditional" Tamil areas of the Sri Lankan north and east, extending to base areas in India and dominating diasporic Tamil communities abroad.

Subsequently crushed by the superior resource mobilization capacity of the state, LTTE responded by further emphasizing terrorism as a method of action. This approach was taken to an extreme. While not forgoing its efforts to create a counterstate, LTTE nevertheless adopted a protracted war stance that settled for support of a rump population, a minority of Tamils, but sufficient to sustain the movement within Sri Lanka, even as essential funding was generated abroad. External factors extended beyond sanctuaries and funding to direct intervention by neighboring India. Contingency entered the picture in the form of an Indian "peacekeeping force" that stopped the likely physical elimination of the Tamil challenge by the Sri Lankan state. Never again was Colombo to prove capable of mustering the resources or energy necessary to deal adequately with the situation.

In its approach, Sri Lanka, as is invariably the case with states facing substate challenges, initially misdiagnosed the situation and responded inappropriately. The targeted Tamil mass base, although alienated, was unwilling to reject participation in the democratic system until the state demonstrated its absolute unwillingness or inability to incorporate and protect them. Indeed, it can be argued that Colombo never, in the long history of the conflict, arrived at a correct understanding of the strategic issues or an adequate response. Still, it did produce a counterinsurgency campaign that was remarkably robust and focused for a Third World nation of, objectively speaking, limited state capacity. An important component of this campaign was the effort to neutralize the tactical use of terrorism by the insurgents.

To examine the case at hand, we shall proceed by first examining the origins (or roots) of the Tamil-Sinhalese conflict. Second, the actions of both sides played a key role in shaping the "terrorist challenge," to which, third, Colombo responded in misguided fashion. External intervention assumed a direct role (the fourth section), which allowed, fifth, the transformation of LTTE from its defensive stance to a full-spectrum threat capable of all forms of warfare. Sixth, Colombo again responded in mistaken fashion, which led to stalemate and, seventh, lessons for the counterterrorist state.

ORIGIN OF THE TAMIL-SINHALESE CONFLICT

As a democracy, Sri Lanka would have seemed theoretically positioned to address popular grievances adequately. A parliamentary system that had (and has) never known an extralegal change of power since independence in 1948; a market economy with a labor force possessing educational attainment and skills; and a bloodless, smooth transition from colonial status under Britain to independence in 1948—all seemed to point toward Colombo having what is often thought necessary (and sufficient) to address an emerging dynamic of internal conflict. Of course, there was much that lurked beneath the surface that was to result in severe conflict.

Sinhalese-Tamil communal conflict had grown progressively worse following departure of the British colonial power, but parliamentary mechanisms had remained intact. It was these mechanisms, however, controlling a highly centralized, unitary state, that assured domination of the polity by the nearly four-fifths majority of Sinhala-speaking (overwhelmingly) Buddhists in a total population of eighteen million (a figure eventually reached during the events to be considered herein). Tamils made up the largest minority—still less than a fifth (17 percent) of the population—and had achieved by the end of the colonial era a dominant position in many key sectors of life, such as the professions and education. They spoke Tamil and were overwhelmingly Hindu. As a group, they increasingly found themselves marginalized in key respects, despite the essential unity of the Tamil and Sinhalese elite. In particular, measures of affirmative action to benefit the Sinhala-speaking, nonelite majority alienated many Tamils, upon whom fell the burden of schemes such as making Buddhism and Sinhala the official state religion and language, respectively.

The rectitude of Sri Lankan government actions is not particularly relevant; they were achieved in a legal, transparent manner through both popular and parliamentary votes that achieved substantial majorities. Of importance, though, is that significant actions were taken in key areas of life (e.g., language, schooling, employment) that provoked passionate responses among all ethnic communities. These responses resulted in violence, of which Tamils were frequently victims. A spiral of escalating conflict saw the growth of Sinhalese chauvinism, a sociocultural phenomenon whereby appeals to Sinhalese Buddhist sentiments were inextricably enmeshed with promises of material and symbolic gains for the underprivileged classes—Sinhala-speaking rural masses who made up some three-quarters of the population—if the Tamils were excluded. Consequently, two major political tendencies of considerable force developed: "the drive for recognition and recompense by the Sinhalese Buddhist majority, and the egalitarian demands of the economically underprivileged strata of society."[4]

These egalitarian demands were represented principally by the non-Marxist socialism of the Sri Lanka Freedom Party (SLFP), a Sinhalese-dominated organization that during the pre-1971 time period dethroned the more market-oriented United National Party (UNP) in the elections of 1956, July 1960, and 1970. The UNP was victorious in 1947, March 1960, and 1965. Yet there was a radical Sinhalese fringe to Sri Lankan socialism, in the form of various Marxist parties. One of these, a splinter from the Communist Party (pro-Peking), or CP(P), was the Janatha Vimukthi Peramuna (JVP; People's Liberation Front), a body, committed to Maoism, that led a 1971 insurgency that was crushed only at the cost of an estimated twenty thousand lives.

Significantly, the coercive structure of the state, based as it was principally on a traditional system of values that was itself falling victim to evolving socioeconomic developments, was quite weak. At a time when the population was more than 12.5 million,[5] there were only 10,605 policemen assigned to 41 small offices and 266 police stations, of which 172 were staffed by 20 or fewer officers. Armament was inadequate and often anti-quated. The military was in a similar state: small, poorly armed and trained, and without combat experience. Authorized strength of the army was 6,578; of the navy, 1,718; and of the air force, 1,397.[6] Fiscal constraints did not allow any substantial augmentation of these numbers. Further, the elite was wary lest too strong a security establishment turn on its masters.

Hence, Sri Lanka was a state remarkably unprepared to deal with even substantial overt protest action, much less subversion and its challenges, whether terrorism or guerrilla action. What followed was a lengthy, almost painful slide into violence for a hitherto relatively peaceful society.

To press for redress of Tamil grievances, a Tamil United Front (TUF)—later adding *Liberation* to become TULF—comprising legal advocacy organizations, was formed in 1972. TULF was oriented toward autonomy, while a leftist-inspired Tamil Students Federation (TSF) called for more radical solutions, such as independence. Predictably, as TSF produced radical splinters at home, radical organizations also began to form among militant Tamil students abroad. These were significant, because they were strongly influenced by Marxism and found in its vocabulary, analytical categories, and explanatory framework a viable explanation for the Tamil situation. Their solution to their "oppression" was to call for "liberation," that is, the formation of a separate socialist or Marxist Tamil state, Tamil Eelam. Membership numbers were small. The Tamil people, whatever their plight, did not readily give their support to "coffeehouse revolutionaries."

Without a mass base, these militants could do little more than plan future terror actions. Police and intelligence documents speak of small, isolated groups of a half- dozen or so would-be liberationists meeting in forest gatherings in Sri Lanka to plot their moves. Actions that occurred, bombings and small-scale attacks on government supporters and police pickets, were irritating but dismissed as the logical consequence of radicalism.

There was method to the upstart schemes, though. By 1975, interrogations demonstrate, the Eelam Revolutionary Organization of Students (EROS), the initial overseas student group seeking Eelam, had made its first contacts with the Palestine Liberation Organization (PLO) through PLO representatives in London. Shortly thereafter, EROS began to send personnel to the Middle East for training. That the PLO was itself not Marxist did not prove a stumbling block, as the issue was framed as one of "liberation from oppression" as opposed to social revolution. Indeed, as the connection matured in the years that followed, another Marxist group (see below), the People's Liberation Organization of Thamileelam (PLOT), forged particularly strong links with George Habash's PLO Marxist splinter, the Popular Front for the Liberation of Palestine (PFLP).[7]

Simultaneously, at home, a proliferation of very small (as few as four individuals), aggressive "liberation groups" took place. Seeking to respond to growing state marginalization of Tamils, especially the requirement of Sinhala proficiency for governmental and educational attainment, alienated Tamil youth lashed out. Assassination attempts against government officials had begun as early as September 1970; bomb making triggered several accidental explosions in workshops in both 1971 and 1972. An early prominent militant, Ponnudarai Sivakumaran of the Tamil New Tigers (TNT), rather than accept capture, killed himself by swallowing cyanide on June 5, 1974, after being cornered during an attempted bank robbery. The methodology came to be the premier symbol of commitment associated with the TNT's successor organization, announced on May 5, 1976, the Liberation Tigers of Tamil Eelam. Its leader was Velupillai Prabhakaran (born November 26, 1954), who had participated personally in the TNT's major actions, including the July 27, 1975, assassination of the Jaffna mayor, Alfred Duriappah, an SLFP member.

Even as such actions escalated—carried out by no more than an estimated fifty militants[8]—the Tamil majority remained overtly committed to resolution of grievances within the parliamentary framework. Yet an escalating series of violent episodes—attacks on the police, seizures of weapons of all types from individuals and government offices, robberies of banks and individuals, thefts of chemicals from schools and explosives from "factories," and attempts to assassinate those seen as "traitors"—led to harsh police actions against alleged militant sympathizers and ultimately, in August 1977, the commitment of the army. Repression set in motion both an inexorable escalation of violence and mushrooming popular support (for "the boys," as the militants were increasingly called) driven by the imperative of self-defense. On May 19, 1978, parliament passed the Proscription of Liberation Tigers of Tamil Eelam and Other Similar Organizations,[9] followed on July 19, 1979, by the more comprehensive Prevention of Terrorism Act (PTA).[10] For all practical purposes, Sri Lanka remained under a state of emergency for the decade and a half that followed.

Such legislation had no impact on the situation. The first attack on the army occurred on October 15, 1981, by which time nine of sixteen police stations in Jaffna were reported closed. The peninsula had become the embryonic counterstate. Parliament amended the PTA on March 11, 1982, to empower the minister of justice to detain suspected terrorists for up to eighteen months without a remand order from a magistrate. By this time, the political ground had shifted substantially. Their inability to impact the situation discredited the TULF leadership, with radical elements increasingly dominant as the voice of the Tamil cause. This voice was fragmented, to be sure; even LTTE, which had the strong leadership provided by Prabhakaran, split into a number of factions that engaged in internecine warfare (particularly important was the departure of Kadirgamapillai Nallainathan, or, as he was more widely known, Uma Maheshwaran, who became the leader of PLOT). Yet all groups shared a commitment to terrorism as a method of action as opposed to a logic of action. Their violence was intended to spur mass mobilization, not as an end unto itself.

Colombo, however, could see only "terrorism," by which it meant terrorism as a logic of action—terroristic acts committed by isolated actors with at best a support base, certainly not the mass base (even if "in waiting") associated with a counterstate. The main arm for combating the threat remained the police, now grown to twelve thousand but still armed, equipped, and deployed for a traditional "watcher" role that could best be termed "presence." Though its Criminal Investigation Division (CID) had within it some highly skilled individuals, these were few and concentrated in the capital, Colombo. The force was overwhelmingly Sinhalese. Forced gradually to abandon their exposed stations, the police gave up what security presence they had, allowing the militants to dominate further the population and to expand the counterstate. Committing the military, the only remaining card left for the state to play, had not done much to rectify the situation, because the military did not have the capabilities for antimilitant action necessary to stop the terror campaign. Indeed, the army's total ground strength was effectively contained in five infantry battalions of five hundred to six hundred men each. The air force and navy were small and not structured as combat forces. The capability for intelligence gathering and surgical application of force was all but lacking.

At this early stage, the militants were still vulnerable and hopelessly divided by issues of ideology and approach. Prabhakaran, for instance, was thoroughly Guevarist, seeing armed action ("guerrilla action") as the key to popular mobilization.[11] Increasingly, the sheer ruthlessness of his will came to dominate the Tamil struggle. Rival groups, as we shall see below, were methodically, systematically wiped out. When Prabhakaran and his fellows could be numbered but in scores, there was an opening for the state. CID had considerable knowledge of the threat but no means to act in an appropriate manner. Response had to be left to the police—who increasingly were unable to defend themselves, much less arrest suspects—or the military, which proved a very blunt instrument indeed. This left action to individual initiative, of which there was a surprising amount, but when casualties began to claim these men or they were marginalized by political concerns, there simply was no second string.

Events, in any case, had taken on a life of their own. On July 15, 1983, Charles Anton, LTTE "military wing" commander, was killed in a firefight with Sri Lankan military personnel in Jaffna. In retaliation, on July 23, again in Jaffna, an ambush executed by an LTTE element left thirteen soldiers dead. Their subsequent funeral in Colombo ignited widespread rioting and looting directed against Tamils. At least 400 persons were killed and 100,000 left homeless; another 200,000–250,000 fled to India. Police stood by, and in many cases members of the armed forces participated in the violence.

This spasm of communal terror served to traumatize the Tamil community and provided LTTE with an influx of new manpower. Thus the ascendancy of radical leadership in the struggle for Tamil Eelam was complete. Even TULF expressed no confidence in the government's efforts to resolve communal difficulties. Only the radical option remained. That option, to be clear, was Marxist-Leninist, as stated directly by the leadership of all the major groups fighting for Tamil Eelam.

NATURE OF THE "TERRORIST" CHALLENGE

Although there may at one point have been as many as forty-two different groups active, they were dominated by just five: LTTE; PLOT, also frequently rendered as PLOTE in the Western press; the Tamil Eelam Liberation Organization (TELO); the Eelam People's Revolutionary Liberation Front (EPRLF); and EROS.[12] A product of Sri Lankan internal contradictions, the groups nevertheless existed within the larger strategic realities of the cold war. Sri Lanka was, at least under the UNP administration so central to events described here, a Western-oriented democracy with a market economy. In contrast, neighboring India was closely linked to the Soviet Union, a democracy with a statist economic approach and a geostrategic view that called for absolute domination of its smaller South Asian neighbors.[13]

Apparently to gain information on developments concerning the Sri Lankan port of Trincomalee, which New Delhi feared was coveted by the West as a base, Indian prime minister Indira Gandhi agreed to a plan by the Research and Analysis Wing (RAW), India's equivalent of the CIA, to establish links with a number of then-small Tamil insurgent organizations.[14] As early as 1982, recorded interrogations demonstrate, RAW became involved in a program of training Tamil terrorists to report on ship movements and Western port calls at Trincomalee. India was not interested in the ideology of those who received its training. PLOT and TELO, both self-professed Marxist entities, were the initial recipients of its largess. Marxism further came to dominate the struggle for Tamil Eelam in the aftermath of the July 1983 riots, when the militant groups—as the only organized Tamil self-defense capacity—assumed the role of protectors of the Tamil community. As manpower flocked to join the struggle, non-Marxist groups were largely absorbed by the avowed Marxists, through either persuasion or coercion.[15] An extensive clandestine counterstate was formed within Sri Lanka, incorporating not only Jaffna but areas in the entire north and east, supported by an extensive network of bases in Tamil Nadu, the fifty-five-million-strong, Tamil-dominated Indian state directly across the narrow Palk Strait from Sri Lanka.

The degree to which counterstate formation was a substantive undertaking depended on the group (e.g., PLOT, being more sophisticated in its Marxism than, say, LTTE, was more systematic in its efforts than not only LTTE but also the other Eelam groups); the area (e.g., Jaffna was more secure for insurgents due to popular support from the overwhelmingly Tamil population, so LTTE, which dominated there, had from early on a significant apparatus and took only minimal steps to conceal it); and the government response (e.g., it was more difficult for the Eelam groups to attempt counterstate construction in the east, where there was strong government presence, than in the north, which was at the end of government reach). In the new post-1983 circumstances, then, what RAW had seen as convenient patrols, useful for the collection of information, mushroomed into small armies. In this, they were further aided by enhanced Indian support. This stemmed from New Delhi's need to respond to domestic pressure to resist Colombo's alleged genocide against the Sri Lankan Tamils—a situation that saw even factions of the Tamil Nadu state government begin to assist the insurgents. Consequently, India expanded the minimal RAW effort and also brought into the fold the other insurgent groups not already under its tutelage, most notably LTTE.[16]

RAW was assisted by other Indian intelligence agencies, such as the National Intelligence Bureau (NIB), and paramilitary forces with the ability to provide training in unconventional warfare, such as the Indo-Tibetan Force (ITBF). Indian officials, at the time, stated privately that their intent was to give the Tamil community a "self-defense capability."[17] It was all too predictable, though, that such an effort, once set in motion, would rapidly escalate beyond India's control. While insurgent manpower did indeed increase rapidly after the trauma of July 1983 and comprised those who fit the classic "grievance guerrilla" profile, the leadership of the Eelam movement came from the original pre–July 1983 Marxist groups. Key figures of all major formations remained those individuals whose designs were much larger than mere self-defense. They were after "liberation" in its Marxist-Leninist sense.[18] Attempts to discern whether groups were "really Marxist," an exercise favored by the Indian High Commission in Colombo during the term of J. N. Dixit, were pointless.[19] The insurgents considered themselves Marxist and drew from Marxist models all that was central to their effort: their strategic analysis of the situation, including vocabulary and analytical categories; their operational approach to waging revolutionary warfare; and their tactics for construction, defense, and expansion of the counterstate.

To ensure that the "grievance guerrillas"—those joining as a result of the repression of the system, real or perceived—shared their analysis of the situation and their aims, the leadership in this period allocated large portions of the daily training schedule to ideological indoctrination.[20] In such sessions, as well as in their public and private pronouncements, the rebels spoke of their fight for Tamil Eelam as involving two struggles. As put by Anton S. Balasingham, number two in the LTTE hierarchy and leading theoretician for the movement, "The political objective of our movement is to advance the national struggle along with the class struggle, or rather, our fundamental objective is national emancipation and socialist transformation of our social formation."[21] Insurgent leaders, then, particularly those of LTTE, which gradually emerged as the leading Eelam organization through brutal use of terror—directed as much at its Tamil rivals as against the Sinhalese security forces—were not interested in adhering to an Indian strategy intended to force Colombo to settle its ethnic dispute, preferably by instituting a framework that recognized Tamil autonomy. They were interested in "liberation."

Predictably, it was difficult to come up with meaningful strength figures for the insurgent groups. It has already been noted that the guerrillas were unable to increase their numbers substantially until after the July 1983 riots radicalized large sectors of the Tamil community, especially the youth, and provided abundant, motivated manpower. In fact, Sri Lankan military intelligence sources noted that in 1975 they carried the number of hard-core insurgents as twenty-five; in July 1983, two hundred "terrorists" were carried on the police order of battle. One year after July 1983, this figure had mushroomed to five thousand and was subsequently put as high as ten thousand, although many counted in the latter figure were not armed. The significance of the number, whether five thousand or ten thousand, lay in the fact that until Sri Lanka could mobilize its manpower pool, the combined insurgents matched, if not exceeded, the strength of the army. Thus they stood a chance—if properly armed, trained, and coordinated—of putting the security forces on the ropes. That they were unable to do so owed far more to their own internal problems than it did to government capacity.

Until the formation of the Eelam National Liberation Front (ENLF) in April 1985, the insurgents engaged in little cooperation and coordination. PLOT remained outside the ENLF group, its representatives and those of LTTE having again, in March, engaged in gunplay to argue their points. Personal differences, as opposed to matters of substance, seemed much at the heart of the matter. All the major groups remained Marxist-Leninist (more on this choice of terminology below), with a vague conception of "people's war" as their model for "making revolution." Likewise, they were all firmly committed to Tamil Eelam in the belief that "liberation" could come only through both an independent Tamil state and the use of Marxist ideology to transform the relations of production. "Our total strategy," noted A. S. Balasingham of LTTE, "integrates both nationalism and socialism into a revolutionary project aimed at liberating our people both from national oppression and from the exploitation of man by man."[22]

Organizationally, insurgent groups utilized the standard Leninist constructs, with politburos, central committees, and the like, but they did not always establish a party element separate from the guerrilla forces themselves. This was particularly true of LTTE, headed by Velupillai Prabhakaran. Despite the prominent role accorded to Balasingham—he was nominally the group's second figure—LTTE remained the organization least committed to a conception of itself as a Marxist insurgency. It was more colored in its approach by its ethnic roots, more oriented toward what it saw as the essence of the struggle, the effort to drive the Sinhalese (blinded though they might be by bourgeois leadership) from the "traditional Tamil homelands." It was not particularly concerned, Balasingham's pronouncements notwithstanding, with the purported overall niche the fight occupied in the global struggle for liberation of the oppressed.[23] The crucial element, LTTE believed, before all others, was to carry the fight to the enemy through combat operations, thereby liberating Tamil Eelam from "Sinhalese fascism." Ideological development and organizational particulars of the future Marxist state would follow.

Tactically, this difference resulted in LTTE (taking ENLF along) being the most active of the insurgent groups in actual fighting. Even when truces were declared during efforts at negotiation, LTTE continued its attacks. It maintained a constant campaign of terror, predictably directed against all Sinhalese targets, including civilians, but also against fellow Tamils. Frequent was the killing, often after torture, of those denounced as informants, traitors, or backsliders. Victims were left tied to or hanging from lampposts, spawning the common use of the terms "lamppost killings" and "lamppost victims" to describe such episodes. These increased in frequency as the conflict advanced, as did bombings and related efforts to inflict damage on human targets and the physical infrastructure, such as the rail system. Far from any attempt to avoid casualties, there was an effort to maximize those affected. This was terrorism, but it remained dedicated to consolidation and expansion of the counterstate, to terrorism as a method of action as opposed to as a logic of action.

PLOT and the other groups (such as those within ENLF) also used terror—and internal purges were a staple of all groups—but PLOT's killings were far more selective and designed to attack the "enemy within." There was an effort to avoid actions that would likely result in reprisals against Tamil civilians, and Sinhalese civilians normally were not indiscriminately attacked.

STATE RESPONSE TO TAMIL INSURGENCY

While an insurgency is normally more dangerous to a government than rebellion or "pure terrorism," the immediate problems for the authorities are much the same: coping with the violent attacks of an armed uprising. By early 1984, therefore, the Sri Lankan military, which previously had been focused on the violent acts of a limited number of actors, which it labeled simply "terrorism," found itself faced with a mass-based uprising and hence the need to engage in counterinsurgency. This it was not in a position to do.

Counterinsurgency first and foremost requires a political response to an armed political campaign, the insurgency. Strategically, the security forces serve as the "shield" behind which the "solution"—the addressing of grievances—is put into effect. Security of the population is the first requirement and necessitates securing of both persons and property, as well as separation of militants from loyal citizens. Insurgent leadership figures invariably are the element pushing ideological solutions (however defined) to grievances; manpower is just as invariably motivated by more pragmatic issues. Operationally, then, the counterinsurgent requirement is for the successive domination of local space (i.e., local areas), within which legitimate government writ is restored. Local action, particularly self-governance linked to microdevelopment initiatives, drives a wedge between the insurgent leadership and followers. Tactics revolve around, on the one hand, fostering democratic capacity and, on the other, engaging in population and resources control. Insurgent armed formations are neutralized through a variety of violent and nonviolent means. All of this action, regardless of level, is dependent on the production of intelligence from an inflow of information from the affected populations and areas.

Evident from the foregoing discussion is just what a conundrum presented itself to the Sri Lankan security forces, for there were no tangible steps taken—although they were considered—to address the fundamental grievances that had produced militancy in the first place. Unable to be the "shield" for the implementation of a "solution," the military, and to a lesser extent the police, was left to carry out the operational effort to successively dominate areas. Tactically, this process had to be carried out against a ruthless foe whose members were quite willing to die for the cause and committed to the use of terrorism as a major weapon. A fundamental strategic requirement, though, regardless of the rectitude of the approach driving the effort to dominate local space, was manpower. This had to be generated. The defense establishment had grown as a result of the 1971 JVP insurgency, but it remained one befitting the island's small size: a fourteen-thousand-man army (twelve thousand regulars and two thousand reserves, or "volunteers," on active duty); a thirty-five-hundred-man air force flying a motley collection of small, fixed-wing aircraft and helicopters; a navy of thirty-five hundred men that crewed thirty-two small craft; and a police force of still roughly twelve thousand assigned to small stations throughout the country. Personnel in all services were poorly trained. Units did not operate as such; the only reservoir of combat experience lay in those older personnel who had participated in the suppression of the 1971 insurgency.

Army combat power originally was centered in a mere five infantry battalions, all of which were under their designated 730-man strength and stationed in company-size cantonments throughout the country.[24] Each line battalion was theoretically the first of three in a regiment, with the other two battalions comprising reservists. In reality, only one regiment had its two "volunteer" battalions. None of the reserve component units were on active duty; all were understrength and armed with outdated weapons. Single armor, artillery, signal, and combat engineer regiments were also understrength battalions. At one time, approximately a third of the "volunteer" personnel were on active duty as individuals to make up for manpower shortages in regular units. Communal disturbances had already stretched the available units so tightly that air force and navy men regularly performed as foot soldiers. Air support was minimal; the navy was a small coastal flotilla.

These, then, were the forces that were called upon to grapple with the complexities of internal war on an island the size of Ireland (or West Virginia, if looking at a U.S. state). They were small, lightly armed and equipped, and minimally trained. Prior to July 1983, when the insurgent movement had not yet taken on new life, a few units were posted to affected areas of the north. They kept occupied running in convoy up and down the main roads. Casualties were few on either side. Still, there were excesses, especially in the first half of 1983, as the tension mounted and the insurgents became more active in their efforts to mount terror and guerrilla attacks. The government was forced to move vigorously to punish abuses, disbanding an entire battalion due to indiscipline.[25] This left just four infantry battalions on the eve of what was to quickly become a war.

After July 1983, the army, deployed in the north in reinforced battalion strength (roughly four companies), found itself subjected to a series of bloody episodes. Even as terrorism was used as a method, a tactic, to dominate the population, guerrilla action, complemented by widespread use of land mines, produced a steady stream of casualties. The security forces rarely saw their assailants. Unable to close with their opponents, the troops reacted in predictable fashion—they all too often gunned down civilians whom they deemed to be implicated. Although the government was probably truthful when it denied that retaliation was official policy, there was a definite callousness toward the population whose "hearts and minds" it purportedly sought to win.

This was hardly surprising. Less than 5 percent of the soldiers were Tamil, less than 3 percent of the officers. Government forces, therefore, saw themselves as cast adrift in a sea of "hostiles," whose language they could not speak and whose customs they did not share—and who, they were convinced, knew precisely where mines were buried and ambushes planned. Such was a dangerously simplistic view, for the average Tamil wanted only to be left alone by all concerned. Yet as the Sinhalese host began to retaliate for its own losses, often burning whole villages (and in one instance in Mannar District gunning down nearly a hundred individuals after a particularly costly ambush), the Tamil masses turned sullenly to the only salvation they saw, the insurgents. Whatever death and destruction was inflicted by the insurgents against declared enemies and spies within their own Tamil community paled next to government depredations. Ironically, most Tamils were neither supporters of Eelam nor "communists," about whose ideology they knew little to nothing.

By the end of 1984, insurgent activity had grown to the point that the counterstate threatened government control of Tamil-majority areas in northern Sri Lanka. The security forces had increased in size and quality of weaponry, but a national concept of operations was lacking. There was serious doubt, in fact, whether some elements of the armed forces in the north, if pressed closely by an insurgent onslaught, would be able to make an orderly withdrawal. Reports forwarded to higher authorities were routinely falsified to put the best possible face on the situation.

The extent to which insurgent capabilities had developed was amply demonstrated in a well-coordinated and -executed attack on November 20, 1984, when a Tamil force of company size used overwhelming firepower and explosives to demolish the Chavakachcheri police station on the Jaffna Peninsula, killing at least twenty-seven policemen defending it. There followed more ambushes of security forces, as well as several large massacres of Sinhalese civilians living in areas deemed by the insurgents to be "traditional Tamil homelands." Use of automatic weapons, mortars, and RPG-7 rocket launchers was reported. All remaining police stations in Jaffna were closed.

Even as these developments took place, it became clear to the authorities that a drastic upgrading of security force capabilities was needed, a task that was accomplished in remarkably short order. Limited involvement of outside powers was initially in stark contrast to the rush to assist that had followed the 1971 JVP outbreak. Rather, Sri Lanka managed largely on its own or by contracting for services. Most significantly, a new police field unit, Special Task Force (STF), was raised under the tutelage of ex-SAS (British Special Air Services) personnel employed by KMS Ltd. STF took over primary responsibility for security in the Eastern Province in late 1984, freeing the army to concentrate on areas of the Northern Province (which included Jaffna). Impeccably trained in the mechanics of counterterrorism and small-unit actions, it had little impact on the situation.[26]

In similar fashion, the government approached Israel on the basis of its demonstrated expertise in counterterrorist operations. In the face of much criticism and amid fears that the lucrative Middle Eastern market for Sri Lankan expatriate labor might be jeopardized, Colombo allowed the establishment of an Israeli Special Interests Section in May 1984, with the United States as the protecting power. Small teams (normally two personnel) from Israel's internal security service, Shin Bet, shortly thereafter arrived to train Sri Lankan personnel in intelligence gathering and internal security techniques. These, as was the case with STF, were largely mechanical solutions to the specific mundane tasks associated with counterterrorism, such as proper search techniques, use of body armor, and neutralization of improvised explosive devices (IEDs). There was no thrust to fit these tactics and technical advances into comprehensive campaigns or strategy. Indeed, the relationship with Israel was not nearly as smooth as was the training itself, particularly given the political complications not only in Sri Lanka's foreign affairs but also in its relations with its large Muslim community. For its part, Israel was essentially looking for a route to renew diplomatic relations, which had been suspended during the Bandaranaike administration (1970–77) and had no desire to become entangled in Sri Lanka's internal fighting. In the end, the value of its counterterrorism advice was of marginal impact, because it addressed terrorism as if it was the logic of action rather than the method it was. Improvements in minor tactics, in other words, could have no appreciable impact in making up for operational and strategic deficiency.

Who said what and to whom may never be known, but there was a basic similarity between the unsuccessful Israeli approach to "counterterrorist" pacification of the occupied Arab territories and that practiced in the early stage of the fighting in Sri Lanka. The "population-as-enemy" philosophy, harsh reprisals, and emphasis on the military to maintain order rather than to function as a shield behind which a political solution could be put in place all were common components of the Israeli and Sri Lankan strategies. So too were the results identical. With their counterstate in Jaffna consolidated, the Sri Lankan insurgents moved in force into areas of the east, which they also claimed as part of Eelam, despite a majority of the population there being non-Tamil. Additionally, they began to operate in Sinhalese-majority areas, attacking the population in acts of terror designed to produce flight from claimed areas of the counterstate.

With its forces deployed in "hot" areas—and having violated the tenet to secure first its own base areas before moving out to engage the enemy—the state was unprepared to meet this new threat. Efforts to increase force strengths further and to purchase new equipment (e.g., a dozen Bell 212 helicopters) did little to improve the serious shortcomings of the security apparatus. Although local forces, comprising minimally armed Sinhalese civilians, were hastily formed, starting in early April 1985, Sri Lanka entered a period of intense violence that culminated on May 14 with an LTTE terror attack on pilgrims in Anuradhapura that left some 180 civilians dead.[27] By mid-1985, then, when a round of peace talks began (see below), the island was in a state of serious disorder, which the security forces proved unable to alleviate.

Most fundamentally, the government was crippled by its inability to set forth a viable political solution within which stability operations could proceed. Military success, therefore, even when gained, was little more than momentary tactical advantage. Regardless of efforts to improve the military posture, there could hence be little impact on the overall poor security climate. Efforts undertaken against terror attacks existed in a strategic vacuum.

Organizationally, there was progress. In the months after July 1983, there was the expected chaos of gearing up for internal conflict. In March 1984, though, it appeared a more ordered approach was at hand. Oxford-educated Lalith Athulathmudalai, a possible successor to President Jayewardene, was named head of a newly created Ministry of National Security, as well as deputy defense minister (Jayewardene himself was defense minister). This effectively placed control of the armed services and counterinsurgency operations under one man. Intraservice coordination improved under a Joint Operations Centre (JOC), as did military discipline and force disposition. Still, it soon became evident that the government effort would continue to be plagued by inefficient planning, unimaginative leadership, and continuing instances of indiscipline.

In the absence of a well-defined socioeconomic-political approach to the problem—a strategy that would cut popular support out from under the Eelam leadership by reversing the process of marginalization—the government's counterinsurgency program rapidly became little more than an attempted exercise in human and organizational engineering. Although the ability of the insurgents to conduct terror attacks in Sinhalese areas was gradually attenuated through a variety of tactical means, such as numerous roadblocks and searches, the same success was not achieved in the major areas of conflict, where the resident Tamil community either offered its allegiance to the insurgents or was cowed into meek obedience. Such a state of affairs, given that the insurgents had been able to gain momentum through decades of state blunders, necessarily meant a protracted struggle. To go on was nevertheless the only viable option open to Colombo. As a democracy, it certainly had the ability to reverse course. Whether it had the capacity remained (and remains) a subject of some debate.

Factions within the government, as well as key military officers, were aware of the critical strategic shortfall in state response to the insurgency (the term was used in internal discussions, although the combatants officially remained "terrorists") but seemed unable to influence policy decisions. It was as though paralysis had set in at every level of Sri Lankan decision making, beginning with President Jayewardene. The most commonly offered explanation for the lack of movement toward a political solution, fear of a Sinhalese backlash, while not a straw man by any means, eventually became a self-fulfilling prophecy and an excuse for inaction. It perversely reinforced what was perhaps the most salient cause of inaction: factionalism within the ruling party. Just as the UNP and SLFP had each played "the ethnic card" against the other to gain electoral advantage, so it was feared within the UNP that positions of significant controversy would open the door for rivals to make their move.

Thus, as the insurgent threat spilled out of Jaffna, the government met it with ad hoc, haphazard schemes. Both privately and publicly, Colombo's spokespersons talked not of the need to solve the various dimensions of the ethnic problem but of their "fight against terrorism." This position was of fundamental import. Focused on armed response to terrorism, counterinsurgency, although waged in name, was not carried out in fact. Colombo ordered its military leaders to go after the guerrillas and to stamp out the violence. There was little movement toward political accommodation that would have isolated the insurgent hard core, the leadership, from the followers. While the security forces were battling the insurgent combatants, essentially no effort was put into the critical task of cutting them off from their mass support. As the insurgents mobilized the target population into their counterstate, the government could not engage in countermobilization because it had no theme or plan about which such action could be based. Instead, it was reduced to overseeing an aggregation of tactical counter-guerrilla and technical counterterrorist moves.

NEW DELHI AND THE EXTERNAL FACTOR

Changes in the Indian political landscape provided some alternatives. The assassination of Indian prime minister Indira Gandhi in October 1984—at the hands of Sikh bodyguards caught up in the backlash that followed New Delhi's Operation Bluestar against terrorists based in Sikhdom's holiest shrine, the Golden Temple of Amritsar—brought to power her surviving son, Rajiv. He promptly carried out a sea change in policy. Lengthy discussions were held with Sri Lankan policymakers to arrive at an approach to the "Tamil problem" acceptable to both Colombo and New Delhi. The insurgents were informed that India would not accept an independent

Tamil state at its back door; Indian covert assistance was scaled back;[28] arms shipments were seized; naval patrols began to stop guerrilla boats attempting to cross the Palk Strait; and the most active insurgent base camps in India were closed down. On June 18, 1985, it was announced that Colombo and the insurgents, bowing to pressure from New Delhi, had agreed to a "cessation of hostilities" and their first face-to-face discussions in an effort to frame a political solution to the conflict.

Five months of desultory talks in Thimphu, the capital of Bhutan, and a truce that never really took hold, led to little of substance. That such would be the result seemed never in doubt to informed observers, for the insurgent leadership was adamant that Eelam was their only acceptable goal, and Colombo was just as adamant that the territorial integrity of the island be preserved. Buttressing its position was the demographic reality that at no time, then or later, did a majority of the Tamil population live in the areas claimed by Eelam. Rather, more than half of all Tamils continued to reside in Sinhalese-dominated areas. Restoring to them their democratic rights, then, as promised under the Sri Lankan legal framework prior to its perversion by ill-considered, chauvinistic measures, was the only way forward. But this could not have been accomplished by talks.

Regardless, Rajiv Gandhi found himself forced to seek political cover. Although New Delhi had upped its profile and finally become a direct participant in the discussions, it was unable to influence the outcome. It paid a high domestic price for its troubles. An upsurge of Dravidian nationalism led to protests in Tamil Nadu and challenges to "Hindi authority." When President Jayewardene told the influential *India Today* in November 1985 that he saw no option to "decisive military action," Gandhi decided to cut his losses. While continuing to express his desire for a diplomatic solution and to send representatives to Colombo for talks, the Indian leader apparently turned the actual handling of the situation back to the same subordinates who had been active throughout the conflict. They proceeded to harangue Colombo at every turn on the need to negotiate with the insurgents, even while supporting them clandestinely.

Policy results were the same: strained relations with Colombo and greater Sri Lankan determination to avail itself of all possible sources of aid. Israel, for instance, even began to fit Sri Lankan security force amputees with artificial limbs. When New Delhi learned of Colombo's use of foreign pilots for training and administrative flights, it warned against external involvement in the conflict. From Colombo's perspective, a more disingenuous position would have been hard to imagine. Violence was again widespread by December 1985.[29] There was considerable irony that insurgent gains occurred even as the divisions within the Eelam movement and the Tamil community itself became more apparent. LTTE turned on its ENLF partners in April and May 1986, all but wiping out TELO, but the government was unable to turn such occurrences to its advantage.

Despite its overwhelming parliamentary majority, the ruling UNP was keenly aware that its dominant position was largely due to electoral mechanics (i.e., winner-take-all voting districts) rather than actual popular dominance. Faced with a situation where a strong opposition was working actively to tap ubiquitous Sinhalese fears and passions, the UNP opted for a path of short-term political expediency and seeming safety. It sought to wear down the insurgents militarily while placing its faith in Indian pressure on them—to be exerted sometime in the future, when, it was assumed, New Delhi would realize the self-destructive folly of backing insurgents based on its own unstable soil. While possible in the short term, such a strategy had little likelihood of long-term success, for it guaranteed that the conflict would remain open-ended, a posture Colombo found difficult to sustain, economically or politically.

Economically, for instance, the 1986 budget contained an estimated deficit of Rs.26,986 million (US$983.1 million) against expenditures of Rs.67,800 million (US$2.47 billion). The Ministry of Defense alone was slated to spend 70 percent over its budgeted amount. These massive outlays, which were beyond the capacity of the economy (built on tea, tourism, and textiles) to endure for long, were heavily dependent on foreign grants and loans. Politically, though, an effective international insurgent propaganda apparatus had so implanted the image of the struggle as one for communal justice, with no ideological component, that Sri Lanka found itself diplomatically on the defensive. Colombo became increasingly isolated from possible sources of material and diplomatic assistance. Major friendly powers, such as the United States and Britain, declined to become more committed to a situation that could only result in a worsening of their already strained relations with India. Neither had they or other nations shown any willingness to move against the expatriate funding that had become the major source of insurgent finances. The result was that Sri Lanka had to proceed alone.

Sources differ on the level of insurgent funding, but the process rapidly grew from reliance on donations from friendly sectors within Tamil Nadu (including state political figures), as well as participation in the drug trade, to use of the substantial Tamil diasporic community (overwhelmingly engaged in "commerce") as the central pillar in the funding profile. Donations were gained both willingly and through extortion (anemic police capabilities within the Tamil communities in the United States, United Kingdom, and Canada ensured that these three sources consistently dominated income generation). Figures in excess of $20 million were regularly cited and seemed entirely plausible, given evidence in terms of weapons and materials purchases. Tamil financing and purchasing mechanisms eventually became very sophisticated, making use of a wide array of techniques, from high- (e.g., Internet) to low-end technology (e.g., couriers).[30]

Nevertheless, states possess inherent capabilities for human and fiscal mobilization that if used properly can provide the wherewithal to wage war. Sri Lanka did just that. Even as the capabilities of the Sri Lankan military occasioned negative comment—and the situation seemed bleak—the security forces generated a credible capacity to coerce.[31] Although it did not put together the necessary campaign plan for ending the insurgency, Colombo did come up with an approach for the *military* domination of insurgent-affected areas. Pacification of areas in the east and near-north, driven by the defeat of guerrilla formations and the creation of a less permissive environment for terror actions (principally through constant roadblocks, cordons, and searches), left only Jaffna as an insurgent counterstate stronghold as 1987 began. The green light for an all-out assault came when a rash of insurgent outrages, including bombings in Colombo and the massacre of Buddhist monks in the east, occurred in April 1987. President Jayewardene responded by ordering the Liberation I offensive in May.

By this time, murderous fighting within the Eelam movement had left LTTE as further dominant. This was significant because, as indicated earlier, LTTE was more militarily oriented than its rivals, increasingly drawing inspiration from a variety of sources in an ever-escalating trajectory of suicide actions.[32] For some years before the Indian invasion, LTTE combatants had worn cyanide capsules around their necks and refused to be taken prisoner.[33] As their position on the Jaffna Peninsula collapsed, the Tigers became even more fanatical, turning to suicide attacks. A "land torpedo," driven by "Miller" (or "Millah," as rendered by Schalk), was used in a suicidal action on July 5, 1997, to demolish the main Jaffna telecommunications center. Its atomized driver joined the growing pantheon of LTTE "martyrs," who were celebrated in regular ceremonies and services—and whose sacrifices even gave shape to the LTTE calendar.[34]

Such tactics, however, could not hold off security force consolidation of its grip on all save Jaffna City. On the verge of launching Liberation II to seize that final Tamil stronghold, where the insurgents had concentrated for a last stand, the Sri Lankans found themselves stymied by India. New Delhi, responding to domestic pressure and making a geostrategic virtue out of its internal dilemma in Tamil Nadu, entered the conflict directly as an Indian Peacekeeping Force (IPKF). Sri Lankan forces returned to barracks, and India assumed directly responsibility for overseeing implementation of a to-be-agreed-on cessation of hostilities. The insurgent groups were pressured to return, cease their armed campaigns, hand over their weapons, and work out a compromise with the state.[35]

Groups other than LTTE proved more prepared to adjust to what one insurgent leader called "the realities of our situation." They structurally reflected the Marxist form of political movements that commanded armed forces. Shelving military plans—complete with turning in their "less useful" weapons—did not rob their liberation campaigns of vitality. They merely prepared to emphasize political organizing. LTTE, in contrast, had increasingly moved away from ideology and saw armed action as the essential component of its campaign. Its efforts to circumvent the agreements resulted in an Indian military assault commencing on October 10, 1987. Conflict quickly became general, with Indian forces endeavoring, as foreigners, to duplicate in the north and east the counterinsurgency campaign previously conducted by the Sri Lankans.[36]

The Indian presence, while having some tactical advantages, was strategically disastrous because it not only reinforced the nationalist aspects of the Eelam appeal among the Tamil mass base but also provoked a Sinhalese nationalist reaction that was tapped by the dormant JVP. The causes that threw up the JVP manpower were the same as those that had produced the 1971 explosion. The new conditions only provided the spark. As the Indians attempted to deal with the Tamil insurgents, the Sri Lankans were forced to move troops south to deal with Sinhalese Maoist insurgents. The failure of the government to resist Indian intervention had prompted widespread rioting in Sinhala-speaking areas and had given the JVP a second lease on life. Exploding nationalist passions resulted in an attempted assassination on August 18, 1987, of President Jayewardene (a later move was made against Rajiv Gandhi, as well, when he arrived in Colombo for discussions). By using terror to murder prominent examples of those who did not comply with their demands, the JVP insurgents gained authority far beyond their numbers. The nation's industrial sector, for instance, thoroughly cowed by a spate of well-selected assassinations, was functioning at a mere 20 percent capacity. Such economic paralysis, in turn, fed the JVP cause. Sri Lanka staggered.[37]

TRANSFORMATION OF LTTE TO FULL-SPECTRUM THREAT

What followed was significant. A change in leadership, with Ranasinghe Premadasa replacing the retiring Junius R. Jayewardene, brought a government approach that again turned the tide. Crucial to this was the employment of the very techniques that had gradually come to be standard in dealing with the Tamil insurgency. Particularly salient was the command-and-control structure that had evolved, because it would continue to be used as the framework for response islandwide, even following the end of the second JVP insurgency.[38] A prerequisite for everything was the continuing evolution of the military, especially the army. Having become a more effective, more powerful organization, it now deployed to areas where, among other things, its members spoke the language of the inhabitants and had an excellent intelligence apparatus. Superimposed on the tactical organization of the army was the counterinsurgency structure itself. Administratively, Sri Lanka's nine provinces were already divided into districts, twenty-two in all, each headed by a government agent (GA), who saw to it that services and programs were carried out. To deal with the insurgency, the GAs were paired with coordinating officers (COs), whose responsibility it became to handle the security effort in the district. Often, to simplify the chain of command, the CO would be the commander of the battalion in the district. The brigade commanders, in turn, acted as chief coordinating officers (CCO) for their provinces[39] and reported to area commanders. Areas 1 and 2 divided the Sinhalese heartland into southern and northern sectors, respectively; Area 3 was the Tamil-populated zone under IPKF control.

Used historically with considerable effect by any number of security forces, particularly the British, this system had the advantage of setting in place security personnel whose mission was to win back their areas. They could be assigned assets, military and civil, as circumstances dictated. Coordinating officers controlled all security forces deployed in their districts; they were to work closely with the GAs to develop plans for the protection of normal civilian administrative and area development functions. For this work, they were aided by a permanent staff whose job it was to know the area intimately. In particular, intelligence assets remained assigned to "coord" headquarters and guided the employment of operational personnel. They did not constantly rotate as combat units came and went. The framework culminated in the JOC. This, though, never really hit its stride as a coordinating body. Instead, manned by senior service officers, it usurped actual command functions to such an extent that it became the military. The service headquarters, in particular army headquarters, were reduced to little more than administrative centers. Attempts to rectify the shortcomings resulted only in a JOC that functioned as a weak supreme command, with the service chiefs rotating as head at three-month intervals. This clumsy arrangement eventually fell by the wayside, too, as operational requirements became more pressing. But the essential confusion of roles remained.

Although often lacking precise guidance from above, local military authorities nonetheless fashioned increasingly effective responses to the JVP insurgency. In contrast to continued unrest in Colombo itself, the rural areas, although unsettled, were gradually brought under control. This was possible because the coordinating officers and operational commanders, older and wiser after their tours in the Tamil areas, proved more than capable of planning their own local campaigns. The Achilles' heel of their efforts, of course, was that in the absence of strategic coordination and operational guidance, each commander had to constantly reinvent the wheel and deal with tactical problems, the ultimate cause of which was beyond his control. He could only ameliorate their local impact. The danger inherent in such a posture was that it could not go on forever.

Intense pressure for local solutions combined with the strains engendered by limited resources and an intense operations tempo to bring about a terrible end to the JVP problem. Put simply, although the process was not systemic, some individuals and units dispensed with the tedious business of addressing grievances, targeted response, and legal process. Those suspected of subversion were simply eliminated. In the process, old and new scores on both sides were settled, although alleged JVP sympathizers certainly accounted for the bulk of the victims. The dead apparently figured at the level of the previous JVP upheaval and included key members of the JVP leadership.[40] In ending the second JVP insurgency, however, the security forces were able to turn their attention again to the Tamil insurgency.

All had not gone well for the IPKF. Grown to eighty thousand men (more than forty infantry battalions), it had proved incapable of dealing with the LTTE challenge. Further, Indian use of non-LTTE Eelam groups as a "Tamil National Army" (TNA) compromised them as quislings, thereby contributing further to LTTE dominance. Tactical errors of force employment ensured that the IPKF would be ineffective in combating LTTE guerrilla and terror tactics. Consequently, by the time of IPKF withdrawal, in January–March 1990, almost three years and several thousand IPKF casualties later, LTTE was more firmly established than it had been upon Indian arrival.[41] This situation was compounded by further LTTE entrenchment during a subsequent Colombo-LTTE negotiation period, which the Tigers used to decimate the forces of the TNA. When LTTE abrogated the talks, renewed hostilities left the security forces facing mobile warfare, with LTTE forces attacking in massed units, often of multiple-battalion strength, supported by a variety of heavy weapons. Deaths numbered in the thousands, reaching a peak in July–August 1991 in a series of set-piece battles around Jaffna. The twenty-five days of fighting at Elephant Pass, a land bridge that connected the Jaffna Peninsula with the rest of Sri Lanka, saw the first insurgent use of armor.

Elsewhere, terror bombings and assassinations became routine. What had seemed a move of desperation, the use of suicide bombers, became instead an LTTE weapon of choice.[42] The Black Tigers, a special unit formed to carry out such attacks (even as regular units pledged not to be taken alive), were joined by a Black Sea Tigers formation directed at naval targets. Women, who already had their own combatant units, joined men in service in the suicide groups. There followed—in a campaign that continued for the remainder of the open conflict—an unrelenting assault on the very glue that held Sri Lanka together. No target was immune, from masses of civilians to political and military figures to troop positions and formations to naval and merchant ships to the holiest of religious shrines (the Temple of the Tooth in Kandy was suicide-bombed in January 1998) to the capital, Colombo, itself. Even national leaders such as Rajiv Gandhi of India[43] and President Ranasinghe Premadasa fell to LTTE bomb attacks (on May 21, 1991, and May 1, 1993, respectively), as did numerous other important figures, such as Lalith Athulathmudalai and members of the JOC upper echelons.[44] Precise numbers—of attacks, attackers, and even victims—remain subject to considerable uncertainty.[45] Of no doubt, though, was the impact on Sri Lanka: again it reeled. Heavy fighting in Jaffna in early 1994, as the security forces attempted to tighten their grip around Jaffna City, resulted in government casualties approaching those suffered by LTTE in the Elephant Pass action. The conflict had been reduced to a tropical replay of the World War I trenches.

Only with the election of a coalition headed by the opposition SLFP in August 1994, followed by the November presidential victory of SLFP leader Chandrika Bandaranaike Kumaratunga, was politics again introduced into the debate on state response to insurgent challenge. The SLFP sweep ended seventeen years of UNP power and led to a three-month cease-fire, during which Colombo sought to frame a solution acceptable to both sides. The effort came to an abrupt halt when LTTE again unilaterally ended the talks by making a surprise attack on government forces. Significantly, the wave of assaults highlighted the military side of the conflict. LTTE techniques included the use of underwater assets to destroy navy ships, as well as the introduction of SA-7 surface-to-air missiles into the conflict. The former involved divers planting underwater demolitions; the latter, the use of the SAMs to down air force transports and later at least one helicopter gunship. Armor and artillery were already in use by both sides. What had begun as a campaign of terror tactics—assassinations, bank robberies, and bombings—had grown to main-force warfare augmented by terror and guerrilla action. LTTE had become a powerful, full-spectrum threat.

INCORRECT STATE RESPONSE TO NEW INSURGENT THREAT

Much more had changed, as well. With the end of the cold war, LTTE quietly dropped all talk of Marxism, although it continued to portray itself as socialist. New Delhi, although still closely linked to Moscow, had seen its patron collapse and cautiously reached out to establish more normal relations with the United States and other supporters of Colombo. There was no objection raised when the United States agreed, in mid-1994, to begin a series of direct training missions conducted by U.S. special forces elements.[46]

New circumstances, in particular a new administration, dictated a review of approach. In mid-1995, therefore, the government held a series of meetings designed to settle on a revised national strategy for ending the conflict.[47] The meetings, of which there were at least three primary sessions, did not go well. A plan for devolution that came close, in all but name, to abandoning the unitary state in favor of a federal system was articulated. Still, while all official bodies basically agreed that LTTE would have to be defeated militarily in order to implement the political solution, there was considerable disagreement on the plan of operations.

On the one side were those who saw no option but to end the LTTE hold on Jaffna, the Tigers' main counterstate area, by direct, conventional assault. The principal advocate of this approach was Anuraddha Ratwatte, a presidential relative and, effectively, minister of defense.[48] He was joined by a body of military officers who felt the effort had to be made. Opposed was an equally distinguished and senior body of officers, both active and retired, who demurred. They cited the considerable success that had been achieved by the systematic domination of areas using force as the security shield behind which restoration of government writ took place. This approach, they argued, while much slower, would be considerably less costly in lives and financial resources and would play to Sri Lanka's strengths, especially the by then well-developed framework for counterinsurgency outlined above. Financial aspects were especially important, because by 1995 interest payments to service government debt were themselves 29.9 percent of current expenditures, with a figure close to 48 percent if amortization and interest payments were considered as a combined figure of true debt cost. High-intensity operations, regardless of purely military considerations, were bound to worsen this financial situation.

So intense became the debate that some critics were sidelined. Army commander Lieutenant General Gerry de Silva, a Sandhurst graduate, found himself very much in the middle. His important contribution after assuming command on January 1, 1994, had been to rationalize the command-and-control structure of a force grown to seventy-six infantry battalions alone (drawn from three sources—active, reserve, and national guard). With even his own staff divided on the merits of a Jaffna assault, he was torn between demands from above that he lead the charge and from below that he back another course of action. The arguments of those sidelined were important, given later developments. They advocated continuing, systematic domination of local areas while taking the battle directly to the insurgents using raids, especially by special operations forces. These were the tactics that had been used successfully in JVP II. The principal weapon for raids was to be a Reserve Strike Force that had been formed in July 1994 as an integral part of refining the command structure. Under it fell the four battalions of what had been the Special Forces Brigade,[49] as well as six infantry battalions, mechanized and airmobile, and three armor battalions. It was a potent, mobile force that could respond in virtually any fashion to a threat anywhere in the country. Rather than being used in the manner intended, however, the force became the spearhead for the approach that came out of the strategy meetings: a conventional response to an unconventional problem.

As a first step, a multidivisional assault on the heavily fortified Jaffna area was ordered. This was carried out successfully. But with no overland link to government positions thus established, the forces in Jaffna became a bridge too far, a classic case of strategic overreach, with LTTE enjoying interior lines. Fiscal overreach was also an issue, as the Jaffna offensive alone was estimated to cost US$500 million to US$750 million in new arms and equipment, as well as operational funding. Intense fighting developed as the Sri Lankan military endeavored to secure its lines of supply and communication from south to north. LTTE adroitly used a combination of main-force and guerrilla units, together with special operations, to isolate exposed government units and then overrun them. These included headquarters elements, with even brigade and division headquarters being battered. In the rear area, LTTE used a suicide truck bomb to decimate the financial heart of Colombo in February 1996, killing at least ninety-one and wounding more than fourteen hundred. Much worse was to come, though, as overextension of forces and an inability to handle the complexities of main-force, conventional operations left the Sri Lankan military badly deployed. A debacle was not long in coming, and on July 17, 1996, an estimated three to four thousand LTTE combatants, using techniques worked out in the 1991 Elephant Pass attack, isolated and then overwhelmed an understrength brigade camp at Mullaitivu in the northeast, inflicting at least 1,520 deaths on the security forces. This exceeded the total death toll for 1994, which had been 1,454,[50] and shattered army morale. Desertion, already a problem, rapidly escalated.[51] There followed stalemate.

LTTE, having only to exist as a rump counterstate that mobilized its young for combat, had demonstrated the ability to construct mechanisms for human and fiscal resource generation that defied the coercive capacity of the state. Estimates in mid-1995 put some 85 percent of the Tamil population living under government control.[52] Yet both recruiting and coercing the young served to fill LTTE ranks. Women made up a growing percentage of combatants, as did the young and the very young.[53] Reports began to surface of children being groomed in isolation for suicide duty.[54] To obtain resources necessary for continuing the conflict, linkages were extended abroad, from whence virtually all funding came (as already discussed), and diasporic commercial ties allowed the obtaining of necessary weapons, ammunition, and supplies.[55] Although the security forces could hold key positions and even dominate much of the east, they simply could not advance on the well-prepared and fortified LTTE positions in the north and northeast, which in any case were guarded by a veritable carpet of mines.

Political disillusionment again followed, increasing as LTTE continued to pull off spectacular terror actions that sapped morale: the commercial heart of Colombo was bombed again on October 15, 1997, with 118 dead and a minimum of 40 wounded. The most sacred Buddhist shrine in the country, the Temple of the Tooth in Kandy (as noted earlier), was attacked by suicide bomb in 1998. Kumaratunga herself narrowly missed following Premadasa as a presidential victim, surviving a 1999 LTTE bomb attack but losing an eye. The Elephant Pass camp that had previously held out against such odds fell in 2000; and in July 2001, a sapper attack on the international airport in Colombo left eleven aircraft destroyed. It was not altogether surprising that in the December 2001 parliamentary elections, the UNP, led by Ranil Wickremasinghe, returned to power.

This left the political landscape badly fractured between the majority UNP and its leader (the prime minister), and the SLFP's Kumaratunga, still the powerful president in Sri Lanka's hybrid system (similar to that of France). That the two figures were longtime rivals, with considerable personal animosity, did not ease the situation. Again, it was changes in the international arena that dealt a wild card. The 9/11 terrorist attacks in the United States and the resulting "global war on terrorism" caused Western countries finally to move to cut off LTTE fund-raising activities on their soil. This was a critical move, because the sheer international scope and global sophistication of LTTE's fund-raising and supply mechanisms had grown beyond the ability of the Sri Lankan state to counter them unilaterally. How, for instance, to prevent the generation of millions of dollars in "donations" in the United States, the United Kingdom, and Canada, the three main sources of cash? How to prevent the buying of arms on the international black market? As it happened, the three countries just named did move, and a heightened awareness of the danger posed to international order by unregulated action such as that carried out by LTTE led to heightened difficulties. Although it is not known if the change was the decisive factor, in February 2002 LTTE suddenly offered the new UNP government negotiations. The government accepted the offer, and an uneasy truce, which has held to the present, commenced.[56]

Talks to arrive at a political settlement were brokered by Norway, but the cessation of hostilities was a very mixed bag. LTTE used the restrictions on Sri Lankan security forces to move aggressively with terror actions into Tamil areas hitherto denied to the group, and rival Tamil politicians were ruthlessly intimidated and assassinated. Throughout Tamil-populated areas, Tamil-language psychological operations continued to denounce the government and the Sri Lankan state, particularly its forces. Internationally, sources of income were adjusted, concealed, and made more difficult to disrupt in the event hostilities needed to be renewed.

LTTE intransigence led the UNP government to flirt with ideas that came close to dismembering the island, even if only de facto rather than de jure. Its major concern was to resurrect the economy, for which a peaceful resolution of the conflict was essential, and even the decades-old emergency provisions were allowed to lapse. Kumaratunga watched uneasily and then moved, in early November 2003, while Wickremasinghe was in Washington meeting with U.S. president George W. Bush. Claiming that the UNP approach was threatening "the sovereignty of the state of Sri Lanka, its territorial integrity, and the security of the nation," she dismissed the three UNP cabinet ministers most closely associated with the talks, dismissed parliament, and ordered the army into Colombo's streets. LTTE watched, but in the April 2004 parliamentary elections, held as a consequence of talks between the dueling Sinhalese parties, the SLFP unexpectedly swept back into power at the head of a United People's Freedom Alliance (UPFA) that included the JVP, still clinging to life and earlier allowed back into the legal mainstream in return for giving up its calls for revolution. Hence the Tigers withdrew from negotiations but did not renew active hostilities.

There was no need to: the "cease-fire" served as the ideal cover for the elimination of all the group saw as standing in its way. This included even the Sri Lankan foreign minister, Lakshman Kadirgamar, an ethnic Tamil;[57] Sarath Ambepitiya, the judge who had sentenced Prabhakaran to two hundred years in jail in absentia for the 1996 bombing of Colombo;[58] and literally hundreds of Tamil politicians and activists (including the misidentified) opposed to LTTE.[59] The latter remained committed to Eelam, whatever the verbiage connected with the peace process, and behaved accordingly.[60] Unable or unwilling to fight back, Colombo dithered as its citizens were murdered, singly and in small numbers. There matters remained as this volume went to press.

LESSONS FOR THE COUNTERTERRORIST STATE

Having arrived at yet another point of apparent stalemate, Sri Lanka would hardly appear a promising case for lessons to be passed on. Still, the sheer complexity of the case presented here and the astonishing level of violence— the lowest figure now used for lives lost during the Tamil insurgency is some sixty-five thousand, which I would hazard is a serious undercount (and to which, of course, must be added as many as forty thousand lost in the two JVP insurgencies)—should serve to highlight the relative success of Colombo in meeting the challenge and continuing on as a viable political and economic entity. Lessons, then, which present themselves include the following.

First, the rule of law is an essential framework within which response must proceed. Whatever the harsh edges of the counterinsurgent campaign, incorporating necessarily a subcampaign to neutralize terrorism as a method of action, the state did not find it necessary to suspend or destroy its democratic system. The rule of law continued, in all its imperfect particulars, and fierce debate raged throughout the contest as to both means and ends that ought to be used and pursued. Certainly the provisions contained in legislation directed against "terrorism" became more stringent, and a legally declared "emergency" remained in force continuously once July 1983 occurred; but the state did not seek to pervert its forms such that it became a police state or a dictatorship. Changes in the forms used (e.g., from a pure parliamentary system to a mixed parliamentary-presidential system) derived largely from the interparty competitive dynamic as opposed to the exigencies of internal war.

Second, a correct strategic approach is the first and foremost requirement of the state in responding to insurgent/terrorist challenge. Although the system remained intact, mistakes of strategic approach and operational implementation were made, beginning with the persistent failure to assess the insurgency in realistic terms appropriate to framing a correct response. Most important, terrorism as a method of action, as one tool among many available to the insurgents, was confused with terrorism as a logic of action, as "pure terrorism," divorced from a grievance-produced mass base. In this, Colombo's experience foreshadows what we often see happening in the "global war on terrorism" (GWOT)—that is, the focus on the symptoms rather than the causes of violence and the misinterpretation of that violence once it has appeared.

What could have arrested the process, of course, was addressing the grievances of the insurgent mass base early on. Although insurgent leaders and followers were spurred by the same injustice, they responded in dissimilar fashion. Leaders sought structural change, revolution, as the route to liberation; followers looked for redress of immediate issues.[61] Had the state early on driven a wedge between the two, what became a profound threat to the security of the state would likely have remained a law-and-order problem. Indeed, it was the very scale of state abuses that galvanized both the Indian and the diasporic Tamil communities to open their hearts and their wallets to the insurgent groups. Even as these latter transformed, becoming ever more violent and divorced from any sense of compromise, their identity as avenging angels remained as a powerful motivating force for alienated Tamils abroad. These could thus lash out vicariously in redress of their own grievances and frustrations.

To focus on the tactical acts of terror, then, was precisely the wrong approach by the state. Certainly repression was a necessary element of response, but the security forces should have been the instrument only for the accomplishment of the political solution. This fact was realized by any number of actors within the conflict, but they were rarely in the right spot at the right time and hence were unable to alter the course once set.

Third, states, even those with limited capacity, can respond to an insurgent/terrorist challenge. It is noteworthy that Sri Lanka, a Third World state with very limited capacity and resources, was able to put together a response that came within a whisker of delivering a knockout punch. Learning and adaptation were constant features of an approach that, even if unbalanced, tilted toward repression as opposed to accommodation and nevertheless proved capable of dealing with not only the complex Tamil insurgent threat—which, to reiterate, incorporated a terrorist subcampaign of staggering proportions—but also two rounds of Sinhalese Maoist upheaval that incorporated a similar level of terrorism. Although any number of criticisms may be leveled at Sri Lanka's imperfect command-and-control arrangements, together with flawed coordination and force deployment, these should not blind us to the reality that Colombo had sought out models, chosen correctly if not wisely, and endeavored to implement its selections. The counterinsurgency structure and procedures used, which emphasized unity of command and long-term presence in affected areas, with security actions designed to neutralize the use of terror, did prove capable of dealing with the situation—but the test was not completed.

It is impossible to say definitively what would have happened in July 1987 had Colombo been allowed to land its hammer blow. One school of thought would hold that in the absence of systemic reform, another round of Tamil insurgency would have arisen, even if the current crop of radical leadership had been eliminated. Another school, though, would point to evidence that populations savaged in the course of a struggle tend to be inoculated against repeat infections. The two rounds of JVP insurgency would seem to support the former, but other cases from abroad—such as the aversion to renewed action that the resurrected Communist Party of the Philippines (CPP) found in former centers of Huk Rebellion recruitment—support the latter.[62]

Fourth, context can be decisive. International forces made moot the issue above, whether the state could have "won." World historical timing obviously matters a great deal in any such situation. The role of India was driven not only by its geostrategic prerogatives but also by its position within the cold war equation. Although Indian sources tend to emphasize New Delhi's need to respond to the domestic forces unleashed by Tamil suppression, evidence supports the conclusion that equal weight was given to perceptions of foreign threat facilitated by purported Sri Lankan fecklessness. That New Delhi had based its actions on a flawed analysis of the situation was cold comfort for Colombo, because it was the three-year IPKF interlude that allowed LTTE not only to recover from its desperate situation in July 1987 but also to move to the mobile-warfare stage of insurgency. Fielding main-force units in conjunction with guerrilla and terror actions, the insurgents emerged in 1990 as a truly formidable force.

So the experience, driven as it was by resistance against foreign occupa-tion, had taken on the characteristics associated with all manner of "wars of national liberation." In these, the goal is invariably to inflict so much death and destruction on the enemy that he decides the campaign is not worth the price being paid. It was entirely logical, then, that no actions were off-limits to LTTE in its quest to inflict pain. Terrorism, although remaining a method of action, emerged ever more prominent as a weapon. LTTE engaged in everything from massacres of Sinhalese communities to bombing cities and temples to executions of prisoners to attempts to use poison gas. Faced with such a foe, the state often responded in kind. It is significant, though, that instances of indiscipline declined dramatically among the security forces as the struggle wore on. From an initial position of feeling terrorized by the security forces, and especially their inability to protect innocent civilians from communal reprisals, the Tamils settled back into Sri Lankan society. Nothing illustrated this more than the con-tinued presence of a majority of the Tamil population within "Sinhalese-controlled territory."

LTTE, which began as an indigenous phenomenon, was quick to recog-nize the inherent advantages to international linkages. From an early flirta-tion with funds generation through participation in the European drug trade to training with the PLO, however, the Tigers moved on to consoli-date a global network capable of generating whatever funds and arms/equipment were necessary to continue the struggle. Until the GWOT altered the international environment, this network proved invulnerable to Sri Lankan action.

Fifth, military force cannot win the campaign, but it can lose it. Little appreciated in any such struggle is an elemental fact: if the security forces will not crack, challengers for state power, whatever damage they may inflict, cannot succeed. Sri Lanka had its fill of problems with desertions and indiscipline, but it also had signal success in using the British regimen-tal model to build and field new units of relative cohesion and effective-ness. Particular efforts were made to maintain morale through a variety of rewards and incentives.

On the other side, the insurgents did the same. Most frightening about LTTE success should be what it tells us about the ability of a radical, institutionally totalitarian movement to recruit, socialize, and deploy manpower so rigidly indoctrinated that combatants prefer death by cyanide or self-destruction to capture. Having gained control of certain areas early on, LTTE was able to recruit manpower at extraordinarily young ages and then guide them in ways such that entire units comprised young boys and girls who had never known alternative modes of existence. In the world created by LTTE leadership, Sinhalese were demons, and a world beyond the insurgent camps did not exist. Even sex lives—especially sex lives—were rigidly controlled by draconian penalties. Combatants knew only their world and each other—and behaved accordingly when unleashed on targets. As relative moderates passed from the leadership scene, those who knew other worlds vanished, their places taken by a hard core who had risen in the movement. They generally spoke no language save Tamil and had limited life experiences. Brutality was simply a weapons system. The ability of the insurgents to keep their manpower isolated was thus an important factor in maintaining control and movement cohesion. The simple lack of alternatives, real or imagined, kept LTTE combatants from defecting.

What was extraordinary was that young people did flee such an environment, balking when faced with instructions to end their own lives, but this did not occur in numbers sufficient enough to make a difference. Although a pronounced decline in the average age of LTTE combatants was noticed as the conflict wore on, at no time did manpower shortages influence insurgent strategy or operations. On the contrary, human wave assaults continued to be the essential tactic of engagements throughout the conflict. Still, the very existence of defectors was evidence that a repentance campaign pushed forward by information warfare is a necessary element in any counterinsurgency.

To what, then, is owed LTTE participation in the present cease-fire? It may be a simple matter of tactics. Prabhakaran has demonstrated a shrewd capacity for combining violent and nonviolent action, armed strikes with information warfare, and local with international action. He may well have simply decided to open up space for a repair of his fund-raising apparatus damaged by the post-9/11 moves against it, or he may have sensed that a Sri Lanka in some disarray as to its own course was ripe for an appeal to a "political solution." The two are not mutually exclusive, and the cease-fire has certainly given LTTE all that it had been unable to acquire through its campaign of political violence: well-nigh complete control over the Tamil population in the area delimited as Eelam. In this sense, it has played its cards shrewdly and is unlikely to resume violence unless the situation changes dramatically. It has no need to: it has used the hunger for normalcy to make the state complicit in meeting its own ends. Nothing could better illustrate the essence of terror as politics by other means.

Sixth, intelligence remains key. Our discussion emphasizes a point made throughout this chapter: the need for extensive information that can produce the basis for action. It is not only tactical, actionable intelligence that is necessary but the knowledge required to formulate strategy and plan campaigns. Sri Lanka developed a reasonably detailed picture of its insurgent foes during the course of its conflicts. This accomplishment allowed it to sustain the fight even in the face of severe reverses. That the state was caught short by LTTE's once again playing the "negotiations card," as it had time and again, only goes to show that there can never be too much knowledge.

This is as true when combating terror as it is with any other form of political violence. Terrorism as a *method of action*, used by LTTE, is not terrorism as a *logic of action*. The two require appropriate responses from the state. Sri Lanka consistently confused them and thus focused on armed repression to the near-exclusion of a comprehensive approach of which repression was but one element. Considerable success was achieved virtually in spite of the approach. More astute assessment and strategy could have resulted in a more viable campaign, with external factors kept in check by finesse in internal application of violence. Hence, when all is said and done, we find ourselves confronted with the often-cited but ever-profound dictum from Clausewitz: "The first, the supreme, the most far-reaching act of judgment that the statesman and commander have to make is to establish . . . the kind of war on which they are embarking; neither mistaking it for, nor trying to turn it into, something that is alien to its nature. This is the first of all strategic questions and the most comprehensive."[63]

NOTES

1. The precise terminology here is that of Michel Wieviorka, "Terrorism in the Context of Academic Research" in *Terrorism in Context,* ed. Martha Crenshaw (University Park: Pennsylvania State University Press, 1995), 597–

606; see also Wieviorka's benchmark *The Making of Terrorism,* trans. David Gordon White (Chicago: University of Chicago Press, 1993).

2. This insightful definition was coined by Larry Cable. See his "Reinventing the Round Wheel: Insurgency, Counter-insurgency, and Peacekeeping Post Cold War," *Small Wars and Insurgencies* 4, no. 2 (Autumn 1993): 228–62.

3. Referred to more commonly by the term "clandestine infrastructure," the concept of the counterstate apparently entered into the literature of internal war in the 1960s. See, for example, Luis Mercier Vega, *Guerrillas in Latin America: The Technique of the Counter-state* (New York: Praeger, 1969). More recently, the concept has been used by Arthur Mitchell, *Revolutionary Government in Ireland: Dail Eireann 1919–22* (Dublin: Gill and Macmillan, 1995), as well as by Gordon McCormick in unpublished work.

4. Robert N. Kearney and Janice Jiggins, "The Ceylon Insurrection of 1971," *Journal of Commonwealth and Comparative Politics* 13, no. 1 (March 1975): 49.

5. The exact figure, as measured in the October 1971 census, was put at 12,747,755.

6. Kearney and Jiggins, "Ceylon Insurrection of 1971," 41.

7. Data summarized in "Terrorist Groups Fighting for Tamil Eelam (Top Secret)" (working document of Intelligence Wing, Counter-terrorism Branch, National Intelligence Bureau [NIB], Colombo, undated but mid-1985). See also M. R. Narayan Swamy, *Tigers of Lanka: From Boys to Guerrillas,* 3rd ed. (Delhi: Konark, 2002), especially 97–101.

8. The premier reference for the formative years of the Tamil insurgency remains Swamy, *Tigers of Lanka.*

9. The government claimed that by July 11, 1979, fourteen policemen had been killed by LTTE and other groups.

10. Text may be accessed at: www.peacebrigades.org/lanka/slppta1979.html.

11. As related by Swamy: "Prabhakaran was furious when the academic [Aton Stanislaus Balasingham, a Marxist academician who eventually became LTTE's second-ranking figure] argued that it was important to politicize people before taking to the gun. 'What people, people, you talk about?' he burst out. 'We have to do some actions first. People will follow us.' When the academic persisted, Prabhakaran commented with undisguised contempt, 'You [armchair] intellectuals are afraid of blood. No struggle will take place without killings. What do you want me to do? You people live in comfort and try to prove me wrong. So what should I do? Take cyanide and die?" See Swamy, *Tigers of Lanka,* 69.

12. The number of groups changed constantly; lists contained in Intelligence Wing files (see note 7) fluctuated. Further discussion, including of personalities, may be found in Thomas A. Marks, *Maoist Insurgency since Vietnam* (London: Frank Cass, 1996), chapter 4.

13. For a recent discussion that places this policy in perspective, see Christian Wagner, "From Hard Power to Soft Power? Ideas, Interaction, Institutions, and Images in India's South Asia Policy," Working Paper no. 26 (Heidelberg: South Asia Institute; Department of Political Science, March 2005). Also useful for its astute assessments of the changing geostrategic environment is C. Raja Mohan, "Beyond India's Monroe Doctrine," *Hindu,* January 2, 2005, Opinion-1.

14. What follows continues to be denied officially by India but has been fairly well documented. Swamy, *Tigers of Lanka* deals with the subject in his chapter 5, "Tamils Get Training." See also the entire volume by Rohan Gunaratna, *Indian Intervention in Sri Lanka: The Role of India's Intelligence Agencies,* 2nd ed. (Colombo: South Asian Network on Conflict Research, 1994). For my own contributions, based on my fieldwork at the time, see Thomas A. Marks, "India Is the Key to Peace in Sri Lanka," *Asian Wall Street Journal,* September 19–20, 1986, 8 (reproduced under the same title in *Island* [Colombo], October 5, 1986, 8; abridged under the same title in *Asian Wall Street Journal Weekly,* September 22, 1986, 25); and Thomas A. Marks, "Peace in Sri Lanka," *Daily News* (Colombo), published in three parts in July 1987: part 1, "India Acts in Its Own Interests," July 6, p. 6; part 2, "Bengali Solution: India Trained Personnel for Invasion of Sri Lanka," July 7, p. 8; and part 3, "India's Political Solution Narrow and Impossible," July 8, p. 6. This same three-part series was published under the same titles in *Sri Lanka News* (July 15, pp. 6–7) and in *Island* as "India's Covert Involvements" (June 28, pp. 8, 10).

15. Even LTTE, although Prabhakaran himself initially held ideology as of little value, required that its recruits undergo political training. "Desmond," for instance, a militant captured in March 1985, spoke of 1981 training at a base in Tamil Nadu that included lessons by three different instructors on "the various wars of the world," on "communism," and "about politics." A fourth instructor taught "firearms." See the NIB file, "Interrogation of Terrorist Suspect Soosaiha Rathnarajah @ 'Desmond,'" SF Headquarters, Vavuniya, April 2, 1985 (Secret). NIB/INT/89.

16. Tamil nationalist sentiments were viewed as especially dangerous, because they had remained a problem in the Indian south ever since the peak of anti-Hindi sentiments in 1964–65. Tamil Nadu's existence as a state was itself a result of the Dravida Munnetra Kazhagham (DMK)-led campaign for a separate Tamil entity. When he took office, Rajiv Gandhi found that the presence in Tamil Nadu of the Sri Lankan insurgents had revived anti-Hindi sentiments and latent Tamil chauvinism. The DMK, which has become the state assembly opposition to the ruling Anna DMK (AIADMK), an offshoot of the old movement, was waging a vigorous campaign to arouse such sentiments and to derive political advantage from them. An excellent consideration of these developments is Manoj Joshi, "On the Razor's Edge: The Liberation Tigers of Tamil Eelam," *Studies in Conflict and Terrorism* 19 (1996): especially 19–42.

17. New Delhi at this point had seen its preferred option, to intervene directly, foreclosed when, in early 1984, its plans for invasion had led to British and U.S. representations strongly warning against such action. Some published sources place Indian preparations at a later date, but my own research finds air and sea assets massed by May 1984 and training of a separate force of "Tamil insurgents," Indian-controlled assets who were to lead the assault in a Bangladesh-like scenario, well under way. At this point, Indian activities had caused a near rupture in relations with Sri Lanka. Details are contained in the works cited above, note 14.

18. Fieldwork, southern India, summer 1984. I discuss this point in greater detail in Thomas A. Marks, "Marxist Tamils Won't Stop at Separatism," *Asian Wall Street Journal,* May 8, 1986, 6 (reprinted as "Tamil Rebels Aim beyond Autonomy," *Asian Wall Street Journal Weekly,* May 26, 1986, 12); Thomas A. Marks, "The Ethnic Roots of Sri Lanka's Ideological Struggle," *Asian Wall Street Journal,* August 12, 1987, 8 (abridged version under the same title in *Asian Wall Street Journal Weekly,* August 31, 1987, 12); and Thomas A. Marks, "Book Review—Stanley Tambiah, *Sri Lanka: Ethnic Fratricide and the Dismantling of Democracy*," *Issues and Studies* 23, no. 9 (September 1987): 135–40. More recently, I have dealt with the subject explicitly in Thomas A. Marks, "Ideology of Insurgency: New Ethnic Focus or Old Cold War Distortions?" *Small Wars and Insurgencies* 15, no. 1 (Spring 2004): 106–27.

19. Dixit's most recent assessment of the Tamil case is contained in J. N. Dixit, ed., *External Affairs: Cross-border Relations* (New Delhi: Roli, 2003), in the chapter "Sri Lanka" (pages 47–96). It is necessary reading, both for its astute analysis as to many matters, as well as its fundamental inaccuracies concerning alleged foreign plots (especially U.S.) to use Sri Lanka as a base from which to threaten India. Revealing is his claim to "definite information" (i.e., intelligence) concerning U.S. motives and actions even as he outlines in detail the shortcomings of the source of those assessments, Indian intelligence agencies, in their efforts concerning Sri Lanka.

20. A nineteen-year-old LTTE guerrilla, following his capture in August 1986, offered the following brief description of such sessions: "The leaders always spoke about Marxism. They wanted a Marxist *Eelam*. That was their main idea." An older, higher-ranking captive, in another discussion, observed, "We were hoping to establish a Tamil socialist state in the north and east."

Fieldwork, Sri Lanka, summer 1986 (both discussions conducted using translators).

21. A. S. Balasingham, *Liberation Tigers and Tamil Eelam Freedom Struggle* (Madras: Political Committee, LTTE, 1983), 42. Consideration of Tamil insurgent ideology has been neglected. Even as fine a work as A. Jeyaratnam Wilson, *Sri Lankan Tamil Nationalism: Its Origin and Development in the 19th and 20th Centuries* (Vancouver: University of British Columbia Press, 2000), has precisely one entry in the index under "Marxist ideology" (page 128; it deals in passing with the Marxism of the EPRLF). Yet in my own fieldwork, when I talked with Tamil insurgent leadership figures, Marxism was the analytical framework within which all analysis took place.

22. Balasingham, *Liberation Tigers,* 42.

23. The precise position of Marxism within LTTE has in many respects been driven by the personal relationship between undisputed LTTE leader Prabhakaran and the decade-older, penultimate figure Balasingham, a relationship sources have variously characterized as son/father or pupil/teacher. That Balasingham has been and remains a committed Marxist is beyond dispute; that Prabhakaran continues to find ideology tedious but perhaps useful up to a point, as long as it is secondary to combat, seems to be a position that evolved over time. In the early years of the movement, as indicated above in note 20, LTTE combatants were required to undergo instruction in Marxism as part of the daily training schedule, but this practice apparently lapsed as the military elements of the struggle became more salient. In my discussions with LTTE combatants and prisoners (who became scarce once suicide became the movement-facilitated alternative to capture), I found not a single insurgent who knew the first thing about Marxism, although they could relate the physical particulars of indoctrination sessions. This was in stark contrast to, for instance, at least some PLOT combatants (and all of the leadership figures).

24. Weaponry was likewise woefully inadequate. There was no single infantry rifle. Even the venerable 1941 .303 Lee-Enfield was in use in some units. Heavier backup was a mix of British, Chinese, Soviet, and Yugoslav arms. For details, see Thomas A. Marks, "'People's War' in Sri Lanka: Insurgency and Counter-insurgency," *Issues and Studies* 22, no. 8 (August 1986): 63–100.

25. In this episode, members of the First Battalion, Rajarata Rifles Regiment, were disciplined after taking retaliatory actions against civilians. In protest against the measures, nearly a hundred other soldiers went on strike and deserted. The entire battalion was consequently disbanded; the deserters, once rounded up, were cashiered, as were key members of the chain of command. The remaining unit members were combined with another understrength regular battalion to form the first unit of an entirely new regiment.

26. Details of STF in Thomas A. Marks, "Sri Lanka's Special Force: Professionalism in a Dirty War," *Soldier of Fortune* 13, no. 7 (July 1988): 32–39.

27. In this attack, a busload of LTTE guerrillas, disguised as soldiers, penetrated Anuradhapura, the site of Sri Lanka's capital from the fourth century BC to the tenth century AD, and opened fire indiscriminately on Buddhist pilgrims paying homage to one of the country's most sacred shrines, the Sri Maha Bodhi, a *bo* tree revered for having been grown from a sapling of the tree under which Buddha attained enlightenment. After first attacking the bus station, the insurgents assaulted worshippers at the shrine itself. All too predictably, in a consequence apparently anticipated by the assailants, attacks on Tamil civilians, at the hands of enraged Sinhalese mobs, followed. Copies of the LTTE report sent to Prabhakaran, both its rough and final drafts, were captured by Sri Lankan security forces. They are chilling in their description of the clinical planning and execution of massacre. Refer to Striking Unit of Victor [LTTE Mannar commander], "Report on the Attack on Sinhalese at Anuradhapura," June 8, 1985, NIB translation (secret).

28. This had grown to substantial proportions and included training a surrogate invasion force (i.e., a force of ostensibly independent Tamils who would provide the political cover for direct Indian intervention). For details, see references in note 14.

29. Details in Thomas A. Marks, "Counter-insurgency in Sri Lanka," *Soldier of Fortune* 12, no. 2 (February 1987): 38–47.

30. Although written a considerable time after the events under discussion, the best single sources are Anthony Davis, "Tamil Tiger International," *Jane's Intelligence Review* (October 1996), 469–73; and Daniel Byman and others, *Trends in Outside Support for Insurgent Movements* (Santa Monica, CA: RAND, 2001).

31. The phrase is again from Cable, *Reinventing the Round Wheel.*

32. I am not aware of any scholarly work that explicitly addresses the origins of all facets of LTTE suicide tactics. Even the introduction of suicide capsules (see discussion in text) is a source of conflicting accounts by LTTE figures from whom one would expect "firsthand" accounts. Most useful, however, are the contributions of Peter Schalk, particularly "The Revival of Martyr Cults among Havar, *Temenos* 33 (1997): 151–90, www.tamilnation.org/ideology/schalk01.htm; and "Resistance and Martyrdom in the Process of State Formation of Tamil Eelam," excerpt from Joyce Pettigrew, ed., *Martyrdom and Political Resistance: Essays From Asia and Europe* (Amsterdam: Centre for Asian Studies; VU University Press, 1997), www.tamilnation.org/ideology/schalkthiyagam.htm. These highlight the salience of Tamil and South Asian elements in the continuing evolution of what Schalk terms "a political movement with religious aspirations." See Schalk, "Revival of Martyr Cults."

33. Schalk, in the illuminating discussion "Resistance and Martyrdom," observes that the May 1984 initiation of cyanide capsules (the glass vials were from Germany, the actual poison from India) took place only after other methods of suicide had been tried but eliminated as unsatisfactory.

34. Full discussion of the cult of martyrs is beyond the scope of this work. Schalk offers the greatest insights. To both of the Schalk works cited above can be added a short but revealing release by the Peace Secretariat of Liberation Tigers of Tamil Eelam, "Remembrance of Martyrs Permeate [*sic*] Nooks and Corners of Tamil Eelam," November 25, 2005, www.ltteps.org/print.ltte?view= 993&folder=2. The date of Miller's death—Day of the Black Tigers—has become one of the two leading commemorative days on the new LTTE calendar. Miller is touted as the first of what would become a growing force in the struggle, the Black Tigers, explicitly committed to suicide attacks (discussion follows in text). The other key LTTE date, November 27—Day of the Great Heroes—is celebrated as Tamil Eelam National Day and honors all those who have died for the cause (i.e., martyrs). That LTTE presently functions as a cult would seem sociologically evident. That it unwittingly seeks to become a religion, as Schalk perceptively notes, would also seem clear.

35. For context, refer to Shankar Bhaduri and Afsir Karim, *The Sri Lankan Crisis* (Delhi: Lancer International, 1990). This work is particularly good for highlighting the difficult situation to which the Indian military found itself hastily committed. My own details of the situation on the ground, including initial Indian casualties, may be found at "Sri Lankan Minefield: Gandhi's Troops Fail to Keep the Peace," *Soldier of Fortune* 13, no. 3 (March 1988): 36–45.

36. Certainly the most poignant aspect of these events was the final delegation that visited the Indian battalion commander with whom LTTE had had daily intercourse, Lieutenant Colonel T. P. S. "Tipi" Brar, headquartered in the Jaffna Fort, to tell him that they understood he was only doing his duty in carrying out orders to attack. Brar, in another of the many ironies of the conflict, was the younger brother of Major General (later Lieutenant General) K. S. Brar, who had commanded Operation Bluestar, the assault on the holiest Sikh shrine, the Golden Temple of Amritsar, then being used as headquarters by Sikh terrorists. India staunchly defended the attack, which provoked widespread upheaval within the Sikh community, even while condemning Sri Lanka's own moves against those legally judged to be terrorists.

37. See C. A. Chandraprema, *Sri Lanka: The Years of Terror—the J.V.P. Insurrection, 1987–1989* (Colombo: Lake House Bookshop, 1991); and my own details in Thomas A. Marks, "In Sri Lanka, Despair Explodes into

Violence," *Asian Wall Street Journal*, August 16, 1989, 6 (abridged version: "Sri Lanka's Despair Breeds Violence," *Asian Wall Street Journal Weekly*, August 21, 1989, 15).

38. For details of "JVP II," see Rohan Gunaratna, *Sri Lanka: A Lost Revolution? The Inside Story of the JVP* (Colombo: Institute of Fundamental Studies, 1990); my own observations in Thomas A. Marks, "Professionals in Paradise: Sri Lanka's Army Gears Up for 'Tiger Hunt,'" *Soldier of Fortune* 15, no. 1 (January 1990): 48–55; and Thomas A. Marks, "Chaos in Colombo: Sri Lanka's Army Awaits Its Marching Orders While Politicians Dither," *Soldier of Fortune* 15, no. 2 (February 1990): 48–55.

39. Only as the conflict progressed did the army place its battalions under permanent, numbered brigades—although these remained continually changing in composition—and its brigades under divisions. In theory, there was a brigade for each of Sri Lanka's nine provinces. These were grouped under three division headquarters, only two of which were operational at this point because the third was designated for the area under Indian occupation.

40. A Sri Lankan general's analysis of the campaign, made directly to me at the time, seems fitting: "We have done terrible things, terrible things."

41. Official IPKF figures are 1,155 dead and 2,984 wounded for the thirty-two-month deployment. See Gunaratna, *Indian Intervention in Sri Lanka,* 315. Many analysts believe that Colombo, determined to see the IPKF depart as quickly as possible, entered into a covert marriage of convenience with LTTE for the express purpose of pressuring New Delhi. Evidence has been rather more scarce than the charge, but a convincing case (for the prosecution) can be made. See, for example, Swamy, *Tigers of Lanka*, 322–32.

42. Considerable irony attaches itself to an "eyes-only" critique, "Assessment of Troops/Terrorist Capabilities in the Jaffna Peninsula," drafted by "a senior infantry major with considerable experience of operations in the peninsula," February 1, 1986. Sent anonymously to his superiors in typescript, it states (page 6): "8c. Suicide Bombers. If a terrorist is capable of taking cyanide when caught, the day will soon dawn when suicide bombers will hit a small detachment like Velvettiturai, Nainativu etc. *(What is meant is that the terrorists will use a vehicle bomb which will be driven into a camp at high speed by a suicidal terrorist and set off in the middle of the camp. TO DESTROY THE ENTIRE ARMY, NAVY AND AIR FORCE IN THE OPERATIONAL AREAS, THEY ONLY NEED 40 SUCH VOLUNTEERS. At the rate the Armed Forces are antagonizing the Tamil Public by their frequent atrocities, we are probably creating persons who will be willing to undertake such tasks)*." (All punctuation in original.)

43. Details in Thomas A. Marks, "Toying with Terrorists: India's Sri Lankan Creation Runs Amok," *Low Intensity Conflict (LIC) International* 1, no. 1 (December 1992): 6–8. Loosely based on the Gandhi assassination is the Santosh Sivan film *The Terrorist* (Phaedra Cinema, 2000). Its misleading letterbox illustration (a ghoul) and label ("she's a natural born killer") notwithstanding (neither have anything to do with the story), the tale itself offers possibly the most insightful exploration available of the suicide bombing dynamic as it appears to function in most areas. Particularly well rendered is the process of Tamil brutalization, whereby the young strike back with all they can muster, the personal sacrifice of the suicide bombing. What is revealed thus accords with what is presented by Robert A. Pape, first in "The Strategic Logic of Suicide Terrorism," *American Political Science Review* 97, no. 3 (August 2003): 1–19; and subsequently in *Dying to Win: The Strategic Logic of Suicide Terrorism* (New York: Random House, 2005).

44. Discussion of this progression, the LTTE units involved, and the ideological underpinnings for the suicide campaign are discussed in R. Ramasubramanian, *Suicide Terrorism in Sri Lanka* (New Delhi: Institute of Peace and Conflict Studies, August 2004). Particularly useful is the comprehensive "Table 3: Suicide Attacks by LTTE in Sri Lanka," 21–25. It lists fifty-eight major suicide attacks through July 7, 2004.

45. Table 3 in Ramasubramanian lists slightly under sixty major suicide attacks. At least ninety-seven LTTE individuals are identified as perpetrators, with a number unknown (e.g., attacks by Sea Tigers often were carried out by groups of unknown strength). This is close to the number of major suicide attacks (sixty-six) listed by the Sri Lanka Army, "World's Top Suicide Killers— Do They Really Have Borders?" (news report, updated September 18, 2001), www.army.lk/News_Reports/September01/news_191_Sep_2001.htm (accessed November 26, 2005). Yet a personal log maintained by a Sri Lankan naval officer with specific service countering LTTE suicide attacks (name withheld at request) claims 232 attacks to early 2005, with 244 Black Tigers deceased, including 53 women (some counts cite fewer than a dozen women). Regardless, any statistics must be used with care. Mia Bloom, *Dying to Kill: The Allure of Suicide Terror* (New York: Columbia University Press, 2005), 93, for example, claims "the LTTE largely aimed at politicians and military targets," but this, although probably true in terms of number of attacks, would not be the case when considering the number of victims, who were overwhelmingly civilian (as reflected in Ramasubramanian's table 3).

46. These were initially scheduled in advance, two per year, as a part of the normal training cycle of the U.S. special operations units concerned. As Sri Lankan needs were further clarified, both individuals and teams returned as dictated by circumstances. Interestingly, these trainers were never threatened by LTTE, much less attacked. Evidence indicates that the insurgents decided not to risk an aggressive U.S. response to an overreaction by LTTE. When all was said and done, U.S. aid would have at most minor tactical impact, while a lashing out by Washington, even if only in the form of increased aid to Sri Lanka, could have operational or even strategic impact.

47. For background and context regarding this effort, including discussion of personalities, see Thomas A. Marks, "Sri Lanka: The Dynamics of Terror," *Counterterrorism and Security* (New Series) 1, no. 1 (1994): 19–23; Thomas A. Marks, "Sri Lanka: Terrorism in Perspective," *Counterterrorism and Security* (New Series) 2, no. 3 (Fall–Winter 1995): 16–19 (reprinted as "Dynamics of Terror in Sri Lanka," *Sunday Times* [Colombo], December 31, 1996, 7; concluded, January 7, 1996, 7); and Thomas A. Marks, "Sri Lanka: Reform, Revolution or Ruin?" *Soldier of Fortune* 21, no. 6 (June 1996): 35–39.

48. He was actually deputy minister, but the president herself was the minister, so Ratwatte ran the security forces. A reserve lieutenant colonel, he had himself recalled to active duty and eventually promoted to four-star rank. This chain of events occasioned considerable controversy.

49. When the early insurgent threat in Sri Lanka was one of terror actions—with attacks including strikes by Tamil groups against Colombo's commercial air links—a small army commando force had been formed. It had but two squadrons, one devoted to rapid-response missions, principally antihijacking, the other to VIP security. As actual hostilities progressed, the commandos found themselves in counterguerrilla operations as well. The shortage of such personnel led to the formation of a separate Special Forces Regiment, primarily for jungle operations. Leaving permutations aside, the end result was that both the commandos and the special forces eventually evolved into forces of two battalions each (these had 450 men rather than the standard infantry 600 to 750 men), organized in a Special Forces Brigade.

50. LTTE filmed the entire operation, which featured suicide personnel clearing defensive minefields by blowing themselves up and defenders overwhelmed by repeated "human wave" assaults. Indeed, the LTTE name for the assault was Operation Oyada Alaikhal, or "endless waves." Details in Paul Harris, "Bitter Lessons for the SLA," *Jane's Intelligence Review* (October 1996): 466–68.

51. Nevertheless, it is noteworthy that at no time did conscription prove necessary. That the recruiting dynamic was driven by what surely is the dominant factor throughout history, lack of viable alternative opportunities, is indeed the finding of Michele Ruth Gamburd, "The Economics of Enlisting: A Village View of Armed Service," in *Economy, Culture, and Civil War in Sri Lanka,* ed. Deborah Winslow and Michael D. Woost (Bloomington: Indiana University Press, 2004), 151–67.

52. Fieldwork, Sri Lanka, June–July 1995.

53. See the very useful statistics in Peter Chalk, "The Liberation Tigers of Tamil Eelam Insurgency in Sri Lanka," in *Ethnic Conflict and Secessionism in South and Southeast Asia: Causes, Dynamics, and Solutions,* ed. Rajat Ganguly and Ian MacDuff (New Delhi: Sage, 2003), 135: "According to informed sources, boys and girls as young as nine years old are now being dispatched to active conflict zones, with intelligence personnel estimating that as many as 60 percent of LTTE cadres are below the age of eighteen. Even if this figure is somewhat exaggerated, conservative assessments of LTTE fighters killed in action reveal that at least 40 percent are between the ages of nine and eighteen. According to Garca Machel, the former first lady of Mozambique who has made a special study of child soldiers for the UN, 20 percent of LTTE injured personnel were between the ages of ten and fourteen during recruitment. While the LTTE has denied such accusations, itself accusing the Sri Lankan military of targeting innocent Tamil children, dedications to the group's war dead, shown every month in propaganda videos, invariably include images of combatants well under the age of eighteen."

54. See interview of S. Manoranjan (Tamil newspaper editor in Sri Lanka) by Joe Rubin of Frontline/World, May 2002, www.pbs.org/frontlineworld/ stories/srilanka/feature.html.

55. Details in Davis, "Tamil Tiger International," 469–73. Davis puts LTTE funding at this point at an estimated $2 million monthly, 60 percent from abroad, principally from Western locales. He further notes: "Perhaps predictably, alleged involvement in the narcotics trade has been a contentious piece of the LTTE financial jigsaw" (page 473). In subsequent research, Byman and others, *Trends in Outside Support,* 41–60, nearly doubled this estimate, citing "at least $50 million a year in operating revenue" from all sources (page 50). Bloom, *Dying to Kill,* 46n5, appears to have misread Byman and others to render "1 million dollars/day," an unrealistic figure. There was no question, however, that LTTE funding mechanisms, by the mid-1990s, had become quite sophisticated. The group even had its own fleet that operated on a global scale. Deception was used skillfully, and in one brilliant operation, the year's supply of mortar shells for the Sri Lankan army was shanghaied by the bold expedient of substituting an insurgent ship for the expected government recipient vessel at an unsuspecting (and culturally clueless) Middle Eastern port.

56. Sri Lanka maintains an official peace process website at www. peaceinsrilanka.org/, while LTTE does likewise at www.lttepeacesecretariat. com/mainpages/n25054.htm, supplementing the peace news on its normal www.eelam.com/.

57. Especially insightful is G. H. Peiris, "Sri Lanka: Deepening Crisis," *South Asia Intelligence Review* 4, no. 5 (August 15, 2005), www.satp.org/ satporgtp/sair/Archives/4_5.htm. *South Asia Intelligence Review, www.satp*.

org, a New Delhi Internet weekly published by the Institute for Conflict Management, is particularly useful for tracking events.

58. See "Gunman Kills Top Sri Lankan Judge," BBC News, November 19, 2004, online version.

59. See figures contained in Somini Sengupta, "Nearly a Year after the Tsunami, Sri Lanka Strife Flares," *New York Times,* November 2, 2005, A3.

60. Capturing this reality well is Philip Gourevitch, "Letter from Sri Lanka: Tides of War," *New Yorker,* August 1, 2005, 53–63.

61. Numerous interviews with prisoners and defectors revealed motivation little different from that of members of other movements: a world of limited options led to a logical "career move." To the extent socialization by the movement had succeeded, the combatant was more motivated and better able to frame his or her response in the appropriate ideological terms. Yet there was little commitment to or knowledge of structural goals (e.g., "socialism") beyond the useful catchall provided by the term *Eelam.* Most heartening was the ability of combatants, once removed from the movement, to experience a regeneration of their basic humanity.

62. In his fieldwork in central Luzon, Ben Kerkvliet found that former Huk areas, having been through an intense round of insurgency in the earlier struggle, had no desire to relive the experience. I discuss these findings and the consequences for CPP strategy in Thomas A. Marks, *Maoist Insurgency since Vietnam,* chapter 3.

63. Carl von Clausewitz in *On War,* cited by Mackubin Thomas Owens, "Same Old Questions: It All Comes Down to Clausewitz," *National Review Online,* September 25, 2001, www.nationalreview.com/comment/comment-owens092501.shtml.

15

JAPAN AND AUM SHINRIKYO

John V. Parachini

Katsuhisa Furukawa

The 1995 poison attack on the Tokyo subway by an obscure religious group marked a new era in terrorism. Seemingly out of the blue, the Aum Shinrikyo ("Aum") did what most government and private experts believed terrorists would eschew: it used a military-grade chemical agent, although with degraded quality, indiscriminately on ordinary citizens with the intent to cause mass murder. Until this attack, most observers assumed terrorists wanted as much public attention with as little death and destruction as they could get away with. A taboo against the use of chemical weapons has been one of the factors constraining states, groups, and individuals from using poison as a weapon. The perpetrators of the Tokyo subway attack violated this taboo repeatedly, justifying killing with poison as a purgative antidote for individuals and organizations that stood in the way of the organization's plans and desires. Aum's leaders justified the organization's violence in religious terms, suggesting that the killing was necessary to protect Aum for the good of humanity and that the victims benefited from death because it purified them of the earthly evils that afflicted them. The combination of religious justification for use and Aum leader interest, perhaps even fascination, with poisons and diseases created the conditions for the group to do the seemingly unthinkable.

Aum typified an emerging profile of groups motivated by religion and seemingly prepared to inflict mass and indiscriminate violence in service of their aims. One scholar presciently noted that religiously motivated terrorism "assumes a transcendent purpose and therefore becomes a sacramental or divine duty [and] arguably results in a significant loosening of the constraints on mass murder."[1] Despite Aum's hundreds of millions of dollars in assets, a membership in Russia three times larger than its Japanese membership, and offices in a number of foreign countries, authorities in Japan, the United States, and Russia did not realize the danger the group posed. Since the Tokyo subway attack, ironically, the danger of the group may have been overdrawn.

Since the Tokyo subway attack, the U.S. government and many other governments around the world have spent considerable sums of money enhancing their capabilities to reduce the consequences of a similar attack. More than a decade has passed since the attack, and fortunately it stands as an aberration rather than a trend. Nevertheless, there is a pervasive fear that al Qaeda, its affiliated groups, or a new terrorist group yet to be identified might seek to harness the deadly potential of unconventional weapons such as poison, disease, or radioactivity. Indeed, numerous statements by Osama bin Laden and his associates, and evidence recovered from al Qaeda facilities in Afghanistan, reveal al Qaeda's considerable interest in obtaining chemical, biological, radiological, or nuclear (CBRN) weapons. However, despite considerable interest, al Qaeda and affiliated or similarly inspired groups have not used unconventional means to achieve their violent ends. Instead, al Qaeda has perpetrated attacks with conventional means and achieved even more catastrophic consequences than the Tokyo subway attack. Aum, in contrast, sought to cause catastrophic violence with unconventional means and caused far less death and destruction.

Evolving political struggles over occupied territories and minorities chafing under imperfectly democratic systems pose one level of terrorist challenge. Groups with both the means and the motive to accomplish catastrophic violence in the service of a twisted worldview pose a fundamentally different challenge. This is precisely the terrorist challenge the Japanese government faced in the case of the Aum Shinrikyo. Much of Japan's modern life is shaped by political events leading up to World War II, Japan's defeat, and its political reconstitution under U.S. stewardship. Japan's postwar rejection of its imperial and expansionist past and its embrace of pluralism, in particular protections for religious freedom, created a fertile environment for a group like Aum to withdraw from the bounds of modern society and chart its own path leading inexorably to conflict.

Despite the novelty of so many aspects of the Aum case, the case provides valuable insights for democratic governments seeking to thwart the deadly designs of religiously motivated subnational groups. Democratic governments of advanced economies will inevitably be challenged by sovereignless subnational collections of people struggling against modernity. Many of these new groups may not look like traditional political organizations or insurgency movements willing to use terrorism as a tactic in their struggle to achieve political or territorial objectives. Like Aum Shinrikyo, these groups may pose the greatest challenge for democratic governments of economically advanced societies and not look anything like secular terrorist groups from the past.

Finally, the Aum case poignantly reveals the challenge democratic societies face when balancing the need of the government to ensure public security and the rights of the citizens to be protected against the vagaries of an insecure state. Japan's prewar authoritarian past contributes to its societal predisposition toward protecting the liberties of its citizens from institutions of government. The mosaic of legal protections Japanese citizens enjoy is both complemented by and an expression of the orderly and structured nature of Japanese society. Japan's highly developed legal structure is also influenced by the country's strong pacifist tendencies, which reached new levels of intensity after 1945. Throughout the Japanese government's struggle with Aum, institutions of government cautiously and deliberately managed issues with the group. Perhaps to a fault, Japanese authorities guarded against government infringement of civil rights of individuals and organizations.

Japan's experience offers important lessons for newly emerging democracies shedding authoritarian pasts as they confront subnational groups bent on mass and indiscriminate violence. Similarly, established democracies that have suspended legal protections, arguing that the extraordinary security demands of the moment require extraordinary measures, may also benefit from an examination of Japan's approach. Japan's authorities followed a rule-of-law approach in the campaign against Aum that should influence how successful counterterrorism campaigns get defined.

Aum's Worldview and Justification for Murder

Aum emerged as one of many new religious organizations in Japan during the 1980s. As the Japanese economy boomed, many young Japanese sought spiritual meaning in these new religious movements. Aum appealed to Japanese youths and others who felt alienated, in part because the group emphasized ascetic living and meditation as a means to greater spiritual attainment. Over the course of eight years, this little-known yoga group became a violent religious cult with ten thousand members in Japan, thirty thousand in Russia, and offices in Germany, Taiwan, Sri Lanka, Australia, and the United States. The group's leader, his religious vision, his followers, and key context-setting aspects of Japan and the world in the 1980s and 1990s were critical factors in the emergence of this group and the violent acts it committed.

In 1986 Chizuo Matsumoto, later known as Shoko Asahara, founded a religious organization, Aum Shinsen no Kai (the Aum Circle of Divine Hermits), with only fifteen members. Asahara's religious vision evolved as a mix of Buddhism, Hinduism, and Christianity and cast both the group and Asahara as forces to save humanity. Members perceived those who impeded their messianic mission as not only a threat to the group but also a threat to humanity. This exalted view of the group's mission, by asserting a higher purpose Aum needed to fulfill, would lead it to justify killing those who sought to impede its efforts.

Shoko Asahara commanded such devotion and control over members that he could successfully order them to do things they ordinarily would not do. Even after Japanese authorities arrested key group leaders for the sarin attack on the Tokyo subway, many members remained devoted to Shoko Asahara and the group. One Aum member stated, "However strongly I felt that there was something strange with Asahara's order, I needed to follow it."[2] Aum's religious doctrine justified murder as a means to save the soul of the person the group felt it needed to kill.[3]

The religious justification for killing rested in part on the belief in a purifying feature of death for Aum's victims. Asahara was also fascinated with the use of poison as a tool for killing. It is not clear exactly how he developed this fascination, but the poetry he wrote praising the virtues of sarin highlights this intense and strange interest in the agent. Thus the combination of Asahara's fascination with sarin, a religious justification for killing, and his exalted sense of himself and the role of Aum created in part the basis for this unprecedented use of a chemical agent by a subnational group.

Several Aum members convicted for the sarin attacks testified that they believed the dispersal of sarin would eventually salvage the souls of the victims. Ikuo Hayashi, one of the people convicted for the sarin attack on the Tokyo subway, believed that ensuring the survival of Aum ensured the protection of the *truth,* which would save humanity.[4] Hayashi believed that victims of the sarin attack would be rewarded for contributing to the survival of Aum, and saving Aum would in turn benefit humanity. Complementing Aum members' belief in the sanctity of killing was a profound sense of fear of their critics and adversaries. In his memoir, Hayashi observed that he and other Aum members believed that "somebody was trying to destroy Aum. Asahara told us that it was a 'shadowy organization' that could even mobilize the United States. We believed in Asahara's words. . . . We also believed that police's investigation was a means to crush the Aum." Therefore, he added, "the dispersal of sarin was a part of our battle against the soldiers of state power," and "we believed that we were driven into a corner and had to strike back."[5] Hayashi's reflections reveal how Aum members felt threatened by authorities and help explain the motivation for a preemptive strike against the police. However, his words do not explain why the group needed to use sarin as opposed to explosives. If Asahara had been fascinated with explosives, would Aum have bombed the headquarters of the Japanese National Police Agency (NPA)? Perhaps part of sarin's appeal to Asahara and his Aum followers was the power that invisible chemical agents gave them. That is, they could take the life out of a person simply by aerosolizing a chemical, and the attack would be hard to trace.

Some Aum members testified that they had engaged in crimes not entirely because of some spiritual belief but also because they feared the consequences if they disobeyed Asahara. Specifically, they feared being killed and being condemned to eternal hell for disobeying Asahara. Yasuo Hayashi, another perpetrator of the sarin incident, acknowledged that dispersing sarin was wrong, but he feared what might happen to him if he disobeyed. He testified, "If I had not obeyed Asahara's order, me and my family would have been harmed. I was scared; I could not disobey the order to disperse the sarin."[6] Yoshihiro Inoue, another conspirator in the attack, also expressed conflicted feelings in his court testimony: "I could not reject Chizuo Matsumoto's order related to the Vajrayana, nor could I quit Aum because I feared that if I had declined Matsumoto's order, I could be killed under the name of *poa.*"[7] Asahara commanded tremendous loyalty from his followers via a combination of religious doctrine and fear. His charismatic control over his followers helps explain how norms or taboos that normally restrain the use of unconventional weapons melted away.

MURDER BECOMES A STANDARD PRACTICE

Aum's spectacular attack on the Tokyo subway with sarin nerve agent was a culmination of a number of violent acts. The group's murders and less-well-known attacks using chemical and biological agents have not been examined in nearly as much detail as the Tokyo subway incident. Examining the events leading up to the Tokyo subway incident reveal "tipping points" in the evolution of the group. Aum's mass and indiscriminate attacks with sarin, first in Matsumoto and later in Tokyo, are the end points of a killing process that started with accidental deaths during the course of bizarre rituals. Then Aum leadership started ordering the murder of members who wanted to leave the organization and people who were opposed to the group. Once members became comfortable with murder as a means of dealing with internal and external opposition, it became easier for them to resort to violence again and again.

In March 1989, the group sought designation as a religious organization to enjoy the benefits of tax exemption. Under Japan's Religious Corporation Law, if a group met certain requirements, it could be designated a religious group and enjoy considerable economic benefits. The Tokyo metropolitan government noted complaints from parents of Aum members, who charged that their children were coerced into joining and "brainwashed" to cease all contact with their families.[8] The Tokyo government regularly rejected applications for religious designation on the grounds that an organization was "antisocial," and some of Aum's practices seemed to fit this characterization. City authorities initially balked at granting Aum status as an approved religious organization. Angered by the hesitation of authorities, Aum members mounted a fierce public lobbying campaign, sending protest letters to city officials and marching outside city hall in white robes. In June 1989, Aum sued the municipal government for malfeasance.[9] Finally, in August, authorities certified Aum as a tax-exempt religious organization, in part because it was "very difficult to present reasons to reject certification."[10] This seemingly innocuous governmental decision may have reinforced for Aum leaders that intimidation tactics work.[11]

The period leading up to Aum's application for designation as a religious organization marked the start of its violence against group members. In October 1988, Teruyuki Majima joined Aum hoping to cure a mental disease with Aum's meditation and training regimen. During one training session, he began to act strangely. Asahara explained Majima's behavior as the result of a concentration of energy in his head and ordered followers to cool him down in cold water.[12] Aum members submerged Majima in a cold-water bath until he died. Shuji Taguchi, a member who witnessed the tragedy and helped Aum's senior leaders secretly burn Majima's body, began to doubt Aum's training and expressed a desire to leave the group.[13] Perhaps fearing that Taguchi would provide information to authorities that would jeopardize the organization's application to be designated a religious organization, Asahara ordered him killed. In early February 1989, weeks prior to Aum's application for designation as a religious organization, Aum members strangled Taguchi before he could leave the group.[14] Asahara justified the killing of defectors and group opponents in religious terms, arguing that in death, the individual was liberated from sins he or she had accumulated in life, particularly the sin of opposing the progress of Aum. Moreover, killing individuals who may have hurt Aum contributed to the eventual good of humanity, because Aum's mission was divine.

Aum committed its next significant murder shortly after receiving its certification as a religious organization. In the fall of 1989, a series of commentators criticized Asahara and Aum practices, stimulating Asahara's sense of paranoia and desire to counter these charges by whatever means possible. On August 3, 1989, Tsutsumi Sakamoto, a human rights lawyer who frequently defended radical leftist groups, negotiated a meeting between parents and their children who had joined Aum.[15] This meeting was the first and last of its kind. Once Aum received its certification as a religious organization, its stance toward Sakamoto and his clients hardened.

Aum members confessed that they had entered Sakamoto's home in the middle of the night and killed him, his wife, and their baby boy. To complicate the anticipated police investigation of the crime, they buried the bodies of the three victims in three different prefectures, which meant that three different police forces would handle the investigation. While parent groups, news organizations, and police were suspicious that Aum might be responsible for the disappearance of Sakamoto and his family, law enforcement authorities were not able to build a sufficient case against the group.

Investigators mistakenly focused on radical leftist groups as potential suspects responsible for Sakamoto's disappearance because Sakamoto had handled many trials for radical leftists.[16] Further confusing the case was how frequently members of religious organizations were also active in radical leftist groups. Additionally, law enforcement authorities failed to appreciate a lead provided by Ichiro Okazaki, one of the perpetrators of the Sakamoto family incident, who secretly sent an anonymous letter to the police. Enclosed in the letter were a map and a picture indicating the location where Sakamoto's baby was buried.[17] The police could not locate the site in the photo and failed to find the body.

In February 1990, Asahara decided Aum should enter electoral politics, expecting that the Japanese electorate would support his list of candidates and catapult the organization to greater national prominence. Aum organized a slate of twenty-five candidates to run as the Shinritoh (Truth) Party in the thirty-ninth general election of the House of Representatives.[18] The slate of candidates engaged in a variety of strange campaign stunts, including parading about wearing masks made in the image of Shoko Asahara and donning elephant heads in honor of a Hindu god. Asahara and other Aum members had delusions that they would take over the Japanese government through the electoral process.

Contrary to Asahara's prediction, Aum's brief foray into legitimate politics ended in abysmal failure and marked a turning point in the group's outlook on its relationship with Japanese society. In April 1990, following the electoral defeat, Asahara announced to his close subordinates for the first time his idea to overthrow the Japanese government and to annihilate the Japanese electorate for committing the "sinful deed" of rejecting Aum in the election.

Aum's establishment of its own governmental structure, parallel to the actual Japanese government, was a sign of trouble to come. It was as though Aum rejected the results of the election and declared itself the government anyway. Aum leaders assumed titles as ministers, similar to those of the Japanese government ministers. Asahara and his close associates had become the government of the world in which they lived. What was not clear at the time was how Aum's desire to seek the arsenal of a state would lead it to do battle with the real state.

AUM GOES GLOBAL AND BUILDS AN ARSENAL FOR BATTLE

The timing of Aum's ascendance corresponded with two international developments that influenced Aum's worldview and its prospects of catalyzing it. The collapse of the Soviet Union and the 1991 Gulf War seemed to confirm some of Shoko Asahara's prophecies about the earthly world beginning to come apart. He prophesied that the apocalypse would occur in 1999 as a result of a global war between major powers. Several Aum members indicated that Asahara and other group leaders were awed by the destructive power they saw in television images from the conflict in the Persian Gulf and were fascinated by the prospect that chemical weapons might be used.[19] The press was filled with stories about the dire economic conditions in the former Soviet Union and the prospect of countries acquiring its poorly guarded weapons and matériel and of former Soviet weapons scientists selling their expertise.[20] These international developments fed the delusional imagination of Shoko Asahara and his close aides.

The economic pressures and instability of the postcommunist era seemed to cause Russian political leaders, scientists, and military personnel to adapt to the new free-market environment by being available for hire. As a result, Aum seems to have been able to buy access to senior political leaders, scientists, military training, and weapons capabilities. According to one analyst, the head of Aum's Russian operation provided "$12 million in payoffs to well-placed officials."[21] Using its considerable assets, Aum exploited the turmoil in Russian political and economic life to expand its membership and get access to the bountiful military capabilities that were for sale in Russia.

As Aum's membership and assets grew, so did its international ambitions. Aum's considerable financial assets resulted from a network of group-owned businesses and medical clinics, as well as contributions from members. The group used these assets to set up numerous branch offices in Japan and abroad and to buy access to senior government officials in foreign countries. Aum opened an office in the United States in 1987 and a European headquarters in Bonn, Germany, in 1991. In 1992 the group launched a "Russian Salvation Tour" and opened its first branch office in Moscow. By 1993 Aum's Russian membership had reached ten thousand, equaling its membership in Japan. The organization also established a trading company in Taiwan and purchased a tea plantation in Sri Lanka and a ranch in Australia.

Throughout this period of dramatic membership expansion and accumulation of wealth, Aum managed a multinational effort to procure equipment and matériel for a robust military buildup. Aum's Russian connections proved the most productive for procuring weapons, equipment, and know-how for Aum's military plans. Serendipitously, Aum sought to expand its membership and build an arsenal at precisely the moment when Russia, after seventy years of religious suppression under communism, experienced a tremendous expansion of interest in new religions.

The full picture of Aum's activities and membership in Russia is still not completely known, but what is known is disconcerting. Its membership grew from ten thousand to more than thirty thousand, and the organization established eighteen different offices, seven of them in Moscow. Different Japanese Aum members visited Russia more than fifty times over the course of a couple of years. In addition to Oleg Lobov, they met with Vice President Aleksandr Rutskoi and parliamentary leader Ruslan Khasbulatov. Aum members also visited the Kurchatov Institute, a nuclear weapons design facility, and a Spetznaz training camp. Aum's Russian membership included former special forces troops, KGB officials, and scientists at defense facilities.

Aum's procurement operations were unprecedented in scale and scope for a nonstate actor. It was able to pursue its weapons procurement activities without much interference, aided by its considerable financial assets, boldness of purpose, and the focus of Russian, Japanese, and U.S. authorities on other security concerns. Russian officials were obliging when the price was right. Japanese authorities did not scrutinize Aum's activities, in large part because of the group's status as an officially sanctioned religious organization. U.S. intelligence attention turned to Aum only after the 1995 Tokyo subway attack. A bizarre but wealthy religious organization avoided the attention of the nations most likely to suffer from its activities: Russia, where it had the largest membership, and the United States, which consistently figured in Asahara's list of forces threatening Aum's existence.

Aum's Biological and Chemical Attacks

A new phase in Aum's operation commenced in the summer of 1993 and evolved until the group's attack on the Tokyo subway. During this period, Aum launched several significant operations using poison or disease.[22]

Examining these three incidents illustrates the evolution of Aum's unconventional weapons capabilities and the government's response.

In the first incident, on June 29 and 30, 1993, residents in the Kameido neighborhood of Tokyo reported foul odors to "local environmental health authorities."[23] Authorities sought to examine the inside of the Aum building, which local residents believed to be the source of the foul odors, but Aum members blocked authorities from entering. Not until two weeks later did officials gain access to the building.[24] By that time, Aum had vacated the building and removed the equipment used to produce the odor. In court testimony, Aum members revealed that the group dispersed "a liquid suspension of *Bacillus anthracis* in an attempt to cause an inhalational anthrax epidemic."[25] Later scientific analysis determined that the material dispersed was anthrax vaccine and thus was not harmful. The foul odor residents smelled probably came from the medium used to grow the strain.

In June 1993, Asahara ordered Masami Tsuchiya, Aum's chief chemist, to research how to produce sarin nerve agent in mass quantity.[26] Tsuchiya succeeded in producing a solution of sarin in August,[27] and Asahara ordered him to start construction of a sarin production facility to produce seventy tons of sarin to disperse over major cities in Japan and the United States.[28] In 1994 Asahara told his key lieutenants, "We have no other option but to throw 70 tons of sarin around Tokyo,"[29] and "there is no other option but to terrorism."[30]

On June 27, 1994, a small group of Aum members traveled to Matsumoto, Japan, and conducted Aum's first mass and indiscriminate attack with a toxic agent. They killed 7 people and injured 144 others when they aerosolized the nerve agent sarin outside a dormitory complex housing three judges presiding over a civil lawsuit contesting Aum's purchase of land.

Initially, local police authorities mistakenly focused on Yoshiyuki Kono, an industrial-machinery salesman, as the prime suspect. He was the first to call for help, probably because his house was near the parking area where Aum released the chemical agent. Authorities discovered significant quantities of chemicals on Kono's property. He explained that he used some of the chemicals for making pesticides for his garden and others for developing photographs.

Japanese criminal investigators failed to connect the pending legal case against Aum and the sarin attack. While Japanese law enforcement authorities in retrospect should be criticized for not "connecting the dots," they may not have been fully aware of what dots to collect in the first place. At the time, the possibility that members of a religious group would attempt to clandestinely kill authorities with a lethal nerve agent to win a civil legal case was hard to imagine.

The difficulties national authorities had in recognizing the importance of the Matsumoto incident stem in part from the different missions of the bureaus within the NPA. The case was initially delegated to the bureau charged with investigating criminal matters rather than the bureau that investigated terrorism and counterintelligence.[31] Thus both national and local law enforcement authorities approached the case as a criminal matter and not an event with broader national security significance.

In July 1994, right after the Matsumoto sarin attack, a strange incident took place near Kamikuishiki, Aum's main communal headquarters. Local residents living near the Aum complex smelled a strange odor and experienced difficulty breathing. Residents reported this incident to the local police, who reportedly took a soil sample.[32]

Finally, in September 1994, soil samples from the area where the incident had occurred were sent for analysis to the National Research Institute of Police Science (NRIPS), part of the NPA.[33] In mid-September, reportedly, the NPA held an important meeting with director-level division officials from several prefecture police headquarters to coordinate measures to counter Aum's illicit activities.[34] At the first formal intergovernmental meeting regarding Aum, the NPA assumed general control of the investigation. Greater cooperation among law enforcement authorities and Japanese military entities proved critical to "collecting and connecting the dots" of evidence on Aum's nefarious activities. First, Japanese Ground Self Defense Force helicopter pilots, who were stationed near Kamikuishiki, noticed a Russian helicopter parked at the Aum complex, reportedly.[35] Second, Nagano prefecture police investigators discovered that a front company run by an Aum member had purchased sarin precursor chemicals and had them delivered to the Aum Kamikuishiki facility.[36] Third, in November 1994, NRIPS's forensic analysis on the soil samples revealed traces of sarin similar to those found in Matsumoto.[37] Finally, law enforcement agencies had sufficient evidence to suspect Aum's involvement in the 1994 Matsumoto attack. Although the police agencies wanted to raid the Aum complex, they still had not collected sufficient evidence for a legal search. In December the prosecutor's office rejected a proposed raid and warned the police agencies to adopt a cautious approach when investigating a religious organization, especially Aum, reportedly.[38] On January 1, 1995, the *Yomiuri* newspaper carried an article reporting how authorities had detected sarin precursor chemicals in soil samples taken from Kamikuishiki facility. Asahara ordered his subordinates to dismantle the sarin production factory and abandon the sarin and semifinished products.[39]

On March 20, 1995, a small group of Aum members released liquid sarin in train cars on several different subway lines in Tokyo. Twelve people died, hundreds of people were seriously exposed to toxic poisoning, almost a thousand people were lightly exposed, and more than five thousand people went to area hospitals fearing they had been exposed. Fortunately, the chemical agent had been hastily prepared, and its purity was only about 20 to 30 percent, which reduced its lethality. Additionally, the liquid agent oozed out of the plastic bags attackers used to transport it and did not disperse very widely in the train cars. Nevertheless, it did disperse enough to create a mass-casualty incident that posed a host of new challenges for Japanese emergency response and media personnel.

The attack on the Tokyo subway fundamentally shifted the Japanese government response from a limited criminal investigation to a nationwide crisis response and investigation. Prior to the Aum case, cooperation between law enforcement authorities and the Japanese Defense Agency (JDA) was limited and in many ways informal. After the attack, the Japanese Ground Self Defense Force (GSDF) deployed chemical units to assist with detection, medical support, and decontamination.[40] Liaison officers were sent to the Tokyo Metropolitan Police Department to facilitate coordination. A formal request for assistance was dispatched from the Tokyo metropolitan governor to the commanding general of the GSDF First Division, which handles all operations related to the national capital. Appropriate personnel were drawn from a variety of military entities, including the Chemical School, and dispatched to the Thirty-second Regiment.[41]

The JDA dispatched a total of sixteen doctors and nineteen other medical personnel to eight different public and private hospitals. Japanese military doctors were deployed to metropolitan hospitals to assist civilian doctors with diagnosis and treatment. Their understanding of nerve agents and treating exposure to them undoubtedly helped reduce the number of severe injuries and perhaps even fatalities.

The Japanese Government's Response to Aum's Subway Attack

Two days after the Tokyo subway attack, Japanese law enforcement officials mobilized an unprecedented number of police personnel to raid twenty-five suspected Aum sites around the country. Twenty-five hundred police personnel, many in protective clothing, sorted and seized a vast array of chemicals at Aum communes. Despite this bold show of force immediately after the subway attack, warrants for the arrest of thirty-eight Aum leaders were not issued until May 15, 1995. The police reportedly waited until they had assembled enough evidence to arrest them with murder charges.[42] The result of gaps in the legal and law enforcement infrastructure was that many key leaders were not arrested for more than forty days, even though authorities knew their whereabouts. Ultimately, forty-one Aum members, including Shoko Asahara, "were arrested on suspicion of murders and making preparations for murders."[43]

Japanese law enforcement authorities arrest people only after they assemble a preponderance of evidence against them, which helps explain the 95 percent conviction rate of those charged with crimes. Further, Japanese police tend to rely on admissions of guilt; their forensic investigations are designed to build a case that leads to a suspect's confession, because such cases are viewed as the most persuasive cases for juries. Given this approach to law enforcement, authorities did not apprehend Asahara and a number of other key figures for weeks after the Tokyo subway incident, even though many of them were hiding in Aum facilities. Asahara was eventually arrested at an Aum facility where he had taken refuge.

In October 1995, the Japanese government revoked Aum's designation as a religious organization and considered applying the 1952 Anti-subversive Activity Prevention Law against it. While a majority of the population supported actions against Aum, the proposal to apply the Anti-subversive Activity Prevention Law caused fierce debate. Some supported the proposal, while others felt it would unduly compromise freedom of religion and other civil liberties.[44] Although Japanese officials and governmental bodies tried to dismantle Aum by applying this law, the Public Security Examination Commission (PSEC), a body affiliated with the Ministry of Justice, rejected this approach.[45] While recognizing that the dangerous components of Aum's religious doctrine and members' belief in Asahara remained unchanged, the PSEC judged that Aum's capabilities, including human resources and physical and financial capabilities, had noticeably decreased as compared with its capabilities before the Matsumoto sarin incident and the Tokyo subway sarin incident. The PSEC judged that Aum had been "shrunken and weakened" and that it had been "transforming itself from a closed, isolated religious group to a religious group spread widely into the society with a purpose of its members to live together."[46]

Many former Aum members who had been arrested previously returned to the successor organization. By the end of 1999, 425 Aum members had been released from jail, and about half of those released returned to Aum.[47] In 1999 the Diet passed the Group Regulation Act, a new law "allowing authorities to monitor and inspect without warrant facilities of groups found to have committed 'indiscriminate mass murder during the past 10 years' and to uncover assets of companies associated with these groups."[48] In January 2000, Aum Shinrikyo renamed itself Aleph and attempted to recast itself beyond a mere name change. Even though the group changed its name, apologized for the Tokyo subway attack, and renounced violence, the PSEC decided to apply the terms of the Group Regulation Act to Aleph members and facilities on the grounds that Aleph also believed in Shoko Asahara and followed Aum's teachings.[49]

The PSEC rejected the 1952 Anti-subversive Activity Prevention Law as the tool to use against Aum for two reasons. First, a former justice minister serving on the PSEC persuasively noted how the 1952 act could endanger civil liberties in a fashion not consistent with current legal and policy practices. The substitute for the 1952 act was the Group Regulation Act, which applied to Aum and the Japanese Red Army because they were the only groups to have committed "indiscriminate murder" in the previous ten years. "Indiscriminate murder" was defined as eight deaths, because this was the lowest number of fatalities in one of the two terrorist acts committed by the Japanese Red Army in the early 1990s.[50] In accordance with this act, Aum/Aleph was placed under continuous surveillance for a three-year period starting in January 2000 and extended in January 2003 and in January 2006. (The PSEC reviews the need to apply the act to particular groups every three years.) The act restricted the use of designated group properties for recruiting that was deemed too aggressive. Every three months, groups were required to file a report with the names and addresses of members. Aum/Aleph filed a lawsuit challenging the act as a violation of the constitutional right to religious freedom, but the Tokyo District Court rejected the suit in June 2001.[51] The act is subject to review in 2005. The second reason the PSEC was reluctant to apply the 1952 law was the belief that Aum and its capacity to undermine public stability had been greatly reduced in size and scope. The PSEC did not view the group as a threat, thereby alleviating the need to apply the severe 1952 law.

At various times since the 1995 subway attack, Japanese authorities have arrested Aum fugitives. As of June 2006, three Aum fugitives remained at large. During an October 1999 search, police discovered an Aum member held in captivity at one of Aum's facilities. Police also discovered materials describing how to create lethal toxic gases, which raised suspicions that Aum members were still plotting attacks with lethal agents.[52] Fumihiro Joyu, who acted as the group's main spokesperson after he was released from prison, alleged that group members were collecting these materials to assist with the trial preparation and not for malicious purposes.[53] The true intentions of the surviving factions and individual Aum members are difficult to assess. The sum of the evidence suggests that at a minimum, some members have continued to function together as an organization and that the group's activities and worldview are evolving. According to the NPA, other members remain devoted to Shoko Asahara.[54]

In several instances, renegade Aum members have operated from abroad in some fashion. In 1998 Toshiyasu Ohuchi, who was wanted for conspiring to kill another Aum member, was expelled from Cyprus.[55] He had had a leading role in Aum's Russia branch and had taken refuge on the island after leaving Russia. Cyprus does not have an extradition treaty with Japan, but Cypriot law enforcement authorities detained Ohuchi, declared him a persona non grata, and expelled him in such a way that Japanese officials could apprehend him.

While Russian authorities closed Aum's Moscow branches in 1995, a core of three hundred followers continued in an underground fashion. In 1999 Dimitry Sigachev, then leader of Aum's Russian activities, plotted to free Shoko Asahara from detention in Japan. In July 2000, Russian law enforcement authorities arrested Sigachev and four coconspirators for plotting to detonate bombs in Kyushu and Okinawa at the time of the G8 Summit.[56] Sigachev received an eight-year prison sentence, and the others received lesser sentences.

In accordance with the Group Regulation Act, the Public Security Investigation Agency (PSIA) conducted "at least 12 on-site inspections of 27

Aum facilities around the country" in 2001.[57] To prevent former members from committing violence prior to the February 27, 2004, sentencing of Shoko Asahara, the agency established "a special investigation headquarters" on January 15, 2004. On February 16, 2004, PSIA personnel inspected eleven Aum facilities, including the main branch's headquarters in Tokyo.[58] These legally sanctioned raids do perform a constraining and deterring function. Like many law enforcement entities around the globe, Japanese police have assumed a much more aggressive style in managing the danger that remaining Aum members might pose. This more forward-leaning approach represents a significant change for most law enforcement bodies, but this is especially true in Japan. When Asahara was sentenced to death in February 2004, there were no incidents.

By April 2004, Aleph claimed to have about 1,650 members, in addition to approximately 300 members in Russia.[59] In 2003 press reports indicated that Aleph had divided into two factions as the result of a power struggle. The main faction, led by Fumihiro Joyu, Aum's former foreign minister and primary spokesman, supported renunciation of the group's past and "drastic reform." This branch occupied facilities in Tokyo's Setagaya Ward, as well as other cities across the country, including Sapporo, Sendai, Yashio, Yoko-hama, Nagoya, Osaka, Kosei, Tokushima, and Fukuoka.[60] Five breakaway factions rejected the reforms of the main branch and are still loyal to Shoko Asahara. One of these was located in Tokyo's Nerima Ward.

When Aleph sought to recast itself with a new name, it also outlined a "drastic reform" of the organization to distinguish itself from its tarnished Aum past. Apologizing for the crimes of Aum was a central feature of Aleph's reform. On January 18, 2000, Aleph released statements by Joyu and Tatsuko Muraoka titled "Outlook on the AUM-Related Incidents and Outline of Drastic Reform."[61] In Joyu's statement, he indicates that "We once again deeply apologize to the victims and bereaved families in the incidents. . . . I believe we have to reform the organization drastically." Muraoka's statement outlined the "drastic reform," which included setting up a liaison committee to handle "compensation for the damages inflicted upon the victims in the Aum-related incidents," transferring organization property and member assets to compensate victims and their families, and "sending apology letters to the victims and bereaved family members in the incidents, paying much attention not to disturb them."

The group decided not to disband, in part so that it would not avoid its responsibility for victim compensation. The group stated that "despite the incidents that should be disapproved of, the practice of yoga has been proved to be beneficial to members." Members also decided "to discard some parts of the teaching." The organization would no longer have a guru, and Asahara would be regarded as the founder but would have only a "spiritual existence" whose importance "will be confined to the subject of meditation." The group pledged to "abandon the parts of the teachings that are considered dangerous." Each member was required to sign an oath stating that he or she "will never exercise the killing or injuring of people . . . even if former representative Shoko Asahara should order him/her to do." In 2005, however, the PSIA concluded that there was sufficient evidence indicating that the group still potentially posed a threat to public security and warranted continued monitoring.[62] As of March 2006, the victims received only 30% of the promised compensation. Reportedly, Joyu's faction agreed in May 2006 to secede from the Aleph to establish a new religious organization.[63]

AFTER SEPTEMBER 11

The September 11, 2001, attacks on the World Trade Center and the Pentagon had a significant impact on how the Japanese government approaches terrorism today. Organizational reforms recommended in the *Intermediate Report of the Administrative Reform Council* enabled Prime Minister Junichiro Koizumi to respond quickly to the events of September 11; Japan was one of the first major allies to express its solidarity with the United States in the immediate aftermath of the tragic attacks.[64] Forty-five minutes after the attacks, Koizumi established a Crisis Management Center at the prime minister's residence. For the first time since the 1998 North Korea Taepodong missile test, Koizumi convened a cabinet-level meeting of the National Security Council.

Rather than stimulating a profound shift in Japanese counterterrorism preparedness, the September 11 attacks were yet another significant event in a series. Many of the organizational and capacity enhancements were well under way before the September 11 attacks, which provided an important sense of added urgency. Following September 11 and the October anthrax letters, Prime Minister Koizumi convened a ministerial-level meeting of the

Council Against NBC [Nuclear, Biological, and Chemical] Terrorism, which had been established in August 2000. An early task for the council was to revise national response plans. When the council met in October 2001, the prime minister used the occasion to urge greater interministerial cooperation and to charge prefectures and cities to establish their "own anti-terrorism countermeasures headquarters."[65]

The September 11 attacks occurred when Japanese and South Korean officials were making security preparations to host the 2002 World Cup matches. These attacks greatly increased the urgency both nations felt to ensure the safety of the matches. Ten different Japanese cities and towns were scheduled to host matches. Prior to the start of the World Cup, Japanese law enforcement and emergency response personnel conducted fifteen different simulation exercises, practicing how to respond to different types of attacks.[66] Officials from both countries were very concerned about the success of this sporting event because of the troubled history they shared from the period of Japanese imperial rule, as well as the necessity of strengthening bilateral ties to deal with North Korean problems. Thus, while the events of September 11 added additional motivation for authorities to take great precautions against the possibility of terrorist threats, Japan had already been steadily increasing its capabilities for a variety of reasons since 1995.

LESSONS FOR OTHER DEMOCRACIES

Japan's approach to counterterrorism has evolved considerably in the past fifteen years. The confrontation with Aum was one of several incidents that combined with broader trends that changed the distribution of authority in the Japanese government. Vesting greater authority in the prime minister's office and the emergence of a more stable governing coalition greatly facilitated a number of important changes in Japanese policy. Prime Minister Junichiro Koizumi capitalized on these trends and has led Japan in a much more assertive direction in terms of domestic and international security.

The first major lesson from Japan's confrontation with Aum relates to the difficulty of responding to the consequences of a surprise attack against civilians with unconventional weapons. Aum's use of sarin on the Tokyo subway underscored how vulnerable modern and open societies are to terrorists determined to inflict mass murder with unconventional weapons.

While Japanese authorities did take some measures to improve forensic and response capabilities, the U.S. government sought to dramatically enhance capabilities throughout the United States to respond to a terrorist attack with unconventional weapons. The combination of the Tokyo subway incident and the Oklahoma City bombing a month later energized the U.S. government to prepare for the worst. Despite having been the victim of the sarin attack, Japan moved at a much more deliberate pace to enhance preparedness for a catastrophic attack. The September 11 attacks boosted Japanese efforts to enhance prevention, response, and consequence management capabilities. The level of danger had to reach a critical threshold, and when it was witnessed on the territory of another state, each government feared an attack on its own territory. U.S. emergency response preparations after the Tokyo subway incident undoubtedly helped in the response to the September 11 attacks. Unfortunately, the lesson many drew from the Tokyo subway incident was the importance of preparing to manage the consequences of an attack with unconventional weapons, not the importance of focusing law enforcement and international assets on preventing such an attack before it occurs.

In 2000, at the G8 Summit in Kyushu and Okinawa, the Japanese government's efforts to deal with NBC terrorism were accelerated. For the first time, decontamination and protection equipment for individual use was distributed, which established a role model to encourage hospitals to make use of similar equipment. The Japanese government distributed similar equipment to 130 hospitals throughout the country. In August a Cabinet NBC Council was established, and in April 2001, the 1999 manual on dealing with NBC terrorism was revised. In the revised manual, each government ministry and agency was tasked with specific assignments.[67] Additionally, the Armed Attack Situation Law was enacted in 2003, followed by the Civil Protection Law in 2004.

The second major lesson is the importance of having the legal infrastructure to reduce the possibility that terrorists might acquire unconventional weapons and to punish them when they do. The pursuit and prosecution of the Tokyo subway attackers underscored the critical importance of having appropriate legal tools available to prosecute perpetrators of crimes that violate taboos and cross thresholds of acceptable societal behavior.

At the time of the Tokyo subway attack, Japan, like many other countries, including the United States, did not have national legislation that enabled it to prosecute people for the possession of chemical and biological weapons. Ten days after the attack, Japan became the first country to ratify the Chemical Weapons Convention (CWC), which required state signatories to pass national implementation legislation making it a crime to produce, stockpile, transfer, or use toxic agents as weapons. As law enforcement authorities pursued Aum suspects and sought to prevent other attacks, they needed a law they could use in the event of another attack. On April 19, the Japanese Diet passed a stopgap piece of legislation, the Law on the Prevention of Human Casualties Caused by Sarin and Other Toxic Substances (Sarin Law). Developing the implementing legislation for the CWC was more complicated and required more time for thorough consideration. On May 5, 1995, the Diet approved the CWC-implementing legislation, known as the Law on the Prohibition of Chemical Weapons and the Regulation of Specified Chemicals, or the CWC Law.

The third lesson from the Aum case is the importance of technical capabilities to handle the forensic and emergency response challenges posed by unconventional weapons. The difficulties Japanese law enforcement authorities had with assessing the implications of some Aum tests, accidents, and initial chemical attacks are similar to the difficulties the U.S. Federal Bureau of Investigation had during the 2001 anthrax letters case. The technical and operational difficulties Japanese law enforcement authorities had when investigating Aum's clandestine chemical and biological program prompted a number of changes in training and procurement. Recommendations to improve police forensic and toxic substance evaluation capabilities were made at several stages during the Japanese government's confrontation with Aum. A number of concrete recommendations were advanced in a 1996 NPA white paper.[68] The Aum case prompted the reorganization of activities at the NRIPS. For example, the institute established a new Office of Extraordinary Cases to handle chemical and biological weapons incidents, increased training for police and investigators in forensic detection, particularly in regard to chemical and biological agents, and procured additional analysis equipment.

The fourth lesson is the importance of a centralized crisis coordination capability serving the key executive leaders of the country. The Japanese took a number of measures over several years to restructure the bureaucratic machinery. A series of natural, accidental, and intentional incidents prompted the Japanese government to make several organizational changes to better manage crisis situations. These incidents included the 1995 Kobe Hanshin earthquake, which killed more than sixty-four hundred people; the 1995 hijacking of an ANA flight; the seizure of the Japanese ambassador's residence in Peru by the Tupac Amaru in 1996–97; the 1998 North Korean launch of the Taepodong missile over Japan; and the 1999 Tokaimura nuclear reactor accident. During each of these incidents, the Cabinet Secretariat supported the prime minister and managed the implementation of the prime minister's policies by ministries and agencies. In 1996 a Cabinet Intelligence and Research Office Situation Center was established to provide the prime minister with around-the-clock information.[69] These initial measures were followed in May 1997 by the *Intermediate Report of the Administrative Reform Council*, which recommended a deputy chief cabinet secretary post be established to handle initial responses to emergencies and coordinate additional measures taken by all ministries and agencies.[70] The new deputy chief cabinet secretary was charged with developing a number of contingency response plans covering the activities of all ministries and agencies.[71] The Intermediate Report also called for the establishment of an Office for Crisis Management in the Cabinet Secretariat to support the deputy chief cabinet secretary.[72] These recommended measures were implemented less than a year later, in April 1998.

On April 10, 1998, the government made a "cabinet decision" on a government response plan on handling a major terrorist incident, which included guidance on the jurisdictional responsibilities, coordination, and decision-making bodies and modalities for governmental response.[73] Legislative support for this change was put in place in June 1999, when the cabinet law was revised to strengthen the role of the prime minister and the Cabinet Secretariat in initiating policies of all types.[74] A further reorganization was undertaken in January 2001 in order to address problems.[75]

With greater emphasis on centralized power dedicated to crisis prevention, response, and consequence management, better coordination resulted among different ministries and agencies and between national and local levels of government. The NPA also announced reforms to better deal with terrorism incidents.[76] The Police Law was amended in June 1998 to ensure that prefectural police were able to handle extensive organized crime swiftly and accurately. Now, prefectural police are authorized to work outside the border of their prefectures when necessary. The NPA director-general now has the authority to give orders and when necessary to direct prefectural police in dealing with special crimes. A new councilor position at the director-general's secretariat was established to be in charge of policies related to scientific investigation of special crimes, strengthening the prefectural police's management in dealing with such crimes.

The NPA embarked on additional reforms designed to improve its capabilities. In April 2000, it established a new organization to manage terrorist attacks, training, special police force units, and interagency coordination. The International Terrorism Response Team was created to better coordinate with foreign law enforcement authorities. The NPA augmented its forensic scientific capabilities by purchasing equipment for protection, detection, and analysis in the event of a chemical terrorism incident and increased its information collection system and analytic capabilities at the NRIPS. In August 2003, the agency announced plans to establish a new public security organization to be responsible for domestic and international terrorism.[77]

The fifth lesson stems primarily from the Japanese government's experience confronting terrorism prior to Aum, but it is relevant for the challenge authorities face when confronting terrorists with absolute or divinely inspired objectives. In the 1970s and 1980s, the Japanese government went to great lengths to avoid any protracted standoffs with terrorists and sought to manage foreign policy in such a way that the prospect of being the object of terrorism was reduced. When the Japanese government confronted hostage situations, frequently perpetrated by the Japanese Red Army (JRA), it sought to resolve the situation peacefully, which periodically meant paying ransom. When members of the JRA hijacked a Japan Airline flight in 1977, the Japanese government paid $6 million in ransom and released eight prisoners.[78] While this approach did free some hostages, even one large payment to the JRA, a group of about only twenty to thirty people, enabled it to survive and periodically strike throughout the 1980s and to make several attempts in the 1990s.

Three factors contributed to a change in Japanese government policy. First, the government's experience with Aum revealed a new type of terrorism that harbored absolutist objectives that were not up for negotiation or resolvable for a price. Second, authorities recognized that the ransom payment to the JRA had helped keep it alive and able to strike again another day. Third, as Japan joined more international agreements on terrorism, officials felt that striking bargains with terrorists to free citizens ran counter to these agreements.[79] A national practice inconsistent with international pledges could not be sustained. The Japanese government altered its policy to seek the "protection of human lives but at the same time without any concession to unlawful demands by terrorists."[80] The "no-concessions policy" was reaffirmed in the 1998 cabinet decision titled On Initial Government Response to Major Terrorism Incident.[81] The Japanese government reaffirmed this policy once again in April 2004, when it refused to give in to terrorists' demands that it withdraw troops from Iraq when three Japanese citizens were kidnapped there. When first confronted with this hostage situation, Prime Minister Koizumi stated, "We cannot give in to the cowardly threats of terrorists."[82] Even the Japanese Democratic Party, which opposed the deployment of forces to Iraq, opposed acceding to the hostage takers' demands. Thus the no-concessions policy is accepted by a wide majority of Japanese political leaders and represents a significant change in government policy.

The sixth lesson this case highlights is the tremendous challenge of balancing the right of legal due process and the need of authorities to take action before a catastrophic attack. In the balance between liberty and security, the Japanese government handled the case of the Aum Shinrikyo with an emphasis on liberty and human rights. The Japanese government's abuses of authority over the citizenry in the 1920s and 1930s have left an enduring legacy of caution on the part of the public security organizations. As one scholar argued, the Japanese government has typically taken a "low-profile approach and patience has been the hallmark" of its counterterrorism policy.[83] Consistent with its post–World War II constitution, the political system, and the predominant view of the body politic, the Japanese government respected the rights of Aum as a religious organization to a degree that is hard to imagine in most other industrialized democratic countries. As a hedge against its past authoritarian practices, the Japanese government countered Aum in a deliberate and restrained fashion.

Japan developed a policy of legally sanctioned preventive searches of Aum's successor organization Aleph. While these searches are not foolproof, they do restrict Aleph's activities; the prospect of a police search hangs over the group at all times. Searches prior to the February 27, 2004, sentencing of Shoko Asahara served to put group members on notice that police were monitoring their activities and could move in on them at any time. Despite fears that Asahara's most devoted followers would take action at the time the court sentenced him to death, there were no incidents.

Japanese authorities have adopted a more aggressive approach toward religious groups of concern while at the same time respecting the limits of their authority. In a 2003 incident, Japanese law enforcement authorities preemptively searched the vehicles of the Panawave cult group for traffic law violations.[84] The Panawave, a cult with a guru who prophesied the destruction of the world on May 15, 2003, has about twelve hundred members, who frequently park their vehicles in public places and get into scuffles with local residents. Like Aum, the group had several facilities in Japan, including a laboratory. On May 14, 2003, a force of three hundred Japanese law enforcement authorities searched the group's facilities and fleet of vehicles. The search warrant accused the group of falsely registering its vehicles under the name of an individual not associated with the group.[85] As of 2004, the group had not been a serious concern, except for the mysterious death of one of its members. In an era when the fear of catastrophic terrorism has led many countries to evoke extraordinary powers in the name of public security and to suspend constitutional protections for some citizens, Japan's deliberateness and patience are noteworthy. The challenge that remains, however, is finding a balance between prudent preemption that has a credible basis of fact and protection against abuses and mistaken efforts.

The seventh lesson the Aum case raises is the challenge of preparing for something unprecedented. In retrospect, it is easier to note the signs of Aum's escalation to mass and indiscriminate murder than it was to interpret unprecedented events as they occurred. In many respects, the Japanese government experienced in 1993–95 what the U.S. government went through in 2001. Both experiences underscore the challenge twenty-first-century democracies face as they attempt to maintain both security and liberty against a subnational collection of people operating globally and bent on waging asymmetric and indiscriminate violence.

The Japanese government was not alone in failing to appreciate the extent of the nefarious activities of a strange but wealthy religious organization. The United States also overlooked or failed to appreciate warnings of Aum's intentions and burgeoning capabilities. On several occasions, Aum radio broadcasts and statements by Asahara threatened violence against the United States, its armed forces, and its president. In court testimony, a Japanese prosecutor argued that some Aum members conspired to smuggle sarin into the United States in order to disperse it in major cities, including New York and Washington, D.C.[86]

Congressional investigators researching Aum's activities reported that in their "discussions with every major U.S. law enforcement and intelligence agency, they all, to a man, and woman, said the Aum was not on their radar screens until Tokyo"—that is, until the sarin attack on the Tokyo subway.[87] One observer, who wondered about the U.S. intelligence community's apparent lack of focus on Aum after the Matsumoto incident, which received extensive media coverage in Japan, asked, "How could our intelligence services, the very people we depend upon to protect us from terrorist threats, not have seen the same thing unless they simply weren't looking?"[88]

Thwarting attacks before plots materialize is a critical challenge for public security authorities in an era when religiously motivated terrorists are willing to conduct mass and indiscriminate killings in service of a perceived divine mission. Shifting the outlook of law enforcement from building a case for prosecution after a crime has been committed to taking preemptive and preventive action is a fundamental change. Not only does the law enforcement culture need to change, but legal guidelines also need to be modified. The challenge democratic societies confront is how to grant authorities the power to act preemptively and yet still maintain sufficient oversight to guard against abuse. The posture of Japanese law enforcement has changed since the Tokyo subway incident, but whether it has changed enough remains an open question. As revealed in 2004, a French al Qaeda operative of Algerian descent entered Japan four times after September 11, despite Interpol and French government alerts. His name was on the watch list of the Japanese Ministry of Foreign Affairs and Ministry of Finance. The operative, Lionel Dumont, appears to have been part of al Qaeda's logistical operation, but he may also have been setting up an al Qaeda cell within Japan.[89]

The string of some twenty-five murders and perhaps some thirty "disappeared" Aum members—who are presumed dead—the seven deaths at Matsumoto, the twelve deaths in the Tokyo subway, plus the hundreds of significantly injured people in both incidents, represent a tragic total. Yet fatality and injury statistics alone do not adequately capture the implications of Aum's violent activities. These events highlight a general concern about public safety and the ability of the Japanese government to preserve it. Japanese authorities responded to these events in a deliberate and determined fashion, which proved too slow for those tragically killed by Aum. Coordination between different agencies of government and segments of the law enforcement and intelligence communities were major shortcomings. Moreover, the failure on the part of many government entities to connect bits of evidence indicating criminal and terrorist activities was a failure of public security. But over a fairly short period, the police arrested more than four hundred Aum members on charges ranging from kidnapping and drug production to murder and the sarin attack. Forty-one Aum members were charged with murder. Almost a dozen of them have been sentenced to death, and most of these cases are moving through the Japanese legal system's appeal process. Additionally, a legally based system of monitoring Aum's successor group and its facilities seems to have reduced the group's opportunity for unlawful and violent actions. Thus, despite some difficulty in recognizing many of Aum's unprecedented crimes, the Japanese government showed that it could adapt and assemble new legal, organizational, and investigative capabilities. In a confrontation with a group willing to commit mass murder with unconventional weapons generally associated with the militaries of states, the Japanese government's accomplishments are worth noting, particularly in a period of heightened concern about terrorism, when officials are predisposed to take aggressive actions first and uphold constitutionally established legal provisions when security is perceived to have been restored.

Notes

1. Bruce Hoffman, "'Holy Terror': The Implications of Terrorism Motivated by a Religious Imperative" (research paper, document P-7834, Santa Monica, CA, RAND,1993).

2. Statement of a leader of Aum's local office in Ibaragi Prefecture, introduced in *A2*, a documentary film produced by Tatsuya Morii in 2001. Translation by the author.

3. See *1996 White Paper on Police* [Heisei 8-nen keisatsu hakusho], by the Japanese National Police Agency [Keisatsuchou], chapter 1, section 1.

4. Ikuo Hayashi, *Aum and Myself* [Oumu to watashi] (Tokyo: Bungei Shunju, 2001), 502–3.

5. Ibid., 445, 455, 463. Translated by the author.

6. See Ryuzo Saki, *Terrorists without a Cause* [Taigi naki terorisuto] (Tokyo: NHK, 2002), 212. Translation by the author.

7. This is a term employed from esoteric Tibetan Buddhism that Asahara reinterpreted as a doctrine to justify killing someone who has committed many sinful deeds before he or she goes to hell. See Ken'ichi Kouhata, *Aum Court*

Trial, vol. 2, part 1, *Guru vs. Followers* [Oumu houtei 2, Guru v.s. shinto jou] (Tokyo: Asahi Bunko, 1998), 42. Translation by the author.

8. Testimony of former Tokyo government official who certified Aum Shinrikyo's status as a religious corporation. See *Records of Court Testimonies,* vol. 2 [Oumu (Kyouso) houte; zenkiroku] (Tokyo: Gendai Shokan, 1997), 194–96.

9. *1996 White Paper on Police,* chapter 1, section 1.

10. *Records of Court Testimonies,* vol. 2 (1997), 194.

11. Ian Reader, *Religious Violence in Contemporary Japan: The Case of Aum Shinrikyo* (Honolulu: University of Hawai'i Press, 2000), 147. See also Kaplan and Marshall, *Cult at the End of the World,* 24.

12. Prosecutor's opening statement in the trial of Kiyohide Hayakawa, March 27, 1996, cited in Ken'ichi Kouhata, *Aum Court Trial,* vol. 1, part 2, *Servants to the Guru* [Guru no shimobe tachi gekan] (Tokyo: Asahi Bunko, 1998), 240–41. See also another prosecutor's interrogation of Chizuo Matsumoto, on October 4, 1995, in Matsumoto's trial, cited in Ken'ichi Kouhata, *Aum Court Trial,* vol. 13, *Maximum Penalty* [Kyokukei] (Tokyo: Asahi Bunko, 2004), 234.

13. Prosecutor's final speech in court on April 24, 2003. See ibid., 234.

14. *1996 White Paper on Police,* 7. See also Kaplan and Marshall, *Cult at the End of the World,* 35–37.

15. Japanese official of the Public Security Investigation Agency, interview with author, February 29, 2004, Washington, DC.

16. Japanese official of the Public Security Investigation Agency, interview with author, October 20, 2003, Washington, DC.

17. See testimony of Hiroshi Ohno, a police inspector of the Kanagawa Prefecture police who was in charge of investigating Okazaki's information, in court on June 29, 1997, cited in *Records of Court Testimonies,* vol. 2 (1997), 273–325.

18. *1996 White Paper on Police,* 5.

19. D. W. Brackett, *Holy Terror: Armageddon in Tokyo* (New York: Weatherhill, 1996), 98.

20. Reader, *Religious Violence in Contemporary Japan,* 181.

21. Kyle B. Olson, "Aum Shinrikyo: Once and Future Threat?" *Emerging Infectious Diseases* 5, no. 4 (July–August 1999): 515.

22. Aum attempted several biological attacks other than the 1993 Kameido case. Tragically, the group did succeed in a few assassinations using various chemical agents, including VX. For a table summarizing Aum's various attacks with chemical and biological agents, see David E. Kaplan, "Aum Shinrikyo

(1995)," in *Toxic Terror: Assessing Terrorist Use of Chemical and Biological Weapons,* ed. Jonathan B. Tucker (Cambridge, MA: MIT Press, 2000), 207–26.

23. Hiroshi Takahashi and others, "Bacillus anthracis Incident, Kameido, Tokyo, 1993," *Emerging Infectious Diseases* 10, no. 1 (January 2004): 117, www.cdc.gov/eid. See also Paul Keim and others, "Molecular Investigation of the Aum Shinrikyo Anthrax Release in Kameido, Japan," *Journal of Critical Molecular Biology* (December 2001): 4566.

24. Takahashi and others, "Bacillus anthracis Incident," 117.

25. Ibid.

26. Decision of the Tokyo District Court on February 27, 2004, cited in *Records of Court Testimonies,* vol. 8 (2004), 190.

27. Prosecutor's final speech in court on April 24, 2003. See ibid., 156. Translation by the author.

28. Testimony of Kazuyoshi Takizawa, formerly in charge of construction of the chemical plant, in court on October 6, 2000, cited in *Records of Court Testimonies,* vol. 6 (2001), 201–3.

29. Decision of the Tokyo District Court on February 27, 2004, cited in *Records of Court Testimonies,* vol. 8 (2004), 193–94.

30. Decision of the Tokyo District Court on February 27, 2004, cited in ibid., 194–95.

31. Former senior official in the cabinet's Office for National Security Affairs, interview with author, January 21, 2004, Tokyo.

32. Iku Aso, *Secret Investigation* [Gokuhi sousa] (Tokyo: Bunshun Bunko, 2000), 42.

33. See ibid., 57. See also Naoya Suzuki, "What Were the Yamanashi Police Doing?" [Yamanashi kenkei wa nani o shita], *AERA,* April 10, 1995, 22; and Hiromichi Ugaya, "Police Rely on Criminals' Confessions More Than Forensic Investigation" [Kagaku sousa yorimo jihaku ga tayori], *AERA,* June 19, 1995, 9.

34. Aso, *Secret Investigation,* 49–54.

35. Ibid., 59–61.

36. Ibid., 62.

37. Ibid., 57.

38. Ibid., 67–71.

39. *Records of Court Testimonies,* vol. 8, 281.

40. Senior Japanese Ground Self Defense Force official, interview with author, January 2004.

41. Ibid.

42. Reiko Inoue, "How X-Day Was Decided" [X Deh wa dou kimatta], *AERA,* May 29, 1995, 15.

43. *1996 White Paper on Police,* 17.

44. Robyn Pangi, "Consequence Management in the 1995 Sarin Attacks on the Japanese Subway System," *Studies in Conflict and Terrorism* 25, no. 6 (November–December 2002): 439.

45. This law was applied to five leaders of radical leftist groups Chukaku and the Bundo-ha Red Army, in 1969. See Peter J. Katzenstein and Yutaka Tsujinaka, *Defending the Japanese State,* Cornell East Asia Series (New York: Cornell University, East Asia Program, 1991), 17.

46. See Ken'ichi Kouhata, *Aum Court Trial,* vol. 4, *Statement of Chizuo Matsumoto* [Matsumoto Chizuo no iken chinjutsu] (Tokyo: Asahi Bunko, 1999), 22–23. Translation by the author.

47. National Policy Agency, *2000 White Paper on Police* [Heisei 12-nen keisatsu hakusho], chapter 5, section 1-1.

48. U.S. Department of State, *International Religious Freedom Report 2002.* Released by the Bureau of Democracy, Human Rights, and Labor, www.State.gov/g/drl/rls/irf/2002/13874.htm. See also Pangi, "Consequence Management," 439.

49. Cited in Ken'ichi Kouhata, *Aum Court Trial,* vol. 11, *Perpetrators of the Assault on Attorney Sakamoto* [Sakamoto bengoshi shugekihan] (Tokyo: Asahi Bunko, 2003), 191–99.

50. Former senior Japanese Cabinet Secretariat official, interview with author, January 2004.

51. Kouhata, *Aum Court Trial,* vol. 11, *Assault on Attorney,* 207–8.

52. "Aum Still a Deadly Threat," *Mainichi Shimbun,* October 9, 1999, 1. "Police Confiscated Aum Toxic Treasure Trove," *Mainichi Daily News,* October 14, 1999.

53. Fumihiro Joyu and Tatsuko Muraoka, Statements made for "Outlook on the AUM-Related Incidents and Outline of Drastic Reform" (Public Relations Department of Aleph, January 18, 2000), http://english.aleph.to/pr/01/html.

54. National Police Agency, Public Security Division [Keisatsuchou, Kouanka], "Regarding a Report on the Status of the Implementation of the Group Regulation Act Applied against a Group That Conducted an Indiscriminate Mass Murder" [Musabetsu tairyou satsujin o okonatta dantai no kisei ni kansuru houritsu no Shikou Joukyou ni kansuru houkoku ni tsuite] (press release, April 16, 2004).

55. "Cypriot Police Arrest Ex-Aum Member over Illegal Stay," *Japan Economic Newswire,* April 17, 1998.

56. Ichiro Mizusawa, "Aum Shinrikyo Boosts Cult-Expansion Efforts," *Tokyo Chian Foramu,* December 1, 2003, 12–21 (FBIS translated text, JPP20031217000030). See also "Russian AUM Cultists Own Up to Planned Japan Terror," *Manichi Daily News,* December 5, 2001.

57. U.S. Department of State, *International Religious Freedom Report 2002.*

58. "Aum Facilities Raided Ahead of Matsumoto's Sentencing," *Daily Yomiuri* (Tokyo), February 17, 2004, 2

59. National Police Agency, Public Security Division, "Report on the Status of the Implementation of the Group Regulation Act."

60. "Japanese Authorities Raid 11 Facilities Related to Doomsday Cult," Kyodo News Service, February 16, 2004.

61. Joyu and Muraoka, "Outlook on the AUM-Related Incidents."

62. Public Security Investigation Agency, "A Request to Extend the Monitoring Period" [Koushin Seikyusho], November 25, 2005.

63. "Joyu's Faction May Establish a New Religious Organization" [Joyuha ga shinkyouden tachiageka], Kyodo News Service, May 2, 2006.

64. Tomohito Shinoda, "Japan's Response to Terrorism" (paper presented at Woodrow Wilson Center, October 16, 2001).

65. Kazuharu Hirano, "The Aum-Shinrikyo Cult and Countermeasures by Japanese Authority: Lessons and Response to Aum-Shinrikyo Affair" (paper for FRS Seminar on Nonconventional Terrorism and the Use of Weapons of Mass Destruction, December 12–13, 2002, Paris, France), 10–11.

66. Japanese National Police Agency senior official, interview with author, January 2004.

67. Deputy chief cabinet secretary for crisis management [Naikaku Kiki Kanri Kan], "Regarding the Response to NBC Terrorism and Other Types of Terrorism Aimed at Mass Murder" [NBC tero sono hoka tairyou sasshou gata tero e no taisho ni tsuite], May 28, 2001.

68. *1996 White Paper on Police,* 22–23.

69. Hirano, "Aum-Shinrikyo Cult and Countermeasures," 8.

70. Administrative Reform Council [Gyokaku Kaigi], *Intermediate Report* [Chukan seiri], May 7, 1997, cited in Bouei Nenkan Kankoukai, *Defense Almanac 1999* [Bouei nenkan 1999] (Tokyo: Bouei Nenkan Kankou Sentah, 1999), 49–50.

71. Hirano, "Aum-Shinrikyo Cult and Countermeasures," 8. See also James L. Schoff, ed., *Crisis Management in Japan and the United States* (Herndon, VA: Brassey's, 2004), 84.

72. Bouei Nenkan Kankoukai, *Defense Almanac 1999,* 24–26.

73. Cabinet Decision [Kakugi kettei], "Regarding the Administration's Initial Response When a Serious Terrorism Incident May Occur" [Juudai tero jiken nado hasseiji no seifu no shodou sochi nitsuite], April 10, 1998, cited in ibid., 51–53.

74. Schoff, *Crisis Management,* 84.

75. Ibid.

76. *1996 White Paper on Police,* chapter 1, section 5-2.

77. National Police Agency, "On organizational Reform of the National Police Agency in 2004" [Heisei 16-nendo ni okeru Keisatsuchou no soshiki kaihen kousou ni tsuite] (press release, August 2003).

78. Peter J. Katzenstein, "Same War—Different Views: Germany, Japan, and Counterterrorism," *International Organization* 57, no. 4 (Fall 2003): 731–60.

79. David Leheny, "Tokyo Confronts Terror," *Policy Review,* December 2001–January 2002, www.policyreview.org/DEC01/leheny_print.html.

80. Hirano, "Aum-Shinrikyo Cult and Countermeasures," 9.

81. Ibid.

82. Joseph Coleman, "Japanese Leaders Explore Option in Wake of Kidnappings in Iraq," Associated Press, April 8, 2004.

83. Katzenstein, "Same War—Different Views," 747.

84. Gary Schaeffer, "Japanese Cult Seeks New Sanctuary after Police Raid," *Independent,* May 2, 2003. See also, "Panawave Sparks Paranoia," *Mainichi Daily News,* December 23, 2003, 8.

85. "Police Raid Bizarre White Cult," *Mainichi Daily News,* May 14, 2003, 1.

86. Prosecutor's final speech in court on December 24, 1999, cited in Ken'ichi Kouhata, *Aum Court Trial,* vol. 9, *Aum's Minister of Intelligence, Yoshihiro Inoue* [Chouhoushou choukan Inoue Yoshihiro] (Tokyo: Asahi Bunko, 2002), 228.

87. Verbal testimony of John F. Sopko, U.S. Congress, Senate, Committee on Governmental Affairs, Permanent Subcommittee on Investigations, *Global Proliferation of Weapons of Mass Destruction,* part 1 (Washington, DC: U.S. Government Printing Office, 1996), 41.

88. Written testimony of Kyle B. Olson, ibid., 111.

89. Norimitsu Onishi, "Japan Arrests Five Who Knew Man Possibly Tied to Qaeda," *New York Times,* May 27, 2004, 10; Isami Takeda, "A Fund Raising Network That Expands throughout the World: What Was al-Qa'ida Doing in Japan?" *Tokyo Chuo Koron,* July 1, 2004, 172–75 (FBIS translated text, JPP20040617000025). See also "Al Qaeda Member Entered Japan 4 Times and Hid in Niigata" [Aru Kaida no menbah ga 4-kai nyuukoku, Niigata Shinai ni senpuku], *Asahi Shimbun,* May 19, 2004.

16

CONCLUSION

Robert J. Art

Louise Richardson

The cases we have examined reveal that there is not one terrorism but many. Terrorism is a tactic that has been adopted by many different groups, in many parts of the world, in pursuit of many different objectives. The terrorist movements we examined operated in mature democracies as well as in new and fragile democracies. They operated in Europe, Asia, the Middle East, Latin America, and North Africa. They fought in pursuit of ethnonationalist, revolutionary, religious, and millenarian objectives. Some have been successfully countered; some have not. Some no longer exist; many do. In all, we have examined the encounters between thirteen governments and about sixteen terrorist groups.

In deriving general patterns from these myriad cases, we find that the lessons we have extracted in and of themselves are not new. What we do claim, however, is that these lessons are now solidly grounded in a careful empirical analysis of a substantial number of disparate cases. Lessons that many analysts had arrived at earlier through an intensive study of their particular cases are now shown to have wider applicability. In short, systematic comparative analysis has validated the claims of more general applicability by previous scholars.

Three important general observations flow from our cases. First, and one that provides grounds for optimism, is that governments' counterterrorist practices improve with time. The Italian, Peruvian, Indian, and British governments, for example, each learned from their mistakes against the Red

Brigades, Shining Path, Sikh terrorists, and the IRA, respectively, and each dramatically improved the effectiveness of its counterterrorism policies. It is our conviction that governments confronting terrorism today have the opportunity to learn from the successes and failures of others. It is also our conviction that it is vital for governments today to learn from the past, because the stakes have become higher than they once were, especially if terrorists acquire weapons of mass destruction. Moreover, we may not have the luxury of time to make our own mistakes and learn from them. Instead, we believe that we can, and that we should, learn from the experiences of other governments.

The second general observation, as the cases in this volume amply demonstrate, is that although the experiences of governments differ, they are alike in one crucial regard: there is no one simple policy prescription—no "silver bullet"—for successfully countering terrorism. This point is obvious, but it needs constant reiteration. There is a tendency to believe, for example, that good intelligence can "solve" the terrorist problem. "If only we can find them, we can eliminate them," so the conviction runs. Clearly, good intelligence, as we make clear below, is crucial in successful counterterrorist campaigns, but good intelligence will enable governments only to find terrorist cells before they act or thwart attacks before they take their toll. But intelligence alone cannot prevent the regeneration and recruitment of terrorists. Other policies are necessary. Moreover, different terrorist movements pose different types of threats in different contexts. As a consequence, terrorism requires a multifaceted response. With the singular exception of Turkey, which was able to engage in the massive use of force and repression, each successful case we examined required a number of policy responses.

The third general observation, and perhaps the most salient, is this: the most successful governmental responses among our cases consisted of both sticks and carrots. Terrorism is unjustified, and the killing of innocent non-combatants reprehensible. The tendency to deal with terrorism only with force and security measures is usually strong, but this understandable temptation must be resisted. Our cases clearly demonstrate that democratic governments that sought simply to obliterate terrorism by force succeeded mostly in making their problems worse. What they ended up doing was simply fanning the flames of discontent and adding to the appeal and ranks of the terrorist groups. On the other hand, when governments moved to address the underlying factors that gave rise to terrorism in the first place, in conjunction with the use of effective coercive policies, they were more likely to succeed. Neither sticks nor carrots worked in isolation from each other. Our cases demonstrate that only an approach that employs both carrots and sticks, and integrates them properly, offers the best hope of successfully countering groups that employ terror tactics to achieve their objectives.

In what follows below, we first address the lessons we have learned about the use of sticks—the "hard" aspects of counterterrorism. Then we address the lessons we have learned about the use of carrots—the "soft" aspects of counterterrorism. Finally, we assess which of these lessons can be of most use in dealing with the transnational jihadist terrorist threats that the United States and its allies face today.

LESSONS ABOUT STICKS

Intelligence

The first and most important rule for successful counterterrorism is "know your enemy," and the key to knowing your enemy is good intelligence. The crucial importance of good intelligence leaps from the pages of every one of our cases. Palmer demonstrates how a small, specialized intelligence agency within the police force was able to achieve what wave after wave of military deployments in the Peruvian countryside could not—the capture of Sendero leader Abimael Guzmán. The decapitation of Sendero proved to be the fatal blow to the movement, whose campaign of Maoist revolution launched a conflict that resulted in sixty-nine thousand casualties.

Ganor shows how Israeli intelligence capability has been crucial to Israel's campaign against Palestinian terrorist groups. He credits the successful development of these capabilities to Israeli familiarity with the Arab language and culture acquired through the many years of Israeli control of the West Bank and Gaza. He argues that this intelligence, which is based on both human sources and advanced technology, has been successfully deployed both defensively and offensively. On the one hand, the intelligence apparatus enabled Israel to prevent and neutralize planned terrorist operations; on the other hand, it provided guidance for targeted killings and air and ground attacks.

Byman's analysis of Israeli action against Hizballah complements Ganor's account. Byman shows that while on a number of occasions, good intelligence led to targeted strikes and kidnappings of Hizballah leaders, because it did not control the territory in which Hizballah operated, Israel found it altogether more difficult to garner good intelligence against Hizballah than against the Palestinian organizations.

Wallace shows how India was able to infiltrate terrorist groups in Punjab and how that infiltration provided good intelligence that in turn had the benefit of weakening the groups by sowing distrust among their memberships. The same occurred in Northern Ireland: Richardson points to a period in which more IRA fatalities were self-inflicted in a search for collaborators than were inflicted by the security forces. Shapiro shows that in France, intelligence was repeatedly used to good effect, although it was not quite good enough to prevent small-scale attacks. Similarly, Calvert argues that in Venezuela, intelligence was the foundation of Betancourt's successful counterterrorist strategy. The fact that Betancourt had emerged from the same political tradition as many of the terrorists greatly facilitated his ability to develop an effective intelligence operation.

Through a painstaking process of developing sources over time, the quality of British intelligence in Northern Ireland improved significantly. Richardson argues that the fiasco of the introduction of internment without trial in 1971 demonstrates the folly of acting prematurely and on faulty intelligence. In an effort to nip the terrorist threat in the bud by rounding up suspected members of the IRA, the British government alienated the Catholic community by applying the policy almost exclusively against the Catholic population and by picking up large numbers of innocent civilians; the IRA leadership, meanwhile, with its own and in this case more reliable sources of intelligence, had escaped across the border to the Republic of Ireland. Years later, when the British government did have good intelligence and might well have been able to round up the leadership of the IRA, even if it could not have won court convictions against them, it did not dare to incur the political cost of reintroducing internment.

Even governments that did not build on intelligence as the centerpiece of their counterterrorist strategy, such as Turkey and Italy, improved the quality of their intelligence over time. In the Italian case, the introduction of *pentiti* legislation (see below) significantly improved the quality of the intelligence acquired, as increasing numbers of *brigatisti* turned in their comrades in return for more lenient sentences.

The absence of good intelligence also contributed to the failure of coun-terterrorism policies in a number of our cases. The Japanese government and its intelligence community completely failed to appreciate the importance, understand the motives, or investigate the extensive assets of Aum Shinri-kyo. Most of all, Japan utterly failed to anticipate Aum's actions. Marks's account of Sri Lanka's counterterrorism policies similarly demonstrates that the government's intelligence community misread the terrorist threat in all its violent parameters and that even when reliable intelligence was available, policymakers failed to act on it in a timely way. Cronin argues that in Chechnya, the Russian government's emphasis on a military response alien-ated the local population and undermined the government's ability to garner intelligence successfully. Finally, in contrast, Waldmann attributes the fail-ure of the Colombian government to develop good intelligence to the gener-ally weak character of the Colombian state and its institutions.

One striking factor that enhanced the effectiveness of intelligence capa-bilities was international cooperation. The Spanish government's campaign against ETA and the British government's campaign against the IRA were immeasurably enhanced once France and the Irish Republic took steps to make cross-border escape more difficult and started sharing intelligence information. Conversely, the ability to slip across a border and acquire sanc-tuary in another country, as Kashmiri separatists were able to do, greatly undermines a state's ability to develop effective intelligence.

In the intelligence realm, U.S. assistance to several of these governments proved to be enormously important. The Turkish government's capture of PKK leader Abdullah Öcalan was only possible due to U.S. intelligence assistance. U.S. intelligence also provided crucial technological assistance to the Peruvian intelligence unit DIRCOTE. Moreover, the United States has constantly helped, although to less apparent effect, the intelligence agencies fighting the FARC in Colombia.

On occasion, crediting foreign governments with valuable assistance—as Britain did with French intelligence in the capture of the Libyan ship the *Eksund*, laden with weapons for the IRA—has the added advantage of solidifying relations between allies and protecting sources. (Although the British publicly credited French intelligence for the capture of the *Eksund*, the ship was actually betrayed by an IRA insider.)

In short, our cases uniformly stress the importance of good intelligence. Moreover, in every one of our cases, it took time to develop good intelligence capacity. It was also easier to develop good intelligence capability when the government controlled the territory in which a terrorist group operated. It also helps to understand the language and culture of the terrorists, and it does not pay to act prematurely on poor intelligence. Finally, our cases point to the crucial importance of international cooperation in countering terrorist movements. The trend for the future is clearly one in which more terrorist groups will be operating outside the territory controlled by their enemies, and this situation will make international cooperation even more important in the future. As a consequence, developing norms and procedures for international intelligence sharing will be a crucial ingredient in any successful counterterrorist strategy.

Coordination of Security Forces

A second conclusion that emerges clearly from our cases is both the importance and the difficulty of coordinating the actions of various security forces. Bureaucratic traditions of defending organizational turf are endemic in governments. A serious effort to coordinate the actions of the different organizations involved in the counterterrorist battle, to ensure sharing of information, effective division of labor, and coordinated action, was a precursor to every successful case we examined. As with the development of effective intelligence capability, this process generally took time. Barkey writes of the importance of training the new units that replaced the forces used in the Turkish government's earlier haphazard action against the PKK. Similarly, Marks describes a gradual improvement in coordination among the various Sri Lankan security forces. Wallace contrasts the difficulties between the military and the police in the earlier period with the coordinated action and intelligence sharing in the later period in the campaign against terrorism in Punjab.

Palmer describes how the various Peruvian forces, in particular military and police forces, were very much at odds with one another in the early days of the Sendero campaign in the 1980s. For some time, the police were on the front lines at the local level and bore the brunt of Sendero attacks, but there was very poor coordination among them in going from intelligence to operations. Later, the principle of establishing emergency zones and the assumption by the military commander of the role of chief political officer introduced coordination at the local and regional levels. In this role, the military commander was the chief coordinator of the other security forces, including the police, who then operated under his control. This process improved in the late 1980s and early 1990s as the military became clearer about what it was trying to achieve and how. Palmer describes how this effective coordination between the military, police, and civilian agencies in the early 1990s permitted the emergence of a shield-and-support strategy, with the military working with civilian agencies to protect emerging micro-development projects.

Israel has had the most experience in confronting a serious terrorist threat and has developed a special coordinating apparatus—the Counter-terrorism Coordination Office within the National Security Council. Ganor describes how cooperation among the security services, military intelligence, the army, and various governmental units produced successful operational results, especially when it came to offensive operations. Israel took the coordination a step further in establishing successful crisis management cooperation between the police and other first-responder units.

Richardson shows how the British government gradually but successfully coordinated the activities of its security forces. Coordination was rendered difficult because of the different standards of behavior of the military and the police, but also because of distrust between British and Northern Irish security forces. Richardson points out that despite significant improvements over time, the behavior of freewheeling agents remained a perennial problem and that some of them showed a tendency to coordinate quite well with extralegal organizations.

In some governments, notably Japan, Italy, France, and Spain, the military was not involved. Coordination among the domestic security agencies nevertheless remained a chronic problem. It was only after the Aum attack that the Japanese government improved coordination among various law enforcement authorities. Similarly, in Italy it took the tragic and humiliating kidnapping and murder of Aldo Moro to force a restructuring of the security forces. Weinberg describes the creation of special units of the state police and the *carabinieri*, headed by Salvatore Genova and Carlo Alberto Dalla Chiesa, respectively, that focused relentlessly on defeating the Red Brigades and finally achieved results. In France, as in Japan, the military was not involved, so the question of coordination became one among law enforcement organizations. Shapiro attributes the successful coordination of government action across law enforcement, intelligence, and the judiciary as perhaps the action most conducive to French success against the GIA.

In examining Venezuela, Calvert describes coordination as both essential and enormously difficult when the government faced a terrorist threat in the cities, a guerrilla threat in the countryside, and the open threat of a military revolt. In contrast, in Chechnya the lack of coordination among the security forces has been an enormous problem for the Russians. Cronin points out how federal and regional security units and the army all appear to be operating on their own—a situation that has on occasion led to terrible losses and has added to the general confusion in Chechnya. In Colombia, too, a weak state was unable to coordinate its forces, with the result that freewheeling paramilitary groups, often with only tenuous relations to the government, waged their own counterterrorism campaigns. The lesson from these cases is crystal clear. It is essential for any government to be aware of the barriers to coordination of its security forces and to make deliberate efforts to overcome whatever impediments exist for such coordination. The impediments are exacerbated in cases in which both the military and the police are engaged in counterterrorist activities, but they also occur between branches of law enforcement just as frequently as between law enforcement and military forces.

Discriminating Use of Force

The temptation to use force in response to a terrorist attack is almost irresistible for any government of any type in any part of the world. The savagery of terrorism and the deliberate violation of codes of behavior that it entails, especially in the deliberate targeting of noncombatants, call for a strong response. Authoritarian governments tend to see a threat to their legitimacy and prowess as defenders of order. Democratic governments also come under intense pressure from the public to react forcefully and not to appear weak to their opponents. Democracies, however, are altogether more restrained than authoritarian governments in their ability to use force. Many authoritarian governments have successfully deployed force against terrorist movements. The history of Latin America is replete with examples, such as the defeat of the ERP and the Montoneros in Argentina and the defeat of the VPR and ALN in Brazil. The wholesale abandonment of human and civil rights that these counterterrorist campaigns entailed is not available to democratic states in responding to threats of domestic terrorism. Democracies are more free to exercise force internationally, however, as the United States has done in Afghanistan and Iraq.

The only case we found in which a democratic or quasi-democratic government successfully deployed the indiscriminate use of force against a terrorist movement was the Turkish defeat of the PKK as described by Barkey. This was a case in which the government, for a variety of reasons, was able to wage a brutal and unrestrained military campaign against the PKK and the Kurdish villages in Turkey that supported it. Far more often, however, our cases show that the military was too blunt an instrument to be successfully deployed against terrorism. Indiscriminate use of force by governments usually had effects opposite to those intended: it made martyrs of terrorists, rallied recruits to the terrorist cause, and caused the uncommitted to lose confidence in the government. Widespread military deployment against terrorists also greatly increased the number of casualties. The Chechnya case is a tragic example of the costs and weaknesses of an exclusive reliance on force to eliminate the threat from terrorism.

Discriminating use of force, of course, is possible only if the security forces are coordinated and are operating with good intelligence. When they are not well coordinated, violence, even if discriminating in its intent, usually appears indiscriminate to victims. Terrorist strategists have long been aware of the value of provoking governmental overreactions that play back into the terrorists' hands. The strategists of ETA have been quite explicit on this point. By committing a terrorist atrocity, they sought to provoke the government into an overreaction. In so doing, ETA sought to win converts to its view that the government was a fascist state determined to trample on the rights of individuals. The decision by the Israeli government to abandon its long-standing policy of destroying the homes of the families of terrorist bombers reflected a recognition of the drawbacks of this approach. Byman describes how Israel's use of massive force against Hizballah in 1993 and 1996 backfired. The action increased popular support for Hizballah, proved a diplomatic disaster after Israel killed refugees at a UN site by mistake, and had little operational impact on the ground. In Northern Ireland, too, the popularity of the IRA rose and fell in keeping with the latest atrocity by the terrorists or the government. Richardson describes how the popularity of the IRA soared after events such as the introduction of internment, Bloody Sunday, and the hunger strikes. IRA popularity waned after bombings that killed women, children, and others uninvolved in politics. Ganor describes how the Israeli High Court, which heard complaints from Palestinians, served as a constraint and ensured greater discrimination in the application of force in the West Bank and Gaza Strip.

Wallace argues that the widespread use of regular, paramilitary, and local forces in the early years led to a counterproductive campaign in both Punjab and Kashmir. He shows how the Indian government learned the hard way—through the fiasco of the first attack on the Golden Temple—the perils of indiscriminate use of force and the advantages of being discriminating. Operation Bluestar in 1984 was conducted by the regular Indian military in the Golden Temple complex in Amritsar. More than one thousand people, including many civilians, were killed. Even moderate Sikhs were outraged, divisions between Hindus and Sikhs deepened, and violence escalated. In contrast, in 1988 Operation Black Thunder was conducted in the same Golden Temple, but with well-trained special forces. The operation caused the deaths of thirty terrorists and no civilians. Moreover, media coverage of the excesses of the terrorists undermined their support. Similarly, Marks shows how futile were the Sri Lankan government's efforts to shift toward what he terms "main-force warfare" against LTTE. In Colombia, according to Waldmann, the state is so weak and there have been so many actors that force has not been discriminating, and violence has been perpetuated. Palmer also shows how the Peruvian government learned to be more discriminating and hence more successful in its application of force. In the 1980s, the military was ignorant of local customs and practices and had no decent intelligence with which to distinguish Sendero supporters from others. After a reassessment in 1989, the military received much better intelligence by using local personnel in field operations, subjected the operational forces to basic human rights training, launched modest civic action programs, and became more careful about inflicting casualties on innocents.

In every one of our cases in which indiscriminate use of force was applied, with the notable exception of Turkey, the policy backfired and over time the governments realized this. The Russian campaign in Chechnya suggests that Russia has still not learned this lesson. In every other case in which the military was deployed, governments learned that focusing force on the perpetrators of the violence, and not more broadly on the communities in which they operated, served to undermine terrorist capability by preventing a flow of recruits to the organization.

Decapitation

While good intelligence, coordination of security forces, and discriminating use of force proved useful in all our cases, some policies were tried in only a few cases. Terrorist groups organize themselves differently; thus policies that work against some groups may not work against others. The policy of decapitation that was practiced in Turkey, Peru, and Japan proved to be an essential ingredient of each state's counterterrorist effort. Conversely, in other cases, most notably in Israel, decapitation did not work at all, and in the case of the Sikhs, it made matters worse. In many other cases, it was never tried. Decapitation means the removal of the leader of the organization. It does not necessarily mean killing him, and indeed in the three most successful cases just mentioned—Turkey, Peru, and Japan—the leader was incarcerated, not executed. Abdullah Öcalan, Abimael Guzmán, and Shoko Asahara were all charismatic leaders and enjoyed centralized power in their respective organizations. In each case their movements could not recover from their removal.[1] Conversely, Palestinian terrorist groups have managed to produce at least one replacement for every leader assassinated or incarcerated by the Israelis. The likely impact of decapitation depends on the role of the leader within the group. The death of Chechen leader Alsan Maskhadov may actually make Russia's goals more difficult to achieve because he was one of the few Chechens with the stature and standing to unite the various Chechen factions. One can imagine how the capture or death of Velupillai Prabhakaran might prove a mortal blow to LTTE, but most terrorist groups have devised a form of leadership that can survive losses of senior leaders by having replacements waiting on the sidelines.

LESSONS ABOUT CARROTS

Our cases demonstrate that Turkey managed to defeat the PKK, and France managed to defeat the GIA, without making concessions either to the terrorists or to the communities from which they derived support. Turkey was able to do so, as mentioned above, because of its ability to rely exclusively on force. France made use of a special court and legal system that gave the government powers that would be politically unacceptable, if not downright unconstitutional, in the U.S. system. These two cases, however, are the outliers. Cronin's account of Russian policy in Chechnya and Marks's account of Sri Lanka suggest that policies that would have alleviated the suffering of the Chechen and Tamil communities might have sapped support from the terrorist movements that operated in their names. In other successful cases, and in some unsuccessful ones, governments attempted to undermine support for terrorists by a range of policies such as social reform, mobilization of moderates, and negotiation—policies that are often gathered under the rubric of a hearts-and-minds approach.

It is not difficult to measure the success of improved intelligence operations; it can be measured in terms of the number of operations prevented or terrorists arrested. Similarly, the success of the use of force is often counted in the number of opponents killed or captured. While we have learned that body counts do not tell the whole story, they are a mechanism for measuring success. In contrast, it is enormously difficult to measure whether a policy of social and economic reform successfully undermines terrorism. Many such policies require a long time horizon and act in concert with other societal influences. That said, many of our authors argue that such soft policies were crucial ingredients in the counterterrorist campaigns of the governments they studied.

Repentance Legislation

An example of a policy that worked in some cases but not in others was the policy of offering to group members incentives for defection—that is, offering lenient treatment in return for a cessation of violence and provision of intelligence. The classic example of this legislation is described by Weinberg in his examination of the Red Brigades and the popularity of the pentiti legislation with members of an organization already under severe pressure. Those who turned state's evidence in turn strengthened the hand of the government by providing it with good intelligence. Spain, Peru, and Venezuela offered similar incentives to members of ETA, Shining Path, and the FALN, respectively, and in each case such legislation provided useful information and undermined morale among the terrorist membership. Richardson describes how a similar effort by the British government to encourage informants through the creation of "supergrass" trials was not as successful and was abandoned in the face of widespread legal challenges to the legitimacy and legality of the policy.

In a number of cases described in the volume, most notably Sri Lanka and Colombia, the policy was introduced and dropped at various points in the conflict with varying degrees of success. A recent similar move by the

Saudi government to offer leniency to Islamist radicals did not elicit much of a response. These cases appear to suggest that the timing of such legislation is important. The opportunity to turn against one's comrades is far more likely to be an attractive proposition to members of an organization facing defeat or under intense pressure than it is to group members who have reason to be confident in their ability to prevail. This judgment appears to be confirmed by the Italian case.

Mobilization of Moderates

In his treatment of the Italian defeat of the Red Brigades, Weinberg points to the essential role played by the Italian Communist Party in undermining support for the brigatisti. Calvert describes Betancourt employing a similar approach in Venezuela. In discussing Punjab, Wallace points to the crucial importance of the 1992 emergence of moderates who contested local and then state and national elections and in so doing succeeded in taking control of the political agenda from the terrorists.

Richardson describes how in Northern Ireland the British government initially sought to strengthen the hand of the SDLP, the moderate Catholic party, as a counterweight to the IRA. Subsequently, Britain continued the approach by attempting to strengthen the hand of the pragmatists within the IRA. In so doing, Britain assisted in the development of Sinn Féin as a major political party (and one that posed the gravest threat to the SDLP) and a political mechanism to pursue the IRA's objectives. In Spain, too, the government initially sought to win support away from ETA by providing concessions to the Basque Nationalist Party. Later, the Spanish government went further in permitting, for a time, the formation of Herri Batasuna as the political arm of ETA. After the March 11, 2004, terrorist attack by Islamist extremists in Spain, the government worked self-consciously to mobilize the Spanish Muslim community. This approach paid dividends on the first anniversary of the attacks, when moderate Muslim clerics in Spain issued a fatwa against Bin Laden as a perversion of Islam.

The policy did not always work. Byman points out that Israel initially tried this tactic in Lebanon in the early 1980s, but the policy actually led to the creation of Hizballah, as radicals within Amal rejected the peace with Israel with enthusiastic backing from Iran and Syria. Similarly, Ganor points out that Israel initially tried to limit community support for terrorist organizations by turning a blind eye to the activities of competitive organizations that were believed to be more moderate and less violent. In the 1970s, Israel permitted the Muslim Brothers to operate in the West Bank and Gaza in an effort to balance Fatah. In 1987 the Muslim Brothers gave rise to Hamas, an even more lethal terrorist organization. Waldmann describes the approach as being used erratically in Colombia.

Some successful counterterrorist approaches did not involve an effort to mobilize moderates. Palmer maintains that the policy was not tried in Peru, and Shapiro argues that it was not attempted in France either. The Japanese government, in reaction to the Aum subway attack, made no effort to mobilize moderate supporters of Aum. On the other hand, Cronin and Marks make clear that an effort to mobilize moderates in Chechnya and Sri Lanka might have mitigated the extent of the violence.

Social Reform

One of the most hotly debated issues among analysts attempting to understand the root causes of terrorism is the question of the relationship of economic factors, particularly poverty, to terrorism. The only consensus is that the relationship is indirect and complex. Nevertheless, that there is a relationship is clear. Most governments, in formulating a counterterrorist strategy, accept as much, and many have attempted to address issues of social reform as a means of undermining support for terrorism. Such policies generally do not have immediate effects and thus are not very attractive to politicians with an eye to the electoral cycle.

A review of our cases suggests a wide range of approaches to the matter of social reform. Turkey and France made no efforts to deal with underlying factors, yet the two governments were successful. On the other hand, the success of the Venezuelan and Peruvian campaigns against terrorism is attributed in large part to government policies addressing social problems. In Northern Ireland and India, the governments did provide funding for social reform efforts, although it is difficult to link these efforts to the success of a counterterrorist strategy.

In the case of the Red Brigades and Aum Shinrikyo, whose supporters by and large did not come from deprived backgrounds, the Italian and Japanese governments were able to defeat the movements without efforts at social reform. On the other hand, Marks attributes the growth of LTTE to the Sri Lankan government's failure to address crucial issues of social reform, whereas Cronin sees the Russian failure to address such issues as entirely in keeping with Russia's futile and brutal military response to the Chechen problem. In its response to Hizballah, Israel made no efforts to create social reform because it did not control the territories in which the terrorists operated. In contrast, after the Israeli occupation of the West Bank and Gaza in 1967, the Israeli government adopted an "open-bridges" policy that allowed residents of these territories to move freely from the West Bank to Jordan and to maintain family and economic ties in neighboring Arab states. In addition to these policies, Israel allowed residents of the territories to join the Israeli workforce. These policies dramatically reduced unemployment in the territories and raised the standard of living. The policies were abandoned during the first intifada (1987).

On the basis of our cases, it is difficult to draw a direct line between policies of social reform on the one hand and success in counterterrorism on the other. Some governments defeated terrorism without social reform policies; some governments could not have defeated terrorism without these policies; and some governments' failure to address social issues has led to a prolongation of conflict. Our cases clearly demonstrate that social privations are a contributing factor to terrorism. Only if it is prepared to ignore international standards of human rights completely, as in Turkey, or if the terrorist group is isolated from the broader community and driven by revolutionary goals, as were the Red Brigades, Aum Shinrikyo, and the GIA, is a government likely to attain success against terrorism without addressing social reform.

Political Engagement

The term *hearts and minds* is often used to describe a range of options, including efforts to engage members of the terrorist recruitment pool politically. Political engagement also extends to negotiating with terrorists. The negotiations can range from indirect meetings in which ground rules for the conflict are set, as in the establishment of red lines between Israel and Hizballah, to the establishment of code words, for instance so that British authorities will know when a bomb threat is a hoax and when it is not. Other political negotiations are far more substantive. In the cases of Northern Ireland and Sri Lanka, such negotiations led to the current peace talks. Similarly, recent negotiations between India and Pakistan have markedly reduced the level of violence in Kashmir.

These kinds of actions appear to have no place in cases of isolated revolutionary organizations such as the GIA, Aum, and the Red Brigades. In the case of a revolutionary organization with a mass base, such as Shining Path, a government can, and in this instance did, successfully employ a hearts-and-minds policy toward potential recruits without entering into negotiations with the terrorist movement itself. Palmer describes the successful establishment of new microdevelopment agencies to direct small amounts of resources to individual projects, concentrated in the two hundred poorest districts of Peru. Unlike the government's other policies of enhanced intelligence, coordination of security forces, and amnesty, which were directed at the terrorists, these development projects were designed to provide direct benefits to the poorest segments of society in order to regain their support for government authority.

In some cases, policies of engagement have been used erratically, as in Colombia and Russia. Cronin describes how negotiations were very much a factor in the first Chechen war, with the signing of the Kasavyurt Accords ending the war. This agreement stipulated that the two parties would resolve the status of Chechnya by 2001, but the second war began in 1999 with Putin's assumption of power and his vigorous adoption of a "no-negotiations" posture. Similarly, Wallace believes that 1985 negotiations between the major moderate Sikh political party and the central Indian government of Rajiv Gandhi, which resulted in an accord, could have avoided a high level of bloodshed and led to an end of the terrorist movement in its early stages. He believes that the failure to implement this agreement greatly contributed to the ensuing violence.

Calvert attributes Betancourt's success to his keeping the primacy of politics constantly at the forefront of his counterterrorist strategy. Marks attributes the prolongation of the Sri Lankan conflict to the government's erratic and uncoordinated attempts to pursue hard and soft policies, which also prevented the government from capitalizing on those times when brutal action by LTTE alienated Tamils. Again, the pattern is not entirely clear-cut, but the cases do point to the importance of pursuing a coordinated strategy of undermining support for terrorism and offering opportunities for political engagement.

LESSONS ABOUT INTERNATIONAL COOPERATION

Finally, our cases demonstrate both how valuable international cooperation can be for a government in its counterterrorism campaign, and how damaging lack of international cooperation can be. Our cases demonstrate how international cooperation can make both sticks and carrots more effective and how the absence of such cooperation can seriously weaken them.

For a variety of reasons, foreign governments have often greatly complicated the task of a government in dealing with its terrorist threat, and our cases provide such examples. Byman shows how support from Syria and Iran for Hizballah greatly increased the movement's strength. Wallace shows that Pakistan's support for Kashmiri separatists has enabled them to win recruits and acquire safe haven. Marks shows how India's role in Sri Lanka greatly exacerbated the problem for the Colombo government. The ability of ETA to flee north to France and of the IRA to flee south to the Irish Republic also increased their effectiveness as terrorist organizations. As these cases demonstrate, the establishment of international norms and procedures to impose sanctions for direct or indirect support for terrorist groups will strengthen the hand of democracies in countering terrorism effectively and will put the onus on governments that fail to live up to these international norms and procedures.

On the positive side, governments can be helpful with regard to the financial support that diasporic communities, such as the Irish in the United States, the Sikhs in North America and the United Kingdom, and the Tamils throughout the world, have provided for their respective separatist movements. International cooperation to stem the flow of financial support to terrorist groups has weakened them by reducing their funding and forcing them to raise funds through criminal activity, which in turn exposes them to risk of capture.

Involvement of outsiders in negotiations, including offers of postconflict foreign investment, has also proven to be a crucial ingredient in the successful negotiation of several important agreements, most notably the Oslo Accords between the Israelis and the Palestinians and the Good Friday Agreement in Northern Ireland. The international community has been a constant advocate for resolution of a number of conflicts, particularly those involving territory, and it has encouraged negotiated resolutions of the Kashmiri and Sri Lankan conflicts. International assistance in funding social reform programs is also quite readily available, whether from other governments, international institutions, or nongovernmental organizations. The Peruvian microdevelopment projects, for example, were largely funded by the Inter-American Development Bank and the World Bank. Waldmann believes that the spiral of violence in Colombia can be broken only through the involvement of the international community, both in addressing the complicating factor of the role of coca production and in providing the means for essential social and economic reform.

The lessons of these cases are that a successful counterterrorist strategy must be tailored to the nature of the movement faced. A simple, one-dimensional strategy is unlikely to be effective. Successful counterterrorist policies require a combination of hard and soft approaches. Moreover, international involvement can greatly strengthen the effectiveness of all policies, whether coercive or conciliatory. Governments that have been successful are those that have a strong intelligence capability, have coordinated their security forces, and have deployed force in a discriminating manner against the perpetrators of violence. Coercive policies directed at the perpetrators are augmented by conciliatory policies addressed to the broader communities from which the terrorists derive support. Successful governments ensure that their coercive policies do not undermine the impact of conciliatory programs, and vice versa. Finally, successful governments must realize that short-term policies cannot be allowed to undermine long-term goals.

Past Lessons and America's Present Challenge

Taken together, our fourteen case-study chapters, which span a forty-year period, constitute a wealth of collective experience about how thirteen democracies have dealt with groups that have employed terrorist tactics against them. Can the lessons we have drawn from these experiences help the United States and its allies in combating the current threats from al Qaeda and its affiliates—now referred to as the international jihadist terrorist network?[2]

Some might want to say no. This network, so the argument goes, has a number of characteristics that, taken together, distinguish it from each of these previous terrorist groups and make it unique to the extent that what worked against those groups will not work against it. Its organization combines features of both a strict hierarchy and a loose network; it has international reach, extensive financial support, technological sophistication, and professional training; and it is willing to inflict large numbers of noncombatant casualties if permitted to. It has, moreover, become much more than an organization; it has been transmogrified into an ideology and a transnational movement. All these attributes, some may argue, set al Qaeda and its affiliates so far apart from almost every other terrorist movement, past and present, that the above lessons we have drawn from previous cases are not relevant for this one.

We do not agree with this view, for two reasons. First, the counterterrorism lessons set forth in this volume, which generally accord with those noted in the few previously existing comparative studies mentioned in the introduction, are the only long-term evidence about counterterrorism campaigns that we have to work with. It therefore makes sense to draw on this evidence and adapt it where necessary to the current situation, especially since almost every one of the groups studied in this volume shares at least one characteristic with al Qaeda and its affiliates, even if none of our cases wholly duplicates them.

Second, and more important, we believe that some of our lessons can be readily applied to the international jihadist terrorist network because terrorist organizations share a number of common characteristics and must perform a number of common tasks if they are to survive and remain effective. For starters, the mixture of political and religious motives that al Qaeda represents is a terrorist trait of many centuries' standing. Similarly, just like other terrorist groups, al Qaeda and its affiliates need to operate under conditions of enormous uncertainty, recruit committed volunteers to replenish their ranks, execute successful attacks to remain viable, and retain passive supporters among the populations in the regions in which they operate. Al Qaeda also needs to ensure its organizational survival, financially and militarily, to be able to communicate internally and move from place to place. Notwithstanding the novel aspects of al Qaeda and its affiliates, they remain organizations dedicated to the use of terrorist tactics, and they employ terrorism strategically to achieve their goals. Because al Qaeda and its affiliates have to attack to ply their trade in the ways that terrorists have previously done, even if on a grander scale, they are therefore susceptible to the counterterrorism techniques that governments have previously used, even if these techniques have to be adapted to the specific characteristics of the international jihadist network. In short, the lessons from the past are useful for the present.

To show why this is so, first we briefly describe the salient characteristics of the international jihadist terrorist network. Then we show how the above lessons can be used to assess what the United States must do with its counterterrorism instruments and policies to meet the challenges posed by al Qaeda and its affiliates. We do not lay out a comprehensive U.S. counter-terrorist strategy; rather, we select from our cases the lessons most applicable to the type of counterterrorist campaign the United States must conduct to be successful against the international jihadist terrorist network.

AL QAEDA AND ITS AFFILIATES

RAND analyst Bruce Hoffman once asked: "Is al Qaeda a concept or a virus? An army or an ideology? A populist transnational movement or a vast international criminal enterprise? All of the above? None of the above? Or, some of the above?"[3] The answer today is probably "all of the above," but the emphasis has to be on the ideological and transnational nature of al Qaeda.[4]

Under the impact of the loss of its base in Afghanistan and under relent-less pursuit by the United States and its allies, al Qaeda, Hoffman has argued, was forced to reconfigure itself from a unitary bureaucratic organi-zation into an ideology and a loose confederation of groups. It has become a true transnational entity that has networked even more than before 2001 with numerous like-minded groups. Al Qaeda today consists of both a core of professional terrorists—what Hoffman terms "al Qaeda central"—and a venture capitalist organization that funds and supports other like-minded groups that resort to terrorism throughout the world.[5] The number of adherents belonging to al Qaeda central—that is, those who have been given the privilege of swearing personal fealty to Osama bin Laden—probably totals only between four hundred and two thousand.[6] The first wave of al Qaeda members came from the Middle East, largely from Alge-ria, Egypt, and Saudi Arabia; trained in al Qaeda's Afghani camps; and fought against Soviet troops there. The second wave of al Qaeda members is increasingly made up of Muslims who moved to western Europe and sec-ond-generation Muslims who were born there. They have lived separate from and segregated from European society, are "born-again Muslims," and have no attachment to a particular country but instead espouse a commit-ment to a universal *ummah* (community).[7]

Membership in groups that are affiliated with, directly tied to, funded by, or inspired by al Qaeda may well number in the several tens of thou-sands, which is the likely strength of the international jihadist terrorist network.[8] Among the most prominent of the al Qaeda–affiliated groups are the following:

- The Abu Sayyaf Group, which seeks to establish an Islamic state in the southern Philippines
- Jemaah Islamiya, which operates largely in Indonesia but seeks to establish a Southeast Asian Islamic state comprising Brunei, Indonesia, Malaysia, Singapore, the southern Philippines, and southern Thailand
- Al-Ittihad al-Islami, which aims to turn Somalia into a fundamentalist Islamic state
- The Islamic Army of Aden-Abyan, which wants sharia law implemented properly in Yemen
- The Salafist Group for Preaching and Combat, operating in Algeria and Europe, which seeks to overthrow the Algerian government and together with the GIA killed more than one hundred thousand Algerians in the 1990s
- Salafiya Jihadiya in Morocco, created by former Afghan mujahideen, as is the case with many al Qaeda–affiliated groups
- Jam'at al-Tawhid W'al-Jihad, Ansar al-Islam, and Asbat al-Ansar in Iraq, which are fighting both the U.S. military and the newly constituted Iraqi government
- The Chechen extremists
- Hizb-I Islamic Gulbuddin, led by Gulbuddin Hikmatyar, operating against U.S. troops in Afghanistan in cooperation with the Taliban
- Lashkar e-Tayyiba and Lashkar I Hhangvi, both based in Pakistan, with the former operating against India to free Kashmir and the latter attacking both westerners and Shias within Pakistan
- The Islamic Movement of Uzbekistan, formed in 1998 with the goal of overthrowing the Uzbekistani secular state and replacing it with an Islamic one[9]

Clearly, each of these groups has its own local agenda, but all buy into a common set of shared beliefs about the United States and the West, together with a common goal—all of which can be said to constitute the shared ideology of the international jihadist terrorist network. The shared beliefs are these: "the West is implacably hostile to Islam; the only way to address this threat and the only language that the West understands is the logic of violence; and jihad is the only option."[10] Because the United States is the leader of the West, it is the prime target. As Bin Laden put it in October 2001, when discussing the 9/11 attack with al-Jazeera journalist Tayseer Allouni: "They [Americans] understand only the language of attack and murder. Just as they kill us, we must kill them, to create a balance of terror. This is the first time in the modern era that terror has begun to reach a point of equilibrium between Americans and Muslims."[11] The common goal of al Qaeda and its affiliated groups is to replace what they see as corrupt and secular Muslim governments with theocracies that would govern according to their own fundamentalist strain of Islam—and would likely be undemocratic and suppress civil liberties. The ultimate goal for many of the jihadists is to establish a new caliphate that would rule over an undivided Islamic realm.[12]

It is these beliefs and goals that bind all these groups in one way or another to al Qaeda and to one another and that enable us to speak of the international jihadist terrorist network. What gives this network its particular potency is that it taps into the many resentments that large numbers of Muslims have about their socioeconomic conditions and the nature of the governments they live under, many of which are repressive and corrupt. It is the resonant chords that the jihadists strike in this larger group of sympathizers that give the jihadists a potentially inexhaustible supply of recruits.

Finally, although the United States and its allies have had successes in their counterterrorist campaigns against al Qaeda and its affiliates, they have not been put out of business. Indeed, the network executed twice as many successful attacks in the three years after 9/11 as it executed in the three years before.[13] According to Gilles Kepel, the purposes of these subsequent attacks were, first, to demonstrate to potential martyrs that al Qaeda was alive and well and, second, to terrorize, demoralize, and split the West.[14] Since 9/11, al Qaeda and jihadist terrorists in general are putting more emphasis than ever on recruitment from the Muslim diasporic community, especially those living in the West. Although the diasporic jihadists may be less capable than those trained in Afghanistan, they appear to be more technologically savvy and just as resolute.[15] Moreover, the Iraq War has served the same functions in the first decade of the twenty-first century that the war in Afghanistan did in the 1980s: as a cause around which to rally and as a training ground for terrorists, but with a twist—the jihadists have become particularly adept at urban terrorist warfare that can be just as easily applied in the United States and Europe as in Iraq and the Middle East.

In sum, al Qaeda today, in the words of Olivier Roy, "is an organization and a trademark. It can operate directly, in a joint venture, or by franchising. It embodies, but does not have the monopoly of, a new kind of violence."[16] Al Qaeda may be the premier organization of the global jihadist terrorist network, but it is not the only one. Today, the international jihadist terrorist network is thriving.

Applying the Lessons

If the international jihadist terrorist network remains a serious threat to the United States and its allies, what advice can we derive from our cases for America's counterterrorism campaign against it? There are three major sets of lessons to be gleaned. The first has to do with international cooperation; the second with the use of sticks; and the third with the political aspects of counterterrorism.

International Cooperation

First and foremost, our cases underline the importance of international cooperation. As important as this was in the majority of the campaigns in this volume, international cooperation is even more vital for the United States today. The governments in our cases were dealing with groups that arose within, and generally stayed within, their own territories, crossed back and forth from their territories to the safety of adjoining states, left their home territories to attack adjoining states, or received financing from their diasporas. Terrorism in these cases was often highly localized. In the current case, the international jihadist terrorist network is, by definition, a global phenomenon, and that requires the United States to operate globally. The war in Afghanistan was the ultimate networking experience for the first generation of al Qaeda members, and many of them then returned to their native countries to found or join the local jihadist groups mentioned above. Al Qaeda is thought to have semiautonomous cells in sixty states around the world, and "past experience has shown that these cells can operate anywhere from Florida to Faisalabad, from Hamburg to Hebron, from New Jersey to Jakarta."[17] There is an Afghan War diaspora, so to speak. Moreover, recruitment for the jihadist network is now worldwide, even if recruits come primarily from a number of specific states around the world. The Jihadists obtain funding from all over the world, and they travel the globe for meetings, recruitment, and operations. The jihadists have gone global.

Because the jihadist network is a global phenomenon, therefore, it takes a global response to deal with it. The United States cannot find the jihadists without the help of other states; it cannot attack them without the cooperation of other states; and it cannot cut off their finances without the help of other states. International cooperation is vital if the United States and its allies are to prevail. Homeland Security Secretary Michael Chertoff put it well: "If we are going to challenge the kind of interdependence that a terrorist network thrives upon, we have to be able to confront the network everywhere it operates, and that means we have to be able to function internationally and do it in partnership with overseas allies."[18]

Nowhere is international cooperation more crucial than in the intelligence area. The United States has allowed its human intelligence ("humint") sources to erode since the end of the cold war and has failed to invest sufficiently in the new types of humint resources that the post–cold war world requires. Its intelligence capabilities are "technology rich" but "humint poor." In particular, the Central Intelligence Agency is woefully lacking in the area and country expertise that the campaign against the international jihadist network requires—analysts with knowledge of the language, culture, and mores of the countries in which the jihadists operate and from which they recruit (apart from countries in Europe), and local agents who can blend in with their compatriots.[19] Under former director George Tenet, the CIA began to redress this humint deficiency, but rectifying it will take time and a serious commitment of resources, because seasoned analysts are not trained overnight, and good local agents are difficult to recruit.[20]

As a consequence, the United States needs the help of other countries' intelligence and security forces to track, penetrate, disrupt, and ultimately take down terrorist cells abroad that seek to harm Americans and our allies abroad and to attack Americans at home. Governments always try hard to develop intelligence about plot-specific plans and targets, but as Paul Pillar states, "Some of what terrorists do will remain, for all practical purposes, unknowable. Some terrorist plots will go undiscovered, and some terrorist attacks, including some major ones, will occur." Therefore, the most valuable thing that counterterrorism intelligence can do is develop information on individual terrorists, their leaders, and their cells. As Pillar has argued, and as the governments in our cases discovered, disruption of terrorist cells is the single most fruitful thing that counterterrorism can do. Disruption of a cell prevents it from launching a terrorist attack, sows suspicion and distrust among other cells, and often leads to the disruption of additional cells through the intelligence that the initial disruption produces. As Pillar puts it: "Most of the counterterrorist successes by U.S. intelligence have involved such disruption."[21]

Even if the United States had all the humint resources it now needs, however, the cooperation of other states would still remain vital.[22] The locals always know their own scene better than foreigners do, and working with local intelligence and police produces synergy effects that cannot be duplicated by working alone. The capture of several key al Qaeda leaders in the past few years in Pakistan demonstrates not only the crucial importance of local knowledge and intelligence but also how great synergy is produced when the United States and a foreign government cooperate. For example, a number of spectacular raids on terrorist cells took place when U.S. intelligence, through satellite tracking of cell phones, was able to pinpoint the location of known terrorists and provided the information to Pakistani security forces, who then conducted a raid. Finally, no matter how good the United States becomes at protecting its borders, they will never be impermeable. As the 9/11 Commission stated in its report: "We do not believe that it is possible to defeat all terrorist acts against Americans, every time and everywhere."[23] Enemies of the United States will find a way to get through, unless they are known beforehand, tracked, and then intercepted before they can execute their acts within the United States. Knowledge—intelligence—about who those bad actors are is one of the best means for creating borders that are as impermeable to terrorist penetration as they can be.

High-Quality Intelligence and the Use of Force

Another set of relevant lessons from our cases concerns three of the "sticks" of counterterrorism. These lessons are the critical importance of coordination and information sharing among governmental intelligence agencies so as to produce high-quality intelligence; the need for the discriminating and controlled use of force; and the mixed record of decapitation for crippling a terrorist group.

With regard to intelligence, the United States possesses a vast and varied intelligence enterprise spread among many agencies, but communication, coordination, and the sharing of information among them have rarely been ideal, especially with regard to counterterrorism. Indeed, in examining the record of the intelligence community before the 9/11 attacks, the *Joint Inquiry* of the House and Senate Intelligence Committees concluded in December 2002:

> Within the Intelligence Community, agencies did not adequately share relevant counterterrorism information, prior to 9/11. This breakdown in communications was the result of a number of factors, including differences in the agencies' missions, legal authorities and cultures. Information was not sufficiently shared, not only between different Intelligence Community agencies, but also within individual agencies, and between the intelligence and the law enforcement agencies.[24]

In particular, the lack of information sharing within the FBI, between agents working on domestic intelligence matters and those working on criminal cases, and between the CIA and the FBI, based on a "firewall" that had grown up in the 1980s and 1990s as a result of law, executive order, and practice, was a severe impediment to tracking terrorists within the United States.[25] As a consequence of this firewall, together with the belief in the summer of 2001 that the major al Qaeda threat was to Americans abroad, no one in the U.S. government was focusing on foreign terrorists who had entered the United States. As the 9/11 Commission recounts:

> The September 11 attacks fell into the void between the foreign and domestic threats. The foreign intelligence agencies were watching overseas, alert to foreign threats to U.S. interests there. The domestic agencies were waiting for evidence of a domestic threat from sleeper cells within the United States. No one was looking for a foreign threat to domestic targets. The threat that was coming was not from sleeper cells. It was foreign—but from foreigners who had infiltrated in the United States.[26]

Clearly, people in the U.S. government are now looking for foreign threats to domestic targets, and more effectively because the U.S. Congress has passed into law most of the recommendations of the 9/11 Commission regarding America's intelligence apparatus.[27] The new legislation creates two important centralizing and coordinating agencies: the Office of the Director of National Intelligence (ODNI) and, under the ODNI, the National Counterterrorism Center (NCTC).[28] The ODNI is to do what the old director of central intelligence was supposed to do but never had the time or real authority to do: coordinate the U.S. intelligence community. The goal is that the NCTC will collect and analyze information about terrorists from both domestic and foreign sources, something the CIA's former Counterterrorism Center did not do.[29] These two reforms are significant steps in the right direction, but much remains to be done. For example, the report of the Robb-Silberman Commission stated in March 2005: "Furthermore, even in the counterterrorism context, information sharing still depends too much on physical co-location and personal relationships as opposed to integrated, [Intelligence] Community-wide information networks."[30] It is also clear that while the FBI has made progress in becoming a better collector and analyzer of intelligence in its domestic counterterrorism role, "it still has a long way to go," and "even FBI officials acknowledge that its collection and analysis capabilities will be a work in progress until at least 2010."[31]

These two changes in America's intelligence apparatus, together with others mandated by Congress, are still in their early stages of implementation, and the degree to which they succeed in accomplishing their stated objectives will depend on how well they are implemented. Nonetheless, if our cases are any guide, these intelligence reforms are important steps in putting America's intelligence apparatus into the shape it needs to be in. Each government that was successful in its counterterrorist campaign found that, in one way or another, it had to improve significantly the quality of its intelligence regarding the group or groups it was combating. Along with enhancing the quality of analysts and improving the ability to penetrate the international jihadist network by infiltrating operatives into it, the coordination of intelligence collection and dissemination is a key step in improving the U.S. intelligence effort. Thus steps the United States has recently taken to improve its intelligence apparatus, particularly efforts to centralize the collection and dissemination of counterterrorism intelligence, accord well with what we have learned from our cases.[32]

With respect to the discriminating and controlled use of force, two points are in order. First, when the United States uses its military power abroad against the jihadist terrorists, it must be certain to do so in as discriminating a fashion as possible, for operations that run the gamut from large-scale military actions to treatment of prisoners. Actions such as the abuse of prisoners at Abu Ghraib and the torturing to death of prisoners in Afghanistan are not only morally reprehensible but also deeply counterproductive politically.[33] As several of our allies found in the cases in this volume, military actions often play right into the hands of the jihadists; for example, U.S. military actions have shown the United States to be exactly as Bin Laden has portrayed it: the United States is out to get Muslims and has a wanton disregard for their lives, and consequently the only thing the West and the United States understand is violence.

Counterterrorism requires the use of force, and there is no way around that. It does not, however, require the indiscriminate use of force, and our cases show how counterproductive the wanton and indiscriminate use of force is to a state's long-term effort to combat terrorism. As Robert Pape concludes in his study of suicide terrorism from 1980 to 2003: "The use of heavy offensive force to defeat today's terrorists is the most likely stimulus to the rise of more."[34] Whatever the arguments both for and against the war in Iraq, from a counterterrorist point of view, the war was a costly mistake. It enabled our enemies to portray us as using indiscriminate force, and it swelled the ranks of local jihadist groups.

The second point with respect to the discriminating and controlled use of force is that because the United States does not face an insurgency at home, it does not have the problem of coordinating the operations of its police and military forces within its home territory, as was the situation for the governments in many of our cases. It does, however, face the problem of coordinating the use of force abroad, especially covert operations, between the Central Intelligence Agency and the Defense Department, especially the latter's Special Operations Forces.[35] Large-scale military actions to go after terrorists, such as taking down the Taliban regime in Afghanistan, are rare. Instead, taking down the current jihadist terrorists abroad requires careful intelligence, diligent police work, and mostly small, covert military operations. Because this is so, it is crucial that the different security agencies conducting military and quasi-military operations abroad do so in tandem with one another. As our cases clearly demonstrate, having different security forces operating in ignorance of one another's operations is a potential recipe for disaster.

Our final lesson regarding the "hard" aspects of counterterrorism is this: Do not count on decapitation to incapacitate the global jihadist terrorist network. Decapitation worked in the Peruvian, Turkish, and Japanese cases because Shining Path, the PKK, and Aum Shinrikyo were highly centralized around one individual. Bin Laden created a different type of organization, one that was more linear, networked, and flatter—one that mirrored the corporate management organizational model of the 1990s and was therefore less dependent for effective functioning on the leader at the top.[36] Bin Laden has also effectively preempted any negative political repercussions that his death may bring about among his immediate followers and the larger audience to which he appeals by making clear publicly that he welcomes martyrdom. Given what he has accomplished thus far, he may well be larger in death than in life. Al Qaeda has also proved resilient in finding new leaders to replace the original ones taken down. In fact, as Bruce Hoffman and Kim Cragin argue, "Mid-level leaders are often more important than top decision makers for the long-term survival of a terrorist organization" because it is the midlevel leaders who carry out the operations and step into leadership roles.[37] Finally, as was made clear earlier, al Qaeda has networked with a collection of like-minded jihadist terrorist groups, most of which are stand-alone entities independent of al Qaeda central, even if they get assistance from it. Taking out the leader of a decentralized, networked organization does not destroy the organization. The 9/11 Commission put the point well:

> Our enemy is twofold: al Qaeda, a stateless network of terrorists that struck us on 9/11; and radical ideological movement in the Islamic world, inspired in part by al Qaeda, which has spawned terrorist groups and violence across the globe. The first enemy is weakened, but continues to pose a grave threat. The second enemy is gathering, and will menace Americans and American interests long after Usama Bin Ladin and his cohorts are killed or captured.[38]

Political Instruments

The third set of lessons we derive from our cases concerns the "softer" aspects of counterterrorism. Our cases clearly demonstrate that most of the time the hard instruments of counterterrorism are not sufficient in themselves to defeat a terrorist threat. This means that effective political policies must also be put into place, along with effective military, intelligence, financial, and economic policies. If the hard instruments of counterterrorism are used to track down and disrupt terrorist cells, then the softer instruments must be used to the following ends: to alleviate conditions that facilitate the emergence of terrorist groups; to turn members of terrorist groups away from the violent to the political; to woo potential terrorist recruits toward political action as a way to deal with their grievances; to strengthen moderates within the larger community so as to create a powerful alternative voice for the political path to change and thus to combat the terrorist ideology; and in general to delegitimize terrorism as a strategy for achieving political objectives within the societies from which it arises. Only this combination of instruments has the best chance to defeat the threat that the United States and its allies now face. The 9/11 Commission summarized the task succinctly: "Our strategy must match our means to two ends: dismantling the al Qaeda network and prevailing in the longer term over the ideology that gives rise to Islamic terrorism."[39]

In devising an effective political counterterrorism strategy, the United States faces two difficulties that most of the governments examined in this volume did not. First, the terrorists who threaten the United States operate from overseas, and therefore the U.S. government must work with Muslim governments and moderate leaders to delegitimize jihadist terrorism. This means, as a consequence, that there are real limits to what the United States can do within foreign societies and to how directly it can do it.

Second, the United States currently has a serious image problem that must be dealt with if its political counterterrorism efforts are to bear fruit. At a time when the jihadist terrorist network has become as much a global ideology and a religious-political movement as it is a networked organization, the United States is more disliked and distrusted in many areas of the world than it has been in more than fifty years, especially among its allies and among those Muslim states whose moderates it must court if terrorism is ultimately to be delegitimized.[40] U.S. unpopularity in the Muslim world in particular is in part a consequence of U.S. wealth, in part a reaction to the pervasiveness of U.S. culture, and most of all a result of U.S. policies in the region. U.S. support of Israel, the deployment of U.S. troops in Saudi Arabia after the Gulf War, the 2003 invasion of Iraq, and the subsequent conduct of the war there have all served to compound U.S. unpopularity in the region. Therefore, any political program to combat the appeal of both al Qaeda and the larger movement that it claims to spearhead must deal with both America's image problem and the appeal that the radical Islamist movement appears to have in the Muslim world. The two are separable to a degree but are also inextricably linked: the United States cannot conduct a successful political campaign against the global jihadists when its standing in the world, especially in the Muslim world, is as bad as it currently is. Consequently, the United States must work to improve its image globally while at the same time working with governments and moderate forces abroad to help delegitimize the global jihadists.[41]

In addition to dealing with these two difficulties, any political counter-terrorism strategy that the United States adopts must incorporate these three elements: (1) a more vigorous public diplomacy in the Muslim and Arab worlds to burnish its general image there and to make better known the valuable things it does in these lands; (2) policies that work unobtrusively but effectively to strengthen moderate Muslims; and (3) targeted political policies aimed at undercutting the appeal that the Islamist radicals and terrorists currently have within segments of the larger Muslim community. There are certainly many more elements for a comprehensive political strategy, but these three seem essential.

The first element is for the United States to strengthen its public diplomacy efforts in the Arab and Muslim worlds.[42] After the cold war ended, the United States allowed its public diplomacy apparatus to wither, much as it allowed the humint resources of the CIA to decline.[43] Even after the United States strengthens its public diplomacy efforts, however, it will take time and the dilution of political conflicts for its image to improve in the Muslim and Arab worlds; but there is basis for optimism that with the proper policies, this can be done. Most opinion polls show that what others object to are the style and policies of the United States, not the values the United States stands for, not U.S. culture, and certainly not Americans per se. Three recent examples demonstrate this point. The State Department's Independent Survey of Arab Publics study showed that anti-Americanism in six Arab countries was due to America's regional policies, especially the perceived bias in favor of Israel in the Israeli-Palestinian conflict, not to U.S. values, religion, or the al-Jazeera factor.[44] The *Djerejian Report* also documents that Arabs and Muslims admire U.S. technology, entrepreneurship, and the values for which the United States stands.[45] Finally, a recent focus group research project conducted in Morocco, Egypt, and Indonesia by the Council on Foreign Relations found that "despite the pervasiveness of anti-Americanism sentiment today, . . . what America says and how America says it can produce a significant shift in Muslim opinion." Thus public diplomacy, when combined with actions that help Muslim societies and a careful scrutiny of U.S. policies in light of their impact on the U.S. counterterrorist campaign, is a good recipe for improving America's image.[46]

The second element of an effective political counterterrorism strategy is for the United States to take steps to bolster Muslim moderates. To the extent feasible, this should be done as indirectly and as unobtrusively as possible. Zeyon Baran expresses the general strategy well: "You do it quietly. You provide money and help create the political space for moderate Muslims to organize, publish, broadcast, and translate their work."[47] Strengthening moderate forces can provide peaceful political alternatives to violence and terrorism for dealing with the legitimate complaints that many moderates have and that drive a very small percentage of Muslims to terrorism. If moderates can offer viable political alternatives to violence, then the replenishment of the terrorist ranks should diminish. Strengthening moderates in the Muslim world is akin to assisting them in creating the elements of a civil society—a free press, civic associations not dominated by the government, an impartial judicial system, modern educational systems—where they do not exist, and strengthening these elements where they do.[48] Democracies work best when a strong civil society functions within them; they do not work well in the absence of it. Social science research teaches that the transition to democratization works best when a strong civil society precedes the creation of a democracy.[49]

The third and most important element in any U.S. political counterterrorism policy is to devise a set of targeted policies that will help mitigate, even if they cannot completely solve, the international conflicts that severely complicate America's relations with the Muslim and Arab worlds. It is important for the United States to do something about the international conflicts over which it can exert some control for many reasons: (1) some conflicts contribute directly to generating terrorists; (2) some add more fuel to the fires of discontent with the United States in the Muslim world; (3) some, because they make the United States "radioactive" in the Muslim world, both alienate the moderates with whom the United States needs to work and undercut the ability of those still willing to work with the United States; (4) some make it more difficult for those governments that want to work with the United States to do so; and finally (5) some give all-too-ready excuses for governments not to work with the United States when they could or to avoid problems that they themselves need to address.

The United States and its allies cannot solve every social, economic, and political problem of the Muslim world nor rectify every grievance that it harbors. On the other hand, the United States and its allies must recognize the stake they have in these conflicts. Therefore, the task for the United States and its allies is to concentrate on those political disputes over which they have some influence, to make visible progress toward solving them, and to be certain not to take steps that create additional irritants in the process. Removing these irritants is not likely to change either the attitude or the dedication of the current generation of jihadists. Neither will it dissuade all the potential recruits of the next generation from replenishing the jihadist ranks. Instead, the goal of the United States and its allies must be to chip away at the problem by working on those issues over which it has some influence. Doing so will remove these issues as jihadist tools of leverage, and that cannot help but strengthen U.S. relationships with moderates and reduce the incentives for some would-be terrorists to join the ranks of the next generation.

Devising a list of policies will require creative thinking, but high on any such list should be the following: the investment of America's political capital toward real and visible progress in solving the Israeli-Palestinian conflict; the offer of America's good offices in helping move the dispute between India and Pakistan over Kashmir toward resolution; and a pledge by the United States not to establish permanent military bases in Iraq. The jihadists use the perceived tilt of the United States against the Palestinians to argue that America is anti-Arab and anti-Muslim. Genuine evenhanded U.S. efforts to solve this dispute will undercut the ability of the jihadists to reap value from the conflict. The Indo-Pakistani conflict over Kashmir serves as a generator of Pakistani jihadist terrorists; therefore, mitigating it may well reduce its value as a terrorist generator. The U.S. invasion of Iraq played right into Bin Laden's hands by enabling him to argue that the United States is in the Middle East to steal Arab oil; therefore, the pledge not to establish permanent military bases will undercut to a degree Bin Laden's claim. None of these targeted policies, nor any other such policies that are devised, are silver bullets. There are no silver bullets in a campaign against terrorism, but making political progress on these and like issues will make a difference.

One final point must be emphasized, however. None of these political instruments will be effective if the United States conducts a unilateral and arrogant foreign policy that is impervious to the interests and concerns of countries throughout the world. Moreover, a policy of invasion and occupation of a Muslim country without the sanction of the United Nations will seriously undercut all the political instruments suggested here. The war in Iraq, as mentioned earlier, was a serious setback for America's campaign against the global jihadist network, and such serious errors in policy must be avoided if success is to be realized.

Conclusion

The United States and its allies probably face a generation's work in combating jihadist terrorism. Its causes are complex and deeply rooted, deriving partly from present social, political, and economic circumstances in the Muslim and Arab worlds, but also from a historical Muslim sense of humiliation at the hands of the West and from the failures of successive Arab leaders to improve the lot of their peoples.

In persevering against the jihadists, the United States must do two difficult things. It must conduct an effective counterterrorism campaign while preserving its democratic freedoms, and it must demobilize the current jihadist terrorists without creating even more. Our cases demonstrate that such campaigns are long and hard, but they can be won if conducted with coordinated and forward-looking policies that combine coercion with conciliation. If the United States and its allies apply the relevant lessons derived from the cases in this volume, they can ultimately prevail.

Notes

1. In the Peruvian case, the government raid that captured Guzmán also captured many members of Shining Path's politburo. In a subsequent raid, the government also seized the movement's computer disks, and this led to further arrests of Shining Path's leadership.

2. See Richard A. Clarke, *Defeating the Jihadists: A Blueprint for Action,* Century Foundation Task Force Report (New York: Century Foundation, Press, 2004), 1.

3. Bruce Hoffman, *Al Qaeda, Trends in Terrorism and Future Potentialities: An Assessment,* RAND P-8078 (Arlington, VA: RAND, 2003), 3, www.rand.org.

4. For an in-depth, although slightly dated, view of al Qaeda, see Rohan Gunaratna, *Inside al Qaeda* (New York: Columbia University Press, 2002). For a more general analysis of the religious motivation of al Qaeda and Bin Laden, see Daniel Benjamin and Steven Simon, *The Age of Sacred Terror: Radical*

Islam's War against America (New York: Random House, 2002), especially chapters 2–4.

5. This description draws from a speech by Bruce Hoffman to MIT's Seminar XXI Program in Washington, DC, on April 4, 2005.

6. The estimate of the core member strength of al Qaeda comes from Clarke, *Defeating the Jihadists,* 16–17.

7. The distinction between the first and second waves, together with the description of the second wave, comes from Olivier Roy, *Globalized Islam: The Search for a New Ummah* (New York: Columbia University Press, 2004), 302–11.

8. This estimate comes from Clarke, *Defeating the Jihadists,* 16–17.

9. This list comes from ibid. See chapter 3 for a full description of each of these groups.

10. Hoffman, *Al Qaeda, Trends in Terrorism,* 10. Hoffman argues that these are the three ineluctable beliefs that stand out from a review of the approximately four thousand websites of the international jihadist network. Hoffman, speech (see note 5).

11. Quoted in Gilles Kepel, *The War for Muslim Minds: Islam and the West* (Cambridge, MA: Harvard University Press, 2004), 118.

12. See Benjamin and Simon, *Age of Sacred Terror,* chapters 2, 3; and Clarke, *Defeating the Jihadists,* chapter 1.

13. Clarke, *Defeating the Jihadists,* 16.

14. Kepel, *War for Muslim Minds,* 123–28.

15. Hoffman, speech (see note 5); and Roy, *Globalized Islam,* chapter 7.

16. Roy, *Globalized Islam,* 294.

17. Michael A. Sheehan, "Diplomacy," in *Attacking Terrorism: Elements of a Grand Strategy,* ed. Audrey Kurth Cronin and James M. Ludes (Washington, DC: Georgetown University Press, 2004), 100.

18. Quoted in Joe Fiorill, "U.S. to Court Europe on 'Security Envelopes,'" *Global Security Newswire,* www.nit.org/d_newswire/issues/2005_5_20.html#2203107.

19. Improving the CIA's human resources in both the analysis and operations divisions was one of the recommendations of the 9/11 Commission. See National Commission on Terrorist Attacks, *The 9/11 Commission Report: Final Report of the National Commission on Terrorist Attacks upon the United States* (Washington DC: U.S. Government Printing Office, 2004), 415. See also Richard A. Best, Jr., *Intelligence Issues for Congress* (Congressional Research Service report, updated March 22, 2005), 45, http://fpc.state.gove/documents/organizatin/45108.pdf.

20. Paul Pillar, "Intelligence," in *Attacking Terrorism,* ed. Cronin and Ludes, 128.

21. Ibid., 118.

22. Richard Clarke reports, however, that whereas only one terrorist snatch from abroad occurred during the Reagan administration, by the mid-1990s these snatches, more properly called extraordinary renditions, were being done on such a routine basis that "all but one of the World Trade Center attackers from 1993 had been found and brought to New York." See Richard A. Clarke, *Against All Enemies: Inside America's War on Terrorism* (New York: Free Press, 2004), 143.

23. *9/11 Commission Report,* 365.

24. *Joint Inquiry into Intelligence Community Activities Before and After the Terrorism Attacks of September 11, 2001* (Report of the U.S. Senate Select Committee on Intelligence and the U.S. House Permanent Select Committee on Intelligence) (Washington DC: U.S. Government Printing Office, December 2002), xvii.

25. For good descriptions of the nature of the firewall that existed, see the *9/11 Commission Report,* 78–80; and David Johnston, "Administration Begins to Rewrite Decades-Old Spying Restrictions," *New York Times,* November 30, 2002, A1.

26. See *9/11 Commission Report,* 263.

27. For the recommendations of the 9/11 Commission on intelligence reform, see ibid., 400–419.

28. The legislation is the Intelligence Reform and Terrorist Prevention Act of 2004, HR 108-796, 108th Congress, 2nd Sess. For useful descriptions of the main features of the congressional legislation, see Philip Shenon, "Next Round Is Set in Push toward Intelligence Reform," *New York Times,* December 20, 2004, A19; Council on Foreign Relations, "Intelligence Reform," December 9, 2004, www.cfr.org/background/intel_reform.php; and Richard A. Best, Jr., *Director of National Intelligence: Statutory Authorities* (Congressional Research Service report, April 11, 2005), www.fas.org/sgp/crs/intel/RS22112.pdf.

29. The Joint Inquiry of the House and Senate Intelligence Committees concluded in December 2002 in finding 9: "The U.S. Government does not presently bring together in one place all terrorism-related information from all sources. While the CIA's Counterterrorism Center does manage overseas operations and has access to most Intelligence Community information, it does not collect terrorism-related information from all sources, domestic and foreign." See *Joint Inquiry into Intelligence Community Activities,* xvii.

30. Commission on the Intelligence Capabilities of the United States Regarding Weapons of Mass Destruction, *Report to the President of the United States, March 31, 2005*, 14, www.wmd.gov.

31. Ibid., 29. See also chapter 10 of the report. Unlike several other countries, the United States has chosen to create a separate counterterrorism intelligence agency and career track within the FBI rather than set up a separate, freestanding domestic counterterrorism intelligence agency. The United States has thus chosen to put both domestic intelligence and law enforcement into one agency, rather than splitting them up. Changing the ethos of an agency whose dominant culture is law enforcement, not counterterrorism, is a slow process. For an analysis of how the United Kingdom, France, Canada, and Australia have structured their domestic counterterrorism security operations, including dedicated domestic intelligence agencies, see Peter Chalk and William Rosenau, *Confronting the "Enemy Within": Security, Intelligence, the Police, and Counterterrorism in Four Democracies* (Santa Monica, CA: RAND, 2004).

32. Other researchers have found similar results. For example, in their survey of seven counterinsurgency and counterterrorism campaigns (Malaya, Kenya, Cyprus, Rhodesia, Northern Ireland, Germany, and Italy), two of which overlap with our cases, Bruce Hoffman and Jennifer Morrison Taw concluded: "Appropriate use of information, the key to any successful counterinsurgency or counterterrorism campaign, depends on three tasks: the acquisition, proper analysis, and perhaps most important, coordination and dissemination of intelligence. This triad can be accomplished only by establishing a centralized, cooperative, and integrative intelligence organization that can channel information effectively to the security forces engaged in tactical operations." See Bruce Hoffman and Jennifer Morrison Taw, *A Strategic Framework for Countering Terrorism and Insurgency,* RAND Note N-3506-DOS (Santa Monica, CA: RAND, 1992), vii–viii, chapter 4. The crucial importance of integrated intelligence was stressed by Lieutenant Colonel Julian Paget in his classic work on counterinsurgency. See Julian Paget, *Counter-insurgency Campaigning* (London: Faber and Faber, 1967), 163–64.

33. The 9/11 Commission recommends that the United States and its friends develop a common approach to the detention and humane treatment of captured terrorists. See *9/11 Commission Report,* 380.

34. Robert A. Pape, *Dying to Win: The Strategic Logic of Suicide Terrorism* (New York: Random House, 2005), 24

35. The 9/11 Commission recommended: "Lead responsibility for directing and executing paramilitary operations, whether clandestine or covert, should shift to the Defense Department." This recommendation was not enacted into law. See *9/11 Commission Report*, 415. For descriptions of the

Pentagon's new and expanded role in covert and clandestine operations under Donald Rumsfeld, see Barton Gellman, "Secret Unit Expands Rumsfeld's Domain," *Washington Post,* January 23, 2005, A1; Mark Mazzetti and Greg Miller, "Pentagon Increases Its Spying Markedly," *Los Angeles Times,* March 24, 2005, A1; Linda Robinson, "Tinker, Tailor, Soldier, Spy," *U.S. News and World Report,* April 25, 2005, 34; and Seymour M. Hersh, "What the Pentagon Can Now Do in Secret," *New Yorker,* January 24, 2005, 40ff, www.newyorker.com/fact/content/?050124fa_fact.

36. Hoffman, speech (see note 5).

37. Bruce Hoffman and Kim Cragin, "Four Lessons from Five Countries" (Santa Monica, CA: RAND, n.d.), 1, www.rand.org/publications/randreview/issues/rr.08.02/fourlessons.html. This short essay is based on a longer study done for the National Security Council in the late 1990s, but unfortunately the larger study is not available.

38. *9/11 Commission Report,* 363.

39. Ibid.

40. For a good overview of the image problems the United States is now experiencing, see Stephen M. Walt, *Taming American Power: The Global Response to U.S. Primacy* (New York: W. W. Norton, 2005), chapter 2. For a recent survey of U.S. standing in Jordan, Syria, Lebanon, Egypt, and the Palestinian territories, see Office of Research, Department of State, "Independent Survey of Arab Publics Shows Bad U.S. Image Based Primarily on U.S. Regional Policy," www.state.gov. Over the past four years, the Pew Research Center for People and the Press has conducted many international surveys of U.S. standing in the world as part of its Global Attitudes Project. These are available at www.people-press.org. See, for example, "Mistrust of America in Europe Ever Higher, Muslim Anger Persists," a nine-country survey, March 16, 2004.

41. For suggestions on how the United States can improve its general global image, see Robert J. Art, *A Grand Strategy for America* (Ithaca, NY: Cornell University Press, 2003), 170–71, 234–38; and Walt, *Taming American Power,* chapter 5.

42. For good suggestions on how to improve U.S. public diplomacy, see Council on Foreign Relations, *Finding America's Voice: A Strategy for Reinvigorating U.S. Public Diplomacy* (Report of an Independent Task Force Sponsored by the Council on Foreign Relations, New York: Council on Foreign Relations, 2003). For recent assessments about the current state of U.S. public diplomacy, see *United States Advisory Commission on Public Diplomacy [this is italicized as if it were a title, but probably the author component of a report? Please advise]*; General Accounting Office, *U.S. Public Diplomacy: State Department Expands Efforts but Faces Significant Challenges,*

September 2003; and General Accounting Office, *U.S. Public Diplomacy: Interagency Coordination Efforts Hampered by the Lack of a National Communication Strategy,* April 2005. Both GAO reports are available online at www.gao.gov.

43. For example, staffing for public diplomacy dropped 35 percent, and funding, when adjusted for inflation, fell 26 percent during the 1980s and 1990s. In 1999 the United States abolished the Voice of America as an independent agency, folded it into the State Department, and severely degraded its effectiveness as a consequence. When examining public diplomacy programs in 2003, the *Djerejian Report* found that "funding for public diplomacy outreach programs comes to only $25 million for the entire Arab and Muslim world—a depressingly small amount." See Advisory Group on Public Diplomacy for the Arab and Muslim World, *Changing Minds, Winning Peace: A New Strategic Direction for U.S. Public Diplomacy in the Arab and Muslim World* (Report of the Advisory Group on Public Diplomacy for the Arab and Muslim World, Washington, DC: October 1, 2003), 25–26. (Hereafter cited as *Djerejian Report.*)

44. See Office of Research, Department of State, "Independent Survey of Arab Publics Shows Bad U.S. Image Based Primarily on U.S. Regional Policy," May 23, 2005, www.state.gov.

45. *Djerejian Report,* 24.

46. Craig Charney and Nicole Yakatan, *A New Beginning: Strategies for a More Fruitful Dialogue with the Muslim World* (New York: Council on Foreign Relations, May 2005), 60, www.cfr.org.

47. Quoted in David E. Kaplan and others, "Hearts, Minds, and Dollars," *U.S. News and World Report,* April 25, 2005, www.usnews.com. This article is the best of those currently out at describing the varied elements of the political strategy that the Bush administration has adopted toward the Muslim world. It is being implemented under the direction of the National Security Council and is called the Muslim World Outreach program.

48. See Clarke, *Defeating the Jihadists,* chapter 5, "Partnering with the Islamic World," for more specific suggestions on how to work with Muslim moderates.

49. For empirical verification of this assertion, see Jack Snyder, *From Voting to Violence: Democratization and Nationalist Conflict* (New York: W. W. Norton, 2000).

INDEX

n following number indicates note

United States Institute of Peace

The United States Institute of Peace is an independent, nonpartisan institution established and funded by Congress. Its goals are to help prevent and resolve violent conflicts, promote post-conflict peacebuilding, and increase conflict-management tools, capacity, and intellectual capital worldwide. The Institute does this by empowering others with knowledge, skills, and resources, as well as by its direct involvement in conflict zones around the globe.

Chairman of the Board: J. Robinson West
Vice Chairman: María Otero
President: Richard H. Solomon
Executive Vice President: Patricia Powers Thomson
Vice President: Charles E. Nelson

Board of Directors

J. Robinson West (Chairman), Chairman, PFC Energy, Washington, D.C.

María Otero (Vice Chairman), President, ACCION International, Boston, Mass.

Betty F. Bumpers, Founder and former President, Peace Links, Washington, D.C.

Holly J. Burkhalter, Vice President of Government Affairs, International Justice Mission, Washington, D.C.

Chester A. Crocker, James R. Schlesinger Professor of Strategic Studies, School of Foreign Service, Georgetown University

Laurie S. Fulton, Partner, Williams and Connolly, Washington, D.C.

Charles Horner, Senior Fellow, Hudson Institute, Washington, D.C.

Seymour Martin Lipset, Hazel Professor of Public Policy, George Mason University

Mora L. McLean, President, Africa-America Institute, New York, N.Y.

Barbara W. Snelling, former State Senator and former Lieutenant Governor, Shelburne, Vt.

Members ex officio

Barry F. Lowenkron, Assistant Secretary of State for Democracy, Human Rights, and Labor

Peter W. Rodman, Assistant Secretary of Defense for International Security Affairs

Richard H. Solomon, President, United States Institute of Peace (nonvoting)

Frances C. Wilson, Lieutenant General, U.S. Marine Corps; President, National Defense University

DEMOCRACY AND COUNTERTERRORISM

This book is set in Adobe Garamond Pro; the display type is Adobe Garamond Pro bold and semibold. The Creative Shop designed the book's cover. EEI Communications, Inc. made up the pages and prepared the index. The text was copyedited by Margaret J. Goldstein and Wesley Palmer. The book was edited by Nigel Quinney, with help from Amy Benavides and Karen Stough.